INDIA DEVELOPMENT REPORT 2017

India Development Report 2017

edited by

S. MAHENDRA DEV

OXFORD
UNIVERSITY PRESS

Oxford University Press is a department of the University of Oxford.
It furthers the University's objective of excellence in research, scholarship,
and education by publishing worldwide. Oxford is a registered trademark of
Oxford University Press in the UK and in certain other countries.

Published in India by
Oxford University Press
2/11 Ground Floor, Ansari Road, Daryaganj, New Delhi 110 002, India

ISBN-13: 978-0-19-948354-9
ISBN-10: 0-19-948354-X

Typeset in 10.5/12.7 Minion Pro
by Tranistics Data Technologies, New Delhi 110 044
Printed in India by Rakmo Press, New Delhi 110 020

Note that $ refers to US dollar unless stated otherwise; tables and figures that do not mention any specific source
are authors' own works; maps are for illustrative purpose only and are not to scale.

Contents

Tables, Figures, and Boxes

TABLES

FIGURES

BOXES

A Statistical Profile of India's Development

Preface

The Indian economy in 2017, with more than 2 trillion dollars of GDP, is different from India in 1991 when the economic reforms were introduced. The country is more globally integrated now as compared to the year when reforms started. The present government has undertaken several reform measures in the last three years. Among others, tax reform in the form of Goods and Services Tax (GST) is a big achievement. Similarly, the Bankruptcy and Insolvency Code promises to make it easier to wind up the falling business and recovery of debts. Appointment of the Monetary Policy Committee is another reform in the monetary sector. The JAM (Jandhan Yojana, Aadhaar and Mobile Number) trinity holds the key for big reform on direct subsidy reforms. The government is pinning its hopes on these three modes of identification to deliver direct benefits to India's poor. Ease of doing business is likely to improve over time. The proposals in Budget 2017–18, particularly on infrastructure, are likely to enhance growth in future. Some of these reforms are expected to improve growth and inclusive development in the next few years.

The Second Advanced Estimates released by the Central Statistical Office reveal that the gross domestic product (GDP) growth would decline from 7.9 per cent in 2015–16 to 7.1 per cent in 2016–17. Similarly gross value added (GVA) in basic prices growth would decline from 7.8 per cent to 6.7 per cent during the same period. In fact, if we consider GVA without agriculture and public administration and defence, its growth in 2016–17 would be much lower than 6.7 per cent. Moreover, present growth is consumption driven. For sustaining growth, investment has to be revived, particularly private investment. In order to increase private investment, the twin balance sheet problem—corporate debt and non-performing assets problem of banks—has to be solved.

In the last 25 years of the reform period, India has done well and one can see significant visible change in economic growth and some of the development indicators. The country has the potential to achieve 8 to 9 per cent GDP growth. In order to have higher and sustainable growth, the country needs to have appropriate policies and implementing systems. There has been slow progress in some areas of development. Six areas which need focus of policy are: (a) infrastructure development; (b) accelerated labour-intensive manufacturing; (c) education and skill of workers for achieving demographic dividend; (d) improved social sector development; (e) achievement of sustainable development; and (f) maximum governance.

The India Development Report (IDR) series provides an independent assessment of the Indian economy including contemporary problems, issues and policies. In addition to the general topics, *India Development Report 2017* (ninth in the series) contains a special section on the Make in India initiative. The chapters in this section deal with issues such as 'make what in India?', 'make where in India?', role of services in manufacturing, evolution of insolvency framework, and policies for the growth of high-technology industries. Other chapters deal with a wide range of issues including monetary policy transmission, new national accounts series, women's empowerment, nutrition, education, labour regulation, and agriculture. The report is divided into two parts. Part I (Chapter 2–10) examines issues and policies in macro, agriculture, and social sectors. Part II (Chapter 11–15) is specifically devoted to trade and industry. I am happy to note that *India Development Report 2017* has special significance as Indira Gandhi Institute of Development Research (IGIDR) has completed three decades since it was established in 1987.

The publication of this IDR has provided us an opportunity to bring the research of IGIDR scholars to a wider audience. Few scholars from other institutes have also contributed chapters to this report. The views expressed in this volume are those of individual authors.

I am grateful to C. Veeramani for coordinating and his contribution to the overview of the report. The chapters were initially presented in a workshop organized at IGIDR. I am thankful to the discussants Vikas Chitre, Manoj Pant, Ravi Srivastava, and Sripad Motiram for their useful comments. All the papers were revised based on their comments. Thanks are also due to all the contributors to this volume and the Economic and Political Weekly Research Foundation (EPWRF) for the statistical appendices. I thank Mahesh Mohan for coordinating the production of the chapters and the Oxford University Press team for editorial support and publication of the report.

S. Mahendra Dev
Director and Vice Chancellor,
IGIDR

Abbreviations

2SLS	Two-Stage Least Squares
4DE	Four Domains of Empowerment
5DE	Five Domains of Empowerment
AAI	Airports Authority of India
AD	Authorized Dealer
ADSORBS	Assessment and Development Study of River Basin Series
AEs	Advanced Economies
AGM	Annual General Meeting
AICTE	All India Council of Technical Education
AIDIS	All India Debt and Investment Survey
AIES	All India Educational Survey
AISES	All India School Education Survey
ALE	Agricultural Labour Enquiry
AMA	Administrative Management Agency
APL	Above Poverty Line
APMC	Agricultural Produce Market Committee
APRAD	Asia Pacific Road Accident Data
AS	Aggregate Supply
AS&FA	Additional Secretary & Financial Advisor
ASDR	Age Specific Death Rates
ASI	Annual Survey of Industries
ASICC	ASI Commodity Classification
BAU	Business as Usual
BECIL	Broadcasting Engineering Consultants India Limited
BMI	Body Mass Index
BOP	Balance of Payments
BPL	Below Poverty Line
BPSI	*Basic Port Statistics of India*
BR	Base Rate
BSE	Bombay Stock Exchange Limited
BSI	Botanical Survey of India

CAB	Cotton Advisory Board
CAD	Current Account Deficit
CAG	Comptroller and Auditor General of India
CAPE	Crop Acreage and Production Estimation
CB	Central Bank
CBHI	Central Bureau of Health Intelligence
CBLO	Collateralized Borrowing and Lending Obligation
CBR	Crude Birth Rate
CBs	Commercial Banks
CCE	Crop Cutting Experiments
CCEA	Cabinet Committee on Economic Affairs
CCI&E	Chief Controller of Imports & Exports
CDR	Crude Death Rate
CDS	Current Daily Status
CEA	Central Electricity Authority
CES	Constant Elasticity of Substitution
CES	Surveys on Consumption Expenditure
CFC	Consumption of Fixed Capital
CGE	Computable General Equilibrium
CIF	Chief Inspector of Factories
cif	Cost, Insurance, and Freight
CIFRI	Central Inland Fisheries Research Institute
CIN	Corporate Identification Number
CIS	Change in Stock
CIWTC	Central Inland Water Corporation
CMA	Cement Manufacturers Association
CMFRI	Central Marine Fisheries Research Institute
CMI	Census of Manufacturing Industries
CMIE	Centre for Monitoring Indian Economy
CMR	Call Money Rate
COINDS	Comprehensive Industry Document Series
COOIT	Central Organization for Oil Industry and Trade
CP	Current Price
CPC	Central Product Classification
CPD	Coordination and Publication Division
CPI	Consumer Price Index
CPI-AL	Consumer Price Index for Agricultural Labourers
CPI-IW	Consumer Price Index for Industrial workers
CRA	Climate Resilient Agriculture
CRR	Cash Reserve Ratio
CRS	Civil Registration System
CSIR	Council of Scientific and Industrial Research
CSO	Central Statistical Organization
CSS	Centrally Sponsored Schemes
CUPS	Control of Urban Pollution Series
CWE	Chief Wage Earner
CWS	Current Weekly Status
CWWG	Crop Weather Watch Group
DADF	Department of Animal Husbandry, Dairying & Fisheries
DBT	Direct Benefit Transfer
DCSSI	Development Commissioner Small Scale Industries

DCU	Departmental Commercial Undertakings
DCU	Discounted Cumulated Utility
DES	Directorate of Economics and Statistics
DGCA	Directorate General of Civil Aviation
DGCI&S	Director General of Commercial Intelligence and Statistics
DGE&T	Directorate General of Employment & Training
DGFT	Directorate General of Foreign Trade
DGHS	Directorate General of Health Services
DGTD	Directorate General of Technical Development
DH	District Headquarters
DIPP	Department of Industrial Policy and Promotion
DISE	District Information System for Education
DLHS	District Level Household and Facility Survey
DME	Directory Manufacturing Establishments
DMI	Directorate of Marketing and Inspection
DOBS	Dwellings, Other Buildings, and Structures
DPD	Data Processing Division
DPEP	District Primary Education Programme
DSIM	Department of Statistics and Information Management
DSO	District Survey Officer
DST	Department of Science and Technology
DSTP	Directorate of Scientific and Technical Personnel
DTR	Daily Trade Returns
EARS	Establishment of an Agency for Reporting Agriculture Statistics
EDE	Emerging and Developing Economies
EDI	Electronic Data Interchange
EGS&AIE	Education Guarantee Scheme & Alternative and Innovative Education
EIAS	Ecological Impact Assessment Series
EMI	Employment Market Information
EMPS	Environment Mopping and Pollution Series
ENI	Estimates of National Income
EPF	Employees' Provident Fund Scheme
EPS	Employees' Pension Scheme
EPWRF	*Economic and Political Weekly* Research Foundation
ESS	European Statistical System
EU	European Union
FAO	Food and Agriculture Organization
FCI	Food Corporation of India
FCRN	Foreign Company Registration Number
FDES	Framework for Development of Environment Statistics
FDI	Foreign Direct Investment
FEE	Foreign Exchange Earnings
FHP	Farm Harvest Prices
FISIM	Financial Intermediation Services Indirectly Measured
FLS	Family Living Survey
fob	Free on Board
FOD	Field Operations Division
FPO	Farmer Producer Organization
FRBM	Fiscal Responsibility and Budget Management
FTA	Foreign Tourist Arrivals
FTSI	*Foreign Trade Statistics of India*

GCES	General Crop Estimation Surveys
GCF	Gross Capital Formation
GDCF	Gross Domestic Capital Formation
GDP	Gross Domestic Product
GER	Gender Enrolment Ratio
GFC	Global Financial Crisis
GFCF	Gross Fixed Capital Formation
GHG	Greenhouse Gas
GIC	General Insurance Corporation
GNP	Gross National Product
GoI	Government of India
GPI	Gender Parity Index
GPN	Global Production Network
GSI	Geological Survey of India
GSS	Government Statistical Service
GST	Goods and Service Tax
GVA	Gross Value Added
GVCs	Global Value Chains
GVO	Gross Value of Output
HBS	Household Budget Survey
HCR	Head Count Ratio
HDPI	Human Development Profile of India
HP	Horizontal Policy
HTM	Held to Maturity
HWMS	Hazardous Waste Management Series
HYV	High Yielding Varieties
IAMR	Institute of Applied Manpower Research
IASI	Inter-American Statistical Institute
IBC	Insolvency and Bankruptcy Code
IBM	Indian Bureau of Mines
ICAI	Institute of Chartered Accountants of India
ICDS	Integrated Child Development Scheme
ICFRE	Indian Council of Forestry Research and Education
ICICI	Industrial Credit and Investment Corporation of India
ICLS	Indian Corporate Law Service
ICPF	Insurance Corporations and Pension Funds
ICPSR	Interuniversity Consortium for Political and Social Research
ICR	Intelligent Character Reading
ICS	Implementation of Crop Statistics
ICSI	Institute of Company Secretaries of India
ICT	Information and Communication Technology
ICWAI	Institute of Cost and Works Accountants of India
IDA	Industrial Disputes Act
IDBI	Industrial Development Bank of India
IEC	Importer and Exporter Code
IFCI	Industrial Financial Corporation of India
IICA	Indian Institute of Corporate Affairs
IIP	Index of Industrial Production
ILO	International Labour Organization
ILS	Indian Labour Statistics
IMF	International Monetary Fund

IMR	Infant Mortality Rate
IMYB	*Indian Minerals Year Book*
IOTT	Input-Output Transactions Table
IR	Indian Railways
IRAD	Indian Road Accident Data
IRDA	Insurance Regulatory and Development Authority
ISI	International Statistical Institute
ISO	Information System Organization
IT	Inflation Targeting
IT	Information Technology
ITC-HS	Indian Trade Classification based on the Harmonized Commodity Description and Coding System
IT-ITES	Information technology and information technology enabled services
IWP	Index of Wholesale Prices
IWT	Inland Water Transport
KP	Constant Price
KVIC	Khadi and Village Industries Commission
LAF	Liquidity Adjustment Facility
LES	Linear Expenditure System
LFPR	Labour Force Participation Rate
LIC	Life Insurance Corporation
LLPs	Limited Liability Partnerships
LPG	Liquefied Petroleum Gas
LULUCF	Land Use, Land-Use Change, and Forestry
MAS	Monthly Abstract Statistics
MCA	Ministry of Corporate Affairs
MCDR	Mineral Conservation and Development Rules
MCLR	Marginal Cost of Funds-Based Lending Rate
MDA	Market Development Assistance
MDG	Millennium Development Goal
MGNREGA	Mahatma Gandhi National Rural Employment Guarantee Act
MHRD	Ministry of Human Resource Development
MIBOR	Mumbai Interbank offered rate
MID	Minor Irrigation Division
MIMAP	Micro Impact of Macro and Adjustment Policies
MIS	Management Information Systems
MISH	Market Information Survey of Households
MMF	Money Market Funds
MMR	Maternal Mortality Rate
MNE	Multinational Enterprise
MOEF	Ministry of Environment & Forests
MOSPI	Ministry of Statistics and Programme Implementation
MOT	Ministry of Tourism
MRTPC	Monopolies and Restrictive Trade Practices Commission
MSF	Marginal Standing Facility
MSFTI	*Monthly Statistics of the Foreign Trade of India*
MSME	Micro, Small, and Medium Enterprises
MSR	Marketed Surplus Ratio
NAAQMS	National Ambient Air Quality Monitoring Series
NABARD	National Bank for Agriculture and Rural Development
NACO	National Aids Control Organization

NAD	National Account Division
NAS	National Accounts Statistics
NBO	National Building Organization
NCAER	National Council for Applied Economic Research
NCDEX	National Commodity Derivatives Exchange
NCERT	National Council of Educational Research and Training
NCFC	National Crop Forecasting Center
NCO	National Classification of Occupations
NCP	National Commission on Population
NCSC	National Crop Statistics Centre
NCV	Net Calorific Values
NDA	National Democratic Alliance
NDCU	Non-departmental Commercial Undertakings
NDE	Non-departmental Enterprises
NDME	Non-directory Manufacturing Establishments
NDP	Net Domestic Product
NDTL	Net Demand and Time Liabilities
NEP	National Environment Policy
NES	National Employment Service
NFHS	National Family Health Surveys
NHB	National Horticultural Board
NIC	National Industrial Classification
NIC	National Informatics Centre
NIEPA	National Institute of Educational Planning and Administration
NKN	National Knowledge Network
NNP	Net National Product
NPA	Non-performing Asset
NPCMS	National Product Classification for Manufacturing Sector
NPISH	Non-profit Institutions Serving Households
NPR	National Population Register
NREGS	National Rural Employment Guarantee Scheme
NRHM	National Rural Health Mission
NRSA	National Remote Sensing Agency
NSC	National Statistical Commission
NSE	National Stock Exchange of India Ltd
NSHIE	National Survey on Household Income and Expenditure
NSI	National Statistical Institute
NSS	National Sample Survey
NSSF	National Small Savings Fund
NSSO	National Sample Survey Organization
NSSO	National Sample Survey Office
NSTMIS	National Science and Technology Management Information System Division
NUEPA	National University of Educational Planning and Administration
OAD	Operational Analysis Division
OAE	Own-Account Enterprises
OAME	Own-Account Manufacturing Enterprises
OEA	Office of the Economic Advisor
OECD	Organization for Economic Co-operation and Development
OLS	Ordinary Least Squares
OMB	Office of Management and Budget
ONS	Office for National Statistics

OPCs	One Person Companies
ORGI	Office of the Registrar General, India
OWS	Occupational Wage Survey
PCS	Private Corporate Sector
pdf	Portable Document Format
PDS	Public Distribution System
PES	Post Enumeration Surveys
PFCE	Private Final Consumption Expenditure
PFRDA	Pension Fund Regulatory and Development Authority
PIM	Perpetual inventory method
PMFBY	Pradhan Mantri Fasal Bima Yojana
PMKSY	Pradhan Mantri Krishi Sinchai Yojana
PMRPY	Pradhan Mantri Rojgar Protsahan Yojana
POL	Petroleum, oil and lubricants
POSB	Post Office Savings Bank
PPP	Purchasing power parity
PSBs	Public Sector Banks
PSU	Particulars of Sample village/Urban Block
PSUs	Public Sector Undertakings
R&D	Research and Development
RBI	Reserve Bank of India
RER	Real Effective Exchange Rate
RERES	Resource Recycling Series
RGI	Registrar General, India
RITES	Rail India Technical and Economic Services
RKVY	Rashtriya Krishi Vikas Yojana
RLE	Rural Labour Enquiry
RMIS	Rationalization of Minor Irrigation Statistics
RMSA	Rashtriya Madhyamik Shiksha Abhiyan
ROC	Registrar of Companies
RR	Reference Rate
RS	Remote Sensing
S&T	Scientific and Technical
SAM	Social Accounting Matrix
SARFAESI	Act Securitisation and Reconstruction of Financial Assets and Enforcement of Security Interest Act
SC	Scheduled Caste
SCC	State Cane Commissioners
SCIS	Standing Committee on Industrial Statistics
SDDS	Standard Data Dissemination System
SDG	Sustainable Development Goal
SDP	State Domestic Product
SDRD	Survey Design and Research Division
SEBI	Securities and Exchange Board of India
SECC	Socio Economic and Caste Census
SFCs	State Financial Corporations
SFTIC	*Statistics of Foreign Trade of India by Countries*
SIC	Standard Industrial Classification
SICA	Sick Industrial Companies (Special Provisions) Act
SIDCs	State Industrial Development Corporations
SIDO	Small Industries Development Organization

SIRO	Scientific and Industrial Research Organization
SITC	Standard International Trade Classification
SLR	Statutory Liquidity Ratio
SME	Small and Medium Enterprise
SPS	Special Performance System
SRS	Sample Registration System
SRTU	State Road Transport Undertaking
SSA	Sarva Shiksha Abhiyan
SSD	Statistical Standards Divisions
SSI	Small-Scale Industries
SSMI	Sample Survey of Manufacturing Industries
SSO	State Survey Officer
ST	Scheduled Tribe
STS	Science and Technology Statistics
SUT	Sustainable Urban Tourism
TADF	Technology Acquisition and Development Fund
TDGDP	Tourism Direct Gross Domestic Product
TDGVA	Tourism Direct Gross Value Added
TFP	Total Factor Productivity
TFR	Total Fertility Rate
TiVA	Trade in Value Added
TPP	Trans Pacific Partnership
TRW	Transport Research Wing
TSA	Tourism Satellite Accounts
TTIP	Transatlantic Trade and Investment Partnership
U-DISE	Unified District Information System for Education
UEE	Universalization of Elementary Education
UFS	Urban Frame Survey
UGC	University Grants Commission
UID	Unique Identification Number
UN	United Nations
UNESCO	U.N. Educational Scientific and Cultural Organization
UNIDO	United Nations Industrial Development Organization
UNSC	United Nations Statistical Commission
UNSD	United Nations Statistics Division
UNWTO	United Nations World Tourism Organization
UPR	Usual Place of Residence
UPS	Usual Principal Status
UPSS	Usual Principal and Subsidiary Status
USA	United States of America
USS	Usual Subsidiary Status
USU	Ultimate stage units
UTI	Unit Trust of India
VDSA	Village Dynamics in South Asia
VP	Vertical Policy
WEAI	Women's Empowerment in Agriculture Index
WHO	World Health Organization
WPI	Wholesale price index
WPR	Worker Population Ratio
XBRL	Extensible Business Reporting Language
ZSI	Zoological Survey of India

Contributors

Runu Bhakta holds a PhD in economics from Indira Gandhi Institute of Development Research, Mumbai and is currently working as a consultant at Ernst&Young with a strong background in economic research on several macro-economic, social, developmental issues, and contemporary public policies.

Sanjoy Chakravorty is professor of geography and urban studies at Temple University and visiting fellow at the Center for the Advanced Study of India at the University of Pennsylvania.

Rupa Chanda is RBI Chair Professor in Economics at the Indian Institute of Management Bangalore where she teaches macroeconomics and international trade.

Tirtha Chatterjee is working as a Research Associate in Indian Council for Research on International Economic Relations (ICRIER), New Delhi.

S. Mahendra Dev is director (vice chancellor), Indira Gandhi Institute of Development Research, Mumbai.

Garima Dhir is a PhD scholar at Indira Gandhi Institute of Development Research, Mumbai.

Ashima Goyal is a professor at the Indira Gandhi Institute of Development Research and a past member of the Monetary Policy Technical Advisory Committee of the Reserve Bank of India.

A. Ganesh-Kumar is a professor at Indira Gandhi Institute of Development Research, Mumbai.

Sunil Mani is the director of Centre for Development Studies, Trivandrum, Kerala.

Abhiroop Mukhopadhyay is an associate professor at the Economics and Planning Unit of the Indian Statistical Institute, Delhi.

G. Mythili is a professor at Indira Gandhi Institute of Development Research, Mumbai.

Karthikeya Naraparaju is an assistant professor in the economics area at the Indian Institute of Management Indore.

Manoj Panda is director at Institute of Economic Growth, Delhi and was earlier in the faculty of Indira Gandhi Institute of Development Research, Mumbai.

Vijay Laxmi Pandey is professor at Indira Gandhi Institute of Development Research, Mumbai.

J. Dennis Rajakumar is the director of Economic and Political Weekly Research Foundation, Mumbai.

Rajeswari Sengupta is assistant professor of economics at Indira Gandhi Institute of Development Research, Mumbai.

Ajay Sharma is assistant professor in economics at Indian Institute of Management Indore.

Anjali Sharma works as a researcher at the Finance Research Group at Indira Gandhi Institute of Development Research, Mumbai.

S.L. Shetty focuses on macro-economic issues in his research endeavours.

D. Suganthi is research associate at System for Promoting Appropriate National Dynamism for Agriculture and Nutrition (SPANDAN), Indira Gandhi Institute of Development Research, Mumbai.

Susan Thomas is faculty at Indira Gandhi Institute of Development Research, Mumbai.

C. Veeramani is associate professor at Indira Gandhi Institute of Development Research, Mumbai.

Preparedness for Make in India and Other Emerging Issues
An Introductory Overview

S. Mahendra Dev and C. Veeramani

INTRODUCTION

India completed 25 years of economic reforms since it embarked on big-bang reforms in 1991. There is no doubt that growth and other macro indicators have been much better since 1991. Growth rates of the gross domestic product (GDP) increased significantly in the post-reform period led by service sector growth. The trend rate of GDP growth in the 25-year reform period has been around 6.5 per cent per annum.[1] The growth rate was nearly 9 per cent per annum during 2003–04 to 2007–09. In the last one and half decades, the economy grew around 7 per cent per annum. Service sector growth was 7 to 9 per cent per annum in the last two and half decades. Industrial growth was the highest in 2000s. On the other hand, agricultural growth in the last one and half decades was lower than those of 1990s and 1980s.

In the last 25 years of reform period, India has done well and one can see significant visible change in economic growth and some of the development indicators.

But, there has been slow progress in some areas. The *India Development Report 2015* discussed six areas for policy focus, which are: (i) infrastructure development; (ii) acceleration of labour-intensive manufacturing; (iii) education and skill of workers for achieving demographic dividend; (iv) improvement of social sector development; (v) sustainable development; and (vi) maximum governance.

After the big-bang reforms of the early 1990s, India has followed a gradualist approach (Ahluwalia, 2002). Gradualism or calibration could be due to two factors. First, it is better to be cautious instead of taking many risks as India cannot afford too many risks with so many poor people. Second, one does not need caution but has to be gradual and slow due to compulsions of the democratic process in a very large and heterogeneous country. One needs consultation and consensus building, which often takes time. A good feature of Indian elections in recent years is that people are voting for development apart from other factors.

The Indian economy, with more than 2 trillion dollars of GDP in 2017, is different from 1991. The country is more globally integrated now as compared to the year when

[1] See Chapter 2 for details on GDP growth rates in the post-reform period.

reforms started. The global financial crisis that originated in the United States of America (USA) in 2008 transmitted to emerging market economies like India. Continued global slowdown had adverse impact on India's economy as the value of exports declined significantly since 2012–13. Currently, India's macroeconomic parameters, such as current account deficit, inflation, fiscal deficit and exchange rate, are under control and stable. India is attracting large inflows of foreign direct investment (FDI).

OUTLOOK FOR THE ECONOMY

Many macro indicators of the Indian economy have improved in the post-reform period. The policymakers should focus now on the six areas mentioned earlier. India has the potential to achieve 8 to 9 per cent GDP growth. In order to have higher and sustainable growth, the country needs to have appropriate policies and systems for implementation. However, present growth is consumption driven. For sustaining growth, investment has to be revived particularly private investment. There is a debt problem for private sector (Government of India, 2016–17). It may take some time for revival of private investment and climate has to be created.

The Second Advance Estimates released by the Central Statistical Office (CSO) show that the GDP growth would decline from 7.9 per cent in 2015–16 to 7.1 per cent in 2016–17. Similarly, growth in gross value added (GVA) would decline from 7.8 per cent to 6.7 per cent during the same period. In fact, if we consider GVA without agriculture and public administration and defence, its growth in 2016–17 would be much lower than 6.7 per cent.

In its April 2017 policy statement, the Reserve Bank of India (RBI) has projected GVA growth to increase to 7.4 per cent in 2017–18 from 6.7 per cent in 2016–17. According to this statement, several favourable domestic factors are expected to increase GDP growth in 2017–18. These are:

First, the pace of remonetisation will continue to trigger a rebound in discretionary consumer spending. Activity in cash-intensive retail trade, hotels and restaurants, transportation and unorganised segments has largely been restored. Second, significant improvement in transmission of past policy rate reductions into banks' lending rates post demonetization should help encourage both consumption and investment demand of healthy corporations. Third, various proposals in the Union Budget should stimulate capital expenditure, rural demand, and social and physical infrastructure all of which would invigorate economic activity. Fourth, the imminent materialisation of structural reforms in the form of the roll-out of the GST, the institution of the Insolvency and Bankruptcy Code, and the abolition of the Foreign Investment Promotion Board will boost investor confidence and bring in efficiency gains. Fifth, the upsurge in initial public offerings in the primary capital market augurs well for investment and growth. (RBI, 2017: 6)

Inflation for the year 2017–18 is projected to average 4.5 per cent in the first half of the year and 5 per cent in the second half (RBI, 2017). Some of the upside risks for inflation are impact of Seventh Central Pay Commission and one-off effects of GST. On the downside, easing of international crude prices and an increase in procurement of foodgrains may be moderating factors for inflation.

On global economic situation, *The Economist* (2017) indicates that the world economy is on the rise. 'Today almost ten years after the most severe financial crisis since the Depression, a broad-based economic swing is at last under way. In America, Europe, Asia and the emerging markets, for the first time since a brief rebound in 2010, all the burners are firing at once' (p. 9). Recession in Russia and Brazil is slowly coming to an end. The April 2017 policy statements of the RBI also highlight some of the positive developments in revival of global economy including USA, Europe, Japan, and the emerging economies (RBI, 2017). There are, however, risks such as high debt in China, protectionist policies of Trump administration, problems in Euro area, and post-Brexit events.

In India, there is some revival in export growth after stagnancy over two years. It has to concentrate on domestic economy apart from creating environment for export growth. Public investment in infrastructure and other areas is crucial as a counter-cyclical measure for reviving the economy. This can also raise private investment. The twin balance sheet problem—overleveraged companies and bad-loan-encumbered banks—needs to be solved (*Economic Survey 2016–17*). The problem of large non-performing assets (NPAs) in public sector banks has to be resolved quickly. One should stick to fiscal deficit targets. Revenue deficit has to be reduced to zero over time. The objectives of both raising public investment and sticking to fiscal deficits can be achieved if non-merit subsidies are removed and disinvestment targets are achieved. On corporate tax, reduction in the rate must be accompanied by reduction in exemptions. This can be used for infrastructure and social sector development.

In order to move to the next stage of economic journey, the *Economic Survey 2016–17* focuses on three things: (i) to remove hesitancy to embrace private sector and protect property rights; (ii) to improve state capacity which is weak particularly in delivery of services like education and health; and (iii) to rectify redistribution, which has been simultaneously extensive and inefficient. 'Further reforms are not just a matter of overcoming vested interests that obstruct them. Broader societal shifts in underlying ideas and vision will be critical' (*Economic Survey 2016–17*: 51).

The present government, led by the National Democratic Alliance (NDA), has undertaken several reform measures in the last three years. Among others, tax reform in the form of Goods and Services Tax (GST) is a big achievement. Similarly, the Insolvency and Bankruptcy Code promises to make it easier to wind up falling business and recover debts. Appointment of the Monetary Policy Committee is another reform in the monetary sector. The JAM trinity (Jan Dhan Yojana, Aadhaar card, and mobile) holds the key for big reform on direct subsidy reforms. The government is pinning its hopes on these three modes of identification to deliver direct benefits to India's poor. Ease of doing business is likely to improve over time. The proposals in Budget 2017–18 (Government of India, 2017–18), particularly on infrastructure, are likely to enhance growth in future. Some of these reforms are expected to improve growth and inclusive development in the next few years.

DEMONETIZATION AND IMPACT ON THE ECONOMY

On 8 November 2016, the Government of India announced that currency notes of high denomination (Rs 500 and Rs 1,000) were being withdrawn from circulation. The main aim of this move was to eliminate black money and to curb counterfeit currency which is used to finance terrorism and drugs and as a conduit for money laundering. The other objective was to move towards cashless economy. The delegalized notes of Rs 500 and Rs 1,000 constitute around 85 per cent of the total currency in circulation and amount to Rs 14 billion. Deposits with banks increased significantly after demonetization.

There are many short-run costs to the people and the economy. Many people, particularly informal sector workers, farmers, and urban poor, depend on cash for their daily transactions. The replacement of cash has taken months. This has led to some hardships for many sections of the population in both rural and urban areas. In its December policy statement, RBI says that downside risks to the economy in the near term could travel through two major channels:

(a) short-run disruptions in economic activity in cash-intensive sectors such as retail trade, hotels & restaurants and transportation, and in the unorganised sector; (b) aggregate demand compression associated with adverse wealth effects. The impact of the first channel should, however, ebb with the progressive increase in the circulation of new currency notes and greater usage of non-cash based payment instruments in the economy. While the impact of the second channel is likely to be limited. (RBI, 2016: 4)

Demonetization is likely to hurt both GDP growth and employment in the short run. Consumption expenditure is likely to drop for people starved of cash. The CSO Second Advance Estimates on GDP and GVA growth for 2016–17 have not captured the impact of demonetization on unorganized sector. The revised estimates may show lower growth in both GDP and GVA for the year 2016–17.

The government recognizes the short-term hardships but banks on medium- to long-term benefits. One of the benefits is moving towards digitization and a cashless economy. Already, the use of digitization for monetary transactions has improved all over India. Another benefit would be increase in taxable income due to rise of funds in bank accounts. Government finances can improve with the increase in taxes on the disclosed income, which is presently unaccounted. This will be known only after scrutinizing bank deposits. The costs of funds for banks will decline with significant rise of deposits.

It may be noted, however, that cash is only one aspect of black economy. Most of the black money is in real estate, gold, foreign accounts, and manipulations in business expenditures. There are several estimates of black economy in India. They range from 25 per cent to 50 per cent of the GDP. Demonetization should be accompanied by several other measures such as reforms in electoral funding, changes in tax administration, reduction in stamp duties, elimination of discretion, police, legal, and other administrative reforms in order to reduce corruption and black economy. The *Economic Survey 2016–17* also discusses a number of follow-up actions needed to minimize the costs and maximize the benefits of demonetization.

POVERTY AND INEQUALITY IN THE POST-REFORM PERIOD

There are two conclusions on trends in poverty in pre- and post-reform period. First one is that a World Bank study by Datt, Ravallion, and Murugan (2016) shows that poverty declined by 1.36 percentage points per annum post 1991, as compared to that of 0.44 percentage points per annum prior to 1991. Their study shows that among other things, urban growth is the most important contributor to the rapid reduction in poverty even in rural areas in the post-1991 period.

Second is that within the post-reform period, poverty declined faster in the 2000s than in the 1990s. The official estimates based on the Tendulkar Committee poverty lines show that poverty declined only 0.74 percentage points per annum during 1993–94 to 2004–05. But, poverty declined by 2.2 percentage points per annum during 2004–05 to 2011–12 (Planning Commission [2013] based on Tendulkar Committee's estimates). Around 138 million people were lifted above the poverty line during this period. This indicates the success of reforms in reducing poverty. Poverty of scheduled castes (SCs) and scheduled tribes (STs) also declined faster in the 2000s. The Rangarajan Committee's report also showed faster reduction in poverty during 2009–10 to 2011–12. Higher economic growth, agriculture growth, rural nonfarm employment, increase in real wages for rural labourers, employment in construction, and social protection programmes contributed for higher poverty reduction in the 2000s, compared to the 1990s.

The evidence shows that inequality increased in the post-reform period. The Gini coefficient, measured in terms of consumption for rural, increased marginally from 0.29 in 1993–94 to 0.31 in 2011–12. There was a significant rise in the Gini coefficient for urban from 0.34 to 0.39 during the same period. However, consumption-based Gini underestimates inequalities. If we use income data from the India Human Development Survey of the National Council of Applied Economic Research (NCAER), the Gini coefficient in income (rural + urban) was 0.52 in 2004–05 and increased to 0.55 in 2011–12. In other words, inequality is much higher in India if we use income rather than consumption. If we consider non-income indicators such as health and education, inequalities between poor and rich are much higher.

AGRICULTURE: CAN WE DOUBLE THE FARM INCOMES?

There is a need for higher agricultural growth and increase in farmers' incomes. The government wants to double farm incomes by 2022. In Budget 2016–17, the finance minister said: 'Government will, therefore, reorient its interventions in the farm and non-farm sectors to double the incomes of the farmers by 2022' (Government of India, 2016–17).

Estimates on changes in farmers' income (farm and non-farm) for 2003 to 2013 (Table 1.1) shows the following. In nominal terms, incomes of the farmers tripled. In real terms, the total income increased only 34 per cent in 10 years. Only in the case of Odisha, farm incomes

Table 1.1 Farmers' Incomes in 2003 and 2013

| | Ratio of Real Monthly Income in 2013 over 2003 | | | | |
States	Wages	Cultivation	Animals	Non-farm	Total Income
Punjab	1.56	1.80	2.39	0.68	1.67
Haryana	1.20	1.85	–	0.57	1.93
U.P.	1.00	1.38	3.76	0.99	1.31
Bihar	1.28	0.80	0.44	0.55	0.83
West Bengal	1.18	0.62	1.44	0.76	0.91
Odisha	1.41	1.79	33.35	1.54	2.08
Chattisgarh	1.25	2.05	1.58	0.00	1.57
M.P.	1.17	1.48	–	0.59	1.75
Gujarat	1.34	1.18	1.84	1.30	1.36
Maharashtra	1.29	1.54	1.82	1.49	1.47
A.P.	1.59	1.56	3.61	1.07	1.64
Karnataka	1.27	1.66	1.92	1.49	1.52
Kerala	1.21	1.43	1.58	1.62	1.36
Tamil Nadu	1.24	1.16	3.93	2.43	1.48
All India	**1.22**	**1.32**	**3.21**	**1.00**	**1.34**

Source: Chandrasekhar and Mehrotra (2016).

doubled. On the other hand, in the case of Bihar and West Bengal, farm incomes declined. Income from cultivation rose only 32 per cent. If we consider income from cultivation and income from farming of animals together it increased by 49 per cent. It is difficult to double this value but not impossible. Income from animal sources and non-farm businesses has high potential and can enhance farmers' income. Therefore, apart from income from farms, the farmers also need non-farm income.

So, what are the drivers of rise in farmers' incomes? Farm income is the product of yields and prices. Both have to be increased along with rise in non-farm income. There are several drivers for rise in farm income (NITI Aayog, 2015). These are: (i) increase in yield or productivity through diversification with rise in high-value crops; animal husbandry and livestock; water efficiency with more crops per drop; new technologies; and efficiency in inputs such as seeds, fertilizers, and credit; (ii) rise in remunerative prices, such as minimum support prices and agricultural marketing; (iii) leasing and titling; (iv) crop insurance and (v) improving the productivity of small and marginal farmers.

A big push for agriculture is required. The distress in agriculture in the last two years is due to two factors: First, crash in the global commodity prices has affected the farmers. Second, there has been a deficit in rainfall for two years in a row—2013–14 and 2014–15—and ten states declared drought last year. These two factors have adversely affected farmers' incomes. Low agriculture growth also affects the prospects of manufacturing and services due to forward and backward linkages. For example, tractor sales have declined in response to lower farm income.

A two-pronged strategy is required for agriculture: (i) raising productivity and incomes of farmers and (ii) coping with risks due to climate change and crash in commodity prices. The following measures are needed to revive agriculture sector.

First, increase in productivity can be achieved through emphasis on investment in infrastructure such as irrigation, rural roads, and electricity. Public investment in rural infrastructure is crucial as private sector does not invest in it. The Pradhan Mantri Krishi Sinchai Yojana (PMKSY) introduced by the present government is in the right direction. There is a need for rise in funding for PMKSY and Rashtriya Krishi Vikas Yojana (RKVY). Apart from funding, water use efficiency has to be increased with better policies on watershed development, groundwater, and involvement of farmers in management of irrigation systems. Use of drip irrigation should be encouraged as it covers ten times the area covered under usual flood irrigation. Main strategy should be to increase water productivity, that is, 'more crops per drop of water'.

Second, climate resilient agriculture (CRA) is needed. To achieve this, three things are highlighted here:

1. There is a need for diversified cropping systems in view of climate related risks. For example, cultivation of pulses can be an important strategy for CRA. Pulses are legumes that improve soil fertility. India has a deficit in the production of pulses and imports from other countries. Thus, diversification to pulse cultivation can lead to a win-win situation in terms of attaining self-sufficiency and raising soil fertility. Year 2016 is the international year of pulses. Government should give incentives to cultivation of pulses, which are largely grown in rain-fed areas. Focus on pulses also reduces food inflation.

2. There is a need for crop insurance, which can be used as one of the policies for risk mitigation and as strategy for CRA. In this context, the recent introduction of Pradhan Mantri Fasal Bima Yojana (PMFBY) by the central government is in the right direction. One expects higher allocation of funds under PMFBY. There are many features in the new crop insurance scheme, which makes it different from earlier schemes. However, crop insurance has not succeeded in many countries. Lessons need to be learnt from these failures. The Mahatma Gandhi National Rural Employment Guarantee Act (MGNREGA) can be useful for asset creation and drought proofing. Studies have shown reduction in vulnerability due to implementation of MGNREGA works and resulted in environmental benefits.

3. The research and extension system is important for promoting CRA. Research leads to development of climate resilient technologies and extension system will promote these technologies among farmers. The research on adaptation and mitigation should cover crops, livestock, fisheries, and natural resource management. India should invest in research and extension in agriculture as technology improvement is crucial for enhancing productivity and conserving natural resources. Thus, investing in research and extension gives high returns.

Third, reforms in fertilizer subsidies are overdue. They should be directly given to farmers. Government should start fertilizer subsidy reforms. The funds thus saved can be provided for investment in infrastructure such as irrigation.

Fourth, there has been a consensus among economists and others on legalizing tenancy. Policy on land tenancy has to be announced. This will lead to access of land for rural population and also increase private investments in agriculture.

Fifth, remunerative prices and development of markets are important for raising the incomes of farmers. Government's idea of creating a national agricultural market, an online platform for selling agricultural produce, will help in better price for farmers. However, much more is needed on the marketing front using value chain approach to connect farmers to input and output markets.

Sixth, there is a need for strengthening of farmer producer organizations (FPOs). One issue is whether the small and marginal farmers are benefiting from FPOs. What are the lessons for FPOs from milk cooperatives? Incentives can be given to commodity-specific FPOs to develop value chains. For example, pulses FPO can be developed on a large scale.

Another issue is agricultural credit. Every year, government announces higher agricultural credit for farmers. Measures have to be taken to increase the formal credit to small and marginal farmers as an RBI committee found that their access to it was limited.

MAKE IN INDIA: FOCUS ON MANUFACTURING AND TRADE

Quality of employment improves with changes in structure of employment from less productive to more productive occupations and sectors. Quality increases with shift from casual workers in the informal sector to regular workers in the formal sector. Productive employment rises if workers in agriculture are shifted to the manufacturing sector.

In this context, the Make in India campaign is in the right direction. The aim is to create 100 million jobs by 2022. As shown by *India Employment Report 2016* (Ghose, 2016) labour-intensive manufacturing is important for quality job creation (particularly in the organized sector). However, there are two related issues: (i) whether employment can rise with manufacturing GDP growth and (ii) what about considering services with 60 per cent of share in GDP for creation of employment?

It is important to examine the prospects of manufacturing, particularly in job creation, in the light of the East Asian experience[2] and in the present context of global

[2] It is well-known that rapid growth of output, export, and employment from the manufacturing sector played a critical role in the economic transformation of East Asian countries.

stagnation. It can be argued here that one has to also include services in the Make in India programme for creation of employment.

Historical experience shows that countries follow agriculture-industry-service sequence in order to obtain higher growth and productive employment. Many East Asian countries including China could increase their manufacturing share in GDP. However, the share of manufacturing employment in China is low (Table 1.2). Japan had peaked share in manufacturing in GDP (36 per cent) and employment (27 per cent) by 1970. In Taiwan, the share of this sector in GDP (33.3 per cent) and employment (32 per cent) peaked by 1990. Similarly Korea has slightly lower share and peaked by 2000. In the case of China, the share of manufacturing in GDP is around 33 per cent now but its share in employment is only 16 per cent.

What are the reasons for low share of the manufacturing sector in employment in China? Early industrializing countries, such as Japan, Korea, and Taiwan, could improve the share in employment. But late industrialization in China, Indonesia, and Thailand resulted rise in share of manufacturing in GDP but not in employment. Employment in manufacturing today is not quite comparable to employment in manufacturing in earlier times. The reason is that manufacturing enterprises used to directly employ staff for a variety of services required but now they outsource them from service enterprises. In other words, employment that counted as manufacturing employment now counts as services employment. To put it another way, manufacturing today generates less direct employment but more indirect employment in services (Ghose, 2015). Employment growth is much more difficult than GDP growth in manufacturing. In India, this sector has been capital intensive.

Table 1.2   Peak Share in Manufacturing Sector in GDP and Employment (Percentage)

Country	Period	GDP	Employment
Japan	1970	36.0	27.0
South Korea	2000	29.0	23.3
Taiwan	1990	33.3	32.0
China	2005	32.5	15.9
Indonesia	2004	28.1	11.8
Thailand	2007	35.6	15.1
India	2011–12	15.7	12.8

Source: NSS (2014) for data on India; Ghose (2015) for the rest of the countries.

Table 1.3   Share of Services in GDP and Employment, 2013
(Percentage)

Country	GDP	Employment
USA	78.6	81.2
Germany	68.4	70.2
France	78.5	74.9
UK	79.2	78.9
Brazil	69.4	62.7
China	46.1	35.7
Japan	72.4	69.7
South Korea	59.1	76.4
India	58.4	26.7

Source: Government of India (2014–15).

Table 1.3 provides the share of services in East Asia and India. Countries, such as Japan, Korea, and Taiwan, have 60 per cent to 80 per cent share of services in both GDP and employment. On the other hand, China, Indonesia and Thailand have around 35 to 45 per cent share of services in both GDP and employment. In all these East Asian countries, the share of services in both GDP and employment are more or less similar. India is an exception to this trend. The country has high share of services in GDP but the share of services in employment is exceptionally low as shown in the Table 1.3. India's share of services in employment is only 26.4 per cent compared to 58.4 per cent share of services in GDP. Thus service sector in India presently is not employment intensive. At the same time, manufacturing sector has low share in GDP (17 per cent) and employment (12.8 per cent). Therefore, the challenges are to raise both GDP and employment growth for manufacturing and employment growth in services.

It may be noted, however, that services generate less employment opportunities for the low skilled. On the other hand, manufacturing can generate substantial employment opportunities for the unskilled workers.

There is hardly any disagreement on the fact that India needs to aim at higher growth of productive employment and decent work, and that the manufacturing sector is critical to growth. Constraints that prevent manufacturing growth need to be addressed in cooperation with states; for example, we need investment, physical infrastructure, skill development, land acquisition, and ease of doing business. Small and medium enterprises (SMEs) and micro, small, and medium enterprises (MSMEs) account for 95 per cent of the total industrial activity in India and can play vital role in boosting employment generation. Estimates suggest that the SME–MSME sector offers maximum opportunities for self-employment jobs after the agriculture sector.

Second, the service sector also need to be promoted as both manufacturing and services are complementary. The indirect employment from manufacturing is created in India cannot ignore services which contributes 60 per cent of GDP.

India has the potential to increase the number of workers in manufacturing and the contribution to the sector for overall growth. But its future development path is unlikely to mimic the one witnessed in East Asia as in Japan, Taiwan, or even in China. Some lessons can be learnt from East Asia. However, India has to forge its own path that will rely on both manufacturing and services as growth engines.

This year's *India Development Report* is divided into two parts. Part I (Chapter 2 to 10) examines issues and policies in macroeconomic, agriculture, and social sectors. Part II (Chapter 11 to 15) is specifically devoted for trade and industry. The overview of both the parts is given in the following sections.

PART I: EMERGING ISSUES IN MACROECONOMICS, AGRICULTURE, AND SOCIAL SECTOR

Macroeconomic Overview

In Chapter 2, Manoj Panda provides an overview of developments on the macroeconomic front in the Indian economy from a medium-term perspective and discusses some of the problem areas that need policy attention. On the whole, the exponential trend growth rate in GDP has been 7 per cent during the 25 years since reform 1991–92 to 2015–16 as against a trend rate of 4 per cent over the quarter century prior to the reforms 1966–67 to 1990–91. India has potential to attain a long term growth rate of 7–8 per cent, though there might be some medium-term fluctuations depending on exogenous factors. While growth in the near future would continue to be service driven, agriculture and industry must grow at higher rates in order to avoid bottlenecks of one type or another.

According to Panda, two short-run problems that policymakers need to address relate to reduced rate of investment rate and decline in exports. Stressed assets of the banking sector may need to be restructured through a new mechanism such as an asset reconstruction company. Banks may also be allowed to convert unpaid loans to equity. For promoting export, a medium-run strategy of exploring new markets and entering into new trade arrangements must be explored so that India can effectively penetrate the global value chain. While employment creation is a sustainable way of removing poverty and improving level of living, attaining full employment may not be a feasible target with rising capital intensity, even in traditionally employment-intensive sectors such as textiles and leather. Some form of social security will then be a necessary ingredient for sustainable growth.

Monetary Policy Transmission

India has deepened money markets in the new century, and formally adopted flexible inflation forecast targeting in 2015. The Central Bank's (CB's) operating target is now a short-term money market rate, the call money rate, and its primary final target is inflation. This follows similar evolution of monetary procedures in many countries. In Chapter 3, Ashima Goyal analyses monetary policy transmission, and assesses its effectiveness in an emerging market like India.

The issue can be broken down into the following: First, how does the repo rate at which the RBI lends in the money market affect the short rate, and then how are the whole range of financial market interest rates, including bank lending rates, affected? Second, how do all these changes affect growth and inflation? The evaluation finds that monetary policy transmission through the structure of interest rates is adequate, although steady improvements are required. The call money rate has closely tracked the repo rate in recent months. The RBI's liquidity response to exogenous liquidity shocks had begun to work, but a longer successful track record is required to establish it. While the transmission to financial interest rates works reasonably, that through bank rates is incomplete and slow. While this is so even in advanced economies, structural restrictions that make for inefficiencies are being reduced as financial repression falls, and by giving banks greater freedom and flexibilities.

Questions remain about how effective transmission channels can be in a country with many features of underdevelopment. Conventional aggregate demand channels may not work well, but CB's actions and communication, which affect inflation and exchange rate expectations, hold more promise. With respect to transmission to the real sector, the real interest rate has a significant impact on aggregate demand and output, while cost push from the exchange rate affects inflation. The continued dominance of supply shocks on inflation suggests that inflation targeting will need to be flexible, but combined with supply-side action from the government, can successfully guide inflation expectations downwards, at minimal output cost. If the government acts on food supply, infrastructure bottlenecks, and generally reduces transaction costs, inflation targeting can reduce inflation expectations. The expectations channel of monetary transmission is likely to be the most effective. Risk proofing against external shocks has improved in India with better fundamentals and continuation on a path of cautious market liberalization. This may protect the transmission of monetary policy from external disruptions and help it better match the needs of the domestic cycle.

New National Accounts Series and GDP Estimation

In January 2015, the CSO brought out the new series of National Accounts Statistics (NAS) with 2011–12 as the base year, replacing the earlier series which had 2004–05 as the base year. Apart from changing the base year, consistent with the most recent international guidelines, the CSO has introduced some major changes in the underlying methodology of estimating GDP and related numbers. These changes have led to major revisions in GDP growth estimation, as also in a number of other related ratios and proportions. For example, according to the new series, economic growth for 2013–14 at constant prices stood at 6.2 per cent compared to 4.8 per cent as per the old series. The industry share in GVA has gone up, while that of services has fallen, and the domestic saving and capital formation rates have gone up.

Chapter 4, authored by J. Dennis Rajakumar and S.L. Shetty, brings out the nature of changes that have occurred in the NAS new series and highlights the key issues in the debate. While appreciating the improvements made by the CSO in terms of the methodology and datasets used for GDP estimation, the authors raise certain questions. They note that contrary to the earlier revisions of 2004–05, the latest visions at the aggregate level, namely GDP/NDP/GNP/NNP[3] measures, in the 2011–12 series have shown absolute declines over the 2004–05 series levels; the 2004–05 estimates of these measures had shown consistently upward revisions over the 1999–2000 estimates. As for the revision at the sectoral level, vastly higher upward revisions are noticed in all the four secondary sector categories in the 2011–12 series compared with the somewhat moderate positive revisions in the 2004–05 series over the 1999–2000 series. The service sector categories, on the other hand,

---

[3] NDP refers to net domestic product; GNP refers to gross national product; and NNP refers to net national product.

have shown significant downward revisions in the latest series.

Despite these differences in levels, the growth rates are uniformly higher in the 2011–12 series as compared with the growth rates revealed in the 2004–05 revisions. This has been so whether at the aggregate level or at the sectoral levels. Even so, the sectoral shares of GDP have changed noticeably. In the 2004–05 revisions, shares of agriculture and industry had fallen; contrariwise, in the latest revision, the shares of these sectors have increased significantly, at the cost of service sector. The gain in secondary sector share and the loss in the service sector share are broadly rooted in the methodology of applying the enterprise approach for the first time and also the application of a more refined 'effective labour input method' for the informal sectors.

Another major difference between the 2004–05 and 2011–12 revisions relates to savings and capital formation by institutional categories. Unlike the 2004–05 revision, the latest revision has produced highly scaled-up estimates of both savings and capital formation in respect of the private corporate sector, which is again related to the radical changes in the data sources referred to above.

The chapter raises a number of questions related to methodology and data: (i) tenability of using GDP at market prices for measuring growth and not GDP at factor cost or GDP at basic prices—the former with large indirect tax components and the latter being historically recognized as important for distributional issues like factor shares; (ii) problems associated with differing use of deflators; and (iii) the method of working out growth rate based on the unrelated reference estimates giving rise to untenable and inflated growth rates.

A radical change introduced in the 2011–12 series in the database relates to the use of corporate sector data based on MCA21, particularly for the manufacturing sector, which has made it possible to shift to the enterprise approach as distinguished from establishment approach.[4] While the level of manufacturing output would be higher because of the coverage of head office contributions to output, Rajakumar and Shetty raise an important question: is it necessary that the growth rates should get accelerated from year to year?

---

[4] With effect from 2010–11, the Ministry of Corporate Affairs (MCA) undertook a major step, to implement an e-Governance programme, popularly known as MCA21, whereby registered companies were required to submit their returns online. The MCA has the objective of covering all registered companies under the programme by 2021.

Diet Diversity, Malnutrition, and Women's Empowerment

Despite India being one of the fastest growing economies in the world, high prevalence of malnutrition in the country, particularly among children and women, is still a great concern. While economic research on nutritional issues in India often focuses mainly on calorie intake, nutritionists are deeply concerned about a range of micro-nutritional deficiencies, including those of essential minerals and vitamins. It is reported that micro-nutrient deficiencies are severe among the children. It is expected that dietary diversification would improve nutritional status of the households. Transformation of agriculture from a cereal-driven to a non-cereal-driven growth is an important feature of the Indian economy since the the the early 2000s. This pattern is reflected in the consumption pattern also. With increasing income, household preferences shift from cereals towards non-cereals and non-grain products. What are the implications of this transition on nutritional outcome?

Some studies have documented that agricultural growth could play a significant role in nutritional outcome only in the early stages; and after a point when the prevalence rate declines, it is argued that malnutrition would be less responsive to growth and hence diversification to non-agriculture is needed for further reduction in malnutrition. If this is true, why is India performing poorly on the nutritional front in spite of faster growth in non-agricultural sector? This is still unresolved.

In Chapter 5, G. Mythili attempts to project consumption and nutritional outcome for the year 2020 under alternative growth scenario using computable general equilibrium (CGE) analysis. The results are expected to provide useful policy directions for improving nutritional intake of poor households. Mythili considers five alternative scenarios, where growth is driven by (i) agriculture; (ii) cereal; (iii) non-cereal crops; (iv) allied agriculture; and (v) non-agriculture. The database for the analysis is the social accounting matrix (SAM) for the year 2007 which was first projected to 2010. The year 2010 has been kept as the base year to project results for 2020 in real terms. The study projects the results for macro-nutrients such as calorie, protein, and fat, and micro-nutrients such as minerals, calcium and iron.

The results indicates that the impressive growth of allied sector, as witnessed in recent years, holds promise for rural sector as the growth driven by this sector improves the intake of nutrients by rural poor population by about 0.5 percentage point to 1 percentage point above the business-as-usual scenario. However for urban poor, it is cereal-driven growth which is more important for enhancing nutrient intake. Specific targeted programmes and implementation of such policies play a key role in achieving target nutrition for the urban poor.

A number of studies show that maternal health, nutritional knowledge, sanitation, and childcare practices are important for nutritional outcomes of children. Women being the primary caregivers of children are central to the decision related to children's nutrition. Women's empowerment has the potential to increase productivity, achieve food security, reduce hunger and improve nutritional outcomes for both children and women. Nearly 77 per cent of the total rural women workforce mostly depends on agriculture. While there is a significant decrease in the percentage of women working as cultivators among the total women workers (33 per cent in 2001 to 24 per cent in 2011), the percentage of women working as agricultural labourers has increased from 39 per cent in 2001 to 41 per cent in 2011 (Census of India, 2011).

Against this backdrop, in Chapter 6, S. Mahendra Dev, Vijay Laxmi Pandey, and D. Suganthi analyse the extent of women's empowerment in agriculture and its effect on household diet diversity for rural Bihar, Jharkhand, and Odisha. They use the data collected under the study, titled Village Dynamics in South Asia (VDSA). The study reveals that in general women's empowerment is low and disempowerment of women is more prominent in Bihar as compared to Jharkhand and Odisha. The results show that the dimensions in which women are disempowered mostly pertained to access to resources, access to assets, decision-making authority over the income, and poor participation in group activities. Nevertheless, the intensity of empowerment varies across the dimensions. Hence, there is a need for targeted policies to reduce gender gap and enhance women's empowerment.

The analysis by Dev, Pandey, and Suganthi in this chapter clearly shows that household diet diversity is significantly and positively affected by gender parity gap, operational landholdings, and possession of number of milch animals. Reduction in income inadequacy for women significantly improves the household diet diversity. From a public policy perspective, labour-saving technologies, livestock development, training, and extension interventions should be targeted towards women. Empowerment of women is a complex dynamic process. Hence, constant efforts are necessary to achieve gender parity and empowerment of women for improved nutritional outcomes.

Agricultural Diversification

Indian agriculture has witnessed dramatic change in the composition of output produced. The production basket has diversified from staples, fibres, spices, and plantation crops to include fruits, vegetables, floriculture, dairy, poultry, meats, fishery, among others. Diversification at the pan-India level, however, masks substantial variations across states. Past studies on agriculture diversification ignore the role of geography and spatial spillovers in influencing diversification across states. In Chapter 7, Tirtha Chatterjee and A. Ganesh-Kumar argue that neighbouring states may interact with each other in several ways; for example, through common agro-climatic factors, river basins and their associated surface irrigation networks, interstate road and rail connectivity, urbanization and marketing avenues that they provide, trade and telecommunication networks, technological spillovers, and labour migration.

Chatterjee and Ganesh-Kumar examine spatial dimensions of agricultural diversification and its determinants for 17 major states in India over the period 1990 to 2010. The analysis provides evidence in favour of wide spatial variation in the extent of diversification across states. States like Andhra Pradesh, Gujarat, Maharashtra, Kerala, Tamil Nadu, Uttar Pradesh, and West Bengal show greater diversification with respect to all India, while Haryana and Punjab show significant concentration.

Using spatial econometric techniques and tests of spatial dependence, they find evidence of significant local spatial dependence across states, except for the states in eastern parts of India. The main channels of spatial spill over are relative prices of horticulture commodities and average daily wage rates of agricultural labour. Therefore, market institutions that affect price formation and degree of market integration across states are critical in affecting agricultural diversification across states. Market integration is perhaps lowest in eastern parts of India and this could be a constraint to their growth. State-specific factors influencing positively on diversification include urbanization, population density, groundwater, and relative price of horticulture, while rainfall deviation from the normal, and wage rate have a significant negative impact.

Education

The importance of education for improving household welfare as well as for promoting economic growth is well understood. Although there has been significant improvement in terms of average years of schooling,

India is falling short of many targets it has set for itself in the area of education. In particular, India is off the track on the target to achieve universal enrolment and completion of primary education. The quality of education is also a major concern. Low primary completion rate may hinder the achievement of sustainable development goal (SDG) of universal secondary enrolment.

In Chapter 8, Abhiroop Mukhopadhyay provides a description of the major trends in the field of education in India. He decomposes human capital into the achievements of various levels of education (literacy, primary, tertiary) by India's adult population and describes how these achievements have changed since the early 1970s. He also provides a state- and district-level analysis of the tertiary education achievement during 2001–2011.

Mukhopadhyay points out that the growth rate of national income is largely affected by the share of tertiary-educated population which works in the service sector. This creates a disconnect between how human capital is evolving and the sectoral composition of India's growth process. One strategy to take full advantage of the mass of school-educated adult population is to kick-start the manufacturing sector, which can take advantage of this population with some basic literacy. If human capital is left to evolve as is dictated by history, then what it will add to the process of economic development will be very little in the medium run. And while overall spatial inequalities may lessen in the long run, this will still leave the worst performing districts lagging way behind. Hence a multi-pronged educational policy intervention is called for, one which goes beyond just giving children the 'right to education'. Perhaps an emphasis on the 'right' education is also called for.

International development goals focus mainly on children's education, and relatively lay less stress on the education of adults. The linkage between adult education and the skill level of labour force is well recognized as a crucial factor determining the overall economic performance of a country. In Chapter 9, Runu Bhakta and A. Ganesh-Kumar take stock of the trends and determinants of adult education in terms of adult literacy rate, percentage of adult population that has completed higher education, and average years of schooling. Further, they examine the trends in the composition of labour supply (in terms of their levels of education attainment and their sectors of employment) and the linkage between adult education attainment and the composition of labour supply.

Using econometric analysis, Bhakta and Ganesh-Kumar project the expected future trends in the composition of labour supply by education levels up to the year 2025–26, under alternative scenarios. Their projections suggest that (i) under all scenarios, the percentage of high-schooled adults and those who completed graduation and above in the labour force would rise; (ii) the illiterate and primary-schooled labour force would shrink in absolute size; and (iii) increasing public expenditure on education (higher education in particular) does help in accelerating the supply of labour with high-school education and above.

Job Security

Jobs with social security forms the basis for achieving 'decent work for all', a key SDG adopted by the United Nations (UN). Using the data of the National Sample Survey Office (NSSO), in Chapter 10, Karthikeya Naraparaju and Ajay Sharma look at the extent of compliance with an important labour regulation in India pertaining to workers' social security: the Employees Provident Fund and Miscellaneous Provisions Act, 1952 (or the EPF Act). Under this regulation, establishments employing 20 or more workers are mandated to provide contributions towards the provident fund of those employees whose wages are below a certain threshold.

Estimates by Naraparaju and Sharma suggest that the evasion of the EPF Act is quite widespread: in 2011–12, 75 per cent (6.6 million) of regular salaried employees earning wages below the threshold and working in establishments employing 20 or more workers have reported to be not receiving provident fund benefits. This has increased sharply from 46 per cent (4.5 million) in 2004–05. These individuals constitute about 10 per cent of the total workforce employed in regular salaried jobs, in the respective years. The authors note that lack of written job contracts is an important correlate of non-compliance with the act.

PART II: SECTOR FOCUS—INDUSTRY, TRADE, AND PREPAREDNESS FOR MAKE IN INDIA

Recognizing the importance of a strong manufacturing sector for employment generation, the current prime minister, Narendra Modi, has recently launched the Make in India campaign with an aim to boost India's manufacturing sector. This campaign aims to transform India as a manufacturing powerhouse by promoting exports, encouraging FDI, improving industrial productivity, and by lowering the barriers to doing business. In this context, some of the pertinent questions are: (i) What are the industries which hold the greatest potential for growth and employment generation? (ii) Where in India will things be made under the new policy direction? (iii) What type of linkages exist between manufacturing and service sectors? (iv) What type of institutions and policies should be created as preconditions for manufacturing growth? The chapters in Part II deal with these questions.

As to the question 'make what in India', in Chapter 11, C. Veeramani and Garima Dhir argue that there are two groups of industries that hold the greatest potential for export growth and employment generation. First, given India's comparative advantage in labour-intensive activities, there exists a huge unexploited export potential in traditional unskilled labour-intensive manufactured products such as textiles, clothing, footwear, and toys. Second, based on imported parts and components, India has a huge potential to emerge as a major hub for the final assembly of a range of products (particularly for electronics and electrical machinery), where the manufacturing process is internationally fragmented and is mainly controlled by multinational enterprises (MNEs) within their global production networks (GPNs).

In certain industries, such as electronics and automobiles, technology makes it possible to sub-divide the production process into discrete stages. In such industries, the fragmentation of production process into smaller and more specialized components allows firms to locate parts of production in countries where intensively used resources are available at lower costs. This geographic splintering of production gives rise to fragmentation-based trade. Labour-abundant countries ('factory economies') like China tend to specialize in low-skilled, labour-intensive activities involved in the production of a final good while the capital and skill-intensive activities are being carried out in countries where those factors are abundant ('headquarter economies'). Thus, international firms might retain skill and knowledge-intensive stages of production (such as research and development [R&D] and marketing) in the high-income headquarters (such as the USA, the European Union [EU] and Japan) but locate all or parts of their production in a low-wage country (such as China, Vietnam, and India).

Although the development of production networks is widespread, their growth in East Asia and China has been particularly impressive. However, India has been locked out of the vertically integrated global and regional supply chains in manufacturing industries. With the increasing wage costs, Chinese firms in the labour-intensive industries are increasingly under pressure and have started looking for other low-cost locations. An important question in this context is: can India become the next workshop of the world? Based on detailed

empirical analyses, Veeramani and Dhir identify a number of specific product categories for which India can emerge as a major hub for final assembly-related activities. At the same time, being a large country with varied resource endowments and skill sets, India has the potential to export a diversified set of parts and components.

Greater integration of domestic industries with global production networks must form an essential part of the Make in India initiative. What is important is the creation of an environment that allows entrepreneurs to freely search and identify opportunities in the vertically integrated global supply chains of various industries. A low level of service link cost—that is, cost related to transportation, communication, and other related tasks involved in coordinating the activity in a given country with what is done in other countries within the production network—is critical for countries to participate in GPNs. Therefore, the policy should focus on reducing India's high service link costs with other countries within the production network. While India has a potential to emerge as a major hub for the final assembly for several industries, it is important to resist the temptation of extending tariff protection for final goods assembly as it will have the detrimental effect of breeding inefficiencies.

Services constitute an integral part of the production and delivery process in the manufacturing sector, from R&D in the initial stages; to transport and distribution following the production stage; to retailing, repair, and maintenance in the final stages, while services such as telecommunications and finance are required at every stage. In the context of India's Make in India initiative and the recent focus on Indian manufacturing, an understanding of these linkages assumes importance. Chapter 12, by Rupa Chanda, is motivated by the need to understand this interdependence between services and manufacturing exports in India. This chapter provides a brief review of the evidence on services as enablers in manufacturing output as well as trade. Next, it discusses the directly visible as well as the invisible, embedded role of services in the Indian economy, through its value-added contribution in manufacturing exports in particular. Chanda shows that the value-added contribution of the service sector to India's gross exports was close to 50 per cent in 2011, significantly greater than the share of services exports in total exports based on balance of payments (BoP) and much greater than in other emerging countries, with modern services contributing more than traditional segments.

Another issue that this chapter deals with is the sub-sectoral nature of the linkage between selected services in India and overall manufacturing exports as well as exports in specific manufacturing segments which are critical for Make in India. The analysis reveals that domestically generated manufacturing content in India's manufacturing exports is low while the contribution of the service sector to overall manufacturing exports is dominated by traditional services. Chanda outlines some key features of the observed trends, that is, the fact that globally competitive segments, such as information technology (IT) services, are not contributing in any significant way to India's manufacturing exports and the very low contribution of R&D and business services to India's manufacturing exports. Overall, the main insight that emerges is that there is potential to create value in India's exports through the integration of services. The unexploited potential may be due to constraints in the manufacturing sector which hinder its ability to draw upon the service sector as well as challenges affecting the service sector, in terms of capacity, quality, regulation, and degree of liberalization and modernization.

The chapter concludes that as India embarks on a range of initiatives to boost its manufacturing sector, a singular focus on manufacturing alone would not be appropriate. Any holistic policy framework must recognize the interdependence between manufacturing and other sectors of the economy. There is scope to increase services content in Indian manufacturing output and exports, but this will require the government to focus on increasing efficiency in India's service sector as an input to the manufacturing sector. A competitive and vibrant service sector should be seen as an enabler for the manufacturing sector and not as a competitor to manufacturing. Such a philosophy should underpin any initiative to bolster Indian manufacturing.

The manufacturing sector consists of a number of disparate industries. One way of grouping them is in terms of their respective employment content and another way is to group them according to their technology content. Although the manufacturing sector in most developing countries are supposed to be dominated by labour-intensive or low-technology industries, Sunil Mani (Chapter 13) argues that there is a need to recognize the importance of high-technology industries.

Given the capital-intensive nature of production, use of proprietary technology, high failure rates, the role of the state in high technology production is very well accepted. There are at least three ways in which the state intervenes in high technology sector. The first mode is a direct one in which the state establishes a state-owned enterprise which then manufactures the high technology product. The second mode is for the state to establish a public R&D programme either exclusively or in partnership with the market, develop the high technology and then transfer it to production enterprises whether owned by the state or by the private sector. The third mode is for the state to craft the ecosystem for high-technology production by having explicit policies and instruments for this to be developed by both public and private sector enterprises. Most industrializing countries such as India have used all the three modes. The first two modes were very popular in the pre-liberalization phase while the third mode is the preferred one in the post-liberalization phase that is characterized by a paring down of state intervention in economic activities.

Mani argues that each high-technology industry requires a specific policy that is crucial for its sustained growth. In short, one size rarely fits all. For example, the most important instrument for the promotion of aerospace industry is public technology procurement, which manifests itself in the form of an offset policy. Such a policy assures a certain amount of demand for the new product, which encourages the manufacturers to be venturesome. On the contrary, for the pharmaceutical industry, the most important policy is the one related to patents. However, a policy for financing R&D and policies on increasing the quantity and quality of science and engineering human resource is important for both the industries. Mani refers to the former set of specific policies as vertical policies (VPs) and the latter set as horizontal policies (HPs). The study proposes to verify the hypothesis of the crucial importance of VPs by taking three successful cases (aerospace, pharmaceutical, and automotive) and one unsuccessful case (telecommunications equipment) from India's manufacturing sector.

In Chapter 14, Sanjoy Chakravorty provides an evaluation of the Make in India initiative from a spatial perspective. The key question being addressed is: where in India will things be made under the new policy direction? In general, a growth-oriented strategy should seek to maximize the comparative advantage of regions. But such a strategy will almost inevitably increase regional inequality. The questions then are twofold: First, is the Make in India initiative built upon good spatial principles that will maximize growth? Second, what are the likely outcomes for comparative regional development? Since there is no evidence yet on the effects of the initiative, this chapter is based on theory from economic geography and the history and effects of past policies.

Chakravorty argues that the Make in India initiative is based on a relatively clear spatial strategy—perhaps the core of the initiative is its spatial strategy. This is rather radical because almost all past industrial policies in India had little or no spatial vision. Make in India focuses primarily on 'industrial corridors' (loosely tied to the smart cities initiative), and secondarily, in fact, rather incoherently, on 'manufacturing clusters'. The initiative pays serious attention to transportation costs but not to external or agglomeration economies. As a result, in some key sectors, especially those that rely on internal scale economies and seek reduced transportation costs, the Make in India initiative has the potential to succeed.

The increasing demand for things (especially for cars and other durable goods) by a rapidly growing and more prosperous population should boost manufacturing in India with or without the Make in India initiative. However, there are serious challenges. Many of these challenges are inherited (such as rising regional inequality, capital-intensity in a labour-abundant society, and distrust of large cities), some are relatively new (such as land acquisition in booming land markets), while others arise from the design of the initiative, especially the overreliance on scale economies and lack of understanding of agglomeration economies. Chakravorty makes two recommendations: First is to 'think small in large'—that is, give serious attention to the potential of the clustering of small firms in large cities (as opposed to enticing large firms to small cities); for example, the textiles, garments, leather, and other small- to medium-scale labour-intensive sectors. Second is to 'innovate for the isolated', especially by focusing on the leading districts in lagging regions (as opposed to the lagging districts in lagging regions). These two approaches are likely to strengthen the second generation of Make in India reforms.

Chapter 15 by Rajeswari Sengupta, Anjali Sharma, and Susan Thomas deals with recent developments with respect to insolvency and bankruptcy law. This law lays down a process by which firms in financial distress can seek a resolution or an exit. The streamlining of procedures, simplification of the insolvency process, and fast-tracking of recovery will have a positive effect on ease of doing business in India. The law is critical for the success of the Make in India initiative as it allows investors to exit from failing investments in a time-bound manner and without needing to freeze funds in long-drawn legal battles. However, Indian framework for corporate insolvency resolution had been fraught with deficiencies in the laws, their procedures, and their implementation, as well as in the capacity and capability of the institutions supporting them. The absence of a coherent and effective mechanism for resolving corporate insolvency has resulted in poor economic and legal outcomes.

Sengupta, Sharma, and Thomas present a brief description of the Insolvency and Bankruptcy Code (IBC), 2016, which is the most recent policy initiative in this field. They argue that this is a clean, modern law that offers a simple, coherent answer to the insolvency resolution problems under the current Indian conditions. The IBC 2016 is different from the labyrinth of extant Indian laws dealing with corporate insolvency, both in principle and in the design of the resolution framework. It is a single, consolidated code for insolvency resolution of all entities unlike the existing laws, such as the Companies Act, 1956, or Sick Industrial Companies (Special Provisions) Act (SICA), 1985, or Securitisation and Reconstruction of Financial Assets and Enforcement of Security Interest Act (SARFAESI Act), 2002, that apply selectively to a certain group of debtors and creditors. Once implemented, the IBC 2016 will supersede all existing legislation pertaining to the insolvency and bankruptcy of firms as well as individuals. The IBC 2016 seeks to achieve the objectives of low time for resolution, higher recovery rate, and higher levels of debt financing across diverse sources. It can potentially change not only the manner in which insolvency is resolved in India, but also the entire credit landscape in the country.

REFERENCES

Ahluwalia, Montek S. 2002. 'Economic Reforms in India Since 1991: Has Gradualism Worked?' *Journal of Economic Perspectives* 16(3): 67–88.

Datt, G., M. Ravallion, and R. Murugan. 2016. 'Growth, Urbanization and Poverty Reduction in India.' Policy Research Working Paper No. WPS7568, World Bank, Washington, DC.

Chandrasekhar, S., and N. Mehrotra. 2016. 'Doubling Farmers' Incomes by 2022.' *Economic and Political Weekly*, 51(18).

The Economist, 'The Global Economy Enjoys a Synchronised Upswing.' 18–24 March, pp. 20–22. Available at http://www.economist.com/news/leaders/21718868-past-decade-has-been-marked-series-false-economic-dawns-time-really-does-feel (accessed on 5 July 2017).

Government of India. 2014–15. *Economic Survey of India 2014–15*. Ministry of Finance.

———. 2016–17. *Economic Survey of India 2016–17*. Ministry of Finance.

———. 2017–18. *Union Budget, 2017–18*. Ministry of Finance, Government of India. Available at http://indiabudget.nic.in/ (accessed on 5 July 2017).

Ghose, Ajit K. 2015. 'Services-led Growth and Employment in India.' In *Labour, Employment and Economic Growth in India*, edited by K. Ramaswamy. New Delhi: Cambridge University Press.

———. 2016. *India Employment Report*. New Delhi: Institute for Human Development.

NSS. 2014. 'Employment and Unemployment Situation in India 2011–12'. NSS Report No. 554., National Sample Survey Office, Ministry of Statistics and Programme Implementation, Government of India.

Planning Commission of India. 2013. 'Press Note on Poverty Estimates 2011–12'. Government of India.

Reserve Bank of India (RBI). 2016. 'Fifth Bi-monthly Monetary Policy Statement, 2016–17'. Mumbai.

RBI. 2017. 'First Bi-monthly Monetary Policy Statement, 2017–18'. Resolution of the Monetary Policy Committee (MPC), Mumbai.

———. 'Monetary Policy Report—April 2017'. Available at https://rbi.org.in/Scripts/PublicationsView.aspx?id=17454 (accessed on 5 July 2017).

PART I
EMERGING ISSUES IN MACROECONOMICS, AGRICULTURE, AND SOCIAL SECTOR

2

Macroeconomic Scenario and Policy Options

*Manoj Panda**

INTRODUCTION

The high growth phase of 8 to 10 per cent recorded in India's national income during 2003–10 has not continued and the earlier anticipation that the economy may again witness a similar high growth phase stands revised downwards. Yet, the overall growth performance of the Indian economy is judged as among the best on a comparative scale across nations in a global environment of economic slowdown. It is being perceived that a potential growth rate of 7 to 8 per cent in gross domestic product (GDP) may be considered as a new normal for India in the medium term. It is possible to realize this potential provided adequate policy measures are adopted in the right direction.

The formation of a new government at the centre with a huge mandate in the mid-2014 election presented a historic opportunity for introducing another generation of economic reforms. Prime Minister Modi has introduced several programmes for the revival of the economy and enhancement of the welfare of the various sections of the population. Such programmes include Make in India, Start-up India, and programmes related to skill development, sanitation, and digitization, among others. His focus on development and spread of entrepreneurial ability of the people has been viewed by many as a

welcome move contributing to long-run sustainability of growth. The government has tried to redesign the institutional architecture in certain spheres. The NITI Aayog has been set up as the think tank of the government for formulating major policy initiatives. The Insolvency and Bankruptcy Code passed by the Parliament is another welcome move providing a framework for time-bound resolution of insolvency of corporates, individuals, and partnership entities. The Reserve Bank of India (RBI) has been mandated to keep inflation within the targeted range and is being assisted by a Monetary Policy Committee to determine the bank's policy rate.

The international economic environment continues to remain vulnerable. Although there are signs of recovery, the global economic slowdown that started with the financial crisis in 2008 has persisted even after eight years. India's GDP[1] in US dollar terms stood at close

---

* The author is thankful to Jyoti Sharma for help in preparing tables and figures.

[1] GDP is the total value of goods and services produced for final use in a country. Although per capita GDP continues to be the single best indicator of level of living in a nation, it is nevertheless a poor indicator of social progress and should be supplemented by other indicators in the sphere of health, education, and environment.

to 2.1 trillion in 2015. Its per capita income at $1,600 is considerably lower than that of other big emerging economies like Brazil, China, Russia, and South Africa whose per capita income stood at about $7,900, $8,500, $9,200, and $6,700 respectively. When adjusted for purchasing power parity[2] (PPP), India's per capita income is about PPP $4,000, but the relative ranking of India among BRICS remains the same. The BRICS countries, which were considered to have possessed huge growth potential before the global crisis in 2008, are struggling to come out of the crisis. The next generation in India aspires to have a better level of living in the coming decades. In order to meet the current global average of $10,000 over the next three decades, it needs to grow at 7 to 8 per cent per year. The government needs to sustain infrastructure and social investment and maintain a policy framework that encourages private investment along with productivity growth.

Against this backdrop, this chapter attempts a review of macroeconomic developments in the Indian economy from a medium-term perspective. The section 'Macroeconomic Developments' documents the major developments in the economy in recent years. The section 'Assessment' makes an assessment of the growth process and discusses certain policy issues for possible action. The final section makes some concluding remarks.

[2] PPP estimates adjust the market price-based nominal dollar estimates by taking into account differences in cost of living and reflects standard of living across countries on a comparable basis.

MACROECONOMIC DEVELOPMENTS

GDP Growth

Figure 2.1 depicts the GDP growth in the Indian economy on a five-yearly average basis[3] during the last 65 years. Since the average growth rate depends on the specific time period chosen, we have depicted a moving average series to get a full picture during the period 1951–52 to 2015–16. The value shown against a particular year gives the average of five years ending against the year shown. The average growth rates fluctuated around 4 per cent before mid-1980s and occasionally touched 5 per cent only to return to the average soon after. It did go up to 5–6 per cent during the second half of the 1980s supported by an aggressive fiscal policy and mild reforms. However, the macroeconomic policy regime followed then nearly broke down in 1991. P.V. Narasimha Rao and Manmohan Singh initiated a set of wide-ranging market-oriented reform measures by abolishing industrial and trade licensing policy and bringing down the import

[3] The new series of GDP in National Accounts has attracted attention of several analysts because the growth rates shown by it, particularly those for the industry, do not appear to be consistent with other indicators such as index number of industrial production and bank credit to commercial sector. A separate chapter in volume deals with this issue. Admittedly, the new series differs from the old one on both methodology and database and is not exactly comparable with the old one. Be that as it may, given our medium- and long-term focus in this chapter, we have extrapolated the old 2004–05 base series using growth rates of the new series.

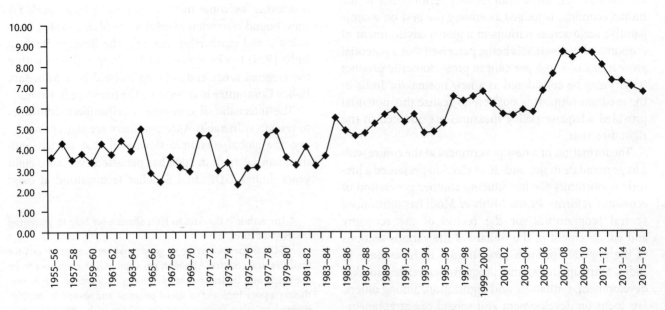

Figure 2.1   Five-Year Moving Average of GDP Growth

tariff and domestic tax rates to more competitive levels. These measures were continued by other governments indicating a broad political consensus. The benefits of economic reforms are clearly visible in the long-term growth rate in aggregate national income.

The average growth rate during the 1990s ranged between 5 per cent and 7 per cent. A decade after the reforms, growth improved further and remained high at 7 to 9 per cent during 2003 and 2010 giving rise to new optimism. However, the global financial crisis hit the economy in 2008 and the annual growth rate dropped to 6.7 per cent. The fiscal stimulus provided then to counter the crisis restored the growth to above 8.5 per cent over the following two years. Since 2011–12, the Indian economy has witnessed a relatively low growth between 6.5 per cent and 7.5 per cent and has not been able to restore the high growth achieved earlier.

On the whole, the exponential trend growth rate in GDP has been 7 per cent during the 25 years since reform 1991–92 to 2015–16 as against a trend rate of 4 per cent over the quarter century prior to the reforms 1966–67 to 1990–91. Analysts broadly agree that India has the potential to attain a long-term growth rate of 7 to 8 per cent, though there might be some medium-term fluctuations depending on exogenous factors.

Agriculture

Agricultural income growth has been low around 3 per cent on a medium- to long-term basis. Known for its supply constraint, it has rarely attained a growth rate of

4 per cent on a five-year average basis (Table 2.1). Even though the growth rate of 3.8 per cent recorded during the last decade has been an improvement over the historical average, food price inflation noticed in recent time means that supply is lagging behind the demand generated by the growth process as well as changing demand patterns.

Agricultural production is shifting in favour of non-foodgrain crops. Foodgrain production has been growing at about 0.5 per cent higher than the population growth rate of 1.3 per cent per annum mostly due to increase in yield rather than area (Figure 2.2). Direct per capita consumption demand for cereals is nearly stagnant and a rise in aggregate demand for cereals is basically due to population growth and an indirect demand for feed to produce protein-based animal products. Of the total net food grains production of 232 million tonnes in

Table 2.1 Decadal and Five-Yearly Growth Rate of GDP and Broad Sectors

Year	GDP	Agriculture	Industry	Service
1951–60	3.94	3.12	6.13	4.04
1961–70	3.75	2.54	5.26	4.56
1971–80	3.16	1.83	4.02	4.18
1981–90	5.40	3.52	6.08	6.54
1991–2000	5.70	2.84	5.56	7.46
2001–2005	6.80	2.75	7.33	8.19
2006–2010	8.62	3.89	8.60	10.09
2011–2015	6.76	3.72	3.04	8.46

Source: CSO.

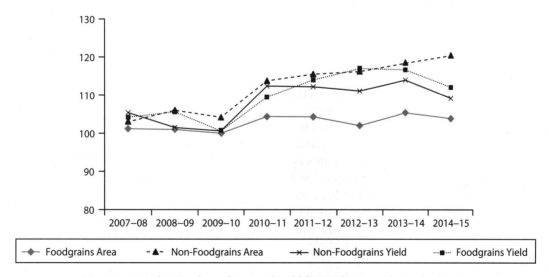

Figure 2.2 Index Numbers of Area and Yield for Foodgrains and Non-foodgrains

Source: Various Editions of the *Economic Survey of India*.

2014, procurement and public distribution accounted for 60 and 44 million tonnes respectively. Cereals exports from India has been about 25 million tonnes on an average during 2010–14 and partly contributed to a decline in government stocks. Despite higher price rise, pulses production has seen sharp fluctuations and is not able to keep pace with demand.[4]

Non-foodgrain output growth has been due to twin factors of rise in area as well as yield. Cotton, tobacco, and potato have been among the fastest growing crops contributing to farmers' income, though sluggish rise in production of oilseeds and sugar has been a matter of concern in recent years.

The consumption pattern in India across all income classes has shifted from cereals to non-cereal food items such as milk and milk products, eggs, fish and meat, and fruits and vegetables which are major sources of protein and vitamins. The increase in household demand for such items has been induced by income gain for all sections of the population in the last decade either directly due to the growth process or indirectly due to the poverty reduction schemes coupled with the relatively elastic demand for them.

The Indian rural economic scene is no longer dependent only on agricultural activities as non-agricultural activities have emerged as the major source of rural income over time. Even in this scenario, agricultural production and investment must receive due consideration to meet consumption and intermediate demand for agricultural products and for managing food inflation which adversely affects the level of living of the people, particularly the low-income group. Technological developments, and consequent land and labour productivity rise, will be important factors for enhancing agricultural growth.

Industry

The industrial sector led the GDP growth during the initial three decades of the development process after Independence with a growth rate of above 5.3 per cent as against overall GDP growth of 3.7 per cent. It laid the foundation for production of basic and capital goods following the Mahalanobis model. The share of industry in GDP increased from 16 per cent to 26 per cent over this period. Industry lost its leading position later on. Industrial share fluctuated between 25 per cent and 28 per cent since 1981. Its growth just kept pace with

GDP growth on a medium-term basis, but was marked by a high degree of volatility in the short run.

The higher industrial value added growth in the revised series of National Accounts Statistics (NAS) with base 2011–12 compared to the growth in physical production as captured by the index number of industrial production has been discussed in several recent papers. While such differences are not new, one component or another of industry exhibits large yearly variations. Industry includes (i) mining and quarrying; (ii) manufacturing; (iii) electricity, gas, and water; and (iv) construction with value added share of 10.4, 58.5, 0.6 and 30.5 per cent, respectively, in 2011–12. As per the new series, total industrial real value added has grown between 4.0 and 7.4 per cent since 2011–12, but mining and quarrying, and construction fell in absolute level in 2012–13 and manufacturing grew by just 0.5 per cent in 2014–15. Construction which absorbs a fairly good proportion of the casual workforce grew at an average rate of only 3.7 per cent from 2012–13 to 2015–16.

Going by the use-based classification in index number of industrial production, the slowdown in manufacturing has been widespread across its subsectors. As Figure 2.3 shows manufacturing output grew at a fairly comfortable rate from 2001 to 2007; growth has been slow in all components except basic goods during 2008–15. Capital goods and consumer non-durables have particularly been more adversely affected.

Services

The service sector has been the major driver of economic growth in India during the last three decades with its share in GDP rising from 38 per cent in early 1980–81 to 53 per cent in 2015–16. The service sector in India employs 31 per cent of the labour force. The sector covers a wide range of activities such as trade, hotels, restaurants, tourism, transport, storage, communication, banking, insurance, business services, real estate, social and personal service, public administration, and defence. Trade, transport, tourism, and personal services contribute substantially to employment generation. Most of the subsectors in services have continued to perform well in recent years except the segments community, social, and personal services.

Services play a key role in the country's exports accounting for above 3.5 per cent of world trade in services with software development as the major exporting sector in India during the last two decades. Software development, communication, and air transport have attracted substantial foreign investment. Business services, which include information technology and

---

[4] It may be noted that some Indian entrepreneurs have started exploring the possibility of pulses production in Africa to meet Indian demand.

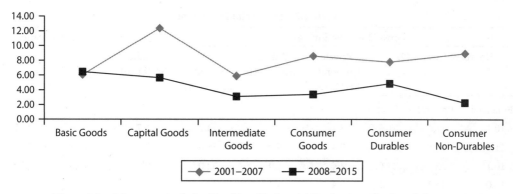

Figure 2.3   Movement in Index Number of Industrial Production: Use Based Category

Source: Various Press Releases, MOSPI, GOI.

information technology enabled services (IT-ITES), continue to rise even after the global crisis contributing to above 5 per cent of GDP and creating large volume of jobs for skilled and semi-skilled manpower.

Within the service sector, 'finance, insurance and business services' has emerged as the largest segment accounting for 40 per cent of income generation in 2015–16 followed by 'trade, hotel, transport and communication' accounting for 36 per cent and 'community, social and personal services' the balance 24 per cent. The network of effective system laid out during the last two decades has revolutionized communication in India and now playing a very important role on the social and work related communication among the people, particularly the youth.

Savings and Investments

Typical of an underdeveloped economy, the gross domestic savings rate in India was 9 to 10 per cent of GDP in the early 1950s. Along with growth, the savings rate too rose slowly to double by the mid-1970s and remained at 20 per cent till the late 1980s rising to 25 per cent in 1999–2000. It further started rising 2003–04 onwards and reached a peak at 36.7 per cent in 2007–08 (Table 2.2). A savings rate of this order was comparable to several East Asian economies, which witnessed a high growth regime and was viewed as a structural break in the Indian economy.

But, savings dropped to 32 per cent in 2008–09 due to the global crisis and has remained around 33 per cent to 34 per cent in recent years. All three sources of savings—household, corporate, and government—contributed to the decline in total savings rate after 2008. The private corporate sector has recovered to 13 per cent of GDP in 2014–15 improving over its earlier peak in 2007. The public sector attained a savings rate of 5 per cent

of GDP in 2007–08, but has mostly remained below 1.5 per cent since then.

Household savings, the largest component of total savings in India, too started recovering but dropped subsequently from 25 per cent in 2009–10 to 19 per cent in 2014–15. Household financial savings has fallen by 3 to 4 per cent of GDP, while physical savings by households recorded an increase. High inflation rate turns real earnings on financial savings negative for households who then allocate larger proportion of their savings into non-productive assets like gold. A low inflation regime assuring 2 to 3 per cent real interest rate for households would encourage higher financial savings by households. The recent policy measures taken for financial inclusion by ensuring banking services to the poor is expected to induce financial savings among the lower income groups, though the total size might not turn out to be large.

The series on gross capital formation rate[5] has stayed above the total domestic savings rate by 1 to 2 percentage points, the difference between the two being financed by foreign savings or net capital inflows. Gross capital formation rate exceeded the domestic savings rate by 4 to 5 percentage points in 2011–12 and 2012–13 indicating a capital inflow driven investment recovery. This recovery did not last long and gross capital formation declined by 3 to 4 percentage points from 2012–13 to 2014–15.

Both public and private sectors have contributed to the aforementioned decline. Public sector investment, which reached 9.4 per cent of GDP in 2008–09, declined subsequently to 7.4 per cent in 2014–15. Private sector investment too declined by more than 2 percentage points from 28.1 per cent in 2007–08. The revised NAS series indicated private investment of 29 per cent and 28 per cent in 2011–12 and 2012–13 respectively, though

---

[5] Gross capital formation includes fixed investment, changes in stocks and valuables besides adjustment for errors and omissions.

Table 2.2 Saving and Investment

Year (1)	Gross Domestic Savings						Gross Fixed Capital Formation			Gross Domestic Capital Formation*
	Household Sector (2)			Private Corporate Sector (3)	Public Sector (4)	Total Savings (2 + 3 + 4)	Public Sector (6)	Private Sector (7)	Total (6 + 7)	
	Financial	Physical	Total							
2000–01	10.1	11.6	21.7	3.7	−1.3	23.7	6.7	16.0	22.7	24.3
2007–08	11.6	10.8	22.4	9.4	5.0	36.8	8.0	24.9	32.9	38.1
2008–09	10.1	13.5	23.6	7.4	1.0	32.0	8.5	23.8	32.3	34.3
2009–10	12.0	13.2	25.2	8.4	0.2	33.7	8.4	23.3	31.7	36.5
2010–11	10.2	12.9	23.1	8.0	2.6	33.7	7.8	23.1	30.9	36.5
2011–12	7.7	15.9	23.6	9.5	1.5	34.6	7.3	27.0	34.3	39.0
2012–13	7.9	14.5	22.4	10.0	1.4	33.8	7.0	26.4	33.4	38.6
2013–14	8.4	12.5	20.9	10.8	1.3	33.0	7.1	24.6	31.6	34.7
2014–15			19.1	12.7	1.2	33.0	7.5	23.3	30.8	34.2

Note: * = GDCF adjusted for errors and omissions
Source: Economic Survey of India (various years); break-down of financial and physical savings of households based on RBI data.

it fell subsequently to 25 per cent in 2014–15. According to Joshi (2016), corporate leverage is high in India as reflected by the highest debt-equity ratio among emerging market economies and major Indian companies are facing a 'debt hangover' due to excessive borrowing during high-growth phase. This subsequently resulted in an increase in stressed assets of the banking system and reduced capacity to lend. Restoration of the investment rate would be an important factor for realizing a higher growth rate for the economy.

Fiscal Developments

The combined expenditure of the central and state governments rose by 2 percentage points of GDP to 28.4 per cent in 2008–09 over 2007–08 (Table 2.3) due to the expansionary fiscal policy followed by the government to overcome the global crisis. It reduced to 27 per cent in 2013–14, but rose again to 28 per cent during 2014–15 and 2015–16 (RE). The central government accounts for a little less than half of the combined central and state government expenditures and the states together the rest.

Revenue receipts of the centre and states together were down to 18.7 per cent of GDP in 2009–10 but recovered to 20.8 per cent of GDP in 2014–15 consisting of tax revenue of 16.6 per cent and non-tax revenue of 4.2 per cent. The centre's tax revenue accounted for 10.8 per cent of GDP (Table 2.4) and the states' taken together another 5.8 per cent.

Under the Indian federal arrangement, the centre transfers a significant portion of the taxes collected by it to the states based on recommendations of the Finance Commission. With the Fourteenth Finance Commission's recommendation for a 10 per cent higher share of states in the divisible pool of revenue, policy attention has shifted to the states in certain schemes and there is a need for greater coordination between the centre and the states.

Gross fiscal deficit of the consolidated government stood at 6.9 per cent of GDP in 2014–15. It had come down to 4.1 per cent of GDP in 2007–08 due to adoption of Fiscal Responsibility and Budget Management (FRBM) target set then, but more than doubled to 8.3 per cent in 2008–09 and further rose to 9.3 per cent in 2009–10 (Table 2.3) indicating that fiscal imbalance after the global crisis was of similar magnitude existed at the time of 1991 crisis. Fiscal consolidation measures adopted subsequently have gradually brought down the fiscal deficit level. Further consolidation is needed since it is currently close to 3 percentage points higher than the 2007–08 level. Revenue deficit, which was as low as 0.2 per cent of GDP in 2007–08, rose to 5.7 per cent in 2009–10 and remains high at 3 per cent in 2015–16 (RE).

Subsidy by central government has come down to 1.7 per cent of GDP in 2015–16 RE. Petroleum and fertiliser subsidies have fallen due to sharp fall in world market prices and orientation towards market-driven prices. Food subsidy went up sharply due to rising

Table 2.3 Receipts and Disbursements of Consolidated General Government (Percentage of GDP)

	1990–91	2000–01	2007–08	2008–09	2009–10	2010–11	2011–12	2012–13	2013–14	2014–15	2015–16 (RE)
Total Receipts (A+B)	26.8	28.7	26.7	27.8	28.5	27.6	27.2	27.8	26.4	27.7	28.0
A. Revenue Receipts (1+2)	18.6	18.1	21.3	19.8	18.7	20.3	18.8	20.2	20.2	20.8	21.0
1. Tax Receipts	15.4	14.6	17.6	16.5	15.2	16	16.0	16.8	16.4	16.6	17.1
2. Non-tax Receipts	3.2	3.5	3.7	3.4	3.5	4.2	2.8	3.4	3.8	4.2	3.9
of which interest receipts	1.1	0.9	0.5	0.5	0.4	0.3	0.3	0.3	0.2	0.3	0.3
B. Capital Receipts	8.2	10.5	5.4	8.0	9.8	7.4	8.5	7.6	6.7	7.0	6.9
1. Disinvestment proceeds	0.0	0.1	0.9	0.0	0.4	0.3	0.2	0.2	0.5	0.3	0.5
2. Recovery of Loans and Advances	0.6	0.5	0.1	0.3	0.2	0.1	0.3	0.2	0.1	0.1	0.1
Total Disbursements (a + b + c)	28.8	28.5	26.4	28.4	28.6	27.5	26.9	28.1	27	28.0	28.1
a. Revenue	22.8	24.8	21.5	24.1	24.4	23.5	22.9	23.9	22.7	23.8	23.6
b. Capital	3.9	2.9	4.5	3.9	3.8	3.4	3.2	3.5	40	3.8	4.2
c. Loans and Advances	2.0	0.9	0.4	0.4	0.4	0.6	0.7	0.6	0.3	0.4	0.4
Revenue Deficit	4.2	6.6	0.2	4.3	5.7	3.2	4.1	3.7	2.4	3.0	2.5
Gross Fiscal Deficit	9.4	9.6	4.1	8.3	9.3	6.9	7.6	7.4	6.3	6.9	6.5

Source: Economic Survey of India (various years).

Table 2.4 Fiscal Parameters of Central Government (as a Percentage of GDP)

Years	2006–07	2007–08	2008–09	2009–10	2010–11	2011–12	2012–13	2013–14	2014–15	2015–16(RE)	2016–17(BE)
Total Expenditure	13.6	15.3	15.8	15.6	15.4	14.9	14.2	13.8	13.1	13.2	13.1
Revenue Expenditure	12.0	11.9	14.2	13.9	13.4	13.1	13.1	12.2	11.6	11.4	11.5
Interest Payments	3.5	3.4	3.4	3.3	3.0	3.1	3.1	3.3	3.2	3.3	3.3
Subsidies	1.3	1.4	2.3	2.2	2.1	2.4	2.4	2.2	2.0	1.9	1.7
Capital Disbursements	1.6	2.4	1.6	1.7	2.0	1.8	1.8	1.7	1.6	1.8	1.6
Capital Outlay	1.4	2.1	1.4	1.5	1.7	1.6	1.4	1.5	NA	NA	NA
Total Tax	11.0	11.9	10.8	9.5	10.1	8.6	8.8	10.2	9.8	10.8	10.8
Direct Tax	5.4	6.3	6.0	5.8	7.3	7.2	7.2	5.6	5.5	5.5	5.6
Indirect Tax	5.7	5.6	4.9	3.8	4.3		4.7	4.6	4.3	5.2	5.2
Non-tax Revenue	1.9	2.1	1.7	1.8	2.8	1.4	1.4	1.7	1.6	1.9	2.1
Gross Fiscal Deficit	3.3	2.6	6.0	6.4	4.8	5.9	5.9	4.5	4.0	3.9	3.5
Revenue Deficit	1.9	1.1	4.5	5.2	1.8	2.8	2.8	1.1	2.9	2.5	2.3

Source: Economic Survey of India (various issues).

Table 2.5   Major Foreign Trade Parameters (as a Percentage of GDP)

Items	1990–91	2000–01	2007–08	2008–09	2009–10	2010–11	2011–12	2012–13	2013–14	2014–15
Export	5.8	9.9	13.4	15.6	13.2	14.5	16.5	16.6	17	15.4
Import	8.8	12.6	20.8	25.4	21.8	22	26.7	27.3	24.5	22.5
Trade Balance	–3	–2.7	–7.4	–9.8	–8.6	–7.5	–10.2	–10.7	–7.5	–7.1
Invisible receipts	2.4	7	12	13.8	11.8	11.4	11.7	12.2	12.4	11.6
Invisible payments	2.4	4.9	5.9	6.3	6	6.4	5.7	6.3	6.3	5.9
Net Invisibles	–0.1	2.1	6.1	7.5	5.8	5	6	5.9	6.1	5.7
Current Receipts	8	16.9	25.4	29.3	25	25.9	28.2	28.8	29.4	27
Current Account Balance	–3	–0.6	–1.3	–2.3	–2.8	–2.6	–4.2	–4.8	–1.7	–1.4
Foreign Investment	0	1.5	5	2	4.7	3.2	2.7	3	1.9	3.7
Debt-GDP Ratio	28.7	22.5	18	20.5	18	18.2	20.9	22.3	23.6	23.8
Debt-Service Ratio	35.3	16.6	4.8	4.4	5.5	4.2	6	6	5.9	5.9
Import Cover of Reserves (in Months)	2.5	8.8	14.4	9.8	11.1	9.6	7.1	7	7.8	8.9

Source: RBI (various years).

difference in procurement price by the Food Corporation of India (FCI) and issue price in public distribution system (PDS). The Food Security Act adopted in 2014 further added to the subsidy bill. Subsidies were introduced to attain specific social objectives but involved large leakages in the delivery system. There is an urgent need to review the subsidy schemes for better targeting. The biometric-based identifiers, initiated by the previous government and continued by the present government, are unique to individuals and are expected to help in better targeting the subsidies.

Foreign Trade

The foreign trade policy changes were at the centre of the structural reform measures in the 1990s. Opening up of the economy to trade and capital flows has played a major role in increasing growth and efficiency during the last quarter century. India's exports rose in an impressive manner from US$ 19 billion in 1990–91 to 310 billion in 2011–12 recording a 17-fold rise in two decades (Figure 2.4). Merchandise trade grew by an average rate of 30 per cent in 2010–11 and 2011–12 indicating

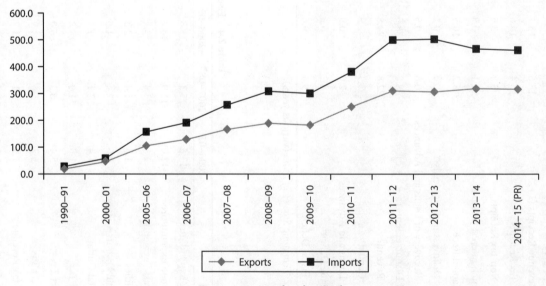

Figure 2.4   Merchandise Trade

Source: RBI (various years).

recovery of trade after the global crisis. However, the recovery did not last long and exports have hardly grown since 2012–13 and in fact have contracted in absolute levels for several months. In 2014–15, merchandise exports accounted for 15.4 per cent of GDP and services another 7.5 per cent. India ranks as the eighth largest service exporter in the world. India's share in world service exports is 3.2 per cent compared to its share of 1.7 per cent in world merchandise exports. Information technology-related exports at $73 billion accounted for 46 per cent of total service exports.

Imports too grew substantially from $28 billion in 1990–91 to $500 billion in 2011–12. It continued around that level in 2012–13 and fell to around 460 billion after that primarily due to a fall in oil prices in the world market. The large jump in imports relative to exports after the global crisis resulted in a trade balance of as high as 9 to 11 per cent of GDP for several years after 2008–09 but reduced to 7 per cent in 2014–15. These large fluctuations in trade balance show the vulnerability of the Indian economy to commodity prices in the world market, particularly to that of oil.

Surplus on invisible transactions amounting to 5 to 6 per cent of GDP has been a great help in financing the trade deficit. Current account deficit (CAD) of 4.2 per cent and 4.8 per cent of GDP in 2011–12 and 2012–13 raised serious concerns about the stability of the foreign exchange market. Several measures were taken by the RBI to curb non-essential imports such as gold and encourage capital flows helping trade deficit to fall. The CAD improved to 1.7 per cent and 1.4 per cent of GDP in 2013–14 and 2014–15, a level well within comfortable levels of net capital flows into India.

It is noteworthy that machinery, transport, and metal manufacturing have emerged as important exports category in recent years with a share of 23 per cent in total exports followed by petroleum products, gems and jewellery, and chemicals with shares of 18 per cent, 13 per cent, and 12 per cent respectively. The import basket is dominated by petroleum, oil and lubricants (POL) accounting for 31 per cent of the total imports followed by capital goods, gold, and electronic goods with shares of 11 per cent, 9 per cent, and 8 per cent, respectively.

Foreign exchange reserves has been around US$360 billion in 2016 Q3 and are currently adequate to provide imports cover of about nine months as against above one year before the global crisis. India's external debt of $486 billion was 24 per cent of GDP in 2015–16. With its entry into the lower middle-income group, the proportion of concessional debt in total debt has declined to

9 per cent in 2015–16 from 23 per cent in 2006–07. The debt service ratio was 9 per cent and short-term debt was 23 per cent of foreign exchange reserves by the end of 2015–16. These ratios are fairly within comfortable zones by conventional wisdom.

While it is a small player in world trade, there is large potential for enlarging merchandise and services exports. Given that exports of goods and services account for about 23 per cent of the total demand in the economy, restoration of the exports performance would be critical for further enhancement of the GDP growth. Joshi (2016) argues that India lost its export competitiveness against its trading partners due to a revised stand in exchange rate policy when real effective exchange rate (RER) was allowed to appreciate in 2009 by about 10 per cent and to remain around that level the following year. Another similar move in 2013 further aggravated the price disadvantage.

Money Supply and Credit

Money supply (M3) grew at about 20 per cent during 2006–07 to 2008–09 during the expansionary fiscal policy phase (Figure 2.5). It was steadily brought down subsequently to reach a growth rate of 10 per cent in 2015–16 when fiscal correction measures were undertaken. Reserve money and broad money grew only by 13 per cent and 10 per cent, respectively, during 2015–16. The money multiplier stood at 5.3 in 2015–16. Growth in bank credit to commercial sector has been low just above 10 per cent since 2013–14. As noted earlier, low growth of bank credit is due to high corporate leverage owing to excess debt in the past on the demand side and reduced capacity to lend on the supply side because of stressed assets of the banks, particularly public sector banks. The possibility of tapering of quantitative easing in the USA has led to capital outflows in 2016. When a similar situation arose in 2013, the RBI had to take exceptional measures to restore stability by containing liquidity.

Inflation

The consumer price index (CPI) inflation was higher than 5 per cent in mid-2016 putting pressure on monetary authorities. One distinguishing feature of inflation in India in recent years is that changes in CPI have been much higher than those in the wholesale price index (WPI) in recent years (Figure 2.6). The CPI for agricultural labourers (CPI-AL), which showed nearly zero growth for a few months in early 2012, rose sharply along with CPI for industrial workers (CPI-IW) at above

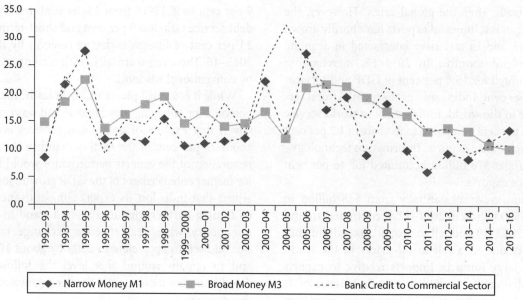

Figure 2.5 Money and Credit

Source: RBI (various years).

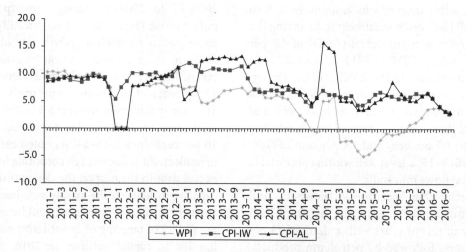

Figure 2.6 Monthly Inflation by WPI and CPI

10 per cent for a good part of end-2012 to mid-2015. The WPI inflation, on the other hand, turned below 5 per cent from mid-2015 and in fact turned negative for several months in 2015–16.

Persistent food inflation is the primary reason for CPI inflation to remain above WPI inflation since food has a larger weight in CPI than WPI. Food inflation is led by items such as milk and milk products, egg, fish and meat, and fruits and vegetables, which are major sources of protein and vitamins. The shift in production pattern

towards these items has not kept pace with demand and a large excess demand has persisted creating upward pressure on prices. A tight monetary policy along with other factors such as fall in international commodity prices, moderation of procurement prices, and slowdown of domestic activities contributed to falling inflation. Policy attention is needed to increase supply of non-cereal food to keep pace with demand.

Prevalence of high inflation for a fairly long time posed a major problem for the RBI. Inflation targeting has been formally adopted by the Parliament for guiding policy rate and a Monetary Policy Committee has been set up jointly by the RBI and the central government. The mean target in terms of CPI movement has been fixed at 4 per cent with the mandate to keep it within a band of +/−2 percentage points of 4 per cent.

Poverty

Since the Indian economy has recorded acceleration in growth from a medium-term perspective, the question finally arises if this growth process has reduced poverty. Since income distribution data are few and far between, the Indian literature on analysis of poverty normally uses consumption distribution data as obtained from the National Sample Survey Organization (NSSO). According to estimates based on the method recommended by the Tendulkar Committee (2009), the head count ratio (HCR)[6] fell from 33.8 per cent in 2009–10 to 25.7 per cent in 2011–12 in rural areas and from 20.7 per cent to 13.7 per cent in urban areas during the same period.

Alternative poverty lines have been worked out by the Rangarajan Committee (2014) which found rural HCR declined from 39.6 per cent in 2009–10 to 30.9 per cent in 2011–12 and urban poverty declined from 35.1 per cent in 2009–10 to 26.4 per cent in 2011–12. Incidence of poverty fell by 7–9 percentage points by both Tendulkar and Rangarajan poverty lines. The poor have thus benefited from overall economic growth in India. A more general result is obtained by Dutta and Panda (2014) who use the Generalized Lorenz Curve and conclude that the observed reduction in incidence of poverty in rural and urban India is independent of the poverty line. The extent of benefits derived by different income groups, though positive, may of course be different.

Employment

India had a total labour force of 476 million according to the Usual Principal and Subsidiary Status (UPSS) in the 2011–12 as per NSSO employment and unemployment survey. The share of females in the total labour force was low at 27 per cent. Elderly population (60 years or more) constituted 8.2 per cent of the total labour force and children (5–14 years old) another 0.8 per cent. The UPSS labour force consists of 441 million by the Usual

Principal Status (UPS) and 36 million by the Usual Subsidiary Status (USS) who were subsidiary workers.[7] The labour force growth has fallen to 1.4 per cent per annum during 1999–2011, from 1.8 per cent during the 1980s. The absolute increase in labour force is about 5.5 million per year.

The structure of employment has been changing slowly compared to the structure of GDP. Agriculture employed 48.1 per cent of total employment in 2011 as against 69.8 per cent in 1980 and 64.8 per cent in 1990. The number of persons employed in agriculture has been falling since 2005. According to Krishna et al. (2016), the maximum growth in employment share has been in the construction sector which accounted for 10.4 per cent in 2011 compared to just 2 per cent in 1980. The service sector's share has increased to 29.1 per cent in 2011 from 16.9 per cent in 1980 and 20 per cent in 1990. Employment growth in manufacturing has been slow and its share increased just by 1 percentage point to 11.4 per cent in 2011 compared to 10.4 per cent in 1980. At a disaggregated level, they find that traditional sectors such as textiles and leather products, wood products, and public administration and defence have experienced a declining share. Besides construction, other notable sectors that gained share are trade, transport and storage, education, and business services.

The growth of working-age population at 2.3 per cent a year is higher than total population growth of 1.7 per cent which gets reflected in the rising share of youth (15–24 years) in the population due to demographic transition. However, Ghose (2016) draws attention to the fact that 'youth bulge' in the labour force has not been visible in India (Figure 2.7). In fact, labour force participation of the youth has declined from 52 per cent in 1983 to 44 per cent in 1999–2000 and further to 32 per cent in 2011–12. The labour force participation of female youth in particular has halved from 30 per cent to 15 per cent since 1983.

Ghose provides several explanations for the fact that the growth in labour force is slower than population growth (1.4 per cent against 1.7 per cent). First, share of students in the working age population (15–59 years)

---

[6] HCR represents the percentage of population below the poverty line.

[7] Many authors prefer UPSS criterion to estimate labour force. The India Employment Report, 2016 (Ghose, 2016) prefers the UPS criterion that excludes the subsidiary work force on the grounds that UPS provides the estimate on an unambiguous and non-overlapping basis. UPSS category, for example, includes students or workers in own households available for only part time work as well as those subsidiary workers who are unemployed by their principal capacity and available for full time work.

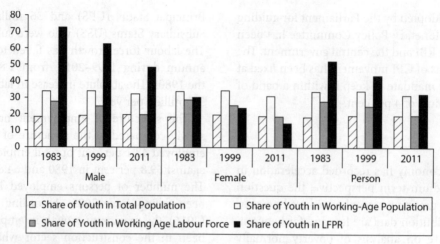

Figure 2.7 Share of Youth (15–24 years) in Population and Labour Force (UPS)

Source: Ghose (2016).

has increased from 9 per cent in 1999–2000 to 13.6 per cent in 2011–12. Second, labour force participation of working age women from the bottom seven expenditure deciles has substantially declined because there existed significant poverty driven participation by them in inferior quality work and increased household income in recent years 'induced and allowed' many women to withdraw from the labour force. Third, there has also been declining participation by the elderly partly due to increased access to social security and other income.

ASSESSMENT

Global Growth Experience

The volume of total production in the world hardly changed substantially before the advent of the industrial revolution. It just kept pace with population growth and all but a small section of the population lived at subsistence level. Population and production changed at about the same rate on a long-term basis. The Industrial Revolution that began in the eighteenth century in Europe raised production capability of the people and initiated economic development. As industrial employment expanded and wages rose due to productivity, more and more people were lifted out of the subsistence level bringing in dramatic changes in their lives by improving consumption of food, health care, education, housing conditions, sanitation, and leisure. Government could afford to provide a certain level of social security to all as its revenue expanded.

The critical factor in the economic development process is sustained growth in per capita production and income over a long period time. The two leading countries in history of global economic development are Britain and the USA. A series of technological innovations in textiles, steam engine, iron and steel, and railways in Britain and electricity, appliances, chemicals, transport, telecommunication, and computers in the USA led to a persistent rise in per capita income over a long period in both countries. Britain and the USA have enjoyed growth over as long as 200 to 300 years, though at a small rate. For example, average per capita income grew by a magnitude of 1.5 per cent to 2.0 per cent per annum over the period 1890 and 2000 and even at lower rates during the previous two centuries (Hudson, 2015). The important feature in this process was continuing growth over a long time. The economic and social management of the industrialization process was of course complex, but level of living of the people rose steadily due to higher real income and low unit cost in several mass consumption goods.

In Asia, the growth process took place at a later stage and attempted to catch up quickly with middle- and even high-income countries because they could use existing technology in the world without depending on their own invention of new technology. They had low-cost labour and material inputs available in plenty in their own country. They penetrated markets in the developed world by supplying manufactured goods having a large demand base at a cheap rate. Japan pioneered the industrialization process in Asia in mid-nineteenth century. While its income per capita rose at a rate of 2 per cent until World War II, it grew very rapidly at above 8 per cent during 1950 and 1973. Later, Korea and China, who entered the growth process in the second half of the twentieth century, too experienced a rapid growth rate. While penetration to markets of developed countries through exports was the common driver of growth in these countries, there were differences in certain important aspects of the growth strategy followed by them. With access to western capital and technology after World War II, Japan applied its management and labour policy, focusing on the domestic market related to reconstruction activities as well as on the external market for manufacturing consumer goods. It slowly shifted to medium and high technology–based manufacturing and consumer electronics. The South Korean government promoted a policy of providing cheap financial capital for investment in exporting sectors focusing on basic goods such as metals and chemicals initially and consumer electronics later. South Korea has experienced a 6 per cent per capita income growth for five decades after 1967. China adopted various state-controlled policies emphasizing on infrastructure, agriculture, and manufacturing after the end of civil war in 1949. It experienced very uneven growth until the mid-1970s but began relaxing its control regime thereafter. It focused on supplying low- and medium-value consumer goods at relatively cheap prices for the western market even as it created domestic demand with very high investment rate of 40–50 per cent of GDP. As the growth process continued for a few decades in these countries and wage rates rose, they found it difficult to be price competitive on low-value products and initiated a gradual reorientation of their growth strategy to move up to more sophisticated higher value manufacturing with certain competitive advantage. While Japan and Korea were relatively small countries by population size, per capita income growth of above 6 per cent for four decades[8] in China, the most populous country in the world changed the overall perception on global economic growth.

It is possible that the growth strategy followed by the Asian countries may not work after reaching a certain maturity and limit. After its catch up with the western countries in level of living, Japan is finding it hard to maintain its export growth since the 1990s. At a high level of income, a convergence in per capita income across countries is expected to take place. The bulk of

incremental demand in high-income countries is for services which are mostly non-tradable or semi-tradable at best. Some of the catch-up countries may not have a natural advantage in exporting services or may need to invest differently on human skills.

The Indian economy was virtually stagnant during the colonial era (Madison, 2006). The economic growth process effectively started in India after Independence and a mixed economy model was adopted. Agricultural production was, by and large, left in private hands, but non-agricultural production and trade involved various license and permit systems. State control for about four decades did not enable the economy to grow very fast. Per capita income grew by less than 2 per cent per annum and doubled in 38 years between 1951 and 1989. It looked as if the Indian economy grew at about the same rate as Britain or the USA did more than a century earlier, when the technological base in the world was narrow. The advantage of reforms initiated in 1991, dismantling the license-permit system could be gauged from the fact that per capita income rose by three times in the 25 years between 1991 and 2015. Although it falls short of the East Asian growth story, growth performance of the Indian economy after the reforms has been commendable, placing the country among the largest growing economies in the world. On the whole, per capita income in India has grown about seven times during the 65-year period, 1951 to 2015.

Prevailing Scenario

The macroeconomic environment prevailing towards end 2016 has been a mildly benign one. There is overall macroeconomic stability reflected by low inflation and low trade deficit. Fiscal deficit has been an area of concern but not above historical peaks. Inflation seems to be under control after remaining high for a few years. Historically speaking, supply deficiency of food items due to drought or rise in imported oil prices has ignited inflation in India. Recent inflation was primarily due to excess aggregate demand built up due to expansionary fiscal policy along with shifting food demand pattern. While tight monetary policy did contribute to reduce excess demand, agricultural supply management needs policy attention for controlling relative prices of non-cereal food items.

The areas of policy intervention in the agricultural sector are well recognized. The package includes infrastructure development to build up cold storage and transportation of perishable goods, supply chain management to link rural producers with urban consumers,

---

[8] If per capita income rises by 6 per cent per annum for 40 years, it means a 10 times rise in the level of living. It is equivalent to a growth of 2.5 per cent for about a century.

and relaxation of Agricultural Produce Market Committee (APMC) rules. There is also the need to develop commercially viable technology for crops such as pulses and maize grown in dry fed areas. On the institutional front, a more vigorous land lease market must be promoted to help a large number of landowners who have migrated from rural areas but continue to hold land. An effective lease market with security of medium-term tenure, without affecting the ownership, could incentivize private investment and help accelerate technological change in agriculture.

Major policy initiatives are needed for reviving the high growth path noticed during 2003–10. Two major problems emerged in recent years have been (i) slowdown in savings and investment rate since 2012–13 on the supply side; and (ii) hardly any growth in exports since 2012–13 and in fact negative exports growth rates for most months during the last two years on the demand side. Given a capital-output ratio of about 4.5 noticed in recent years, the investment rate needed to support a growth rate of 8 per cent would be about 38 per cent with the current level of productivity rise. Both private and public components of savings need to rise by a couple of percentage points of GDP. Household savings have been the largest component of total savings in India and comparable to that of other emerging countries, but corporate and government savings rates have been significantly low. The current emphasis on low inflation and fiscal inclusion would help raising household financial savings as discussed earlier. Fiscal instruments have also played a major role in determining the savings behaviour of households. Limits for tax-induced financial savings instruments have remained stagnant for long and it is time to raise them to take care of inflation. In fact, a rethinking is needed on an earlier abandoned policy initiative to exempt financial savings and annual earnings on them from taxation and tax the earnings on maturity only if not redeployed in investment. A general 'exempt-exempt-tax' rule of this nature would in principle mean equal treatment of investment across potential instruments available to households.

Government savings fell when a large volume of counter-cyclical fiscal stimulus was adopted in 2008. However, the quality of expenditure deteriorated as most of the stimulus went to raise government consumption expenditure. Fiscal consolidation adopted later increased government investment to some extent. High inflation and the consequent response in terms of high interest rate regime have affected the cost structure of the corporate sector reducing their savings. A macroeconomic regime of low inflation and low interest rates could help

in raising corporate savings and investment. Further, confidence of business on the long-term demand conditions in the economy will no doubt guide the animal spirit of business towards investment.

The falling external demand has adversely affected production and jobs in several sectors such as garments, leather, and gems and jewellery. Measures to reversing this large unfavourable effect on the economy would be included, among other things, for quicker movement from the ports and improving competitiveness by working through industry bodies and export promotion councils. Success of the Make in India initiative to expand manufacturing capability in the country would depend on removal of several bottlenecks related to land acquisition, power supply, connectivity, transportation, and trade facilitation. Service exports that are not so dependent on physical infrastructure have a higher share of 2.7 per cent in global trade.

Another point in this context is that a good proportion of global trade is likely to flow through the regional trade agreements channels such as Trans Pacific Partnership (TPP) and Transatlantic Trade and Investment Partnership (TTIP). India must be more aggressive in joining some regional cooperation arrangement so that it does not remain isolated in the new global trade regime. It must improve the global competitiveness of Indian industry to take advantage of emerging scenario. Two important factors in this connection are: (i) tackling persistent infrastructure problem by a drastic reduction in the time taken for movement of raw materials to the factory and from the producing factory to the external demand centre, and (ii) a competitive exchange rate management by adopting a regime of 'managed float' that provides incentives to exporters.

On the fiscal front, early implementation of the goods and service tax (GST) could help in providing some amount of fiscal space through expansion of the tax base and plugging in the loopholes in tax administration. The government has vigorously pursued the introduction of a major indirect tax reform and GST is certainly a big-ticket reform that could change the conventional framework of government revenue collection.

Moderate transfer payment may be regarded as a necessary condition for sustaining growth in a liberal democracy. The government has taken several steps for expanding and restructuring of welfare expenditure in several ways by financial inclusions by opening as many as 220 million new bank accounts under the Jan Dhan Yojana with moderate insurance coverage. The Aadhar card, which was started by the previous government and continued by the present, is based on biometric technology and would greatly help to identify the beneficiaries.

The sharp fall in oil price from above $120 a barrel in March 2012 to below $50 by January 2015 meant large savings for the government due to reduced subsidies for fuel and fertilizers providing necessary space for new schemes by about 0.5 per cent of GDP without raising additional revenue. More importantly, it created the right environment for giving up the administered price mechanism for petroleum and diesel and a shifting to market-determined prices. Liquefied Petroleum Gas (LPG) subsidies are credited to the bank accounts of the targeted beneficiaries based on Aadhar identification. The prime minister's appeal to higher income consumers to surrender their LPG subsidy succeeded in inspiring several million consumers to do so.

The developments on the employment front show that India actually has not so far derived demographic dividend. A rise in share of working-age population by itself does not imply demographic dividend, which requires that the number of employed people must rise faster than the population in order to reduce the dependency ratio and raise the savings–investment rate. The dependency ratio (number of persons supported per worker) has actually risen from 2.6 in 1983 to 2.7 in 1999–2000 and to 2.8 in 2011–12. Thus, the so-called demographic dividend has not yet been reaped in India. In order to reap this benefit, employment must grow faster than the population to absorb potential job seekers in the labour force. Further, if suitable jobs are made available for the section of the population that has withdrawn from the labour force because of earlier poverty driven engagement in inferior jobs, most of them may re-enter the labour force.

We need to recognize that progress on human development is an integral component of economic growth with one feeding on the other (Mehrotra, 2016). India's track record on health and education in sectors has been dismal. Public expenditure on health is only 1.3 per cent of GDP while other countries spend several times more. This results in large out-of-pocket expenses by individuals and often is a major reason why the households that have crossed above the poverty line slide back below. The government should provide reasonable health care to all. It may attempt to double the health expenditure as a proportion of GDP from current level of 1.3 per cent over the next five years. If basic health facilities can be created in every panchayat utilizing the educated unemployed, the government will also be generating large volume of employment in the public sector.

Turning to education, right to education has emphasized only on student enrolment and not on quality of education. Several studies show that the quality of education in public schools, with the exception of a small fraction, has deteriorated over the years. Only one or two teachers manage four-to-five classes in many schools. While government expenditure by itself will not raise the quality, there is no doubt that a minimum number of teachers needs to be employed to maintain differences in different standards. Such a move too has large employment potential.

Industry has often complained of an inadequate supply of skilled labour. Proper training of youth after their education is possible only with a joint collaboration of industry and government. It is industry that knows the various types of skill requirements in the right volume. Government may collaborate in these types of initiatives because of the public-good nature of such trainings.

CONCLUSION

This chapter aimed at providing an overview of developments on the macroeconomic front in the Indian economy from a medium-term perspective and discussed some of the problem areas that need policy attention. The 25 years after the reform have witnessed an additional growth rate of 2.5 per cent over the previous 25 years. The average growth rate of about 7 per cent during the quarter-century in the post-reform period includes high growth phase of 8–10 per cent per annum for several years. Since the growth path is not a linear one, episodes of similar high-growth phase would be needed to realize the perceived potential average of 7 per cent per year. While growth in the near future would continue to be service driven, agriculture, and industry must grow at a higher rates in order to avoid bottlenecks of one type or another.

Two short-run problems relate to reduced rate of investment and decline in exports. Stressed assets of the banking sector may need to be restructured through a new mechanism such as an asset reconstruction company. Banks may also be allowed to convert unpaid loans to equity. With the introduction of GST, government might have attained some additional fiscal space for expanding public investment. Exports may be provided incentives through exchange-rate management; but a medium-run strategy of exploring new markets and entering into new trade arrangements must be explored so that India can effectively penetrate the global value chain.

The government's current move for financial inclusion will provide the necessary flexibility to reconfigure the subsidy regime. While employment creation is a more sustainable way of removing poverty and improving level of living, attaining full employment may not be a feasible target with rising capital intensity even in traditionally employment-intensive sectors such as textiles and leather. Some form of social security will then be a necessary ingredient for sustainable growth. Feasible options are government directly creating temporary jobs similar to the national rural employment guarantee scheme for the educated or semi-educated youth (say, in the health and education sectors) and unemployment insurance. Adoption of a universal direct benefit transfer to all households for complete poverty removal advocated by some scholars (Joshi, 2016) might not be feasible at this stage of development unless all prevailing subsidies are removed. However, replacement of certain specific subsidies by direct benefit transfer (DBT) is a desirable move.

REFERENCES

Das, D. K., A. A. Erumban, Suresh Aggarwal, and S. Sengupta. 2015. 'Productivity Growth in India under Different Policy Regimes.' In *The World Economy: Growth or Stagnation?* edited by D. Jorgenson, M. P. Timmer, and K. Fukao. Cambridge University Press.

Dutta, Bhaskar, and Manoj Panda. 2014. 'Social Welfare and Household Consumption Expenditure in India—2004–05 to 2011–12.' *Economic and Political Weekly* 49 (31).

Ghose, Ajit K. 2016. *India Employment Report 2016*. New Delhi: Institute for Human Development and Oxford University Press.

Hudson, Edward A. 2015. *Economic Growth: How It Works and How It Transformed the World*. Delaware: Vernon Press.

Joshi, Vijay. 2016. *India's Long Road: The Search for Prosperity*. Penguin Allen Lane.

Krishna, K. L., Suresh Chand Aggarwal, Abdul Azeez Erumban, and Deb Kusum Das. 2016. 'Structural Changes in Employment in India, 1980–2011.' Working Paper No. 262, Centre for Development Economics, Delhi School of Economics, Delhi.

Kumar, Rajiv. 2016. *Modi and His Challenges*. New Delhi: Bloomsbury.

Mehrotra, Santosh. 2016. *Realising the Demographic Dividend: Policies to Achieve Inclusive Growth in India*. New Delhi: Cambridge University Press.

Panagariya, Arvind. 2008. *India: The Emerging Giant*. New York: Oxford University Press.

Planning Commission. 2014. *Report of the Expert Group to Review the Methodology for Measurement of Poverty*. Chaired by C. Rangarajan. New Delhi: Planning Commission, Government of India.

Reserve Bank of India. Various Years. *Handbook of Statistics on the Indian Economy*.

World Economic Forum. 2016. *The Global Competitiveness Report 2013–14*. Geneva.

3

Monetary Policy Transmission in India*

Ashima Goyal

INTRODUCTION

This chapter studies monetary policy transmission in an emerging market (EM) like India, and assesses its effectiveness. Questions asked are: what are the central bank's (CB) intermediate targets, how does it affect them, and how do those in turn affect its final target variables? Intermediate targets could be monetary variables or interest rates and final targets could be some combination of growth and inflation. As India has deepened money markets in the new century, and formally adopted flexible inflation targeting[1] in 2015, its operating target is now a short-term money market rate such as the call money rate (CMR), and its primary final target is inflation. This follows a similar evolution of monetary procedures in many countries.

* The chapter was presented as a paper at the IGIDR IDR conference and gained from audience comments. In particular, I thank the referee Professor Chitre for very detailed and useful comments, and Reshma Aguiar for excellent assistance.

[1] An agreement on monetary policy framework was signed between the central government and the RBI on the 20 February 2015. The inflation target was set at 4 per cent plus minus 2 per cent. The RBI will have failed to meet its target after a deviation of more than three quarters in either direction. It is required to publish an inflation report every six months giving its inflation forecast for a period of 6 to 18 months ahead, on the basis of which it will calibrate its policies (see http://www.finmin.nic.in/reports/MPFAgreement28022015.pdf).

The issue can be further broken down into two: First, how the repo rate at which the Reserve Bank of India (RBI) lends in the money market affects the CMR, and then how the whole range of financial market interest rates, including bank lending rates, are affected. Second, how do all these changes affect real rates, growth, and inflation?

With respect to the second, questions remain about how effective transmission channels can be in a country with many features of underdevelopment. We argue conventional aggregate demand channels may not work well, but CB actions and communication that affect inflation and exchange rate expectations hold more promise. These important channels are also explored. A range of interventions can directly affect exchange rates especially in thin emerging and developing economies (EDE) markets. They also have a role in transmission and in reducing external risks to transmission. The 'aggregate demand', 'expectation', and 'cost push' channels of monetary transmission are each analysed and their contribution in the ongoing Indian policy cycle assessed.

The remainder of the chapter is structured as follows: the section 'Transmission in Theory' analyses the theory of monetary transmission; the section 'Financial Sector Transmission' examines monetary policy procedures that affect short rates in a first stage; the next section 'Transmission to Bank Loan Rates' examines further transmission from short to long rates of interest; the section 'The Second Stage: Impact on the Real Sector' takes up transmission to the real sector; the section 'Insulating Monetary Transmission from External Shocks' considers how to insulate transmission from external shocks before the last section concludes.

TRANSMISSION IN THEORY

Box 3.1 summarizes the general channels of policy transmission, which comprise of the aggregate demand, expectation, and cost push channels. The aggregate demand channel is the traditional channel, which is the focus of textbooks. It consists of the effect of the interest rate, asset prices, exchange rate, and credit on demand. When CB action affects the price and amount of short-term liquidity, this affects the rate at which banks lend to each other in the short-term money market. For example, if the CB changes its repo rate at which it lends to banks in the short-term money market, this affects the cost of borrowing and works its way through a variety of market short-term interest rates. Transmission across the maturity spectrum affects long-term interest rates. Since prices are sticky, real interest rates change and affect investment and other interest sensitive components of aggregate demand. In the short-run, aggregate demand affects output more than prices as in the first channel shown in Box 3.1. This is the real interest channel.

The short-term interest rate mainly affects capital flows, exchange rates, and other asset prices. It is the longer term interest rates that affect aggregate demand. Smoothing short-term interest rates can lower volatility in asset prices and yet allow the CB to directly affect demand through the long-term rate. If the short-term interest rate is expected to rise in the future, for example, the long-term rate will rise more. So the long-term rate can be affected with a smaller current change in the short-term rate. It is especially so if forward-looking behaviour dominates, since then discounted future values determine current values of key variables, such as exchange rates.

A change in nominal interest rates also affects exchange rates. A rise in domestic nominal interest rates raises the relative return to domestic assets attracting foreign inflows. The domestic currency appreciates in nominal terms and, because of sticky prices, in real terms also. This reduces the demand for domestic goods and raises the demand for foreign goods—exports fall and imports rise, thus reducing domestic output.

A rise in nominal interest rates makes bonds more attractive relative to equity, since both the expected dividend flow and their present discounted value will fall.

Arbitrage reduces the value of other real assets such as real estate for similar reasons. This fall in wealth reduces household spending and output. This is the asset channel.

Box 3.1 Monetary Transmission Channels

- Aggregate demand channels
  - Real interest rate

    $$re\uparrow \Rightarrow M\downarrow \Rightarrow r\uparrow \Rightarrow I\downarrow \Rightarrow AD\downarrow \Rightarrow Y\downarrow$$

  - Exchange rate (floating)

    $$re\uparrow \Rightarrow M\downarrow \Rightarrow i\uparrow \Rightarrow NFI(i)\uparrow \Rightarrow S\downarrow \Rightarrow Q\downarrow \Rightarrow AD\downarrow \Rightarrow Y\downarrow$$

  - Credit

    $$re\uparrow \Rightarrow M\downarrow \Rightarrow Credit\downarrow \Rightarrow AD\downarrow \Rightarrow Y\downarrow$$

  - Wealth

$$re\uparrow \Rightarrow M\downarrow = i\uparrow \Rightarrow \left. \begin{array}{c} \text{Equity prices}\downarrow \\ \text{Asset prices}\downarrow \end{array} \right\} \text{Wealth}\downarrow \Rightarrow \left. \begin{array}{c} I\downarrow \\ C\downarrow \end{array} \right\} \Rightarrow Y\downarrow$$

- Cost shock from the exchange rate
  - Own exchange rate

    $$S_t\uparrow \Rightarrow CPI_t\uparrow \Rightarrow \pi^e_{t+1}\uparrow$$

  - Exchange rate policy; intervention, signalling
  - External rates

$$i^w\uparrow \Rightarrow S^w\downarrow \Rightarrow S_t\uparrow \left\{ \begin{array}{l} \Rightarrow \text{Intermediate goods price}\uparrow \\ \Rightarrow CPI^e_t\downarrow \Rightarrow \begin{array}{c} W^e_{t+1}\uparrow \\ \\ P^e_{t+1}\uparrow \end{array} \Rightarrow \pi^e_{t+1}\uparrow \end{array} \right\} \Rightarrow \pi^e_{t+1}$$

- Expectations channel
  - Inflation expectations

    $$re\downarrow \Rightarrow M\uparrow \Rightarrow \pi^e_t\uparrow \Rightarrow W^e_{t+1}\uparrow \Rightarrow \pi^e_{t+1}\uparrow$$

  - Country risk

$$S^e\uparrow \left\{ \begin{array}{l} \Rightarrow \text{Intermediate goods price}\uparrow \\ \Rightarrow CPI^e_t\uparrow \Rightarrow \begin{array}{c} W^e_{t+1}\uparrow \\ \\ P^e_{t+1}\uparrow \end{array} \Rightarrow \pi^e_{t+1}\uparrow \end{array} \right\}$$

Notation:

AD: Aggregate demand; M: Money Supply; re: Repo rate; r: Real, i: Nominal interest rate; I: Investment; Y: Output; NFI: Net foreign inflows; Q: Real exchange rate; S: Nominal exchange rate Rs/US\$; S^w: World nominal exchange rate; i^w: World nominal interest rate; π^e_t: Expected inflation; W_{t+1}: Wage rate in t+1; CPI: Consumer price index; WPI: Wholesale price index; P_{t+1}: Implicit GDP deflator in t+1.

In addition to demand and price, liquidity, or availability, also affects the generation of credit. Credit market imperfections, such as credit rationing, imply the quantity of credit as well as its price matters for aggregate demand. This is the credit channel. In an EDE with a large informal credit market, however, a change in the price of formal credit can have a magnified effect on the price and availability of informal credit, increasing the relevance of the interest rate.

In the short term, aggregate demand is expected to affect output more than price, but the traditional view is that in the longer term it affects only price. Money affects prices and its rate of growth affects inflation. Most economies have ongoing positive rates of money growth and inflation. Other monetary transmission channels can also directly affect inflation and therefore prices.

The exchange rate affects traded goods prices which directly enter consumer prices, as well as prices of key imported intermediate goods such as fuel, depending on the pass-through. If a rise in import prices raises wages and other costs of production, it leads to further rounds of inflation. This is the 'cost shock channel' of transmission. Imported goods affect the consumer price index (CPI) and CPI inflation, if there are second-round effects, with a shorter lag than the aggregate demand channel. The impact of the exchange rate on the CPI rises in an EDE once agriculture becomes a traded good. It is large also in an economy dependent on intermediate imports such as oil.

Apart from the effect of the interest rate on the exchange rate, CBs in EMs can also affect the exchange rate through different types of intervention and signalling. Movements in foreign interest and exchange rates that affect domestic exchange rates would also have similar effects on domestic inflation. Shocks to foreign exchange rates and prices are also part of the cost channel. An appreciation would directly reduce prices apart from its effect through aggregate demand.

Box 3.1 also presents the 'expectation channels'. The policy regime and its credibility will affect inflation and exchange rate expectations. Over time, inflation-targeting regimes often succeed in anchoring inflationary expectations independently of aggregate demand.[2] Then, despite a rise in some relative prices such as oil or food, the second-round rise in wages does not take place, and inflation does not rise. In inflation-targeting regimes, aggregate demand is not allowed to exceed potential output.

The exchange rate is also an asset price, so capital flows, domestic and global fragility affect exchange rate expectations. A rise in country risk leads to expected depreciation. So expectation-induced volatility can also have all the above cost push effects. As costs rise, so can future inflation.

We next examine how effective these channels are in the Indian context and their role in the current cycle. We first assess monetary procedures and the transmission of primary liquidity to financial markets, before turning to transmission from the financial to the real sector.

FINANCIAL SECTOR TRANSMISSION: MONETARY POLICY PROCEDURES AND INTEREST RATES

Due to the rapid pace of globalization and financial innovations even in EDEs, interest rates have begun to play a larger role in monetary transmission compared to monetary aggregates. Moreover, demand for broad money becomes unstable and enhancement in its supply from commercial banks more flexible, so that targeting monetary aggregates becomes difficult and the attempt causes high volatility in interest rates.[3] As interest rates become more flexible and responsive to CB action, more sensitive and fast as signals of potential imbalances, transmission through financial market rates rises. The size of foreign exchange, bonds, equity, and other asset markets, which are very sensitive to interest rates, rises. These are the major reasons for a shift to interest rates as operating targets.

Even so, other channels of transmission, such as credit, continue to be important, although more open and unified financial markets lower the effectiveness of direct credit controls. In line with these trends, the Chakravarty Committee (RBI, 1985) suggested moving towards a greater role for interest rates in monetary policy procedures. Now forward-looking behaviour becomes more important and markets are interested in guessing the CB's response to uncertainty and macroeconomic shocks. Thus, transparency becomes a major issue.

After liberalization in the early 1990s most interest rates stopped being administered, and the short policy rates became more effective policy instruments. The statutory liquidity ratio (SLR) and cash reserve ratio (CRR) rates peaked (at respectively 37.25 and 14.75) in the early

---

[2] After the global financial crisis (GFC) inflation did not fall in the West despite a slowdown. IMF (2013) attributes this partly to the better anchoring of inflation expectations.

[3] As the reviewer Professor Chitre pointed out, research suggests demand for money defined more precisely, and controlling for other financial asset prices, may be stable. However, this quantity is difficult to target. The Indian experience of the 90s was one of repeatedly missing money supply targets set.

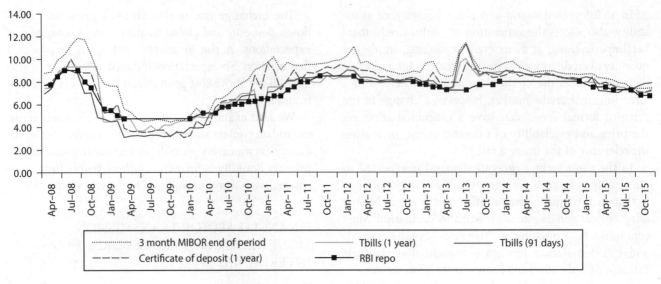

Figure 3.1   Transmission of RBI Repo Rates

Source: RBI. *Database on the Indian Economy.*[5]

1990s, and then were brought down, with some reversals, as the repressed financial regime was dismantled. In 2016, they were at 21.5 and 4 per cent respectively. The liquidity adjustment facility (LAF) implemented around 2002 helped fine-tune domestic liquidity and money markets slowly became more sophisticated. The LAF matured and was actively used after 2004. By this time, most of the sector refinance facilities had been wound up.[4] The RBI absorbed liquidity at the announced reverse repo and injected it at the repo rate.

Volatility in the RBI's target variable, the CMR, was much lower after the mid-1990s. The collateralized borrowing and lending obligation (CBLO) market rapidly grew to be the largest because of prudential limits on bank borrowing in the call money market. The latter was made a pure inter-bank market. The weighted average CMR was the operating target because truly liquidity-constrained banks had to borrow in the overnight or call money market so the CMR was the first to reflect monetary tightening. Although liberalization initially increased the volatility of rates in a thin market, it eventually brought down volatility, as markets deepened, to levels prevailing when rates were tightly administered. Now rates came through a complex market process (Goyal, 2014).

[4] In response to a request to revive credit allocation to critical sectors, the then RBI Deputy Governor Subir Gokarn replied the system was now too complex for the RBI to make such detailed interventions. The Chakravarty Committee (RBI, 1985) had also highlighted inefficiencies and waste credit allocation and rationing had caused.

Figures 3.1 to 3.3 show how money markets transmitted policy impulses through market rates in the period after 2000. Figure 3.1 shows how the short policy rate, the RBI repo, influenced longer maturity rates through the term structure, demonstrating one leg of active monetary transmission through rates.

Figure 3.2 shows the gap between the liquidity injection rate (Repo) and absorption rate (Reverse Repo) and whether the target CMR remained within this band. The CBLO rates are also shown in Figure 3.2. While open market buying and selling of government bonds or foreign exchange was meant to address long-term changes in money demand, the LAF was for adjustment to short-term fluctuations in liquidity. Since lending in the LAF was based on collateral, market rates were above the upper band during periods of tight liquidity when collateralizable securities were exhausted as in 2010–11. However, for much of the early period, rates hugged the lower band as the RBI used the LAF to absorb excess liquidity generated by large foreign inflows. There were large autonomous changes in liquidity due to forex inflows, variations in government cash balances held with the RBI and banks behaviour. Continued use of blunt CRR changes also added to jumps in liquidity. The RBI was not able to forecast and fine-tune liquidity sufficiently to keep the CMR in the middle of the band.

[5] Available at https://dbie.rbi.org.in/DBIE/dbie.rbi?site=home (accessed on 3 July 2017).

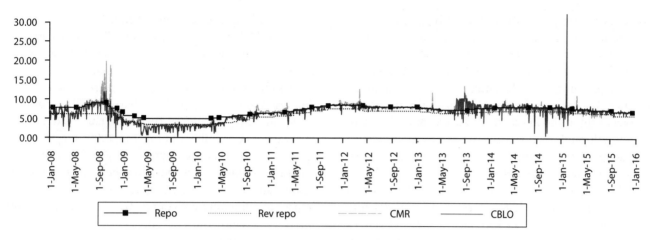

Figure 3.2   Daily Policy Rates: 2008–15

Source: RBI. *Database on the Indian Economy.*[6]

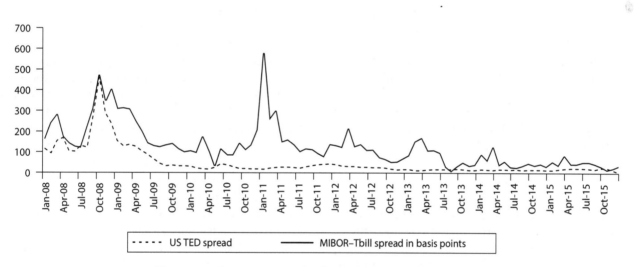

Figure 3.3   Comparing US and Indian Risk Spreads (in Basis Points)

Source: RBI, *Database on the Indian Economy* and Board of Governers of the Federal Reserve System.[7]

There was also insufficient appreciation that now policy had to act through the cost of funds or a shifting of the band, rather than through tight or surplus liquidity. A liquidity squeeze was not compatible with keeping interest rates within the band. In the initial stages policy changed both price and quantity variables in the same direction. The volatility of call money rates, although reduced, was still appreciable since they could jump from one edge of the band to the other.

Following recommendations in RBI (2011) some of the issues were sought to be addressed by making the repo rate the signal of the policy stance, as the single policy rate, with a marginal standing facility (MSF) fixed at 100 basis points above and absorption at 100 basis points below the repo rate. The MSF would make liquidity available up to 1 per cent of the SLR in addition to lending through the repo. Steps were also taken to improve liquidity forecasting and reduce transaction

[6] Available at https://dbie.rbi.org.in/DBIE/dbie.rbi?site=home (accessed on 3 July 2017).

[7] Available at https://dbie.rbi.org.in/DBIE/dbie.rbi?site=home and http://www.federalreserve.gov/releases/h15/data.htm, respectively (accessed on 3 July 2017).

costs in accessing liquidity from the RBI, so as to allow fine-tuning of liquidity requirements and smoother adjustment of market rates. Such fine-tuning became all the more imperative with the decision to keep liquidity at the injection mode. The latter was the international practice and was thought to enhance pass-through. With markets kept at the injection mode, accommodation of liquidity through repo was constrained by an indicative restriction of 1 per cent of net demand and time liabilities (NDTL) of commercial banks.

Following a new report (RBI, 2014), RBI moved to shift markets to variable rate term repo by restricting borrowing in the fixed rate LAF repo to 0.25 per cent of NDTL with 0.75 made available through term repos. An active term repo market was expected to improve market resilience to liquidity shocks with less dependence on the RBI, as well as provide benchmarks for financing a wider range of market products.[8] However, banks were reluctant to depend too much on each other since, in the absence of a benchmark rate, bilateral rates could rise too much.

As the RBI moved to an accommodating stance and began cutting rates in 2015, keeping the system in the liquidity deficit mode was found to be hampering pass-through of rate cuts. After episodes of severe liquidity shortages in 2016, the RBI committed to remove the liquidity deficit together with a narrowing of the repo reverse-repo band. The latter implied rates would not drop by too much, even if they fell towards the reverse repo rate. Moreover, past success in keeping call rates near the repo rate in deeper markets implied softer liquidity need not imply large interest rate fluctuations. Some research also suggests transmission is better when rates and quantity of liquidity work in the same direction.

Figure 3.3 shows the TED spread, the difference between the three-month US T-bill and the three-month London Eurodollar Deposit Rate, and the Indian equivalent of the TED spread, the Indian 91-day T-bill yield minus the thee-month Mumbai Interbank offered rate (MIBOR). The difference between the interest rates on interbank loans and on risk-free, short-term government debt (T-bills) is an indicator of rising counterparty risk, or of tightening liquidity in the interbank market.

The US TED spread remains generally within the range of 10 and 50 bps (0.1 per cent and 0.5 per cent), except in times of financial crisis. A rising TED spread often precedes a downturn in the US stock market.

In India, however, these spreads were large even in non-crisis times and peaked sharply during periods when liquidity was tight. That they narrowed during the years of large inflows in the mid-2000s suggests that spreads are partly due to tight liquidity or the inability to fine tune liquidity in response to shocks in government cash balances and in foreign capital flows. There is a large impact of a liquidity demand or supply shock in a thin market. Therefore, the TED spread can be used as a test of liquidity management.

Narrowing TED spreads suggests some improvement after 2014. Even so, more remains to be done. Although they were smaller, peaks still occurred. There was a sharp peak in April 2015, when the CBLO rates also jumped sharply above the LAF band. The CBLO and CMR volatility increased over September 2013 to May 2015 before coming down again to earlier levels.

Curdia and Woodford (2010) argue that in advanced economies (AEs), a change in spreads has implications for optimal monetary policy. Changes in the spread due to liquidity shocks have to be reduced or compensated for through lower rates, together with vigilant prudential policy to prevent bubbles. A larger, persistent spread in EMs indicates a requirement for further reform to remove distortions that raise spreads, such as the inability to predict liquidity shocks or the absence of a benchmark rate—but to the extent large spreads imply the average level of lending rates is higher there should be a downward bias to policy rates. Liquidity tightening and use of the interest rate defence also have a larger impact in thin markets, and should be used cautiously. A rise in rates is magnified many times through the informal credit market.

TRANSMISSION TO BANK LOAN RATES

There is a large literature on interest rate pass-through by banks. This pass-through is especially important in EDEs where banks dominate the financial sector. Pass-through is generally incomplete and faster in the upward direction. Banks solve an inter-temporal problem under adverse selection and moral hazard. This affects banks' loan interest rates and their spread over deposit interest rates. Banking structure, competition, and ownership, all affect outcomes. In India there are additional issues such as the role of public sector banks (PSBs), regulatory issues (such as CRR, SLR, and

---

[8] After a transitional period, the operating target was to shift to the 14-day term repo; the reverse repo was to approach the repo, with the floor of the LAF corridor now provided by a non-collateralized remunerated standing deposit facility. Apart from market development, this was conditional on better government cash management (shifting to an independent debt office), and better liquidity assessment with daily reporting by banks.

held to maturity [HTM], which allows banks to avoid marking-to-market their GSECs (Government securities), and priority-sector lending.

Ansari and Goyal (2014a) examine post–financial-reform interest rate pass-through for Indian banks after controlling bank-specific factors, regulatory and supervisory features, market structure, and macroeconomic factors. They find the several factors commercial banks consider, apart from the policy rate, limit policy pass-through. More competition reduces policy pass through but it can improve monetary transmission provided managerial efficiency rises. Reform had mixed effects on commercial banks' loan pricing decisions. While managerial inefficiency raised rates and spreads, product diversification reduced both. Costs of deposits are passed on to loan rates. Regulatory requirements raise loan rates and spreads. Since spreads are high in India, lending rates are much higher.

Pass-through is incomplete even in the long run with considerable heterogeneity across retail products and banks ownership. Banks' balance sheet structure, size, liquidity, and capitalization matter. Large, illiquid, well-capitalized banks and those heavily involved in inter-bank lending change their rates more rapidly and reflect more of market conditions in their rates in the long run. Banks with large non-performing assets would therefore require re-capitalization for more effective pass-through. Public sector banks adjust more slowly under expansionary monetary condition and vice versa. There can be a trade-off between regulation and effectiveness of the transmission mechanism and competitiveness of the loan market. Banks may be subsidizing loans by investment in risk-free government securities. Although the SLR has been reduced, banks continue to hold excess SLR, reducing loan supply and therefore pass-through.

Reforms removed restrictions on bank loan rates in phases. Under the benchmark prime lending rate instituted after the 1990s reform, corporates could bargain for rates below prime rates while small borrowers were charged higher rates. So from 1 April 2010, the Base Rate (BR) system was adopted. As a minimum lending rate, it was an average cost of funds based floor rather than a cap rate. Banks could determine their own base rate and the actual lending rates that were based on it. The base rate was expected to increase credit flow to small borrowers at lower rates. Although still not an optimal price, it was also expected to lead to faster and more transparent monetary transmission, since it was forward looking as compared to the prime rate, which reflected the past cost of funds. The BR was linked to deposit rates of one-year tenor since 80 per cent of loans were of one-year tenor.

Ansari and Goyal (2014b) found that the base rate had an inbuilt upward bias because it did not allow for arbitrage across finer product categories. For example, overhead cost need not be charged to investment income in the base rate system, and lower short-term treasury yields could be deducted to arrive at the base rate although a higher yield was earned on longer-term treasuries. In comparison with the optimal loan interest rate, the base rate was found to have an upward bias in the range of 150 to 300 basis points. If the marginal cost of loans is lower than the average cost, the optimal loan rate would be below the base rate. Due to its upward bias, the base rate could impose a suboptimal excess loan pricing structure on the banking system.

In 2015, RBI cut its benchmark rate by 125 basis points. Banks reduced their median term deposit rate by 83 basis points but median base rates came down only 60 basis points. In December, therefore, RBI announced a move to a marginal cost of funds-based lending rate (MCLR) starting 1 April 2016.[9]

The main difference is the calculation of marginal cost under MCLR which is determined largely by deposit rates and repo rates. Differentiation based on loan tenor, funding composition and strategies will improve loan pricing, compared to computing base rates for all loans on the same deposit rate as earlier. For example, a five-year loan based on one-year MCLR will be able to adjust without mismatch as policy rates change. Banks' short-tenure loans could be priced to compete with the commercial paper market, whose rates of growth in the current cycle far exceeded that of bank credit because of faster pass-through. Other flexibilities for banks are the option to stay with the base rate system for existing loans, and exemptions for certain categories of loans. This will reduce the immediate impact on profits. Existing borrowers can negotiate a move to an MCLR linked loan. Interest rates must be reset at least once a year in line with a pre-announced schedule.

---

[9] The components of MCLR are: (i) Marginal cost of funds = 92% × Marginal cost of borrowings + 8% × Return on net worth. Marginal cost of funds includes deposits and borrowings, with 8 per cent weight for tier I equity. Borrowings include those from the RBI at the repo rate; (ii) Negative carry for mandatory CRR, calculated as: Required CRR × (marginal cost)/(1 − CRR); (iii) Operating costs excluding charged services; and (iv) Tenor premium. Banks will publish an MCLR for different tenors—overnight loans, one-month, three-months, six-month and one-year loans. A Board mandated spread, based on uniform criteria, will be charged to customers on the internal benchmark determined on these four criteria (RBI, 2015).

The MCLR has potential to reduce response time and enhance pass-through, since marginal cost of funds is expected to be below average cost based base rates by at least 50 basis points. Despite this, since banks gain flexibility and corporates more options, profitability can improve. New margins of adjustment and innovation become available. However, by June 2016 average fall in base rates stayed at 60 basis points although the RBI had cut the repo rate by another 25 basis points. Banks used the flexibility they had to raise the risk premium for higher tenor loans, although short-term loan rates fell, keeping average loan rates unchanged. Companies' borrowing-cost did fall, however, as they borrowed more through cheaper commercial paper (RBI, 2016). Banks have to be forced to reveal their optimal rates, since they arbitrage any set formula.

THE SECOND STAGE: IMPACT ON THE REAL SECTOR

We next examine transmission to the real sector. First, how do real interest rates change and how do these affect aggregate demand? Real interest rates have historically shown considerable variation as change in nominal rates differed from that in inflation. Over 1990Q4 to 2012Q1 the real call money rate calculated as the difference between the nominal rate and one period ahead non-food manufacturing (core) inflation averaged 3.1 with a high of 22 and a low of −13 in the 1990s.[10] The range fell in recent years but was still high. The standard deviation fell from 6.4 in the period before 2003Q1 to 4.3 for the period after. Aggregate demand estimations that use the interest rate gap (the difference between the real and natural interest rate) find a higher interest elasticity of demand (−0.21) similar to that in AEs (Goyal and Arora, 2016).

As retail credit markets deepen, the interest elasticity of aggregate demand rises. In 2010, for example, low policy rates of interest helped stimulate growth at above 10 per cent. With inflation targeting and further market development, changes in real rates of interest will be smaller but more effective.

Many backward sectors less integrated with modern financial systems do reduce the reach of monetary policy but more openness greatly raises its impact. Once agriculture becomes a traded good, the nominal exchange rate affects agricultural prices; this affects wages and prices throughout the economy, since food is a major part of the consumption basket.

The pass-through to the real sector has been formally estimated in a number of structural VARs that analyse the effect of monetary shocks on target and other intermediate financial variables. The general problem with these estimations is that past results need not be valid in a new inflation targeting regime.

For the more recent period these models use interest rates as the policy instrument. Identification of exogenous shocks and inclusion of relevant variables are required to prevent theoretically inconsistent results known as puzzles. For example, if supply shocks are not included in the variables, a rise in inflation due to these shocks could be attributed to a rise in policy interest rates. The recursiveness assumption is useful to identify primary monetary shocks, since a CB typically observes some variables it reacts to, and its actions affect its targets with a lag. Recursive identification imposes the CB's reaction function, assuming that variables entering it (such as growth and inflation) are affected by monetary policy only with a lag.

Mishra and Mishra (2012) impose such an assumption and find results are theoretically consistent with an interest rate rather than a monetary aggregate as the policy instrument. The interest rate channel has a stronger effect on demand, the exchange rate affects inflation, and supply shocks have a major role. Khundrakpam and Jain (2012) find monetary policy impacts output with a lag of two-to-three quarters and inflation with a lag of three-to-four quarters, the impact persisting for 8-to-10 quarters. The CMR interest rate channel is the strongest. It accounts for about half of the total impact of monetary shocks on output growth and about one-third of the total impact on inflation. But effect of CMR on output is two-to-three times greater than its effect on inflation. The exchange rate has an insignificant impact on output growth, but has a non-negligible impact on inflation. Results are not significant for all measures of inflation and for different sample periods. Although the interest rate channel is the most important channel for monetary policy transmission in India, transmission is weakened because of structural issues such as supply-side shocks from food and oil.

There is strong evidence in India that the impact of tightening is first on output not on inflation implying the short-run aggregate supply (AS) is elastic. Most regression estimates of the AS find a low coefficient on the output gap variable in AS regression (Goyal, 2015a). With more exact measurement of the supply-shock

---

[10] The range would be even higher if more volatile headline inflation (that includes commodity prices) is used to calculate the real interest rate.

variable, the coefficient of the output gap falls (Goyal and Tripathi, 2015). The significance of supply shocks (Goyal and Arora, 2016) suggests the AS is, however, subject to frequent upward shifts. For example, oil and food price shocks raise intra-marginal costs also. Theoretical derivation from a dual economy macroeconomic DSGE model confirms this (Goyal, 2011). In it the long-run AS is also elastic but still subject to cost push. This conclusion is supported by NSSO unemployment survey results that show double-digit unemployment in some skill categories. Youth unemployment is at 30 per cent, but infrastructure and other bottlenecks raise costs of production. In an economy undergoing a growth transition, with easier movement between traditional and modern sectors, structural unemployment becomes cyclical.

Such a structure of aggregate demand and supply suggests the most effective monetary transmission may be through the expectation channel, especially if coordination with the government reduces cost push. This would allow monetary tightening to be mild, reducing the output sacrifice of disinflation. Under flexible forecast, inflation targeting policy rate movements can continue to be based on multiple indicators, while giving a more focused signal, since all the variables that affect inflation are relevant for an inflation-targeting CB.

We examine transmission in the current accommodating phase of monetary policy, evaluating the channels presented in Box 3.1. Domestic and international research shows transmission through changes in aggregate demand to be weak in low-income countries (Mishra and Montiel, 2012). In addition, transmission of the policy impulse tends to be weaker during softening cycles. As Stiglitz wrote—you can pull on a thread but not push on it. An unusual aspect of the current phase is that accommodation is combined with the attempt to anchor inflation at low levels.

High-interest elasticity of demand for categories such as consumer durables and housing implies the interest rate channel will work but is slow, because of banks' reluctance to cut loan rates in a softening cycle. However, bank costs will come down as they reduce interest rates on new deposits and public sector bank non-performing assets (NPAs) are resolved. The move to marginal cost pricing of loan rates gives banks more flexibility. Apart from a lack of demand and continuing high loan rates, NPAs also limit a rise in credit to corporates, but debt issues are restricted to a narrow set of infrastructure firms. Private and foreign banks balance sheets are relatively healthy but they tend to concentrate on retail credit. Transmission is also working through markets as corporates shift borrowing to cheaper commercial paper.

Measures were also announced to stimulate the corporate bond market, thus reducing pressure on banks.

The exchange rate is another aggregate demand transmission channel. As policy rates fall, a floating exchange rate should depreciate, raising net export demand. However, as a softening cycle raises expected growth, equity inflows can actually rise, appreciating the exchange rate, unless they are absorbed in reserves. However, Indian interest rates are normally much higher than those in the rest of the world. Debt inflows are limited by caps, not by the interest differential. Therefore, the real exchange rate channel also does not work in a textbook fashion. The interest rate impact on exchange rates is weak. The mature floating exchange rate insulates macro-policy from the external sector. If the interest rate rises, higher capital inflows tend to appreciate the real exchange rate and lower demand thus contributing to monetary tightening.

In India, however, the nominal exchange rate channel is likely to be more effective as a cost push channel, since it affects the cost of intermediate goods and food imports. However, this channel is also limited because the depreciation required to keep the exchange rate competitive limits cost-reducing appreciation. Moreover, global risk-on risk-off shocks can cause too much variation in directions unrelated to the needs of the domestic cycle. Volatility reducing intervention can sometimes damp changes in exchange rates too much.

Exchange rate targets, such as a fixed or a crawling peg, however, have normally not done well in EMs. They do serve as an explicit nominal anchor fixing the inflation rate for traded goods. In particular, pegging the exchange rate of a high-inflation country to that of a low-inflation country can serve as a credible commitment to low inflation. But the disadvantages are: giving up autonomy of domestic monetary policy; transmission of external shocks as domestic interest rates change with foreign; real appreciation that harms exports; and suppression of feedback on the monetary policy stance from sensitive FX markets. It can encourage domestic firms to make excessive short-term international borrowing, resulting in financial fragility and crises. The perceived risk for foreign investors is also lowered. If EM currencies only depreciate over time as the pegged rate is adjusted downwards, this provides a safe one-way bet and encourages speculation.

The aggregate demand channel primarily works by affecting quantities—that is, output—since prices tend to be sticky in the short run. It affects prices over a longer horizon. But in economies that have persistent positive inflation rates, prices are changing more

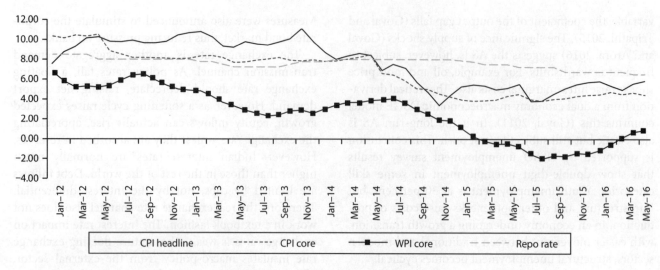

Figure 3.4 Inflation Trends and Policy Rates

Source: Asian Bonds Online, Figure 4: Effect of Fed Taper in three countries.[12]

continuously—there is an underlying trend expected inflation rate. Future demand and cost shocks and past inflation behaviour feed into this.

In a credibly disinflating economy, the inflation expectation channel of monetary transmission is likely to be the most effective. In India, household expectations respond to food and commodity prices more than to a demand squeeze. Double-digit food price inflation over 2007–13 raised consumer inflation expectations.[11] Food price inflation affects expectations, in the downward as well as upward direction. Psychological factors make double-digit food inflation salient, giving it a larger impact—it leads to second round persistent effects on inflation. Low food inflation becomes a non-inflationary relative price change. Over 2014–15, there was a sharp downward revision in household inflation forecasts after many years of double-digit expected inflation. Sticky core inflation also fell, following that in headline CPI (Figure 3.4).

Despite two sub-par monsoons in 2014 and 2015, the impact on food inflation, except on pulses, was less than expected, indicating some structural improvements in agriculture. These possibly include improvements infra-

structure, marketing, moderation of wage growth, and low growth in cereal support prices. The latter may have encouraged diversification to producing vegetables and proteins. In 2016, there was a large increase in acreage under pulses. Soft international food prices also capped domestic price increases. A mid-2016 spike in food prices is likely to be transient since it is restricted to a few commodities.

Using the expectation channel requires clear and strategic use of communication. In inflation targeting (IT) regimes, the policy rate has to rise with expected inflation. With forward-looking behaviour, if the policy rate rises at least as much as inflation, the real interest rate is positive and cumulative cycles of rising inflation are prevented. However, for IT to be consistent, it must reduce policy rates with a fall in expected inflation. This is necessary to develop understanding of how IT works.

The RBI's inflation forecast can play an important role in further downward shifts. A credible forecast can be a major focal point because information tends to be thin in a developing economy. Therefore, these should not show a systematic upward bias that could come from not adequately revising past forecasts. The inflation report must clearly show how changed data affects the inflation forecast, and why deviations occurred from past forecasts. Papadamou, Sidiropoulos, and Spyromitros (2015) show that a more transparent monetary policy makes the transmission mechanism more

[11] The wholesale price index food articles averaged above 10 per cent in this period, with frequent peaks of double-digit inflation.

[12] Available at https://asianbondsonline.adb.org (accessed 3 July 2017).

effective, even in EMs, reducing the need for an aggressive policy rate. If the inflation forecast is falling, a fall in interest rates is consistent with disinflation. Not cutting it feeds the perception that the RBI is behind the curve, and boosts political lobbies. The argument that inflation was high for so long, therefore, a tight monetary policy is required for as long is a typical example of backward-looking policy, as is being stuck in a high-inflation forecast when inflation is falling. After the global financial crisis, there was too little tightening. Too much now will not correct the earlier error—it will only make another one.

In countries like India, moreover, there is also a large share of backward-looking behaviour (Goyal and Tripathi, 2014, 2015). In such circumstances, if in waiting for data change is delayed too long, macroeconomic instability can occur because of lags in the system. Moreover, since the aggregate demand channel contributes little to reducing inflation, too high real interest rates impose unnecessary costs. Figure 3.4 shows the large real interest imposed on firms as the policy repo rate swung from being below CPI headline to above it. The WPI core (non-food manufacturing) is the relevant index to calculate the real interest rate facing firms. This real interest rate was always positive and widened to double digits as the 2014 commodity price fall reduced both core and headline inflation but the repo rate was not reduced adequately. Space available to reduce it, consistent with inflation targeting, in end-2014 and early-2015 was not utilized.

Since commodity price shocks are favourable, the government is also undertaking some supply-side measures, and the RBI has adopted flexible inflation forecast targeting, there is a real opportunity to guide and anchor inflation expectations downwards, despite rate cuts that help some growth recovery. A cut need not indicate giving up on the inflation fight—only fighting it intelligently. The latter requires policies to be allocated to the task where they are most effective. Fiscal actions must bear the brunt of the inflation fight, while monetary policy sustains demand. Flexible inflation targeting allows giving some weight to growth. In any case, rate cuts are consistent with inflation targeting if inflation is coming down.

INSULATING MONETARY TRANSMISSION FROM EXTERNAL SHOCKS

A major risk for monetary transmission is if global risk-driven capital flow surges create excess exchange rate volatility and impact the domestic interest rate, contrary to the needs of the domestic cycle. Another is high debt and its sensitivity to interest and exchange rate volatility. Under perfect capital mobility and a fixed exchange rate, monetary policy autonomy is lost. The world real interest rate determines the interest rate. Under floating exchange rates, the latter is supposed to absorb the shock, but too much exchange volatility affects interest rates. In intermediate regimes, both can vary.

During global risk-off periods there were outflows from EMs unrelated to their own cycles. For example, the 19 largest EMs saw outflows of $0.5 tn 2008/09 and $1 tn over 2014–15. During risk-on periods over July 2009 to June 2014, $2 tn flowed in. While the reasons were largely global, domestic macroeconomic vulnerabilities contributed.

These vulnerabilities have reduced for India. Since risks are going to continue, the best response would be to ensure fundamentals remain strong, and then focus interest rate policy on the domestic cycle. Excess exchange rate volatility can be moderated according to the experience gained in 2013 of the most effective types of intervention (Goyal, 2015b). Capital mobility is rarely perfect, and the CB also has real power to affect exchange rate expectations and risk perceptions.

If the exchange rate is managed in a shifting 5 per cent band it will help markets discover the equilibrium real exchange rate. Mild nominal exchange rate variation in the short-term can help stabilize CPI inflation as part of a flexible inflation target, while avoiding large fluctuations in both exchange and nominal interest rates. This, together with smoothing short-term interest rates, will lower volatility of asset prices, but allow sufficient variability in nominal interest rates to reach the target real interest rate.

The literature largely finds capital controls do not work: they create distortions and evasion, an open current account with two-way movement is more stable. However, the Indian experience suggests that calibrated restrictions on inflows can be very helpful.

The EM corporate dollar debt rose from $1.7 tr in 2008 to $4.3 tr 2015. However, partly because of limits on foreign borrowing, Indian corporate debt is the lowest among EMs. Private sector external debt rose to $105 bn from $59 bn in 2008. Debt was concentrated in large infrastructure firms, but even so, debt-equity ratio was around 1. For 4,388 non-government non-financial public limited companies, however, the ratio was only 0.44 in 2013–14 (Rajakumar, 2015).

The IMF reports a steep rise in total non-financial corporate EM debt to 74 per cent of GDP in 2014 from 45 per cent in 2005. China, Turkey, and some Latin

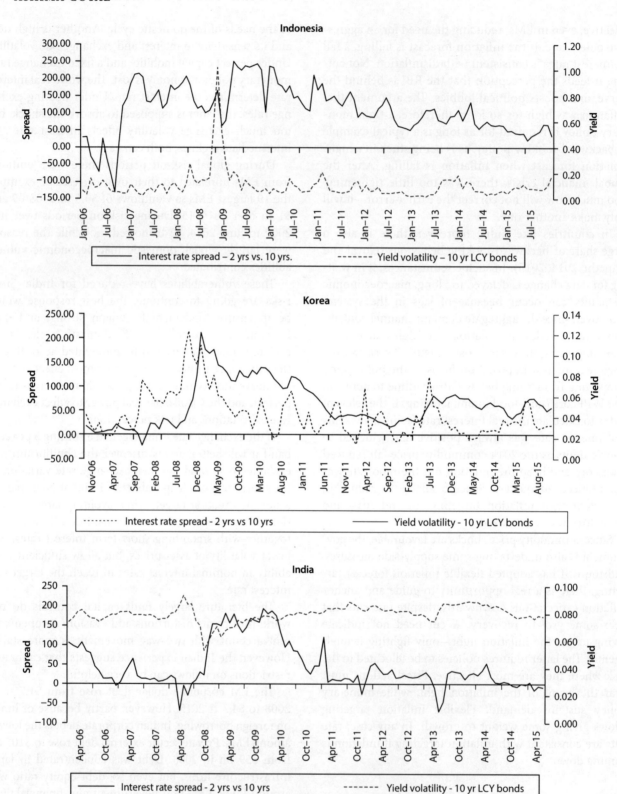

Figure 3.5 Effect of Fed Taper in Three Countries

Source: RBI. *Database on the Indian Economy*, Figure 5: Inflation Trends and Policy Rates.[13]

[13] Available at https://dbie.rbi.org.in/DBIE/dbie.rbi?site=home (accessed on 3 July 2017).

American countries saw the most change over 2007–14. In India, the rise was large in absolute terms but still low as a ratio to GDP (14 per cent) compared to China's 164 per cent.

A careful sequencing between domestic market development and foreign entry helped limit risks and volatility. Some EDEs opened out to foreign investment in local currency bonds after the global crisis. The logic was that with these, currency risk is borne by foreign investors. However, outflows can still raise interest rate volatility. Fluctuations in the yield of Indian ten-year local currency bonds and changes in the spread between ten- and two-year bonds were less than in more open developed and less developed EDEs during the outflows provoked by the threatened rise in US Fed rates in the summer of 2013 (Figure 3.5 and Table 3.1).

There tend to be mechanical EM sell-off driven outflows in periods of global risk-on. However, the Indian experience in 2008, 2011, and 2013 is inflows tend to return, if prospects are robust, and the share of risk-sharing capital is larger. Therefore, capital-flow management that restricts types of inflows is effective. Caps on riskier types of capital flows can rise gradually as domestic markets deepen. The limit for debt inflows was $81 bn in 2016, with a larger share for long term investors. The limit on foreign holding of Gsecs is to rise from $30 bn to $60 bn by 2018 (5 per cent of stock) in stages even as domestic retail holding is encouraged.

There are two views on ongoing global risks: One that the normalization of US monetary policy is factored in, and the rise in rates will be a non-event, since skittish inflows have already left. The second expects widespread turbulence, liquidity shortages, and outflows from emerging markets. The Fed rate rise, and normalization of US monetary policy will test India's strategy of risk proofing—strengthening macroeconomic fundamentals,

restricting excess volatility of exchange and interest rates, and sequencing of restrictions on capital flows. If excessive volatility of exchange and interest rates is avoided, the accommodative path can continue without interruptions.

CONCLUDING REMARKS

Our evaluation finds monetary policy transmission through the structure of interest rates is adequate, although steady improvements are required and continue. The call money rate has closely tracked the repo rate in recent months, suggesting the mixture of market deepening and RBI liquidity response to exogenous liquidity shocks had begun to work, but a longer successful track-record is required to establish it. While the transmission to financial interest rates works reasonably, that through bank rates is incomplete and slow. While this is so even in AEs, structural restrictions that make for inefficiencies and wide spreads are being reduced as financial repression falls, and by giving banks greater freedom and flexibilities.

With respect to transmission to the real sector, also the real interest rate has a significant impact on aggregate demand and output, while cost push from the exchange rate affects inflation. The continued dominance of supply shocks on inflation suggests that inflation targeting will need to be flexible, but combined with supply-side action from the government, can successfully guide inflation expectations downwards, at minimal output cost. If the government acts on food supply, infrastructure bottlenecks, and generally reduces transaction costs, inflation targeting can reduce inflation expectations, limiting cost-push items such as wage-rise and exchange rate depreciation, even as monetary policy remains accommodative. The expectations channel of monetary transmission is likely to be the most effective.

Risk proofing against external shocks has also improved in India with better fundamentals and continuation on a path of cautious market liberalization. This may protect the transmission of monetary policy from external disruptions and help it better match the needs of the domestic cycle.

Table 3.1   EM Bond Markets 2014

	S. Korea	Indonesia	India
Percentage of GDP	75	15	54
Size: US $ bn	1701	124	1200
Share of foreign investors (%)	10.6	38	4
10-yr yld vtn taper-on 2013 (%)	6.3	17.4	1.3

Source: Asian Bonds Online.[14]

[14] Available at https://asianbondsonline.adb.org (accessed on 3 July 2017).

REFERENCES

Ansari, J., and A. Goyal. 2014a. 'Banks Competition, Managerial Efficiency and the Interest Rate Pass-through in India.' In *Risk Management Post Financial Crisis: A Period of Monetary Easing (Contemporary Studies in Economic and Financial Analysis, Volume 96)*, edited by

J.A. Batten, and N.F. Wagner. United Kingdom: Emerald Group Publishing Limited, Chapter 15, 317–39.

Ansari, J., and A. Goyal. 2014b. 'Optimality of Base Rate System of Loan Pricing of Developing and Emerging Market Economies: An Evaluation.' *Banks and Bank Systems*, 9(3): 74–82.

Curdia, V. and M. Woodford. 2010. 'Conventional and Unconventional Monetary Policy'. *Federal Reserve Bank of St. Louis Review*, 92 (4, July/August): 229–64.

Goyal, A. 2011. 'A General Equilibrium Open Economy Model for Emerging Markets: Monetary Policy with a Dualistic Labor Market.' *Economic Modelling*, 28(2): 1392–404.

———. 2014. *History of Monetary Policy in India since Independence. Springer Briefs in Economics.* India: Springer.

———. 2015a. 'Understanding High Inflation Trend in India.' *South Asian Journal of Macroeconomics and Public Finance*, 4(1): 1–44.

———. 2015b. 'External Shocks.' In *India Development Report 2015*, edited by S. Mahendra Dev. New Delhi: IGIDR and Oxford University Press, 36–51.

Goyal, A. and S. Arora. 2016. 'Estimating the Indian Natural Interest Rate and Evaluating Policy', *Economic Modelling*, 58: 141–53. November.

Goyal, A., and S. Tripathi. 2014. 'Stability and Transitions in Emerging Market Policy Rules.' *Indian Economic Review* 49(2): 153–72.

———. 2015. 'Separating Shocks from Cyclicality in Indian Aggregate Supply.' *Journal of Asian Economics* 38 (June): 93–103.

International Monetary Fund (IMF). 2013. 'The Dog That Didn't Bark: Has Inflation been Muzzled or was it Just Sleeping?' In *World Economic Outlook: Hopes, Realities, Risks.* (Chapter 3), 79–96.

Khundrakpam, J.K., and R. Jain. 2012. 'Monetary Policy Transmission in India: A Peep Inside the Black Box.' *RBI Working Paper Series No. 11.* Available at https://www.rbi.org.in/scripts/PublicationsView.aspx?id=14326 (accessed December 2015).

Mishra, A., and V. Mishra. 2012. 'Inflation Targeting in India: A Comparison with the Multiple Indicator Approach.' *Journal of Asian Economics* 23(1): 86–98.

Mishra, P., and P. Montiel. 2012. 'How Effective is Monetary Transmission in Low-Income Countries? A Survey of the Empirical Evidence.' *IMF Working Paper 12/143.* Washington: International Monetary Fund.

Papadamou, S., M. Sidiropoulos, and E. Spyromitros. 2015. 'Central Bank Transparency and the Interest Rate Channel: Evidence from Emerging Economies.' *Economic Modelling*, 48 (August): 167–74.

Rajakumar, J.D. 2015. 'Are Corporates Overleveraged?' *Economic and Political Weekly*, 50(44): 115–18.

Reserve Bank of India (RBI). 1985. *Report of the Committee to Review the Working of the Monetary System* (S. Chakravarty, Chairman). Bombay: RBI.

———. 2011. *Report of the Working Group on Operating Procedures of Monetary Policy* (Chairman: D. Mohanty). Bombay: RBI. Available at https://www.rbi.org.in/Scripts/PublicationReportDetails.aspx?UrlPage=&ID=631 (accessed in June 2016).

———. 2014. *Report of the Expert Committee to Revise and Strengthen the Monetary Policy Framework* (Chairman: Urjit Patel). Bombay: RBI. Available at https://rbidocs.rbi.org.in/rdocs/PublicationReport/Pdfs/ECOMRF210114_F.pdf (accessed in June 2016).

———. 2015. *Interest Rates on Advances.* Available at https://www.rbi.org.in/Scripts/NotificationUser.aspx?Id=10179&Mode=0 (accessed on 3 July 2017).

———. 2016. *Annual Report 2015–16.* Bombay: RBI. Available at https://rbi.org.in/Scripts/AnnualReportPublications.aspx?year=2016 (accessed on 3 July 17).

4

New National Accounts Series

An Exposition and Key Issues in the Debate

J. Dennis Rajakumar and S.L. Shetty[*]

THE BACKDROP

India's National Accounts Statistics (NAS) series has a long pedigree and is one of the most massive statistical exercises undertaken in the world. Some of the most well-known names in the post-Independence economic history of the country—P.C. Mahalanobis, D.R. Gadgil, V.K.R.V. Rao, Moni Mukherjee, and B.S. Minhas—had played a significant role in laying the foundation for India's NAS. The system, as it has got evolved over decades, has also been the end result of intertwining of hundreds of primary statistics sourced to myriad administrative statistical reportings and periodical surveys.

In building the structure, adopting appropriate concepts, and employing diverse sources of data, the Indian statistical system, as in the case of the systems of all United Nations (UN) member states, has derived its inspiration from the UN System of National Accounts (UN SNA)—first published in 1953 and updated thrice over thereafter in 1968, 1993, and 2008. Until the latest revision, India had used the broad conceptual contours of 1968 SNA which itself was a major attempt and all member governments had adopted it for achieving international comparisons of their NAS. No doubt, India did make some changes 'to the extent data were

available' based on SNA 1993 in the 1999–2000 base year revision and those based on SNA 1993 and 2008 in the 2004–05 base year revision, but they were truly peripheral and indistinguishable in the totality of NAS numbers.[1] It is only now—in the latest series—that the Central Statistics Office (CSO) has made concerted attempts to follow the SNA 2008, which is largely an updated version of the SNA 1993, and the changes introduced in the latest 2011–12 series based on SNA 2008 have been quite substantial, so much so that they have become very distinguishably large and a new beginning in the data set.

In order to supplement the efforts of Advisory Committee on NAS (chairman: K. Sundaram), five

[*] The authors would like to thank Vikaschandra Chitre for his comments on the earlier version of the draft.

[1] In the 1999–2000 base year revision, a new category, 'valuables', was included in gross capital formation (GCF) but outside gross fixed capital formation (GFCF). In the 2004–05 series, some more changes were affected, such as revising the life tables of assets, using the user cost approach in estimating the services of owner occupied houses, and using the construction component and machinery/transport outlay of defence capital account as capital formation.

subcommittees[2] with chairmen and members drawn from official circles and academia, were appointed and their recommendations were duly considered while rebasing the NAS from 2004–05 prices to 2011–12 prices.

Thus, at the outset, it is important to appreciate the efforts made by the CSO in observing guidelines provided in the UN SNA and internationally followed best practices, while at the same time making efforts to improve quality of statistics by relying on new data sets and improved methodology.

Periodic changes in the base year are an essential aspect of a healthy statistical system because shifting of base year reflects structural changes taking place in the economy over time. Intervening between the first official estimates with base year 1948–49 and the latest with the base year 2011–12, there had been six base year changes in India's NAS. While affecting the base year changes, the statistical authorities take advantage and introduce firmer methodology, seek to capture newer and better quality data sets and improve the presentation. Such changes were done in all the base revisions in the past but the attention that the latest revision from 2004–05 to 2011–12 base series has attracted, is unparalleled.[3] This has happened because the CSO has shown greater degree of dynamism this time by going far beyond the customary changes in the methodology employed and the data sources used.[4] As we allude to them in the chapter, we emphasize that the changes introduced have been far

more radical and they have resulted in equally radical changes in varied aspects of the NAS numbers—the levels and sectoral compositions as well as the reported growth. The objective of this chapter is to present an exposition of the conceptual and methodological changes introduced and newer data sources used and also their implications for the estimates of various NAS numbers followed by the growth scenario depicted by the new numbers.

KEY COMPONENTS OF RADICAL CHANGES INTRODUCED

Comprehensive reviews of the existing database as well as the methodology of compilation and implementation, to the extent feasible, of the international guidelines in this regard have been the key objectives of the 2011–12 revision exercise. The substantive changes largely following the UN SNA thus introduced add up to a radically improved set as presented in Box 4.1.

The Choice of 2011–12 as Base Year

As NAS relied on Population Census for certain vital information such as labour inputs, the choice of base year generally coincided with the census year, which was the case until the 1990s. But, because the Gulf War had adversely impacted the economy in 1990–91, the NAS was rebased to 1993–94. In line with the recommendation of the National Statistical Commission to rebase economic variables once in every five years, CSO had done a similar exercise in 1999–2000 and then in 2004–05. The next revision was due in 2009–10, but that year was not considered as normal year in view of the global slowdown following financial crisis of 2008 and the quality of employment statistics collected was found to be unsatisfactory; the CSO had chosen the year 2011–12 to rebase NAS using the new Employment and Unemployment Survey (EUS) conducted with July 2011–June 2012 as the reference period.

Conceptual Changes

Shift to Alternative Measures of Value Added and to GDP at Market Prices

Under the new NAS series, some radical changes have been introduced in the use of value added measures, based as they are on the UN SNA. First, for the national

---

[2] These subcommittees covered (i) System of Indian National Accounts (chairman: A.C. Kulshreshtha) (ii) Agriculture and Allied Sectors (chairman: S. Mahendra Dev); (iii) Private Corporate Sector including PPPs (chairman: B.N. Goldar); (iv) Unorganised Manufacturing and Service Sectors (chairman: K. Sundaram); and (v) Private Final Consumption Expenditure (chairman: A.K. Adhikari).

[3] Elucidation of changes introduced and their implications have been discussed in a series of recent research contributions, particularly in the reputed social journal *Economic and Political Weekly*: EPW Research Foundation (2015), Goyal (2015), and Rajakumar, Sawant, and Shetty (2015. Adoption of gross domestic product (GDP) at market prices in place of erstwhile GDP at factor cost for measuring real growth has been questioned by Shetty (2015). Besides, a number of issues have been discussed, such as data sets and method of blow-up related to estimates of corporate sector (Nagaraj, 2015a; Rajakumar, 2015; Rao, 2015); size of manufacturing output (Goldar, 2015; Nagaraj, 2015a; Mazumdar, 2015); size of unorganized sector's output (Nagaraj, 2016); possibility of using double deflation method (Dholakia, 2015; Rajakumar and Shetty, 2015); size of revision in NAS successive rounds (Rajakumar, 2016; Rajakumar and Shetty, 2016a, b); and size of output of Reserve Bank of India (Bhuyan, 2016).

[4] Alagh (2015), who was the Minister of Statistics in the mid-nineties, noted that the CSO at that time was less dynamic and

had opposed adopting global standards. However, we do not have fuller details of the debate he has had with the statisticians then.

Box 4.1   Major Departures in NAS New Series

A. *Conceptual changes*
 1. Introduction of gross value added (GVA) and related aggregates at basic prices.
 2. Adoption of gross domestic product (GDP) at market prices as GDP instead of GDP at factor cost as the aggregate income measure and a measure for deriving the economy-wide real growth.

B. *Classificatory changes at sectoral level*
 3. Separate estimates of various aggregates for institutional sectors introduced for the first time in the Indian NAS; the sectoral categories are public non-financial corporations; private non-financial corporations; public financial corporations; private financial corporations; general government; and households including NPISH.
 4. Refinement in the coverage of institutional categories such as the separation of quasi-corporations from the household sector and adding them to the corporate sector.

C. *Improvements in coverage of sectors*
 5. Use of MCA 21 e-governance data for a comprehensive set of over 5.3 lakh companies instead of the Reserve Bank of India (RBI) sample study of around 4,500 companies;
 6. The coverage of financial corporations has been expanded to include a number of financial and capital market enterprises such as all mutual funds, stock brokers and stock exchanges, and pension funds as well as financial regulatory authorities, namely, Securities and Exchange Board of India (SEBI), Insurance Regulatory and Development Authority (IRDA), and Pension Fund Regulatory and Development Authority (PFRDA).
 7. A substantially improved coverage of local bodies and autonomous institutions under the general government (comprising central and state governments, as well as local bodies and autonomous institutions).

D. *Methodological changes in compilation*
 8. Shifting to the enterprise approach from the establishment approach, the head office operations have been allocated to the non-financial corporations in the mining and manufacturing sectors.
 9. Adoption of effective labour input method (ELI method) instead of the bland labour input method (LI method) for a majority of unincorporated enterprises.
 10. Fixed capital formation have been compiled for four categories of assets (earlier two categories) in order to distinctly account for intellectual capital and cultivated biological resources.
 11. A few other important changes such as (i) Financial Intermediation Services Indirectly Measured (FISIM) based on the reference rate approach; (ii) the output of RBI entirely treated as non-market at cost as part of public corporations unlike previously treating its issue department as non-market and part of general government and banking department as market and as part of the public financial sector; and (iii) the GVA estimates for the unorganized financial services (moneylenders) based on specific field surveys rather than the blanket one-third approach.

E. *Consequential changes in the dissemination of data series*
 12. No data series are published on GDP at factor cost at the aggregate level or at the sectoral level; instead, published are (i) GDP at market prices only at the aggregate level; (ii) GVA at basic prices both at the aggregate and sectoral levels; (iii) key macro aggregates for 11 sub-sectors; (iv) similar key aggregates for six institutional categories; (v) sector-wise gross capital formation; (vi) four categories of fixed capital formation; and (vii) various components of private final consumption expenditure.

Source: Compiled by authors

---

economy as a whole, the concept of gross domestic product (GDP) at market prices is preferred instead of GDP at factor cost. Both SNA (1993) and SNA (2008) have argued that GDP at factor cost is essentially a measure of income and not output (SNA, 1993: 154 and SNA, 2008: 104). This is so because GDP at factor cost, which can be arrived at by adjusting gross value added (GVA) at basic prices for net production taxes (defined further in the chapter), has no observable vectors of prices and outputs that define the production process. Hence, GDP at market prices is considered appropriate as GDP for measuring real growth at the aggregate level. The CSO

has, thus, ceased to publish data series on GDP or GVA at factor cost under the new series as a separate macro identity.

But, even the UN SNA (2008) has conceded the importance of factor cost estimates. It has said that GVA at factor cost 'is essentially a measure of income; it represents the amount remaining for distribution out of GVA, however defined, after the payment of all taxes on production and the receipt of all subsidies on production' (p. 104). SNA (2008) goes on to affirm that GDP, as defined in the SNA, is such that an identity exits between a measure built on value added, a measure built on income, and one based on final expenditures—the three ways to reach a GDP measure. Further, 'value added represents the contribution of labour and capital to the production process' (p. 103). Hence, the importance of factor cost estimates lies in the study of these distributional issues (we discuss this later in the section 'GDP as a Measure of Income').

Incidentally, though the CSO does not provide the aggregate annual series of GDP at factor cost, we have been able to derive them from the data available on production taxes net of production subsidies. We have now designated them as GVA at factor cost.[5]

Introduction of an Innovative Concept of GVA at Basic Prices

Second, at the sector level and for the national economy as a whole, what is now published is GVA at basic prices. It is perceived that production taxes, like land revenue and stamps and registration fees, are absorbed in the reported value of production and hence, what we eventually get are GVA at basic prices, that is, value added at factor cost plus production taxes less production subsidies.

To dilate a while, prevalence of total indirect taxes in an economy is divided into two categories: (i) taxes on products consisting of all value added type taxes (VAT), import, and export duties; and (ii) 'other taxes on production'.

This classification is done depending upon whether an indirect tax is paid on the factors of production employed or whether it is paid on per unit of output involved.

Taxes on products are, thus, taxes that are payable on sale, transfer, leasing, or delivery of goods and service. In the Indian context, these consist of union excise duties, state excise duties, sales tax, service tax, electricity consumption and sales tax, entertainment tax, hotel receipts tax, interest tax, custom duties, and expenditure tax.

Other taxes on production, on the other hand, are not related to products per unit or any such size of sale, transfer, or delivery; they are charged regardless of the transaction size involved. The UN SNA 2008 (para 7.97) has classified them under these categories: (i) taxes on payroll or workforce; (ii) recurrent taxes on land, buildings, or other structures; and (iii) business and professional license fees.

In the Indian context, the CSO (2015a) has included following taxes as production taxes:

1. fringe benefit tax
2. land revenue
3. stamps and registration fees
4. estate duty
5. banking cash transaction tax
6. taxes on vehicles, and
7. other taxes and duties on commodities and services

New Devices Used for Deflating Indirect Taxes and Subsidies

As explained in the section 'GDP as a Measure of Income', the use of GDP at market prices for measuring real growth raises an important question of the measure including indirect taxes net of subsides. The nominal growth in GDP would get inflated if indirect tax base is expanded. Such an exaggerated increase has to be obviated while working out the real growth in GDP, which calls for applying an appropriate deflator for the net indirect taxes. SNA (2008: paras 14.150, 15.175) has set out how (i) specific taxes levied on volume of a product, and (ii) ad valorem taxes levied on product values, have to be deflated. Apparently, using this recommendation, the International Monetary Fund (IMF) Mission in India which gave recommendations on the new NAS series, prescribed a statistical framework which 'mandates only the real growth in the underlying indirect tax base is included in calculating GDP at market prices' (Sen, 2015). This is done by ensuring that indirect tax collections due to an increase in indirect tax rates is reflected as a rate of change in price. Thus, for specific taxes, any change in the rate of specific tax is a price increase (SNA, 2008: para 14.150) and the volume effect is strictly limited to changes in the quantity of item purchased. For the ad valorem cases, the volume measure is calculated with tax rates from the base year. Sen (2015) opines that collection rate increases be considered as a price effect; likewise new taxes be treated as price changes. As a result of these methods of deflation, the influence of indirect tax increases gets almost diluted from the real GDP growth. But, as we point out later, this deflating method only obviates the possible double counting at the real GDP level but it cannot negate the double counting charge at the nominal GDP level.

Emphasis on Value Added and Not Output

In defending the new NAS series, senior officials of the statistical system have vociferously argued that what

---

[5] See, for details, http://www.epwrfits.in, NAS module (accessed on 20 June 2017).

GDP captures is value added and not output. This has always been the case but, a few fresh occurrences in the new series have brought the differences to the forefront. First, as brought up later in this chapter, the use of corporate sector data as distinguished from the Annual Survey of Industries (ASI) data or the physical growth in the Index of Industrial Production (IIP) has produced higher sets of valued added numbers. Both IIP and the ASI capture information from establishments at the plant level, whereas the corporate data provide such information for an entire enterprise owning the plant, including other establishments and their head office operations dealing in post-manufacturing value added through marketing, trading, and other services. Second, subsequent to the introduction of the new series, the economy's inflation represented by Wholesale Price Index (WPI) and Consumer Price Index (CPI), particularly the former, has decelerated, leading to the deceleration in the rates of change in deflators which, in turn, has resulted in higher growth of value added in real terms. This has also come about because input prices have fallen more than their output prices, leading to higher value added. Finally, there are three or four key elements in the calculation of value added: physical value dimension, per unit price of output, per unit price of intermediate inputs, and efficiency in the use of inputs due to technological changes. It is claimed that being sensitive to the underlying factors in the value added measurement, the new series reflects the combined results of all of these elements.

Data on Key Aggregates for Institutional Sectors for the First Time

Yet another key feature of the new series is the publication —for the first time—of key macroeconomic aggregates in respect of six institutional sectors, as described in Box 4.1. As in the past series, savings and capital formation are made available at different levels under these categories. In addition, GVA at basic prices by institutional categories are also provided. More importantly, the coverage of sectors has undergone significant changes, as noted further.

The most significant compositional change relates to the private corporate sector that has now been enlarged. Previously, private corporate sector was defined to include non-government joint stock companies registered under the Companies Act, 1956 and cooperative institutions (CSO, 2012: 199). Under the new series, private corporate sector additionally includes business enterprises registered under the Limited Liability Partnership (LLP) Act, 2008 as well as quasi-corporations (QCs) maintaining books of accounts but not necessarily having been registered either under the Companies Act or LLP Act (CSO, 2015b: 15). The QCs may be proprietary concerns, which were hitherto included under household sector and also cooperatives. Inclusion of these sub-institutional categories can place estimates of private corporate sector on the higher side compared to old series, with a corresponding decline in the estimates for the household sector. The estimates for private corporate sector are presented separately under two subcategories: private financial corporations and private non-financial corporations.

Improvements in Coverage of Sectors

Use of MCA 21 Database for Corporate Sector

In sourcing of new data sets, the use of MCA 21 database for the private corporate sector stands out as the most outstanding change. Traditionally, the population estimates of savings and capital formation of the corporate sector were derived using the Reserve Bank of India's (RBI) studies of non-government non-financial public limited companies (NGNF PLC) and NGNF private limited companies (NGNF PTC). Since these studies are based on sample companies, they had to be scaled up using blow-up factors—ratio of paid-up capital (PUC) of population to the PUC of sample companies. In the 1950s and 1960s, these sample companies used to account for a major chunk of PUC of their respective population groups. For instance, the coverage of NGNF PLC, in terms of total PUC of the NGNF PLC, used to be about 80 per cent in the 1960s and 65 per cent in the mid-1980s. In the case of NGNF PTC, the coverage was 35 per cent in the 1950s which declined to about 13 per cent in the mid-1980s. With major policy reforms introduced since the early 1990s, there has been a phenomenal rise in the growth of private sector companies and consequently, the coverage of RBI sample companies has declined sharply in the last two and a half decades or so (Rajakumar, 2015). The RBI's studies coinciding with the new NAS base year of 2011–12 had NGNF PLC and PTC accounting for 30.5 per cent and 6.8 per cent, respectively, of PUC of their population.

Thus, with the coverage of RBI studies in terms of PUC deteriorating, concerns have been raised time and again on the reliability of estimates based on their blow-up factor (Rajakumar, 2003; Nagaraj, 2009; Rangarajan HLC Report, 2009). In the early 1980s, the Working Group on Savings, chaired by K.N. Raj (Government of India, 1982), had endorsed the use of data set of RBI sample companies and blow-up method for estimating corporate savings and capital formation because of the large coverage at that point in time, though recommended use of representative sample for PTC. Rangarajan High Level Committee (Ministry of Statistics and Programme Implementation, 2009) recommended using a larger set of companies so as to improve the reliability of the estimates.

Until then, the Companies Act had mandated all registered companies to file manually annual reports with the Registrars of Companies (ROC) after their annual general meetings. Such filings were, however, far from satisfactory. The National Statistical Commission (2001) observed that only 47 per cent of registered companies filed their returns for 1997–98 by March-end 1999. Therefore, in order to cover all registered companies and following the advancement in telecommunications technology, the Ministry of Corporate Affairs (MCA) undertook a major step—to implement an e-governance programme, popularly known as MCA 21,[6] whereby registered companies were required to submit their returns online.

With effect from 2010–11, MCA 21 has been made mandatory[7] for corporate filing in a web platform known as XBRL (Extensible Business Reporting Language) for four classes of companies—companies listed in any stock exchange in India and their India subsidiaries, companies having PUC Rs 5 crore and above, companies with a turnover of Rs 100 crore and above, and companies required to file their returns in 2010–11 through the XBRL platform. Filings by other companies have to be done through another web platform known as Form 23 CA/ACA,[8] which collates financial information in a simpler e-form. The LLP firms are also covered by MCA 21 portal, but they need to file through LLP Form from 2012–13.

With considerable success being achieved in terms of the number of registered companies e-filing their returns, the MCA 21 has become a preferred data set over the erstwhile sample-based RBI studies and as such CSO has decided to use the same for NAS purposes.

Apart from MCA 21 data, yet another improvement has been introduced for the corporate sector data. In the earlier series, in the initial years of advance and provisional estimates (PE), the manufacturing sector output was being measured through IIP. In the new series, for Advance Estimates (AE), IIP growth estimates for some quasi-corporate and unorganized segments, supported by data available from listed companies for the first three quarters, are used, while, for the PE, IIP for some sectors such as mining and quarrying and the information available from company finance studies of RBI supplemented with the information available from the advance filing of corporate accounts, that is, in respect of listed companies under stock exchanges (Bombay Stock Exchange and National Stock Exchange) (CSO, 2016b), are used to derive the value added data, as explained further.

The Process of Blowing-up or Scaling-up

But the problem of full coverage continues to remain. By the time CSO begins to retrieve information from MCA 21, it is very unlikely that all companies would have completed e-filing. At the time of the release of NAS new series in January 2015, for the first two years 2011–12 and 2012–13, CSO could cover about only 5.24 lakh non-financial companies through online reporting of forms 23ACA/AC and 31,636 companies through XBRL reporting, though there were close to 7.5 lakh and 8.3 lakh active companies in those years, respectively (MCA, 2014). In order to account for the uncovered companies, CSO uses traditional blow-up procedure by deriving population PUC based on active companies, defined to include all those companies which have filed their returns at least once in the last three years.[9] Those covered companies had accounted for 85 per cent of population PUC (CSO, 2015). Thus, though a large number of companies have been covered, the blow-up procedure was not completely dispensed with.[10]

There is yet another catch in the application of this blowing-up procedure. As rightly desired by Sinharay,

---

[6] It is called thus because MCA has the objective of covering all registered companies under the programme by 2021.

[7] Vide MCA Circular No. 16/2012 dated 06/07/2012. MCA 21 has several dimensions of taxonomy for filing based on the revised Schedule IV to the Companies Act (MCA, 2014).

[8] While Form 23ACA collects information relating to profit and loss account, the Form 23CA collects from balance sheets (CSO, 2015b).

[9] RBI works out coverage based on the population PUC supplied by the MCA (formerly by Department of Company Affairs).

[10] At the time of release of NAS new series in January 2015, CSO had used a single blow-up factor for both NGNF PLC and NGNF PTC. Rajakumar (2015), besides pointing out how such procedure could give rise to overestimates, argued in favour of working out estimates separately for NG PLC and NG PTC using separate blow up factors and then combine them to arrive at the population estimates. Also see Rao (2015). This procedure has now been followed in the first revised estimates for 2014–15 released in January 2016 (CSO, 2016).

Table 4.16 Investment Rate (at Current Prices)

Items	2004–05			2011–12		
	1999–2000 Series	2004–05 Series	Differences	2004–05 Series	2011–12 Series	Differences
	As % of GDP at market prices					
Gross Fixed Capital Formation						
Public Sector	6.4	6.9	0.5	7.1	7.3	0.2
Private Corporate Sector	9.5	9.1	−0.4	9.4	11.2	1.8
Household Sector	12.5	12.7	0.2	15.2	15.7	0.5
Total	28.4	28.7	0.3	31.8	34.3	2.6
Gross Capital Formation						
Public Sector	6.9	7.4	0.5	7.7	7.5	−0.2
Private Corporate Sector	10.8	10.3	−0.4	10.1	13.2	3.1
Household Sector	12.7	13.4	0.8	15.8	15.9	0.1
Total	30.3	31.2	0.9	33.6	36.7	3.0
	As percentage to total					
Gross Fixed Capital Formation						
Public Sector	22.5	24.1	1.5	22.3	21.4	−0.9
Private Corporate Sector	33.5	31.8	−1.7	29.7	32.7	3.0
Household Sector	44.0	44.2	0.2	48.0	45.9	−2.1
Total	100.0	100.0	0.0	100.0	100.0	0.0
Gross Capital Formation						
Public Sector	22.7	23.8	1.1	23.0	20.5	−2.4
Private Corporate Sector	35.5	33.1	−2.4	30.1	36.1	6.0
Household Sector	41.8	43.1	1.3	46.9	43.4	−3.6
Total	100.0	100.0	0.0	100.0	100.0	0.0

output is dissected into seed, feed, and wastage, exports net of imports, and change in stock based on some thumb rules and past evidences and the balance is treated as household consumption expenditure. Similarly, GFCF is derived from production data based on capital goods data in the IIP. Second, the consumption component of production-side data are valued differently; in food items, ex-farm price for product method and retail price for some part of consumption. This is done in the absence of direct data on expenditures on a regular basis. Third, expenditure side data entail more projections and rules of thumb rate calculations than production-side data for measuring GDP. Finally, it should be recognized that even if independent expenditure side data were available for household consumption and fixed capital formation, there is no guarantee that such data would agree with production-side data. It is the experience of statisticians the world over that some source differences always give rise to differences in estimation. For instance, field survey data on consumption or on capital formation do not entirely tally with the production data reported from

the farms and the factories as gathered by the official agencies.

Before we conclude this section, we may look at the estimates of discrepancies for different years under the two NAS series and at different stages of revisions in the new series (Table 4.17).

A few key observations can be made on these data. First, the size of discrepancies has been considerably reduced in the new series as compared with that in the 2004–05 series, which suggests that the new data sources or the methodology of estimation or both are an improvement over the previous data sources and methods. Second, for almost all the years since 2011–12, the sizes of discrepancies have narrowed as more data become available when estimates move from AE stage to PE stage, from PE stage to First Revised Estimates (FRE) stage, and finally to final or Second Revised Estimates (SRE) stage. Finally, however, as highlighted earlier, there are some noticeable differences in discrepancies as between the current price series and constant price series. One reason for this appears to be the differences

Table 4.17   Varying Pictures of 'Discrepancies' (Rupees, Crore)

A. Comparisons of 2004–05 & 2011–12 Estimates

	2011–12	2012–13	2013–14		2014–15
2004–05 Series	135,220	324,505	266,992		–
2011–12 Series	(–) 28,667 (SRE)	80,227 (SRE)	40,206 (SRE)		44,168 (FRE)

B. Discrepancies at Different Stages of Estimation (New Series at Current Prices)

	2011–12	2012–13	2013–14		2014–15
2011–12 Series	(–) 28,667 (SRE)	80,227 (SRE)	40,206 (SRE)		44,168 (FRE)
	(–)1,13,242 (SRE)	63,439 (SRE)	(–)58,373 (FRE)		(–) 98,678 (PE)
	–	–	–		(–)146,174 (AE)

C. Discrepancies at Current and Constant Prices (New Series)

2011–12 Series (Latest)	2011–12	2012–13	2013–14	2014–15	2015–16
Current Prices	(–) 28,667	80,227	40,206	44,168	9,135 (PE)
Constant Prices	(–) 28,667	70,586	(–)44,117	(–)35, 284	214,843 (PE)

in the method of estimation for capital formation and GVA, the one based on MCA 21 and the other continues to be based on ASI data.

KEY FEATURES OF GROWTH SCENARIO EMERGING FROM THE NAS NEW SERIES

There are certain distinct features of growth that are discernible in the new series; they have also been highlighted earlier. To enumerate them briefly,

1. Although GVA, at basic prices, and GDP, at market prices, have grown on annual basis, there is seen a distinct contrast in current and constant price estimates; while growth at current prices has been falling, that at constant prices has been rising during the past four years 2012–13 to 2015–16 (Table 4.18). As a result of these contrasting trends, the differences between the growth rates of both GDP and GVA, at current prices, and those at constant prices, have considerably narrowed down over the years. This phenomenon can be attributed to the falling trends in GDP or GVA deflators. This peculiar feature of the new series can be traced to the behaviour of WPI, which has an overwhelming influence on the GDP deflators and which has been behaving in a parallel fashion with such deflators.

2. Another distinctive feature of the new series is the unusually large revisions affected in successive updating of GDP and GVA estimates. Unlike in the 2004–05 series, the revisions subsequent to the 2011–12 series have been much larger, and

as explained further, this has much to do with alterations in the database, particularly for the manufacturing sector. The AE and PE are based on IIP and advance filing of corporate accounts with stock exchanges. For the FRE, apart from IIP for mining, the results of a larger sample of common companies (say, 3 lakh companies) are applied. As explained further, because of the divergent sources of data and varied sizes of companies, the estimates undergo substantial revisions and hence, we have proposed (i) corporate results be obtained by adopting the principle of stratified sampling instead of the simple random sampling method, and (ii) the final growth rates be obtained by relating the likes with likes so that the growth rates are not worked out in a period over the latest available.

3. There has been a phenomenal rise in government collection of indirect taxes in 2015–16—it grew by 19.4 per cent at current prices, but by 7.5 per cent at constant prices indicating a larger rise in its deflator. The changes in the deflator of taxes on products normally reflect changes in tax rates and collection rates of indirect taxes and, thus, the relatively higher growth of deflator of indirect taxes in 2015–16 shows that government has collected more revenue by taxing products and raising taxes. Also, it has been repeatedly emphasized by the government and CSO spokespersons that declining oil prices was the major cause for India's GDP growing at 7.9 per cent in Q4 of 2015–16. Anant, for instance, was quoted as saying thus: 'Insofar as the growth

Table 4.18 Key Aggregates of National Accounts (Base Year 2011–12)

Item	At Constant (2011–12) Prices					At Current Prices				
	2011–12	2012–13	2013–14	2014–15	2015–16	2011–12	2012–13	2013–14	2014–15	2015–16
Growth Rates										
GVA at factor cost		5.4	6.5	7.1			13.5	12.9	10.6	
GVA at basic prices		5.4	6.3	7.1	7.2		13.6	12.7	10.5	7.0
Taxes on Products		9.5	5.3	8.0	7.5		18.9	13.5	12.4	19.4
Subsidies on Products		12.7	−7.9	4.8	−5.6		21.5	−2.3	8.1	−5.7
GDP at market prices		5.6	6.6	7.2	7.6		13.9	13.3	10.8	8.7
Consumption of Fixed Capital		10.0	9.2	8.3	7.2		15.6	13.1	11.2	8.7
Private final consumption exp.		5.3	6.8	6.2	7.4		15.5	14.8	10.5	12.3
Govt. final consumption exp.		0.5	0.4	12.8	2.2		9.6	8.6	18.4	5.4
Gross capital formation		6.8	−1.9	6.3			12.9	1.8	9.3	
Gross fixed capital formation		4.9	3.4	4.9	3.9		10.8	7.3	7.9	3.3
Exports of goods and services		6.7	7.8	1.7	−5.2		13.8	17.0	0.2	−5.4
Imports of goods and services		6.0	−8.2	0.8	−2.8		14.5	2.6	1.3	−5.6
GNDI							13.6	13.2	10.6	8.5
Gross Saving							11.2	10.7	10.5	
Net Saving							9.3	9.6	10.2	
As % of GDP at market prices										
GVA at factor cost	92.7	92.5	92.4	92.3		92.7	92.4	92.1	91.9	
GVA at basic prices	92.8	92.6	92.3	92.2	91.9	92.8	92.6	92.1	91.9	90.4
Taxes on Products	10.2	10.6	10.4	10.5	10.5	10.2	10.6	10.7	10.8	11.9
Subsidies on Products	3.0	3.2	2.8	2.7	2.4	3.0	3.2	2.7	2.7	2.3
Consumption of fixed capital	10.5	10.9	11.2	11.3	11.3	10.5	10.7	10.6	10.7	10.7
Private final consumption exp.	56.2	56.0	56.1	55.6	55.5	56.2	57.0	57.7	57.6	59.5
Govt. final consumption exp.	11.1	10.6	9.9	10.4	9.9	11.1	10.7	10.2	10.9	10.6
Gross capital formation	39.0	39.4	36.2	35.9		39.0	38.6	34.7	34.2	
Gross fixed capital formation	34.3	34.1	33.0	32.3	31.2	34.3	33.4	31.6	30.8	29.3
Valuables	2.9	2.8	1.5	1.6	1.5	2.9	2.8	1.4	1.5	1.4
Exports of goods and services	24.5	24.8	25.1	23.8	20.9	24.5	24.5	25.3	22.9	19.9
Imports of goods and services	31.1	31.2	26.9	25.2	22.8	31.1	31.2	28.3	25.9	22.5
Discrepancies	−0.3	0.8	−0.4	−0.3	1.9	−0.3	0.8	0.4	0.4	0.1
Gross Saving to GNDI						33.8	33.0	32.3	32.3	
PFCE to NNI	63.4	63.8	64.1	63.5	63.4	63.4	64.6	65.5	65.3	67.5

is concerned, it is substantially on account of the subsidy compression. That is the major factor in the increase' (*Economic Times*, 2 June 2016). A more pertinent question is not asked as to what do subsidies have to do with working out the real growth? We trace it to the root of the problem, which is that it is improper to take the concept of GDP at market prices to measure the real GDP growth in the economy (discussed further in the next section).

4. A peculiar development is seen in the new series which concerns the phenomenon of *discrepancies*. As rightly pointed by Anant (*Economic Times*, 2 June 2016), discrepancies are inherent in the Indian NAS in which the methodology and data sources differ for the production-side of the GDP estimates (which is the principal estimate) with expenditure-side estimates, the most of which are projected and extrapolated from the available base data. Our issue is not with the large size of

discrepancies as some commentators perceive it. On the other hand, what we are intrigued by are the differences in *discrepancies* as between the current and constant price estimates and also as between the successive revised estimates. To cite two instances, first, *discrepancies* have been (–) Rs 44,117 crore, (–) Rs 35,284 crore, and (+) Rs 214,843 crore, respectively during 2013–14, 2014–15, and 2015–16 at constant prices. In contrast, these *discrepancies* have all been positive but not so large at current prices; they are Rs 40,206 crore, Rs 44,168 crore, and Rs 9,135 crore for these three years, respectively. The second instance concerns the changes effected in the sizes of discrepancies in the successive revisions of the NAS data series. For instance, the AE for 2015–16 at constant prices gave a figure of Rs 58,745 crore as *discrepancies*, but at the next stage of PE, the size of *discrepancies* has shot up to Rs 214,843 crore—nearly four-fold. A more intriguing trend is seen in the successive revisions effected for the year 2014–15 in its constant price estimates: (–) Rs 10,656 crore in AE; (+) Rs 43,491 crore in PE; and (–) Rs 35,284 crore in the FRE. In a subsequent section, we have speculated on the possible causes for these *discrepancies*, broadly attributing them to (i) different deflators used, (ii) differing sources of data for the private corporate sector, and (iii) corrections in the sizes of *discrepancies* with the flow of better information at successive stages of revision.

5. Persistent falling trends in the domestic capital formation to GDP and savings to GNDI ratios appear a distinct feature of the new NAS series (Figure 4.1). Contrasted to this is the steady increase in the growth rate. Interestingly, this macro-perspective gets sorted out if the growth measurement is altered to reference points with likes over likes—an important justification for comparing comparable estimates as proposed in the section under 'reference points for estimating growth'.

HOW REAL ARE THE GDP GROWTH ESTIMATES THEMSELVES?

Under this enquiry, we raise three issues: one, whether GDP at market prices can be considered an appropriate measure of income; two, are the deflators used appropriately; and, three, what should be the reference period or base estimates for working out growth for the recent periods?

GDP as a Measure of Income

Gross domestic product is essentially a value added concept. Once the final goods are adjusted for intermediate consumption, what we get is the value added that constitutes, by foolproof economic logic, as the earnings of land, labour, and capital, that is, factor shares. The

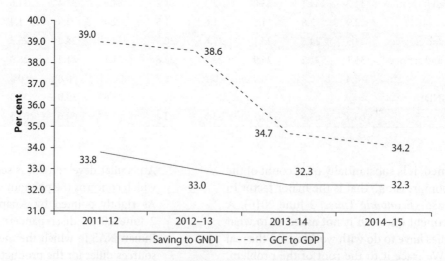

Figure 4.1   Trends in GCF and Gross Savings Rates

Source: Author's calculation based on data extracted from EPWRF India Time Series[20]

[20] Available at www.epwrfits.in (accessed on 3 July 2017).

contention that GDP, at factor cost, has no observable vectors of prices and output is factually correct, but it is only a technocratic argument and it misses out on the analytical thrust of GDP as a value added measure. That is, this measure of GDP at factor cost automatically gets quantity and price counterparts in measures of final goods and intermediate goods used to derive the value added. It does not require the rates of wages, interest, rent, and profit to derive such value added numbers. Factor cost valuation is, thus, an analytical construct in-built in the production approach. A genuinely accurate measure of real growth, and also the one close to measuring social welfare should, thus, be GDP at factor cost—a historically accepted concept, and not GDP at market prices which are influenced by the presence of indirect taxes and subsides, as argued earlier.

The new NAS series has embraced the use of GDP at market prices, that is, GVA *plus* indirect taxes net of subsidies, as the true measure of GDP. The authorities have done this by falling in line with the 1993 and 2008 UN SNA. We have probed into the genesis of this adoption. A detailed study traces this development to the writings of the US Department of Commerce without closer examination of its economic significance (Shetty, 2015). Comparing GDP at market prices against GDP at factor cost, well-known economists have given this judgment: 'addition of indirect taxes to factor costs would result in double-counting and an exaggerated national product total' (Kuznets, 1951). The US system has accepted that GDP 'is still the best measure of market value of goods and services, it is not necessarily a measure of welfare or even a significant measure of standards of living' (Greenspan, 2000). For us, GDP should indeed be a welfare measure, a true measure of the people's standards of living, not just a market-based commercial or accounting concept. With that understanding, distributional issues concerning the income shares of labour and capital are capable of being analytically addressed through the concept of GDP at factor cost and not through the concept of GDP at market prices. By accepting the US Department of Commerce's view, the UN SNA has grievously erred and departed from the most valid concept of GDP at factor cost—a welfare measure. Such an approach using GDP at market prices alone has harmed the analytical construct of the true national income measure. It included indirect taxes net of subsidies. A legitimate question is not asked as to how growth can be raised by increasing indirect taxes. But the fact is that in a nominal GDP growth of 8.7 per cent during 2015–16 against 10.8 per cent growth during 2014–15, there has been a 19.4 per cent increase in indirect taxes or 11.9 per cent increase in indirect taxes net of subsidies.

For real GDP, to an extent, the method of deflating indirect taxes may arrest the exaggerated growth in nominal terms. That is, CSO deflates the indirect taxes levied on quantity of products by extrapolating using volume indices of products; for those levied on values of products, it uses volume index with tax margin from the base year; and new taxes and collection rate increases are treated as price changes. With this method of using volume changes for deflation of indirect taxes, it is claimed that the real growth in GVA at basic prices and GDP at market prices become, by and large, similar for which there is some evidence in the growth rates. The growth rates at current prices during 2015–16 were 7.0 per cent in GVA and 8.7 per cent in GDP, with a difference of 1.7 percentage points, that is, far higher than those in the previous years. This difference was reduced to 0.4 percentage point in the same measures at constant prices—very similar to the earlier three years.

The import of this methodology used for measuring the deflators for product taxes has manifested itself in differing growth rates of implicit deflators of various NAS aggregates as presented in Table 4.19. The growth rate of implicit deflators of both GVA and GDP moved in tandem till 2014–15 with only marginal differences, but in 2015–16 they have diverged considerably by about 1.5 percentage points. The implicit deflator of product taxes remained marginally higher than GDP deflator over the years but in 2015–16, this divergence has considerably widened. While the implicit GDP deflator grew at 1 per cent in 2015–16 against 3.3 per cent in 2014–15, the implicit deflator of taxes on products grew at 13 per cent in 2015–16, compared to 4 per cent in the previous year. The divergence in the growth rates of GVA and GDP in 2015–16 in nominal terms, but not in real terms, as also their respective deflators in the same year should, thus, be attributable to the novel deflator method employed for product taxes. While this deflator method is indeed novel and helps to correct the artificially inflated nominal GDP growth due to indirect taxes, it does not obviate the basic objection to the use of an inappropriate concept of GDP for measuring real growth (Rajakumar and Shetty, 2016b).[21] Most importantly, the expansion of nominal GDP due to the inclusion of indirect taxes tends to overestimate the size of per capita GDP—an economic welfare measure.

[21] These two paragraphs have been a verbatim summary of ideas contained in the earlier study, namely, Rajakumar and Shetty (2016b).

Table 4.19   Annual Percentage Variations in Implicit Deflators of Selected NAS Aggregates

Year	GVA at Basic Prices	GDP	Taxes on Products	Subsidies on Products	Private Final Consumption Expenditure	Government Final Consumption Expenditure	Gross Fixed Capital Formation	Changes in Stock	Valuables	Exports of Goods and Services	Imports of Goods and Services
2012–13	7.8	7.9	8.6	7.8	9.7	9.0	5.7	6.7	5.4	6.6	8.0
2013–14	6.0	6.2	7.8	6.0	7.5	8.2	3.8	4.1	3.0	8.6	11.8
2014–15	3.2	3.3	4.0	3.2	4.0	5.0	2.9	1.8	2.4	−1.4	0.5
2015–16	−0.5 (−0.1)	1.0 (1.1)	13.0	−0.5	4.8	2.9	−1.6	0.4	−4.2	−0.3	−0.1

Source: Rajakumar and Shetty (2016b).

At this stage, it is necessary to recognize that the complex system of national accounts is capable of diverse analytical constructs, each of which has its own importance. First, there is the supply and use tables (SUT) framework for balancing supply and demand. Such balancing exercise involves the reconciliation of discrepancies that arise between the production side and the expenditure side due to the use of disparate data sources.[22] This is obviously done at GDP at market prices as the following final results suggest (Table 4.20). The GDP figures at current market prices contain over 7 per cent of indirect taxes which, by no stretch of imagination, can form part of real GDP estimation.

Second, GDP, at factor cost, which measures the value added as the contributions of labour, capital, and other factors in the production process. The measure so derived represents true value added as it is not coloured by the presence of any items outside the contributions of factors of production. This is the true economic welfare measure particularly when GDP is converted to per capita terms.

Finally, there is the *Consolidation Accounts of the Nation* which provides a comprehensive accounting framework integrating complex economic activities including capital finance and external transactions accounts, put together in the form of a set of national accounts for depicting the overall picture of the economy.

Each of these has independent analytical importance serving different purposes. It is necessary to recognize that it is improper to apply one measure to another which is unrelated. The balancing exercise under SUT is done at market prices but that does not qualify for measuring

[22] In the latest SUT built for 2011–12 and 2012–13, 'the balancing exercises were undertaken till the discrepancy between *supply* and *use* was reduced to around 3%' (CSO, 2016). Thereafter, there is no option but to adopt what has come to be known a RAS (automatic row-column prorate adjustments), and thus, equalize the production and expenditure sides.

Table 4.20   GDP by Expenditure and Production Approaches from Supply and Use Tables

			(Rupees, Crore)
	2011–12	2012–13	Increase in Per Cent
Reconciled Data			
Output	17,822,309	19,916,206	
Intermediate Consumption	9,654,721	10,644,823	
Product Taxes			
Less Subsidies	485,987	577,765	
Import Duty	143,396	163,556	
Total Indirect Taxes	629,383	741,321	7.0
GDP	8,796,971	10,012,704	13.8
GVA	8,167,588	9,271,383	13.5
As % of NAS (2016) given below			
GDP	100.70	100.62	
GVA	100.75	100.69	
Earlier Reported Estimates (NAS 2016)			
GDP	8,736,039	9,951,344	13.9
GVA	8,106,656	9,210,023	13.6

Source: CSO (2016).

real growth or for working out per capita income—an economic welfare measure. The latter has to be done at factor cost.

Appropriateness of Deflators

In the new NAS, there has arisen a major source of distortion in deflators, that is, vastly divergent behaviour of WPI and CPI insofar as annual inflation rates are concerned. The GDP deflators themselves are a conglomerate, based on individual deflators used for final goods consisting of consumption and capital goods and services; they sometimes cover output value indices, or

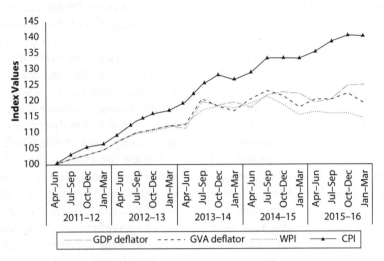

Figure 4.2   Movements in Price Indices

Source: Author's calculation based on data extracted from EPWRF India Time Series[24]

WPI or CPI themselves.[23] The WPI is based on wholesale price quotations of producers of domestically produced commodities such as basic, intermediate, and final goods and does not reflect taxes on products. The CPI has market price as the reference point but its basket comprises consumption items of goods as well as services, and as such, they absorb product taxes and subsidies. This may also include prices of imported goods, if they are consumed. Given these structural differences in the coverage of various indices and their weighing diagrams, some differences may be noticed amongst different price indices (Figure 4.2). However, the GDP deflators under new series move mostly in tandem with WPI.

While rebasing NAS, how has CSO relied on both CPI and WPI for deflating output of a number of commodities? The CPI used for 2011–12 series has been indexed to a recent period, that is, 2012, whereas the WPI still has price weights of 2004–05. If the structure of primary articles and manufactured output has undergone changes by 2011–12, the WPI weighing diagram would also have got altered. The failure to use price weights of more recent point in time is likely to impact estimates at constant prices, if composite price indices have been used as deflators—indeed that has been the case.

The question is not one of any inappropriateness of deflators; rather due to the peculiarity of the situation since the third quarter of 2011–12, the differing behav-

iour of CPI and WPI have contributed to the aberrations in the behaviour of deflators.

Reference Points for Estimating Growth

Moving on to the third issue, namely, the relevant reference period or base estimate to arrive at the current growth, we first discuss various phases by which CSO releases estimates of national income. First, CSO releases AE of a given financial year much before the closure of the financial year, sometime in the second week of February of that year, PE on the last day of May of the next year, FRE on the last Friday of January of the succeeding financial year, and finally SRE in the last quarter of the second succeeding year.[25] As at present, under the NAS new series, we do not have a single year for which GDP estimates are available through these four rounds of estimation. We do have AE, PE and FRE for 2014–15 and, FRE and SRE for 2013–14.

Rajakumar (2016) has observed that for the year 2013–14, SRE of real GDP and GVA are about 0.8 and 0.9 percentage point, respectively, lesser than their respective FRE. While FRE of GDP in 2014–15 is 0.9 percentage point lower than its PE, it is about one percentage point lower compared to AE. A similar trend is noticed in the case of FRE of GVA which is less than its corresponding PE and AE. Differences are not much between PE and AE in 2014–15 and 2015–16. Thus, there is not

---

[23] This is done in the absence of a Producers Price Index (PPI) which is universally accepted as the correct measure and which is said to be CSO's ultimate goal.

[24] Available at www.epwrfits.in (accessed on 3 July 2017).

[25] The release date for AEs has been advanced by a month in 2016 in view of advancing of presentation of the *Union Budget*.

much change between AE and PE, but a major revision happens between PE and FRE and further between FRE and SRE.

The root cause of this differences is that data sources radically change as we move from AE and PE to FRE and from FRE to SRE. As explained in Table 4.21, AE and PE have the same data sources, namely, IIP for some purposes and advance filing of corporate accounts with stock exchanges, but for FRE and SRE, the corporate sector data sources are 3 lakh common companies and 5.25 lakh companies, respectively. As explained in the earlier sub-section, the blowing-up in such situations are quite distinct and different; hence, we see divergent results.

Looking at it differently, as shown in Table 4.22, there are persistent declines in the estimates of GDP and GVA (both at current and constant prices) from one successive stage to another, from AE to PE, from PE to FRE, and finally from FRE to SRE. The implications of such persistent downward revisions are significant in two ways: first, lower estimates of GDP or GVA in each of the successive steps of estimation get hidden from the public glare. What gets highlighted is the inflated growth over the lowest estimate of the previous year. Thus, when PE is published for 2015–16, the growth rate is worked out over the latest estimates available for 2014–15, that is, the FRE for that year. But, the fact that the FRE of that year is a considerably reduced figure gets ignored. Between the PE and FRE that year, there was a reduction of 0.9 per cent in GDP at constant prices or that of 1.0 per cent in GVA at constant prices. Thus, if PE of 2015–16 is compared with the PE of 2014–15, we get a real GDP growth of 6.6 per cent; it is when we compare the PE of 2015–16 over FRE of 2014–15 that we get a real GDP growth of 7.6 per cent which is officially published and publicized.

Such revisions may be attributed to a variety of data sets resorted to in different phases of estimation. Data sets, for instance, used for estimating manufacturing GVA of private corporate sector, which contributes nearly two-thirds to total manufacturing GVA, is not very different for AE and PE but there are significant dif-

ferences between PE and FRE and between FRE and SRE (Table 4.22). Given this, should we consider the latest estimate available for the previous year as the reference point? Given the enormity of revisions arising from taking recourse to different data sets at different points of estimates, we contend that comparing latest estimates of GDP of a given year over the latest estimates of its preceding year may be less desirable; such a comparison would imply comparison of data which are non-comparable.

We are conscious of the fact that with the arrival of firmer data, the quality of estimates improves such that PE results appear better than AE, FRE results are better than SRE, and SRE results are better than FRE results. When we say better, we emphasize it as significantly better because the improvements of one stage over the other are sizeable such that they cannot be ignored while relating them for growth rate purposes. Here, we are also conscious of the fact that the preceding year's data become the benchmark estimates for moving forward the growth estimates. But, such benchmark yardstick becomes valid when the basis of revision does not radically change from one phase of revision to another. But, in the new series, the relevance of the benchmark gets completely negated.

We have concrete evidence for the successive results being significantly different from each other. This evidence is self-explanatory as detailed in the new methodology and data sources used for the new series (CSO, 2015b). In particular, this is relevant for 'the non-financial private corporate sector which contributed about 32 per cent of total GVA in the economy for the base year 2011–12' (Sinharay et al., 2015) and about 76 per cent of the manufacturing GVA. There are two components of this evidence. First, as cited earlier, the filing of accounts by the companies and their use for the NAS is a dynamic process—a process by which the number of companies covered goes on increasing. As per the methodology, there is the necessity of scaling up. It is this size of scaling up that gets reduced as the coverage improves. When a majority of the MCA 21 data are covered, the scaling up is just 15 per cent; this is for the SRE. For the

Table 4.21   Phase-wise Data Availability for Manufacturing Sector

Type of Estimates	Data Sources	
	2004–05 series	2011–12 series
Advance Estimates (AE) Provisional Estimates (PE)	Index of Industrial Production (IIP)	IIP + Advance filing of corporate accounts
1st Revised Estimates (FRE)	IIP	IIP + MCA 21
2nd Revised Estimate (SRE)	Annual Survey of Industries (ASI)	MCA 21 + Non-corporate ASI

Source: CSO (2015c).

Table 4.22 GVA and GDP Estimates at Different Stages of Revisions

(Rupees Crore)

Date of Revision	2011–12				GVA of Manufacturing (Current Prices)
	Total GVA		Total GDP		
	Current	Constant	Current	Constant	
January 2015	8,195,546	8,195,546	8,832,012	8,832,012	1,482,158
February 2015	8,195,546	8,195,546	8,832,012	8,832,012	
January 2016 (SRE)	8,106,656	8,106,656	8,736,039	8,736,039	1,409,986
	(−0.99)	(−0.99)	(−0.99)	(−0.99)	(−4.9)
	2012–13				
	GVA		GDP		
	Current	Constant	Current	Constant	
January 2015	9,252,051	8,599,224	9,988,540	9,280,803	1,654,084
February 2015 (FRE)	9,252,051	8,599,224	9,988,540	9,280,803	
January 2016 (SRE)	9,210,023	8,546,552	9,951,344	9,226,879	1,573,632
	(−1.00)	(−0.99)	(−1.00)	(−0.99)	(−4.9)
	2013–14				
	GVA		GDP		
	Current	Constant	Current	Constant	
January 2015	10,477,140	9,169,787	11,345,056	9,921,106	1,808,370
February 2015 (FRE)	10,477,140	9,169,787	11,345,056	9,921,106	
January 2016 (SRE)	10,380,813	9,084,369	11,272,764	9,839,434	1,714,730
	(−1.0)	(−1.0)	(−1.0)	(−1.0)	(−6.2)
	2014–15				
	GVA		GDP		
	Current	Constant	Current	Constant	
February 2015 (AE)	11,689,705	9,857,672	12,653,762	10,656,925	1,991,191
May 2015 (PE)	11,550,240	9,827,089	12,541,208	10,643,983	19,84,173
	(−1.2)	(−0.3)	(−0.9)	(−0.1)	(−0.4)
January 2016 (FRE)	11,472,409	9,727,490	12,488,205	10,552,151	1,845,541
	(−0.7)	(−1.0)	(−0.4)	(−0.9)	(−7.0)

Note: Figures in brackets are percentage variations over the preceeding stage.

FRE, wherein about 3 lakh companies are covered, the scaling up would be more than 50 per cent. And finally, at the lowest level end of coverage at the AEs and PEs, the scaling up would be around 70 per cent or more. Such differing scaling up would of course have differing contributions to the end results.

The second attribute of the dynamic process of corporate accounts filing relates to the differing growth rates emerging from the nature of companies filing accounts at successive stages. On this, a neat set of data has been presented in Sinharay, Kumar, and Anant. (2015). It is brought out therein how, for instance, the rates of increases in GVA have been found to be in ascending order in relation to their relative size (23AC/ACA, XBRL non-list, and XBRL listed), that is, smaller companies are growing relatively far higher than bigger companies.

Comparison of apples over apples and not apples over oranges

Therefore, though unconventional, we propose to compare PE of 2015–16 over PE of 2014–15 and contrast it with the usual practice of taking PE over FRE (Table 4.23). A difference in the growth rate of real GDP, by about one percentage point, is noticed from 7.6 per cent to 6.6 per cent if we use PE of 2015–16 over PE of

Table 4.23   Comparison of Growth Rate Using Different Reference Estimates

Sr. No.	Sectors	At Constant Prices		At Current Prices		As % of Total GVA in 2015–16 at Current Prices
		2015–16 PE over 2014–15 PE	2015–16 PE over 2014–15 FRE	2015–16 PE over 2014–15 PE	2015–16 PE over 2014–15 FRE	
1	Agriculture, forestry and fishing	1.3	1.2	6.5	4.9	15.4
2	Mining and quarrying	12.5	7.4	15.5	4.7	3.1
3	Manufacturing	2.6	9.3	0.5	8.1	17.5
4	Electricity, gas, etc.	1.2	6.6	14.9	10.8	2.2
5	Construction	11.7	3.9	9.5	1.3	8.5
6	Trade, hotels, etc.	4.9	9.0	3.5	6.6	19.2
7	Financial services, real estate, etc.	11.6	10.3	6.8	7.4	21.6
8	Public administration	6.1	6.6	11.6	12.1	12.6
9	GVA at basic price	6.1	7.2	6.3	7.0	100.0
	GDP at market price	6.6	7.6	8.3	8.7	

Note: Full nomenclatures:
4. Electricity, gas, water supply and other utility services
6. Trade, hotels, etc., comprised: Trade, hotels, transport, communication and services related to broadcasting.
7. Financial services, real estate, etc., comprises: Financial, real estate and professional services.
8. Public administration includes: Public administration, defence and other services
Source: Based on data extracted from CSO (2015b and 2016b).

2014–15. So is the case with real GVA, the growth of which gets corrected from 7.2 per cent to 6.1 per cent. Such change is discernible across-the-board except in agriculture and public administration. Real GVA of manufacturing sector (constituting 17.5 per cent of total GVA), wherein the corporate sector blowing-up is the most important, witnessed a steep decline from 9.3 per cent to 2.3 per cent if we consider PE over PE, whereas in the case of construction sector growth improves from 3.9 per cent to 11.7 per cent. Sectors such as trade, hotel, and so on, contributing 19.2 per cent to economy-wide GVA, also record a dip from 9.0 per cent growth to 4.9 per cent. Considering the sizeable nature of differences in the growth indicators from phase to phase, it is advisable to compare what may be said as apples over apples rather than apples over oranges.

Benchmark to Indicator Method for Data Revisions

We are aware that the aforementioned proposition of comparing PE of one year with PE of the previous year for working out annual growth rates instead of comparing PE against FRE of the preceding year as done now by the CSO, has been questioned by Anant (2016c). He has done so on the grounds that, based on 'Bench Mark to Indicator' method as a procedure recommended by the UN SNA for the revision of SNA series, the benchmark estimates are the previous year's FREs. Thus, according

to Anant, 'Comparing PE of the current year with PE of previous year is therefore methodologically inappropriate as the benchmark estimates on which the indicator growth is applied are different. Further, use of non-standard approaches is inconsistent with the fundamental principles of official statistics.'

This is an important statement as periodic revisions have to be undertaken to provide continuous and timely time series. But, our contention is that if the new data sources used at the stages of PE are far removed from, and inconsistent with, the firm final data set, the intervening results may have serious questions of credibility. With a view to examining the issue raised by Anant (2016c) closely, we have delved into a number of authoritative sources, such the Eurostat and European Central Bank (Branchi, Haine, Horvath, Kanutin, and Kezbere, 2007), OECD and Eurostat (McKenzie, undated), IMF (Carson, Khawaja, and Morrison, 2004), UN SNA 2008,[26] and the *SNA News and Notes*[27] ... all of which provided guidelines broadly on the 'good practices for revision policies'

[26] See paragraphs 15.45 to 15.50, 18.11 to 18.13, 18.33 and 18.37 to 18.39 of UN SNA (2008).

[27] SNA News and Notes is an information service of the Inter-Secretariat Working Group on National Accounts (ISWGNA). In the *SNA News and Notes* of May 2000, there was a sub-section on 'Implementing the 1993 SNA: How to Deal with Revisions'. In it, there is a detailed description of the 'Bench-Mark Indicator' approach. See Hexeberg (2000).

both for short-term and long-term revisions of official statistics, primarily National Accounts; they have discussed at length the 'Bench-Mark to Indicator' approach on which Anant (2016c) has based his critique of our proposition.

Guidelines on Data Revisions

We have done this extensive coverage because the issue raised by Anant (2016c) is an important one. In this literature, a number of issues have been posed and guidelines set out for revisions of official statistics. In this respect, the CSO's approach to adopting *revision cycles* should be commended as it has been observing all general principles of good governance in statistics as set out in the IMF Working Paper and other documents referred to previously; its approach has been very transparent providing advance information on the revision calendars as prescribed by the IMF's special data dissemination standards (SDDS) and general data dissemination system (GDDS). However, the revisions involved in the latest NAS and the resultant growth rates in GDP disseminated have raised some misgivings when we juxtapose the results against the guidelines contained in the above literature. In the maze of issues that the above literature, we identify those that are of direct relevance to the justification of the proposition made by us.

First, as part of the OECD/Eurostat study referred to here, a case study of the revisions of Dutch estimates of GDP volume growth was made. That study had the following distinct question posed:

It is an interesting question, whether estimates before and after a benchmark revision should or should not be compared to each other. On the one hand, it may be argued that comparing estimates based on different definitions or concepts is like comparing apples and oranges, on the other hand, one may argue that users are still interested in the continuity of time series even if there has been a benchmark revision. If benchmarking results in large changes, that will be of concern to the users. (Hoven, 2008: 3)

Second, in this respect, we reproduce a key principle the IMF Working Paper has set out which may appear common place but very significant in the context of the revisions effected in the CSO's new NAS series. The IMF paper states,

On Accuracy: Although they [policy makers] want timely data on which to base their decisions, they do not want to take a decision based on data that are likely to change substantially in the next month or next quarter (Hoven, 2008: 10).

It is in this context, we recall former RBI Governor D. Subbarao's statement as to how he was confronted with the fluctuating GDP numbers and how difficult it was to formulate monetary policy:

The poor quality of data is compounded by frequent and significant revisions, especially in data relating to output and inflation which are at the heart of monetary policy. As governor Y.V. Reddy put it with his characteristic wit, everywhere around the world, the future is uncertain: in India, even the past is uncertain. It is this data uncertainty under which the Reserve Bank has to make policy; it does not have the luxury of waiting until the past becomes crystal clear. Flawed data was also the culprit behind the 'stagflation' puzzle we had encountered in 2012 when growth moderated steeply from 8.9 per cent in 2010–11 to 6.9 per cent in 2011–12 even as inflation remained elevated. … It now turns out that there was no puzzle, after all. Subsequent data revisions tell us that growth had not slowed as sharply as indicated by real-time data, which explains both the presence of high inflation and absence of any stagnation (Subbarao, 2016: 54–55).

As displayed in the data presented in Tables 4.22 and 4.23 earlier, there have been downward revisions in each of the four years 2011–12 to 2014–15 from AE to FRE in real GDP numbers and more so, in GVA of the manufacturing sector. For instance, if the RBI were to formulate monetary policy based on PE or even FRE, they would assume certain real GDP growth or certain manufacturing growth, which finally turns out to be significantly lower. There is a definitive reason which has contributed to this, that is, the shifting data sources for the GVA estimation of the manufacturing sector, as elucidated earlier.

Finally, the most forceful reason advanced by Anant (2016c) for questioning our proposition of PE over PE, is the 'Benchmark-Indicator Approach'. For this, as cited earlier, Anant has argued that for the PE of 2015–16, 'the benchmark estimates are the previous year's First Revised Estimates'. We beg to differ here. If the nature of source data used for the two sets of estimates are qualitatively different, the benchmark estimates do not have to be the previous year's FRE. When the database for the two sets of results, PE and SRE, are significantly different and when there is concrete evidence of the end results in terms of growth rates being different, there is no justification for following that strategy. Our considered view is that when the situation of step-by-step revisions are taking place and the finality of estimates for a year are yet to be reached, the CSO should disseminate GDP and sectoral growth rates based on benchmark estimates of comparable sets rather than non-comparable sets. In this respect, we have an authoritative guidance set out in the *SNA News and Notes* (Hexeberg, 2000) which has deliberated at length precisely on the subject of 'the benchmark indicator approach'. To quote this source:

Generally benchmarking means combining a time series of data (indicator) with more reliable level-data from one or several benchmark years for the same variable. In the benchmarking process the benchmark(s) solely determine the overall level of the series, while the indicator determines the (short-term) movements. Thus, only the movements, and not the overall level, of the indicator are of any importance. In the context of conducting major revisions the indicator may be:

- the old national accounts estimates for the series;
- the original source data for the series;
- recompiled source data for the series;
  or
- a related series'. (Hexeberg, 2000: 9)

To elaborate on the proposition made here, the first three attempts of the revision cycle—AE, PE, and FRE—are based on data which are conjunctural in nature. The time series arising out of them should be segregated from the time series based on SRE and final estimates. In those conjunctural series, the growth rates to be published and advocated for the use of economic policy formulation should be likes over likes and not apples over oranges. This proposition should be placed as an official arrangement for growth estimates.

CONSEQUENCES OF ADOPTING MCA 21 DATA

The use of MCA 21 database, besides aiding to follow enterprise approach, has been perceived to overcome the basic problem associated with building up population estimates for private corporate sector, as they contain data of more than 5.5 lakh active companies compared to erstwhile narrow database of RBI company studies based on a fewer thousands. The problem lies in the way a company is classified under an industry group or under a state based on Corporate Identity Number (CIN) code and the use of blow-up factors to arrive at population estimates.

The CIN is a 21-digit alpha-numeric code assigned to each of a company by the Registrar of Companies (ROC) at the time of registration. It is a unique code intended to facilitate tracking variety of information that a company holds with ROC. First digit is a character that indicates if a company is listed (L) or unlisted (U). Next five digits provide description of economic activity (or industry) that a company has been engaged with (belong to). Next two alphabets denote the state in which the company is registered (for instance, KL for Kerala). This is followed

by four digits of the year of incorporation, usually a calendar year. Next three alphabets denote type of ownership (for instance, GOI for Companies owned by Government of India, SGC for Companies owned by State Government, PLC for Public Limited Company and PTC for Private Limited Company).[28] Further, finally, the last six digits are the registration number (ROC code) issued by ROC to a company at the time of its registration. Thus, the CIN reveals several information of a company that is of interest to national income accounting such as industry group or state or ownership type.

The problem is that once a company has been issued a CIN code, it remains unchanged. The ROC may change CIN code, provided the company makes a fresh application to that effect. This can pose problem for estimating output, and thereby, value added of an industry. Consider a company that has been set up as one belonging to the industry of electrical goods or auto components manufacturing. If the company eventually becomes a trading company, its value of output will still be captured under the original industry code. This can potentially complicate the understanding of the structure of the economy.

While CIN code reveals the state in which a company has been registered, it may so happen that most of the company's activities may be spread across the country or concentrated in a state other than where it has been registered. Relying on CIN code for estimating output in these states could be misleading.[29] The use of MCA 21 data, thus poses unprecedented challenges for estimating state domestic products.

Moreover, the use of blow-up factor for uncovered companies could lead to overestimate if uncovered companies do not exist (and therefore, do not comply with the e-filing requirements) and, as pointed out by Nagaraj (2015b), due to the presence of companies, primarily PTC, not actively engaged in economic activities. We concede that it is not the role of the country's statistician's to determine the working status of registered companies, but we cannot ignore the chances of upward bias inherent in the blow-up method.

---

[28] Other abbreviations used in the CIN code include the following: FLC for Financial Lease Company as Public Limited; FTC for Subsidiary of a Foreign Company as Private Limited Company; GAP for General Association Public; GAT for General Association Private; NPL for Not For Profits License Company; ULL for Public Limited Company with Unlimited Liability and ULT for Private Limited Company with Unlimited Liability.

[29] Barman (2016) has pointed out the need for collating data at the district level. This may not be useful to estimate domestic product at the state level.

Need to Adopt the Principle of 'Stratified Sampling' Rather Than 'Simple Random Sampling' approach to derive corporate results

These discussions of MCA 21 database in the above two sub-sections, particularly concerning the issues of blowing-up for the uncovered companies, raises an important methodological question. At present, the CSO adopts a method which is derived from the simple random sampling technique. That is, if 85 per cent of the companies based on PUC is covered, the resultant numbers are scaled up by another 15 per cent irrespective of the size or any other characteristics revealed for the balance companies.

What is important is to stratify the companies based on at least their sizes and when weights are assigned based on such stratification, the eventual results would very likely improve. An important stratification method that the CSO adopted at their FRE for 2014–15 (CSO, 2016) was the use of separate scaling factors for 'public limited companies' and 'private limited companies' in the MCA 21 database instead of a common scaling factor used earlier.

The issue of the private corporate sector calls for a more robust application of the principle of stratified sampling based on the sizes of companies within both the sets of companies rather than the simple random sampling method. This is possible to be adopted as the PUC series are available for the uncovered companies. The stratification can be done on the basis of the size of PUC in respect of both covered and uncovered companies separately for private limited and public limited companies.

MCA 21 Data Require an Independent Audit

As brought out earlier, one of the most conspicuous aspects of the new NAS series has been the use of MCA 21 database in respect of corporate enterprises in a much more comprehensive manner than hitherto. This database has substituted the earlier data uses in two key respects. First, it has replaced the use of RBI sample studies on different types of corporate sector generating estimates for certain key components of NAS, particularly corporate savings and investment. Second, it has facilitated the application of *enterprises* approach to the corporate sector replacing, as far as possible, the *establishment* approach, which is inherent in the data produced by the ASI data.

The ASI collects data from individual factories serving as independent *establishments*, whereas companies serve as umbrella *enterprises* harbouring one or more establishments. When such companies are classified in the MCA 21 database as *manufacturing companies* statistically possessing more than 50 per cent of output value from manufacturing activities, their overall level of manufacturing output would be higher than what the ASI data depict. Apart from that, such manufacturing companies also provide post-manufacturing value added generated through marketing or trading as well as other services. As emphasized by the government (MOSPI, 2015), 'This component of value added was earlier being excluded from GDP because it was not covered in ASI, although the concerned enterprises belonged to the manufacturing segment.'

Intriguing Results

Be that as it may, the manufacturing GVA and their annual growth rates in the new NAS series have produced peculiar results, particularly when they are compared with similar results of the 2004–05 series. As may be seen from Table 4.24, the new series have radically altered the sector's growth scenario. For instance, the earlier reported manufacturing growth in real terms of 1.1 per cent for 2012–13 has been pushed up to 6.2 per cent under the new method or for 2013–14, from (–)0.7 per cent to 5.3 per cent. Or for the latest two years, when IIP has registered growth rates of 2.8 per cent in 2014–15 and 2.4 per cent in 2015–16, the new series places the manufacturing growth at constant series for these years at 5.5 per cent and 9.5 per cent, respectively. When confronted with such a scenario, the officials have rightly defended the new official series by arguing that IIP provides growth rates of physical output, whereas the NAS provides such growth rates in value added estimates. However, it deserves to be noted that whenever the ASI data were used even in the 2004–05 series, the data were dependent on value added estimates and not physical output figures. At the same time, the new series has a few other kinds of improvements that has made a significant difference from the previous series. First, the new system captures better the coverage of small and medium industries. With a substantially wider coverage of as many as 5.24 lakh companies, the representation for smaller companies increases. Further, as Sinharay, Kumar and Anant (2015) bring out, the inclusion of smaller companies, which have shown higher growth in GVA than larger companies, has contributed to an upward revision of manufacturing growth. Second, the services rendered by head offices of manufacturing enterprises are captured through MCA 21 data unlike in the ASI.

These are all valid arguments but the moot question is: do they justify such metamorphic alterations in the growth rates as 1.1 per cent becoming 6.2 per cent or (–)0.7 per cent becoming 5.8 per cent (Table 4.24)? We have attempted a tentative analysis of this data, as shown in Table 4.25. We have tried to make an estimate of the possible size of GVA attributable to head office (HO) operations, that is, the post-manufacturing marketing or trading and other services produced by the enterprises. These estimates show that such GVA contributions have not only been very large—as much as ranging from 26 per cent to 38 per cent of the pure manufacturing GVA, but also their proportions have jumped from 25.9 per cent in 2011–12 to 35.3 per cent in 2012–13 and further to 38.6 per cent in 2013–14. This implies that the growth rates in such contributions have been phenomenal, that is, by 40.4 per cent in the first year and by another 15 per cent in the next year.

These suggest that not only the level of aggregate GVA including HO operations appear much higher than the GVA generated as per ASI data but also the contributions of such HO operations grow at phenomenally high rates. It is these contributions that catapult the manufacturing GVA growth rate, in the examples given here based on ASI data availability, from 3.1 per cent to 10.8 per cent in 2012–13 and from 5.7 per cent to 8.3 per cent in 2013–14. On the face of it, such upward revisions appear unrealistic not only in the levels of GVA but also in successive growth rates. Hence, it is necessary for the CSO to take a fresh look at these data, if necessary, by undertaking a special independent audit of the MCA 21 data which has contributed to these misgivings.

Table 4.24   Manufacturing GVA: New Series Compared with 2004–05 Series

	Growth at Current Prices		Growth at Constant Prices		GVA Share in Total GDP	
	2004–05 Series	2011–12 Series	2004–05 Series	2011–12 Series	2004–05 Series	2011–12 Series
2011–12	–	–	–	–	14.7	18.1
2012–13	6.9	11.6	1.1	6.2	14.1	17.9
2013–14	2.2	9.3	(–) 0.7	5.8	12.9	17.3

Source: MOSPI (2015)

SUMMING UP

Undoubtedly, the latest revision exercise has been very commendable and the methodological changes and changes in the coverage of data are indeed praiseworthy.

The welcome change includes the use of data sets for a large number of companies instead of a limited sample, broadening the coverage of private corporate sector and inclusion of new asset items under capital formation. However, different building blocks do raise questions of credibility.

Table 4.25   GVA of the Manufacturing Sector

(Rupees, Crore)

	Part A: GVA of Organized Manufacturing						Part B: GVA of Total Manufacturing (Organized Plus Unorganized)
Year	Public Sector[1]	Private Corporations[2]	Total Corporate Sector [2+3]	ASI (GVA at Current Prices)[3]	Derived GVA on Account of Head Office Operations [4–5]		
(1)	(2)	(3)	(4)	(5)	(6)		
2011–12	1,31,973	10,98,467	12,30,440	9,76,939	2,53,501	[25.9]	14,09,986
2012–13	1,32,864	12,30,222	13,63,086	10,07,280	3,55,806	[35.3]	15,73,632
	(0.7)	(12.0)	(10.8)	(3.1)	(40.4)		(11.6)
2013–14	1,38,184	13,37,727	14,75,911	10,65,111	410,800	[38.6]	17,14,730
	(4.0)	(8.7)	(8.3)	(5.7)	(15.5)		(9.0)

Notes: (i) Figures in round brackets are annual percentage increases (ii) Figures in square brackets are col. (6) as a proportion of col. (5), that is, Head Office (HO) operations are as percentage of ASI GVA.

[1] These cover general government, Departmental Enterprises (DE) and Non-Departmental Enterprises (NDE)

[2] These include Quasi-Corporations (QC)

[3] Includes public & private limited companies, NDEs, proprietary & partnership factories, Hindu Undivided Families (HUFs) & Khadi and Village Industries Commission (KVIC), etc.

First, corporate sector and its data, especially those attributed to the activities of the HO. One cannot overlook the corporates' motivation relating to taxes, transfer pricing, and capital market orientation. Influence of these factors will impact corporate accounting, and hence, there is need for scrutinizing the content and quality of MCA 21 database.

Second, changes affected at successive rounds of revisions lead to the question of what should be considered as the reference estimates for arriving at growth rates for later periods. We need to consider working out growth rates based on comparable estimation, that is, PE over PE, FRE over FRE, and SRE over SRE.

Third, the tenability of the implied use of 'simple sampling technique' for scaling up purposes in respect of the corporate sector results, appears suspect; it calls for a closer look.

Fourth, dichotomy between the declining trend in savings and investment rate and rising growth rate, complicate the understanding of the emerging macro-economic relationship under the new series. They do not tie up. This once again calls for reconsideration of the reference estimate for working out growth rates because we find that our approach to deriving growth rates based on comparable estimation resolves this issues to a great extent.

Fifth, the divergence between the trend in the growth rate of industry as per IIP and under NAS new series also leads one to wonder why not consider reconstruction of IIP side-by-side with rebasing of NAS.

Sixth, use of WPI with old weighing diagram as deflators undermine its appropriateness. Every time the NAS is rebased, price indices should be also rebased. More so, given the fact that GDP measures output at market prices, WPI may be irrelevant and inappropriate as deflator. A way to overcome this problem is to construct a producers' price index (PPI).

Finally, the misgivings about the nature of the new estimates arise from a number of other concerns such as the need for the application of double deflation method in manufacturing and the method of reconciling production-side and consumption-side estimates The statistical establishment is now admittedly engaged in producing what are called *Back Series* of National Accounts for which it would apply the same method and data sources with which many academicians have become uncomfortable. Therefore, we are constrained to suggest the appointment of an independent expert group to examine afresh all the issues that have arisen in the recent revision of National Accounts and offer recommendations to set the matter right.

REFERENCES

Alagh, Y.K. 2015. 'The Alarming Investment Slide.' *Business Line*, 10 June.

Anant, T.C.A. 2015. 'Don't Compare New GDP Data Series with Old.' *Economic Times*, 14 April.

———. 2016. 'Government Making Efforts to Reduce Discrepancies in GDP Data.' *Economic Times*, 3 June.

———. 2016a. 'Discrepancies are Inherent Part of Expenditure Side of GDP as of Now.' *Business Standard*, 2 June.

———. 2016b. 'IIP has Limitations as a Representative of Aggregate Growth in Manufacturing.' *The Hindu*, 20 June.

———. 2016c. 'Discrepancies in GDP Data.' A reply to the EPW Editorial on the latest data on India's GDP Series, *Economic and Political Weekly* 51 (30, 23 July): 4–5.

Barman, R.B. 2016. 'Rethinking Economics, Statistical System and Welfare: A Critique with India as a Case.' *Economic and Political Weekly* 51 (28, 9 July): 46–56.

Bhuyan, P. 2016. 'Measurement of Central Bank Output Methodological Issues for India.' *RBI Working Paper Series WPS (DEPR): 06, 2016*, Reserve Bank of India, Mumbai.

Branchi, M., H.C. Dieden, W. Haine, C. Horvath, A. Kanutin, and L. Kezbere. 2007. Analysis of Revisions to General Economic Statistics, *Occasional Paper Series No. 74*, October. European Central Bank, Frankfurt.

Carson, C.S., S. Khawaja, and T.K. Morrison. 2004 'Revisions Policy for Official *Statistics*: A Matter of Governance.' *IMF Working Paper No. WP/04/87*, May.

Central Statistics Office. 2012. *National Accounts Statistics Sources and Methods 2012*, Ministry of Statistics and Programme Implementation, New Delhi.

———. 2015. 'No Room for Doubts on New GDP Numbers.' *Economic and Political Weekly* 50 (16, 18 April): 86–89.

———. 2015a. *Changes in Methodology and Data Sources in the New Series of National Accounts: Base Year 2011–12*, Ministry of Statistics and Programme Implementation, New Delhi, 26 June.

———. 2016. '*First Revised Estimates of National Income, Consumption Expenditure, Saving and Capital Formation 2014–15*', Press Note, 29 January.

———. 2016a. '*Advance Estimates of National Income 2015–16 and Quarterly Estimates of Gross Domestic Product for the Third Quarter (Q3) 2015–16*', Press Note, 8 February.

———. 2016b. '*Provisional Estimates of Annual National Income, 2015–16 and Quarterly Estimates of Gross Domestic Product for the Fourth Quarter (Q4) 2015–16*', Press Note, 31 May.

Dholakia, H.R. 2015. 'Double Deflation Method and Growth of Manufacturing: A Comment.' *Economic and Political Weekly* 50 (41, 10 October): 88–90.

EPW Research Foundation. 2015. 'New Series of National Accounts: A Review.' *Economic and Political Weekly* 50 (7, 14 February): 74–78.

Goldar, B. 2015. 'Growth in Gross Value Added of Indian Manufacturing 2011–12 Series vs 2004–05 Series', *Economic and Political Weekly* 50, (21, 23 May): 10–13.

Government of India. 1982. *Capital Formation and Saving in India 1950–51 to 1979–80, Report of the Working Group on Savings* (chairman: K.N. Raj), Reserve Bank of India, Bombay.

Goyal, A. 2015. 'Measuring Indian Growth Why the Data should be Doubted Less.' *Economic and Political Weekly* 50 (32, 8 August): 66–70.

Greenspan, A. 2000. 'Remarks'. In Bureau of Economic Analysis, at the Press Conference *January 2000 Survey of Current Business* 'GDP: One of the Great Inventions of the 20th Century', at the http://www.bea.gov/scb/pdf/BEAWIDE/2000/0100od.pdf (accessed on 14 December 2016).

Hexeberg, B. 2000. 'Implementing the 1993 SNA: Backward Revision of National Accounts Data.' *SNA News and Notes* 11, May: 8–10.

Hoven, L. 2008. 'Using Results from Revisions Analysis to Improve Compilation Methods: A Case Study on Revisions of Dutch Estimates of GDP Volume Growth.' *Contribution to the joint OECD/Eurostat Task Force on 'Performing Revisions Analysis for Sub Annual Economic Statistics'*, May 30. Accessed at the https://www.oecd.org/std/40309550.pdf (accessed on 30 November 2016).

Kuznets, S. 1951. 'Government and National Income'. In *Income and Wealth*–Series I, edited by Erik Lundberg, International Association for Research in Income and Wealth, Bowes & Bowes, Cambridge.

———. 1959. *Six Lectures on Economic Growth*. New York: The Free Press of Glencoe.

Mazumdar, S. 2015. 'Manufacturing Growth in the New GDP Series.' *Economic and Political Weekly* 50 (24, 13 June): 120–21.

McKenzie, R. undated. 'OECD/Eurostat Guidelines on Revisions Policy and Analysis', *Summary report of the OECD/Eurostat Task Force on 'Performing Revisions Analysis for Sub-Annual Economic Statistics'*. Accessed at the http://www.oecd.org/std/40315564.pdf (6 December 2016).

Ministry of Corporate Affairs. 2014. *58th Annual Report on the Working & Administration of the Companies Act, 1956 Year ended March 31, 2014*, Government of India, New Delhi.

Ministry of Statistics and Programme Implementation (MOSPI). 2009. *Report of the High Level Committee on Estimation of Saving and Investment* (chairman: C. Rangarajan), Government of India, New Delhi.

———. 2015. *'New Series Estimates of National Income, Consumption Expenditure, Saving and Capital Formation (Base year 2011–12)'*, Press Note dated 30 January.

———. 2015a. *'Understanding the New Series of National Accounts: Frequently Asked Questions'*, Accessed from www.mospi.gov.in (accessed on 8 April 2016).

Nagaraj, R. 2009. 'Is Services Sector Output Over-Estimated? An Inquiry.' *Economic and Political Weekly* 44 (5, 31 January): 40–45.

———. 2015. 'Growth in GVA of Indian Manufacturing.' *Economic and Political Weekly* 50 (24, 13 June): 117–20.

———. 2015a. 'Size and Structure of India's Private Corporate Sector: Implications for the New GDP Series.' *Economic and Political Weekly* 50 (45, 7 November): 41–47.

———. 2016. 'Unorganized Sector Output in the New GDP Series: Why Has It Shrunk?' *Economic and Political Weekly* 51 (14, 2 April): 24–27.

Nagaraj, R. and T.N. Srinivasan. 2016. 'Measuring India's GDP Growth: Unpacking the Analytics & Data Issues behind a Controversy that Refuses to Go Away'. *India Policy Forum 2016*, National Council of Applied Economic Research (NCAER), New Delhi, 12–13 July.

National Statistical Commission. 2001. *Report of the National Statistical Commission*, (chairman C. Rangarajan), Government of India, New Delhi, 5 September http://mospi.nic.in/Mospi_New/upload/css_12.html (accessed on 30 August 2016).

Rajakumar, J. Dennis. 2003. 'How Real Are Estimates of Corporate Investment?' *Economic and Political Weekly* 38 (22, 31 May–6 June): 2155–58.

———. 2015. 'Private Corporate Sector in New NAS Series Need for a Fresh Look.' *Economic and Political Weekly* 50 (29, 18 July): 149–53.

———. 2016. 'Estimates of High GDP Growth in 2015–16 Not Entirely Convincing.' *Economic and Political Weekly* 51 (26 and 27, 25 June): 117–20.

Rajakumar, J. Dennis and S.L. Shetty. 2015. 'Gross Value Added Why Not the Double Deflation Method for Estimation?' *Economic and Political Weekly* 50 (33, 15 August): 78–81.

———. 2016. 'Some Puzzling Features of India's Recent GDP Numbers.' *Economic and Political Weekly* 51 (2, 9 January): 79–82.

———. 2016a. 'Continuous Revisions Cast Doubts on GDP Advance Estimates.' *Economic and Political Weekly* 51 (10, 5 March): 70–74.

Rajakumar, J. Dennis, V.B. Sawant, and A. Shetty. 2015. 'New Estimates of Saving and Capital Formation: Larger Number in a Declining Trend.' *Economic and Political Weekly* 50 (12, 21 March): 64–66.

Rao, S.K.G.K. 2015. 'Mystery of Private Corporate Sector Saving.' *Economic and Political Weekly* 50 (22, 30 May): 158–162.

Sen, P. 2015. 'The Three Unanswered Questions in GDP Data.' Interview in *Live Mint*, 2 September.

Shetty, S.L. 2015. 'Factor Cost Basis of GDP is Fundamental for Measuring Real Growth and Not GDP at Market Prices', A paper presented at the *34th Annual Conference of the Indian Association for Research in National Income and Wealth* held during 20–21 November 2015 at IGIDR, Mumbai.

Sinharay, A., A. Kumar, and T.C.A. Anant. 2015. 'Decoding the GVA Growth Rate.' *Business Standard*, 29 July.

Subbarao, D. 2016. *Who Moved My Interest Rate?: Leading the Reserve Bank of India Through Five Turbulent Years.* Gurgaon: Penguin Books.

United Nations. 1968. *A System of National Accounts 1968,* Studies in Methods, Series F No.2, Rev.3, United Nations: 52–53.

United Nations. 1993. *A System of National Accounts 1993,* United Nations.

———. 2008. *A System of National Accounts 2008,* United Nations.

5

Consumption and Nutritional Implications of Alternative Growth Scenario for India*

G. Mythili

INTRODUCTION

Transformation of agriculture in both production and consumption in the last two decades is quite prominent in the Indian economy. On the supply side, agriculture has moved away from predominantly cereal-led growth during the 1950s to 1980s towards non–cereal- and livestock-driven growth. In the last two decades, there is a drastic fall in the growth of cereals output and in contrast, livestock and non-cereal agricultural commodities, particularly fruits and vegetables, registered a significant increase in the growth of output. On the other hand, consumption patterns of households have also undergone changes, showing more preferences towards non-cereals, particularly pulses, fruits and vegetables, and milk and milk products.

Globalization is the key reason for bringing in dietary changes in consumption, which in turn has brought in necessary changes in the supply system, for example, large supply chains (Pingali and Khwaja, 2004). Past studies have also identified higher living standard and urbanization as the major drivers of changing consumption pattern. With increasing income, household preferences shift from cereals towards non-cereals and non-grain

products. The analysis of the composition of total calories intake by grains, non-grains, and animal products revealed that the contribution of grain (including pulses) to total calorie intake has declined from 71 per cent to 63 per cent from the 1980s to 2000s; the non-grain products' (excluding animal products) contribution has increased from 22 per cent to 28 per cent during the same period (Amarasinghe et al., 2007). It is also reported that the cereal consumption is fast decreasing annually in rural areas. This is particularly evident in rice consumption. The data of the National Sample Survey Organisation (NSSO) round of surveys revealed that the rural per capita rice consumption has recorded a fall of 0.5 per cent annually since 1993–94. Total cereal consumption per capita between 2005 and 2010 has declined by about 1 per cent. It is expected that fruits and vegetables would prominently figure in future consumption. What are the implications of this transition on nutritional outcome? It is expected that dietary diversification would improve the nutritional status of the households. The crucial question is 'what is the outcome for the poor?' Malnutrition is still a great concern for India. While economic research

* I received financial support for this study from SPANDAN project funded by Bill Melinda Gates Foundation and coordinated by IGIDR. I am very grateful to the sponsors. I also thank the review team of IDR for their constructive comments on an earlier draft.

on nutrition issues in India often focuses mainly on calorie intake, nutritionists are deeply concerned about a range of micro-nutritional deficiencies, including those of essential minerals and vitamins. It is reported that micronutrient deficiencies are severe among the children. Surveys of National Nutrition Monitoring Bureau (NNMB) indicated Indian children are consuming micronutrients less than half of the recommended norms (Radhakrishna, 2006). In the age group of one-to-three years, the ratio of average intake to 'recommended daily allowance' of rural Indian children is only 13 per cent for Vitamin A, 33 per cent for iron, and 30 per cent for calcium; similar statistics for the age group four to six years is , 16 per cent for Vitamin A, 35 per cent for iron, and 45 per cent for calcium (Gopaldas, 2006).

Regional analysis for India shows that in the year 2005–06, the prevalence of anaemia among women has recorded highest in the eastern states (more than 60 per cent in West Bengal, Jharkhand, and Assam) and is relatively high in other states as well. Kerala scores best with only about 32 per cent of women suffering from any form of anaemia (Gulati et al., 2012). In the policy paper addressing the issue of micronutrient deficiencies, the Indian National Science Academy (2011) has reported that iron deficiency (anaemia) is the most important public health issue—though some of the vitamin deficiency diseases such as beri beri (thiamine–vitamin B1 deficiency) and scurvy (vitamin C deficiency) are slowly vanishing, osteoporosis in adults , particularly in women after menopause due to calcium and vitamin D deficiency, is the next common disease after anaemia. The report further points out that cereal–pulses based Indian diets are deficient in micronutrients. It is characterized by low intake of income-elastic foods such as vegetables, fruits and foods of animal origin, which are rich in iron, calcium, and vitamins.

Given the importance of micronutrients in the context of health, and its neglect in the economic literature on nutrition, the present chapter intends to focus more on micronutrients. The chapter attempts to project consumption and nutritional outcome for the year 2020 under an alternative growth scenario using Computable General Equilibrium (CGE) analysis. The purpose is to make a comparison of nutritional outcome of different sources of growth. The results are expected to provide useful policy directions for improving nutrition intake of poor households.

The plan of the chapter is as follows: Some important findings of past studies have been discussed in the section 'literature on agriculture–nutrition linkages'. The status of base year production and consumption of major food products in India along with nutritional status is presented in the section 'status of production, consumption and nutrient-intake'. This is followed by a description of the methodology used in the present study and the scenario in the section 'methodology'. The section 'results of alternative scenarios' presents the scenario results followed by a discussion. The final section concludes the chapter.

LITERATURE ON AGRICULTURE–NUTRITION LINKAGES

Agriculture being the source of livelihood for about two-thirds of the population both directly and indirectly, the slowdown of agriculture since the 1990s has had a negative impact on rural income. The government has launched various programs to tackle this problem; deserving of particular mention is the National Rural Employment Guarantee Scheme (NREGS), an employment-guarantee program. There are studies which came out with varied results on whether the programs proved beneficial to the rural poor, and whether rural labour wage increase might have an adverse effect on agriculture. However, the link between agriculture growth and malnutrition is still a point for debate. Though growth, in general, is considered a favourable factor for increasing nutritional status, there are studies which maintain that agricultural growth could play a significant role only in the early stages. In addition, after a point, when the prevalence rate declines, it is argued that malnutrition would be less responsive to growth and hence diversification to non-agriculture, a particularly promising sector, is needed for further reduction in malnutrition (Ecker et al., 2012). However, the findings of these studies confirm that the child malnutrition could not be contained with mere growth channels, and it requires a specifically designed program which targets child nutrition.

Dev (2012) argues that there are three entry points through which the agriculture–nutrition link is established, namely inclusive growth, women in agriculture, and food prices. This study has highlighted the need for convergence between sectors and the role of institutions and policies in bringing in convergence.

Kadiyala et al. (2014) have examined different pathways linking agriculture and nutrition based on available research studies. Six major pathways have been identified in this chapter. The three pathways which can directly link agriculture and nutrition are: agriculture as a provider of home food, namely self-consumption of own produce; agriculture as a source of income for those with marketable surplus which then can be used for spending on alternative commodities which are nutritionally richer; macroeconomic impacts of agricultural growth which could influence the relative prices depending on the structure of growth and hence could change the diet composition depending on the price elasticity of demand. The indirect links are related to involvement of women in agriculture, which can influence intra-household allocation of food, health, and care—particularly childcare—and finally nutritional status of mothers engaged in agriculture influencing child nutrition.

The study finds fairly good evidence for some of the linkages. For instance, the ownership of land and cultivation of diversified crops and livestock asset ownership have a positive link with nutritional outcome. The pathway of agriculture as a source of income is found to be associated with calorie intake and dietary diversity. That livestock ownership has a significant influence on nutrition has also been supported by Carletto et al. (2015). Focusing on household-level impacts, the findings of the study also supports the notion that household crop production has a positive impact on dietary pattern and nutrition.

With more studies reporting the existence of a steep slope in the relationship between income and calorie intake, Kadiyala et al. (2014) opined that this finding has brought to fore an interesting paradox. If income is one important determinant of dietary quality, then it is a puzzle that nutritional outcomes are showing very slow and marginal improvement during the period of faster economic growth. One reason could be unequal distribution of income growth and lesser improvement in poor households with regard to consumption of micronutrient rich food.

As regards the next set of pathways between price changes and consumption pattern, the relation typically depends on whether the rural poor are net purchasers or producers of food. One finding that came out is the regions of higher food prices also reported higher rural wage growth. The findings also pointed out that increase in the prices of main staples have, in fact, spiked the protein consumption, which is a favourable nutritional outcome. The finding of the analysis of pathway between women in agriculture and intra-household decision-making have clearly established that women's asset ownership and the mothers' decision-making power impact the children's nutritional outcome in a positive manner (Bhagowalia et al., 2012; Swaminatha et al., 2012).

Empirical evidence indicates a significant correlation between increased food production, farming incomes, and better nutrition among rural labourers which in turn increase labour productivity among the rural working poor (Dasgupta, 1998). Nutritional improvement is, in fact, found to contribute to further increases in labour productivity in both current and future generations

(Hazell and Haddad, 2001). Heady et al. (2011) highlighted some of the reasons that limit agriculture's impact on nutrition, namely socio-economic factors such as gender inequality, intra-household inequality, and some public-targeted programs. For instance, the nationwide Integrated Child Development Scheme (ICDS) seems to have little impact on malnutrition due to its poor coverage and targeting (Gragnolati et al., 2005), and due to the absence of intervention during pre-natal and post-natal stages. It was also reported that India has the lowest public health care expenditure per capita in Asia; also the proportion allotted to preventive interventions is one of the lowest (Deolalikar, 2008; Jha and Laxminarayan, 2009). It was argued by Heady et al. (2011) that more than the disconnect between agriculture and nutrition, the disconnect between nutrition and policies related to health, education, and infrastructure might be playing a bigger role in explaining low improvement in malnutrition. This study has emphasized that agriculture could only be treated as one component in a multidimensional strategy aimed at nutrition improvement.

Using regression analysis, Thirtle et al. (2001) have examined the impact of agricultural productivity (land, labour, and total factor productivity) on nutritional outcome across countries. It is found that a 1 per cent increase in productivity (output per unit of land) leads to an increase in daily energy supply of 5.3 per cent and a decrease in the count of under-weight children under five of 0.42 per cent. Increasing supply that leads to a decline in food prices would directly result in an increase in real income for net food-buying households and hence more resources would be available for spending. This could bring in a potential increase in consumption of staple foods or more nutritionally rich foods.

Analysing the relative dominance of income and price effects, Gaiha et al. (2010) have found that for protein consumption, income effects outweigh the relative price effects. The non-linear nature of the relationship between agricultural growth and calorie intake has also been highlighted in a few studies. At the low level of calorie consumption, agriculture-led growth of the economy has a high impact on calorie consumption; but after a level, the influence of agricultural growth is declining (Headey, 2011). It is also found that dietary diversity is helped by non-agricultural growth.

Stressing the need for developing a more useful index to indicate nutritional status, Deaton and Drèze (2009) argue that calorie consumption alone could not represent nutritional status, as calorie requirement widely varies with respect to different sections of population depending on varying level of activities. This chapter emphasizes the need for considering micronutrients in arriving at a nutrition indicator. Gulati et al. (2012) have conducted a quantitative analysis to ascertain the linkage between agricultural performance and malnutrition. The study first computed the Combined (Adult and Child) Normalized Malnutrition Index (CNMI) using the data of the National Family Health Survey 3 (NFHS-3) survey for the year 2005–06. The study has found a significant negative relationship between agricultural productivity/ income and malnutrition.

There are very few studies in the Indian context using the general equilibrium framework. Panda and Ganesh-Kumar (2008) examined the impact of trade liberalization on nutritional outcome using the CGE model. Three nutrients fat, calories, and protein were considered for the simulation analysis. The study concluded that trade reforms were not really working with respect to increasing the nutritional status of bottom 30 per cent of the population. In fact, this percentile group recorded a decline in the calorie and protein intake though intake of fats recorded an increase. It also emphasized that food security impacts of any policy reforms must be given specific attention. Pauw and Thurlow (2010) conducted an analysis for Tanzania using the CGE model. The scenario analysis gave the result that promoting agricultural growth, especially the commodity maize, greatly strengthens the growth–poverty relationship and enhances households' caloric availability. Using a regionalized dynamic CGE model, the study has found that there is no significant relation between agricultural growth and nutrition outcomes and this has been attributed to slow growth of food crops and livestock. The study finally identified that low yield, constraints on post-harvesting stages of processing, and marketing and barriers to import substitution for major food crops are the major obstacles for nutrition improvement.

A survey of past studies revealed that there are no systematic analyses linking growth with micronutrient outcome within general equilibrium framework. This study fills this gap.

STATUS OF PRODUCTION, CONSUMPTION, AND NUTRIENT INTAKE

To understand the magnitude of transformation between 2005 and 2010, some production and consumption statistics are given in Tables 5.1 to 5.3. The data in Table 5.1 depicts a steep increase in the production growth of fruits, vegetables, milk and dairy products, and fish. The annual increase in the production of these products are

Table 5.1   Production of Food Products and Its Growth

Food Products	2004–05 (Million Tons)	2009–10 (Million Tons)	Annual Growth Rate from 2004–05 to 2009–10 (%)
Rice	83.13	89.09	1.40
Wheat	68.64	80.80	3.32
Bajra	7.93	6.50	−3.88
Jowar	7.24	6.70	−1.54
Maize	14.17	16.72	3.36
Pulses	13.13	14.66	2.23
Foodgrains	198.36	218.10	1.92
Fruits	50.95	71.51	7.02
Vegetables	101.43	134.10	5.74
Milk and Milk Products	92.6	112.540	3.98
Edible Oil	8.097	8.398	0.73
Fish	6.30	7.85	4.48
Poultry Eggs (Millions)	45,200	59,800	5.75
Meat Products	2.2	4.5	15.38

Source: Author's calculation.[1]

in the range of 4 per cent to 15 per cent against a meagre increase of 1.9 per cent for foodgrains.

It is quite evident from the consumption data (Table 5.2) that diversification of diet is taking place increasingly. People consume less of foodgrains and more and more of products such as vegetables, fruits, milk products, and meat products. Fruit consumption in the agricultural crop sector has registered a maximum annual growth of 7.85 per cent in the rural areas. Among the allied sectors, poultry consumption has gone up by about 19 per cent annually in rural areas. Meat products come next with a 15 per cent and 12 per cent annual increase in urban and rural areas respectively.

Nutrient intake per capita presented in Table 5.3 clearly indicate a declining trend from 2000 to 2010 for calories and protein. However, the fat intake shows an increasing trend. In the five-year period from 2005–10, it has recorded an annual increase of about 3 per cent to 4 per cent.

In the existing studies, more attention has been given to major nutrients such as calories, fat, and protein. The micronutrients, which are important for the overall

[1] Based on the data extracted from www.indiastat.com (last accessed on 29 January 2016).

Table 5.2   Monthly Per Capita Consumption of Food Products

Food Products	2004–05 (Kg)	2009–10 (Kg)	Annual Percentage Change from 2004–05 to 2009–10
Cereals—Rural	12.12	11.34	−1.32
Cereals—Urban	9.94	9.38	−1.15
Pulses—Rural	0.71	0.65	−1.75
Pulses—Urban	0.82	0.79	−0.74
Vegetables—Rural	4.68	6.3	6.13
Vegetables—Urban	5.05	6.4	4.85
Fruits—Rural	0.329	0.48	7.85
Fruits—Urban	0.743	0.9	3.91
Milk and Milk Products—Rural	4.01	4.18	0.83
Milk and Milk Products—Urban	5.21	5.64	1.60
Edible Oil—Rural	0.48	0.63	5.59
Edible Oil—Urban	0.66	0.82	4.44
Fish—Rural	0.201	0.27	6.08
Fish—Urban	0.206	0.24	3.10
Poultry—Rural	0.05	0.12	19.14
Poultry—Urban	0.085	0.18	16.19
Eggs—Rural (in Numbers)	1.01	1.73	11.36
Eggs—Urban (in Numbers)	1.72	2.67	9.19
Meat Products—Rural	0.047	0.084	12.31
Meat Products—Urban	0.070	0.142	15.20

Source: Author's calculation from the data of NSSO reports.

Table 5.3   Per Capita Daily Intake of Calories, Protein, and Fat

Nutrient	2004–05		2009–10		Annual Percentage Change from 2004–05 to 2009–10	
	Rural	Urban	Rural	Urban	Rural	Urban
Calories (Kcal)	2047	2020	2051	1957	−0.27	−0.93
Protein (Grams)	55.8	55.4	55.0	53.5	−0.14	−0.55
Fat* (Grams)	35.4	47.4	41.6	52.5	4.26	3.38

Note: *Fat intake for 2009–10 represents 2011–12 statistics.

Sources: 1) www.Indiastat.com; 2) Deaton and Drèze, 2009.

nutritional status, need more attention as there is a higher prevalence of malnutrition in micronutrients in India. This study attempts to focus on both macronutrients and micronutrients. We have projected the consumption and nutritional outcome for 2020 under alternative growth scenario and the projection is made for three major nutrients, namely calories, fat, and protein,

and three micro nutrients, namely calcium, minerals, and iron.

METHODOLOGY

The chapter uses the CGE model of recursive dynamics to project results for the future years with reference to 'Business as Usual' (BAU) and alternative scenarios using GAMS software. The basic model adopts the one by Panda and Ganesh-Kumar (2008) for production and consumption structure and has made extensions in a number of sectors and factors. Panda and Ganesh's model is a static CGE model based on the modified Social Accounting Matrix (SAM) for the year 2003–04 as prepared by Saluja and Yadav (2006). The specific features of the model are: intermediate demands follow Leontief's input–output coefficients and the sectoral value added follows the constant elasticity of substitution (CES) production function. Capital and labour supply are fixed. The model has five factors and ten household classes, five each for rural and urban. Households' preferences are specified through a linear expenditure system (LES) system of demand, which has the standard properties of floor-level consumption independent of income, and the other component varies with respect to income. Rest of the world is a single entity in the model and the trading partners are combined as one entity. It also has the specific feature of Armington[2] specification where the imports, exports, and domestic goods are treated as imperfect substitutes for the same good.

To suit our analysis, the following adjustments have been made in the present model.

Agricultural Sectors

In the existing model, the agricultural sector comprises 14 subsectors—10 for crops and 4 for allied sectors such as dairy, fishing, poultry, and other animal products. In the crop sector, coarse cereals are combined into one sector. Since the present analysis focuses on consumption and nutrition, individual crops in the combined coarse cereals, namely bajra, jowar, maize, and others have been separated and the total crops sector is extended from 10 to 13 sectors.

Factor Market Disaggregation

The existing model has only five factors—four for labour, rural–urban further divided by skilled and unskilled, and one for capital. Our model has split capital into land, agricultural capital, and non-agricultural capital. This was perceived as important for the recursive dynamics where the growth in land and agricultural capital widely differ from that of non-agricultural capital. Hence, to inject growth in the capital, it has become necessary to have these types separately.

Household Classification

The existing SAM has five household classes each for rural and urban areas based on the consumption expenditure. The modified SAM aggregated top two and bottom two household classes to make only three household classes each for rural and urban areas. This was carried out to make the model more meaningful for the future years. There may be households who shift from one group to another over time, and the model is not capable of updating this. The clubbing of finer groups will result in minimum errors.

The following are the final household groups. The classification is based on three expenditure classes each

for rural and urban areas and was based on the following monthly per capita expenditure percentiles:

Category 1: Less than 30 per cent (poor)
Category 2: 30 per cent–70 per cent (middle)
Category 3: More than 70 per cent (rich)

The model is solved only for relative prices and the wholesale price index was chosen as numeraire.[3]

Dynamics

The model follows 'recursive dynamics' for future projections, wherein inter-period changes are analysed through a series of temporary equilibria. Parametric changes are fed into the model to take it to future years. The parametric changes are considered for capital, population growth, labour, total factor productivity, certain behavioural parameters, government expenditure, and foreign inflow and outflow. With 2006/07 as the base year, we first simulated the model parameters for 2009/10 and keeping this as the base, the results were simulated for 2019/20.

India is witnessing rise in younger population. Based on population projections for India, the share of working-age population in total population is expected to increase for the next three decades or so. This demographic transition points to higher labour growth due to augmented supply of labour. The total labour endowment was projected taking into account not only the demographic dividend but also the rural-urban migration effect.

The growth rates of labour supply and population implemented in the dynamic block is provided in Table 5.4.

---

[2] The demerit of this specification is gain from trade cannot be fully realized.

[3] The model is only in real terms (absence of money in the model). This means inflationary effects are not included. The change in prices reflect only the effects of reallocation of capital and labour across sectors depending on demand and supply of factors triggered by external shocks as defined in the scenario.

Table 5.4   Population and Labour Growth Rate Parameters Used in the Model

Population/Labour	Annual Growth Rate from the Base Year (Percentage)
Population—Rural	0.82
Population—Urban	2.38
Labour—Rural	1.43
Labour—Urban	2.50

Source: Author's calculation using the parameters released by the Office of the Registrar General and Census Commissioner, India, 2011.

Social Accounting Matrix (SAM)

To study the effect of various policy targets on agriculture in the general equilibrium model, a SAM for 2006/07 of India based on the detailed SAM developed by Panda and Ganesh-Kumar (2008) was used. The SAM has been modified with respect to number of sectors, factors, and household groups as discussed earlier in the methodology. The final SAM comprised 35 sectors, 7 factors of production and 6 categories of households.

The 35 sectors comprised 17 sectors from agriculture, one sector of primary products, 4 sectors of agro-processing, 7 sectors of manufacturing and 6 sectors of services. The SAM was constructed at market prices of the commodities in 2006/07. The model projects the data for the year 2009–10 in the first stage and using this as the base year, the model projects the results for different scenario for the year 2020. The sectoral classification is presented in Appendix 5A.

Scenario Description

Base year is 2009–10 and the projection is made for 2019–20

BAU: 8 per cent real GDP annual growth
Scenario 1: Agriculture[4]-led growth
Scenario 2: Cereal-led growth
Scenario 3: Non-cereal[5]–led growth
Scenario 4: Allied agriculture–led growth
Scenario 5: Non-agriculture–led growth

---

[4] Agriculture includes allied agriculture. Allied agriculture consists of milk and milk products, poultry, other animal products, and fish.
[5] Excludes allied agriculture sector.

The baseline scenario is built with 8 per cent real GDP annual growth. Since the *Economic Survey* reported 7.6 to 8 per cent real GDP growth, this is a realistic assumption. The scenarios were built by introducing 1 per cent higher growth in the respective sectors as compared to the BAU scenario. The growth is initiated through Total Factor Productivity (TFP). The results of all the scenarios maintain overall real GDP annual growth of 8.5 per cent. For agriculture-led, cereal-led, and non-cereal led growth, the respective growth injected is 1 per cent more than that of BAU. However, for allied agriculture and non-agriculture–led growth, 1 per cent higher growth in the respective sectors causes real GDP growth far exceeding the specified range rendering the results non-comparable. Hence, for the last two scenarios, the growth stimulus is less than 1 per cent so that the overall real GDP stays at 8.5 per cent.

RESULTS OF ALTERNATIVE SCENARIOS

The impact of alternative sources of growth on income, consumption, and nutrient intake are examined in this section.

The results of agriculture-led, non-agriculture–led and sub-sector–led growth (Table 5.5) indicate that agriculture-led growth imparts more growth to the sub-sectors in agriculture due to higher multiplier effects. It is also noted that a small push to agriculture has a far greater impact on non-agriculture than vice versa. This result has a significant policy implication.

Income

The results on real income and wages by household groups are presented in Tables 5.6 to 5.8.

Table 5.5 Sectoral Real GDP Growth—Annual Growth Rate Percentage from 2010–20

Sectors	Baseline (Annual Real GDP Growth = 8%)	Agriculture-Led Growth	Cereal-Led Growth	Non-cereal (Crops)–Led Growth	Allied Agriculture Sector–Led Growth	Non–Agriculture–Led Growth
GDP Growth	8.0	8.5	8.5	8.5	8.5	8.5
Agriculture and Allied	5.3	6.3	5.8	5.9	6.0	5.8
Non-agriculture	8.4	8.9	8.9	8.9	9.0	9.2
Cereal	3.9	5.0	4.9	4.4	4.1	4.0
Non-cereal (Crops)	5.2	6.3	6	6.2	6.4	5.6
Allied Agriculture	6.2	7.0	6.1	6.4	6.5	7.0

Note: The sectoral composition of cereal, non-cereal, and allied agriculture in agriculture are 20 per cent, 49 per cent and 31 per cent respectively in the base year 2010.
Source: Author's calculation.

Table 5.6 Real Income Composition (Percentage), 2020

Households	Baseline	Agriculture-Led Growth	Cereal-Led Growth	Non-cereal (Crops)-Led Growth	Allied Agriculture Sector–Led Growth	Non-agriulture–Led Growth
Rural Poor	5.2	6.1	5.7	5.4	5.2	5.1
Rural Middle	14.6	16.6	15.7	15.3	14.9	14.4
Rural Rich	40.8	42.5	41.1	41.4	41.9	40.6
Urban Poor	2.5	2.3	2.5	2.5	2.4	2.5
Urban Middle	8.5	7.7	8.2	8.2	8.2	8.6
Urban Rich	28.4	24.7	26.9	27.2	27.4	28.8

Source: Author's calculation.

Table 5.7 Real Income Per Capita—Annual Growth Rate Percentage from 2010–20

Households	Baseline	Agriculture-Led Growth	Cereal-Led Growth	Non-cereal (Crops)-Led Growth	Allied Agriculture Sector-Led Growth	Non-agriculture–Led Growth
Rural Poor	5.5	7.7	6.6	6.3	6.8	5.8
Rural Middle	6.2	8.3	7.0	7.1	7.4	6.5
Rural Rich	7.1	8.4	7.3	7.7	7.8	7.4
Urban Poor	3.1	3.3	3.2	3.4	3.4	3.7
Urban Middle	3.9	3.9	3.8	4.1	3.9	4.4
Urban Rich	4.7	4.4	4.5	4.9	4.6	5.2

Source: Author's calculation.

Table 5.8 Real Wages (for 2010 = 1 for all classes)—Projection for 2020

Sectors	Baseline	Agriculture-Led Growth	Cereal-Led Growth	Non-cereal (Crops)-Led Growth	Allied Agriculture sector–Led Growth	Non-agriculture–Led Growth
Rural Unskilled	1.78	2.03	1.91	1.90	1.93	1.82
Rural Skilled	1.64	1.73	1.70	1.70	1.70	1.7
Urban Unskilled	1.4	1.41	1.39	1.40	1.40	1.47
Urban Skilled	1.4	1.39	1.39	1.41	1.39	1.47

Source: Author's calculation.

Composition of real income across six groups of households indicates that the overall agriculture growth provides higher benefits to rural households (Table 5.6). Particularly, percentage of income of rural poor in the total income was pushed up from 5.2 per cent in the BAU scenario to 6.1 per cent in the scenario of agriculture-led growth. Urban poor income proportion has not changed much in any scenario as compared to baseline. Real income per capita shown in Table 5.7 further corroborates this result.

Increase in real wages across four groups of labour, namely rural skilled, rural unskilled, urban skilled, and urban unskilled, confirm that the uniform overall growth of agriculture generates more income for rural unskilled (Table 5.8). However if we focus on subsector-led growth within the agricultural sector, then allied agriculture turns out to be the crucial sector for increase in wages for rural poor.

Consumption

The base year monthly per capita grain consumption classified according to three household groups indicates that coarse cereal consumption is less prevalent in urban than in rural areas. The difference in the grain consumption between rich and poor is prominent in the consumption of pulses, which is a major source of protein. The data supported diet diversification towards non-cereals of urban households as indicated by the fact that total intake of cereals is higher in rural than urban for all groups of households (Table 5.9).

The results of consumption of different commodities in real terms under different scenario are presented in Tables 5.10 to 5.14.

Table 5.9 Base Year Per Capita Monthly Consumption of Cereals and Pulses 2009–10 (in Kg)

Foodgrains	Rural Poor	Rural Middle	Rural Rich	Urban Poor	Urban Middle	Urban Rich
Rice	6.15	6.18	6.05	4.75	4.79	4.39
Wheat	3.72	4.30	5.02	4.25	4.39	4.42
Jowar	0.32	0.31	0.28	0.28	0.17	0.10
Bajra	0.12	0.30	0.33	0.12	0.10	0.05
Maize	0.22	0.22	0.17	0.03	0.02	0.01
Total Cereals	10.62	11.43	11.96	9.48	9.57	9.05
Pulses	0.48	0.60	0.80	0.54	0.76	0.96

Source: NSSO (2009–10).

Cereal consumption is impacted by agriculture-led growth in rural and non-agriculture–led growth in urban as expected (Table 5.10). However, in rural areas, this could be attributed to the own-consumption effect. Coarse cereal consumption does not show much variation across scenarios in urban rich category. However allied agriculture-led growth is equally important for coarse cereal consumption (Table 5.11).

Allied agriculture sector–led growth assumes significance when we turn to fruits and vegetables and pulses consumption (Tables 5.12 and 5.13). We have noted that vegetables and fruits consumption display a high-income effect.

It is also noted that increase in the growth in the consumption of fruits and vegetables for middle-income groups exceed that of rich households. This is attributed to the low base-level consumption of poor and middle as compared to the rich. It basically shows the 'inverted U shape' type of relation between percentage increase in the consumption of these items and income.

Table 5.10 Cereal Consumption in Real Terms—Annual Growth Rate Percentage from 2010–20

Households	Baseline	Agriculture-Led Growth	Cereal-Led Growth	Non-cereal (Crops)-Led Growth	Allied Agriculture Sector–Led Growth	Non-Agriculture–Led Growth
Rural Poor	3.7	5.1	4.6	4.2	4.2	3.7
Rural Middle	3.0	4.1	3.7	3.7	2.6	2.8
Rural Rich	3.1	4.0	3.6	3.5	3.1	3.1
Urban Poor	3.5	3.9	3.6	3.8	3.1	4.5
Urban Middle	3.3	3.5	3.2	3.4	3.0	3.5
Urban Rich	2.7	2.7	2.7	2.7	2.6	2.8

Source: Author's calculation.

Table 5.11 Coarse Cereal Consumption in Real Terms—Annual Growth Rate Per Cent from 2010–20

Households	Baseline	Agriculture-Led Growth	Cereal-Led Growth	Non-cereal (Crops)–Led Growth	Allied Agriculture Sector–Led Growth	Non-agriculture–Led Growth
Rural Poor	5.3	6.8	6.2	5.7	6.8	5.7
Rural Middle	1.9	1.2	1.4	1.2	1.4	1.2
Rural Rich	2.6	3.0	2.7	2.7	2.8	2.7
Urban Poor	3.4	3.5	3.7	3.6	3.7	3.8
Urban Middle	1.8	1.8	1.9	1.8	1.9	1.8
Urban Rich	3.3	3.3	3.3	3.3	3.3	3.5

Note: Coarse cereals like maize finds larger use as animal feed consumption and the figures in the tables represent only human consumption. However, we find that the middle class of rural and urban areas use less coarse cereals for consumption in all the scenarios including the baseline. This could be partly due to regional variation in the cultivation of concerned coarse cereals which are used more for animal feed and the percentage of middle income group of the region to the total; moreover this pattern is found in the base year SAM of 2006–07 also, which is reflected in the subsequent years' scenario results.
Source: Author's calculation.

Table 5.12 Pulses Consumption in Real Terms—Annual Growth Rate Percentage from 2010–20

Households	Baseline	Agriculture-Led Growth	Cereal-Led Growth	Non-cereal (Crops)–Led Growth	Allied Agriculture Sector–Led Growth	Non-agriculture–Led Growth
Rural Poor	5.1	6.8	6.2	6.0	6.7	5.2
Rural Middle	4.4	5.7	5.1	5.2	5.4	4.4
Rural Rich	5.0	6.0	5.5	5.7	5.6	4.9
Urban Poor	4.9	4.6	4.8	4.9	4.9	5.5
Urban Middle	4.5	4.5	4.4	4.7	4.5	4.8
Urban Rich	4.5	4.5	3.4	3.5	3.3	3.5

Source: Author's calculation.

Table 5.13 Vegetables and Fruits Consumption in Real Terms—Annual Growth Rate Percentage from 2010–20

Households	Baseline	Agriculture-Led Growth	Cereal-Led Growth	Non-cereal (Crops)–Led Growth	Allied Agriculture Sector–Led Growth	Non-agriculture–Led Growth
Rural Poor	3.7	4.9	4.9	5.4	6.8	4.3
Rural Middle	4.5	5.7	5.4	6.6	7.7	5.1
Rural Rich	4.4	5.2	5.0	6.2	6.8	4.9
Urban Poor	4.2	5.1	5.0	5.1	4.7	4.6
Urban Middle	5.9	6.5	6.2	6.8	6.3	6.3
Urban Rich	6.0	5.3	4.8	5.2	5.0	4.9

Source: Author's calculation.

Table 5.14 Milk and Milk Products Consumption in Real Terms—Annual Growth Rate Percentage from 2010 to 2020

Households	Baseline	Agriculture-Led Growth	Cereal-Led Growth	Non-cereal (Crops)–Led Growth	Allied Agriculture Sector–Led Growth	Non-agriculture–Led Growth
Rural Poor	9.8	10.8	8.7	10.3	10.6	11
Rural Middle	8.4	9.4	7.1	8.9	8.6	9.4
Rural Rich	7.0	7.3	5.7	7.2	6.6	7.9
Urban Poor	1.0	1.2	3.8	1.6	3.6	3.1
Urban Middle	4.3	4.2	4.8	4.6	5.2	6
Urban Rich	4.0	3.6	3.9	3.9	4.0	4.8

Source: Author's calculation.

Consumption of milk and milk products is projected to have the highest growth compared to all other products, more than 10 per cent in some scenarios for rural poor (Table 5.14). Very low base-year consumption is also one reason why the rate of growth is higher. Allied agriculture and non-agriculture–led growth seem to be important for rural poor and middle-income groups.

Nutritional Outcome

Projected output, income, and consumption figures are directly available in the model results as these are endogenous variables. However, nutrient variables are to be computed from the consumption figures. Nutrient content of each food published by the Indian Council of Medical Research (ICMR) have been used to first compute the nutrient intake corresponding to individual food item from the projected consumption. Then the weighted average of each nutrient intake has been arrived at using ratio of consumption of each food in the total in the base year as weights.

Agriculture and non-agriculture–led growth, respectively, improves nutritional outcome in rural and urban areas as expected. However, the nutritional implication of sub-sectoral–led growth within agriculture has thrown some interesting results between rural and urban and between rich and poor (Figures 5.1 to 5.6). Major nutrients such as calories and protein increase by 1 percentage point more under allied agriculture–led growth than that of baseline; for micronutrients such as minerals and iron, the increase is more than 1.5 percentage points.

While development of allied agriculture turned out to be most important for rural poor, the urban poor benefits more in terms of nutrient intake when the growth is led by the cereal group. This may be attributed to the fact that expansion of the cereal sector could enhance the quantity distributed by the public distribution system on which majority of urban poor depend for their

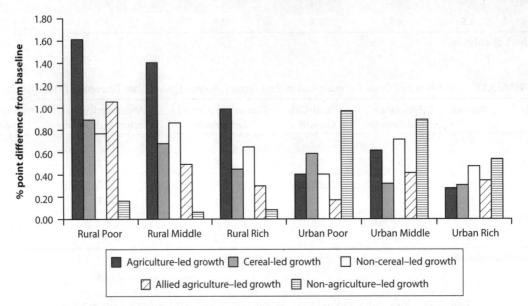

Figure 5.1   Calorie Intake Per Cent Change from Baseline in Alternative Scenario

Source: Author's calculation.

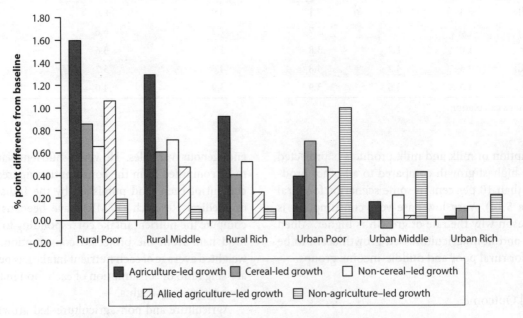

Figure 5.2   Protein Intake Per Cent Change from Baseline in Alternative Scenario

Source: Author's calculation.

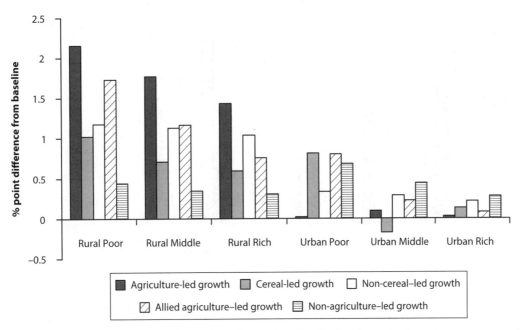

Figure 5.3   Fat Intake Per Cent Change from Baseline in Alternative Scenario

Source: Author's calculation.

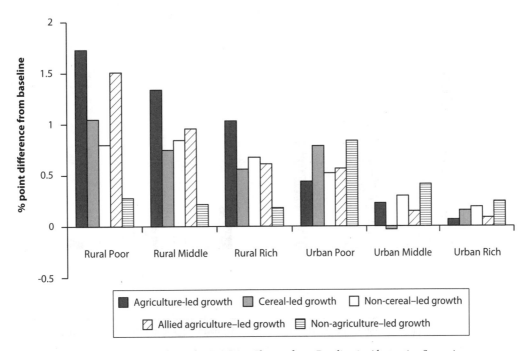

Figure 5.4   Minerals Intake Per Cent Change from Baseline in Alternative Scenario

Source: Author's calculation.

consumption. For rural and urban poor, the next important sector is the non-cereal sector, which includes vegetables, fruits, and pulses and oilseeds, for nutrient intake. The high value added scope of fruits and vegetables and the huge supply chain in the provision of these products could be attributed to this result. Although this sector is

highly labour intensive in production, the amount of job creation in the value added stage is also promising due to its long supply chain process.

Considering the fast growth that has been witnessed in fruits, vegetables, dairy and other animal products, and the prospects for better growth in the future, it is

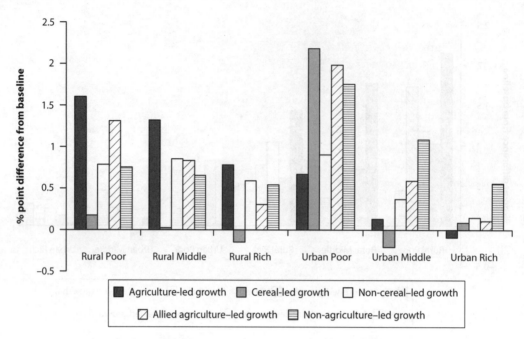

Figure 5.5   Calcium Intake Per Cent Change from Baseline in Alternative Scenario

Source: Author's calculation.

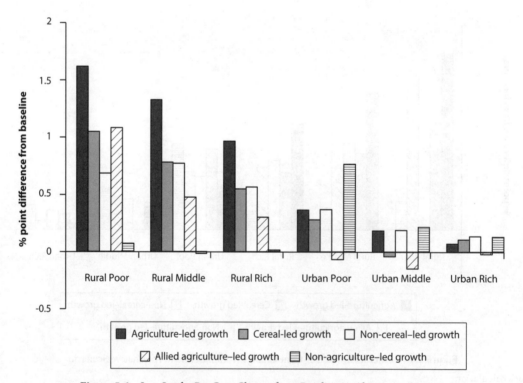

Figure 5.6   Iron Intake Per Cent Change from Baseline in Alternative Scenario

Source: Author's calculation.

promising for the rural households whose nutrient intake increase by about 0.5 to 1 percentage points more as compared to BAU. Middle-income groups also benefit more from the development of these sectors. Calcium

intake of urban poor grows more than that of rural poor in allied agriculture-led growth due to significant growth in milk consumption in this scenario. This is an exception.

CONCLUSION

This study examined the impacts of alternative growth scenario on consumption of food products and nutrition using general equilibrium framework. The results of alternative scenario confirmed that nutrient intake will improve for rural poor if the allied agriculture sector is given more attention for expansion. However, for urban poor, within agriculture sub-sectors, cereal-led growth assumes significance. This could be due to their inability to satisfy their minimum grain intake. However, the scope for cereal-led growth is very limited in the short run unless a dramatic yield growth of cereals is expected in the near future with the technological advances. Hence it is a policy challenge to improve nutrient intake of urban poor to the desired level. Our results also endorsed the existing findings that consumption of high value added products such as fruits and vegetables and milk and milk products which are nutritionally rich in micronutrients, are highly income elastic. Our findings confirmed that the continuing present trend in the output growth of non-cereal and the allied agricultural sector can have far-reaching implications in improving the nutritional status of the rural poor. However, it is questionable if this would help urban poor to the expected level and hence specific targeted programmes may be needed. The institutions implementing policies play a key role in linking growth with target nutrient level.

APPENDIX 5A

Table 5A.1   Sectors in Social Accounting Matrix (SAM)

Number	Sectors	Number	Sectors	Number	Sectors
	Agriculture		Industry		Services
	Crops				
1	Paddy	18	Primary Products	30	Electricity
2	Wheat			31	Water Supply
3	Jowar		*Agro-processing*	32	Transport Services
4	Bajra	19	Sugar	33	Storage and Warehouse
5	Maize	20	Vegetable Oil	34	Trade
6	Other Coarse Cereals	21	Other Food Products	35	Other Services
7	Pulses	22	Beverages and Tobacco		
8	Sugarcane		*Manufacturing*		
9	Oilseeds	23	Textiles and Garments		
10	Cotton	24	Petroleum Products		
11	Fruits	25	Fertilizers		
12	Vegetables	26	Pesticides		
13	Other Crops	27	Manufacturing 1 (Labour Intensive)		
	Allied	28	Manufacturing 2 (Capital Intensive)		
14	Milk and Milk Products	29	Construction		
15	Poultry and Eggs				
16	Other Animal Products				
17	Fishing				

REFERENCES

Amarasinghe, U. A., T. Shah, and O. P. Singh. 2007. 'Changing Consumption Patterns: Implications on Food and Water Demand in India.' Research Report 119. Colombo: International Water Management Institute.

Bhagowalia, P., D. D. Headey, and S. Kadiyala. 2012. 'Agriculture, Income, and Nutrition Linkages in India: Insights from a Nationally Representative Survey.' IFPRI Discussion Paper 01195. Washington, DC: International Food Policy Research Institute.

Carletto, G., M. Ruel, P. Winters, and Alberto Zezza. 2015. 'Farm Level Pathways to Improved Nutritional Status: Introduction to the Special Issue.' *Journal of Development Studies* 51(8): 945–57.

Dasgupta, P. 1998. 'The Economics of Poverty in Poor Countries.' *Scandinavian Journal of Economics* 100(1): 41–68.

Deaton, A., and J. Drèze. 2009. 'Food and Nutrition in India: Facts and Interpretations.' *Economic and Political Weekly* 44(7): 42–65.

Deolalikar, A. 2008. 'Malnutrition & Hunger.' Copenhagen Consensus 2008 Perspective Paper. Copenhagen: Copenhagen Consensus Centre.

Ecker, Olivier, C. Breisinger, and Karl Pauw. 2012. 'Growth is Good, but Is Not Enough to Improve Nutrition.' In *Reshaping Agriculture for Nutrition and Health*, edited by Fan Shenggen and R. Pandya-Lorch. Washington, DC: International Food Policy Research Institute, Chapter 6.

Gaiha, R., R. Jha, and V. S. Kulkarni. 2010. 'Demand for Nutrients in India, 1993–2004.' ASARC Working Papers form the Australian National University. Canberra: Australia South Asia Research Centre.

Gopaldas, Tara. 2006. 'Hidden Hunger: The Problem and Possible Interventions.' *Economic and Political Weekly* 41(34): 3671–74.

Gragnolati, M., M. Shekar, M. Das Gupta, C. Bredenkamp, and Y.-K. Lee. 2005. 'India's Undernourished Children: A Call for Reform and Action.' Health, Nutrition and Population (HNP) Discussion Paper. Washington, DC: World Bank.

Gulati, A., A. Ganesh Kumar, G. Shreedhar, and T. Nandakumar. 2012. 'Agriculture and Malnutrition in India.' *Food and Nutrition Bulletin* 33(1): 74–86.

Hazell, P., and L. J. Haddad. 2001. 'Agricultural Research and Poverty Reduction.' Food, Agriculture and the Environment Discussion Paper 34. Washington, DC: International Food Policy Research Institute.

Headey, Derek. 2011. 'Turning Economic Growth into Nutrition-sensitive Growth.' 2020 Conference paper 6, Leveraging Agriculture for Nutrition and Health. New Delhi, India, 10–12 February.

Headey, Derek, A. Chiu, and Suneetha Kadiyala. 2011. 'Agriculture's Role in the Indian Enigma: Help or Hindrance to the Undernutrition Crisis?' Discussion Paper 01085. Washington, DC: International Food Policy Research Institute.

Indian National Science Academy. 2011. *Micro-nutrient Security for India-Priorities for Research and Action*. New Delhi: Science Policy Cell.

Jha, P., and R. Laxminarayan. 2009. *Choosing Health: An Entitlement for all Indians*. Toronto: Centre for Global Health Research.

Kadiyala, S., J. Harris, H. Headey, S. Yosef, and S. Gillespie. 2014. 'Agriculture and Nutrition in India: Mapping Evidence to Pathways.' *Annals of the New York Academy of Sciences*, Vol. 1331, December, pp. 43–56.

Mahendra Dev, S. 2012. 'Agriculture–nutrition Linkages and Policies in India.' IFPRI Discussion Paper 01184. Poverty Health and Nutrition Division. Washington, DC: International Food Policy Research Institute.

NSSO. 2009–10. *Level and Pattern of Consumer Expenditure, 2009–10*. NSS 66th Round. Ministry of Statistics and Programme Implementation, Government of India.

Panda, M., and Ganesh-Kumar, A. 2008. 'Trade Liberalization, Poverty and Food Security in India.' Working Paper WP-2008-013. Mumbai: Indira Gandhi Institute of Development Research.

Pauw, Karl, and J. Thurlow. 2010. 'Agricultural Growth, Poverty and Nutrition in Tanzania.' IFPRI Discussion Paper 00947, Development Strategy and Governance Decision, January.

Pingali, Prabhu, and Y. Khwaja. 2004. 'Globalisation of Indian Diets and the Transformation of Food Supply Systems.' ESA Working Paper No. 04–05. Agricultural and Development Economics Division. The Food and Agricultural Organisation of the United Nations.

Radhakrishna, R. 2006. 'Food Consumption and Nutritional Status in India: Emerging Trends and Perspectives.' Working Paper 2006–008 Mumbai: Indira Gandhi Institute of Development Research.

Saluja, M.R., and Bhupesh Yadav. 2006. *Social Accounting Matrix for India 2003–04*. Gurgaon: India Development Foundation.

Swaminatha, H., R. Lahoti, and J. Y. Suchitra. 2012. 'Women's Property, Mobility, and Decisionmaking: Evidence from Rural Karnataka, India.' IFPRI Discussion Paper 01188. Washington DC: International Food Policy Research Institute.

Thirtle, C., X. Irs, L. Lin, V. Mckenzie-Hill, and S. Wiggins. (2001) 'Relationship between Changes in Agricultural Productivity and the Incidence of Poverty in Developing Countries', Report No. 7946. London: Department for International Development.

6

Women's Empowerment in Agriculture
Implications on Nutrition in India[1]

S. Mahendra Dev, Vijay Laxmi Pandey, and D. Suganthi

INTRODUCTION

Despite rapid economic growth, the percentage of undernourished and stunted children in India is strikingly high. The stunting rate among children in India is more than 38 per cent, which is relatively higher than that in other developing countries (for example, China: 10 per cent; Nepal: 37 per cent; and Bangladesh: 36 per cent). Approximately 18.6 per cent children aged less than 3 years are underweight and nearly 69.5 per cent children aged between 35 months and 6 years suffer from anaemia (Raykar et al., 2015). The recent data from the fourth National Family Health Survey (NFHS-4) revealed that the prevalence of underweight is more common among rural children than among their urban counterparts (Ram et al., 2016). Moreover, the interstate variation in the nutritional status of stunting among children aged less than 5 years is extremely pronounced, ranging from 48 per cent in Bihar to 27 per cent in Tamil Nadu. Similarly, the mortality rate for children aged less than 5 years is also relatively high—Madhya Pradesh recorded a mortality rate of 65 deaths per 1,000 live births (Ram et al., 2016).

Experts opine that the decline rate of stunting among children aged less than 5 years was relatively low from 1992–93 to 2005–06, with 1.2 per cent per year. However, the decline rate intensified from 2006 to 2014, with 2.3 per cent per year. This decline rate is comparable to that of Bangladesh (2.3 per cent) but lower than that of Nepal (3.3 per cent) (Raykar et al., 2015). The literature on health has highlighted the relevance of maternal health, nutritional knowledge, sanitation, and childcare practices for improved nutritional outcomes of children. Recognizing the multidimensional aspects of undernutrition, agriculture has been identified as one of the crucial sectors (Gillespie, Harriss, and Kadiyala, 2012). The existing literature has determined six pathways through which agriculture can influence the nutritional outcomes (Kadiyala et al., 2014).

Agriculture is not only a major sector for achieving food security but also a primary source of employment in India, as nearly 52 per cent of the workforce is engaged in agriculture and allied activities. The livelihood of rural women workforce primarily depends on agriculture. Nearly 77 per cent of the total rural women in workforce are employed in this sector, of which approximately 29 per cent work as cultivators and 49 per cent as agricultural labourers (GoI, 2011). The corresponding

[1] The chapter was written as part of the 'System of Promoting Appropriate National Dynamism for Agriculture and Nutrition (SPANDAN)', an initiative by the Bill & Melinda Gates Foundation. An earlier draft of this chapter was presented at International Conference on Applied Economics and Policy 2017, University of Malaya.

figures for rural men are 35 per cent and 34.4 per cent, respectively (GoI, 2011). There is a significant decrease in the percentage of women working as cultivators in the total women work force from 33 per cent in 2001 to 24 per cent in 2011. However, the proportion of women working as agricultural labourers has increased from 39 per cent in 2001 to 41 per cent in 2011 (GoI, 2011). Thus, the women in agriculture are more likely to be labourers than cultivators. This may be because, women, in general, are deprived of access to assets, resources, and agricultural inputs (Agarwal, 1994; Kabeer, 1999).

Women have both direct and indirect links with children's nutritional outcomes; the direct being the childcare practices and the indirect being the child's birth weight (Ramalingaswami, Jonsson, and Rohde, 1996; Smith et al., 2003). Women, as mothers or other female members of the household, are the primary caregivers of children and are central to the decision-making related to child nutrition. Therefore, the low status of women increasingly contributes to the poor nutritional outcomes of the children (Smith et al., 2003). Low level of women's empowerment is present indiscriminately across different classes and castes in India (Malhotra and Schuler, 2005); many studies have argued that empowerment is the basic right of women (Kishor and Gupta, 2004). By recognizing the relevance of women's status and gender aspects for improving nutritional outcomes, the three out of six agriculture–nutrition pathways have emphasized the importance of women's empowerment (Kadiyala et al., 2014). This is also reflected in the millennium development goals (MDGs) adopted in 2003 that promote women's empowerment and gender equality.

Empirical narratives on gender dimensions argue that women's empowerment has the potential to increase agricultural productivity, achieve food security, reduce hunger, and improve nutritional outcomes of both children and women (Hoddinott, 1997; Pandey, Dev, and Jayachandran, 2016; Quisumbing et al., 1995; Smith et al., 2003). Further, empirical evidence had shown that women's empowerment improved the nutritional outcomes of children, household food security, and agricultural productivity (Kishor, 1995, 2000; Kishor and Gupta, 2004; Smith and Haddad 2000). For instance, in Côte d'Ivoire, women's share of cash income significantly increased the share of household food budget (Duflo and Udry, 2004; Hoddinott and Haddad, 1995). Similarly, Doss (2006) discovered that, in Ghana, women's share of farmland significantly increased the household food expenditure and Allendorf (2007) reported low underweight trend among children of mothers who owned land. More recently, Sraboni et al. (2014) revealed that in Bangladesh, women's

empowerment had a significant effect on household diet diversity and calorie availability but not on the adult body mass index (BMI). Moreover, the mother's control over resources considerably influenced not only nutritional but also educational outcomes (Hallman, 2003; Quisumbing, 2003; Skoufias, 2005; Yoong, Rabinovich, and Diepeveen, 2012). Another strand of literature argued that women tend to be more competent producers with high productivity than the men if the resources were redistributed from men to women (Kilic, Palacios-Lopez, and Goldstein, 2013; Peterman, Behrman, and Quisumbing, 2010). These findings suggest that women are major stakeholders in agriculture–nutrition interventions and their empowerment is consequential for nutritional outcomes.

Moreover, dynamic changes in the agriculture sector, such as new marketing institutions, changes in commodity preferences, climate change, and changes in the composition of the rural workforce because of the migration of male members, increase the workload and pose serious challenges for women in agriculture. In addition, these changes increase the vulnerability of resource-constrained rural women and undermine the agenda of sustainable inclusive growth (World Bank, 2009). Similarly, gender roles and socio-cultural norms affect the distribution of resources between men and women (Agarwal, 1997; Kishor, 1999), intra-household food allocation, restrictions on mobility, and suppression in household decision-making (Kabeer, 1999; Kishor and Gupta, 2004), has implications on nutritional and developmental outcomes (Mahmud, Shah, and Becker, 2012; Sraboni et al., 2014).

Against this backdrop, this chapter constructs a Women's Empowerment in Agriculture Index (WEAI) for India using the Alkire–Foster methodology and investigates the extent of women's empowerment in the agricultural domains (Alkire et al., 2013). In addition, this chapter examines the effect of women's empowerment in agriculture on household diet diversity for rural Bihar, Jharkhand, and Odisha, using data from the Village Dynamics in South Asia (VDSA) study using instrumental variable approach. The structure of the chapter is as follows: the next section discusses the definition and measurement of empowerment; the subsequent two sections present the data and empirical framework; results are discussed in the fourth section, and last section gives the conclusion.

DEFINITION AND MEASUREMENT OF EMPOWERMENT

According to Alkire et al. (2013), the notion of empowerment is subjective and influenced by contextual factors. They provide a detailed discussion of the different definitions postulated by various researchers. However, the construction of the WEAI is on the basis of the definition proposed by Kabeer (1999: 437), according to whom empowerment implies 'expanding people's ability to make strategic life choices, particularly in contexts in which this ability had been denied to them'. This definition broadly covers the three dimensions of empowerment: resources, agency, and achievements.

In earlier studies, women's empowerment measures were an aggregate country-level metric that used proxy indicators, which failed to capture the regional diversity and socio-economic status of the people (Alkire, 2005; Alsop, Bertelsen, and Holland, 2006; Kishor and Subaiya, 2008; Narayan, 2005). Some of the often used proxy indicators were women's education and workforce participation. Since women's empowerment plays an important role in agricultural productivity and nutritional outcomes of children, these measures were criticized for having several limitations: they were indirect measures of empowerment and focused only on domestic and not economic spheres of women's lives. Moreover, most metrics on gender equity lacked agriculture-related indicators and the measures to monitor agricultural development were gender blind; therefore, the requirement for metrics measuring gender equity in agriculture has been appropriately articulated in the available literature (Kishor and Subaiya, 2008; Malhotra and Schuler, 2005).

The 'Women's Empowerment in Agriculture Index (WEAI) is a new survey-based index designed to measure the empowerment, agency, and inclusion of women in the agricultural sector' (Alkire et al., 2013: 72). The index is based on individual-level data collected from the primary male and female within the same household. The WEAI comprises two sub-indices. The first sub-index indicates the percentage of women who are empowered in the five domains of empowerment (5DE) in agriculture: production, resources, income, leadership, and time allocation. Among the women who are not empowered, the index also reflects the percentage of indicators wherein women have adequate achievements. The second sub-index, the gender parity index (GPI) represents the gap between women and men for those households that lack gender parity. Hence, the WEAI is an aggregate index that presents the extent of women's empowerment within households and communities and the extent of gender differences within households.

Measuring Women's Empowerment in Agriculture

The objective of WEAI was to account for contextual factors affecting agency and empowerment and, therefore, the indicators were domain specific instead of a single indicator to denote agency in all possible domains. These five domains were measured using ten indicators. Table 6.1 presents detailed definitions and corresponding weights of these indicators. The

Table 6.1   Modified Definitions of Indicators and the Weights Used for the Construction of WEIA using VDSA Data

Domain	Indicator	Definition of the Indicators	Weight Used
Crop Production	Input in productive decisions	Sole or joint decision making over inputs (food and cash-crop farming)	1/8
	Autonomy in production	Who (sole or joint) influences the utilization or management of inputs (food and cash-crop farming)? Captures respondent's ability on decision making but not motivation	1/8
Resources	Ownership of farm assets	Sole or joint ownership of land, livestock and machinery (no household assets)	1/12
	Purchase, sale, or transfer of farm assets	Decision making regarding the above owned assets	1/12
	Access to and decisions on credit	Access to and participation in decision making concerning credit	1/12
Farm Income	Control over use of farm income	Who (sole or joint) influences the utilization or management of output (crop main production, sale quantity, and income)?	1/4
Leadership qualities	Group membership	Whether respondent is a member of any organization (Panchayat members and SHGs)	1/4

Note: Please refer Alkire et al. (2013) and Sraboni et al. (2014) for original definitions of domains and indicators.

details of the construction of each indicator involved in the WEAI are illustrated in Alkire et al. (2013), which comprehensively discuss that the choice of the domains and indicators reflects the definitions and aspects related to women's empowerment available in the literature.

Alkire et al. (2013: 75) argued that 'The WEAI was constructed to create a simple, intuitive, and visible headline figure that can be compared across places and time.' This framework has the potential to capture the diversity and dynamic features of agriculture–gender relations and to monitor the gradual progress. Women are considered empowered if they achieve adequacy across multiple indicators and surpass a certain threshold. The study further stated that empowerment is a complex dynamic process; individual indicators in isolation may not be sufficient to analyse the process accurately. Moreover, the Alkire–Foster methodology permits the decomposition of the constituent domains and facilitates focus on domain-specific adequacy requirements. Hence, the index can identify the domains and indicators wherein women are empowered or disempowered. This is crucial from a public policy perspective because it provides an incentive for domain-specific targeted interventions to improve women's empowerment.

DATA AND METHODOLOGY

This study used the VDSA household-level data[2] collected under the aegis of the Bill and Melinda Gates Foundation through a survey conducted by the National Centre for Agricultural Economics and Policy Research (NCAP; now ICAR-NIAP [Indian Council of Agricultural Research–National Institute of Agricultural Economics and Policy Research]), from July 2012 to June 2013, for three Indian states (Bihar, Jharkhand, and Odisha). In each state, data was collected in two districts, covering two villages in each district. The survey was not aimed at measuring women's empowerment in agriculture. However, many questions related to agriculture and gender relations were posed to the head of the household and their spouse, if they were not available, then to the next decision-maker and their spouse within the same household. Hence, the WEAI framework in this study collected information, which is not exactly the same, but similar to the WEAI framework suggested by Alkire et al. (2013). Therefore, the VDSA data set was adapted by

changing the definitions and weights accordingly, which are reported in Table 6.1 (columns 5 and 6). Although the definition of certain indicators may not be exactly identical, the VDSA data set broadly captures the same, if not all, aspects.

Data Limitations

The entire analysis was based on dual-adult households. Therefore, families, where one primary member was absent (that is, the primary member was a widow or widower), were not considered for the construction of the index. Other limitations were that the data for Bihar was available only for two villages and this data had much information missing. The reason for missing information was not clear, that is, whether it was because of no response or no participation. Hence, the households with missing information were excluded from the analysis. The participation in group membership was extremely low because, in most cases, the children, not the head of the households, were members of voluntary organizations. However, if we considered household participation instead of member participation, the group participation scores might have considerably increased.

The information regarding time use did not have a 24-hour recall and leisure activities were also not measured; hence, the workload and leisure indicators were excluded from the analysis and the weights were adjusted accordingly. Due to the non-availability of information regarding the empowerment of mothers of children aged less than 5 years, the association between mother's empowerment and nutritional outcomes of children could not be tested.

EMPIRICAL FRAMEWORK

Scoring the WEAI

As previously mentioned, the WEAI comprises two sub-indices: one measures empowerment in the 5DE and the other measures the GPI within the household. The weights of the 5DE and GPI sub-indices are 90 per cent and 10 per cent, respectively. The total WEAI score is the weighted sum of the 5DE and GPI. Any improvement in either the 5DE or the GPI increased the WEAI. This 5DE index appraises whether women or men are empowered across the five domains associated with the WEAI.

Since the data was available for only four domains (data for 24-hour recall and time use was not available),

---

[2] See http://vdsa.icrisat.ac.in/vdsa-database.aspx, last accessed on 3 January 2016.

we calculated the four domains of empowerment (4DE) and accordingly modified the weights from the original index (Table 6.1). The construction was initiated by calculating the inadequacy score for each individual, which is the weighted inadequacies across all indicators.[3] The disempowered individuals were identified on the basis of their inadequacy score greater than 25 per cent. This is equivalent to having adequacy in three out of the four domains. Subsequently, four domains of disempowerment index M_o were constructed similarly to Alkire and Foster (2011).

$$M_o = H_p * A_p,$$

where H_p is the headcount ratio and A_p is the intensity (or breadth) of disempowerment.

$$4DE = 1 - M_o$$

$$4DE = H_e + H_p(A_e),$$

$$H_e = (1 - H_p)$$

$$A_e = (1 - A_p),$$

where H_e is the empowered headcount ratio and A_e is the average adequacy score of disempowered individuals.

The 4DE measures were computed separately for both the primary male and female in a dual-adult household. This enabled the comparison of empowerment in agriculture between men and women in the same household and is embodied in the GPI, a relative inequality measure.

$$GPI = \{1 - (H_{GPI} * I_{GPI})\}$$

where, H_{GPI} is the percentage of women who lacked gender parity with their male counterparts and among those who lacked parity, I_{GPI} is the extent of empowerment inequality between women and their spouses.

Correlation with Other Household Characteristics

The empowerment measure was used to obtain the correlation with other household and individual characteristics. Therefore, the association between empowerment and individual characteristics, such as age group, education, BMI score, and landholding, was examined. The BMI score was computed for each adult individual and was grouped into the following three categories: below, normal, and above BMI status. For landholdings, farmers were divided into four categories, namely marginal, small, medium, and large, depending on the size of the

land.[4] Additionally, the correlation between empowerment and autonomy in other aspects of household decision-making were also examined.

Cramer's V and the phi coefficient were computed to measure the correlation between empowerment and individual characteristics. In addition, Pearson's chi-square and Fisher's exact test were performed to assess the statistical significance of the correlation between empowerment and household/individual characteristics. The null hypothesis is that the rows and columns in a two-way table are independent.

Regression Analysis

The effect of women's empowerment on household diet diversity was investigated by estimating the following model:

$$hd = \beta_0 + \beta_1 E + \beta_2 x + \beta_3 h + \varepsilon,$$

where hd is the household diet diversity score variable, $\beta_1 = 0, 1,..., 3$ are coefficients to be estimated, x is a vector of individual-level characteristics, h is a vector of household-level characteristics, and ε is an error term.

Even though we computed various women's empowerment measures, the focus is on women's empowerment relative to men, captured by the gender parity gap. The gender parity gap was computed by considering the difference between the men's and women's 4DE scores for only those households that did not have gender parity. It was assumed that women's empowerment within the household might improve the household diet diversity, which might subsequently affect women's empowerment through other confounding factors that affect both women's empowerment and household diet diversity. An instrumental variable technique to rectify potential endogeneity bias was performed using the ivreg2 procedure in Stata13 (Baum, Schaffer, and Stillman, 2010; StataCorp, 2011).

Variables

The definitions and expected signs of variables used in the regression analysis are presented in Table 6.2. The dependent variable used for the analysis is household diet diversity score, which is the number of food groups consumed using 24-hour recall of household food consumption data. The score was computed following FANTA (Food and Nutrition Technical Assistance) index (Food and Agriculture Organization of the United Nations [FAO], 2011), where food was classified into 12 categories. The main independent variable included is the gender parity

---

[3] Details of construction of the WEAI is available in Alkire et al. (2013).

[4] Farmers having farms of the sizes <1, 1–2, 2–4, and 4–10 hectares were classified as marginal, small, medium, and large farmers, respectively.

Table 6.2   Definitions of Variables Used and Their Expected Signs

Variables	Definition	Expected Sign
Household diet diversity score	Different categories of food items consumed by the household in a month. The score was obtained following FANTA index	
Gender parity household dummy	Household having gender parity is given '0' and '1' otherwise	'−'
Education of the head of the household	Years of education of the household head	'+'
Education of the main female member	Years of education of the main female member	'+'
Household size	Number of family members in the household	'−'
Crop diversity index	Different crops produced by the household in a year. And the index was obtained by the Simpson index framework	'+'
Number of milch animals	Number of goats, sheep, cows and buffaloes owned by the household	'+'
Operational landholding	The size of the operating land holdings	'+'
Instruments		
Age difference	Difference of age between the male and female members	'−'
Education difference	Difference of years of education between the male and female members	'−'
Freedom of mobility	This variable takes value '1' if the woman decides whether to step out and '0' otherwise	'+'

household dummy; households with gender parity were rated '0' and those without were rated '1'. The other independent variables included are education level of the head, household size, operational landholdings, and years of education of the primary female member of the household, crop diversity index, and a number of milch animals possessed by the households. The crop diversity index captures the diversity in the production basket of the household. The number of milch animals includes the number of goats, sheep, cows, and buffaloes owned by the household, which was assumed to affect household diet diversity through the agriculture–nutrition pathway of agriculture as a source of food. The instruments used were age and education differences between the primary male and female of the household. In addition to these, a dummy variable capturing the decision related to women's mobility was used. This variable took the value '1' if the woman decided to step out of the house and '0' otherwise.

RESULTS

Table 6.3 displays the results of the WEAI for the total sample. The WEAI is 0.714 which is the weighted average of two sub-indices, the 4DE, and GPI. For women, of the total sample, approximately 70 per cent are disempowered and have inadequate achievements in 41 per cent of the domains (average inadequacy score). However, for the men, the numbers are more satisfactory; less than 20 per cent of the men are disempowered and their accomplishment inadequacy is just 5 per cent. At the same time, approximately 64 per cent of the women lack

gender parity with their spouse in the household. The empowerment gap between men and women within the households is relatively high at 48 per cent. The overall GPI for the total sample is 0.698.

Subsequently, a state-wise analysis was performed to observe the differences in the performance. The WEAI for Bihar is lowest (0.258) among the three states. In Bihar, the empowerment headcount ratio is 11.9 per cent and 95.2 per cent, for the women and men respectively. In addition, women have poor achievement in 83.3 per cent of the domains, whereas men have poor achievement in only 1.8 per cent of the domains. The GPI revealed that only 19 per cent of the women have gender parity with their spouse. The gender empowerment gap between women and men is as high as 92.3 per cent in Bihar.

In Jharkhand, approximately 44 per cent of the women and 69 per cent of the men are empowered. Women lack achievement in 27 per cent of the domains, whereas the men lacked in only 10.4 per cent of the dimensions. The GPI revealed that approximately 42.3 per cent of the women are at par with their spouse. Thus, the empowerment gap between women and men is 36 per cent, which is relatively less compared to that in Bihar. The GPI of Jharkhand is 0.847, which is reasonably better compared to that of Bihar.

In Odisha, approximately 22 per cent of the women and 96 per cent of the men are empowered. Moreover, the disempowered women are inadequate in 37 per cent of the domains, whereas the men have inadequacies in only 1.2 per cent of the dimensions. At the same time, the GPI revealed that nearly 77.4 per cent of the women

Table 6.3   Results of WEAI for Total Sample and Individual States

Indices	Total Sample		Bihar		Jharkhand		Odisha	
	Women	Men	Women	Men	Women	Men	Women	Men
Disempowered Headcount (H) (%)	69.6	16.1	88.1	04.8	55.8	30.8	77.4	03.6
Average Inadequacy Score (A) (%)	40.8	05.5	83.3	01.8	27.1	10.4	36.6	01.2
Disempowerment Index (Mo)	0.284	0.009	0.734	0.001	0.151	0.032	0.283	0.000
Empowered Headcount (H) (%)	30.4	83.9	11.9	95.2	44.2	69.2	22.6	96.4
4DE Index $(1-M_0)$	0.716	0.991	0.266	0.999	0.849	0.968	0.717	1.000
Gender Parity Inadequate Households (%)	63.5		88.1		42.3		77.4	
Average Empowerment Gap (%)	47.5		92.3		36.1		29.5	
GPI	0.698		0.187		0.847		0.772	
WEAI	0.714		0.258		0.849		0.722	
Number of Observations	230	230	42	42	104	104	84	84

Source: Computed by the authors using VDSA data, in line with Alkire et al. (2013).

experienced gender parity with their spouse. The empowerment gap between women and men is 30 per cent, which is less compared to that in both Bihar and Jharkhand.

Domain-Specific Achievements

The domain-specific contribution to the women's disempowerment measure (Table 6.4) indicates inadequate empowerment in group membership in a voluntary organization (51.6 per cent). Nearly 41 per cent of the women did not have access to credit and lacked decision-making authority over credit. Furthermore, approximately 44 per cent of the women lacked access to assets and 25 per cent have limited control over decision-making related to assets. Nevertheless, domain-specific contribution to the men's disempowerment measure is relatively different from that of the women. Most of the men had access to resources, decision-making authority over agricultural production, and control over income than the women. Simultaneously, men are more disempowered in group membership.

The results for the state-wise decomposition analysis are reported in Tables 6.5–6.7. For Bihar, the decomposition analysis reveals that more than 65 per cent of the women lacked empowerment in most of the domains. In addition, particulars of domains indicate that more than 20 per cent of the contribution emerged from all the domains, which was strikingly higher than the configuration of men's inadequacy in empowerment. The men are empowered in access to resources, control over income, and decision-making authority over production processes. However, the primary difference is that the men are more disempowered in group membership than the women.

Table 6.4   Decomposition by Dimension and Indicator for Total Sample

Total Sample	Ownership of Assets	Decision-making for Assets	Access to and Decisions on Credit	Input in Productive Decisions	Autonomy in Production	Control over Use of Income	Membership
Women							
Censored Headcount	0.435	0.252	0.409	0.217	0.261	0.335	1.000
% Contribution Indicators	7.450	4.321	7.003	5.610	6.732	17.278	51.608
% Contribution by Dimension	18.773			12.341		17.278	51.608
Men							
Censored Headcount	0.004	0.004	0.152	0.000	0.000	0.004	0.878
% Contribution Indicators	0.154	0.154	5.398	0.000	0.000	0.465	93.830
% Contribution by Dimension	5.706			0.000		0.465	93.830

Source: Computed by the authors using VDSA data, in line with Alkire et al. (2013).

Table 6.5   Decomposition by Dimension and Indicator for Bihar

Bihar	Ownership of Assets	Decision-making for Assets	Access to and Decisions on Credit	Input in Productive Decisions	Autonomy in Production	Control over Use of Income	Membership
Women							
Censored Headcount	0.786	0.643	0.690	0.857	0.881	0.881	1.000
% Contribution	7.553	6.180	6.638	12.410	12.754	25.509	28.956
% Contribution by Dimension	20.371			25.164		25.509	28.956
Men							
Censored Headcount	0.024	0.024	0.024	0.000	0.000	0.000	0.405
% Contribution	1.845	1.845	1.845	0.000	0.000	0.000	94.465
% Contribution by Dimension	5.535			0.000		0.000	94.465

Source: Computed by the authors using VDSA data, in line with Alkire et al. (2013).

Table 6.6   Decomposition by Dimension and Indicator for Jharkhand

Jharkhand	Ownership of Assets	Decision-making for Assets	Access to and Decisions on Credit	Input in Productive Decisions	Autonomy in Production	Control over Use of Income	Group Membership
Women							
Censored Headcount	0.298	0.260	0.442	0.077	0.058	0.125	1.000
% Contribution	6.492	5.655	9.634	2.523	1.892	8.200	65.604
% Contribution by Dimension	21.780			4.416		8.200	65.604
Men							
Censored Headcount	0.000	0.000	0.298	0.000	0.000	0.010	0.990
% Contribution	0.000	0.000	9.005	0.000	0.000	0.875	90.120
% Contribution by Dimension	9.005			0.000		0.875	90.120

Source: Computed by the authors using VDSA data, in line with Alkire et al. (2013).

Table 6.7   Decomposition by Dimension and Indicator for Odisha

Odisha	Ownership of Assets	Decision-making for Assets	Access to and Decisions on Credit	Input in Productive Decisions	Autonomy in Production	Control over Use of Income	Group Membership
Women							
Censored Headcount	0.429	0.048	0.226	0.071	0.202	0.321	1.000
% Contribution	8.802	0.978	4.645	2.096	5.938	18.861	58.680
% Contribution by Dimension	14.425			8.034		18.861	58.680
Men							
Censored Headcount	0.000	0.000	0.036	0.012	0.012	0.000	0.976
% Contribution	0.000	0.000	1.186	0.595	0.595	0.000	97.624
% Contribution by Dimension	1.186			1.191		0.000	97.624

Source: Computed by the authors using VDSA data, in line with Alkire et al. (2013).

In Jharkhand, the domain-specific contribution to the women's disempowerment measure reveals that they are weakly empowered in group membership in a voluntary organization (65.6 per cent) and ownership of assets (22 per cent). Nearly 44 per cent of the women did not have access to credit and have inadequate decision-making authority over it. However, most of the men have access to resources, decision-making authority over agricultural production, and control over income than the women. However, the men face inadequate empowerment in group membership.

Finally, for Odisha, the component domains reveal that more than 43 per cent and 23 per cent of the women and men are disempowered due to lack of access to resources and credit, respectively. Furthermore, domain-specific share shows that the women have less control over income and group membership, whereas the men are empowered in access to resources, control and decision-making authority over income, and production processes. Similar to the other two states, the men had an inadequate empowerment in group membership.

Even though the data is not representative of the district or state, it provides useful insights into the condition of women in comparison to men. In Bihar, a high percentage of the women are disempowered and lack adequacy across all domains. With respect to gender empowerment gap, the women suffer more in Bihar compared to other states.

Correlation with Other Individual and Household Characteristics

The results for the correlation between empowerment and other household characteristics are presented in Table 6.8. For the total sample, the BMI is significantly associated with women's empowerment in agriculture.

Table 6.8 Correlation between Empowerment and Individual and Household's Characteristics

Characteristics	Empowerment (%)			
	Women		Men	
	Empowered	Disempowered	Empowered	Disempowered
Age Group				
Less than 18 Years	0	1	0	0
	(0)	(100)	(0)	(0)
18–40 Years	35	68	55	5
	(33.98)	(66.02)	(91.67)	(8.33)
Above 40 Years	35	91	138	32
	(27.78)	(72.22)	(81.18)	(18.82)
Total	70	160	193	37
	(30.43)	(69.57)	(83.91)	(16.09)
Cramer's V	0.08		0.13	
Pearson Chi^2 (statistic and p-value)	1.47	0.48	3.62	0.057
Fisher's Exact (p-value)		0.525		0.066
Education				
Illiterate	42	76	41	11
	(35.59)	(64.41)	(78.85)	(21.15)
Primary	14	39	59	8
	(26.42)	(73.58)	(88.06)	(11.94)
Secondary	13	42	65	15
	(23.64)	(76.36)	(81.25)	(18.75)
High Secondary	1	3	28	3
	(25)	(75)	(90.32)	(9.68)
Total	70	160	193	37
	(30.43)	(69.57)	(83.91)	(16.09)

(Cont'd)

Table 6.8   *(Cont'd)*

Total Sample Characteristics	Empowerment (%)			
	Women		Men	
	Empowered	Disempowered	Empowered	Disempowered
Age Group				
Cramer's V	0.12		0.12	
Pearson Chi^2 (statistic and p-value)	3.14	0.37	3.21	0.361
Fisher's Exact (p-value)		0.371		0.376
BMI				
Below Normal <18.5	27	66	62	19
	(29.03)	(70.97)	(76.54)	(23.46)
Normal 18.5–24.9	39	70	112	16
	(35.78)	(64.22)	(87.5)	(12.5)
Above Normal >25	4	24	19	2
	(14.29)	(85.71)	(90.48)	(9.52)
Total	70	160	193	37
	(30.43)	(69.57)	(83.91)	(16.09)
Cramer's V	0.15		0.15	
Pearson Chi^2 (statistic and p-value)	5.01	0.082	5.15	0.076
Fisher's Exact (p-value)		0.076		0.097
Land class				
Marginal <2.5	49	96	124	21
	(33.79)	(66.21)	(85.52)	(14.48)
Small 2.5–5	13	40	41	12
	(24.53)	(75.47)	(77.36)	(22.64)
Medium 5–10	8	18	22	4
	(30.77)	(69.23)	(84.62)	(15.38)
Large >10	0	6	6	0
	(0)	(100)	(100)	(0)
Total	70	160	193	37
	(30.43)	(69.57)	(83.91)	(16.09)
Cramer's V	0.136		0.117	
Pearson Chi^2 (statistic and p-value)	4.27	0.234	3.123	0.373
Fisher's Exact (p-value)		0.263		0.442

Note: Figures are for total sample.
Source: Computed by the authors using VDSA data, in line with Alkire et al. (2013).

Most of the empowered women have a normal BMI status than the disempowered women, who are more likely to have the below normal BMI status. By contrast, age is significantly associated with the men's empowerment in agriculture. A majority of the men are above 40 years of age and have low empowerment percentage. However, the younger men have more empowerment than the older men. Similarly, the BMI status is significantly associated with the men's empowerment in agri-

culture. Most of the empowered men have normal BMI than the disempowered men, who have below normal BMI status.

The results presented in Table 6.9 reveal the correlation between empowerment and decision-making authority in household-related decisions. Women who are empowered in the 4DE have significantly high decision-making authority over other aspects. For instance, women empowered in agriculture have decision-making

Table 6.9   Correlation between Empowerment and Answers to Decision-making Questions

Decision-making in Other Indicators	Empowered		Phi Coefficient	Pearson Chi^2		Fisher Exact	Missing
	Yes	No		Statistic	p-value	p-value	Indicator
Percentage of Women Who Feel They Can Make Decisions regarding							
Children Marriage	88.6	63.8	0.294	19.83	0	0	31
Contraception Usage	71.4	61.9	0.273	17.18	0	0	49
Education of Children	0	0					
Expenditure on Healthcare	0	0					
Household Maintenance	98.5	83.1	−0.217	10.87	0	0	0
Number of Children	0	0					
Women Stepping Out of the House	87.1	54.4	0.316	22.97	0	0	3
Percentage of Men Who Feel They Can Make Decisions regarding							
Children Marriage	82.32	17.68	0.202	9.38	0.009	0.015	31
Contraception Usage	80.25	19.75	0.172	6.846	0.033	0.02	50
Education of Children	84.62	15.38	0.158	5.768	0.056	0.12	8
Expenditure on Healthcare	84.3	15.7	0.168	6.478	0.039	0.081	4
Household Maintenance	86	14	0.147	4.947	0.026	0.031	0
Number of Children	83.72	16.28	0.162	6.052	0.049	0.16	14
Women Stepping Out of the House	84.21	15.79	0.054	0.679	0.712	0.599	3

Note: Figures are for total sample.
Source: Computed by the authors using VDSA data, in line with Alkire et al. (2013).

authority over contraception usage, household main-tenance, children's marriages, and stepping out of the house. Even the men, who are empowered in agriculture, have significant decision-making authority over all aspects except decision-making related to women stepping out of the house.

Intrahousehold Patterns of Empowerment

Similar to that of Alkire et al. (2013), intra-household comparisons were possible due to the availability of the data for both the primary male and female of the same households. The 4DE values differ substantially across states. For instance, Jharkhand has the highest 4DE score for the women (0.849), whereas Bihar has the lowest (0.266). For the men, scores are generally high and differed marginally across states.

The GPI is highest for Jharkhand and lowest for Bihar. Even though 58.5 per cent of the women have parity with their spouses in Jharkhand, among the households which lacked parity, the gap was is 36 per cent. By contrast, in Odisha, only 22.6 per cent of the women have parity and the gap is 29 per cent, which is lower than Jharkhand. For Bihar, both the indicators are poor—only 11.9 per cent of the women have parity and the gap is 92.3 per cent.

The results for intra-household patterns of 4DE are presented in Table 6.10. Bihar has the highest percentage (86 per cent) of households with disempowered woman

Table 6.10   Household-wise Empowerment Patterns

Household Characteristic	Bihar	Jharkhand	Odisha
Both woman and man are empowered (number of households)	4	44	19
	9.5%	42%	22.6%
Both woman and man are disempowered (number of households)	1	30	3
	2.4%	29%	3.6%
The woman is disempowered; the man is empowered (number of households)	36	28	62
	86%	27%	74%
The man is disempowered; the woman is empowered (number of households)	1	2	0
	2.4%	2%	0

Source: Computed by the authors using VDSA data, in line with Alkire et al. (2013).

and empowered man, and only 2.4 per cent of the households have the reverse (empowered woman and disempowered man). However, in Jharkhand, the percentage of households having disempowered woman and empowered man is the lowest (27 per cent). Moreover, the proportion of both the woman and man empowered or disempowered in the same household, is highest in Jharkhand than in the other states. This is also reflected in the high GPI of Jharkhand.

Results of Determinants of Household Dietary Diversity

Summary statistics for the variables employed in the regression analysis are reported in Table 6.11. The results for the determinants of household diet diversity score are presented in Table 6.12. Column 1 in Table 6.12 presents the ordinary least squares (OLS) estimates. The result reveals that the gender parity gap is highly significant

Table 6.11 Summary Statistics

Variables	Number of Observations	Mean	Standard Deviation	Minimum	Maximum
Age of head of the household (years)	230	50.048	12.949	22	77
Education of the head of the household (years)	229	5.707	4.527	0	17
Age of the primary male (years)	230	48.622	11.989	20	75
Education of the primary male (years)	229	5.786	4.559	0	17
Age of the primary female (years)	230	43.526	11.762	17	72
Education of the primary female (years)	229	3.079	3.713	0	15
Household size (in numbers)	230	5.913	2.635	2	18
Number of food crops	230	2.374	1.530	1	9
Number of milch animals	230	2.061	1.757	0	10
Household diet diversity score	230	0.748	0.116	0.139	0.896
Gender parity gap (dummy)	230	0.634	NA	0	1

Source: Computed by the authors using VDSA data.

Table 6.12 2SLS Regression Analysis for Household Diet Diversity

Household Diet Diversity Score	OLS		2SLS	
	Coefficient	Robust standard errors	Coefficient	Robust standard errors
Gender parity dummy	−0.035**	0.015	−0.356**	0.159
Operational landholdings	0.002	0.002	0.009*	0.005
Education of the head of the household	0.001	0.002	0.006	0.004
Household size	−0.009***	0.002	−0.014***	0.005
Number of milch animals	0.015***	0.005	0.012*	0.007
Education of the primary female	−0.006***	0.002	−0.003	0.004
Crop Diversity	0.004	0.031	−0.006	0.062
Constant	0.806***	0.021	0.975	0.092
Observations	199		199	
			Statistic	p-value
Endogeneity test p, Ho: exogenous			12.45	0.0004
Kleibergan-Paap rk LM statistic under identification test			6.211	0.102
Kleibergan-Paap rk Wald F statistic weak identification test			1.773	13.91
Hensen J Statistic over-identification			3.107	0.212

Note: *, **, *** represents 10%, 5% and 1% level of significance respectively.
Source: Computed by the authors using VDSA data.

and negatively correlated with the household diet diversity score. The two-stage least squares (2SLS) estimates in Column 3 reveal that after instrumenting the endogenous variable, the lesser the gender parity gap the more is the household diet diversity score. This suggests that when women have an equal say in the household decision-making, the household diet diversity improves. This is consistent with the finding of a previous study (Smith et al., 2003): if the bargaining power within the household is in favour of women, household welfare outcomes improves. The 2SLS estimates are higher than the OLS estimates, implying that neglecting the endogeneity of gender gap variable would have underestimated the impact of increased women's empowerment on the household diet diversity. The diagnostic tests are reported at the end of Table 6.12. The endogeneity test reveals that the gender parity gap dummy variable is endogenous and needs to be instrumented. The over- and under-identification test results confirms that the instruments used are valid and the models are exactly identified.

Further, a number of milch animals possessed by the households and operational landholdings significantly and positively influenced the household dietary diversity, possibly through wealth or income effect. However, the crop diversity index and household head's education level are insignificantly associated with household diet diversity. Household size has a significant negative impact, implying that higher the number of members, lower the household diet diversity.

CONCLUSION

Women are the major stakeholders in the agriculture–nutrition interventions and their empowerment is consequential for improved nutritional outcomes and inclusive economic growth. This study reveals that women's empowerment, in general, is low and disempowerment of women is more prominent in Bihar compared to Jharkhand and Odisha. Moreover, the gender parity gap is high. The study shows that domains wherein women are mostly disempowered pertained to access to resources, access to assets, decision-making authority over income, and poor participation in group activities. Nevertheless, the intensity of empowerment varies across the domains. Hence, there is a need for targeted policies to reduce gender gap and enhance women's empowerment.

Furthermore, our analysis clearly reveals that the household diet diversity was significantly and positively affected by gender parity, operational landholdings, and

a number of milch animals possessed by the household. As women contribute 50 per cent to 90 per cent of the labour inputs for livestock rearing (GoI, 2007), the programmes of livestock development, training, and extension interventions should also be targeted towards women.

Women's representation in terms of agriculture labourers has been increasing; however, they face serious barriers because of the prevailing gender bias in accessing credit, inputs, extension services, and markets. Moreover, women are denied property rights to land and other productive resources, and, therefore, overcoming these barriers through various policy initiatives has become a necessity. Women's empowerment is a complex dynamic process (Alkire et al., 2013) and requires constant support to achieve gender parity and empowerment of women for improved nutritional outcomes of children and women.

REFERENCES

Agarwal, B. 1994. *A Field of One's Own: Gender and Land Rights in South Asia*. Cambridge, United Kingdom: Cambridge University Press.

———. 1997. '"Bargaining" and Gender Relationships: Within and Beyond the Household'. *Feminist Economics* 3 (1): 1–51.

———. 2010. 'Rethinking Agricultural Production Collectives'. *Economic and Political Weekly* 45 (17): 64–78.

Allendorf, K. 2007. 'Do Women's Land Rights Promote Empowerment and Child Health in Nepal?'. *World Development* 35 (11): 1975–88.

Alkire, S. 2005. 'Quantitative Studies of Human Agency'. *Social Indicators Research* 74(1): 217–60.

———. 2007. 'Measuring Agency: Issues and Possibilities'. *Indian Journal of Human Development* 1 (1): 169–78.

Alkire, S., and J. Foster. 2011. 'Counting and Multidimensional Poverty Measurement'. *Journal of Public Economics* 95 (7): 476–87.

Alkire, S., R. Meinzen-Dick, A. Peterman, A. Quisumbing, G. Seymour, and A. Vaz. 2013. 'The Women's Empowerment in Agriculture Index'. *World Development* 52: 71–91.

Alsop, R., M. Bertelsen, and J. Holland. 2006. *Empowerment in Practice from Analysis to Implementation*. Washington, DC: World Bank.

Baum, C.F., M.E. Schaffer, and S. Stillman. 2010. ivreg2: Stata Module for Extended Instrumental Variables/2SLS, GMM and AC/HAC, LIML and K-Class Regression. USA: Statistical Software Components, Boston College, Department of Economics.

Cain, M.T. 1984. 'Women's Status and Fertility in Developing Countries: Son Preference and Economic Security'. World Bank Staff Working Paper No. 682, World Bank, Washington, DC.

Doss, C. 2006. 'The Effects of Intra-Household Property Ownership on Expenditure Patterns in Ghana'. *Journal of African Economies* 15 (1): 149–80.

Duflo, E., and C. Udry. 2004. 'Intra-household Resource Allocation in Cote d'Ivoire: Social Norms, Separate Accounts, and Consumption Choices'. NBER Working Paper No.w10498, National Bureau of Economic Research, Cambridge, MA.

Food and Agriculture Organization of the United Nations (FAO). 2011. *Guidelines for Measuring Household and Individual Dietary Diversity*. Rome: Food and Agriculture Organization of the United Nations.

Gillespie, S., J. Harris, S. Kadiyala. 2012. 'The Agriculture–Nutrition Disconnect in India, What Do We Know?'. IFPRI Discussion Paper No. 01187, June, International Food Policy Research Institute, Washington, DC.

Government of India (GoI). 2007. *Report of the Working Group on Gender Issues, Panchayat Raj Institutions, Public Private Partnership, Innovative Finance and Micro Finance in Agriculture*. New Delhi: Planning Commission, Government of India.

———. 2011. Census. Registrar General of India, Government of India, New Delhi.

———. 2014. Indian Labour Statistics. Ministry of Labour and Employment, Government of India, New Delhi.

Haddad, L., J. Hoddinott, and H. Alderman. 1997. *Intra-household Resource Allocation in Developing Countries: Models, Methods, and Policy*. Baltimore, MD: Johns Hopkins University Press.

Hallman, K. 2003. 'Mother-Father Resources, Marriage Payments, and Girl–Boy Health in Rural Bangladesh'. In *Household Decisions, Gender, and Development: A Synthesis of Recent Research*, edited by A.R. Quisumbing, 115–20. Baltimore, MD: Johns Hopkins University Press.

Hoddinott, J. 1997. 'Water, Health, and Income: A Review'. Food Consumption and Nutrition Division Discussion Paper No. 25, International Food Policy Research Institute, Washington, DC.

Hoddinott, J., and L. Haddad. 1995. 'Does Female Income Share Influence Household Expenditures? Evidence from Cote d'Ivoire'. *Oxford Bulletin of Economics and Statistics* 57 (1): 77–96.

Kabeer, N. 1999. 'Resources, Agency, Achievements: Reflections on the Measurement of Women's Empowerment'. *Development and Change* 30 (3): 435–64.

Kadiyala, S., J. Harris, D. Headey, S. Yosef, and S. Gillespie. 2014. 'Agriculture and Nutrition in India: Mapping Evidence to Pathways'. *Annals of the New York Academy of Sciences* 133: 43–56.

Kilic, T., A. Palacios-Lopez, and M. Goldstein. 2013. 'Caught in a Productivity Trap: A Distributional Perspective on Gender Differences in Malawian Agriculture'. World Bank Policy Research Working Paper No. 6381, World Bank, Washington, DC.

Kishor, S. 1995. 'Autonomy and Egyptian women: Findings from the 1988 Egypt Demographic and Health Survey'. Occasional Papers No. 2, Macro International, Calverton, USA.

———. 1999. 'Women's Empowerment and Contraceptive Use in Egypt'. Paper presented at the Annual Meetings of the Population Association of America, March, New York.

———. 2000. 'Empowerment of Women in Egypt and Links to the Survival and Health of Their Infants'. In *Women's Empowerment and Demographic Processes: Moving Beyond Cairo*, pp. 119–56, edited by H. Presser, and G. Sen. New York: Oxford University Press.

Kishor, S., and K. Gupta. 2004. 'Women's Empowerment in India and its States: Evidence from the NFHS'. *Economic and Political Weekly*. 39 (7): 694–712.

Kishor, S., and L. Subaiya. 2008. *Understanding Women's Empowerment: A Comparative Analysis of Demographic and Health Surveys Data*. DHS Comparative Reports No. 20. Calverton, MD: Macro International.

Mahmud, S., N.M. Shah, and S. Becker. 2012. 'Measurement of Women's Empowerment in Rural Bangladesh'. *World Development* 40 (3): 610–19.

Malhotra, A., and S.R. Schuler. 2005. Women's Empowerment as a Variable in International Development'. In *Measuring empowerment: Cross-Disciplinary Perspectives*, edited by D. Narayan, 219–46. Washington, DC: World Bank.

Miller, B.D. 1981. *The Endangered Sex: Neglect of Female Children in Rural North India*. Ithaca, NY: Cornell University Press.

Narayan, D., ed. 2005. *Measuring Empowerment: Cross-disciplinary Perspectives*. Washington, DC: World Bank.

Pandey, V.L., S.M. Dev, and U. Jayachandran. 2016. 'Impact of Agricultural Interventions on the Nutritional Status in South Asia: A Review'. *Food Policy* 62: 28–40.

Peterman, A., J. Behrman, and A. Quisumbing. 2010. 'A Review of Empirical Evidence on Gender Differences in Non-Land Agricultural Inputs, Technology, and Services in Developing Countries'. IFPRI Discussion Paper No. 975, International Food Policy Research Institute, Washington, DC.

Quisumbing, A.R., ed. 2003. *Household Decisions, Gender, and Development: A Synthesis of Recent Research*. Washington, DC: International Food Policy Research Institute.

Quisumbing, A.R., and K. Hallman. 2005. 'Marriage in Transition: Evidence on Age, Education, and Assets from Six Developing Countries'. In *The Changing Transitions to Adulthood in Developing Countries: Selected Studies, Panel on Transitions to Adulthood in Developing Countries*, edited by C.B. Lloyd, J.R. Behrman, N.P. Stromquist, and B. Cohen, 200–69. Washington, DC: Committee on Population, Division of Behavioural and Social Sciences and Education, National Academies Press.

Quisumbing, A.R., L.R. Brown, H.S. Feldstein, L. Haddad, and C. Pena (eds). 1995. *Women: The Key to Food Security*.

Washington, DC: International Food Policy Research Institute.

Ram, F., B. Paswan, S.K. Singh, H. Lhungdim, C. Sekhar, A. Singh, W.D. Bansod et al. 2016. 'Demographic and Health Trends in India (2005–06–2015–16) Results from Phase 1 of NFHS-4'. *Economic and Politically Weekly* 51 (14): 79–83.

Ramalingaswami, V., U. Jonsson, and J. Rohde. 1996. 'Commentary: The Asian Enigma'. In *The Progress of Nations 1996*. New York: United Nations Children's Emergency Fund.

Raykar, N., M. Majumdar, R. Laxminarayanan, and P. Menon. 2015. *India Health Report: Nutrition 2015*. New Delhi: India Public Health Foundation of India. Accessed 24 March 2016, http://www.transformnutrition.org/wp-content/uploads/sites/3/2016/05/INDIA-HEALTH-REPORT-NUTRITION_2016.pdf

Sraboni, E., H. Malapit, A. Quisumbing, and A. Ahmed. 2014. 'Women's Empowerment in Agriculture: What Role for Food Security in Bangladesh?'. *World Development* 61: 11–52.

Skoufias, E. 2005. 'PROGRESA and its Impacts on the Welfare of Rural Households in Mexico'. Food Consumption and Nutrition Division Discussion Paper No. 139, International Food Policy Research Institute, Washington, DC.

Smith, L.C., U. Ramakrishnan, A. Ndiaye, L. Haddad, and R. Martorell. 2003. 'The Importance of Women's Status for Child Nutrition in Developing Countries'. IFPRI Research Report Abstract No. 131, International Food Policy Research Institute, Washington, DC.

Smith, L., and L. Haddad. 2000. 'Explaining Child Malnutrition in Developing Countries. a Cross-Country Analysis'. IFPRI Research Report No. 111, International Food Policy Research Institute, Washington, DC.

StataCorp. 2011. Stata Statistical Software: Release 12. College Station, TX: StataCorp LP.

World Bank. 2009. *Gender in Agriculture Sourcebook*. Washington, DC: World Bank.

Yoong, J., L. Rabinovich, and S. Diepeveen. 2012. *The Impact of Economic Resource Transfers to Women versus Men: A Systematic Review*. Technical Report. London: EPPI-Centre, Social Science Research Unit, Institute of Education, University of London.

7

Spatial Aspects of Production Diversification in Indian Agriculture

Tirtha Chatterjee and A. Ganesh-Kumar

INTRODUCTION

Indian agriculture has witnessed dramatic change in the composition of output produced. The production basket has diversified from staples, fibers, spices, and plantation crops to fruits, vegetables, floriculture, dairy, poultry, meats, and fishery. Diversification is seen in terms of value of output and value added but less so in terms of acreage allocation.

Past studies, such as Birthal et al. (2013); Joshi et al. (2004); Rao, Birthal, and Joshi (2006), show that diversification is largely driven by changes in demand by households and growing importance of agro-processing, hotels and restaurants sectors. Household demand shows clear change away from cereals to high-value products—fruits, vegetables, dairy products, poultry, meat, and fishery. Also, there has been a rise in demand for processed foods and eating out.

Diversification at the all India level masks variations at the state level. Some states are more diversified than others. The focus of earlier studies have mostly been at the national level, though some have examined diversification at the state level also, such as Birthal et al. (2013); Joshi et al. (2004); Singh and Sahoo (2007). Factors identified as influencing diversification include rainfall; infrastructure, especially irrigation and rural connectivity; agricultural marketing institutions; agricultural credit; and urbanization. These studies, however, have overlooked the role of geography and spatial spillovers in influencing diversification at the state level. They have considered states as absolute units and have typically included state-level rainfall as the most important (often the only) geographic/climatic factor influencing diversification. These studies do not allow any possibility of spatial interaction/spillovers across them.

The significance of role of relative spatial dependence on agriculture in general, that is, impact of geographic location of regions with respect to each other on land use, deforestation patterns, farming decisions, and land price volatility, is gaining popularity in recent years (Benirschka and Binkley, 1994; Florax, Voortman, and Brouwer, 2002; Irwin and Bockstael, 2002; Nelson and Hellerstein, 1997; Schmidtner et al., 2011). In reality states are not isolated geographic units, but interact with each other in several ways through agro-climatic factors that are common across states, river basins and their associated surface irrigation networks, interstate road and rail connectivity, urbanization and marketing avenues that they provide, trade and telecommunication networks, technological spillovers, and labour migration, among others. Ignoring these potential interstate linkages can result in incomplete/biased inferences on factors that affect diversification at the state level (Anselin, 1988).

The impact of geographic factors, in particular relative geography, on diversification within agriculture has, to our best possible knowledge, not been studied in the empirical literature on Indian agriculture. From a policy perspective, agricultural diversification towards high-value commodities is known to have positive impacts on farm income and accelerates poverty reduction (Birthal et al. 2008; Birthal et al. 2013; Birthal, Roy, and Negi 2015). Besides, several high-value agricultural commodities, such as dairy products, fruits and vegetables, eggs, meat, and fishery, are beneficial from a nutritional perspective also (Herforth 2010; Jones et al. 2014). Given these, it is important to understand the nature of geographic/spatial spillovers on agricultural diversification so that policies that exploit the interstate linkages can be designed to accelerate diversification.

This chapter looks at spatial aspects of agricultural production diversification[1] in India, considering 17 major states over the period 1990–91 to 2010–11, which are Andhra Pradesh, Assam, Bihar, Gujarat, Haryana, Himachal Pradesh, Jammu and Kashmir, Karnataka, Kerala, Madhya Pradesh, Maharashtra, Odisha, Punjab, Rajasthan, Tamil Nadu, Uttar Pradesh, and West Bengal. Data on the newly formed states of Jharkhand, Chhattisgarh and Uttaranchal have been merged with their parent states Bihar, Madhya Pradesh, and Uttar Pradesh, respectively, to maintain uniformity in the panel data set. These 17 states accounted for approximately 85 per cent of gross cropped area (GCA), 90 per cent of gross domestic product (GDP), and approximately 98 per cent of value of output from agriculture in 2010–11. The analysis has been done at the state level because of paucity of data on several explanatory variables at a lower level of geographical units, such as districts. It is conceivable that spatial dependence is stronger at a lower level of geographical aggregation. However, we believe evidence of significant spatial channels at the state level will make the case stronger.

In this chapter we cover the three broad sub-sectors—agriculture and allied activities, forestry, and fishing—

while assessing diversification. Towards understanding the spatial dimensions of agricultural diversification in India, we first examine the shares of different sub-sectors in the aggregate domestic product and value of output, at both the national and state levels. Further, we also look at the trends in the shares broad crop groups in the total crop output and gross cropped acreage, and similarly for individual items in the value of livestock output. In order to measure the extent of diversification, we compute the Simpson's index of diversification (SID; discussed later) at both national and state level. Further, we compare how individual states fare in comparison to the all India levels.

In order to understand the determinants of diversification and in particular the role of geography in this context we use spatial econometric methods that help incorporate spatial spillovers/dependence through a spatial weight matrix (SWM). We relate the diversification indices to various factors that existing studies have identified as important in this regard after incorporating spatial spillovers.

The next section examines the trends in agricultural diversification in the county as a whole and at the state level. In particular, it examines where states stand in comparison to the national-level picture in terms of diversification. The third section attempts to identify some factors affecting diversification at the state level. In particular the role of geography in this regard is studied here. The last section provides some concluding remarks.

TRENDS IN AGRICULTURAL DIVERSIFICATION

Trends at the All India Level (Sum of States)

As mentioned earlier, we consider 17 major states over the period 1990–91 to 2010–11. We begin by examining trends in the shares of the broad sub-sectors—agriculture and allied activities, forestry, and fishing—in overall agriculture. Specifically, we look at the shares in gross value added and gross value of output. Next, we examine the share of major crops groups such as cereals, pulses, and oilseeds in the total value of crop output and also their shares in the gross cropped acreage in the country. We then study the trends in the shares of major animal products, such as milk, egg and chicken meat, wool, dung, silk, and bovine and ovine meat, in the value of livestock output. Finally, SID is calculated for each of the major variables for each year in the study period. This allows us to capture the trends in diversification at the all India level.

---

[1] Diversification has been defined in several ways in literature. 'Livelihood diversification' is defined as the process by which rural families construct a diverse portfolio of activities and social support capabilities in order to survive and to improve their standard of living (Ellis, 1998). This includes income diversification and risk diversification. This chapter focuses on the determinants of production diversification.

The data for the analysis has been compiled from various published sources. Value of output, gross domestic product, and gross state domestic product for the 17 states at 2004–05 series have been collected from databases of National Account Statistics, Ministry of Statistics and Programme Implementation (MOSPI), Government of India and EPW Research Foundation (EPWRF), respectively. Data on crop-wise and total gross cropped acreage at the national and state levels has been taken from Land Use Statistics, Ministry of Agriculture, Government of India.

One of the characteristics observed in the data is that the state-level information does not add up to the national totals as reported in these official data sources. Hence, to ensure consistency in the analysis, we use the sum of these states as the 'national' total in the analysis here.

The shares of agriculture and allied activities, forestry, and fishing in the total agricultural GDP (GDP-AGRI) are plotted in Figure 7.1. It is seen that these shares have remained more of less steady over the last two decades. We find that agriculture and allied activities contributes approximately 85 percent of GDP-AGRI while forestry 10 per cent and fishery comprises of only 4 per cent. Share of agriculture and allied activities can be seen to be declining somewhat over the years and this has been gained by forestry with share of fishery remaining more or less constant.

Turning to value of agricultural output, from Figure 7.2 we see that once again agriculture and allied activities accounts for the major chunk, although it has come down somewhat over the years from approximately 70 per cent in 1999 to 60 per cent in 2010. As in

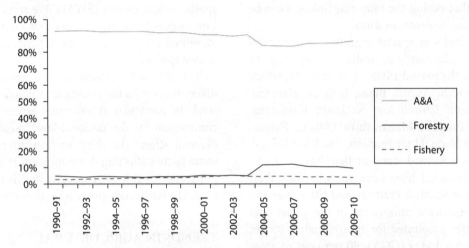

Figure 7.1   Share of Sub-sectors in Agricultural GDP (in per cent)

Source: Authors 'calculations based on data from EPWRF database.

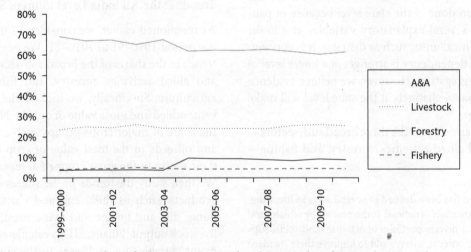

Figure 7.2   Share of Sub-sectors in Agricultural Gross Value of Output (in per cent)

Note: State-level data on value of output of forestry and fishing is available only 1999 onwards. Hence the above plots start from 1999.
Source: Authors' calculations based on data from MOSPI.

the case of GDP-AGRI, forestry has gained share over time, while the shares of livestock and fishery have remained almost steady over the years.

To get a more disaggregate picture, we look at the shares of major crop groups in the total value of crop output (Figure 7.3). Here we see some significant churn over the years. Cereals as a group continues to occupy the first rank, though its share has gone down over the years from around 35 per cent in the early 1990s to around 29 per cent to 30 per cent by 2010. On the other hand, fruits and vegetables have gained significant share over the years from about 17 per cent in 1990 to 28 per cent in 2010, which is almost the same as that of cereals. Sugar and pulses have steadily lost shares, while the share of other crop groups have remained more or less stable.

To assess if the allocation of land resources is commensurate with the share of different crops groups in value of output, we plot the shares of various crop groups in the GCA in Figure 7.4. One can see a decline in area allocated to cereals and a corresponding rise in area allocated to other crops though there is no striking change in the percentage allocated to any individual crop group. This indicates that some reallocation of land seems to be happening in the country.

Nevertheless, the pace of this reallocation is not commensurate with the changes in the shares of the major crop groups in the total value of crop output. Strikingly, cereals account for more than half of the total GCA, even though their share in value of output is only about 30 per cent. In contrast fruits and vegetables occupy only about 5 per cent (up from about 3.5 per cent in early 1990s) of cropped area though they contribute nearly the same amount as cereals in terms of the value of output. Sugar crops form the second highest share with approximately

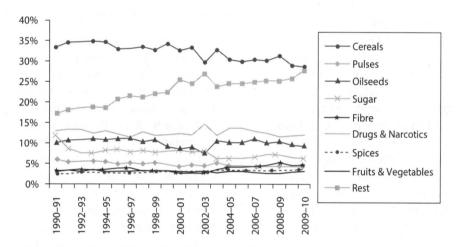

Figure 7.3   Share of Major Crop Groups in the Total Value of Crop Output (in per cent)

Source: Authors' calculations based on data from MOSPI.

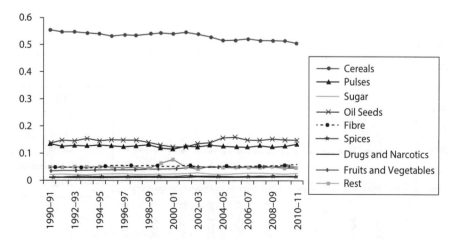

Figure 7.4   Share of Crop Groups in Gross Cropped Area (in per cent)

Source: Authors' calculations based on data from Land Use Statistics, Ministry of Agriculture.

15 per cent of the land allocated to sugar related crops. The third highest share comprises pulses with approximately 13 per cent of land devoted to different types of pulses. All other crop groups occupy the remaining approximately 15 per cent of GCA. The contrasting trends in the shares of value of output and cropped area indicates some amount of stickiness in the land allocation patterns.

Turning to livestock products, Figure 7.5 plots the trends in the share of major items in the total value of livestock output. It is seen that milk accounts for over 60 per cent of value of livestock products. Meats come second at about 20 per cent. The remaining items account for the balance. No significant trend is seen in the shares of these items over the years. As seen earlier, livestock as a group has maintained steady shares in the total value of agricultural output and GDP-AGRI, suggesting that this sub-sector has grown roughly at about the same rate as agriculture as a whole.

In order to assess the extent of diversification, we compute SID, which is defined as: $I = 1 - \sum s_j^2$ where $s_j = X_j / \sum X_j$ is the share of group j in the total for a variable of interest X. For example, in the case of total value of agricultural output, j would refer to each of its constituent groups—agriculture and allied activities, forestry, and fishing. The index ranges from 0 to 1, with 0 indicating complete specialization and 1 when there is complete diversification. The attractiveness of SID is that it accounts for both richness in the number of groups and evenness in the distribution of the constituents in the total.

Here we compute the SID for GDP-AGRI, agricultural gross value of output, total value of crop output, GCA, and total value of livestock output. For each of these variables, SIDs are computed for every year since 1990 (except for agricultural gross value of output where we compute SID from 1999), with the constituent groups for each of these variables are as indicated in the Figures 7.1 to 7.5. Trends in these SIDs are plotted in Figure 7.6. Diversification is highest in the case of total value of crop output though the index does not show any trend (rising/ falling). Diversification in acreage, although the second highest and shows a rising trend, is significantly lower than that in crop output. At the other end, diversification is lowest in the case of GDP-AGRI though it is showing a positive trend over the years. Livestock output is the only one that shows a declining value of SID indicating greater specialization within this group. As seen earlier, milk and meats dominate this group, and their shares are increasing over time.

Diversification Trends at the State Level

To examine the levels and trends in the diversification at the state level, SIDs are computed for each of the five variables as given in Figure 7.6 for the 17 major states considered in this study, treating them as separate geographical units. Further, to facilitate comparison the ratio of the state-specific SID value to that of the corresponding all India SID value is computed. A value greater/(less) than 1 for this ratio indicates that the diversification in a particular state is more/(less) than that at the national level. This allows us to rank the states according to their diversification relative to all India. It must be mentioned here that the all India SID values are not an average of the state-level SIDs.

Trends in the SIDs for the five variables for each of the 17 states are reported in the Appendix 7A. For the purpose of exposition, we examine the ranks of the states

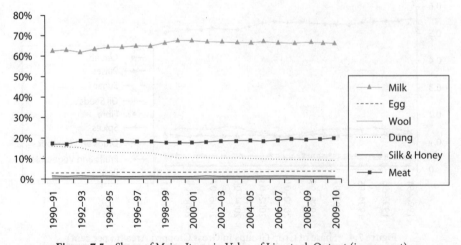

Figure 7.5   Share of Major Items in Value of Livestock Output (in per cent)

Source: Authors' calculations based on data from MOSPI.

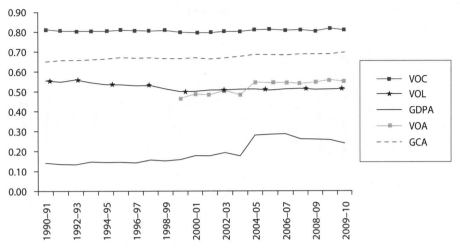

Figure 7.6   Diversification Indices

Notes: (i) VOC – diversification in value of crop output.
(ii) VOL – diversification in value of livestock output.
(iii) VOA – diversification in value of overall agricultural output.
(iv) GDP-AGRI – diversification in GDP-AGRI; (v) GCA – diversification in GCA; and (vi) State-level data on value of output of forestry and fishing are available only from 1999 onwards.
Source: Authors' calculations based on data from sources mentioned earlier.

for three time points—1990, 2000, and 2010. This gives a snapshot of the trends in the spatial variation in the degree of diversification.

We begin first with GSDP from agriculture (GSDPA) in Figure 7.7. Over the years, broadly the same set of states remains more diversified than all India. In 1990, ten states—Himachal Pradesh, Odisha, Jammu and Kashmir, West Bengal, Maharashtra, Kerala, Madhya Pradesh, Assam, Gujarat, and Karnataka—were more diversified than all India. The set of states was slightly different as Assam, Gujarat, and Karnataka were no longer more diversified than all India and their places were filled by Andhra Pradesh, Bihar, and Tamil Nadu. In 2010, once again ten states were more diversified with Assam and Karnataka taking their positions back and Andhra Pradesh and Tamil Nadu losing theirs. Among all, seven states— Kerala, Himachal Pradesh, Odisha, West Bengal, Madhya Pradesh, Jammu and Kashmir, and Maharashtra—have always been more diversified than all India. Over the years, the extent of diversification has come down for as the most diversified state, Himachal Pradesh which was approximately 2.5 times more diversified than all India in 1990, in 2010 although retained its position was only 1.7 times that of all India. The least diversified states have been Punjab and Haryana for all the three years.

Figure 7.8 gives the spatial variation in diversification in total value of output from agriculture relative to that of all India for the two years. In 2000, ten states—Kerala,

Jammu and Kashmir, Himachal Pradesh, Andhra Pradesh, West Bengal, Rajasthan, Gujarat, Madhya Pradesh, Tamil Nadu, and Bihar—were more diversified than that of All India. In 2010, eight states—Andhra Pradesh, Jammu and Kashmir, Kerala, Bihar, Tamil Nadu, Rajasthan, West Bengal, and Himachal Pradesh—were more diversified than all India. Eight states—Andhra Pradesh, Jammu and Kashmir, Kerala, Bihar, Tamil Nadu, Rajasthan, West Bengal, and Himachal Pradesh—have been more diversified relative to all India in both the years. Madhya Pradesh and Gujarat were more diversified in 2000 but not so in 2010. Once again, like in the case of GSDPA, the set of states which are more diversified than all India broadly remains the same in both the years.

Spatial variation in diversification in value of crop output relative to all India is shown in Figure 7.9. Only three states—Gujarat, Maharashtra, and Andhra Pradesh—were more diversified than All India in 1990. By 2000, Karnataka, Tamil Nadu, and Madhya Pradesh also joined the ranks of the above three state in being more diversified than All India. However, there seems to have been a reversal in this trend and, by 2010, only Maharashtra, Karnataka, and Gujarat remained more diversified than All India. Thus, overall Gujarat and Maharashtra are the only two states which have always been more diversified than all India. However, even these states have been only somewhat more diversified than all India (SIDs less than 10 percentage points). On the other

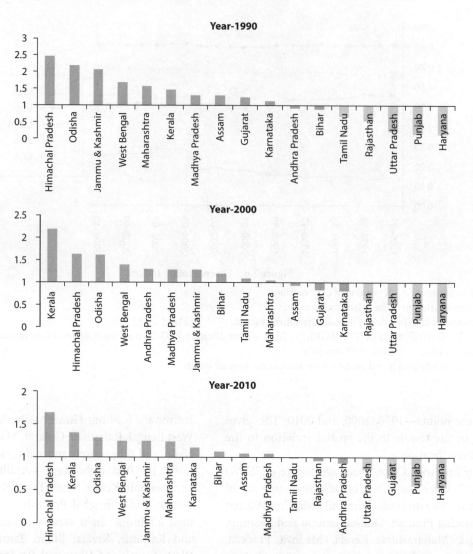

Figure 7.7   Spatial Variation in Diversification in Gross State Domestic Product from Agriculture Relative to All India
Source: Authors' calculations based on data from sources mentioned earlier.

hand, several states show significant specialization with their SIDs being more than 10 percentage points lower than that of all India. In particular, Bihar, Haryana, Himachal Pradesh, Jammu and Kashmir, Odisha, Punjab, and West Bengal showed far lower SIDs than all India.

Figure 7.10 gives the spatial variation in diversification in GCA relative to all India. We find that in 1990, seven states—Kerala, Gujarat, Tamil Nadu, Rajasthan, Karnataka, Andhra Pradesh, and Maharashtra—were more diversified than all India in 1990. Odisha was as diversified as all India in 1990. In 2000, apart from the same seven states Madhya Pradesh turned out to be more diversified than all India. Odisha was less diversified than all India in 2000. The same set of seven states once again are more diversified than all India in 2010. The set of states which are more diversified than all India in the

three years have remained exactly the same. The extent of diversification has declined over the years. For example, in 1990, Kerala (the most diversified state) was 20 percentage points more diversified than all India, in 2010 Gujarat (the most diversified state) was approximately 15 percentage points more diversified than all India.

Figure 7.11 gives the spatial variation in diversification in value of livestock output relative to all India. In 1990, nine states—Andhra Pradesh, West Bengal, Karnataka, Tamil Nadu, Uttar Pradesh, Kerala, Odisha, Assam, and Jammu and Kashmir—were more diversified than all India. In 2000, seven states—Odisha, West Bengal, Uttar Pradesh, Andhra Pradesh, Kerala, Assam, and Bihar—were states with higher diversification than all India. In 2010, nine states—Odisha, West Bengal, Uttar Pradesh, Tamil Nadu, Andhra Pradesh, Jammu and

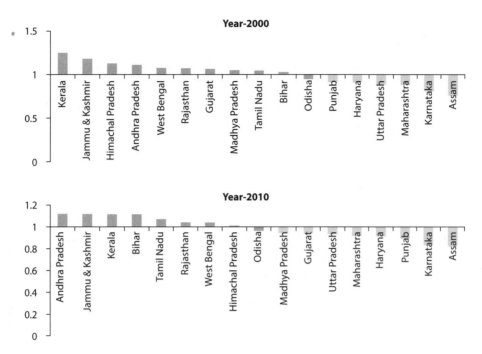

Figure 7.8   Spatial Variation in Diversification in Total Value of Output from Agriculture Relative to All India

Note: State-level data on value of output of forestry and fishing are available only from 1999 onwards. Hence the above charts are for only 2000 and 2010.

Source: Authors' calculations based on data from sources mentioned earlier.

Kashmir, Assam, Kerala, and Karnataka—showed higher diversification than all India. The set of states which have always been more diversified than all India are Andhra Pradesh, West Bengal, Uttar Pradesh, Odisha, Assam, and Kerala. Further, there has been a systematic increase in the extent of diversification relative to all India in these states. For instance, in 1990, Andhra Pradesh (the most diversified state) was approximately 15 per cent more diversified than all India. In 2000 and 2010, Odisha (the most diversified state) was approximately 30 percentage points more diversified than all India in both these years. Here we should note that the diversification index for livestock output for all India has declined.

SOME FACTORS DRIVING DIVERSIFICATION

Findings of Past Studies

Joshi et al. (2004) study the patterns, trends, and determinants of diversification across South Asia using SID for crop, livestock, and fishery subsectors and find that diversification has increased in almost all the countries in South Asia, except Bangladesh, Nepal, and Bhutan, which are less diversified than the others. They found that for India, although there is spatial variation in the nature of diversification, it is picking momentum with a purpose

of augmenting incomes rather than a coping or risk-mitigating strategy. They use area under crops to compute SID for crops and value of output for the other sectors for 19 states in India between 1980–81 and 1998–99. They find that income, roads, and markets increase the level of diversification in favour of horticultural crops, while irrigation decreases the same. Further, they find that the relative profitability of horticultural crops to other crops increases diversification. However, they find that rural literacy has a negative relationship with diversification. For the livestock sector, they find relative profitability, small landholders, income, and urbanization as positive drivers, while irrigation is negatively related.

Rao, Birthal, and Joshi (2006) use a modified tobit model on district-level data between 1980 to 1998 and find that urbanization, roads, and veterinary institutions have a positive and significant relationship with high-value agriculture (dependent variable is share of output from high-value commodities, such as fruits, vegetables, milk, meat, and eggs, in total value of output). On the other hand fertilizer, tractors, and high-yield-value crops have a negative relationship.

Singh and Sahoo (2007) study 15 states between 1990 and 2002 and find that share of horticulture and livestock sectors in total agricultural output has significantly increased during the period. They find spatial variation

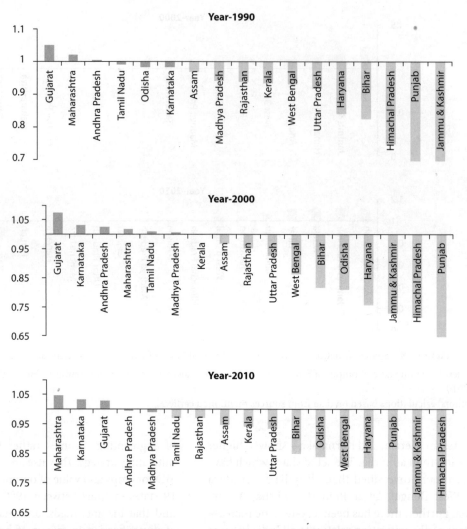

Figure 7.9   Spatial Variation in Diversification in Value of Crop Output Relative to All India
Source: Authors' calculations based on data from sources mentioned earlier.

in these sectors and that all states except Punjab, Haryana, Rajasthan, and Kerala have diversified. They use fixed effects regression to confirm that urbanization, per capita income, road, number of tractors, and small size of holdings have positive relation with SID, while rural literacy, irrigation, and fertilizer use have a negative coefficient. The study also finds beta convergence across states in terms of diversification.

Birthal et al. (2013), using state-level and household-level data, find that small holders are more likely to diverse towards high-value crops. Through their state-level analysis, they find that apart from that per capita income, average land size, markets, and prices of fruits and vegetables relative to cereals increase diversification. They find a negative relation between roads and diversification. Their household-level analysis also shows a pro small-holder bias towards high-value crops. But they

find that small holders play a higher role in vegetables rather than fruits cultivation. Singh, Kumar, and Singh (2006), using OLS estimate the determinants of diversification measured using area under crops from 1990 to 2000 and found that roads, villages electrified, value of agricultural output, and population per net sown area reduce diversification, while fertilizer consumption increase diversification.

As is evident, the above studies have considered states as absolute units and have overlooked the possibility of spatial interaction/spillovers across them. As argued earlier, spatial spillovers across states can arise due to the fact that states are not isolated geographic units but are interlinked across several dimensions, such as agro-climatic factors, natural endowments (river basins), infrastructure, marketing networks, and flow of labour. Not accounting for these potential interstate linkages can

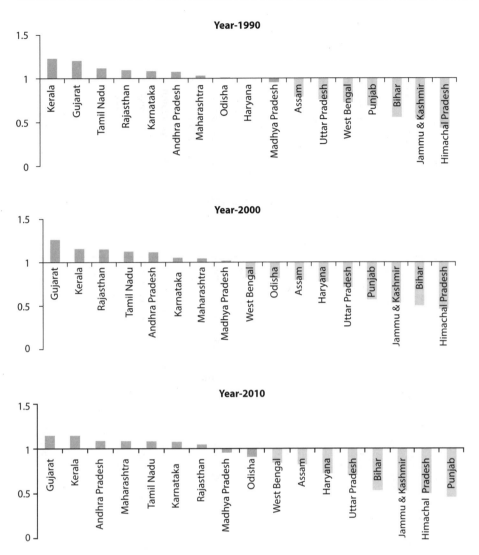

Figure 7.10   Spatial Variation in Diversification in Gross Cropped Area Relative to All India
Source: Authors' calculations based on data from sources mentioned earlier.

result in biased inferences on factors that affect diversification at the state level. Here we use spatial econometric methods to account for such spatial spillovers affecting agricultural diversification across states.

Spatial Dependence in Agricultural Diversification

Spatial dependence is said to occur when observations of a particular spatial unit is dependent on observations of its neighbours. It implies that there exists a relationship between what happens at different points or locations in space. The underlying idea driving the influence of geographical location is that forces driving regional–agricultural performance could exhibit significant geographical dependence because of reasons such as agro-climatic zones being spread over multiple regions,

and spillover of information and technology, trade, and transportation infrastructure into neighbouring regions. Due to the interplay of these and many other factors, regions act like interacting agents and we therefore need to empirically specify a structure to this spatial dependence which can be modelled on the basis of a number of theoretical frameworks as discussed in Anselin (2002).

Channels, such as road and irrigation infrastructure and urbanization, might have potential spillover effects across neighbouring states, which, in turn, create spatial spillover in demand- and supply-side factors, thereby driving the production basket of the states. These factors do not abruptly stop influencing the production behaviour because of the geographical limits of the state. Therefore, it is conceivable that diversification in a state

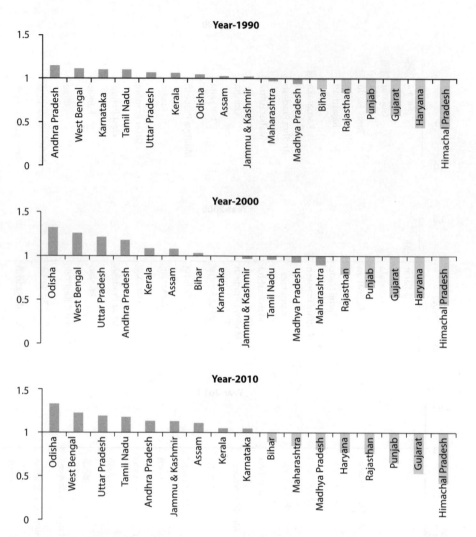

Figure 7.11   Spatial Variation in Diversification in Value of Livestock Output Relative to All India

Source: Authors' calculations based on data from sources mentioned earlier.

is driven by that of its neighbouring states through all these channels. So, our hypothesis is that along with other state-level factors, the level of production diversification in the neighbouring states plays a vital role in the diversification pattern of the state itself.

Econometrically, spatial dependence is quantified through an SWM. The SWM is the first step in spatial econometric analysis. It defines the structure of interaction between states and therefore defines the extent of spatial relationship and spillovers across states. Each observation (region) appears both in rows and columns. Hence the non-zero elements on each row of the matrix define the 'neighbourhood' of the corresponding spatial unit. The element w_{ij} expresses the intensity of the interaction between locations i and j.

The decision of classifying as to what constitutes a neighbour can vary. Not much guidance is available in

literature on defining SWMs. However, any form must satisfy two basic rules, that of being finite and non-negative (Anselin, 1988). 'W' is therefore a symmetric matrix and can be defined on the basis of context of the study. By convention, the diagonal elements are set to zero, $w_{ii} = 0$. The most common definition is simply one of contiguity: if two units share a common border, they are neighbours. We use this contiguity-based matrix for our analysis and give weight 1 if states are contiguous to one another and 0 if they are not. The SWM is then row-standardized so that sum of all the entries in a row equals 1. This ensures that the spatially weighted variable is the average of the values of the variable of all the neighbours wherein the weights are defined by the definition of W.

The first step in the analysis is to detect spatial dependence in the sample. Spatial dependence is typically detected using Global and local Moran's I-tests. Both these statistics measure the degree of dependency among observations in a geographic space. If these tests reject the null of absence of spatial dependence, then spatial modelling should be used to explain the behaviour of the data. Global Moran's I-test statistics for the presence of global spatial dependence among the spatial units are given by:

$$I = \frac{n}{\sum_i \sum_j w_{ij}} \frac{\sum_{i=1}^{n} \sum_{j=1}^{n} w_{ij}(x_i - \bar{x})(x_j - \bar{x})}{\sum_{i=1}^{n}(x_i - \bar{x})^2}, \qquad (1)$$

where n is the number of regions, w_{ij} is the element of the weight matrix W, x_i is the value of the variable at region i and $\bar{x}$ is the cross-sectional mean of x. Values range from −1 (indicating perfect dispersion) to +1 (perfect correlation). A value of 0 indicates a random spatial pattern. For statistical hypothesis testing, Moran's I-values can be transformed to Z-scores in which values greater than 1.96 or smaller than −1.96 indicate spatial autocorrelation that is significant at the 5 per cent level. A significant correlation statistic indicates presence of spatial dependence. It is a measure of overall clustering of data. Spatial autocorrelation that is more positive than expected from random indicate the clustering of similar values across geographic space, while significant negative spatial autocorrelation indicates that neighbouring values are more dissimilar than expected by chance.

These global tests, however, overlook local spatial dependence. It is possible that for a given year, global spatial detection tests indicate no spatial relation, while local spatial tests indicate strong dependence across some regions in the total set of regions. The local Moran's I-tests allow for decomposition of global indicators. Global spatial analysis or global spatial autocorrelation analysis yields only one statistic to summarize the whole study area. In other words, global analysis assumes homogeneity. If that assumption does not hold, then having only one statistic does not make sense as the statistic should differ over space. However, if there is no global autocorrelation or no clustering, we can still find clusters at a local level using local spatial autocorrelation. Local Indicators of Spatial Association (LISA) evaluate the clustering in individual units by calculating local Moran's I-values for each spatial unit and evaluating the statistical significance for index of each region (I_i). Hence, to have a better idea on local spatial dependence, local Moran's I-tests are used. For each location, these values compute its similarity with its neighbours and test whether the similarity is statistically significant.

For each location, local Moran's I-test statistics can be computed and this is given by:

$$I_i = \frac{(x_i - \bar{x}) \sum_j w_{ij}(x_j - \bar{x})}{\sum_i (x_i - \bar{x})^2 / n}. \qquad (2)$$

Under the null hypothesis of no spatial dependence, both the Global and local Moran's I-test statistics asymptotically follow a standard normal distribution. For each location, these values allow for the computation of its similarity with its neighbours and also to test its significance.

We test for global and local spatial dependence in the diversification across states for value of crop output and value of livestock output, since the underlying data are available from 1990 onwards only for these two variables. The results of these test are reported in Table 7.1. The results from global Moran's I-tests show presence of significant spatial dependence across states in India for all the years. Results of Local Moran's I-tests also show that southern, western, and north-western states have had a consistently high spatial dependence among themselves for all the years. This gives us the empirical basis for further spatial modelling.

Spatial Regression Model of Agricultural Diversification

Once spatial dependence is detected, the estimation framework must control for the same. For that we use a spatial lag framework wherein the levels of the dependent variable depend on its levels in neighbouring regions. This implies that dependent variable of a particular location is dependent on the dependent variable of its neighbours. The value of the dependent variable is therefore jointly determined with that of its neighbouring regions. In this case, a spatially lagged dependent variable is added to the right hand side in a standard regression model of the dependent variable on a set of explanatory variables. The spatial regression model is written as:

$$y_{it} = \alpha_i + \rho W y_{it} + \beta X_{it} + \varepsilon_{it}, \qquad (3)$$

where y is the dependent variable, X are the exogenous variables, Wy is the spatially weighted (lagged) dependent variable and ρ is a scalar spatial lag coefficient and ε follows a normal zero, one distribution. The above model is estimated using the maximum likelihood framework as the presence of spatially lagged dependent variable results in the OLS being biased and inconsistent (Anselin, 1988; Elhorst, 2013).

A significant ρ coefficient indicates that spatial dependence matter. In such a situation, the X variables

Table 7.1   Results of Global and Local Moran's I-test

Year	Global Moran's I-Statistic	States with Significant Local Moran's I-test Statistic
1990	0.610***	TN, AP, GUJ, KAR, MAHA, HP, PUN, JK
1991	0.661***	GUJ, TN, KAR, JK, MAHA, AP, HAR, HP, PUN
1992	0.640***	JK, KAR, TN, MAHA, AP, HAR, PUN, HP
1993	0.651***	GUJ, KAR, AP, TN, MAHA, HAR, JK, HP, PUN
1994	0.690***	KER, AP, TN, MAHA, HAR, KAR, JK, HP, PUN
1995	0.535***	GUJ, HAR, TN, PUN, MAHA, AP, HP, KARN
1996	0.475***	JK, TN, MAHA, PUN, HP, KAR, AP
1997	0.643***	MP, TN, KAR, GUJ, AP, MAHA, HAR, JK, PUN, HP
1998	0.611***	GUJ, TN, AP, JK, MAHA, HAR, KAR, HP, PUN
1999	0.635***	KER, GUJ, TN, AP, JK, KAR, MAHA, HAR, HP, PUN
2000	0.624***	GUJ, KER, AP, TN, HAR, JK, MAHA, KAR, HP, PUN
2001	0.634***	KER, GUJ, AP, TN, HAR, JK, MAHA, KAR, HP, PUN
2002	0.510***	KER, JK, AP, TN, HAR, HP, MAHA, KAR, PUN
2003	0.566***	KER, HAR, TN, AP, JK, MAHA, KAR, PUN, HP
2004	0.558***	MAHA, HAR, AP, TN, KAR, JK, PUN, HP
2005	0.617***	TN, HAR, AP, MAHA, KAR, JK, PUN, HP
2006	0.656***	HAR, GUJ, TN, AP, MAHA, KAR, HP, JK, PUN
2007	0.650***	MP, HAR, TN, GUJ, AP, KAR, MAHA, JK, PUN, HP
2008	0.677***	MP, GUJ, TN, HAR, AP, MAHA, KAR, JK, HP, PUN
2009	0.605***	MP, HAR, TN, MAHA, KAR, AP, HP, JK, PUN
2010	0.572***	TN, HAR, MP, KAR, MAHA, AP, HP, JK, PUN

Notes: ***indicates p < 0.01, implying spatial dependence.
Source: Authors' calculations.

for a particular state *j* have two types of effects, direct and indirect. The direct effect refers to the impact that a change in X value for a state j has on the y values for that state. The indirect effect refers to the influence of X value for state *j* has on the y values of state *i* via the influence that y_j has on y_i.

Following this approach, we specify the following fixed effects panel regression in the maximum likelihood framework to identify the factors driving state-level diversification from 1990 to 2010:

$$Div_{it} = \alpha_i + \rho WDiv_{it} + \beta X_{it} + \varepsilon_{it}, \qquad (4)$$

where Div_{it} is diversification index of each state, i in year, t. $WDiv_{it}$ is the spatially weighted diversification index, with W being the SWM described earlier, X_{it} is the set of all state-level factors which drive diversification in the state, α_i controls for the unobserved state-specific effects in our models and ε_{it} is the error term in our regressed models. We also include year-specific effects in our estimated models.

Our dependent variable is SID in the total value of output in agriculture over both crops and livestock over the period 1990 to 2010. The sub-groups considered here are cereals, pulses oilseeds, sugar, fibre, drugs and narcotics, spices and condiments, fruits, vegetables and floriculture, rest of agriculture products, milk, meat, wool and hair, eggs, dung, silk, and honey.

With regard to the explanatory variables, we consider both demand- and supply-side factors as explanatory variables in our analysis. The demand-side factors are: per capita income (in rupees), share of urban geographical area in total geographical area of the state, and population density. The supply-side factors are: share of ground irrigation in net area irrigated in the state, share of gross area irrigated in total cropped area of the state.

We control for road infrastructure and average daily wages of farm labour. To control the impact of prices in the diversification pattern of the state, we control for ratio of price deflators for each agriculture and livestock product group to cereal price deflator. We use price deflators, owing to lack of data on farm gate prices for each of the agriculture and livestock product groups that we consider in our analysis. We further control for rainfall shocks in our estimation framework through absolute deviation of actual rainfall from normal rainfall in each year. State and year fixed effects control for all other unobservable factors which might influence their diversification behaviour.

The data on the explanatory variables for the analysis has been compiled from various published sources. Annual state-level data on share of ground irrigation in net irrigated area has been taken from *Land Use Statistics* (various years). Data on gross area irrigated and total cropped area has been collected from *Land Use Statistics* (various years). Data on rural and total road length (in kms) has been collected from *Statistical Abstract of India* and *Basic Road Statistics* (various years). The actual and normal rainfall data was compiled from *Statistical Abstract of India* (various years). Data on rural and total population, total geographical area, and urban geographical area was collected from census and interpolated for the years between two consecutive censuses. Price deflators have been computed for all livestock and agricultural product groups as a ratio of value of output of those products at current prices and constant 2004–05 series. State-level agricultural wage rate (rupees per day) was collected from *Agricultural Wages of India* (GoI

various years). Data on GSDP at 2004–05 prices has been collected from Economic and Political Weekly Research Foundation (EPWRF) database.

Table 7.2 reports the estimation results for two sets of models, with and without spatially lagged dependent variable. The results clearly show that diversification in a state is significantly spatially dependent on the extent of diversification of its neighbours (column (5)). Amongst the explanatory variables, urbanization (the ratio of urban geographic area to total geographic area in a state), population density, groundwater, rainfall deviation from normal, relative price of horticulture, and wage rate are significant drivers of agricultural diversification in states. Amongst these, wage rate and rainfall deviation from normal have a negative impact, while the rest of them have a positive impact.

Given the significance of the spatial dependence, we can say that the values of these explanatory variables for a state j affect not just the extent of diversification within that state, but also to some extent the diversification seen in its neighbours. The direct and indirect effects as well as the total effect of these explanatory variables are also reported in Table 7.2. This clearly shows that only two of

Table 7.2   Estimation Results, 1990–2010

Explanatory Variables	Non-spatial Model	Spatial Model		
		Direct Effect	Indirect Effect	Total Effect
(1)	(2)	(3)	(4)	(5)
Road density Total road per rural population (km)	−1.867	−1.704	−0.190	−1.894
Per capita GSDP (Rs)	−0.004	−0.004	−0.001	−0.005
Ratio of urban geographic area to total geographic area	0.011*	0.010*	0.001	0.011*
Population density	3.03e−06***	3.03e−06***	3.37e−07	3.37e−06***
Ratio of groundwater irrigation in total net irrigated area	0.021**	0.020***	0.002	0.023***
Ratio of gross irrigated area to total cropped area	0.017	0.022	0.003	0.025
Absolute deviation of actual rainfall from normal rainfall	−0.0002*	−0.0001*	−0.00002	−0.0002*
Ratio of horticulture price deflator to cereal price deflator	0.023***	0.022***	0.002*	0.024***
Average daily agricultural labour wage rate (Rs)	−0.0002***	−0.0002***	−0.00002**	−0.0003***
Spatially lagged diversification				0.110**
State effects	Yes	Yes	Yes	Yes
Year effects	Yes	Yes	Yes	Yes
Constant	0.798***			
R^2	0.42			
N	357			357
AIC	−1889.787			−1891.686
BIC	−1843.254			−1841.275
Ll	956.8935			958.8428

Notes: *p < 0.1; **p < 0.05; ***p < 0.01.
Source: Authors' calculations.

the explanatory variables—relative price of horticulture and wage rate—have significant indirect effects on diversification.

It is conceivable that the spatial role of prices and wage rates arise from the demand of agricultural commodities across state boundaries. For example, studies such as Minten, Rearden, and Vandeplas (2009) and Reardon (2012) find that potato supply chains are spread over geographic boundaries of states. Potatoes produced in Bihar and Agra (Uttar Pradesh) are sold in retail and wholesale markets in New Delhi. This shows that the spatial impacts of prices cut across more than just immediate neighbours. All the other explanatory variables such as urbanization, population density, groundwater, and rainfall deviation from normal, have only direct effects on diversification.

On the demand side, population density, capturing the overall size of the market and urbanization are positive drivers of agricultural diversification. It is plausible that per capita income is not significant in our models as it does not capture the market size. It is at best a proxy for high-value market centres, whereas population density is a proxy for geographic concentration and higher density makes markets more attractive. Further, transportation cost of reaching customers in concentrated markets is likely to be much lower than that of spread over markets. For example comparing the absolute population numbers and population density for states we find that although absolute population number for north-eastern states[2] is 2.6 times that of National Capital Region (NCR)[3], the population density of NCR and north-eastern states is 11,267 and 178 per square km, respectively, making the NCR a much larger and more attractive market than the North East.

On the supply side, greater availability of groundwater irrigation has a positive impact on diversification. The significant negative coefficient of wage indicates that high wages tends to reduce the set of profitable commodities, which would then channelize resources to a narrower set of commodities thereby increasing specialization/concentration in just a few commodities. In contrast, higher relative price of horticultural products tends to encourage diversification as they become even more profitable inducing farmers to go for such high-value crops.

CONCLUSIONS

In this study we examined the spatial dimensions of agricultural diversification in India, covering 17 major states,

over the period 1990 to 2010. We computed SID at the national and state levels for agricultural GDP, value of output from agriculture, value of crop output, GCA and value of livestock output. At the all India level, diversification is highest in the case of total value of crop output, though the index does not show any trend over time. Diversification in acreage, although the second highest and shows a rising trend, is significantly lower than that in crop output. At the other end, diversification is lowest in the case of GDP-AGRI though shows a positive trend over the years. Livestock output is the only one that shows a declining value of SID indicating greater specialization within this group.

We also found that there is significant spatial variation in the extent diversification across states. Barring a few, in most states the extent of agricultural diversification is not much from that seen at the all India level. By and large, Andhra Pradesh, Gujarat, Maharashtra, Kerala, Tamil Nadu, Uttar Pradesh and West Bengal showed greater diversification in crop and/or livestock output than all India. At the other end, Haryana and Punjab show significant concentration in agriculture.

We also examined the determinants of diversification in Indian agriculture, and in particular the role of geographic/spatial spillovers in that context. We did this using spatial econometric method. We found that there clear evidence of spatial dependence in agricultural diversification across states. Spatial regression models also showed that diversification in a state is positively influenced by the extent of diversification in its neighbours. We found that urbanization, population density, groundwater, and relative price of horticulture have a positive effect on diversification, while rainfall deviation from normal, and wage rate have a significant negative impact. Our results show that amongst the explanatory variables, only relative price of horticulture, and wage rate have significant spatial spillovers on diversification. The rest of the explanatory variables have only state-specific impact.

From a policy perspective, our findings that only price variables (of horticulture and of labour) have both direct and indirect and hence spatial impacts suggest that market institutions that affect price formation are critical in affecting agricultural diversification. To an extent the literature has also recognized the importance of market institutions and price formation on agricultural diversification. What those studies have overlooked is that their impacts are not confined only within the state boundaries, but have significant spillovers for neighbouring states as well. This all more stresses the importance of developing and strengthening agricultural marketing institutions through meaningful reform measures.

[2] North-eastern states are Arunachal Pradesh, Assam, Manipur, Meghalaya, Mizoram, Nagaland, Sikkim, and Tripura.

[3] The population density of the national capital region (NCR) is 16,787,941 while that of the entire north-eastern India is 43,793,686 (Census 2011).

APPENDIX 7A: DIVERSIFICATION INDICES OF STATES RELATIVE TO ALL INDIA

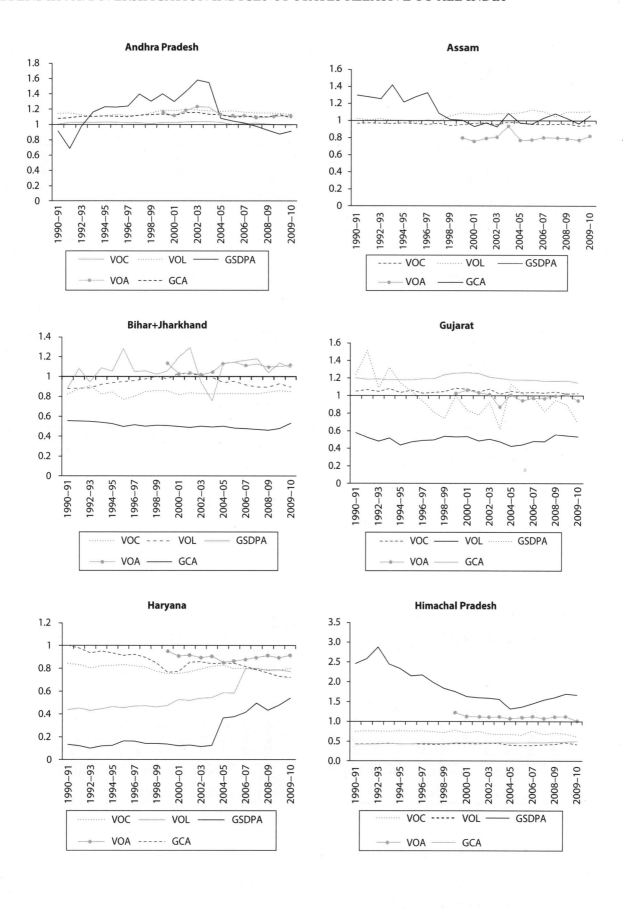

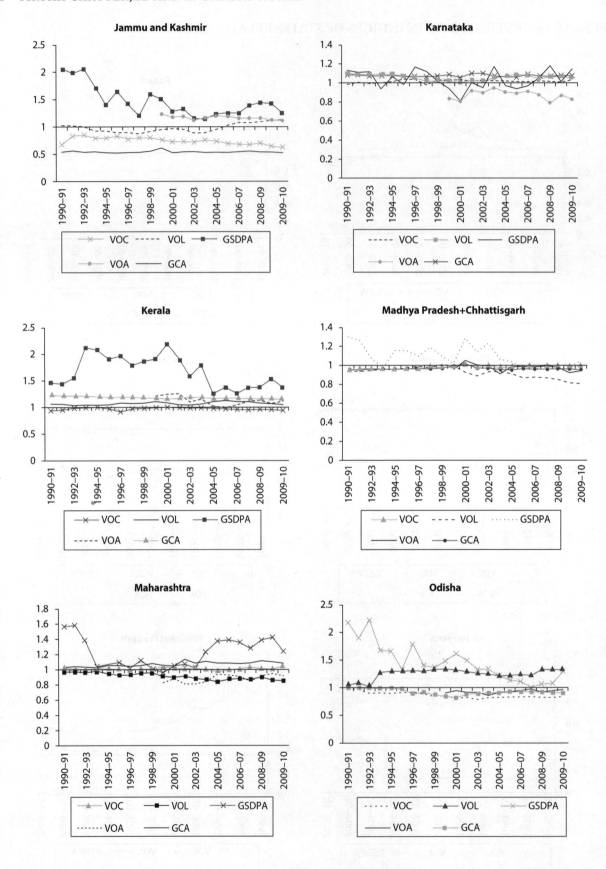

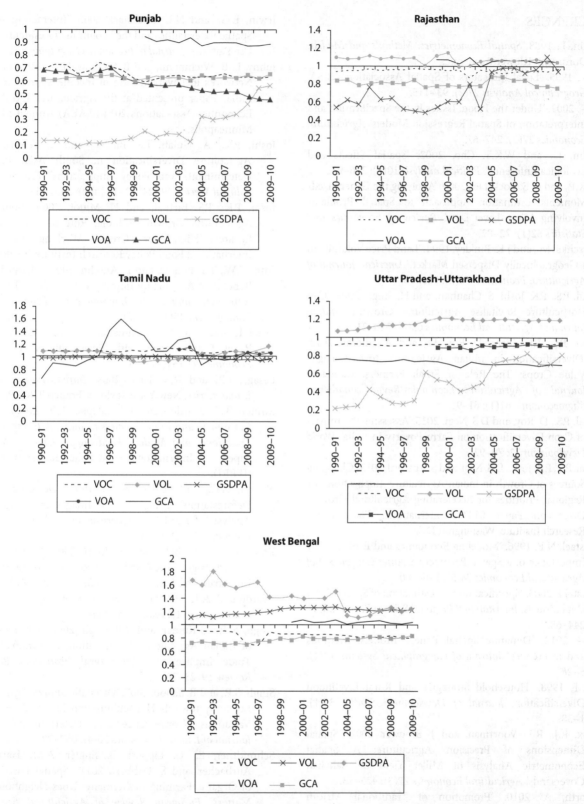

Notes: (i) VOC: diversification in value of crop output; (ii) VOL: diversification in value of livestock output; (iii) VOA: diversification in value of overall agricultural output; (iv) GSDP: diversification in GSDP from agriculture; (v) GCA: diversification in GCA; (vi) all are expressed as ratios to their respective all India diversification index values; (vii) State-level data on value of output of forestry and fishing are available only from 1999 onwards. Hence VOA starts from 1999.

Source: Authors' calculations based on data from various sources mentioned in the main text.

REFERENCES

Anselin, L. 1988. *Spatial Econometrics: Methods and Models.* Dordrecht: Kluwer Academic.

——. 1995. 'Local Indicators of Spatial Association—LISA'. *Geographical Analysis* 27(2): 93–115.

——. 2002. 'Under the Hood: Issues in the Specification and Interpretation of Spatial Regression Models'. *Agricultural Economics* 27(3): 247–67.

Anselin, L., and W.K.T. Cho. 2002. 'Spatial Effects and Ecological Inference'. *Political analysis* 10(3): 276–97.

Bell, K.P., and N.E. Bockstael. 2000. 'Applying the Generalized-Moments Estimation Approach to Spatial Problems Involving Micro-Level Data'. *Review of Economics and Statistics* 82(1): 72–82.

Benirschka, M., and J.K. Binkley. 1994. 'Land Price Volatility in a Geographically Dispersed Market'. *American Journal of Agricultural Economics*: 76(2): 185–95.

Birthal, P.S., P.K. Joshi, S. Chauhan, and H. Singh. 2008. 'Can Horticulture Revitalise Agricultural Growth?'. *Indian Journal of Agricultural Economics* 63(3): 310–21.

Birthal, P.S., P.K. Joshi, D. Roy, D., and A. Thorat. 2013. 'Diversification in Indian Agriculture toward High-Value Crops: The Role of Small Farmers'. *Canadian Journal of Agricultural Economics/Revue canadienne d'agroeconomie* 61(1): 61–91.

Birthal, P.S., D. Roy, and D.S. Negi. 2015. 'Assessing the Impact of Crop Diversification on Farm Poverty in India'. *World Development* 72: 70–92.

Birthal, P.S., P.K. Joshi, D.S. Negi, and S. Agarwal. 2013. 'Changing Sources of Growth in Indian Agriculture: Implications for Regional Priorities for Accelerating Agricultural Growth.' Discussion Paper 01325. International Food Policy Research Institute, Washington DC.

Bockstael, N.E. 1996. 'Modeling Economics and Ecology: The Importance of a Spatial Perspective'. *American Journal of Agricultural Economics* 78(5), 1168–80.

Elhorst, J.P. 2003. 'Specification and Estimation of Spatial Panel Data Models'. *International Regional Science Review* 26(3): 244–68.

——. 2012. 'Dynamic Spatial Panels: Models, Methods and Inferences.' *Journal of Geographical Systems* 14(1): 5–28.

Ellis, F. 1998. 'Household Strategies and Rural Livelihood Diversification'. *Journal of Development Studies* 35(1): 1–38.

Florax, R.J., R.L. Voortman, and J. Brouwer. 2002. 'Spatial Dimensions of Precision Agriculture: A Spatial Econometric Analysis of Millet Yield on Sahelian Coversands'. *Agricultural Economics* 27(3): 425–43.

Herforth, A. 2010. 'Promotion of Traditional African Vegetables in Kenya and Tanzania: A Case Study of an Intervention Representing Emerging Imperatives in Global Nutrition.' Available at https://ecommons.cornell.edu/handle/1813/17139 (accessed on 6 July 2017).

Irwin, E.G., and N.E. Bockstael. 2002. 'Interacting Agents, Spatial Externalities and the Evolution of Residential Land Use Patterns'. *Journal of Economic Geography* 2(1): 31–54.

Johny, J., B. Wichmann, and B. Swallow. 2014. 'Role of Social Networks in Diversification of Income Sources in Rural India.' Paper presented at the Agricultural and Applied Economics Association's 2014 (AAEA) Annual Meeting, Minneapolis.

Joshi, P.K., A. Gulati, P.S. Birthal, and L. Tewari. 2004. 'Agriculture Diversification in South Asia: Patterns, Determinants and Policy Implications'. *Economic and Political Weekly* 39 (24, 12–18 June): 2457–67.

Joshi, P.K., P.S. Birthal, and N. Minot. 2006. 'Sources of Agricultural Growth in India: Role of Diversification towards High-Value Crops.' Working paper 98. International Food Policy Research Institute (IFPRI).

Kim, C.W., T.T. Phipps, and L. Anselin. 2003. 'Measuring the Benefits of Air Quality Improvement: A Spatial Hedonic Approach'. *Journal of Environmental Economics and Management* 45(1): 24–39.

Lee, L.F., and J. Yu. 2010. 'Estimation of Spatial Autoregressive Panel Data Models with Fixed Effects'. *Journal of Econometrics* 154(2): 165–85.

Lesage, J.P., and R.K. Pace. 2009. *Introduction to Spatial Econometrics.* New York: Taylor & Francis/CRC Press.

Minten, B., T. Reardon, and A. Vandeplas. 2009. *Linking Urban Consumers and Rural Farmers in India: A Comparison of Traditional and Modern Food Supply Chains.* Working paper 883. International Food Policy Research Institute (IFPRI).

Nelson, G.C., and D. Hellerstein. 1997. 'Do Roads Cause Deforestation? Using Satellite Images in Econometric Analysis of Land Use'. *American Journal of Agricultural Economics* 79(1): 80–8.

Rao, P.P., P.S. Birthal, and P.K. Joshi. 2006. 'Diversification towards High Value Agriculture: Role of Urbanisation and Infrastructure'. *Economic and Political Weekly* 2747–53.

Reardon, T. 2012. *The Quiet Revolution in Staple Food Value Chains.* Asian Development Bank.

Singh, N.P., R. Kumar, and R.P. Singh. 2006. 'Diversification of Indian Agriculture: Composition, Determinants and Trade Implications'. *Agricultural Economics Research Review* 19: 23–36.

Singh, S.P., and B. Sahoo. 2007. 'Diversification of Agricultural Economy towards Horticulture and Livestock: Regional Variations, Convergence and Determinants'. *Indian Journal of Labour Economics* 50(4): 657–72.

Schmidtner, E., C. Lippert, B. Engler, A.M. Häring, J. Aurbacher, and S. Dabbert. 2011. 'Spatial Distribution of Organic Farming in Germany: Does Neighbourhood Matter?' *European Review of Agricultural Economics* 39(4): 661–83.

Weiss, M.D. 1996. 'Precision Farming and Spatial Economic Analysis: Research Challenges and Opportunities' *American Journal of Agricultural Economics* 78(5): 1275–80.

8

Human Capital and the Economy
Where Are the Tertiary Educated?

Abhiroop Mukhopadhyay

INTRODUCTION

Conventional wisdom on economic growth and development emphasizes the role of human capital. In a country where poverty still abounds despite reasonably high growth rates, education is envisaged as a path out of penury for many. The idea that education is important for the micro-economy of household welfare as well as the growth of the macroeconomy, has spawned many policy interventions over the years. The overbearing thought process, in recent years, has been that giving access to basic schooling to all, as espoused by the Right to Education (RTE), would go a long way in not only raising the human capital of the nation, but also leading in the medium and long run to economic growth.

Though India has taken impressive strides in increasing the average years of schooling over time, it is falling short of many targets it has set for itself. A report of the United Nations (UN), 'India and the MDGs (Millennium Development Goals)', points out that '[l]atest data suggest that India is off-track on the targets to achieve universal enrolment and completion. Large numbers of children still remain out of school and fail to complete primary education. The quality of education is also a

major concern.'[1] The report goes on to say that the low primary completion rate may hinder the next Sustainable Development Goal (SDG) of universal secondary enrolment.

Even if the progress of education has not been as envisaged, many development policy discourses cite the improvement in some of the indicators of human capital, such as falling illiteracy and an increase in primary schooling enrolment, as a success in itself, largely inspired by Amartya Sen's seminal insight that one needs to endow individuals with capabilities to increase their welfare. While this welfarist imperative cannot be denied, it is also important that one keeps an eye, in the shorter run, on what constitutes this progress of human capital and what it might mean for growth and development of an economy.

In this chapter, we provide a rich description of what has constituted the progress of education in India. In particular, we decompose human capital into the achievements of various levels of education (literacy, primary, tertiary) by India's adult population and describe

---

[1] Available at http://in.one.un.org/img/uploads/India_and_the_MDGs.pdf (accessed on 31 August 2017), page 7.

how these achievements have changed over the last 40 years. Motivated by recent literature which shows that only a share of population with tertiary education matters for economic development and growth of India, we provide a state- and district-level analysis of the tertiary education achievement of the population: its spatial heterogeneity and temporal pattern. In particular, we highlight the progress over the last decade. This path of enquiry raises many interesting questions about the tertiary educated—whether they all live in urban areas. What industries are these people employed in? What is the gender composition of the tertiary educated? Are the proportions of population who are tertiary educated very unequal across states and districts? How much of this is because of differences between states? Has this changed over the years? Does history play a big role in the evolution of this share?

The answers to these questions inform our discussion on whether regional convergence can be achieved through human capital. This naturally leads us to ask what can be done to raise the tertiary education achievement of the population. This brings us back to the point raised by the UN report on poor primary schooling quality and we provide suggestive evidence on how this may impact tertiary education achievement.

In the next section titled 'Human Capital: Some Stylized Facts', we provide some stylized facts about human capital and the achievement of different levels of education by the adult population. The rationale for a disaggregated lens on human capital is provided in the section titled 'Macroeconomic Returns to Human Capital', where we discuss which achievement level matters for growth and development. In a sub-section therein, we provide the link between human capital and growth by looking at where people with different levels of human capital are employed. Section titled 'Tertiary Education Achievement' focuses on tertiary education achievement of districts of India: its spatial and temporal patterns. The section 'Tertiary Education Completion and School Age Learning Levels' explores the link between the learning levels of children who are in the school going age and the attainment of tertiary education. We conclude with a short discussion of our results in the last section.

HUMAN CAPITAL: SOME STYLIZED FACTS

The human capital of a nation embodies the total capital embodied in its people. This broad definition includes both education and health of the population. In this chapter, we focus more narrowly on education when we talk about human capital. A popular proxy for human capital is the stock of education in the adult population (defined as those with age above 25 years: see, for example, Barro and Lee, 2013).[2] An accurate measure of this stock is the quality adjusted years of education. However, for India, data on the quality of education is available only for those in the school going age group. Hence, a temporal lens on human capital necessarily involves looking at an imperfect measure: the average years of education. With that caveat in mind, we explore, to begin with, the evolution of the average years of education from 1971 to 2011. This data is sourced from the Census of India. The census reports the number of people who have completed various stages of education. To calculate average years of schooling, a few assumptions are required. We assume that those who report that the highest level they have competed is literate without education level (formal as well as informal) or below primary have three years of education; those who have completed only primary and only middle schooling have five and eight years of education, respectively. We club those who have completed only matric, only higher secondary, and those with technical/non-technical diplomas, not amounting to a degree, and ascribe 10 years of education to them. Lastly, those who have completed graduate degrees (or diplomas equivalent to degrees) have 15 years of education.[3]

The average years of schooling among the adult population has risen from 1.72 in 1971 to 5.03 in 2011 (Figure 8.1). This reflects an annual growth rate of 2.6 percentage points. In comparison, the advanced world, on an average, has shown an increase in average years of education from 7.3 (1970) to 11.29 (2010); the Latin American countries from 3.44 to 7.7; the South Asian countries, as a whole, have moved from 1.29 to 4.57 (Barro and Lee, 2013).

This growth reflects the changing proportions of adult population that have completed various education levels. It is important to look at this in the context of various strategies that education policies have targeted over the years. Education policies were more education-level neutral for most parts of 1960s and 1970s with a general aim at lowering illiteracy. However, with a push towards improving access to lower levels of schooling (primary) in the 1986 New Education Policy (NEP), together with

---

[2] An alternate cut off for defining the adult population is 15 years of age. However, this would imply that we partially count the human capital accumulation of those who are still not old enough to go for tertiary education (http://www.barrolee.com/papers/Barro_Lee_Human_Capital_Update_2011Nov.pdf).

[3] Alternate assumptions do not change the tenor of the discussion that follows.

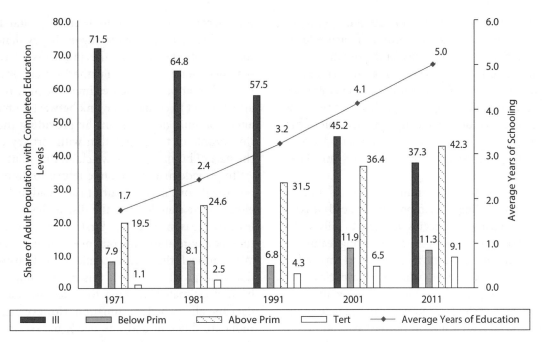

Figure 8.1 Evolution of Human Capital: 1971–2011

Source: Author's calculation (Census of India, 1971, 1981, 1991, 2001, 2011).

the pressure of meeting MDGs, there was a focus towards getting children into primary and middle schools in the 1990s and 2000s.

In line with these various strategies to improve education outcomes, we divide the adult population into four groups: those who are illiterate (*Ill*), those who have some schooling but have not completed primary school (*Below-Prim*), those who have completed some level of schooling above primary but have not gone on to complete graduate degrees (*Above-Prim*), and those who have completed graduate degrees/tertiary education (*Tert*). The movement of the adult population from *Ill* to *Below-Prim* largely reflects a small increment in education levels. While the benefits of making people literate cannot be underestimated, this increase also reflects a failure of the education system to sustain interest of the population to stay into schools. In essence, it often reflects that a child was enrolled in school but then quickly dropped out. The increase in the share of adult population in *Above-Prim* reflects a reasonable amount of schooling, often enough to provide some returns in the labour market. The increase in *Tert* reflects a substantial increase in human capital (though it may not always embody the skills that the labour market is looking for).

The evolution of the education of the adult population based on these classifications is presented in Figure 8.1. A 34.25 percentage point fall in illiteracy rates over the period 1971 to 2011 has been accompanied by

a 3.39 percentage point rise in the share of those with *Below-Prim*, a 22.79 percentage point rise in the share of those with *Above-Prim*, and a 8.06 percentage point rise in the share of those with tertiary education. This implies that for the whole period, going to some lower level of schooling and no far accounts for around 9.90 per cent of the rise in literacy while *Above-Prim*, accounts for around 66.56 per cent of the rise and the remaining 23.54 per cent of the rise is because of an increase in adult population with competed tertiary education.

A period-wise break up reveals the impact of some of the changing strategies. If we consider the period 1971 to 1991, 85 per cent of the fall in illiteracy (14 percentage points) is accounted for by the rise of *Above-Prim* while 22.8 per cent is on account of *Tert*. The proportion of those with *Below-Prim* in fact falls 1.1 percentage points over the period. This is in contrast to the period 1991 to 2011. Now, while *Tert* accounts for 24 per cent of the fall in illiteracy (20 percentage points), not too different from the previous period, *Above-Prim* accounts for only 53.67 per cent with the remaining 22.27 per cent explained by the rise in population with *Below-Prim*.

Before delving into this further, let us explore another important dimension related to the measurement of human capital. Recall that the rise in average years of schooling is 3.3 years (a rise from 1.72 in 1971 to 5.03 in 2011). What accounts for this rise when decomposed by the education classifications discussed above? To do this, we multiply each share with the corresponding years of education and calculate the proportion of each education completion level that accounts for the rise in average years of schooling. This exercise reveals a simple interesting observation. Given that tertiary education embodies a much larger amount of human capital, the 24 per cent rise in *Tert* accounts for a much larger 37 per cent of the rise in average years of schooling over the period. Some low-grade schooling (*Below-Prim)* contributes only 3 per cent of the rise.

The purpose of this accounting exercise is not to point out that schooling is unimportant. Instead, it is to highlight that education strategies that lead to only some low-grade schooling completion—an emerging feature of the labour force—do not contribute much to this index of human capital. Moreover, while we have classified low-grade schooling to include only those below primary school completion, a similar argument can be made about those who drop off with just some primary education.

The arguments presented so far assume that the various education-level completions matter for economic development and growth and they do so in an ordered manner. This is a non-trivial assumption in the narrative of how human capital is an investment into growth and development. The assumption may not be true: for example, if an economy has diminishing economic returns to incremental years of education, then there may not be a big difference if one were to make improvements, for example, in tertiary education completion rates as compared to, say, merely school completion rates. This is a pertinent query, given the evidence in the past on such concave returns to human capital at the micro level (Psacharopoulos, 1994). Since tertiary education completion may be tough to achieve, the benefits to increasing tertiary education achievement have to be quantified to defend such an assumption.

Hence, in the next section, we delve deeper and ask the following questions: does the rising proportion of those with below primary schooling reflect an economically relevant increase in human capital? The same question can be asked more broadly and posed as a second query: given that the share of adult population with schooling and no higher accounts for the larger proportion of the rise in literacy, does this change lead to growth and development at the macro level?

MACROECONOMIC RETURNS TO HUMAN CAPITAL

An evaluation of the benefits of education to the macroeconomy implicitly needs one to calculate the macroeconomic returns to human capital for India. In this section we provide suggestive evidence, pointing out, on the way, to the problems of calculating macroeconomic returns. Further, we cite some recent research that provides an estimate of such returns. We also attempt to connect the link between human capital and economic development by providing the occupation profile of the population with tertiary education, the part of human capital we claim that matters.

To provide macroeconomic returns of human capital on growth, one needs to turn to sub-national analyses—either at the state level or the district level. There are at least two reasons to do so: First, to calculate the magnitude of any relationship, one needs enough data points. With annual time series data on nation-wide gross domestic product (GDP), this relationship would not be well estimated. Moving to states provides us more data and allows better estimation. However, states across India are different and one needs to take into account this heterogeneity. Comparison across states, for example, may not be a valid exercise. Hence, studies that try to estimate the relationship between gross state domestic product (GSDP) and a state's human capital need to work with times series data for each state in a combined longitudinal analysis. Such panel analysis takes into account individual state heterogeneity as well as time-varying variables that capture the other variables that also affect both GSDP and human capital.[4]

Using state-level data from 1960 to 2000, Castelló-Climent and Mukhopadhyay (2013) show that a one-year increase in average years of education increases the growth rate by 0.05. Since the average annual GSDP growth rate during this period was around 0.02, this reflects a rather large effect of average years of education on GDP. Recall, however, that the annualized growth rate of average years of education has only been 0.026. Starting from a base of 5.1 average years of education in 2011, an increase of one year to six will take about seven years, at the current rate of progress of education.

Which part of human capital drives this correlation between growth and human capital? To investigate this further, one can investigate the correlation between growth and proportions of those with *Above* or *Below Prim* and *Tert* (after taking into account other variables). This analysis reveals a very interesting insight. If one keeps the share of tertiary-educated people in adult force the same, an increase in the share of people with *Above*

---

[4] For example: Population, Rainfall, Urbanization, Development Expenditures. There is also need for considering the reverse causality: that areas with high growth attract human capital.

or *Below Prim* education level results in *no* increments in growth. The only impact on growth comes from the share of the population that completes tertiary education.[5] An alternate way to say this is that if India lowers illiteracy rates by sending children to school, but not ensuring that they clear graduate level education, this has no impact on growth rates. This does not imply that one needs to think about only tertiary education. Rather, it makes us think more seriously about what education policies will graduate people through university and technical institutes.[6]

A large part of the explanation of the primacy of tertiary education completion as being the main driver of Indian growth is the historical pattern of what has constituted this growth. An analysis involving decomposition of total growth into growth of the primary (largely agriculture), secondary (largely manufacturing), and tertiary (services) sector reveals that while some schooling has an impact on the growth of the secondary sector, only tertiary education completion has an impact on the tertiary sector. These sectoral results also reconcile, to some extent, the observation that some schooling has micro returns (in terms of income) but no macro returns. To elaborate, labour with some schooling are employed in manufacturing and earn some economic returns. However, since the sector does not show dynamism, this part of human capital correlates weakly to overall economic growth. This story is important to keep in mind, as it suggests an alternate route to growth that largely bypasses the need to graduate people through university: that of artificially stimulating the manufacturing sector. These results suggest that the current education system with low tertiary graduation rates may still be able to contribute to this sector. But policy interventions to stimulate the manufacturing sector are yet to put this sector on a strong growth trajectory. Given that reality, it is perhaps instructive to think more about increasing the share of adult population with tertiary education.

Table 8.1 Industry Classification of Tertiary Educated (25+)

Industry	India	Male	Female	Rural	Urban
Agriculture Forestry and Fishing	7.21	10.69	0.81	21.22	1.3
Construction	1.82	2.65	0.29	1.73	1.86
Manufacturing	7.86	11.17	1.78	5.27	8.96
Mining and Quarrying	0.54	0.83	0.02	0.32	0.64
Services	48.26	60.4	25.94	43.75	50.16
Not Working	34.31	14.26	71.16	27.71	37.09

Source: Author's calculations: NSSO 68th Round.

In Which Sector Do Tertiary Educated Work?

We have assumed a mechanism through which those with tertiary education affect development and growth: that involving the service sector. To investigate this further, we source information from the 68th round of the National Sample Survey Organisation (NSSO) for the year 2011–12[7] and calculate the industry profile of those with tertiary education (Table 8.1). Consistent with our assumption, around 48 per cent of those with tertiary education work in the service sector.[8] This proportion is around 60 per cent for adult males. For adult females, who are more likely not to work (given their low labour force participation rate), services still forms the most likely activity for those who do work (at around 26 per cent of the whole female population).[9] Services also account for 44 per cent of those in the rural areas with tertiary education as well as more than 50 per cent of those in urban areas. Interestingly, around 21 per cent of tertiary educated in rural areas are in agriculture. In contrast, only 19.65 per cent of the adult population with some schooling work in the service sector. This proportion is 13 per cent in rural areas whereas it is 31 per cent in the urban sector. A somewhat large component of school educated in urban areas work in the manufacturing sector (14 per cent).[10]

Given the large representation of service industry among the tertiary educated, we delve further into composition of activities that constitute the service sector for

---

[5] The same argument is borne out when one uses district level data to explore the same correlation. Only tertiary education completion correlates with District GDPs or other correlates of development: for example, night lights. These results can be obtained from Castelló-Climent, Chaudhuri, and Mukhopadhyay (2015). This chapter estimates the causal impact of tertiary education on development using the variation in tertiary education induced by where catholic missionaries settled in India by the early 20th century.

[6] It is important to point out that economic growth is only one rationale for educating people. Hence, the arguments in the chapter have limited implications on the basic rationale for educating people, even if that means they get only some schooling.

[7] July 2011–June 2012.

[8] We follow NIC-2008 classification.

[9] The high proportion of those with tertiary education not working, especially among women, does not necessarily reflect a waste of human capital. Educated women, for example, contribute more to the human capital of children, and thus, their capital is a critical input in the future human capital of the nation.

[10] This number is 21 per cent for just school educated males in urban areas.

Table 8.2   Decomposition of the Service Sector for Tertiary Educated (25+)

	India	Male	Female	Rural	Urban
Accommodation and Food Services	1.7	1.9	0.7	0.9	1.9
Administrative and Support Services	2.7	3.0	1.7	1.2	3.3
Education	29.2	23.1	55.1	47.2	22.5
Finance and Insurance Activities	9.3	9.6	7.6	6.4	10.3
Health and Social Work	5.9	5.1	9.4	5.3	6.1
Information and Communication	7.5	7.7	6.6	1.6	9.6
Other	2.7	2.9	2.2	3.2	2.6
Professional, Scientific, and Technical Services	5.7	6.2	3.6	3.7	6.4
Public Administration and Defense	10.6	11.7	6.0	10.0	10.8
Real Estate Activities	1.0	1.2	0.0	0.4	1.2
Transportation and Storage	4.8	5.7	1.1	3.4	5.4
Wholesale and Retail Trade	19.0	22.0	6.1	16.6	19.9

Source: Author's calculations: NSSO 68th Round.

this population (Table 8.2). Around 30 per cent of the tertiary educated work in education. This is largely driven by tertiary educated females, 55 per cent of whom are in this line of work. However, 23 per cent of tertiary educated males are also in education. The other big industry that accounts for tertiary educated men is wholesale and retail trade. Public administration, health services, and finance services are the other big industries that employ tertiary educated. Given the large presence of the education and public administration sector in the list, a natural question is whether public sector hires most of the tertiary educated. However, only 36 per cent of tertiary educated work in the public sector, though the number is higher at around 46 per cent in the rural economy.

A question that immediately comes up, given the typology of rural/urban and male/female presented earlier, is whether the rural sector or females account for any significant proportion of tertiary educated. For example, it may be argued that most tertiary completed people stay in urban places. We, therefore, calculate, from the census, the share of rural tertiary educated among the total. This proportion is not insignificant at 36.6 per cent. To alleviate fears that small rural settlements in big cities drive these results, we drop all districts with overall urbanization rates greater than 90 per cent. The average share of rural among the tertiary educated rises to 37.8 and allays fears that urban villages drive our results.

Another argument that may crop up is that rural households often include, as household members, people whom they think are part of their family, despite best attempts by enumerators to follow a strict rule of residency duration to define a household. This is often complicated by the recent trend of short-term migration

which makes recalling the exact number of days that a member stays in a household difficult. This argument implies that the tertiary educated are often misclassified as rural when they are in fact urban. Moreover, even if the recall is perfect, there may be conceptual problems on how to count people who live in rural places but work in nearby urban centres. However, this concern is misplaced. Around 89 per cent of rural tertiary educated work in rural areas, whereas only 11 per cent go to work in urban areas. On the other hand, 5 per cent of the urban tertiary educated go to the rural areas for work. This establishes that rural areas do account for significant proportion of tertiary educated and one cannot leave them out of the story. In fact, we take the stand that it may be misleading to carry forward the urban-rural typology since many rural areas now have urban features (Chandrasekhar, 2014). So we drop this distinction for the rest of our discussion.

How important is to include tertiary educated females in the analysis, especially given their low labour force participation rate? While the share of females who are tertiary educated is low at 6.7 per cent (as compared to 11.4 per cent for males), females account for 36 per cent of the tertiary educated in the country. Hence, any account of human capital without keeping count of female tertiary education completion is incomplete. Hence, in what follows, we look at the share of tertiary educated of a population that includes both men and women.

With this in mind, we focus next on the spread of the share of tertiary educated population across states and districts, and its growth over both the short as well as long term.

TERTIARY EDUCATION ACHIEVEMENT

If growth is indeed explained partially by tertiary education achievement, then it is the distribution of this component of human capital across the country that has implications about the inequalities in sub-regional growth and development. In this section, we seek to chronicle the spatial heterogeneity of the proportion of adult population with completed tertiary education in 2011. Moreover, we explore whether there is convergence or persistence over time.

Spatial Heterogeneity

To explore the extent of spatial heterogeneity, we use a district as the unit of analysis. Using census data from 2011, we plot the proportion of districts with a particular share of tertiary education completion (Figure 8.2).[11] As the figure shows, there is great degree of inequality

[11] The proportion of districts is weighted by their adult population.

between districts. For almost a quarter of districts, the share of adult population who have completed tertiary education is less than 6 per cent; the median district has only 7.5 per cent of its population with tertiary education. However, at least 5 per cent of districts have more than 21 per cent tertiary education completion rates (for a GIS depiction, see Figure 8.3).

How much of this variation between districts is driven by state-level factors? Given that provision of education is an item on state list, perhaps, the variation in district level tertiary completion rates reflect state differences. A decomposition of the total district-level differences (variation) into what are within-state differences and what are between-state differences can answer this question. Results show that as much as 38 per cent of the variation is because of differences between states, whereas the remaining 62 per cent is because of within state differences.

The relatively high variation across states is a source of concern, given the somewhat divergent growth rates between states of India that is well documented (Bandyopadhyay, 2012). To elaborate further, one can imagine a

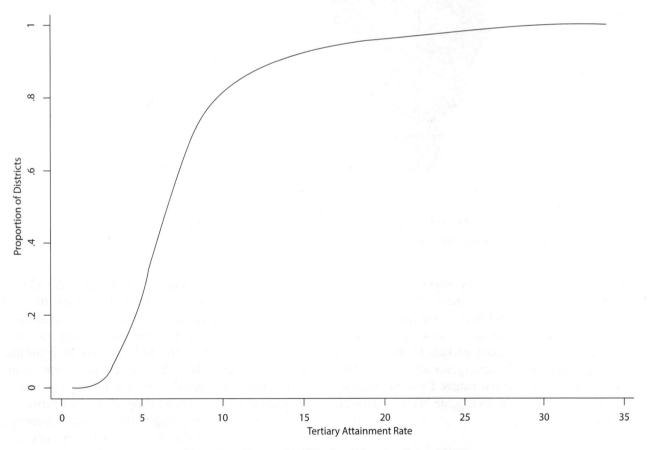

Figure 8.2   District-Level Tertiary Education Shares (2011)

Source: Author's calculation (Census of India, 2011).

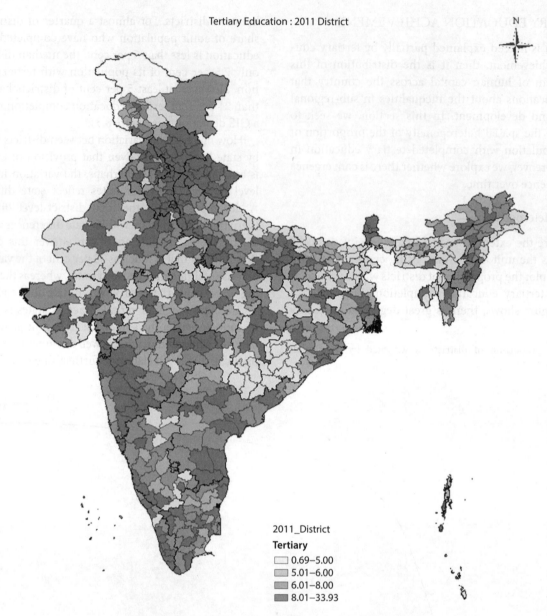

Tertiary Education : 2011 District

2011_District
Tertiary
☐ 0.69–5.00
☐ 5.01–6.00
☐ 6.01–8.00
☐ 8.01–33.93

Figure 8.3 Spatial Distribution of Tertiary Completion Rates

Source: Author's calculation (Census of India, 2011).

model of development driven by migration of tertiary educated workers to particular states. This can generate income that is then sent back to the home state so that incomes equalize across states. However, remittance income from tertiary educated workers, if any, seems to be playing a limited role in convergence across states. The evidence on this is somewhat patchy. Even the premise that tertiary educated workers migrate between states is not documented.[12]

[12] Available evidence suggests that migration between states is low.

The importance of looking at a district as the relevant unit of analysis can be undermined by an extension of the argument made here: that there can be specialization within a state. Tertiary-educated workers migrate within a state to the urban centres and that accounting for that will reduce appreciably how much intra-state differences explain the total difference in tertiary completion rates. To check for this, we drop the highest urbanized district in each state. Doing so does reduce, somewhat, the proportion of difference attributable to intra-state differences but it is still a very high 56 per cent. Hence, differences induced by highly urbanized districts are only a small part of the story and substantial heterogeneity exists even when we do not take them into account.

Interestingly, in contrast, within state differences account for only 38 per cent of the differences in only some schooling completion (*Below Prim + Above Prim*). Hence, state-level differences explain the bulk of the differences in the success in getting people from being illiterate to some level of schooling.

How have the inequalities in tertiary completion rates between districts changed over the years? Since the number of districts has gone up over the years, we need to combine districts to a unique vantage to make valid comparisons. We do so by considering 1971 boundaries.[13] A convenient way to look at whether inequalities have increased or decreased over years is to

look at Lorenz curves (Figure 8.4). To elaborate further, consider the total of all tertiary-completion rates across all districts. The Lorenz curve then plots the proportion of districts on the horizontal axis and the proportion of total of all *Tert* on the vertical axis. The diagonal represents equal distribution of tertiary completion rates across districts: for example, 50 per cent of the total of all tertiary completion rates are accounted for by 50 per cent of the districts.[14] The area between this diagonal and each curve represents the level of inequality over the time. Hence, more the Lorenz curve is below the diagonal, greater the inequality. As can be seen in

---

[13] This necessary entails dropping some districts since it is not always possible to recreate old districts. In addition, data is missing for some states for particular census years. Given this, we are able to consistently follow 250 districts of 1971 vintage (without missing data concerns, this number would be 267 (Kumar and Somanathan, 2011).

[14] Strictly speaking, it is hard to interpret what the total of tertiary attainment rate across districts means. An alternative way would be to add the number of individuals who have completed tertiary education across districts and to calculate what proportion of districts accounts for different proportions of this total. While this has a clearer intuitive meaning, this is subject to the criticism that it does not take into account the difference in population across districts and the differential spatial growth of this population over time.

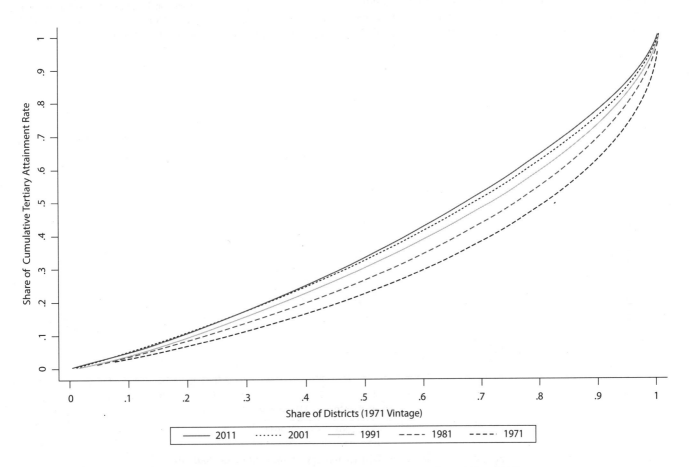

Figure 8.4   Lorenz Curves: District Tertiary Attainment Rates (1971–2011)

Source: Author's calculation (Census of India, 1971, 1981, 1991, 2001).

Figure 8.4, the Lorenz curve has been shifting inwards towards the diagonal representing that inequality across districts has been falling over time. The districts with poorer *Tert* in 2011 account for a larger proportion of the cumulative sum of *Tert* than 1971. Part of the explanation for this is that the bottom districts have increased *Tert* faster than the top districts. This can also be gleaned from Table 8.3 wherein the Gini coefficients are reported. The Gini has almost halved from 0.44 in 1971 to 0.25 in 2011, reflecting a reduction in inequality across districts. However, the rate of decline has slowed down over the years. While Gini fell from 0.44 in 1971 to 0.36 in 1981, it only fell by 0.02 from 0.27 in 2001 to 0.25 in 2011.

One possible explanation could be that there is a base effect: that it was much easier to raise *Tert* when the initial levels were low even at the top, but it has become harder to raise *Tert* in the top districts with the passage of time. For example, in 1971, the average share of adult population with completed tertiary education was 13.16 per cent among the top 1 per cent of districts; in 2001 this average was around 23 per cent. This share (in 2001) is around the nationwide average share of completed tertiary education for many advanced countries (United Kingdom: 18.8, Japan: 19.9, Canada: 27.7,

Table 8.3   Gini of Share of Adult Population with Completed Tertiary Education

Years	1971	1981	1991	2001	2011
Gini	0.44	0.36	0.30	0.27	0.25

Source: Author's calculations: 1971–2011 Census.

Australia: 25.2).[15] The modest increase in the Gini due to such slowdown would imply some convergence, which is not totally undesirable.

In order to evaluate this explanation, we consider data only from 2001 and 2011 where we construct districts of 2001 vantage (for 2011 data). The results of this analysis suggest that the comments made here regarding slowdown of lowering inequality are true for this decade but that one needs to be nuanced while claiming convergence. In fact, using data from districts of 2001 vantage suggest that the fall in the Gini is even lower: from 0.327 in 2001 to 0.314 in 2011. Figure 8.5 reveals that the Lorenz curve for 2011 does not lie entirely below

[15] The top 1 per cent districts on India far exceed the average rate for France: 12.1, Germany: 16.1, Italy: 8.0, and Spain 17.0 while it is much lower than for the US: 30.9 and Korea: 34.8.

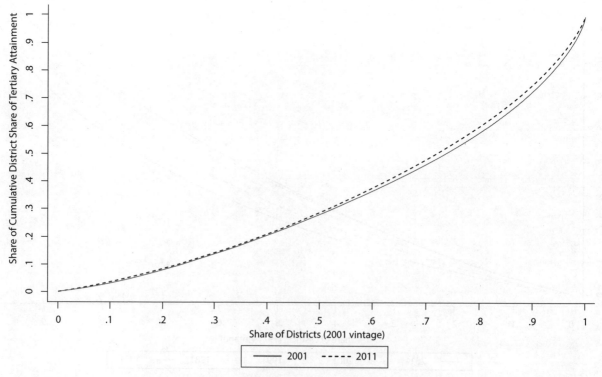

Figure 8.5   Lorenz Curves: District Tertiary Attainment Rates (2001–10)

Source: Author's calculation (Census of India, 2001, 2011).

the Lorenz curve for 2001. At best, one can say that the bottom half of districts of India (in performance) have not changed their share in the cumulative share of total. This story is reaffirmed if one looks at the average share of completed tertiary education for various percentiles for both the years (Table 8.4). For example, the bottom 1 per cent districts have only 0.2 percentage points more

share between 2001 and 2011. All percentiles below and equal to the 50th percentile show a change that is around 1 percentage point. On the other hand, all percentiles above 50th percentile show a much larger change. In fact, the table (and Lorenz curve) suggests that it is the improvements of districts that are in the 50th to 75th percentile that drives the decline in Gini.

Table 8.4   Percentile Averages of District Share of Tertiary Education 2001–11

Percentile	Average Share of Competed Tertiary Education		
	2001 (%)	2011 (%)	Difference (2011–01)
1	1.54	1.74	0.2
5	2.3	3.25	0.95
25	2.73	3.83	1.1
50	4.61	5.06	0.45
75	6.51	9.03	2.52
90	9.92	13.61	3.69
95	13.59	17.73	4.14
99	23.44	27.76	4.32

Source: Author's calculations: 2001 and 2011 Census.

Temporal Persistence

In the previous section we have shown that bottom 50 per cent of the districts have not improved their outcome of the share of completed tertiary education as much as the top. However, that does not necessarily imply persistence. For example, the list of bottom percentile districts may be changing over time. This churn would imply some dynamism. As a first step, we examine the persistence of the share of *Tert* between 2001 and 2011. Figure 8.6 provides a scatter plot between the share of completed tertiary education in 2001 and 2011. The 45 degree line reflects a situation where there were no changes from 2001. A linear regression fit is also provided. The relationship shows high degree of persistence. The correlation between the

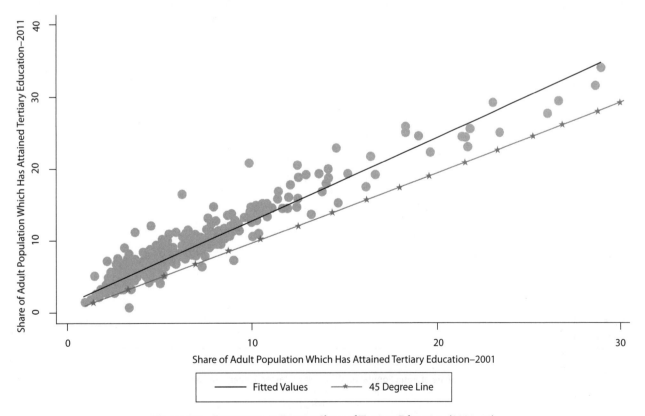

Figure 8.6   Persistence in District Share of Tertiary Education (2001–11)

Source: Author's calculation (Census of India, 2001, 2011).

two is as high as 0.95. A simple regression yields that if between two districts the difference between the share of completed tertiary education was 1 percentage point in 2001, that difference is 1.15 percentage points in 2011.

While we have shown in the section 'Spatial Heterogeneity' that few pockets of high tertiary education or urbanization do not affect the tenor of our results, concerns may still linger that it is the top that drives all these results. To see whether this is indeed the case, we drop districts that lie in the top 10 percentile of districts in 2001. This does not alter the qualitative results: in fact, now 1 percentage point difference in 2001 results in a higher difference of 1.27. As a matter of fact, this result stays more or less the same even if we consider only the bottom 50 per cent of the districts in 2001.

How much of this is driven by history? The education of the adult population is a stock accumulated over many years. Figure 8.7 shows that there is persistence even we compare 1971 to 2011 (districts of 1971 vintage).[16] The correlation between the two is 0.79. That is very high for a period of 40 years. Is it then this historical stock of tertiary

educated people who are driving our results of persistence? Perhaps things have changed a lot in recent times.

To investigate whether the recent trends in tertiary education completion are different from the past, we concentrate only on the cohort aged 25 to 34. These are the new stock of people that join the adult population between any two census rounds. We focus on the 2001 and 2011 censuses. Figure 8.8 shows that the district level persistence is equally high in this cohort. The correlation between the two years is 0.87. Districts with a 1 percentage point difference in the share of tertiary completion in this age cohort in 2001 would see a 1.17 percentage point difference in 2011. Again, the natural question is, how much does the inclusion of some districts with a large proportion of tertiary educated young people (highly urbanized districts) drive the persistence story. To investigate this we drop all districts with greater than 50 per cent urbanization rates in 2001 (the top decile of districts in terms of urbanization). Figure 8.9 plots the relationship of the share of completed tertiary educated between the two years. As can be seen, the persistence is equally high. The correlation between the two years is still 0.8.[17]

---

[16] We have omitted 1971 districts where the share of tertiary education completion is greater than 10 per cent. This is largely to show that the positive correlation is not driven by high tertiary educated areas in 1970s (like metro cities).

[17] The degree of persistence is lower for the top districts than for districts at the bottom. Hence, there is a slight lowering of inequality over time.

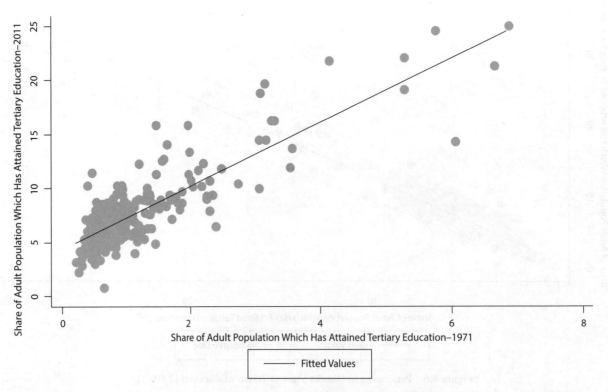

Figure 8.7   Persistence in District Share of Tertiary Education (1971–2011)

Source: Author's calculation (Census of India, 1971, 2011).

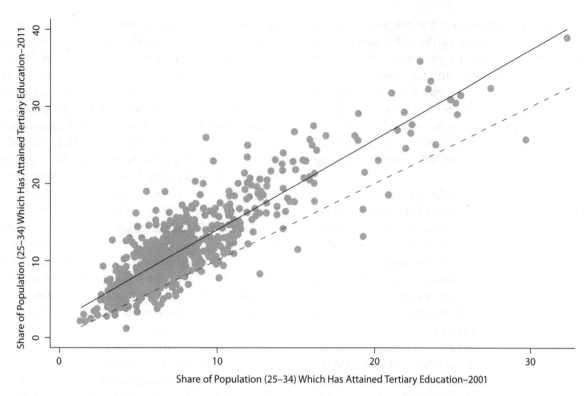

Figure 8.8   Persistence in District Share of Tertiary Education (Ages 25–34) 2001–11.

Source: Author's calculation (Census of India, 2001, 2011).

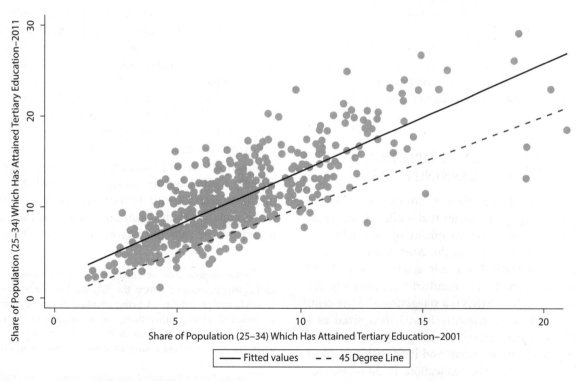

Figure 8.9   Persistence in District Share of Tertiary Education (Ages 25–34). Urbanization Rates Less than 50 Per Cent: 2001–11

Source: Author's calculation (Census of India, 2001, 2011).

There is then persistence and it is not just driven by the educational achievement of the older generations. That does not imply that the past does affect recent achievements: for example, attitude towards higher education, or the capacity to pay for it can depend crucially on the past. But at the very least, this implies that regional inequality cannot be reduced through the spatial distribution of human capital, given the current trends in education together with the sectoral make up of our growth process.

So what can be done to redress the regional (district level) inequality in the share of completed tertiary education? As explained earlier, some natural regional inequality in share of education completion will always exist as metro cities provide agglomeration advantages (Das, Ghate, and Robertson, 2015). However, as we have seen, inequalities still exist even among less urbanized regions and any regionally balanced growth would require a reduction in disparities in the medium run.

There can be many policies that can be used to address this problem. There can be policies addressed explicitly towards higher education. However, such policies addressed towards older cohorts may already be too late an intervention. Completing tertiary education is not just about getting higher education right: instead, perhaps, the correct way to think about it is as a barometer to measure how the whole process of educating an individual, which starts from schools, culminates into a stock of human capital.

With this in mind, we turn to the important point raised by the UN in its evaluation of India's progress on the MDGs. We ask if there is any relationship between the learning levels among school age children and tertiary education completion.

TERTIARY EDUCATION COMPLETION AND SCHOOL AGE LEARNING LEVELS

It has been remarked by those examining issues on the efficacy of school programmes that while school enrolment has risen over time, the quality of those educated is very poor. For example, in the *2013 Annual Status of Education Report* (ASER) which is facilitated by the NGO Pratham, the proportion of standard 1 children who are not able to recognize letters is a staggering 47.3 per cent.

The problem of low quality is well recognized as a critical issue facing primary schooling in India. However, here we extend this argument and look at this problem through the lens of tertiary education. To do so, we correlate the district-level quality of education of the age-group 10 to 16 in 2008, obtained from an ASER survey,

with the district share of population in the age group 25–29 who have completed tertiary education. To elaborate further, the exercise is to investigate if the state of knowledge of math and vocabulary of children in school has any relationship with what their tertiary outcomes are when they reach the relevant age. An ideal exercise would follow the same cohort over the years but that would need longish panel data sets. Here we make the plausible assumption that there is a fair bit of persistence in district-level learning levels and that these levels in 2008 can proxy for the learning in the district over the preceding decade.[18] Since ASER surveys are conducted only for rural India, we explore this correlation only for rural India.[19] We base our indicator of learning levels on the district level proportion of children aged 10 to 16 who can do simple subtraction (math) and the share of such children who can read without hesitation a passage pitched at a level that is apt for class 1 (vocabulary).

In Figures 8.10 and 8.11, we present the relationship between the variables of interests. It is clear that there is a significant correlation between basic math and vocabulary knowledge among students, on the one hand, and the share of population with complete tertiary education. Further analysis shows that a 1 per cent increase in the share of children who can do subtraction would lead subsequently to a 0.6 per cent increase in the share of population aged 25–29 who complete tertiary education. The correlation between vocabulary and tertiary education is larger. A 1 per cent increase in the vocabulary indicator leads to a 1.3 per cent increase in *Tert* for the 25–29 age group. These are fairly large effects if one keeps in mind that there are many reasons why a student may not complete tertiary education. In fact, an argument can be made that while the lack of basic subtraction and vocabulary are poor reflection of what children learn in schools, they do not ultimately matter so much for tertiary education completion since there are many other hurdles to translate knowledge picked up from schools into tertiary education completion. For example, wealth constraints as well as poor access to universities may themselves negate the advantage of

---

[18] An analogous exercise is done in Khanna and Mukhopadhyay (2015) where, using data from the National Sample Survey round in 2011, the probability of being enrolled in tertiary education is modelled, among other things, as a function of the relevant cohort's primary school level math and vocabulary knowledge when they were young (using an earlier round of ASER data). Results are similar.

[19] To omit the influence of any urban village, we omit all urban districts where the share of urban population is greater than 90 per cent.

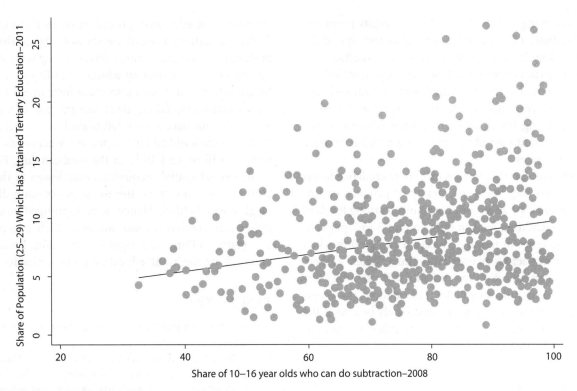

Figure 8.10   School Age Learning Levels and Share of Population Which Has Attained Tertiary Education (Ages 25–29). Rural Districts 2011

Source: Author's calculation (ASER, 2008; Census of India, 2011).

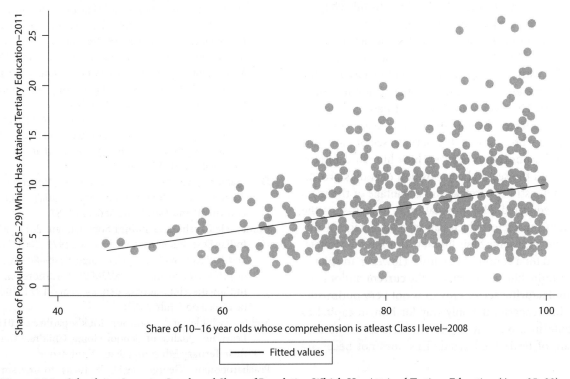

Figure 8.11   School Age Learning Levels and Share of Population Which Has Attained Tertiary Education (Ages 25–29)— Rural Districts 2011

Source: Author's calculation (ASER, 2008; Census of India, 2011).

good schooling quality. However, our results point out that the district-level average state of knowledge of the children does have a lingering impact on whether they complete tertiary education. One must add here that our results merely show correlations: however, a causal interpretation is very plausible in this context and implies that improving the quality of primary education may be an important part of the story to get higher tertiary completion rates.

While this correlation does give some credence to the emphasis on improving the quality of primary education, one must strike a cautionary note: learning levels of school age children explain only around 5 to 7 per cent of the outcomes of tertiary education completion when one compares across all districts of India.[20] Hence, there may be other education instruments that can affect tertiary education outcomes better. For example, the access to centres of higher education must surely be one of the important policy interventions. But more research is needed to throw light on this issue.

CONCLUSION

Over the last decade, India has seen fast-paced growth but it has often been described as jobless. At the same time, there has been a rise in human capital as measured by the average years of schooling. In this chapter, we have delved deeper into the composition of human capital and chronicle the evolution of achievement of various levels of education. We found that the growth of population with just some level of schooling has been the most dynamic aspect of human capital accumulation in recent years. However, growth rates of national income are largely affected by the share of tertiary educated population, who work in the service sector and this creates a disconnection between how human capital is evolving and the sectoral composition of India's growth process. One strategy to take full advantage of the mass of school educated adult population is to kick-start the manufacturing sector which can take advantage of this population with some basic literacy. This kind of strategy has worked for a country like China. However, in spite of Make in India kind of initiatives, the current outlook for the manufacturing sector growth is not very optimistic. Given this scenario, the only way for human capital to contribute in a big way to growth rates is to increase the share of tertiary educated. This does not necessar-

ily imply that education policies need to focus only on higher education. Instead we show evidence that suggests that increasing learning levels among school-going age children is not only an education policy to meet the SDGs, rather that it is an important instrument through which human capital can be an integral part of a growth strategy. If human capital is left to evolve as is dictated by history, what it will add to the process of economic development will be very little in the medium run. Further, while overall spatial inequalities may lessen in the long run, this will still leave the worst performing districts lagging way behind. Hence, a multipronged education policy intervention is called for, one which goes beyond just giving children the right to education. Perhaps an emphasis on the 'right' education is also called for.

REFERENCES

ASER. 2013. 'Annual Status of Education Report (Rural).' January.

Barro, Robert, and Jhong Wha Lee. 2013. 'A New Data Set of Educational Attainment in the world, 1950–2010.' *Journal of Development Economics* 104: 184–98, September.

Bandyopadhyay, S. 2012. 'Convergence Club Empirics: Evidence from Indian States.' *Research on Economic Inequality* 20: 175–20.

Castelló-Climent, Amparo and Abhiroop Mukhopadhyay. 2013. 'Mass Education or a Minority Well Educated Elite in the Process of Growth: The Case of India.' *Journal of Development Economics.* 106(November): 303–20.

Castelló-Climent, Amparo, Latika Chaudhuri, and Abhiroop Mukhopadhyay. 2015. 'Tertiary Education and Prosperity: Catholic Missionaries to Luminosity in India.' IZA Discussion Paper No. 9441, October.

Chandrasekhar, S. and Ajay Sharma. 2014. 'Growth of the Urban Shadow, Spatial Distribution of Economic Activities, and Commuting by Workers in Rural and Urban India.' *World Development* 61: 154–66.

Das, Samarjit, Chetan Ghate, and Peter Robertson. 2015. 'Remoteness, Urbanization and India's Unbalanced Growth.' *World Development* 66: 573–87.

Kumar, Hemanshu and Rohini Somanathan. 2011. 'Mapping Indian Districts across Census Years, 1971–2001.' *Economic and Political Weekly* 46(32, 6 August): 69–88. Available at http://www.epw.in/journal/2009/41-42/notes/mapping-indian-districts-across-census-years-1971-2001.html (accessed on 5 July 2017).

Mehta, Twinkle, and Abhiroop Mukhopadhyay. 2015. 'Can Learning Quality of School Going Children Determine their Tertiary Education Status?', mimeo.

Psacharopoulos, George. 1994. 'Returns to Investment in Education: A Global Update.' *World Development* 22(9, September): 1325–43.

---

[20] Learning levels seem to explain a lot more once we account for state level differences.

9

Adult Education and Composition
of Labour Supply in India

Runu Bhakta and A. Ganesh-Kumar

INTRODUCTION

Education has long been considered an instrument for economic and social development (Schulz, 1988; Tilak, 2003). Growth theories describe several mechanisms through which education influences economic growth in both short and long run. Mankiw, Romer, and Weil (1992) show that education increases human capital inherent in the labour force, which enhances productivity and promotes growth in the long run. Lucas (1988) and Romer (1990) identified the role of education in innovation and creation of new technologies resulting in higher economic growth; whereas Barro (2001) identified two channels through which education generates higher growth for the economy. First, education as a primary component of human capital facilitates the absorption of superior technologies from leading countries; and second, a country with higher ratio of human capital to physical capital achieves higher growth rate by increasing the quantity of physical capital accordingly. Other studies have shown that investment in education yields more return on growth than investment in physical capital (Blaug, Layard, and Woodhall, 1969; Tilak, 1987).

The post-World War II growth experience of the East Asian countries brought out the importance of mass primary and higher education programme pursued by government to facilitate the process of economic development in the long run. Here, Japan, Taiwan, and Korea attained higher economic growth in the 20th century through technological advancement which was possible by expanding education, skills, and acquisition of knowledge. The success of South East Asian countries that followed on reinforces the importance of education for economic growth.

With very high levels of illiteracy among adults in India, the need for public action is only too evident. The Government of India (GOI) has initiated several educational programmes with an emphasis towards adults. The basic objective of these adult education (AE) programmes is to provide education to those who have lost the opportunity and have crossed the age of formal education. Towards this, the National Adult Education Programme (NAEP) was launched in 1978 with an objective to eradicate illiteracy among adults of the age group 19–35. It was initiated not only to promote literacy skills to persons belonging to the economically and socially deprived sections of the society, but also to create awareness and raise functional capabilities among them. Again in 1988, National Literacy Mission (NLM) was initiated to literate adults in the age group of 15–35. The programme was started in 502 districts.[1]

In order to make the AE programme more effective, the GOI has extended the Total Literacy Campaign (TLC) with the Post Literacy Campaign (PLC) under the ninth plan to have a better impact in the society. Towards this, more Jan Shikshan Sansthans (JSS), that is, Institute of People's Education (IPE), are developed for conducting skill upgradation in the areas of programmes of non-formal and AE for neo-literate people. It provides academic and technical support to district-level institutions in both urban and rural areas. In 2001, they extended this policy to 593 districts out of which 160 districts are covered under TLC, 264 under PLC, and 152 under the Continuing Education Programme (CEP).[2] The policy has been extended to remaining districts under the Tenth Plan. Till 2005, around 1,274.5 lakh people got literate through the NLM, out of which 60 per cent were females and 35 per cent were from scheduled castes (SC) and scheduled tribes (ST).[3] The CEP establishes Continuing Education Centres (CEC) and Nodal Continuing Education Centres (NCECs), which provide learning opportunities and facilities such as library, reading room, learning centres, sports centres, cultural centres, and other programmes catering to individual aptitude.

Several non-profit non-governmental organizations (NGOs) were set up to provide similar platform with an objective to enhance AE and provisioning skill development programmes. The central government had provided several incentives and financial support to these NGOs for running literacy, post-literacy, and CEPs.

Under the Eleventh Five Year Plan (2007–12), the GOI had formulated an extensive and comprehensive National Skill Development Mission (NSDM) which had a three-tier institutional structure, namely (i) Prime Minister's (PM's) National Council, (ii) National Skill Development Coordination Board (NSDCB), and (iii) National Skill Development Corporation (NSDC). The core objective of the mission was to create 500 million skilled people by 2022 through skill systems.[4] In continuance with the previous programmes, the GOI has initiated the Skill India campaign in 2015 to provide training to about 40 crore people in different fields by 2022. The campaign includes NSDM, National Policy for Skill Development and Entrepreneurship (NPSDE), Rural India Skill (RIS), Pradhan Mantri Kaushal Vikas Yojana (PMKVY), and the Skill Loan Scheme (SLS). The NSDM will provide the institutional framework at the centre and state level to implement all skill development programmes. The NPSDE is initiated with an objective to improve quality in existing skill development programmes. It aims to provide a common platform to all skill activities existing in the country and to align them in a standard platform and link them with demand centres. This initiative provides clarity in the process of linking the skill development efforts across the country within the existing institutional arrangements. It has also linked skills development to improved employability and productivity. In this regard, the NSDC provides funding to build large and profit-making vocational training centres. The objective of the PMKVY is to encourage the development of employable skills and to enhance the efficiency and productivity in their employment. This policy gives monetary incentives and awards to offer them effective learning during their training. The SLS is initiated to provide financial support through loan to the youth who want to take any vocational/skill training in the country. Keeping in mind the rural-urban gap in educational outcomes, the GOI has initiated another programme with an emphasis towards rural India namely Rural India Skill (RIS). This policy provides training to the unemployed rural youth in various disciplines and groomed to employable level, especially from the interior and remote villages.

To some extent, these policies have had the desired effects. Literacy rate among adults rose steadily from 60.4 per cent in 1999–2000 to 75.7 per cent in 2011–12. Nevertheless, about one in five adult males and one in three adult females remain illiterate in the country. In 2011–12, only one in ten persons in the country had completed higher education and the average years of schooling amongst adults is an abysmal 6.7 years. All these summary statistics show that the country has a very long way to go in enhancing the education attainment of its adult citizens.

Whatever be the extent of progress in AE, its impact on the composition of labour supply is not well understood. To the best of our knowledge, Planning Commission (2008) provides the only available set of estimates of the labour supply by education levels. In that report, education composition of a particular age cohort 'x to x+5' at time t is assumed to be the same as that of the age cohort 'x-5 to x' at time t-5, thereby ignoring the impact, if any, of mortality and migration on the education composition.

---

[1] http://mhrd.gov.in/adult-education
[2] http://planningcommission.nic.in/plans/planrel/fiveyr/10th/volume2/v2_ch2_6.pdf.
[3] http://mhrd.gov.in/adult-education.
[4] http://12thplan.gov.in/12fyp_docs/9.pdf.

By this approach, estimates of labour force by education attainment is arrived at for the year 2009–10 using the data on the percentage of population at each level of education attainment in each age cohort for the year 2004–05 from the NSSO. Based on the values for 2004–05 and 2009–10, the estimates for 2007 are worked out through linear interpolation and these interpolated values are carried forward for 2012.

This procedure, while being simple to implement, does not help understand how the progress in AE attainment feeds into labour supply by the level of education qualification in the country. From a policy perspective, it would be useful to understand how public spending on (higher) education affects education attainment of adults, and, in turn, its impact on the composition of the labour force. In this chapter we attempt to bridge this gap in the literature. Towards this, our analysis in this chapter consists of three parts as follows.

First, we assess the trends in AE in the country through three widely used indicators of education attainment, namely, literacy rate, percentage of population that has completed higher education, and average years of schooling. We use the individual-level information contained in the data from the NSSO for four quinquennial rounds namely, 55th (1999–2000), 61st (2004–05), 66th (2009–10), and 68th (2011–12) to analyse the trends in adult educational achievements across states. We then review the literature on the determinants of AE in India. In particular, we discuss in detail the findings of a recent study on the determinants of AE attainment by Bhakta (2015).

Second, we examine the trends in labour supply by their level of education qualification. For this, again, we use the NSSO data of employment of labour by education qualification in various sectors of the economy.

Third, we carry out a projection exercise wherein we forecast the supply of labour by their education qualification using the econometric models of the determinants of AE attainment estimated by Bhakta (2015). We come up with forecasts of the labour supply composition under alternative scenarios on public expenditure on education sector, and in particular, higher education.

The rest of this chapter is organized as follows: The trends and determinants of AE are studied in the section 'Trends and Determinants of Adult Education', while the trends in labour supply composition is discussed in section 'Trends in Labour Supply Composition'. In the next section, 'Projecting Labour Supply Compositions', we describe the projection exercise that we carry out, the scenarios, and the results of this exercise. Finally, some concluding remarks are provided in the last section.

TRENDS AND DETERMINANTS OF ADULT EDUCATION[5]

Target Group, Indicators, and Data Source

Target Group

We examine the educational attainment of young adults in the age group of 18–40 years for women and of 18–45 years for men. In 2011–12, this age group constituted about 75 per cent of the total working population (authors' calculations based on NSSO data, 2011–12). This age group includes bulk of the target group of population (which is 15–35 years of age) for the NLM of the GOI. The age group we consider is also important from economic point of view as the returns to education is likely to be high for this particular age group since they are likely to remain in the labour force much longer than older adults. Besides, the probability of getting higher education after these age limits is relatively low in the Indian context where very few older adults enrol for higher education. Additionally, Bhakta and Ganesh-Kumar (2014) show that as per the National Family Health Survey (NFHS) data, about 95 per cent parents with a child below five years of age belong to this age group, and hence, their education attainment is important for non-economic reasons too, in particular, for its positive spillovers on health and education of children. For all these reasons, this age group is considered as the target population for the study.

Indicators

Education attainment has been measured in several ways by various researchers and agencies. Tilak (1979) developed a composite educational development index for India using enrolment and educational cost data in 1974–75. In the *Human Development Report* of 1990 published by the United Nations Development Programme (UNDP), the human development index includes an 'education index', which is a weighted average of literacy rate and mean years of schooling. In 1995, the mean years of schooling was replaced by gross enrolment ratios of primary, secondary, and tertiary enrolment ratios. Tilak (1999) analysed the inter-state variations in stock and flow of human capital in India applying gender disparity index or Sopher's index, index of deprivation, and educational development and financing. Rani (2007) constructed an educational development index that combines enrolment, total institutions, and teachers in secondary education for 1990–91 and 2003–04. Further,

---

[5] This section draws extensively from Bhakta (2015).

she developed an educational performance index for the years 1991–92 and 2000–01 based on the rate of transition from upper primary to secondary education, the cumulative dropout rate from class 1 to 10, the percentage of students who appeared in the secondary education examination, and percentage of students who passed out of the secondary education.

While these composite indices metrics are useful to assess the overall educational attainment/performance of adult population, they do not lend themselves easily to capture the impact of progress in education on the composition of labour force. Hence, instead of constructing a composite index, we consider three separate and simpler measures to capture the level of educational attainment of adult population, namely literacy rate, percentage of adults who have completed higher education, and average years of schooling (AYS). The AYS is calculated as

$$AYS = \sum_{i=1}^{k} P_i \times YS_i$$

where 'i' refers to each level of education which varies from 1 to k, P_i is the percentage of population that has completed ith level of education, and YS_i is the years of schooling to complete the particular level of education.

As is well known, literacy rate (LR) captures the basic educational attainment in a state/country (Drèze and Sen, 1995; *Human Development Report*, 1990). While literacy is the starting point in a person's educational progress, skill development requires several years of schooling much beyond primary school level. In general, it may not be unreasonable to assume that the potential for skill development in a person improves with the number of years of schooling, with those completing higher education being particularly well placed to acquire skills that are in demand in the labour market. We examine the percentage of adults who have completed higher education (PAHE) to assess the progress in skill development among adults in the country. Additionally, we use the AYS also as it captures the overall educational attainment including primary, secondary, and tertiary levels of education (Barro and Lee, 1993, 2010).

We use these three metrics with caution here. For sure, all three of them provide only a quantitative assessment of the progress in AE. None of them capture the qualitative aspects of education. This has been a matter of concern at all levels of schooling and higher education in India. Several studies have shown that children who have completed primary school are found to be lacking in basic literacy and elementary math skills (see Annual Status of Education Report (Rural), various years published by ASER Centre/PRATHAM). Similarly, firms

cutting across industries and services have also been pointing out that the students who have completed high school and even graduates are not 'readily employable' (see National Employability Report for various sectors various years published by Aspiring Minds; ICEF Monitor, 2015) and require substantial training at huge cost to the employers to render them productive (NASSCOM). Several reasons that plague the quality of the education system are inadequate public investment in physical infrastructure, overcrowded classrooms, short-staffed faculties, inadequately trained teachers, unattractive incentive structure, poor governance and accountability systems, socio-economic factors that inhibit effective inclusion, and so on. A detailed examination of these factors is beyond the scope of this study. Given the scope of our chapter, namely, to examine the linkage between AE and composition of labour force, we restrict ourselves to a quantitative assessment of the educational achievements for adults in India here using the aforementioned three measures.

Data Source

We have used household level data from the NSSO for four quinquennial rounds namely, 55th (1999–2000), 61st (2004–05), 66th (2009–10), and 68th (2011–12), to analyse the trends in adult educational achievements across states. The NSSO data provides information on the education status of each individual in the household under nine categories, namely, not literate, literate without formal schooling, below primary school, primary school, middle school, secondary school, higher secondary school, graduate, and postgraduate and above.

To calculate LR across states, we have considered those individuals who have either completed primary education or literate without formal schooling. The PAHE is measured as total population that has completed either graduation in any subject or has any kind of technical education divided by total population in the particular age group. The AYS is calculated by first assigning values to the eight education categories in the NSSO data. Total years required to complete the corresponding education level are assigned as follows: First, the aforementioned categories are reclassified into broader categories, namely, no schooling, below primary and literate without formal schooling, completed primary schooling, middle school, secondary schooling, higher secondary schooling, and higher education. Second, to quantify the years of schooling of adults who are literate without formal education, we assigned them 2.5 years of schooling and combined them with those who attended school but could not complete primary education. Third, the adults who attended middle schools are given 7.5 years of schooling and the category 'higher education' comprises individuals who are graduate, postgraduate, and above; and we combined them and assigned 15 years of schooling.

We compute these metrics of education attainment of adults for 26 states namely, Andhra Pradesh, Arunachal Pradesh, Assam, Bihar, Delhi, Goa, Gujarat, Haryana, Himachal Pradesh, Jammu and Kashmir, Karnataka, Kerala, Madhya Pradesh, Maharashtra, Manipur, Meghalaya, Mizoram, Nagaland, Odisha, Punjab, Rajasthan, Sikkim, Tamil Nadu, Tripura, Uttar Pradesh, and West Bengal. We have combined Jharkhand, Chhattisgarh, and Uttaranchal with their original states, Bihar, Madhya Pradesh, and Uttar Pradesh, respectively.

Trends and Patterns in AE in India

Literacy rate in the country as a whole rose steadily from 60.4 per cent in 1999–2000 to 75.7 per cent in 2011–12. Progress in LR was fastest at 1.4 per cent between 2004–05 and 2009–10 (Table 9.1). Male LR has been higher than female LR all through. The latter, however, has been increasing more rapidly and consequently gap between the two has narrowed down noticeably, from about 25 percentage points in 1999–2000 to about 17 percentage points in 2011–12. Nevertheless, it is sobering to note that only two in three adult women are literate in the country even in 2011–12.

Turning to PAHE, it is distressing to note that in 2011–12, just about 1 in 10 persons in the country has completed higher education as defined here. Unlike LR, the gender gap in PAHE is much lower at just about 4 percentage points. Given the substantial illiteracy in the country, and also very low PAHE, the AYS is also quite low in the country at about 6.7 years in 2011–12, with the average for males (females) being 7.6 (5.7) years. Based on these, one can safely say that the country has a very long way to go in improving the educational attainment of its citizens.

Educational attainment in terms of LR, PAHE, and AYS of people in rural and urban areas are given in Table 9.2. In 2011–12, about 70 per cent (87 per cent) of rural (urban) population were literate. Indeed, the gap in LR between rural and urban areas has steadily declined over time, from 27 percentage points in 1999–2000 to about 17 percentage points in 2011–12. In contrast, the picture with regard to higher education is distressing. In 2011–12, a little less than 6 per cent of rural population had completed higher education, whereas in urban areas about 23 per cent of the population were either graduate or had completed some technical education. Further, the

Table 9.1   Gender-wise Educational Indicators of Young Adults across NSS Rounds

	Level				Per Year Increase (%)		
	1999–2000	2004–05	2009–10	2011–12	2004–05	2009–10	2011–12
LR (%)							
Male	72.7	77.7	82.7	84.2	1.0	1.0	0.8
Female	47.8	54.6	63.9	67.0	1.4	1.9	1.5
Total	60.4	66.3	73.4	75.7	1.3	1.4	1.2
Male-Female Difference	24.9	23.1	18.7	17.2	−0.4	−0.9	−0.8
PAHE (%)							
Male	8.2	10.1	12.2	13.1	0.4	0.4	0.5
Female	4.6	5.8	7.7	9.0	0.3	0.4	0.6
Total	6.41	8.0	10.0	11.1	0.3	0.4	0.6
Male-Female Difference	3.7	4.3	4.5	4.1	0.1	0.04	−0.2
AYS (years)							
Male	5.9	6.6	7.4	7.6	0.1	0.2	0.1
Female	3.6	4.4	5.3	5.7	0.2	0.2	0.2
Total	4.8	5.5	6.3	6.7	0.1	0.2	0.2
Male-Female Difference	2.3	2.2	2.1	1.9	0.01	0.03	0.1

Source: Author's calculations based on the NSS data.

Note: Per-year increase is the average increase over the inter-round years. For example, the values for 2004–05 are the average increase in the five years between NSS Rounds 1999–2000 and 2004–05, and so on.

Table 9.2   Rural-Urban Variation in Educational Indicators of Young Adults across NSS Rounds

	Level				Per Year Increase (%)		
	1999–2000	2004–05	2009–10	2011–12	2004–05	2009–10	2011–12
LR (%)							
Rural	53.0	59.6	67.9	70.5	1.3	1.7	1.3
Urban	80.1	83.5	86.7	87.5	0.7	0.7	0.4
Total	60.5	66.3	73.4	75.7	1.2	1.4	1.2
U-R Difference	27.1	23.9	18.8	17.0	0.6	1.0	0.9
PAHE (%)							
Rural	2.9	4.0	4.9	5.9	0.2	0.2	0.5
Urban	15.6	18.4	22.3	22.8	0.5	0.8	0.2
Total	6.4	8.0	10.0	11.1	0.3	0.4	0.6
U-R Difference	12.7	14.4	17.4	16.9	−0.3	−0.6	0.3
AYS (years)							
Rural	3.8	4.5	5.3	5.7	0.2	0.2	0.2
Urban	7.5	8.1	8.8	8.9	0.1	0.2	0.1
Total	4.8	5.5	6.3	6.7	0.1	0.2	0.2
U-R Difference	3.7	3.6	3.5	3.3	0.02	0.0	0.1

Source: Author's calculations based on the NSS data

Note: Per year increase is the average increase over the inter-round years. For example, the values for 2004–05 are the average increase in the five years between NSS Rounds 1999–2000 and 2004–05, and so on.

rural-urban gap in PAHE has widened during the period by over 4 percentage points. Not surprisingly, AYS in rural areas is lower at 5.7 years in 2011–12 compared to 8.9 years in urban areas. The rural-urban gap in AYS has

declined slightly, reflecting the faster progress in LR in rural areas than urban areas.

The spatial progress in LR across states is shown in Figure 9.1. The LR varies substantially across the states,

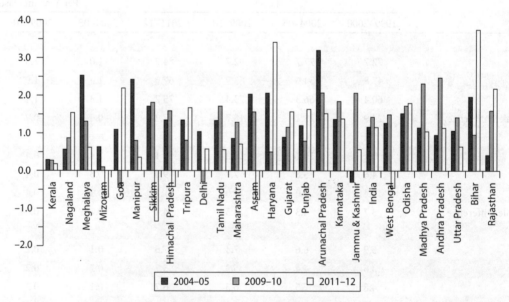

Figure 9.1   Per Year Increase in Literacy Rates across States (Per Cent)

Source: Author's calculations based on the NSS data.

Note: The states are sorted in descending order of their literacy rates in 2011–12. The per-year increase is the average increase over the inter-round years. For example, the values for 2004–05 are the average increase in the five years between NSS Rounds 1999–2000 and 2004–05, and so on.

both in terms of the level and progress over time. In 2011–12, for instance, Kerala is almost completely literate (98 per cent) while in Rajasthan barely two-thirds of the population is literate (63 per cent). Over the years, the progress in LR also shows substantial variation across states. Bihar, Madhya Pradesh, Rajasthan, and Uttar Pradesh (BIMARU states) have some of the lowest LR in the country, averaging about 66 per cent, in 2011–12. However, these states have experienced a steady increase in total LR over time, though their progress has somewhat weakened in later rounds. The North-Eastern states, in general, report a very high LR (around 90 per cent), though some of them, namely, Sikkim, Mizoram, and Assam, experienced a drop in LR between 2009 and 2012.

The progress in PAHE is shown in Figure 9.2, which ranks the states in decreasing order of PAHE in 2011–12. It is seen that the ranks of the states in 2011–12 in terms of PAHE is quite different from that of LR in the same year. Unlike LR, several states are ranked below the national average most of which also have low LR. The progress over time also shows substantial variation across states. Per year increase in PAHE is highest between 2009–10 and 2011–12, with the sole exception of Sikkim, which witnessed a fall between these two years. Further, the progress in PAHE is also high in general for the leading states that already report a higher than national average

PAHE, suggesting that the gap between the leading and trailing states could be widening. This could have adverse impact on the skill distribution, and hence, the income-earning potential of the people across states.

Figure 9.3 presents the progress in AYS across states. Again, it is seen that the set of states with less than national average AYS are the ones with low LR and/or low PAHE. As in the case of PAHE, per year increase in AYS is also highest between 2009–10 and 2011–12 with Sikkim again being the sole exception. Further, the progress in AYS is higher for the leading states than the trailing ones.

Determinants of AE

There are several studies in the literature that pertain to the factors affecting literacy rates, secondary, and higher secondary level education among children in India (Badr, et al., 2012; Case and Deaton, 1999; Joshi and Rao, 1964; Mason and Khandker, 1995; Rani, 2007). However, to the best of our knowledge, hardly any study exists, both in the international and Indian context that systematically assesses the factors that determine the level of educational attainment of adults. One recent study that does this is by Bhakta (2015). In this section we first summarize the findings of this study with regard to the determinants of AE.

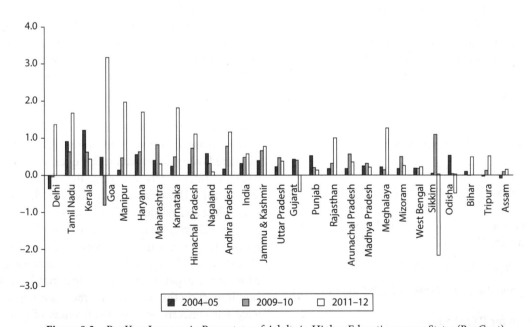

Figure 9.2 Per Year Increase in Percentage of Adults in Higher Education across States (Per Cent)

Source: Author's calculations based on the NSS data.

Note: The states are sorted in descending order of their percentage of population completed higher education in 2011–12. The per-year increase is the average increase over the inter-round years. For example, the values for 2004–05 are the average increase in the five years between NSS Rounds 1999–2000 and 2004–05, and so on.

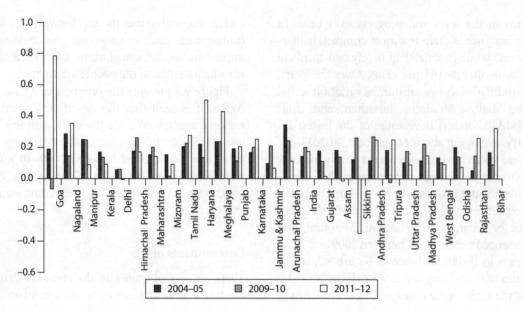

Figure 9.3   Per Year Increase in Average Years of Schooling across States (Years)

Source: Author's calculations based on the NSS data.

Note: The states are sorted in descending order of their average years of schooling in 2011–12. The per-year increase is the average increase over the inter-round years. For example, the values for 2004–05 are the average increase in the five years between NSS Rounds 1999–2000 and 2004–05, and so on.

Bhakta (2015) develops a set of econometric models to study the factors that affect education attainment of adults in India as measured by the three indicators—LR, PAHE, and AYS—described earlier. Econometric models are then developed for (i) per year increase in literacy rate among adults (PYILR), (ii) per year increase in the percentage of population that completed higher education (PYIHE), and (iii) per year increase in the average years of schooling (PYIAYS), as follows.

The equation for PYILR is given as:

$$PYILR_{ij} = \alpha_{1ij} + \beta_{11}PubExp_{ij} + \beta_{12}EcoCharP_{ij}$$
$$+ \beta_{13}SocChar_{ij} + \beta_{14}Demo_{ij} + \beta_{15}Infras_{ij} + \varepsilon_{1ij} \quad (1)$$

The equation for per year increase in the percentage of population completed higher education (*PYIHE*) is given as:

$$PYIHE_{ij} = \alpha_{2ij} + \beta_{21}PubExp_{ij} + \beta_{22}EcoCharP_{ij}$$
$$+ \beta_{23}SocChar_{ij} + \beta_{24}Demo_{ij} + \beta_{25}Infras_{ij} + \varepsilon_{2ij} \quad (2)$$

The equation for PYIAYS is given as:

$$PYIAYS_{ij} = \alpha_{3ij} + \beta_{31}PubExp_{ij} + \beta_{32}EcoCharP_{ij}$$
$$+ \beta_{33}SocChar_{ij} + \beta_{34}Demo_{ij} + \beta_{35}Infras_{ij} + \varepsilon_{3ij} \quad (3)$$

The explanatory variables in each equation capture five broad dimensions—public expenditure in education (*PubExp*), economics characteristics (*EcoChar*), social characteristics (*SocChar*), demographics (*Demo*), and infrastructure (*Infras*). Several variables are considered under each of these five dimensions. For details of these variables and their data source, see Bhakta (2015). The study used 69 observations comprising three NSS rounds, namely, 2004–05, 2009–10, and 2011–12, as the time period 1999–2000 is dropped off to calculate the per year increase in subsequent round. These models are estimated using panel data techniques, allowing for state level and time effects to control the effects of unobservable factors. Hausman test is done to choose between fixed effect and random effect models.

Table 9.3 presents the estimated results of two separate models for per year increase in literacy rates from Bhakta (2015). Model 1 explicitly shows that percentage of total educational expenditure in AE does not have a significant impact on the statewise literacy rate, supporting the wide-felt concern on the effectiveness of public policy with regard to adult literacy. It may be due to the fact that government is spending merely around 1 per cent of total education expenditure on AE. Thus, the government has to enhance total coverage to a significant percentage of

Table 9.3 Labour Force by Education-Level Across NSS Rounds

	Rural + Urban					Rural					Urban				
	1993–94	1999–2000	2003–04	2009–10	2011–12	1993–94	1999–2000	2003–04	2009–10	2011–12	1993–94	1999–2000	2003–04	2009–10	2011–12
Total number of persons (millions)	496.8	588.6	643.7	707.8	763.0	367.7	429.1	467.8	502.1	530.8	129.1	159.5	176.4	205.5	232.4
ILPE labour (%) (% of total persons)	70.3	64.7	61.0	53.3	51.3	78.0	72.9	69.1	61.4	59.4	48.3	42.5	39.6	33.3	32.8
SE labour (%) (% of total persons)	25.7	30.3	32.1	38.3	39.3	20.4	25.0	27.6	34.7	36.1	40.9	44.5	43.8	47.2	46.8
HE labour (%) (% of total persons)	4.0	5.1	6.9	8.4	9.4	1.6	2.1	3.3	3.9	4.6	10.8	13.0	16.5	19.5	20.3
Not in labour force (% of total persons)	35.4	38.2	36.3	42.9	44.1	31.4	34.3	32.3	39.6	41.3	46.7	49.0	47.1	51.2	50.7
ILPE labour (% of not in labour force)	66.4	61.5	57.2	50.4	48.0	75.5	70.9	66.7	59.1	56.1	49.0	43.7	40.0	34.0	32.9
SE labour (% of not in labour force)	30.7	34.6	37.4	42.6	44.5	23.8	27.9	31.3	38.0	40.5	44.0	47.3	48.4	51.3	52.0
HE labour (% of not in labour force)	2.9	3.9	5.4	6.9	7.5	0.7	1.2	2.0	2.9	3.4	7.0	9.0	11.6	14.6	15.1
Employed (% of total persons)	63.4	60.4	62.2	55.9	54.7	67.7	64.8	66.6	59.5	57.7	50.9	48.6	50.6	47.2	47.6
ILPE labour (% of employed persons)	73.5	67.8	64.2	56.2	54.7	79.9	74.8	71.1	63.6	62.3	49.3	42.6	40.5	33.3	33.4
SE labour (% of employed persons)	22.2	26.9	28.5	34.8	35.0	18.3	22.9	25.4	32.2	32.7	37.2	41.2	39.5	42.8	41.7
HE labour (% of employed persons)	4.2	5.4	7.3	9.0	10.3	1.8	2.3	3.6	4.2	5.0	13.5	16.3	20.0	23.9	24.9
Unemployed (% of total persons)	1.2	1.4	1.5	1.2	1.2	0.8	1.0	1.1	0.9	1.0	2.4	2.4	2.4	1.6	1.7
ILPE labour (% of unemployed persons)	14.8	18.6	19.3	16.4	17.3	17.3	18.7	24.9	18.9	21.4	15.4	15.3	13.5	12.1	12.5
SE labour (% of unemployed persons)	62.8	58.4	50.0	49.8	44.1	63.9	62.2	51.9	53.6	48.3	59.6	57.1	46.9	44.8	38.8
HE labour (% of unemployed persons)	22.4	23.0	30.7	33.7	38.6	18.8	19.1	23.2	27.5	30.3	25.0	27.6	39.6	43.1	48.8

Source: Author's calculations based on the NSS data

illiterate people through such literacy mission and they have to implement this programme more effectively to get a significant impact on literacy rate.

In Model 2, public expenditure on AE is dropped as it is insignificant in Model 1. The result shows that the per year increase in percentage of population in backward castes (SC and ST) have negative impact on the improvements in literacy rates per year. Thus, social status still plays a significant role in India. Evidence suggests that students from SC and ST community are being neglected in schools and other social platforms, which has a negative impact on their enrolment and completion of education and, hence, on overall literacy rates.

Demographic pattern is an important determinant of LR. States with a greater proportion of population from older age group show lower progress in LR. The percentage of rural households with own land also turns out to be an important determinant of LR. In rural India, households without land are mostly in economically and socially vulnerable state with credits and other liabilities. Thus, the proportion of rural households with land

indirectly captures their economic ability to afford basic education level from formal schooling.

The percentage of registered manufacturing in total manufacturing is identified as a demand pull factor which motivates them to attain at least minimum level of education. The LR is increasing annually at a diminishing rate which is captured by the year dummies with the coefficients 1.16 and 1.67 in 2009–10 and 2011–12, respectively.

The estimated results for per year increase in PAHE is given in Table 9.4. Here public policy is found to be effective in increasing educational attainment of young adults. The proportion of educational expenditure in higher education has significant impact on the annual increase in the percentage of population completed higher education.

The results also suggest that states with higher growth in Hindu population experiences lower increase in percentage of population completed higher education annually. Similarly, social status plays a critical role here, as per year increase in percentage of ST population has negative impact on higher education.

Table 9.4 Trends in ILPE Labour Across NSS Rounds

	1993–94	1999–2000	2003–04	2009–10	2011–12
Rural + Urban					
Total Persons (millions)	349.2	380.7	392.8	377.0	391.3
Not in Labour Force (%)	33.5	36.3	34.0	40.7	41.3
Unemployed (%)	0.3	0.4	0.5	0.4	0.4
Employed (%)	66.3	63.3	65.5	59.0	58.3
Agricultural (% of employed)	73.7	72.2	69.2	64.7	60.6
Non-Agricultural (% of employed)	26.3	27.7	30.8	35.3	39.5
Rural					
Total Persons (millions)	286.8	312.9	323.4	308.3	315.1
Not in Labour Force (%)	30.4	33.3	31.2	38.1	39.0
Unemployed (%)	0.2	0.2	0.4	0.3	0.4
Employed (%)	69.4	66.4	68.4	61.6	60.6
Agricultural (% of employed)	82.5	81.3	78.1	73.4	70.1
Non-Agricultural (% of employed)	17.5	18.6	21.8	26.6	29.9
Urban					
Total Persons (millions)	62.4	67.8	69.9	68.5	76.3
Not in Labour Force (%)	47.4	50.4	47.5	52.2	50.9
Unemployed (%)	0.8	0.9	0.8	0.6	0.7
Employed (%)	51.9	48.7	51.7	47.2	48.5
Agricultural (% of employed)	19.4	15.0	14.7	13.5	11.3
Non-Agricultural (% of employed)	80.6	85.0	85.3	86.6	88.6

Source: Author's calculations based on the NSS data

Taking sex ratio in a state as a proxy for women empowerment, the results show that an increase in sex ratio has positive impact on educational progress. Data shows that female education is growing at a higher rate than the male population, which may have a positive effect on the overall progress in education in a state where the sex ratio is increasing as compared to others. Dependency ratio, which captures the economic burden on households, shows a negative significant coefficient.

Percentage of gross state domestic product (GSDP) in industry and services is included in the model to capture the demand pull effects on education. It is seen that an increase in the percentage of GSDP in industry and services has a positive impact on the completion rate of higher education.

Table 9.5 gives the estimated results for per year increase in average years of schooling. Here, per year increase in per capita real expenditure on education is significant at 1 percentage level. Thus, public education policy is effective in improving overall educational outcome across states. Amongst the social and demographic

variables, only the percentage of ST population is found to be important in determining annual progress in AYS. Result suggests that states with greater percentage of ST population have slow progress in AYS.

Then the share of GSDP in industry and services has positive impact on the overall educational progress which can be explained as a demand side impact on education. Greater share of GSDP in industry and services increases the demand for educated labour, which has a significant impact on the educational attainment in India. Additionally, annual increase in percentage of households with irrigated land in rural areas has positive impact on educational improvements as the increase in the share of irrigated land captures the economic development of those households which are engaged in agriculture sector. Such development improves income of those households and offers them an opportunity to afford educational services. Moreover, increase in total number of higher/secondary schools and colleges per area has positive impact on educational improvements. This may be due to the fact that increase in the number

Table 9.5   Trends in SE Labour Across NSS Rounds

	1993–94	1999–2000	2003–04	2009–10	2011–12
Rural + Urban					
Total Persons (millions)	127.8	178.2	206.3	271.2	300.1
Not in Labour Force (%)	42.2	43.7	42.4	47.8	50.0
Unemployed (%)	3.0	2.7	2.3	1.5	1.4
Employed (%)	54.8	53.6	55.3	50.7	48.7
Agricultural (% of employed)	43.5	43.6	44.9	44.6	41.4
Non-Agricultural (% of employed)	56.4	56.4	55.1	55.4	58.8
Rural					
Total Persons (millions)	75.0	107.1	129.1	174.1	191.4
Not in Labour Force (%)	36.6	38.3	36.7	43.4	46.4
Unemployed (%)	2.6	2.4	2.1	1.5	1.3
Employed (%)	60.8	59.3	61.2	55.2	52.3
Agricultural (% of employed)	63.6	63.1	62.3	61.4	57.7
Non-Agricultural (% of employed)	36.5	36.9	37.7	38.6	42.3
Urban					
Total Persons (millions)	52.9	71.0	77.3	97.0	108.8
Not in Labour Force (%)	50.2	52.0	51.9	55.7	56.3
Unemployed (%)	3.5	3.1	2.5	1.6	1.4
Employed (%)	46.3	44.9	45.5	42.8	42.3
Agricultural (% of employed)	6.3	4.8	6.0	6.0	5.6
Non-Agricultural (% of employed)	93.7	95.2	94.0	94.1	94.4

Source: Author's calculations based on the NSS data

of schools and colleges improves the accessibility of the education facilities in each place which improves total enrolment and completion in those places and people are more willing to send their children to school if it is closer to their homes.

TRENDS IN LABOUR SUPPLY COMPOSITION

In this section we examine the trends in the composition of labour supply in terms of the educational attainment of the labour force. For this we use the household-level data from the NSSO on Employment-Unemployment for four quinquennial rounds, namely 55th (1999–2000), 61st (2004–05), 66th (2009–10), and 68th (2011–12). The NSSO data provides information on the education status of each individual in the household as well as their labour force participation and whether or not they are employed as well their sector of employment.

Towards this, we first map the education level of the individuals to three types of labour based on their education attainment and then track their labour force participation, employment status, and the sector of employment. As mentioned earlier, there are nine categories as per the NSSO data—not literate, literate without formal schooling, below primary school, primary school, middle school, secondary school, higher secondary school, graduate, and postgraduate and above. Based on these nine categories we define the three labour types as follows:

1. Labour that is illiterate/has completed education up to primary school level (ILPE labour). This type of labour includes five education categories: not literate, literate without formal schooling, below primary school, primary school, and middle school.
2. Labour that has completed schooling up to secondary/higher secondary level (SE labour).
3. Labour that has completed higher education (HE labour) consisting of graduates and postgraduate and above.

Table 9.6 presents the size and distribution of adults according to these three labour types in the country as

Table 9.6   Trends in HE Labour across NSS Rounds

	1993–94	1999–2000	2003–04	2009–10	2011–12
Rural + Urban					
Total Persons (millions)	19.8	29.7	44.6	59.6	71.6
Not in Labour Force (%)	25.7	29.4	28.4	35.4	35.1
Unemployed (%)	6.9	6.3	6.5	4.7	5.0
Employed (%)	67.4	64.3	65.2	59.9	59.9
Agricultural (% of employed)	13.4	14.3	14.3	12.4	12.3
Non-Agricultural (% of employed)	86.6	85.7	85.8	87.5	87.7
Rural					
Total Persons (millions)	5.9	9.0	15.3	19.7	24.3
Not in Labour Force (%)	14.6	19.0	19.5	29.4	30.3
Unemployed (%)	9.8	8.8	8.0	6.7	6.5
Employed (%)	75.6	72.2	72.6	64.0	63.2
Agricultural (% of employed)	36.0	38.1	33.9	31.8	30.5
Non-Agricultural (% of employed)	64.0	61.8	66.0	68.2	69.5
Urban					
Total Persons (millions)	13.9	20.7	29.2	40.0	47.3
Not in Labour Force (%)	30.5	34.0	33.1	38.4	37.6
Unemployed (%)	5.6	5.1	5.6	3.6	4.1
Employed (%)	63.9	60.9	61.3	57.9	58.3
Agricultural (% of employed)	2.0	2.1	2.0	1.9	2.1
Non-Agricultural (% of employed)	98.0	97.9	98.0	98.1	97.8

Source: Author's calculations based on the NSS data

a whole and in rural and urban areas. It is seen that the total number of adults in the country in 2011–12 stood at 793 million, a rise of about 266 million from 1993–94. About two-thirds of them were in rural areas (531 million) and a third in urban areas (232 million). Over these years, in the country as a whole, there has been a significant reduction in the percentage of ILPE labour, from about 70 per cent in 1993–94 to 51 per cent in 2011–12 reflecting improving educational attainments in the country. Nevertheless, the size of this labour type actually rose to about 417 million in 2011–12 as against 349 million in 1993–94. All through, the percentage of ILPE labour in rural areas is much higher (59 per cent in 2011–12) than in urban areas (33 per cent in 2011–12). However, the reduction in the percentage of ILPE labour in rural areas has been somewhat larger (19 percentage points on a much larger base) than in urban areas (15.5 percentage points). The slower reduction in this labour type could partly be due to migration from rural areas to urban areas. Commensurate with the reduction in the percentage of ILPE labour, there has been a rise in the percentage of SE labour and HE labour over these years. In terms of absolute numbers, in 2011–12 there were 300 million SE labour and 72 million HE labour in the country. It is also seen that urban areas have a larger percentage of SE labour and HE labour than rural areas. Yet, it is sobering to note that less than 5 per cent of adults in rural areas are HE labour as defined earlier.

About 44 per cent of adults in the country were not in labour force in 2011–12, a rise from about 35 per cent in 1993–94.[6] At 51 per cent, this percentage is 10 percentage points higher in urban areas than in rural areas. In 1993–94, two-thirds of the persons not in labour force were ILPE labour type, which has declined over the years to about 48 per cent in 2011–12. In contrast, the percentage of SE labour and HE labour not in labour force has risen in the country. Similar trends are seen in rural and urban areas, though the percentages of SE labour and HE labour not in labour force is relatively higher in urban areas than their corresponding figures in rural areas.

Turning to employment, in 2011–12 about 55 per cent of the all adults (57 per cent in rural and 48 per cent in urban) were employed. Commensurate with the rise in persons not in labour force, employment percentages have fallen over time in the country as a whole and in rural and urban areas. Indeed, the fall in employment

between 1993–94 and 2011–12 is quite sharp (10 percentage points) in rural areas than in urban areas (about 3 percentage points). Much of this fall in the percentage of adults employed seems to have occurred in the 2000s. As in the case of total persons and persons not in labour force, a larger percentage of the employed adults are ILPE labour type (55 per cent in 2011–12). This is followed by SE labour (35 per cent) and HE labour (10 per cent). Further, the trends in the composition of employed persons are also similar to that of total persons and persons not in labour force; that is, the percentage of ILPE labour amongst the employed is declining while that of SE labour and HE labour is rising. The trends and patterns in rural and urban areas are similar qualitatively, though the percentages vary across them.

In contrast, the situation with regard to unemployed persons is dramatically different. First of all, unemployment rate is quite low in the country as a whole and does not exhibit any significant trend. Rural unemployment rates are slightly lower, while urban unemployment rates are somewhat higher, and neither of them shows any trend. A majority of the unemployed in the country are SE labour, followed by HE labour. Over time, the percentage of HE labour amongst the unemployed has been rising while that of SE labour is declining. The pattern and trends in both rural and urban areas are quite similar, with some variations in the magnitudes.

Trends in the ILPE labour in the country and in rural and urban areas are shown in Table 9.7. In 2011–12, 41 per cent of ILPE labour was not in labour force. This percentage has, in fact, been rising over time. While unemployment rates amongst ILPE labour is very low and does not exhibit any trend, employment rate has been falling over time and stood at 58 per cent in 2011–12. A majority of ILPE labour was employed in agriculture, though the share of agriculture has been declining over time. In rural areas, agriculture employed a much higher percentage of ILPE labour (70 per cent in 2011–12), while in urban areas an overwhelming majority (89 per cent in 2011–12) of ILPE labour was employed in non-agriculture.

The number of SE labour has been rising in the country (Table 9.8) and stood at 300 million in 2011–12. As with ILPE labour, the percentage not in labour force has been rising, and in 2011–12, only half of them were in labour force. Unemployment rates are slightly higher for SE labour than ILPE labour, though this has been declining over time. In 2011–12, about 41 per cent of the employed were in agriculture and the rest in non-agriculture. The picture across rural and urban areas is similar qualitatively, except that agriculture accounts for

---

[6] For a discussion of the reasons for the rise in persons not in labour force see Rangarajan, Kaul, and Seema (2011).

Table 9.7   Determinants of Per Year Increase in Literacy Rate (PYILR)

Variable	Model 1	Model 2
Per Year Increase in Percentage Expenditure in Adult Education	0.0001	
Per Year Increase in Percentage of ST Population	−0.3788***	−0.3580***
Per Year Increase in Percentage of SC Population	−0.25143*	−0.2588*
Per Year Increase in % of Population in 30–45 Years of Age Group	−0.25697**	−0.2237**
Registered Manufacturing as a Percentage of Total Manufacturing	0.01097**	0.0103**
Percentage of Rural HHs with Own Land	0.0197***	0.0174***
Year 2009–10	−1.3586***	−1.1071***
Year 2011–12	−1.8860***	−1.6482***
State Dummies	Yes	Yes
No. of observations	69	69
Root MSE	0.938	0.951
R-Square	0.748	0.734
Adjusted R-Square	0.715	0.704
F Value	22.48***	24.18***

Source: Bhakta (2015).

Table 9.8   Determinants of Per Year Increase in Percentage of Population Completed Higher Education (PYIHE)

Variable	Model
Percentage of Educational Expenditure in Higher Education	0.0032*
Per Year Increase in Percentage of Hindu Population	−0.1348*
Per Year Increase in Percentage of ST Population	−0.2251***
Per Year Increase in Sex Ratio	0.0086*
Per Year Increase in Dependency Ratio	−0.3348***
Per Year Increase in Percentage of GSDP in Industry and Services	0.0593***
State Dummies	Yes
No. of observations	69
Root MSE	0.528
R-Square	0.613
Adjusted R-Square	0.562
F Value	12.12***

Source: Bhakta (2015).

Table 9.9   Determinants of Per Year Increase in Average Years of Schooling (PYIAYS)

Variable	Model
Per Year Increase In Per Capita Educational Expenditure	0.0001***
Per Year Increase In Percentage of ST Population	−0.0314***
Per Year Increase In % of HHs with Irrigated Land in Rural Areas	0.0127***
Per Year Increase In Dependency Ratio	−0.0846***
Per Year Increase in No. of Higher/Secondary Schools and Colleges Per Area	3.9581*
Percentage of GSDP in Industry and Services	0.0019***
Year 2009–10	−0.0523*
Year 2011–12	−0.0793**
State Dummies	Yes
No. of observations	69
Root MSE	0.096
R-Square	0.828
Adjusted R-Square	0.802
F Value	32.21***

Source: Bhakta (2015).

relatively greater share of employment in rural areas than in urban areas.

The picture with respect to HE labour is somewhat mixed. The trends in the size of HE labour as well as the percentage not in labour force have been rising similar to ILPE labour and SE labour (Table 9.9). Unlike the latter two, however, urban areas have more HE labour than rural areas. Further, unemployment rate is highest for HE labour though it has been declining over time and stood at 5 per cent in 2011–12. The most important difference is in the sector of employment. In the country as a whole, about 88 per cent of HE labour is employed in non-agriculture in 2011–12. Even in rural areas, 70 per cent of HE labour is employed in non-agriculture, while in urban areas this percentage is almost 98 per cent. While in rural areas, the percentage of HE labour in non-agriculture is rising in urban areas, this percentage has been quite stable over time.

PROJECTING LABOUR SUPPLY COMPOSITIONS

As mentioned earlier, Planning Commission (2008) provides projections of the growth in labour force in the country between the years 2002 and 2022. To the best of our knowledge, these are the only available forecasts of the growth in total labour force in the country. We use this information to first project the total labour force in the country between 2011–12 and 2025–26. We then use the econometric relations estimated by Bhakta (2015) described in the section 'Determinants of Adult Education' to project the proportion of ILPE labour, SE labour, and HE labour in the total to determine the size of the labour force by education level.

The Planning Commission forecasts the annual rate of growth in the labour force at five yearly intervals: 2.28 per cent between 2002 and 2007; 1.92 per cent between 2007 and 2012; 1.60 per cent between 2012 and 2017; and 1.23 per cent between 2017 and 2022. These estimates suggest a slowdown in the growth of the labour force between 2012 and 2017, and further between 2017 and 2022, for the intervening years we specify a linear reduction in the annual growth rate of labour force to the above levels. For the years beyond 2021–22, we use a linear reduction in the annual growth rate of labour force at the same rate as in 2017–2022.

We proceed as follows to project the proportion of ILPE labour, SE labour, and HE labour in the total. For the base year 2011–12, the initial composition of labour supply across labour types is calculated from the NSS data for that year. These initial shares are then updated for each subsequent year using the econometric relations of Bhakta (2015) discussed in the section titled 'Determinants of Adult Education' under certain simplifying assumptions.

1. We assume that the proportion of HE labour (ls) is assumed to increase by the annual increase in PAHE as projected by the equation for *PYIHE* (Equation 2 in the section titled 'Determinants of Adult Education').
2. Similarly, we assume that the proportion of SE labour (lss) increases by the annual growth in AYS as projected by the equation for *PYIAYS* (Equation 3 in the section titled 'Determinants of Adult Education').
3. Finally, the proportion of ILPE labour is obtained residually as 1-*ls*-*lss*.

As the econometric relations for *PYIHE* and *PYIAYS* show public expenditure in education as a significant driver of education attainment, it allows us to specify alternative scenarios on government policy with respect to education. This allows us to capture the potential impact that government policy on education can have on the levels of educational attainment in the country,

and hence, on the composition of the labour supply and overall economic performance of the country.

These econometric relations also show that the proportion of non-agricultural sector in gross domestic product (GDP) is an important pull factor hastening progress in adult education attainment. Here we assume that the share of non-agricultural GDP will increase at the same rate as in the year 2011–12. While projecting *ls* and *lss*, we keep all other variables in the econometric relations such as social and demographic characteristics constant at their base year levels.

We make the projections under the following four scenarios:

1. Business as Usual (BAU): Growth rate of SE labour and HE labour are estimated from the historical data using the models estimated by Bhakta (2015).
2. Policy Scenario 1: Increase in educational expenditure in higher education by 10 per cent.
3. Policy Scenario 2: Increase in educational expenditure in higher education by 20 per cent.
4. Policy Scenario 3: Increase in educational expenditure in higher education by 30 per cent.

The projected shares of the labour types in each of these scenarios are given in Table 9.10 to Table 9.13. Looking first at the BAU scenario, it is seen that there is a steady progress in the share of the labour force that has completed either secondary or higher education. Over the 15 year horizon, 2011–12 to 2025–26, the share of SE labour and HE labour together in the total labour force is expected to rise from about 45 per cent to about 65 per cent. Indeed, during this period, HE labour is expected to rise faster by about 66 per cent albeit from a lower base while SE labour could rise by about 35 per cent over their respective shares in 2011–12. Correspondingly, the share of ILPE labour falls to about 35 per cent in 2025–26.

More significantly, the size of ILPE labour is expected to shrink in absolute size by 85 million from 417 million in 2011–12 to about 332 million in 2025–26, even as the size of total labour force is projected to rise by 174 million during this period. Alongside, the rising share of SE labour and PE labour coupled with rising size of total labour force implies that the supply of these two types of labour is expected to expand by 178 million and 81 million, respectively, over the 15-year period.

The projections in the three scenarios essentially give a similar picture. In all these policy scenarios, the share and size of both SE labour and HE labour expands while ILPE labour contracts. These changes, however, are

Table 9.10   Projected Labour Force by Type—BAU Scenario

Year	Total Labour Force (millions)	Share of Labour by Type			Total Labour Supply by Type (millions)		
		ILPE-labour	SE-labour	HE-labour	ILPE-labour	SE-labour	HE-labour
2011–12	763.0	54.7	35.0	10.3	417.1	267.4	78.5
2012–13	777.6	53.4	35.9	10.8	415.0	278.8	83.8
2013–14	792.1	52.0	36.7	11.3	411.7	291.0	89.3
2014–15	806.2	50.6	37.6	11.8	408.2	303.2	94.9
2015–16	820.2	49.3	38.5	12.3	404.1	315.5	100.5
2016–17	833.8	47.9	39.3	12.7	399.5	328.0	106.3
2017–18	847.2	46.6	40.2	13.2	394.4	340.7	112.1
2018–19	860.1	45.2	41.1	13.7	388.6	353.5	118.0
2019–20	872.6	43.8	42.0	14.2	382.2	366.4	124.0
2020–21	884.6	42.4	42.9	14.7	375.3	379.3	130.0
2021–22	896.1	41.0	43.8	15.2	367.7	392.4	136.0
2022–23	907.2	39.6	44.7	15.7	359.6	405.5	142.1
2023–24	917.7	38.2	45.6	16.1	350.9	418.7	148.2
2024–25	927.9	36.8	46.6	16.6	341.6	432.0	154.3
2025–26	937.5	35.4	47.5	17.1	331.8	445.3	160.4

Source: Authors' calculations.

Table 9.11   Projected Labour Force by Type—Policy Scenario 1

Year	Total Labour Force (millions)	Share of Labour by Type			Total Labour Supply by Type (millions)		
		ILPE-labour	SE-labour	HE-labour	ILPE-labour	SE-labour	HE-labour
2011–12	763.0	54.7	35.0	10.3	417.1	267.4	78.5
2012–13	777.6	53.4	35.9	10.8	415.0	278.8	83.8
2013–14	792.1	52.0	36.7	11.3	411.7	291.0	89.3
2014–15	806.2	50.5	37.7	11.8	407.4	303.9	94.9
2015–16	820.2	49.2	38.6	12.3	403.2	316.3	100.6
2016–17	833.8	47.8	39.4	12.8	398.5	328.9	106.5
2017–18	847.2	46.4	40.3	13.3	393.2	341.6	112.4
2018–19	860.1	45.0	41.2	13.8	387.3	354.5	118.3
2019–20	872.6	43.6	42.1	14.3	380.8	367.4	124.4
2020–21	884.6	42.2	43.0	14.7	373.7	380.5	130.4
2021–22	896.1	40.8	43.9	15.2	366.0	393.6	136.5
2022–23	907.2	39.4	44.8	15.7	357.6	406.8	142.7
2023–24	917.7	38.0	45.8	16.2	348.8	420.1	148.8
2024–25	927.9	36.6	46.7	16.7	339.4	433.5	155.0
2025–26	937.5	35.1	47.7	17.2	329.4	446.9	161.2

Source: Authors' calculations.

Table 9.12   Projected Labour Force by Type—Policy Scenario 2

Year	Total Labour Force (millions)	Share of Labour by Type			Total Labour Supply by Type (millions)		
		ILPE-labour	SE-labour	HE-labour	ILPE-labour	SE-labour	HE-labour
2011–12	763.0	54.7	35.0	10.3	417.1	267.4	78.5
2012–13	777.6	53.4	35.9	10.8	415.0	278.8	83.8
2013–14	792.1	52.0	36.7	11.3	411.7	291.0	89.3
2014–15	806.2	50.4	37.8	11.8	406.6	304.7	95.0
2015–16	820.2	49.1	38.7	12.3	402.3	317.1	100.7
2016–17	833.8	47.7	39.5	12.8	397.5	329.8	106.6
2017–18	847.2	46.3	40.4	13.3	392.0	342.6	112.6
2018–19	860.1	44.9	41.3	13.8	386.0	355.5	118.6
2019–20	872.6	43.5	42.2	14.3	379.4	368.5	124.7
2020–21	884.6	42.1	43.1	14.8	372.1	381.7	130.8
2021–22	896.1	40.6	44.1	15.3	364.3	394.9	137.0
2022–23	907.2	39.2	45.0	15.8	355.8	408.2	143.2
2023–24	917.7	37.8	45.9	16.3	346.8	421.5	149.4
2024–25	927.9	36.3	46.9	16.8	337.2	435.0	155.7
2025–26	937.5	34.9	47.8	17.3	327.1	448.5	161.9

Source: Authors' calculations.

Table 9.13   Projected Labour Force by Type—Policy Scenario 3

Year	Total Labour Force (millions)	Share of Labour by Type			Total Labour Supply by Type (millions)		
		ILPE-labour	SE-labour	HE-labour	ILPE-labour	SE-labour	HE-labour
2011–12	763	54.7	35.0	10.3	417.1	267.4	78.5
2012–13	777.6	53.4	35.9	10.8	415.0	278.8	83.8
2013–14	792.1	52.0	36.7	11.3	411.7	291.0	89.3
2014–15	806.2	50.3	37.9	11.8	405.8	305.4	95.0
2015–16	820.2	48.9	38.8	12.3	401.4	318.0	100.8
2016–17	833.8	47.5	39.7	12.8	396.4	330.6	106.8
2017–18	847.2	46.1	40.5	13.3	390.9	343.5	112.8
2018–19	860.1	44.7	41.4	13.8	384.7	356.5	118.9
2019–20	872.6	43.3	42.4	14.3	378.0	369.6	125.0
2020–21	884.6	41.9	43.3	14.8	370.6	382.8	131.2
2021–22	896.1	40.5	44.2	15.3	362.6	396.1	137.4
2022–23	907.2	39.0	45.1	15.8	354.0	409.5	143.7
2023–24	917.7	37.6	46.1	16.3	344.8	423.0	150.0
2024–25	927.9	36.1	47.0	16.8	335.1	436.5	156.3
2025–26	937.5	34.6	48.0	17.3	324.8	450.1	162.6

Source: Authors' calculations.

only marginal. For instance, in 2025–26, the projected size of HE labour ranges between 160.4 million (BAU) to 162.6 million (Scenario 3). Similarly, the projected size of the SE labour and ILPE labour too does not vary much across the scenarios. This suggests that the efficacy of public expenditure in education as an instrument for bringing about dramatic changes in the AE attainment, and hence, on the composition of labour force by education level could be limited. An important weak link here is the quality of education across all levels—primary, secondary, and higher that was mentioned earlier in the section 'Trends and Patterns in AE in India'. The challenge really is to bring about a dramatic improvement in the education system as a whole in the country in order to raise the education attainment of adults, both quantitatively and qualitatively.

CONCLUSIONS

The impact of progress in AE on the composition labour force by education attainment is not well understood in the Indian context. We have tried to address this gap in the literature in this chapter. Towards this, we first examined the trends and determinants of AE in India followed by the trends in labour-supply composition. We then carried out an exercise to project the labour supply by education level based on progress in AE attainment under different scenarios.

We examined the trends in the education attainment of young adults in the age group 18–40 years for women and 18–45 years for men using data from the NSSO for four quinquennial rounds namely, 55th (1999–2000), 61st (2004–05), 66th (2009–10), and 68th (2011–12). Education attainment was assessed in terms of LR, PAHE, and AYS. We found that that even though the country has made substantial progress in AE levels since the country became independent from colonial rule, nevertheless, substantial distance still remains to be covered. In 2011–12 in the country as a whole, one in four adult Indians remain illiterate, only 1 in 10 adult Indians has completed higher education, and the average years of schooling of adults is a very low at 6.7 years. We find that education attainment in terms of all the three indicators is higher for males than for female, though this gender gap, especially in literacy rate, has been narrowing over the years. Between rural and urban areas, the gap in LR and AYS has narrowed while that in PAHE has widened. Across states, all three indicators exhibit substantial variation in their levels and show uneven progress over time. The gap across states in LR has narrowed somewhat while in PAHE and AYS, it has widened. Based on

a review of the literature shows we find that qualitatively too the Indian education system has not been very efficient in turning out well trained labour force that is readily employable as pointed out in several studies in the past.

Turning to the determinants of AE, we find that the literature in India is scanty at best. A recent study on this is by Bhakta (2015) who has estimated econometric models to explain the annual growth in LR, PAHE, and AYS using the NSSO data across states. The results of this study show that social status still plays a crucial role in the society in determining actual progress in educational outcomes. While the share of expenditure in higher education is an important determinant of PAHE, expenditure on AE does not have significant impact on LR. She also finds that share of GSDP in industry and services and percentage of registered manufacturing are important demand pull factors that encourage education. Besides, percentage of rural households with irrigation facility is important to have better progress in education sector possibly via its impact on improving rural livelihood.

After examining trends and determinants of AE, we then studied trends in the composition of labour supply using NSSO data for the four quinquennial rounds mentioned earlier. For this we classified labour into three types based on their level of education attainment: (i) ILPE labour, (ii) SE labour, and (iii) HE labour. We find that between 1993–94 and 2011–12, though ILPE labour has declined from about 70 per cent of labour force to about 51 per cent reflecting an improvement in the literacy levels, nevertheless, the size of ILPE labour increased from 349 million to 417 million reflecting the growth in population and total labour force. The share of ILPE labour is higher in rural areas than in urban areas, though it has declined significantly in the former than in the latter. The slower reduction of ILPE labour in urban areas can be attributed to rural to urban migration. In 2011–12, the SE labour was about 300 million strong while HE labour was about 72 million. In rural areas, less than 5 per cent of the labour is HE labour. About 44 per cent of adults were not in labour force, of which nearly half of them were ILPE labour. Over time, more SE labour and HE labour are opting to stay away from labour force in both rural and urban areas. Over half the employed in 2011–12 are ILPE labour, though over time, the shares of SE labour and HE labour in total employment are rising. However, a majority of unemployed adults are SE labour and HE labour types and their shares have been increasing over time even though unemployment rate is quite low and stable at about 1 per cent to 1.5 per cent over the years. In terms of sector of employment, agriculture in the mainstay of ILPE labour and SE labour in rural areas, while in urban areas majority of them are in the non-agriculture sectors. In contrast, for the HE labour non-agriculture sectors are the main source of employment in both rural and urban areas.

Finally, we carried out an exercise to project the composition of labour force by education level under alternative scenarios over 15-year period of 2011–12 to 2025–26. For this we use the econometric models of the determinants of AE attainment estimated by Bhakta (2015) under certain simplifying assumptions. Specifically, we assume that the shares of HE labour and SE labour increase at the same rate as PAHE and AYS, respectively as projected by the econometric models of Bhakta (2015) and the proportion of ILPE labour being residually determined. Projections are made under a BAU scenario and three policy scenarios wherein public expenditure on higher education is raised by 10 per cent, 20 per cent, and 30 per cent, respectively over the levels in BAU scenario. Our results show that ILPE labour declines as a share in the total labour force and in absolute levels over the forecast period in the BAU and all three policy scenarios. In the BAU scenario, by 2025–26, ILPE labour accounts for only 35 per cent of the labour force and its size declines to about 332 million from 55 per cent and 417 million in 2011–12. Correspondingly, both SE labour and HE labour gain share, the latter at a faster rate, and grow in absolute size as well. In the BAU, the share and size of SE labour is 48 per cent and 445 million in 2025–26, and that of HE labour is 17 per cent and 160 million, respectively. Across alternative scenarios on public expenditure in higher education, we find that the projected size of all the three types of labour does not vary much. This, we think, reflects the low efficacy of education system in the country in general, and of public expenditure in higher education in particular, in bringing about dramatic improvements in the AE attainment, and hence, on the composition of labour force by education level.

The fall (rise) in the absolute size of the IPLE labour (SE labour and HE labour) may be expected to bring about a dramatic change in the structure of the labour market conditions in the country. The country could witness a growing (perhaps desirable) scarcity of IPLE labour for low-end/low-wage manual work across all sectors, while the supply of 'semi-skilled' and 'skilled' labour force would expand. This, in turn, would force all sectors to adapt their labour demand through appropriate changes in their production technologies. These changes

in both supply and demand would, in turn, cause the wage rates for these three types of labour to change.[7] At a macro-level, the challenge for government policy is to ensure that the transition in the labour market remains smooth. In particular, the rate at which demand for educated labour expands needs to be commensurate with the expansion in the supply of such labour. This is critical for maintaining social and political stability and for sustaining high economic growth over a fairly long period.

REFERENCES

Badr, M., O. Morrissey, and S. Appleton. 2012. 'Determinants of Educational Attainment in Mena.' *CREDIT Research Paper* 12(3): 1–38.

Barro, R.J. 2001. 'Human Capital and Growth.' *American Economic Review* 91(2): 12–17.

Barro R.J. and J.W. Lee. 1993. 'International Comparisons of Educational Attainment.' Journal of Monetary Economics 32(3): 363–94.

_____. 2010. 'A New Data Set of Educational Attainment in the World, 1950–2010.' NBER Working Paper 15902, National Bureau of Economic Research, Cambridge, MA.

Bhakta. R. 2015. 'Educational Attainment of Young Adults in India: Measures, Trends & Determinants.' WP-2015-034, Indira Gandhi Institute of Development Research, Mumbai.

Bhakta, R. and A. Ganesh-Kumar. 2014. 'Linkages between Parental Education, Utilization of Health Care Facilities and Health Status of Children: Evidence from India.' WP-2014-036, Indira Gandhi Institute of Development Research, Mumbai.

Blaug, M., P.R.G. Layard, and M. Woodhall. 1969. *The Causes of Graduate Unemployment in India*. London: Allen Lane the Penguin.

Drèze, J. and A. Sen. 1995. *India: Economic Development and Social Opportunity*. New Delhi: Oxford University Press.

Human Development Report. 1990. *The United Nations Development Programme (UNDP)*. New York: Oxford University Press.

ICEF Monitor. 2015. Available at http://monitor.icef.com/2015/10/indias-employability-challenge/ (accessed on 17 March 2016).

Lucas, R.E. 1988. 'On the Mechanics of Economic Development.' *Journal of Monetary Economics* 22: 3–42.

Mankiw, N.G., D. Romer, and D. Weil. 1992. 'A Contribution to the Empirics of Economic Growth.' *Quarterly Journal of Economics* 107(2): 407–37.

[7] Quantifying these impacts would require an economy-wide model such as a computable general equilibrium (CGE) model that characterizes both the supply and demand side of the market for different types of labour. Such an analysis is beyond the scope of this chapter.

Planning Commission. 2008. *Report of the Working Group on Labour Force & Employment Projections Constituted for the Eleventh Five Year Plan (2007–2012)*, Planning Commission, Government of India, New Delhi.

Rangarajan, C., P.I. Kaul, and Seema. 2011. 'Where Is the Missing Labour Force?' *Economic and Political Weekly*, 46(39): 68–72.

Rani, P.G. 2007. Secondary Education in India: Development and Performance, Working Paper, NIEPA, New Delhi. Available at http://www.esocialsciences.com/ (accessed on 7 July 2017).

Romer, P. 1990. 'Endogenous Technological Change.' *Journal of Political Economy* 99(5, part 2): S71–S102.

Tilak, J.B.G. 1979. 'Interstate Disparities in Educational Development in India.' *Eastern Economist* 73(3): 140–46.

_____. 1987. *Economics of Inequality in Education*. New Delhi: Sage Publications/Institute of Economic Growth.

_____. 1999. 'Emerging Trends and Evolving Public Policies on Privatisation of Higher Education in India.' In *Private Prometheus: Private Higher Education and Development in the 21st Century*, edited by P.G. Altbach, pp. 113–35. Westport: Greenwood Publishing.

_____. 2003. 'Higher Education and Development.' In *The Handbook on Educational Research in the Asia Pacific Region*, edited by J.P. Kleeves and R. Watanabe, pp. 809–26. Dordrecht: Kluwer Academic Publishers.

10

Labour Regulations and Worker Welfare
The Case of Provident Fund in India

Karthikeya Naraparaju and Ajay Sharma

INTRODUCTION

The impact of labour regulations on economic activity has been an issue of considerable interest in academic as well as policy circles in the Indian context. Some of the aspects being debated include the question of whether, and to what extent, labour regulations hamper the growth of jobs in India's formal sector. Two characteristic features of this literature and the debate surrounding it stand out: first, the relative overemphasis on select aspects of labour regulations pertaining to job security provisions (in particular, the Chapters V-A and V-B of the Industrial Disputes Act, 1947 [IDA][1]); second, the relative under-emphasis on the extent and nature of compliance with the labour regulations.

The excessive focus on select labour laws pertaining to job security provisions, such as the IDA, has come at the cost of a relative neglect of the impact of other labour regulations on worker welfare that, given their lower firm-size thresholds (for a firm to come under their ambit) combined with the preponderance of small-sized firms in the Indian economy, affect a much larger set of firms and workers employed in them. Further, before we look at the impact of labour regulations, it is pertinent to ask the extent to which these regulations are complied with on the ground. For, in the absence of such evidence, the 'regulation debate takes place in a purely theoretical setting, which may not match reality on the ground' (Chatterjee and Kanbur, 2015: 394). Given that regulations are weakly enforced in developing countries such as India, it is surprising that there has not been an adequate emphasis on arriving at the estimates of non-compliance with India's labour laws.[2]

In this chapter, we attempt to fill this gap by looking at compliance with an important labour regulation pertaining to workers' social security: the Employees Provident Fund and Miscellaneous Provisions Act, 1952 (hereafter, EPF Act), and specifically the Employees' Provident Fund

[1] For a detailed discussion on the features and impact of Chapter V-A and V-B of Industrial Dispute Act, 1947, the readers are referred to Bhattacharjea (2006) and Ahsan and Pagés (2009) and the references therein.

[2] Chatterjee and Kanbur (2015), a notable exception in this regard, provides the estimates of non-compliance with India's Factories' Act 1948 that applies to all manufacturing enterprises employing 10 or more workers with electricity or 20 or more workers without electricity.

Scheme, 1952 (hereafter, EPF) and the Employees' Pension Scheme, 1995 (hereafter, EPS) that were formulated under the EPF Act. Under these schemes, establishments employing 20 or more workers are mandated to provide social security contributions towards the provident fund (a pension and contingency fund) of those employees whose wages are below a certain threshold. In addition, workers enrolled in EPF are also required to contribute a share of their earnings to their fund.

We focus on the EPF Act for the following reasons: First, unlike the IDA or the Factories' Act, 1948 which are applicable only to the manufacturing sector, the EPF Act has wider coverage in terms of the sectors of work, and is mandatory to workers employed in any establishment employing at least 20 workers and not earning more than the threshold wage.[3] Second, the government's latest initiative for employment generation in the formal sector, the Pradhan Mantri Rojgar Protsahan Yojana (PMRPY), has brought the EPF Act into sharp focus. Launched in August 2016, the PMRPY aims to incentivize job creation for semi-skilled and unskilled workers by providing a partial subsidy on employers' contributions to the provident fund of all new employees earning up to Rs 15,000 per month, for a period of three years. For establishments in the labour-intensive textiles sector, the entire employer contribution to such workers' EPF is subsidized.[4] Such an initiative demonstrates the policymakers' belief in EPF's potential in delivering social security to workers. Moreover, it is consistent with the objective of achieving 'decent work for all', a key sustainable development goal adopted by the United Nations.

The government's initiative has come in the backdrop of a debate on the extent to which EPF is helpful to the workers. On the one hand, the EPF enables workers' access to social security. On the other hand, it is argued that the mandatory contributions under EPF impose a substantial pecuniary burden on the labourers, reducing their monthly 'take-home' earnings and thus might be counter-productive for worker welfare (Government of India, 2016; Sabharwal, 2014). Even before one looks into the relative merits of these arguments, in order to match these concerns with ground realities, it is important to know the extent and nature of compliance with the EPF Act. The objective of this chapter is to provide

such estimates and also look at the correlates of non-compliance with EPF Act.

The rest of this chapter is organized as follows: in the next section, 'The Employees Provident Fund: A Brief Overview and Data', we briefly describe the features of the EPF and EPS schemes and the data we use to arrive at our estimates. In the section 'Non-Compliance with the EPF Act: Estimates, Trends, and Covariates', we look at the trends in compliance with these schemes between 2004–05 (when worker-level survey data on access to work-related social security first became available) and 2011–12 (the latest year for which the data is available). In this section, we also look at the correlates of non-compliance with EPF Act, discuss how these relate to the concerns raised on its design, and suggest avenues for future research. In the section 'Discussion and Conclusion' we conclude by looking at the policy implications of our study.

THE EMPLOYEES PROVIDENT FUND: A BRIEF OVERVIEW AND DATA

In India, in order to provide social security to workers earning wages below a certain threshold (revised to Rs 15,000 per month or less, with effect from 1 September 2014) and working in enterprises employing more than a certain threshold number of workers (currently at 50 or more workers for cooperatives without power and 20 or more workers for all other establishments), the national government enacted the EPF Act. At present, the EPF Act is applicable to the whole of India, except for the state of Jammu and Kashmir. As in many other former British colonies, the provident fund in India combines workers' and employers' contributions to create individual savings accounts for the workers (Fields, 2012: 27). These accounts are meant to provide for the workers' retirement, resignation, and in the case of premature death, provide for the workers' family members. Further, under certain circumstances, workers can make a partial withdrawal from the EPF in the case of specific expenses such as house construction, illness, children's higher education, and marriage. Thus, EPF serves multiple purposes as a retirement as well as contingency fund. The amount payable at the end of the employment (either due to resignation, premature death, or retirement) includes the contribution made by the employee, the employer, and the interest accumulated on these contributions.

The reason for mandating a low-wage threshold for eligibility under the EPF Act is to cover workers who are more vulnerable to income and consumption shocks and are less likely to avail social security provisions, such

---

[3] Since September 2014, the wage threshold has been revised to Rs 15,000 per month. Prior to this, it was at Rs 6,500 per month.

[4] See 'Scheme Guidelines for Pradhan Mantri Rojgar Protsahan Yojana (PMRPY)'.

as pension funds and insurance, on their own. Some important features of this scheme are as follows: First, the employer as well as employee has to contribute some proportion of wages to the EPF.[5] Currently employees contribute 12 per cent of their wages.[6] The employers match the employees' contributions (subject to a maximum ceiling of wages of Rs 15,000 per month); out of the employer's 12 per cent contribution, 8.33 per cent goes into the worker's pension account under the Employees' Pension Scheme and the remaining 3.67 per cent is allocated to the worker's provident fund account.

The EPF Act also specifies that establishments (that come under the ambit of the act) can be exempted from providing contributions to the EPF and EPS, if they provide their employees (who come under the purview of the act) with an alternative provident/pension fund that, in the opinion of the government, has no less favourable contribution rates and benefits to the employees as compared to the EPF and EPS (Section 17 of the EPF Act, 1952).

Data

Given the illegality of non-compliance with labour regulations, it is difficult to obtain estimates of evasion from a direct survey of enterprises. However, we can discern such phenomena by looking at the responses given by the employees in a labour force survey. Since 2004–05, the quinquennial National Sample Surveys on Employment and Unemployment Situation (NSS) have captured data on workers' (self-reported) access to various social security provisions by the employers. In addition to health and maternity benefits, this also includes employers' contributions to employees' pension and various provident funds including, General Provident Fund, Contributory Provident Fund, Public Provident Fund, and Employees Provident Fund.

We use data from the 2004–05 (the 61st round) and 2011–12 (68th round) quinquennial NSS surveys to arrive at estimates of non-compliance with the EPF Act. If employees coming under the purview of the act by virtue of their wages and the size of their firm claim to be not receiving any provident fund or pension payments, we interpret this as non-compliance with the

act.[7] Thus, while computing our estimates we consider only those employees who are employed in a firm that employs 20 or more workers. Further, we do not consider workers employed in the state of Jammu and Kashmir because they do not come under the purview of the EPF Act. Moreover, we also exclude workers employed in cooperatives, trusts, and non-profit firms, due to lack of identification for eligibility under the EPF Act.[8]

Although the EPF Act is applicable to any employee 'who is employed for wages in any kind of work, manual or otherwise, in or in connection with the work of an establishment and who gets his wages directly or indirectly from the employer' (Section 2, Clause (f) of the EPF Act), we only consider those workers who are classified as 'regular salaried or wage workers' in the NSS dataset. The reason we exclude casual labourers is because there was some ambiguity with regard to the employers' liability in contributing provident fund payments to casual workers, at least until the time of the latest NSS survey in 2011–12. This ambiguity is evident from court judgments delivered in 2014 mandating employer contributions under the EPF Act for casual labourers (*Indian Express*, 2014).

Between 1 June 2001 and 31 August 2014, the wage threshold specified for coming under the purview of EPF Act was Rs 6,500 per month. Both the NSS surveys we are using were conducted during this period and we use weekly total wages (cash and kind) for regular salaried/wage employees given in the surveys and scale it up appropriately to arrive at the individual's monthly wage. This monthly wage is then used to compare with the threshold of Rs 6,500. For determining eligibility under EPF, the following components of an employee's wage are considered: 'basic wages, dearness allowance (including the cash

[5] For the purpose of the EPF, wages are defined as those including basic wages, dearness allowance (including the cash value of any food concession), and retaining allowance (if any) payable to the workers (see Chapter V of the EPF).

[6] The contribution rate for those working in sick or loss-making establishments is 10 per cent of their wages.

[7] Although the EPF Act grants exemptions to a few establishments from contributing to the provident and pension funds set up under the Act, this exemption is predicated on the employer contributing to an alternative fund whose benefits are no less favourable to the workers than provided by EPF. Hence, lack of employer contribution to *any* provident or pension fund of a worker implies non-compliance with the EPF Act.

[8] For cooperatives which do not use power, the size threshold for applicability of the EPF Act is 50 or more workers. The NSS data on enterprise size is interval based and consists of the following five categories: less than 6 workers; 6 and above; 10 and above but less than 20; 20 and above; not known. Given this, we cannot discern establishments with 50 or more workers from the data. Since the categories for the type of enterprises in the data club cooperatives with trusts and non-profit firms, we would have to exclude all of them from the analysis. In all, about 3 per cent of regular salaried workers in 2011–12 worked in cooperatives, trusts, and non-profit institutions.

value of any food concession) and retaining allowance (if any)' (Paragraph 29 of The Employees' Provident Fund Scheme, 1952). On the other hand, wages calculated in the NSS surveys include other components too (for example, bonus and prequisites[9]). Thus, by applying the threshold of Rs 6,500 on wages calculated from NSS, we could be *underestimating* the proportion of those coming under the purview of EPF Act by virtue of their wages.

The other caveat to be kept in mind while interpreting our estimates of evasion is the following: under the act, once an employee earning less than the wage threshold and working in an establishment employing more than 20 workers comes under its purview, his/her employer is mandated to contribute to the provident and pension funds regardless of whether, over time, the wage of the employee has risen above the threshold. Due to data constraints, we will not be able to capture evasion of provident fund contributions to those employees whose current wage is above the threshold but their wages when they first started working was below the threshold. We will be able to capture evasion for only those employees whose *current* earnings (as reflected in the respective NSS surveys) are less than the wage threshold.

NON-COMPLIANCE WITH THE EPF ACT: ESTIMATES, TRENDS, AND COVARIATES

In India, there were about 57.3 million regular salaried workers constituting 15 per cent of total labour force in 2004–05. This has increased to 74.3 million or about 18.7 per cent of the total labour force in 2011–12.[10] Analysing the distribution of regular salaried workers by the wage and firm-size thresholds specified under the EPF Act, we find that in 2004–05 (2011–12), around 75 (51) per cent of workers were earning wages less than Rs 6,500 per month whereas 25 (49) per cent of the workers were earning above the wage threshold. In absolute terms, workers earning below the wage threshold of Rs 6,500 have decreased from 40.5 million to 35.6 million between 2004–05 and 2011–12, whereas number of workers above the wage ceiling have increased by more than two and a half times from 13.2 million to 34.9 million during the same period.[11] This trend should not be surprising

given that over a period of seven years the growth in the nominal wages of the workers, due to inflation and other factors, would have pushed the wages of a greater proportion of them above the constant nominal wage threshold of Rs 6,500. The proportion of those employed for less than Rs 6,500 per month has come down across small (firms employing less than 20 workers) as well as the relatively large firms (employing 20 or more). Further, all those workers who join the workforce with a salary of more than Rs 6,500 per month during this period were automatically excluded from the applicability of the act. In other words, by not changing a nominal wage threshold over a period of 13 years (between June 2001 and August 2014), the wage criteria for coming under the purview of the act has been consistently diluted over time.

Coming to the second criterion of number of workers employed in a firm, we observe that share of workers employed in firms with number of workers being twenty or more, has increased from 37 per cent (16.5 million) to 41 per cent (26.3 million) between 2004–05 and 2011–12. Consequently, there was a small reduction in the share of regular workers employed in firms with less than 20 workers from 63 per cent in 2004–05 to 59 per cent in 2011–12.

Next, we analyse the incidence of provident fund provision by the employers of regular salaried workers and its trend during the period of analysis. We find that between 2004–05 and 2011–12, the incidence of provision of provident fund (PF) by employers[12] has decreased from 41.5 per cent to 38.2 per cent for the regular salaried workers; but in absolute terms the number of individuals accessing PF contributions from employers has increased from 21.7 million to 25.8 million during the respective period. A rise in the *proportion* of regular workers *not* accessing employers' PF contributions could be happening for multiple reasons: first, these workers might not be coming under the purview of the EPF either because they are joining a firm whose size is smaller than 20 workers, or because they are joining the workforce with a starting monthly wage greater than Rs 6,500. On the other hand, there could be an increase in the incidence of evasion of the EPF Act over time, wherein among those mandated

---

[9] Source: Chapter 4 of the supporting documents of the 61st and 68th rounds.

[10] We consider only usual principal activity status of the worker while calculating these numbers.

[11] Since some regular workers have not reported data on their wages, these numbers do not add up to 57.3 million and 74.3 million in 2004–05 and 2011–12 respectively.

[12] The term Provident Fund (PF) will include employers' contribution to General Provident Fund, Contributory Provident Fund, Public Provident Fund, Employees Provident Fund, etc. (Source: Chapter 4 of supporting documents of the 61st and 68th NSS rounds on employment and unemployment). If the worker does not receive contribution to any of these, it automatically implies he/she is not receiving EPF contributions.

to receive the PF contributions, a greater number of workers are not receiving them in 2011–12 as compared to 2004–05. Next, we look at these possibilities in detail.

Non-compliance with the EPF Act

We analyse compliance with the EPF Act by looking at the distribution of the incidence of employer contribution to PF for regular workers by the wage and firm size thresholds. We categorize regular workers into the following four groups: (i) workers employed in *small firms* (less than 20 workers) and earning *less than or equal to* Rs 6,500 per month; (ii) workers employed in *large firms* (20 or more workers) and earning *less than or equal* to Rs 6,500 per month; (iii) workers employed in *small firms* (less than 20 workers) and earning *more than* Rs 6,500 per month; and (iv) workers employed in *large firms* (20 or more workers) and earning *more than* Rs 6,500 per month. Workers in category (i) are not mandated to receive employers' PF contributions due to small firm size, whereas those in category (iii) and (iv) are not mandated to receive PF due to their wages being higher

than the threshold.[13] Therefore, only workers in category (ii) are mandated under the act to be receiving employers' contributions to PF.

In Table 10.1, we analyse the distribution of regular salaried workers across these four categories and the proportion of those receiving employers' provident fund contributions within each category, for the years 2004–05 and 2011–12.[14] For ease of interpretation, we will briefly explain the table's arrangement: the first row of data

[13] This is to be noted with the caveat that some employees whose current wage is above the threshold might have started their career with a wage below the threshold wage and hence come under the purview of the Act. However, data limitations imply that we will not be able to identify such employees.

[14] One point to be noted here is that the numbers provided in the earlier section in the context of workers' distribution by access to provident fund, wage threshold, and firm size, might slightly differ from those mentioned in Table 10.1. This is because there are some workers who have not provided information on all three of these indicators in the survey. In Table 10.1 only those workers who provide information for all three aspects are considered for analysis.

Table 10.1   Distribution of Regular Salaried Workers by Provident Fund Provisions for 2004–05 and 2011–12

Eligibility Criteria for Provident Scheme			Provident Fund/Pension Provisions Provided or Not					
			2004–05			2011–12		
Wage Ceiling (per Month)	Number of Workers in a Firm	Category	Yes	No	Total	Yes	No	Total
Less than or equal to Rs 6,500	Less than 20	(i)	2,998,737	21,359,870	24,358,607	1,322,985	21,680,971	23,003,956
			12%[#]	88%	100%	6%	94%	100%
			7%[*]	48%	55%	2%	35%	37%
Less than or equal to Rs 6,500	More than or equal to 20	(ii)	4,884,125	4,195,548	9,079,673	2,139,064	6,352,497	8,491,561
			54%	46%	100%	25%	75%	100%
			11%	10%	21%	3%	10%	14%
More than Rs 6,500	Less than 20	(iii)	2,975,231	499,633	3,474,864	6,994,859	6,897,987	13,892,846
			86%	14%	100%	50%	50%	100%
			7%	1%	8%	11%	11%	22%
More than Rs 6,500	More than or equal to 20	(iv)	6,576,914	559,684	7,136,598	12,772,089	4,226,191	16,998,280
			92%	8%	100%	75%	25%	100%
			15%	1%	16%	20%	7%	27%
	Total		17,435,007	26,614,735	44,049,742	23,228,997	39,157,646	62,386,643
			40%	60%	100%	37%	63%	100%
			40%	60%	100%	37%	63%	100%

Notes: [#] This number denotes the share of workers, in category (i) in the respective year, who have access to provident fund.
[*] This number denotes the share of regular salaried workers, in category (i) in the respective year, who have access to provident fund.
Source: Authors' calculations using unit level data from NSSO Surveys.

gives the absolute number of workers estimated in the respective category and year; the second row depicts the category-wise distribution of access to PF contributions in each year (thus adding up to 100); whereas the third row indicates the share of total regular salaried workers in a particular category in that year (all the third row percentages in a year together add up to 100). Therefore, the table provides information about all three indicators, that is, wages, size of the firm in which the regular workers are employed, and whether they received PF contributions by the employer.

The total number of regular salaried workers considered in our analysis has increased from 44.05 million to 62.4 million over the period 2004–05 and 2011–12. However, the share of workers with access to PF contributions, across all categories, has decreased from 40 to 37 per cent. Considering workers who are mandated to receive PF contributions under the act, that is, category (ii), we observe that they constituted 21 per cent of total regular salaried workers in 2004–05, which decreased to 14 per cent by 2011–12. Moreover, the absolute number of workers for whom PF payments are mandatory has also decreased from 9.08 million to 8.5 million during the same period. As discussed, this could be a result of not changing the nominal wage threshold over time and thus lowering its value in real terms. Even without a rise in real wages, if workers' wages are just inflation-indexed, the number of workers earning less than the nominal wage of Rs 6,500 reduces over time. This effect is evident from Table 10.1 where we see that an increase in the number of workers is occurring in the higher wage categories of (iii) and (iv). In both the lower wage categories (i) and (ii), we see a *reduction* in the number of workers over time.

Looking at category (ii), what is surprising though is that while the total number of workers under this category has decreased, the number of those not receiving PF contributions has actually *increased* during this period from 4.2 million to 6.4 million individuals. Consequently, the share of workers receiving PF contribution within category (ii) has decreased from 54 per cent to 25 per cent between 2004–05 and 2011–12. In other words, the incidence of non-compliance with the EPF Act has increased from 46 per cent to 75 per cent during this period.

Moreover, while a dilution of the wage threshold implies that fewer number of workers come under the purview of the EPF Act in 2011–12, since the rate of non-compliance with the act has increased over time, the proportion of workers whose PF payments are being evaded among all regular salaried workers has remained constant at about 10 per cent in both 2004–05 and 2011–12.

When we look at the type of enterprises where workers whose PF payments are evaded are employed, we see that in 2011–12 (2004–05) about 40 (34) per cent were employed with public and private limited companies, about 39 (36) per cent were employed with male proprietary establishments and about 9 (13) per cent were employed with government/public sector establishments.

Based on the two-digit National Industrial Classification code, we find the following industries to be employing more than 5 per cent of workers whose payments are evaded in 2011–12: manufacturing of products such as wearing apparel (7 per cent in 2011–12; 9 per cent in 2004–05), non-metallic mineral products (6 per cent in 2011–12; 3 per cent in 2004–05), textiles (6 per cent in 2011–12; 12 per cent in 2004–05), food products (6 per cent in 2011–12; 5 per cent in 2004–05), and leather and related products (5 per cent in 2011–12; 5 per cent in 2004–05), other sectors include education (5 per cent in 2011–12; 6 per cent in 2004–05) and waste collection activities (5 per cent in 2011–12; zero in 2004–05).

Such a large incidence of non-compliance with the act raises the important question of what it is that could be the reason for this phenomenon. Some have argued that such vast non-coverage could reflect the fact that these workers are employed on a contractual basis. Chakraborty (2016), for instance, shows that in the organized manufacturing sector, there has been a steady increase in the proportion of factories employing contract workers, from 23.01 per cent in 2003–04 to 33.48 per cent in 2010–11 and that the share of total non-wage benefits paid to workers in this sector has declined between 1999–2000 and 2011–12. However, contractual employment in itself does not preclude workers from being eligible for provident fund contributions. The Employees Provident Fund Act's definition of an 'employee' eligible for provident fund payments includes those who are employed through a contractor.[15] Given this, employing on a contractual basis by itself does not absolve the employer from contributing towards provident fund. What is plausible, though, is that the contract employees do not have any written proof of their employment contract with the employer. This way, employers could avoid any obligation towards these payments.

---

[15] As per Subsection 2 (f) (i) of The Employees' Provident Funds and Miscellaneous Provisions Act, 1952, the definition of an employee includes those 'employed by or through a contractor in or in connection with the work of the establishment'; also see Section 8A of the Act on the recovery of employer's contribution from the contractor and related issues.

Job Contracts and EPF

In this subsection, we explore the conjecture that job contracts do play an important role in the provision of PF. We argue that a written job contract between an employee and the employer acts as a proof of employment. As a result, this contract can be used by the employee to claim various benefits from the employer as mandated by various government legislations. Moreover, the contract can also be invoked in a court of law in case of any dispute. Thus, an employer who would like to evade mandatory social security contributions to its employees would want to ensure that the latter do not have proof of employment to claim the benefits.

Before we turn towards the evidence on this plausibility, it is important to note that the incidence of lack of written job contracts is quite widespread, regardless of whether the workers are eligible to receive provident fund payments or not. This can be seen from Table 10.2, where we analyse the distribution of workers with job contracts across the aforementioned four categories [that is, (i), (ii), (iii), and (iv)]. Overall, we observe that the share of regular salaried workers with job contracts is quite low and has actually decreased from 39 per cent to 34 per cent between 2004–05 and 2011–12, although in absolute numbers, it has increased from 17 million to 22 million in the same period. Looking at the disaggregated picture, we observe that while the incidence of job contracts has decreased across all the categories, among those workers for whom the PF scheme is mandated, that is, category (ii), the incidence of job contracts has had the greatest relative decline: from 48 per cent to 24 per cent in the period of analysis (see Table 10.2). For both the years, we see that incidence of job contracts is lower in low-wage categories (i and ii) than in relatively high-wage categories (iii and iv). This is the pattern we also see with respect to the provision of PF contributions in Table 10.1: high-wage workers were more likely to receive PF than low-wage workers, regardless of the firm size threshold. This pattern is robust across various wage deciles of regular salaried employees, not just at the wage threshold cut-off, as is evident from Figures 10.1 and 10.2.

Table 10.2   Distribution of Regular Salaried Workers by Job Contracts for 2004–05 and 2011–12

Eligibility Criteria for Provident Scheme			Has a Job Contract or Not					
			2004–05			2011–12		
Wage Ceiling (per Month)	Number of Workers in a Firm	Category	Yes	No	Total	Yes	No	Total
Less than or equal to Rs 6,500	Less than 20	(i)	4,299,075	20,068,207	24,367,282	2,918,047	20,846,748	23,764,795
			18%[#]	82%	100%	12%	88%	100%
			10%[*]	46%	55%	5%	32%	37%
Less than or equal to Rs 6,500	More than or equal to 20	(ii)	4,403,901	4,677,550	9,081,451	2,082,029	6,653,778	8,735,807
			48%	52%	100%	24%	76%	100%
			10%	11%	21%	3%	10%	14%
More than Rs 6,500	Less than 20	(iii)	2,638,783	837,254	3,476,037	6,126,818	8,253,232	14,380,050
			76%	24%	100%	43%	57%	100%
			6%	2%	8%	10%	13%	22%
More than Rs 6,500	More than or equal to 20	(iv)	5,681,503	1,456,458	7,137,961	10,915,954	6,396,272	17,312,226
			80%	20%	100%	63%	37%	100%
			13%	3%	16%	17%	10%	27%
	Total		17,023,262	27,039,469	44,062,731	22,042,848	42,150,030	64,192,878
			39%	61%	100%	34%	66%	100%
			39%	61%	100%	34%	66%	100%

Notes: [#] This number denotes the share of workers in category (a) in the respective year, who have access to job contract.

[*] This number denotes the share of regular salaried workers, in category (a) in the respective year, who have access to job contract.

Source: Authors' calculations using unit level data from NSSO Surveys.

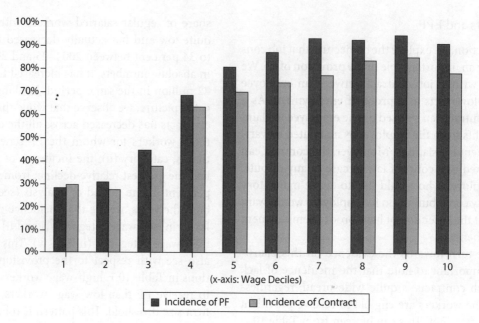

Figure 10.1   Incidence of PF and Job Contract among Regular Salaried Workers, 2004–05

Source: Author's own calculations.

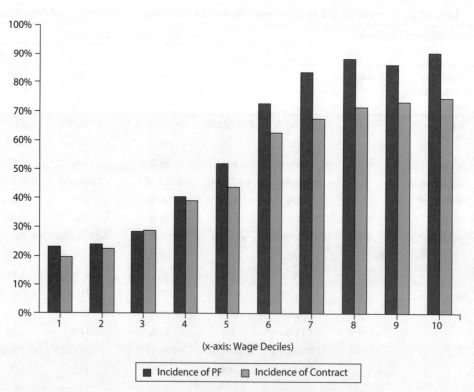

Figure 10.2   Incidence of PF and Job Contract among Regular Salaried Workers, 2011–12

Source: Authors' own calculations.

Different factors could be at play at each category that results in this phenomenon: first, firms employing workers in category (i) could be less productive (because of their small size), and though they do not come under the purview of EPF Act, it is conceivable that they do not provide a job contract to evade some other labour regulation that is binding on them but they cannot afford to comply with it; second, a large proportion of workers in category (iii) are employed with the government/public sector (44 per cent in 2011–12) making them more likely to possess a written job contract and have access to PF. Similarly, though we cannot underpin any causal relationship between job contracts and access to PF, we explore how non-compliance with the EPF Act is correlated with the incidence of job contracts.

In Table 10.3, we look at those eligible for receiving PF payments (that is belonging to category (iii) in Tables 10.1 and 10.2) and categorize them based on whether they have access to PF and possess a written job contract.[16] We see that among those who have access to PF about 46 per cent have access to job contract, although this has reduced sharply from about 70 per cent in 2004–05. On the other hand, among those who do not have access to PF, 84 per cent do not have a job contract, and this has increased from 76 per cent in 2004–05. The correlation between lack of access to social security in general and no job contracts has also been noticed with older data (NCEUS, 2007: 39).

[16] The total number of individuals mentioned in category (iii) in Tables 10.1 and 10.2 and those mentioned in Table 10.3 do not match because there are some individuals who have not given information about both PF and job contract. Only those individuals who give information on both are considered for Table 10.3.

Are Mandated Benefits Themselves the Culprit?

While we see that there is a strong correlation between eligible workers not receiving provident fund payments and lack of written job contracts for these workers, there could be multiple pathways through which this might be occurring.

Let us first consider the employer's perspective. For a small enterprise, registering its employees under the EPF entails a substantial pecuniary burden in the form of contributions towards their provident funds and other administrative costs. In a study, a substantial number of firms (35 per cent) found dealing with EPF-related regulations challenging. These were particularly great for small firms without dedicated administrative units to deal with regulatory compliance issues (Government of India, 2016: Volume 1, Chapter 10, 150).

In addition, even if these costs are assumed to be insignificant, the procedure of registration under the EPF scheme and the consequent inspections that it invites might expose the enterprise to other labour regulations such as the Employee State Insurance Act, 1948 (ESI) and, for manufacturing enterprises, the Factories Act, 1948. This is particularly the case since the firm size thresholds for coming under the purview of these three regulations are similar. The additional resources required to comply with these labour regulations might act as an additional disincentive for small firms to register under the EPF Act and garner unwarranted attention from the enforcement authorities.

Given all of this, firms can respond by choosing to stay out of the ambit of the regulation by reducing their size such that it is below the threshold and the regulation does not apply to them. Alternatively, to the extent that the enforcement is imperfect such that larger firms are more likely to be inspected than smaller firms (Almeida

Table 10.3 Distribution of Regular Salaried Workers Eligible for PF by Job Contracts for 2004–05 and 2011–12

Has Access to PF or Not	Has a Job Contract or Not					
	2004–05			2011–12		
	Yes	No	Total	Yes	No	Total
Yes	34,10,819	14,72,692	48,83,511	9,84,264	11,50,926	21,35,190
	70%	30%	100%	46%	54%	100%
No	9,92,916	32,02,632	41,95,548	10,27,885	53,24,612	63,52,497
	24%	76%	100%	16%	84%	100%
Total	44,03,735	46,75,324	90,79,059	20,12,149	64,75,538	84,87,687
	49%	52%	100%	24%	76%	100%

Source: Authors' calculations using unit level data from NSSO Surveys.

and Ronconi, 2016), firms can evade as long as their size is not too high relative to the threshold and they do not have any written job contract with the workers. However, to the extent that regulation forces an evading firm to stay smaller than its 'natural' size, there are inefficiencies being created.

From the employee's perspective, Sabharwal (2014) argues that the mandated contributions towards provident fund and employee state insurance payments by workers earning salaries at the lower end of the wage distribution imposes a substantial burden (up to 45 per cent of their gross salaries in some cases, as per his estimates) on the immediate finances of these workers. For workers earning as low as Rs 6,500 a month or less, this leaves them with too little cash for their immediate expenses. A related concern is the issue of the incidence of EPF contributions: while both employees and employers are mandated to contribute, the extent to which the burden falls on either of them is determined by the relative elasticities of labour supply and demand. If labour demand is more elastic than labour supply, the employer might partly offset its contributions to EPF by reducing the total wages paid to the employee (Government of India, 2016: Volume 1, Chapter 10, 149).

Although these contributions are, in principle, going to be eventually paid back to these workers when they retire, the poor service delivery of the agencies managing these benefits might make the workers unwilling to contribute a substantial portion of their salaries to these agencies. *Economic Survey (2015–16)* cites a study based on a survey conducted through phone at 'one of India's largest contract labour companies'. About 70 per cent of the respondents said that they would prefer receiving cash instead of contributing part of their salary into their EPF account (Government of India, 2016: Volume 1, Chapter 10, 149). The reasons given for such preference were that they prefer spending cash sooner and that the transaction costs associated with withdrawing their EPF monies were high. As evidence that suggests these high transaction costs, the survey also reports that a large number of EPF accounts (about 9.23 crore out of 15 crore accounts) are inoperative, accounting for about Rs 44,000 crore.

Anticipating difficulties in accessing these funds when they need them, workers might insist that the employer pay them their entire gross salary. The employers might oblige, but in turn, to avoid coming under the scrutiny of the enforcement authorities, take care that there is no written proof that they employ the worker. Thus, the burden of the mandated benefits might unintentionally drive the workforce towards informal employment. This,

of course, is over and above those who, in order to avoid making these contributions, chose to work in informal enterprises that are smaller than the mandated threshold of firm size.

While the aforementioned mechanism seems plausible, further investigation is required to understand whether this is indeed the reason behind a substantial proportion of workers not being covered in social security payments, though being eligible for them. Even if the mechanism is true, we need to be careful about drawing implications for policy. First, the suggestions given by Sabharwal (2014) and the *Economic Survey* that there is a need to improve EPF by, inter alia, facilitating competition by giving employees a choice to either save in other private alternatives as well as easing the procedures for compliance for the employers, are welcome. In fact, this is one of the reforms announced by the government in its special package for the textiles sector and the same should be extended to all the sectors.

Second, if the workers' desire to have higher net incomes is driving them towards informalization, then subsidizing wages might be explored wherein the government pitches in with the social security contribution for workers employed in small firms. Scholars have also been arguing for the need to incentivize employment generation by restructuring subsidies given to firms towards the labour they employ rather than the current system of subsidizing capital owners (*Financial Express*, 2016). This can be complemented with assistance towards developing workers' skills and access to technology for these firms under schemes such as the recently launched Technology Acquisition and Development Fund (TADF), so that these firms raise their productivity and grow out of the need to access these subsidies in the long-run. In this light, the government's latest scheme, PMRPY, to subsidize employer's contribution to EPF for those earning less than Rs 15,000 per month for the first three years is a step in the right direction. While the scheme is directed towards employers, this can incentivize them to pass on some of the benefits in the form of higher wages to the workers.

More importantly of course, we need further research to convincingly establish that workers are willing to give up benefits, and the extent to which they are willing to do this, in order to have higher net incomes. Lower take up of social security schemes such as the EPF could actually be a result of slack enforcement. Evidence from other contexts suggests that, with better enforcement, workers are willing to pay for mandated benefits by receiving lower wages (Almeida and Carneiro, 2012). In the Indian context, better enforcement of labour regulations, universalizing social security, and removal wage ceiling for schemes such as the EPF have been some of the demands of the labour unions.[17] This suggests that a better designed and well enforced provident fund scheme will promote greater access to social security for the workers.

DISCUSSION AND CONCLUSION

Many commentators have argued that India is at the cusp of a distinct advantage: its favourable demographic profile implies that a large proportion of its population is going to be in the working age group for the next few decades. If India is to leverage this 'demographic dividend' for enhancing its economic growth and reducing poverty, then generating adequate number of productive jobs is going to be crucial. Consequently, the thrust of several initiatives of the government is on incentivising job creation in the formal sector.

While ensuring that there are adequate job opportunities, it is imperative that there is access to work-related social security. This will ensure that these workers have adequate means to self-finance their retirement expenses and do not burden the state when its demographics turn relatively less favourable. Jobs with access to social security is also consistent with the United Nations' goal of achieving decent work for all, an important landmark in the evolution of the nature of work across the world. While the Indian democracy has ensured that various worker-related social security measures are legislated, evidence on the extent of compliance with such regulations is relatively scant. In this chapter, we have looked at the compliance with one such regulation: the EPF Act.

Our estimates suggest that the evasion of the EPF Act is quite widespread: in 2011–12, 75 per cent (6.3 million) of regular salaried employees earning wages below the threshold and working in establishments employing 20 or more workers have reported to be not receiving provident fund benefits. This has increased sharply from 46 per cent (4.2 million) in 2004–05. These individuals constitute about 10 per cent of the total workforce employed in regular salaried jobs, in the respective years. We find that lack of written job contracts is an important correlate of non-compliance with the act.

We then explored the various plausible reasons for such high non-compliance. From the employer's

perspective, a major impediment towards contributing mandated provident fund payments could be the associated costs. However, given the normative nature of the objectives of such regulations (for example, ensuring retirement corpus), it is neither desirable nor practically possible to dilute them. In this context, it is important that the government takes note of suggestions about subsidizing labour in place of its hitherto practice of subsidizing capital, particularly if India has to leverage its demographic dividend. In this light, the government's latest initiative to subsidize employer's contribution to EPF for those earning less than Rs 15,000 per month is a step in the right direction. Such measures, combined with better enforcement of the regulation, could bring more workers into the fold of formal employment. An important initiative being proposed by the government, which could improve enforcement, is mandating written job contracts for workers to establish a proof of their employment (*The Hindu*, 2016).

We also see that not indexing the wage threshold with inflation has meant that the regulation has become less stringent over the years, leaving many workers out of its ambit. In order to avoid this, the wage ceiling needs to be indexed to inflation. Further, there needs to be uniform criteria, in terms of firm size and wage threshold, for all welfare-related labour regulations (such as EPF and ESI). This is not only advantageous to the workers but also eases employers' transaction costs of complying with the regulations.

More fundamentally, one of the most pressing challenges before the Indian economy is to increase firm productivity so that firms generate jobs and can afford contributing towards mandated benefits. It is increasingly being realized that the path towards creating productive job opportunities, as traditionally followed by the developed countries, may no longer be so straightforward. In particular, the industrial history of developed countries in Europe, the USA, as well as in East Asia, has shown us that development has always been accompanied in the initial stages by tremendous growth in the manufacturing sector, which is later followed up with a pick-up in the service sector. A recent and most successful example of this model is China. However, as Rodrik (2015a) has argued, developing countries across the world are rapidly de-industrializing such that the share of value-added and employment engaged in manufacturing is peaking at increasingly lower levels of per capita incomes. Amirapu and Subramanian (2015) show this phenomenon to be taking place in nearly all states of India, including its manufacturing hubs of Gujarat, Maharashtra, and Tamil

[17] See Centre of Indian Trade Unions, available at http://citu-centre.org/index.php/component/k2/item/75-12-point-charter-of-demands

Nadu. Instead of formal jobs, informal employment in the trade, services, and low-productive manufacturing sector has emerged as a refuge for those transitioning out of agriculture. Given this, the challenge, as Rodrik (2015b) notes, is to strike a balance between democratically mandated worker welfare benefits, such as the EPF, while a significant proportion of the economy's labour force is still engaged in low-productive occupations.

REFERENCES

Ahsan, A., and C. Pagés. 2009. 'Are All Labor Regulations Equal? Evidence from Indian Manufacturing.' *Journal of Comparative Economics* 37(1): 62–75.

Almeida, R., and P. Carneiro. 2012. 'Enforcement of Labor Regulation and Informality.' *American Economic Journal: Applied Economics* 4(3): 64–89.

Almeida, R., and L. Ronconi. (2016). 'Labor Inspections in the Developing World: Stylized Facts from the Enterprise Survey.' *Industrial Relations: A Journal of Economy and Society* 55(3): 468–89.

Amirapu, Amrit, and Arvind Subramanian. 2015. *Manufacturing or Services? An Indian Illustration of a Development Dilemma*. Washington, DC: Center for Global Development and Peterson Institute.

Bhattacharjea, A. 2006. 'Labour Market Regulation and Industrial Performance in India: A Critical Review of the Empirical Evidence.' *Indian Journal of Labour Economics* 49(2): 211–32.

Centre of Indian Trade Unions. '12 Point Charter of Demands.' Available at http://citucentre.org/index.php/component/k2/item/75-12-point-charter-of-demands (accessed on 3 September 2016).

Chakraborty, S. 2016. 'Wages and Non-wage Benefits in Organised Manufacturing.' *Economic and Political Weekly* 51(3): 81.

Chatterjee, U., and R. Kanbur. 2015. 'Non-compliance with India's Factories Act: Magnitude and Patterns.' *International Labour Review* 154(3): 393–412.

Fields, G.S. 2012. *Working Hard, Working Poor: A Global Journey*. USA: OUP.

Financial Express. 2016. 'Need to be Careful about how We Count GDP, says Raghuram Rajan.' Available at http://www.financialexpress.com/article/industry/banking-finance/need-to-be-careful-about-how-we-count-gdp-raghuram-rajan/203740/ (accessed on 7 February 2016).

Government of India. 2016. *Economic Survey 2015-16*. New Delhi: Government of India.

Indian Express. 2014. 'Don't Withhold PF of Construction Workers: Delhi HC to Employers.' 24 September.

National Commission for Enterprises in the Unorganised Sector (NCEUS). 2007. *Report on Conditions of Work and Promotion of Livelihoods in the Unorganised Sector*. New Delhi: Government of India.

Rodrik, Dani. 2015a. 'Premature Deindustrialization.' *Journal of Economic Growth* 21(1): 1–33.

————. 2015b. 'The Evolution of Work.' Project Syndicate, 9 December. Available at http://www.project-syndicate.org/print/workers-rights-developing-economies-by-dani-rodrik-2015-12 (accessed on 5 February 2016).

Sabharwal, M. 2014. 'Pains of the Pay Cheque.' *Indian Express*, 25 November.

'Scheme Guidelines for Pradhan Mantri Rojgar Protsahan Yojana (PMRPY).' Available at http://www.labour.nic.in/whatsnew/scheme-guidelines-pradhan-mantri-rojgar-protsahan-yojana-pmrpy (accessed on 28 August 2016).

The Hindu. 2016. 'Appointment Letters to be Made Mandatory Soon.' 26 June.

PART II
SECTOR FOCUS: INDUSTRY, TRADE, AND PREPAREDNESS FOR 'MAKE IN INDIA'

11

Make What in India?

C. Veeramani and Garima Dhir

INTRODUCTION

Since the 1980s, there has been a turnaround in India's gross domestic product (GDP) growth performance. Yet, the process of structural change, in terms of transferring large pools of surplus labour from agriculture to non-agriculture, has been very slow. Agriculture accounted for, on average, about 18.1 per cent of India's GDP during 2011–13, but employed about 48.9 per cent of the total workforce in 2011 (*Economic Survey of India*, 2014–15). The growth process in China and other East Asian countries followed the conventional pattern of shifting labour from agriculture to labour-intensive manufacturing. By contrast, India has been skipping the intermediate stage of industrialization and directly moving to the final stage of services led growth.

A natural question is: why manufacturing? Historical evidence from difference parts of the world demonstrates the indispensable role that industrialization plays in the economic development process of countries. The experience of East Asian countries, in particular, shows that export-led industrialization is crucial for the attainment of sustained employment generation and poverty reduction. Recognizing the importance of a strong manufacturing sector for employment generation, the prime minister launched the 'Make in India' campaign with an aim to boost India's manufacturing sector. This campaign aims to transform India as a manufacturing powerhouse by promoting exports, encouraging Foreign Direct Investment (FDI), improving industrial productivity, and lowering the barriers to doing business. The government hopes to create 100 million jobs by 2022 and to increase the share of manufacturing in GDP to 25 per cent.

In this context, several questions have been asked, begging for answers that are theoretically founded and empirically substantiated. What are the industries which hold the greatest potential for growth and employment generation? What should be the nature of trade policy: should we pursue an 'ultra-export promotion strategy' or a neutral policy which favours neither the domestic nor the export market?[1] Should the government pursue an activist industrial policy by selectively promoting some industries or just play the role of a neutral facilitator? What roles do multinational corporations play and what kind of synergies can they establish with domestic companies? On the basis of evidence garnered from trade data analysis and literature, this chapter tries to provide answers to some of these questions.

---

[1] 'Ultra-export promotion strategy' involves subsidizing exporters with cheap inputs as well as an undervalued exchange rate (Bhagwati, 1978). It is generally argued some of the successful East Asian countries, including China, have followed this strategy.

As to the question of what to make in India, we argue that given our comparative advantage in labour-intensive activities and the imperative of creating employment for a growing labour force, there are two groups of industries that hold the greatest potential. First, there exists a significant unexploited export potential in India's traditional unskilled labour-intensive manufactured products such as textiles, clothing, footwear, toys, and so on (see Veeramani and Dhir, 2016 for a detailed analysis of this sector). Second, based on imported parts and components, India has a huge potential to emerge as a major hub for final assembly in a range of products, where production process is internationally fragmented and is mainly controlled by multinational enterprises (MNEs) within their global production networks (GPNs). In general, these products are not produced from start to finish within a given country. Based on the available literature, Athukorala (2011) has identified seven product groups where GPN- and fragmentation-based international trade is most prevalent. These product groups, referred to as 'network products' (henceforth NP), include office machines and automatic data processing machines (SITC 75), tele-communication and sound recording equipment (SITC 76), electrical machinery (SITC 77), road vehicles (SITC 78), professional and scientific equipment (SITC 87), and photographic apparatus (SITC 88).

Using highly disaggregated six-digit Harmonized System (HS) level trade data, this chapter provides a comparative descriptive analysis of the trends and patterns of India's exports of NP. We compare India's performance with that of China and selected developing countries from Southeast Asia. The selected countries include China, South Korea, Malaysia, Singapore, Thailand, and Vietnam. Based on export intensity indices, the chapter provides a list of specific NPs at the six-digit HS level where India's unexploited export potentials are the greatest.

The rest of the chapter is organized as follows. The next section provides a brief discussion on the concept of GPNs. The section 'Export Growth Performance and Domestic Value Added Share of Exports: General Overview' provides a general overview of India's merchandise export growth performance and domestic value added share of India's exports. 'Exports of Network Products' deals with trends and patterns of NP exports from India in a comparative perspective. In this section, using export intensity indices, we also identify the major NPs (at the six-digit HS level) where India has unexploited export potential. Finally, the last section concludes and discusses the policy implications.

CONCEPT OF GLOBAL PRODUCTION NETWORKS

Worldwide reduction in tariff barriers and technology-led decline in the costs of transportation and communication has made it possible to unbundle the production processes in several industries, with various stages occurring in different countries. Rapid growth of international fragmentation, notably since the 1980s, has led to a major change in the nature and pattern of world trade. Countries increasingly engage in trade by specializing in particular stages of good's production sequence or tasks rather than in final goods. Trade in parts and components (P&C) have grown much faster than trade in final goods as intermediate products cross national borders multiple times during the production process (see, for example, Athukorala, 2012; Baldwin and Lopez-Gonzalez, 2013; Feenstra, 1998; Hummels, Ishii, and Kei-Mu, 2001). The type of trade that results from interconnected production processes involving a sequential, vertical trading chain stretching across many countries, is described under various terminologies such as fragmentation trade, trade in NP, trade in middle products, task trade, and vertical specialization trade.

It is important to distinguish primary and conventional intermediate commodities and inputs (such as coal, timber, iron ore, iron and steel, rubber, primary chemicals, and so on) from fragmentation-based P&C (see Hummels, 2002 for this distinction). The latter appears further along the production chain and forms a layer between primary inputs and final consumer goods. Unlike in the case of primary and conventional intermediate inputs, international exchange of fragmentation-based P&C does not occur in organized markets. Trade in fragmentation based P&C generally takes place through a network of intra- and inter-firm relations rather than in an arms-length manner. Trade in primary and conventional intermediate inputs is usually explained by the natural resource endowments of exporting countries whereas the activities of MNEs are an important determinant of trade in fragmentation based P&C.

The concept of GPN has been developed as a way to analyse the complex link between a lead or a key firm and its suppliers in different countries.[2] Growth of GPN

[2] The concepts of global commodity chain (GCC) and global value chain (GVC) have also been used to describe the interconnected production process in a given industry across countries. Compared to GPN, the conceptualization of GCC/GVC is more restricted, focusing on the governance of inter-firm transactions and on the linear structures with sequential stages in the value chain. The GPN is a broader framework encompassing both

implies that trade involves not only the exchange of end products but, increasingly, of P&C that go into making them. Each country specializes in a particular fragment of the production process based on its comparative advantage, which, in turn, is determined by factor intensity of fragments and differences in factor prices across countries.

In certain industries, such as electronics and automobiles, technology makes it possible to sub-divide the production process into discrete stages. In such industries, fragmentation of production process into smaller and more specialized components allows firms to locate parts of production in countries where intensively used resources are available at lower costs. This geographic splintering of production gives rise to fragmentation-based trade. Labour-abundant countries ('factory economies') like China tend to specialize in low-skilled labour-intensive activities involved in the production of a final good while capital- and skill-intensive activities are being carried out in countries where those factors are abundant ('headquarter economies'). Thus, international firms might retain skill- and knowledge-intensive stages of production (such as Research and Development [R&D] and marketing) in the high-income headquarters (for example, the USA, EU, and Japan) but locate all or parts of their production in a low wage country (for example, China and Vietnam).[3]

Although the development of production networks is widespread, their growth in East Asia and China has been particularly impressive.[4] Export promotion policies of China, since the early 1990s, relied heavily on a strategy of integrating its domestic industries with regional and GPNs. This led to a remarkable increase in the share of NP, particularly electrical machinery, in its export

basket. Reflecting the differences in comparative advantage, the more advanced East Asian countries (Japan, South Korea, and Taiwan) became large exporters of P&C while low wage countries like China specializes in final assembly.

However, India has been locked out of the vertically integrated global and regional supply chains in manufacturing industries. Krueger (2010: 424) notes that 'India has not succeeded in attracting foreign investors to use India as an export platform in many of the unskilled-labour intensive industries that have been attracted to east and southeast Asia'. Athukorala (2014) notes that India has so far failed fitting into GPNs in electronics and electrical goods, which have been the prime movers of export dynamism in China and other high-performing East Asian countries. A number of large MNEs in electronics and electrical goods industries have set up production bases in India, but they are mainly involved in production for the domestic market. However, in the case of automobile industry, studies suggest a steady growth in India's integration with GPNs (Athukorala, 2014; Tewari and Veeramani, 2016). A number of leading automobile companies have established assembly plants in India and some of them have begun to use India as an export base within their global production networks. Since the early 2000s, India's exports of assembled cars (completely built units) have increased at a much faster rate than automobile parts (Athukorala, 2014). Overall, though India's exports of assembled vehicles recorded some growth, the country remains as a minor player in fragmentation based trade, particularly in electronics and electrical goods.

EXPORT GROWTH PERFORMANCE AND DOMESTIC VALUE ADDED SHARE OF EXPORTS: GENERAL OVERVIEW

Export Growth Performance

During the first decade of economic reforms (1993–94 to 2001–02), India's merchandise exports in dollars grew at the rate of about 8 per cent a year. This is slightly better than the average growth rate of 7 per cent a year in the 1980s but pales in comparison with the growth rate of 18 per cent a year in the 1970s (Veeramani, 2012). Table 11.1 shows the average annual growth rates of India's merchandise and services exports for various sub-periods during 2000–01 to 2015–16. Based on export growth performance, two different phases can be identified during the post-2000 period: (i) a relatively long period of high growth from 2000–01 to 2011–12, and (ii) the

---

intra- and inter-firm relationships, both linear and non-linear linkages, and all relevant sets of actors.

[3] This pattern is clearly evident from analysis, based on World Input Output Database (WIOD), by Baldwin and Lopez-Gonzalez (2013). It is found that China's participation in international supply chains lies heavily in labour-intensive final assembly while the high-income countries specialize in the production of technologically sophisticated P&C within the value chain. Based on the technological asymmetry in the international production network, Baldwin and Lopez-Gonzalez make the distinction between 'headquarter economies' and 'factory economies'. They note that '… firms in the headquarter economies (mostly the US, Japan and Germany) arrange the production networks while factory economies provide the labour' (Baldwin and Lopez-Gonzalez, 2013: 19).

[4] Though not as dynamic as the ones in East Asia, strong production networks also exist in Europe (for example, between Germany and Hungary/Czechoslovakia) and North America (for example, within NAFTA).

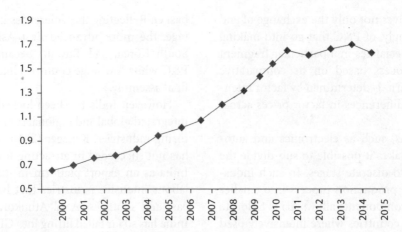

Figure 11.1   India's World Market Share in Merchandise Exports (Per Cent)

Source: Authors' estimation using data extracted from WTO website[5]

Table 11.1   Growth Rates of India's Merchandise Exports (Valued in $ Million, Percentage)

Period	Oil	Non-Oil	Total
2000–01 to 2011–12	39.8	18.4	20.4
2000–01 to 2005–06	45.2	18.1	19.8
2006–07 to 2011–12	21	17	17.6
2012–13 to 2015–16	–19.6	–0.9	–4.1

Source: Authors' estimation using data from Reserve Bank of India (RBI, various years).

more recent period of negative growth from 2012–13 to 2015–16. The first phase (2000–01 to 2011–12) is further divided into two equal sub-periods of six years each: 2000–01 to 2005–06 and 2006–07 to 2011–12.

In stark contrast to the first decade of the reforms, India's merchandise exports recorded an exceptionally high growth rate of 20 per cent a year during 2000–01 to 2011–12 (Table 11.1). During this period, oil exports grew faster than non-oil exports; share of the former in total merchandise exports increased steadily from virtually zero in 1999–2000 to about 20 percent by 2012–13. India's share in world exports of merchandise increased steadily from 0.66 per cent in 2000 to 1.65 per cent in 2011 (Figure 11.1). Yet, India's world market share is paltry compared to over 10 per cent for China in 2011.

Since 2012, India's merchandise exports plummeted with a negative growth rate of 0.9 per cent per annum. The

decline has been particularly steep for oil exports with a negative growth rate of almost 20 per cent in current US dollars. While India's share in world merchandise exports remained, more or less, unchanged since 2012, China's market share recorded a consistent increase accounting for nearly 14 per cent of world exports in 2015.

Composition of Exports

The composition of Indian exports shows an anomaly in that, despite being a labour-abundant country, the fast-growing exports from India are either skilled labour intensive or capital intensive. While the share of capital-intensive products increased consistently from about 32 per cent in 2000 to nearly 53 per cent in 2015, the share of unskilled labour-intensive products declined from about 30 per cent to 17 per cent (Veeramani, 2016).[6] This type of specialization is an anomaly in a country like India with large pools of unskilled labour. Due to its idiosyncratic specialization, India has been locked out of the vertically integrated global supply chains in many manufacturing industries. It is almost tautological to state that export growth that is driven by capital- and skill-intensive industries cannot be sustained in a capital scarce but labour-abundant economy.

The disproportionate bias of its export composition towards capital- and skill-intensive products have provided India with a comparative advantage in relatively poorer regions (such as Africa) but at the cost of losing

---

[5] Available at https://www.wto.org/english/res_e/statis_e/merch_trade_stat_e.htm (accessed on 10 July 2017).

[6] Capital intensive products accounted for only a quarter of India's exports in 1993 (Veeramani, 2012).

market shares in the richer countries. Products from India with high technology and skill content are unlikely to make inroads to the quality-conscious richer country markets. These products, however, might enjoy a competitive advantage in the relatively poorer countries. At the same time, rich country markets provide a huge potential for labour-intensive exports from developing countries such as India. Thus, specialization out of traditional labour-intensive products implies a general loss of India's export potential in advanced country markets.[7]

In the past, high-income OECD (Organisation for Economic Co-operation and Development) countries accounted for a major share of India's export basket. However, their dominance has declined considerably over the last two decades. The aggregate share of these markets in India's merchandise exports decreased from 58.2 per cent in 1992 to 38.6 per cent in 2015. On the other hand, India's market share in low and middle income countries increased steadily from 18.4 per cent in 1992 to 35.8 per cent in 2015. For China, the share of high-income OECD countries increased sharply from 37.7 per cent in 1992 to 62 per cent in 2000 and then declined to 47.5 per cent in 2015. Despite the decline during the last decade, China's trade orientation in high-income OECD countries remains significantly higher than that of India. Contrary to the general perception, there exists a great potential for India to expand and intensify its export relationships with the traditional developed country partners. However, this would necessitate greater participation in GPNs and a realignment of India's specialization on the basis of its true comparative advantage in labour-intensive process and product lines.

Domestic Value Added Content of Gross Exports

The extent of a country's participation in GPN can be gauged by measuring vertical specialization—that is, the amount of imported inputs embodied in goods that are exported (see Box 11.1). Multi-country production networks imply that intermediate inputs cross borders several times during the manufacturing process, and trade is recorded (in gross terms) at each time this happens. Ideally, trade statistics should be collected and reported on value added basis rather than in gross terms. However, unlike the recording of domestic transactions, trade data are usually collected and reported as gross flows at each border crossing rather than the net value added between border crossings. This leads to double (or multiple) counting. Thus, published trade data overstates the domestic value added content of exports. Countries with greater participation in GPNs are expected to show lower domestic value added content of exports.

Box 11.1 Measurement Vertical Specialization

Vertical specialization occurs when (i) a good is produced in two or more sequential stages, (ii) two or more countries provide value added during the production of the good, and (iii) at least one country must use imported inputs in its stage of the production process, and some of the resulting output must be exported. Following Hummels et al. (2001), vertical specialization in country k, and sector i is given as:

$$vs_{ki} = \left(\frac{m_{ki}}{y_{ki}}\right) x_{ki}$$

where

m_{ki} = imported intermediates in country k, and sector i
y_{ki} = gross output of country k, and sector i, and
x_{ki} = gross exports from country k, and sector i.

Vertical specialization can thus be seen as the import content of exports expressed in value terms. Aggregating across sectors i for country k, and taking into account imported inputs used *indirectly* in production of an exported good, vertical specialization in country k (that is, the share of aggregate imported intermediates embodied in a country's aggregate exports) can be shown in matrix notation as:

$$VS_k = uA^M \left[I - A^D\right]^{-1} X/x_k$$

where u is $1 \times n$ vector of 1's, A^M is the $n \times n$ imported coefficient matrix (elements a_{ij} of this matrix denotes imported inputs from sector i used to produce one unit of sector j's output), A^D is the $n \times n$ domestic coefficient matrix, I is the identity matrix, X is an $n \times 1$ vector of exports, x_k is a scalar that denotes the aggregate value of exports from country k and n is the number of sectors. The numerator of the above equation measures all the imported inputs that are needed to produce the exports of country k from all n sectors. Dividing this by the amount of aggregate exports yields the share of country k's exports attributable to imported inputs—that is, the share of foreign value added in exports.

---

[7] An illustrative example will make this point clearer. India's exports of passenger motor vehicles (SITC 7810), a capital and skill-intensive product group, increased remarkably from USD 102 million in 2000 to USD 5,392 million in 2015, registering an annual growth rate of 34 per cent. In 2015, high-income OECD countries accounted for only 22 per cent of Indian exports of passenger motor vehicles while low and middle income countries accounted for 68 per cent. On the other hand, India's exports of apparel (SITC 84), a traditional labour-intensive group, grew at a much lower rate of 9 per cent per annum during 2000–15. In 2015, while high-income OECD countries accounted for 64 per cent of India's exports in this category, low and middle income countries accounted for just 12 per cent.

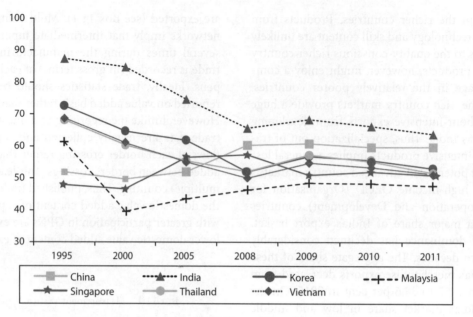

Figure 11.2   Domestic Value Added Share of Manufactured Exports (Per Cent)

Source: OECD TiVA Database

Based on OECD's Trade in Value Added (TiVA) database, Figure 11.2 reports domestic value added share of gross exports (domestic share) between 1995 and 2011 for India and a number of comparator countries from East and Southeast Asia.[8] Domestic value added share of gross exports is a measure that illustrates how much value added is generated throughout the economy for a given unit of exports. The lower the ratio the higher the foreign content and so the higher the importance of imports to exports.[9]

As far as changes over time are concerned, it is evident from Figure 11.2 that the domestic share has declined for India, Korea, Malaysia, Thailand, and Vietnam. In contrast, China's domestic share shows some increase while that of Singapore remained broadly stable. Turning to values for the year 2011, the countries with the lowest domestic shares include Malaysia (47.6 per cent), Singapore (51 per cent), Vietnam (51.2 per cent), Thailand (51.7 per cent), and Korea (53.1 per cent). China has

recorded a value of 59.9 per cent while India's domestic share has been the highest throughout the period (63.9 per cent in 2011, down from 87.4 per cent in 1995). India's domestic share values suggest that while the country's integration with GPNs has increased over the years, the level of its integration remains significantly below that of other countries.

It must be noted that the calculation of value added content of exports is usually based on the assumption that production techniques and input requirements are the same for exports and domestically absorbed final goods. This assumption would overstate the value added content of exports for countries such as China and Mexico that have large export processing sectors (Koopman, Powers, Wang, and Wei, 2010; Johnson and Noguera, 2012). For example, in China, processing exports account for about half of overall exports. For countries with large processing exports, it is appropriate to compute domestic shares adjusting for processing trade. Estimates for the year 2004 by Johnson and Noguera (2012) confirm that once processing exports are separately taken into account, the domestic shares fall substantially from 0.70 to 0.59 for China and from 0.67 to 0.52 for Mexico. The domestic shares reported in Figure 11.2 are without adjusting for processing trade and hence, could underestimate the extent of production sharing for countries such as China.

Figure 11.3 shows domestic shares across different manufactured product groups for the year 2011. It is evident that India's domestic share is higher than that of

---

[8] TiVA Database: http://stats.oecd.org/Index.aspx?DataSet Code=TIVA2015_C1 (data extracted on 12 Feb 2016 04:44 UTC (GMT) from OECD Stat).

[9] Input-output (I-O) tables, used for the estimation of domestic share, are usually published at typically long time intervals (usually every five years). For example, the latest I-O table available for India is for the year 2007–08. Therefore, the times series estimates of domestic share are generally obtained using interpolated and extrapolated I-O structure.

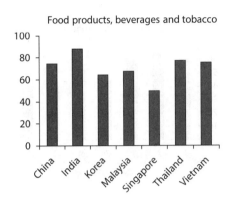

Food products, beverages and tobacco

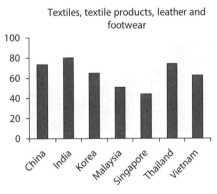

Textiles, textile products, leather and footwear

Wood and products of wood and cork

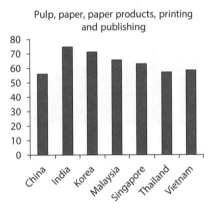

Pulp, paper, paper products, printing and publishing

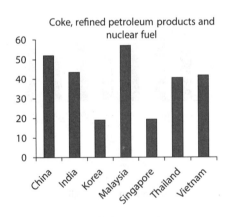

Coke, refined petroleum products and nuclear fuel

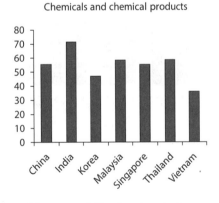

Chemicals and chemical products

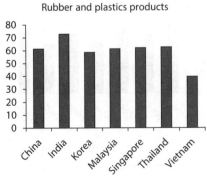

Rubber and plastics products

Other non-metallic mineral products

(Cont'd)

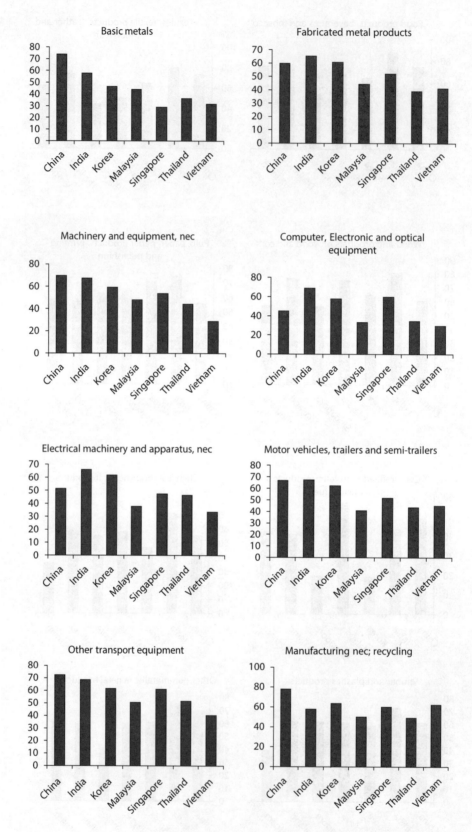

Figure 11.3   Domestic Value Added Shares of Exports across Product Groups (Percentage)

Source: OECD TiVA database

other countries for most of the product groups, with the notable exception of coke, refined petroleum products and nuclear fuel, base metals and manufacturing nec (not elsewhere classified) and recycling. China records higher domestic shares than India for base metals, machinery and transport equipment nec, other transport equipment, and manufacturing nec and recycling.

As can be seen in Figure 11.2, product groups with the lowest values of domestic shares include highly import dependent sectors such as refined petroleum products, base metals, and fabricated metal products. These sectors mainly use primary and conventional intermediate inputs such as coal, iron ore, iron and steel, and so on. The group of NP, in Figure 11.2, broadly corresponds to 'computer, electronic and optical equipment', 'electrical machinery and apparatus nec', 'machinery and equipment nec' and 'motor vehicles, trailers and semi-trailers'. Fragmentation-based trade is most prevalent in these sectors, which is reflected in their relatively low domestic value added shares. In contrast, domestic shares are found to be relatively high in sectors such as 'food products, beverages and tobacco', 'wood products', 'paper products', and so on.

Table 11.2 shows the changes in domestic shares across product groups for India and China during the period 1995–2011. Between 1995 and 2011, India's domestic shares have declined in all product groups, with magnitude of the decline being relatively high for sectors using conventional intermediate inputs (coke, refined petroleum products, and nuclear fuel; manufacturing nec, recycling, basic metals, and fabricated metal products) as well as for NP (motor vehicles, trailers and semi-trailers; electrical machinery and apparatus, nec; machinery and equipment, nec and computer, electronic and optical equipment). For China, in contrast, domestic shares have increased in several product groups, notably in NP. The recent increase in China's domestic shares notwithstanding, domestic value added content of India's exports remains significantly higher than that of China for most of the product groups. Further, when comparing the domestic shares of India with China, we must keep in mind the possibility that the values reported in Table 11.2 could be an overestimation for China as they are unadjusted for processing exports.

Table 11.2 Domestic Value Added Shares of Exports Across Product Groups (Percentage)

Product Groups	India				China			
	1995	2000	2005	2011	1995	2000	2005	2011
Food products, beverages, and tobacco	92.8	92.2	88.6	87.9	61.1	64.7	74.8	74.6
Textiles, textile products, leather, and footwear	90.2	90.4	85.0	80.2	56.7	61.8	69.1	73.5
Wood and products of wood and cork	92.0	90.5	86.2	80.5	65.3	62.3	72.1	60.6
Pulp, paper, paper products, printing, and publishing	85.9	84.9	79.7	74.7	26.8	31.8	50.1	56.1
Coke, refined petroleum products, and nuclear fuel	73.4	57.1	54.5	43.4	41.8	39.2	48.0	52.0
Chemicals and chemical products	85.9	86.5	78.3	71.4	43.7	44.4	53.6	55.4
Rubber and plastics products	84.6	88.1	78.6	72.9	49.2	49.7	55.7	61.4
Other non-metallic mineral products	84.2	77.4	77.6	75.5	78.5	77.1	73.0	70.0
Basic metals	81.5	74.1	68.2	57.9	74.5	72.3	72.7	73.8
Fabricated metal products	83.7	77.4	71.4	65.3	51.4	50.9	59.5	59.8
Machinery and equipment, nec	83.7	81.4	73.2	67.4	60.0	61.0	65.2	69.6
Computer, Electronic, and optical equipment	84.6	78.8	72.3	68.8	26.3	22.5	31.2	45.0
Electrical machinery and apparatus, nec	84.9	80.5	73.4	66.0	30.3	31.8	43.2	51.4
Motor vehicles, trailers and semi-trailers	87.2	82.1	77.7	67.5	41.8	46.0	58.9	66.9
Other transport equipment	83.9	78.6	74.8	68.5	62.9	66.0	64.3	72.4
Manufacturing nec; recycling	83.7	82.3	72.8	57.6	71.9	74.1	74.1	77.7

Source: OECD TiVA Database

EXPORTS OF NETWORK PRODUCTS

Empirical Approach and Data

As discussed, being a labour-abundant country, India enjoys significant comparative advantage in the assembly of NP. To what extent has India been successful in exploiting this comparative advantage? In order to provide an answer to this question, this section deals with a descriptive analysis of India's export trends and patterns in NP. To place the discussion in a proper comparative perspective, the analysis also covers China and selected countries from Southeast Asia.

While the measures of trade in value added are useful for understanding the extent of vertical specialization, these indicators are not appropriate for tracking a country's actual performance in fragmentation-based exports. For one thing, the input-output (I-O) tables, used for the estimation of trade in value added, are usually published at typically long-time intervals (usually every five years). For example, the latest I-O table available for India is for the year 2007–08.

Another option for the purpose at hand is to rely on published trade data at a detailed level of disaggregation. This approach helps us in tracing the growth and pattern of fragmentation based exports by constructing suitable indicators at the aggregated and disaggregated level using the latest available data on trade flows. The customs classification, however, does not give us a straightforward way of partitioning trade data on the basis of clear conceptual categories related to fragmentation based trade. We, therefore, follow Athukorala's (2011) observation that the only practical way is to focus on the specific product categories in which fragmentation trade is heavily concentrated. He argued that GPN and fragmentation-based trade are most prevalent in a group of products referred to as 'network products' (NP).

Following this approach we build a disaggregated dataset on network products using the United Nations (UN) Comtrade database that we concorded with the UN-Broad Economic Categories (BEC) system to separate out P&C from assembled end products (AEP). To build this dataset, we first identified codes at the six-digit level of the Harmonized System (HS) of trade classification that corresponded with the group of NP.[10]

This yielded a total of 576 product codes at the six-digit HS level. We next identified and separated about 241 codes related to P&C within NP using the BEC system of classification. The value of *assembly trade* (that is, AEP) was approximated as the difference between the total value of trade in NP and the value of trade in P&C within this category.[11]

Trends and Patterns of NP Exports

Figure 11.4 shows the trends in the values (USD Billion) of NP exports from India and comparator countries during the period 2000–14. India's NP exports increased from about 2 billion dollar in 2000 to 24 billion dollar in 2014. Though India's exports of NP grew at the rate of about 22 per cent per annum during the period 2000–14, the dollar value of its exports for the year 2014 (24 billion) is miniscule compared to that of other countries: China (932 billion), Korea (258 billion), Singapore (162 billion), Malaysia (88 billion), Thailand (81 billion), and Vietnam (47 billion).

Of the total exports of 24 billion dollars by India in 2014, AEP accounted for a higher proportion (14 billion) compared to P&C (10 billion). The importance of P&C exports in relation to AEP varies significantly across countries. This can be seen clearly in Figure 11.5, which depicts the share of the two groups in the national export baskets of different countries for the period 1990–2014. Relatively richer countries such as Singapore and Malaysia show significantly higher share of P&C than end products. For Korea, however, the two groups account for broadly similar shares. On the other hand, relatively low wage countries (China, Vietnam, and India) record higher share of AEP as compared to P&C. While P&C accounted for higher share than AEP in Thailand's exports until the mid-2000s, the pattern got reversed since then. Similarly, for India, P&C accounted for slightly higher share than AEP until the mid-2000s, but the latter started occupying higher position since then. In general, it may be noted that low wage countries enter into NP by specializing in labour-intensive assembly activities. Over the years, as wage rates go up and workers acquire new skills, exports of P&C expand while low-end assembly activities witness a relative decline. While India's exports of AEP have shown some growth

---

[10] The concordance table between HS-1988/92 and SITC codes corresponding to NP, available in World Integrated Trade Solution (WITS), is used for this purpose.

[11] Therefore, at the 6-digit HS level, the total number of AEP within the category of NP is 335 (= 576 – 241).

NP Exports

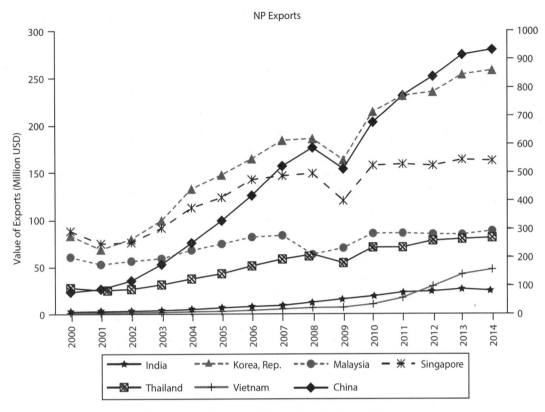

Figure 11.4 Exports of Network Products, USD Billions

Source: Authors' estimation using data extracted from COMTRADE-WITS. http://wits.worldbank.org/ (accessed on 10 July 2017).

in recent years, the country is still in the nascent stage of assembly line production.

Table 11.3 reports the share of each country in world exports of NP as well as the share of NP in each country's total merchandise exports for 2000 and 2014. That India is relatively a minor player in NP is evident from the fact that in 2014 its exports account for a meager 0.5 per cent in world exports of NP, up from 0.1 per cent in 2000. By contrast, exports from China accounted for close to 20 per cent of world exports in 2014, followed by Korea (5.4 per cent), Singapore (3.4 per cent), Malaysia (1.8 per cent), Thailand (1.7 per cent), and Vietnam (1 per cent). Between 2000 and 2014, the market shares of Malaysia and Singapore experienced a decline while other countries, most dramatically that of China, recorded an increase. China's market share has increased phenomenally for both P&C and AEP. However, being a major assembly hub, AEP record significantly higher market share than P&C in both the years for China. That Vietnam is emerging as an important hub for assembly related activities is evident from the fact that its share in the world exports of AEP increased

from almost nil in 2000 to 1.2 per cent in 2014. For both P&C and AEP, Vietnam recorded significantly lower market share than India in the year 2000. However, the world market share for Vietnamese products (both P&C and AEP) stands more than double than that of India in 2014.

These trends can also be seen by referring to the shares of NP in national export basket. While the share of NP in India's export basket increased from 5 per cent in 2000 to 7.7 per cent in 2014, it remains abysmally lower than those of other countries. For the year 2014, NP accounted for 40 per cent or more in the export baskets of Korea, China, and Singapore; 35 per cent or more in the export baskets of Malaysia and Thailand; and about 31 per cent of Vietnam's exports. Between 2000 and 2014, the share of NP in national export basket has increased for China, Vietnam, and India while other countries recorded a decline. Growth in the share of NP in the export baskets of China, Vietnam, and India has been mainly driven by AEP while the share of P&C remained broadly unchanged in these countries. Looking at the pattern across countries and over the years, it is clear that

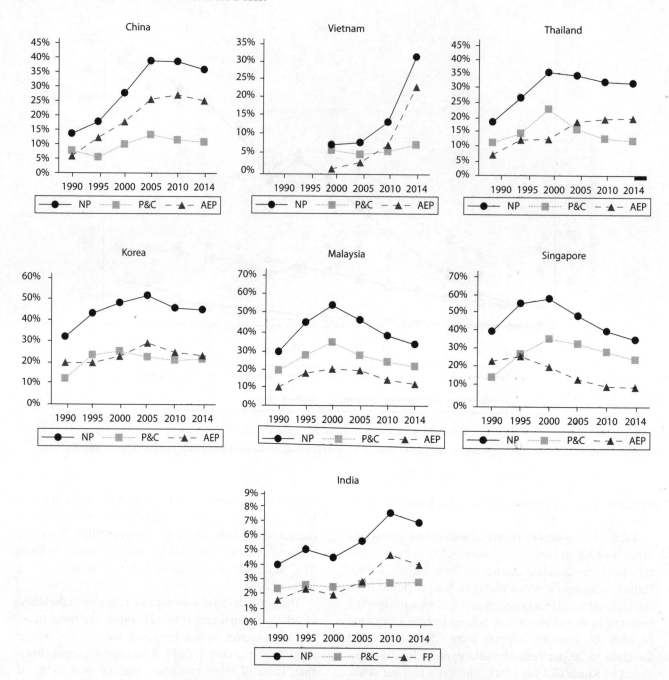

Figure 11.5   Share of NP, P&C, and AEP in National Export Basket

Source: Authors' estimation using data extracted from COMTRADE-WITS. http://wits.worldbank.org/ (accessed on 10 July 2017).

there exists significant opportunities for India to expand its exports of NP, particularly AEP.

The distribution of NP exports, as shares of national export basket, across the two-digit SITC groups is depicted in Figure 11.6. It is evident that the relative importance of different product groups varies significantly across countries and over time. The export basket of Malaysia and Singapore are highly concen-

trated in electrical machinery (SITC 77) while China and Korea depicts greater diversification. For China, SITC 77 and SITC 76 (telecommunication and sound recording equipment) records the largest export share (about 12 per cent in 2014 for each) closely followed by SITC 75 (office machines and automatic data processing machines). Together, these three product groups accounted for about 34 per cent of China's merchandise

Table 11.3 Exports of NP: Share in World Exports and Share in National Export Basket

	Total	P&C	AEP	Total	P&C	AEP
		2000			2014	
Share in World Exports of NP						
China	3.71	2.91	4.38	19.57	15.20	22.33
India	**0.10**	**0.13**	**0.08**	**0.51**	**0.55**	**0.49**
Korea	4.02	4.61	3.53	5.41	6.74	4.58
Malaysia	2.91	4.03	1.96	1.84	3.06	1.08
Singapore	4.25	5.85	2.90	3.40	6.23	1.63
Thailand	1.32	1.87	0.86	1.69	1.66	1.72
Vietnam	0.05	0.10	0.02	0.99	0.65	1.20
Share in Each Country's Total Merchandise Exports						
China	30.72	11.01	19.70	39.81	11.94	27.87
India	**5.01**	**2.80**	**2.21**	**7.68**	**3.19**	**4.49**
Korea	48.20	25.26	22.94	45.00	21.63	23.37
Malaysia	61.10	38.74	22.36	37.49	24.04	13.46
Singapore	63.67	40.12	23.55	39.57	27.97	11.60
Thailand	39.64	25.63	14.01	35.45	13.39	22.06
Vietnam	7.83	6.34	1.49	31.26	7.92	23.34

Source: Authors' estimation using COMTRADE-WITS database

exports in 2014. As far as Korea is concerned, the export composition is somewhat different from that of China though SITC 77 still holds the largest share (17 per cent in 2014). As expected, road vehicles (SITC 78) account for a significant share (about 13 per cent in 2014, next to SITC 78) in Korea's export basket while the share of SITC 75 is relatively small. Together, SITC 76, 77, and 78 account for about 37 per cent of Korea's total merchandise exports in 2014. Vietnam's exports are highly concentrated in SITC 76, accounting for 18 per cent of its total merchandise exports.

The main product groups in India's export basket include SITC 78, accounting for 4.3 per cent of exports in 2014, and SITC 77 with a share of 2 per cent. India's export growth of NP between 2000 and 2014 has been mainly brought about by SITC 78, mainly AEP within this group. India's export share in SITC 77, the most important category for several comparator countries, is extremely small. There exists a significant potential for India to emerge as a hub for electrical machinery manufacturing and assembly. At the same time, being a large country with varied resource endowments and skill sets, India has the potential to export a diversified set of NP, as seen in the case of China.

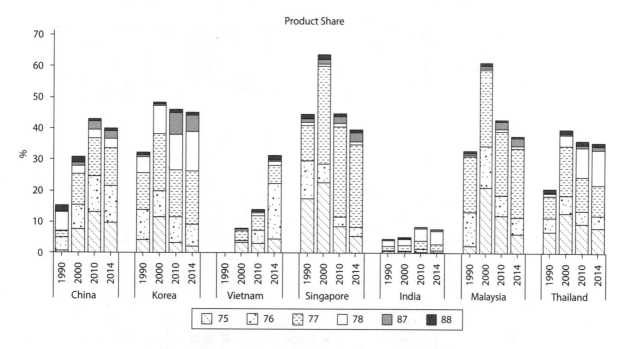

Figure 11.6 Composition of Network Product Exports (Per Cent)

SITC 75: Office machines and automatic data processing machines
SITC 76: Telecommunication and sound recording equipment
SITC 77: Electrical machinery
SITC 78: Road vehicles
SITC 87: Professional and scientific equipment
SITC 88: Photographic apparatus
Source: Authors' estimation using COMTRADE-WITS database

Figure 11.7 shows the geographical direction of exports, separately for P&C and AEP. That India is locked out of the regional production network in Asia is abundantly clear from these graphs. For all countries, except for India, East and Southeast Asian region accounts for an overwhelmingly large share of P&C exports. Furthermore, there is no evidence to show that India is improving its participation in the regional production network over the years: in fact, the share of East and Southeast Asia in India's exports of P&C declined from 21 per cent in 2000 to 17 per cent in 2014. For the year 2014, the share of East and Southeast Asia region in the total exports of P&C stands at above 75 per cent for Vietnam, above 60 per cent for Malaysia, Korea, and Thailand, and

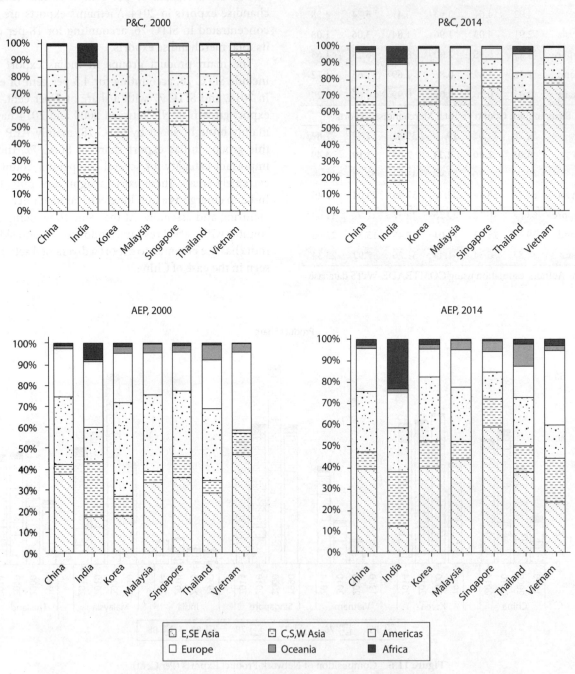

Figure 11.7   Geographical Direction of Exports, P&C, and AEP

Source: Authors' estimation using COMTRADE-WITS database

Notes: E, SE Asia: East and Southeast Asia

C,S, W Asia: Central, South and West Asia

about 55 per cent for China. Europe accounts for the largest share of India's P&C exports (27 per cent) closely followed by Americas (24 per cent) and 'Central, West and South Asia' (21 per cent).

For the category of AEP too, the geographical direction of India's exports is strikingly different from that of comparator countries. 'Central, West and South Asia' accounts for the largest share of India's exports of AEP (26 per cent) closely followed by Africa (23 per cent). Between 2000 and 2014, the share of Africa increased remarkably from 8 per cent to 23 per cent while the share of Europe and East and Southeast Asia declined significantly. This pattern clearly indicates that much of the recent growth observed in India's AEP exports, mainly road vehicles, is driven by the demand originating from the African region. In contrast, for the comparator countries, East and Southeast Asia region provides the major market for AEP (except for Vietnam, for which Europe accounts for the largest share). Traditional rich country markets like Americas and Europe accounts for a relatively smaller share in India's exports of AEP (37 per cent in 2014) compared to China (48 per cent), Korea (43 per cent), Malaysia (43 per cent), and Vietnam (51 per cent).

Contrary to the general perception, there exists a great potential for India to expand and intensify its export relationships in NP with traditional developed country partners. While India's exports of assembled cars have increased significantly since the early 2000s, it is important to note that Indian made automobiles are unlikely to make inroads into the traditional richer country markets, though they enjoy a competitive advantage in the relatively poorer regions such as Africa. In order to exploit the potential in rich country markets, India needs to strengthen its participation in global and regional production networks in a wide range of NP (especially electrical machinery and electronics) while also building on its existing strength in automobile assembly. It is important to keep in mind that the absolute size of rich country markets continue to remain much larger compared to that of poor country regions and that it is crucial to tap this market.

INDIA'S EXPORT POTENTIAL IN NP: ANALYSIS BASED ON EXPORT INTENSITY INDICES

Empirical Approach and Methods

How do India's exports of NP to a given destination region (r) compare with the structure of competing country group's (c) exports to the region r? Is India supplying products that are important to a given destination region, and are there opportunities that India is missing and can

potentially grow into? Is India's export of a given NP (p) under-represented or *biased* against a given destination region as compared to India's exports to other regions and world as a whole? To help answer these questions and to identify the products (p) and markets (r) where India has unexploited export potentials, we estimate export intensity indices as defined below.

$$EI_1 = \frac{S_{ipr}}{S_{cpr}} \qquad (1)$$

where

$$S_{ipr} = x_{ipr} \Big/ \sum_p x_{ipr}$$

(India's export of network product p to destination region r (x_{ipr}) divided by India's total manufactured exports to destination region r)

$$S_{cpr} = x_{cpr} \Big/ \sum_p x_{cpr}$$

(Competing country group's export of network product p to destination region r divided by competing country group's total manufactured exports to destination region r)

We consider two competing country groups: (i) the set of developing countries from Asia and (ii) the whole group of developing countries (that is, the set of low and middle income countries). The list of destination regions (r) considered for the analysis include: (i) Africa, (ii) Americas, (iii) Central, South, and West Asia, (iv) East and Southeast Asia, (v) Europe, and (vi) Oceania.

A value greater than 1 for EI_1 indicates that the share of p in India's total manufactured exports to a given region is larger than the corresponding share of the competing country group; values less than 1 are suggestive of unexploited export potential for India in a given product p and in a given market r.

We also estimate another export intensity index, as defined below.

$$EI_2 = \frac{S_{ipr}}{S_{ipw}} \qquad (2)$$

where

$$S_{ipw} = x_{ipw} \Big/ \sum_p x_{ipw}$$

(India's world export of network product p (x_{ipw}) divided by India's total manufactured exports to world w).

The value of EI_2 index indicates whether or not India's export of product p is under-represented or *biased* against a given region r relative to India's exports of p to world as a whole. A value greater than 1 for EI_2 indicates that the share of p in India's total manufactured exports to a given region exceeds the share of p in India's total manufactured exports to the world; values less than 1 are suggestive of unexploited export potential for India.

In order to make sure that we end up identifying the products which are important for world trade as well as for the destination region under consideration, we apply two separate stages of data filtering. First, we exclude those six-digit HS codes with less than 0.05 per cent share in total world exports of NP for the year 2014. As a result, the total number of HS codes was reduced from 576 to 271, of which 123 codes belong to the group of AEP while the remaining 94 codes represent P&C. It must be noted that the 271 codes, left after filtering, still account for 96 per cent of total world exports of NP. Second, we exclude those 6-digit HS codes with less than 0.05 per cent share in the total import of NP by a given destination region, r.

Identification of Products and Markets with Export Potential

Table 11.4 provides the number of AEP (six-digit HS codes) where values of EI_1 are found to be equal to or greater than 1, with the group of Asian developing countries as the competing group. Table 11.5 provides similar results for P&C. Similar results corresponding to the values of EI_2 is reported in Table 11.6 and 11.7 respectively.[12] These tables also report the shares of each SITC two-digit group in world exports of NP as well as

12 To save space, results with all developing countries as the competing group are not reported, but are available with the authors. The results remain broadly the same for the two sets of competing country groups.

Table 11.4   Number of Assembled End Products (Six-Digit HS Codes) where Values of $EI_1 \geq 1$ for 2014

| SITC | Share in World NP Exports | No. of Products (Six-Digit) | No. of Six-Digit Codes with $EI_1 \geq 1$ | | | | | | Extensive Margin |
			Africa	Americas	Central, South, and West Asia	East Southeast Asia	Europe	Oceania	
75	8.6%	6	0	0	0	0	0	0	0%
76	11.9%	20	1	1	1	1	1	2	6%
77	6.1%	34	4	3	1	3	2	1	7%
78	19.7%	24	8	6	9	2	6	2	23%
87	6.7%	29	12	6	5	7	5	8	25%
88	1.7%	10	0	0	3	1	1	1	10%
Total	54.7%	123	25	16	19	14	15	14	
Extensive Margin			20%	13%	15%	11%	12%	11%	14%

Source: Authors' Estimation Using COMTRADE-WITS Database

Table 11.5   Number of P&C Products (Six-Digit HS Codes) where Values of $EI_1 \geq 1$ for 2014

| SITC | Share in World Exports | No. of Products (Six-Digit) | No. of Six-Digit Codes with $EI_1 \geq 1$ | | | | | | Extensive Margin |
			Africa	Americas	Central, South, and West Asia	East Southeast Asia	Europe	Oceania	
75	2.7%	2	1	1	0	1	1	1	42%
76	4.0%	5	0	0	1	0	0	0	3%
77	23.5%	51	14	7	10	11	15	12	23%
78	8.6%	19	4	7	6	7	6	4	30%
87	1.5%	10	4	2	1	1	5	6	32%
88	0.7%	7	0	1	1	0	0	2	10%
Total	41.0%	94	23	18	19	20	27	25	
Extensive Margin			24%	19%	20%	21%	29%	27%	23%

Source: Authors' Estimation Using COMTRADE-WITS Database

Table 11.6 Number of Assembled End Products (Six-Digit HS Codes) where Values of EI$_2 \geq$1 for 2014

SITC	Share in World Exports	No. of Products (Six-Digit)	No. of Six-Digit Codes with EI$_2 \geq$1					
			Africa	Americas	Central, South, and West Asia	East Southeast Asia	Europe	Oceania
75	8.6%	6	2	1	3	5	1	2
76	11.9%	20	6	6	8	8	1	3
77	6.1%	34	11	5	11	11	13	4
78	19.7%	24	19	3	16	3	2	3
87	6.7%	29	11	13	6	12	13	5
88	1.7%	10	0	1	3	6	1	2
Total	54.7%	123	49	29	47	45	31	19
Extensive Margin			40%	24%	38%	37%	25%	15%

Source: Authors' estimation using COMTRADE-WITS Databas

Table 11.7 Number of P&C Products (Six-Digit HS Codes) where Values of EI$_2 \geq$1 for 2014

SITC	Share in World Exports	No. of Products (Six-Digit)	No. of Six-Digit Codes with EI$_2 \geq$1					
			Africa	Americas	Central, South, and West Asia	East Southeast Asia	Europe	Oceania
75	2.7%	2	1	1	0	1	1	1
76	4.0%	5	0	0	1	0	0	0
77	23.5%	51	14	7	10	11	15	12
78	8.6%	19	4	7	6	7	6	4
87	1.5%	10	4	2	1	1	5	6
88	0.7%	7	0	1	1	0	0	2
Total	41.0%	94	23	18	19	20	27	25
Extensive Margin			24%	19%	20%	21%	29%	27%

Source: Authors' estimation using COMTRADE-WITS Database

the number of HS-six digit codes within each of the SITC two-digit group.

The 'extensive margin' reported in these tables for each destination region and for each SITC two-digit groups is defined as follows.

'Extensive margin' for destination region r

$$= \frac{\text{Number of HS 6-digit codes with } EI_1 \geq 1 \text{ for region } r}{\text{Total number HS 6-digit codes}}$$

For example, in Table 11.4, the extensive margin for Africa for the year 2014 = 25/123 ≈ 20 per cent

'Extensive margin' for a given SITC group:

$$= \frac{\begin{array}{c}\text{Number of HS 6-digit codes with } EI_1 \geq \\ 1 \text{ for a given SITC group across all regions}\end{array}}{(\text{Number of HS 6-digit codes}) \times (\text{Number of destination region})}$$

For example, extensive margin for SITC 78 for the year 2014 = 33/(24×6) ≈ 23 per cent.

Extensive margins can be computed analogously with respect to EI$_2$, our second measure of export intensity (see Tables 11.6 and 11.7).

Referring to Table 11.4, it can be seen that, among the two-digit groups, AEP corresponding to SITC 78 accounts for 20 per cent in world exports of NP, followed by SITC 76 (accounting for 12 per cent world NP exports) and SITC 75 (9 per cent of world NP exports). In terms of the number of products (HS six-digit codes), however, SITC 77 ranks at the top followed by SITC 87, SITC 78, and SITC 76. Together, the 123 selected AEP, account for about 55 per cent total world exports of NP.

Among the different SITC groups, extensive margin is found to be the highest for SITC 87 (25 per cent) followed by SITC 78 (23 per cent) and SITC 88 (10 per cent). Within SITC 87, the number of HS codes with

$EI_1 \geq 1$ found to be the largest for Africa (12) followed by Oceania (eight) and East and Southeast Asia (seven). Within SITC 78, the number of cases with $EI_1 \geq 1$ are the largest for Central, South, and West Asia (nine) followed by Africa (eight). Among the various destination regions, the extensive margin is found to be the largest for Africa (20 per cent) followed by Central and South West Asia (15 per cent). Overall, for all regions and commodity groups taken together, the extensive margin for AEP stands at 14 per cent for the year 2014. The results remain broadly the same when we consider the group of all developing countries as the competing group though the overall extensive margin is found to be slightly lower at 12 per cent.

P&C corresponding to SITC 77 account for 24 per cent of total world exports of NP while P&C of SITC 78 account for only 9 per cent of world NP (Table 11.5). This pattern is in contrast with that observed in Table 11.4 for AEP where SITC 78 and SITC 76 accounted for the largest shares in world exports. Together, the 94 selected P&C account for 41 per cent of world exports of NP. As far as P&C are concerned, SITC 77 and SITC 78 are the largest categories, not only in terms of their share in world exports, but also with respect to the number of six-digit products. The overall extensive margin for P&C (23 per cent) is higher than that for AEP (14 per cent).

The purpose of estimating EI_1 is to assess whether or not India holds an export potential by comparing India's export structure with that of a competing country group. Our second export intensity measure EI_2 is used to assess export potential from a different perspective—that is, to see whether or not India's export is *biased* against a given destination region r relative to India's overall exports to the world. Tables 11.6 and 11.7 report the number of HS codes with $EI_2 \geq 1$ for AEP and P&C, respectively.

The results in Table 11.6 shows that India's exports of AEP is biased in favour of Africa (with an extensive margin of 40 per cent) and Central, South, and West Asia (with an extensive margin of 38 per cent) and biased against Oceania, Americas, and Europe.[13] Therefore, the assembly related exports from India are primarily targeted in low and middle income countries in Africa and Asia while significant potential exists to expand exports to traditional rich country markets. The high export intensity in Africa and Central, South and West Asia is primarily driven by AEP corresponding to SITC

78 (Road Vehicles). When it comes to P&C, India shows a greater export bias in favour of Europe and Oceania (primarily driven by SITC 77) and against Americas and other Asian countries (see Table 11.7).

Finally, based on EI_1 index, we attempt to identify the major products at the six-digit HS level where India has an unexploited export potential. Table 11.8 reports EI_1 for all six-digit codes corresponding to assembled end products and Table 11.9 gives similar list for P&C. Shares of each product in world exports of NP for the year 2014 are reported in both the tables. These tables include only those HS codes accounting for at least 0.5 per cent in world NP exports. Referring to both the tables, it is clear that, with some exception within SITC 78 and SITC 87, India holds unexploited export potential for almost all products and across all destination markets.

It can be seen that only three products record $EI_1 \geq 1$ across all destinations: these products are (i) HS 870322 (automobiles with reciprocating piston engine of cylinder capacity exceeding 1000cc but not exceeding 1500cc.); (ii) 901890 (other instruments and appliances of medical science); and (iii) 901890 (other instruments and appliances of medical science). The first two of them correspond to SITC 78 while the third one corresponds to SITC 87. The products grouped under HS 870322 mostly include small passenger cars. For HS 870323 (Automobiles, spark ignition engine of 1500–3000 cc), which includes mostly bigger passenger cars, the $EI_1 \geq 1$ for two destination regions—Africa and Americas. For this category, India holds a potential to expand exports to other destination regions, particularly in Asia. For HS 870332 (Vehicles; compression-ignition internal combustion piston engine, diesel or semi-diesel, cylinder capacity exceeding 1500cc but not exceeding 2500cc), India has shown high export intensity with respect to Africa, Americas, and Central, South, and West Asia while there exists a significant potential to penetrate into other regional markets.

CONCLUSION AND POLICY IMPLICATIONS

With increasing wage costs, Chinese firms in the labour-intensive industries are under pressure and have started looking for other low-cost locations. An important question in this context is: can India become the next workshop of the world? This chapter argues that the industries which hold the greatest potential for growth and employment generation in India include: (i) traditional labour-intensive products and (ii) NPs, particularly labour-intensive assembly. Within the group of NP, India's present strength primarily lies in assembly related activities given its vast manpower.

---

[13] Extensive margin in Table 11.6 is obtained by dividing the number of HS codes with $EI_2 \geq 1$ by total number of HS codes corresponding to assembled end products. For example, extensive margin of 40 per cent for Africa is obtained by dividing 49 by 123.

Table 11.8 Values of EI_1 and World Exports Shares across HS Six-Digit Codes, AEP, 2014

HS Code	Product Description	SITC Code	Share in World NP Exports	Africa	Americas	Central, South, and West Asia	East and Southeast Asia	Europe	Oceania
847120	Digital computers with CPU and input-output units	75	3.4%	0.1	0.0	0.0	0.0	0.0	0.0
847193	Storage units, whether or not presented with the rest of a system	75	1.6%	0.1	0.0	0.0	0.0	0.0	0.0
847191	Digital computer CPU with some of storage/input/output	75	1.5%	0.1	0.0	0.2	0.0	0.0	0.0
847192	Input or output units, whether or not presented with the rest of a system and whether or not containing storage units in the same housing	75	1.4%	0.0	0.0	0.0	0.1	0.0	0.0
847199	Automatic data processing machines and units, nes	75	0.6%	0.3	0.0	0.1	0.1	0.1	0.2
852520	Transmit-receive apparatus for radio, TV, etc.	76	4.9%	0.3	0.0	0.2	0.0	0.0	0.0
851782	Telegraphic apparatus, nes	76	2.5%	0.1	0.1	0.1	0.3	0.1	0.1
852810	Colour television receivers/monitors/projectors	76	1.9%	0.0	0.3	0.1	0.1	0.0	0.0
852110	Magnetic tape-type video recording & reproducing apparatus	76	0.7%	0.0	0.0	0.0	0.1	0.0	0.0
850440	Static converters, nes	77	1.1%	0.4	0.3	0.2	0.6	0.5	0.4
854380	Electrical machines and apparatus, nes	77	0.6%	0.1	0.1	0.1	0.0	0.1	0.5
870323	Automobiles, spark ignition engine of 1500-3000 cc	78	5.8%	1.2	11.1	0.2	0.2	0.1	0.1
870332	Vehicles; compression-ignition internal combustion piston engine (diesel or semi-diesel), cylinder capacity exceeding 1500cc but not exceeding 2500cc	78	3.0%	0.9	8.6	1.3	0.1	0.0	0.1
870324	Vehicles; spark-ignition internal combustion reciprocating piston engine, cylinder capacity exceeding 3000cc	78	2.6%	0.0	0.0	0.0	0.0	0.0	0.0
870322	Vehicles with spark ignition internal combustion reciprocating piston engine, of a cylinder capacity exceeding 1,000 cc but not exceeding 1,500 cc.	78	1.6%	5.0	4.0	3.3	5.0	2.7	10.1
870421	Vehicles; compression-ignition internal combustion piston engine (diesel or semi-diesel), for transport of goods, (of a gvw not exceeding 5 tonnes), nec	78	1.0%	0.8	0.5	1.0	0.4	0.0	0.1
870333	Vehicles with compression ignition internal combustion piston engine (diesel or semi-diesel), of a cylinder capacity exceeding 2,500 cc.	78	0.8%	0.3	0.0	1.0	0.0	0.3	0.0
870120	Tractors; road, for semi-trailers	78	0.7%	0.1	0.0	0.4	0.7	0.2	0.0
870431	Gas powered trucks with a GVW not exceeding five tonnes	78	0.6%	0.0	0.0	0.0	#	0.0	0.0
901380	Optical devices, appliances and instruments, nec	87	1.6%	0.1	0.0	0.0	0.0	0.0	0.0
901890	Other instruments & appliances of medical science	87	1.0%	1.6	1.2	1.3	2.2	1.0	1.4
901839	Needles, catheters, cannulae and the like, nes	87	0.5%	3.5	2.2	1.6	0.9	1.4	0.3
901020	Apparatus and Equipment for photographic laboratories, nes	88	0.5%	#	0.1	0.0	0.0	0.0	0.0

Source: Authors' estimation using COMTRADE-WITS data.

Note: # refers to those cases that do not meet the cut-off.

Table 11.9 Values of EI_1 and World Exports Shares across HS Six-Digit Codes, P&C, 2014

HS Code	Product Description	SITC Code	Share in World NP Export	Africa	Americas	Central, South, and West Asia	East and Southeast Asia	Europe	Oceania
847330	Parts and accessories of data processing equipment nec	75	2.6%	0.1	0.1	0.0	0.1	0.0	0.2
851790	Parts of line telephone/telegraph equipment, nes	76	2.6%	0.3	0.2	0.2	0.2	0.6	0.0
852990	Parts for radio/tv transmit/receive equipment, nes	76	1.1%	0.0	0.1	0.4	0.1	0.4	0.1
854219	Monolithic integrated circuits, nes	77	10.1%	0.2	0.0	0.0	0.0	0.0	0.0
854140	Photosensitive/photovoltaic/LED semiconductor devices	77	1.2%	0.1	0.2	0.0	0.1	0.4	0.0
853710	Boards, panels, consoles, desks and other bases; for electric control or the distribution of electricity	77	1.0%	0.9	0.5	0.7	1.7	0.3	1.3
853400	Electronic printed circuits	77	1.0%	0.0	0.5	0.1	0.0	0.9	0.9
853690	Electrical apparatus; n.e.c. for switching or protecting electrical circuits, for a voltage not exceeding 1000 volts	77	0.8%	1.0	0.8	0.4	0.3	1.2	2.8
854430	Insulated electric conductors; ignition wiring sets and other wiring sets of a kind used in vehicles, aircraft or ships	77	0.7%	0.2	0.1	0.2	0.2	3.9	1.4
853890	Electrical apparatus; parts suitable for use solely or principally with the apparatus of heading no. 8535, 8536 or 8537	77	0.7%	1.5	2.0	1.4	0.9	2.1	3.3
854459	Electric conductors, for a voltage >80V but not exceeding 1000 v	77	0.6%	0.1	0.1	0.1	0.1	0.1	0.1
854441	Electric conductors fitted with connectors for a voltage not exceeding 80 v	77	0.6%	0.1	0.0	0.1	0.1	0.1	0.1
870899	Motor vehicle parts nes	78	2.2%	2.3	4.6	2.5	4.0	3.4	1.8
870829	Vehicles; parts and accessories, of bodies, other than safety seat belts	78	1.4%	0.3	0.2	0.1	0.2	0.2	0.1
870840	Vehicle parts; gear boxes and parts thereof	78	1.3%	0.2	2.0	1.0	2.7	1.2	0.5
870839	Other brakes & servo-brakes & parts thereof	78	0.6%	0.1	0.4	0.2	0.5	0.7	0.5

Source: Authors' estimation using COMTRADE-WITS data.

Note: There are no product codes within SITC 87 and 88 with share greater than 0.5 per cent.

Based on imported parts and components, India has a huge potential to emerge as a major hub for final assembly in several industries, particularly in electronics and electrical machinery. Since this strategy involves processing or assembly of imported parts and components, the net domestic value added per unit of exported good would not be very high. However, since the scale of operations is usually very large, the total domestic value addition from these activities could be considerably high, contributing to large scale employment generation.

What needs to be done at the policy level to exploit India's potential in NP? A number of studies suggest that a low level of service link costs—costs related to transportation, communication, and other related tasks involved in coordinating the activity in a given country with what is done in other countries within the production network—is critical for countries to participate in GPN. Supply disruption in a given location due to shipping delays, power failure, political disturbances, labour disputes, and so forth, could disrupt the entire production chain. Clearly, the policy should focus on reducing India's high service link costs with other countries within the production network.

Assembly processes within production networks require not only trainable low-cost unskilled labour but also a lot of middle-level supervisory manpower. For example, when Apple employed about 700,000 factory workers in China, it also employed 30,000 engineers on-site to supervise those workers (Isaacson, 2011). This implies that skill development policy should be actively followed by both the central and state governments.

While GPNs in several industries are primarily controlled by big MNEs, local firms and micro, small, and medium enterprises (MSMEs) play a significant role as subcontractors and suppliers of intermediate inputs to MNEs. An example of such relationship in the Indian context is that of firms in auto ancillary industries supplying components to larger auto makers. A number of studies from East and Southeast Asian countries suggest that local firms and MSMEs actively participate in production networks. Typically, the lead firm in the production network is supported by a small number of preferred first-tier suppliers. These first-tier firms, in turn, are supplied by other firms, forming a tiered structure consisting of large and small enterprises. In general, it is easier for MSMEs in low-income countries to enter a network as a lower tier supplier of highly labour-intensive components. Over time, the MSME firm may try to move up the tiers by upgrading the value-added content of their activities.

The MSMEs involvement with lead MNEs can occur in traditional labour-intensive industries as well as in NP. However, the nature of this relationship can vary significantly in these two groups of industries. Traditional industries such as garments, footwear, and toys are important examples for MNE-MSME linkage via buyer-driven network, where the lead firm concentrate in design, branding, and marketing while the physical production takes place in MSMEs and other firms in the network. In contrast, producer-driven network is more prominent in the case of NP, such as electronics, computers, automobiles, and so on. In producer-driven networks, while many transactions are done inside the vertically integrated company, the lead firm also establishes business relations with external firms, which are often long-lasting and intensive.

Greater integration of domestic industries with GPN must form an essential part of the Make in India initiative. What is important is the creation of an environment that allows entrepreneurs to freely search and identify opportunities in the vertically integrated global supply chains of various industries. While India has a potential to emerge as a major hub for final assembly in several industries, it is important to resist the temptation of extending tariff protection for final goods assembly as it will have the detrimental effect of breeding inefficiencies. A level playing field should be created for different types of business entities—domestic, foreign, and joint ventures. The domestic market for goods should be as contestable as is the export market for competing suppliers from around the world.

We argue that an outward-looking, but not an ultra-export promoting, strategy should be an integral part of the Make in India initiative. As pointed out by Rajan (2014) an ultra-export promotion strategy, which 'involves subsidizing exporters with cheap inputs as well as an undervalued exchange rate', is unlikely to be effective at this juncture (Rajan, 2014: 6). An outward-looking strategy which favours neither the domestic nor the export market is neutral (Bhagwati, 1978). For the Make in India initiative to be successful, it is important to ensure duty-free access to imported inputs irrespective of whether these inputs are used for producing for the domestic market or for the export market. In order to avoid the danger of inefficiencies, the domestic market for all products, intermediate or final, should remain contestable by foreign products and by foreign investment.

A neutral trade policy along with the absence of distortions and rigidities in other markets (in particular, factor markets) would ensure greater specialization in accordance with comparative advantage. This process of specialization in itself would induce faster export growth without any need for subsidizing exporters.

REFERENCES

Athukorala, Prema-chandra. 2011. 'Production Networks and Trade Patterns in East Asia: Regionalization or Globalization?' *Asian Economic Papers*, 10(1): 65–95.

————. 2012. 'Asian Trade Flows: Trends, Patterns and Prospects.' *Japan and the World Economy* 24(2): 150–62.

————. 2014. 'How India Fits into Global Production Sharing: Experience, Prospects, and Policy Options.' In *India Policy Forum 2013/14*—National Council of Applied Economic Research and Brookings Institution, edited by Shekhar Shah, Barry Bosworth, Arvind Panagariya, pp. 57–116. Sage.

Baldwin, Richard, and Javier Lopez-Gonzalez. 2013. 'Supply-Chain Trade: A Portrait of Global Patterns and Several Testable Hypotheses.' NBER Working Paper No. 18957.

Bhagwati, Jagdish N. 1978. 'Anatomy and Consequences of Exchange Control Regimes.' *National Bureau of Economic Research* 1(10). Available at http://www.nber.org/books/bhag78-1 (accessed on 10 July 2017).

Feenstra, R.C. 1998. 'Integration of Trade and Disintegration of Production in the Global Economy.' *Journal of Economic Perspectives* 12(4): 31–50.

Government of India. 2014–15. *Economic Survey of India 2014–15*. Ministry of Finance.

Hummels, D. 2002. Book Review for 'Fragmentation: New Production Pattern in the World Economy' by S.W. Arndt and H. Kierzkowskei. *Journal of Economic Geography* 2: 368–69.

Hummels, D., J. Ishii, and Kei-Mu Yi. 2001. 'The Nature and Growth of Vertical Specialization in World Trade.' *Journal of International Economics* 54(1): 75–96.

Isaacson, Walter. 2011. *Steve Jobs*. New York: Simon & Schuster.

Johnson, R.C., and G. Noguera. 2012. 'Accounting for Intermediates: Production Sharing and Trade in Value Added'. *Journal of International Economics* 86(2): 224–36.

Koopman, R., W. Powers, Z. Wang, and S. Wei. 2010. 'Give Credit where Credit Is Due: Tracing Value Added in Global Production Chains.' NBER Working Paper No. 16426. Available at http://www.hkimr.org/uploads/publication/49/ub_full_0_2_297_wp-no-31_2011-final-.pdf (accessed on 10 July 2017).

Krueger, Anne O. 2010. 'India's Trade with the World: Retrospect and Prospect.' In *India's Economy: Performance and Challenges*, edited by Sharkar Acharya and Rakesh Mohan, pp. 399–429. New Delhi: Oxford University Press.

Rajan, Raghuram. 2014. 'Make in India, Largely for India.' Talk delivered at the Bharat Ram Memorial Lecture on 12 December 2014 in New Delhi. Available at https://www.rbi.org.in/Scripts/BS_SpeechesView.aspx?Id=930 (accessed on 10 July 2017).

RBI. Various years. Handbook of Statistics on Indian Economy. Available at https://www.rbi.org.in/scripts/annualPublications.aspx?head=Handbook%20of%20Statistics%20on%20Indian%20Economy (accessed on 10 July 2017).

Tewari, Meenu and C. Veeramani. 2016. 'Network Trade and Development: What Do Patterns of Vertically Specialized Trade in ASEAN Tell Us about India's Place in Asian Production Networks?' *Global Economy Journal* 16(2 June).

Veeramani, C. 2012. 'Anatomy of India's Merchandise Export Growth, 1993–94 to 2010–11.' *Economic and Political Weekly* 47(1): 94–104.

Veeramani, C. and Garima Dhir. 2016. 'India's Exports of Unskilled Labour Intensive Products: A Comparative Analysis.' In *International Trade and Industrial Development in India: Emerging Trends, Patterns and Issues*, edited by C. Veeramani and R. Nagaraj. Orient Blackswan.

12

Services for Indian Manufacturing

Rupa Chanda

INTRODUCTION

Over the past decade, there has been a clear thrust on the manufacturing sector for ensuring sustainable growth and employment creation in India. Recent initiatives such as Make in India and Skill India, platforms such as the National Manufacturing Competitiveness Council and the efforts of institutions such as the National Skills Development Corporation highlight this concerted focus on manufacturing and on addressing the many challenges that plague this sector. The vision, as declared under the Make in India programme, is to raise the contribution of manufacturing to 25 per cent of GDP from its stagnant and low share of around 16–17 per cent of GDP, to increase the sector's growth to 12–14 per cent per annum over the medium term and to create 100 million additional manufacturing jobs by 2022. The government also aims to increase domestic value addition and technological depth in manufacturing as well as increase the global competitiveness of India's manufacturing.[1]

While the significance of the manufacturing sector in terms of GDP growth, employment creation, trade and investment flows, and skilling cannot be questioned, thereby warranting focused attention on this sector, a point that is not sufficiently highlighted in policy discussions is the fact that manufacturing is not independent of other segments of the economy. In particular, the value added contribution of services in manufacturing output and exports is often not adequately recognized or valued and rather the manufacturing sector is seen as competing for resources with the services sector. However, such a view is very narrow. Services constitute an integral part of the production and delivery process in the manufacturing sector, from research and development and product design in the initial stages to transport and distribution following production to retailing, repair, and maintenance in the final stages while services such as telecommunications and finance are required at every stage. Individual manufacturers typically require a full spectrum of services.

Background and Motivation

With growing global demand for more sophisticated products and business offers, with a global production and business environment that is characterized by outsourcing, production sharing, fragmentation, off-shoring and specialization, and with growing pressure to cut costs, improve efficiency and deepen customer relationships, manufacturing companies have become more and more reliant on access to cheap, reliable, and quality services.

---

[1] Available at http://www.makeinindia.com/policy/national-manufacturing (accessed on 5 March 2016).

Developments in services such as information and communications technology (ICT), logistics, and financial intermediation have enabled increased geographic dispersion of manufacturing production by reducing trade and coordination costs. As a result, manufacturing companies worldwide are increasingly using and also providing a growing and more diverse mix of services, either in-house or through offshore or on-shore outsourcing arrangements. In some sectors such as computer and electronic products, intermediate services inputs may constitute close to 50 per cent of expenses (USITC, 2013: Chapter 3, 3–1). Business services such as legal, accounting, advisory, data processing, and ICT services in particular have come to constitute a growing share of intermediate inputs for manufacturing firms. According to the WTO *Annual Report 2014* and several recent studies by the OECD and governments, this trend can be termed as the 'servicification' or 'servicizing' of manufacturing (National Board of Trade, 2010; OECD, 2015; USITC, 2013).

The corollary to this growing interdependence between services and manufacturing is the fact that restrictions on the ability to deliver or buy services and the lack of a competitive service sector may ultimately restrict manufacturing production and trade by raising costs, reducing efficiency, and hurting competitiveness, directly and indirectly. Hence, the existing regulatory and business environment in the service sector, issues of skilling and standards in services, and technological and infrastructural conditions in services can significantly impact the growth and competitiveness of the manufacturing sector. Trade and investment liberalization of services and steps to enhance productivity in services are thus of importance to manufacturing firms as consumers and procurers of services and increasingly as providers of services alongside products. It, therefore, follows that any policy to boost manufacturing must necessarily look beyond this sector and, first, recognize its existing and potential linkages with services; and second, identify and address the bottlenecks, which prevent effective realization of these linkages.

In the context of India's Make in India initiative and the recent focus on manufacturing, an understanding of these linkages assumes importance, particularly because services have been the main driver of growth in the Indian economy in recent decades, constitute around 60 per cent of India's GDP, and make a significant direct contribution to India's exports.[2] India is also recognized globally for its competitiveness in certain services such as information technology and business process outsourcing. It is thus imperative to examine to what extent, in which areas, and in what manner Indian manufacturing has drawn upon India's services sector, particularly with respect to manufacturing exports. This chapter is motivated by need to focus attention on this interdependence between services and manufacturing exports in India and to assess how both these sectors, not any one alone, can serve as twin pillars for growth and development.

The discussion is primarily based on trade in value added terms, that is, how much domestic value added is generated by the exports of a good or service in a country. Such a perspective is useful as conventional gross trade statistics do not reveal the value added content of exports and to what extent this value added is foreign or domestic in origin. In the context of services, this is particularly important as gross trade statistics significantly underrepresent the value added share of services content in a country's exports as goods industries require significant intermediate inputs of both domestic and foreign services. An analysis based on trade in value added terms can help highlight the role of services trade and foreign direct investment policies as well as measures to improve service sector efficiency in enhancing export competitiveness in goods industries. Such an analysis can also enable identification of weak links in the services to manufacturing value chain, where policy support may be needed.[1]

Chapter Outline

Following this introduction, the section 'Servicification: Brief Overview of the Evidence' provides a brief review of the evidence on services as enablers in manufacturing output as well as trade. The section 'Servicification Trends in Indian Manufacturing' goes on to discuss the directly visible as well as the invisible, embedded role of services in the Indian economy, through its value added contribution in manufacturing exports in particular. The section 'Decomposing Services Contributions to Manufacturing Exports' examines the sub-sectoral nature of this linkage between selected services in India and overall manufacturing exports as well as exports in specific manufacturing segments which are critical for the Make in India programme. The discussion in the third and fourth sections is based on the OECD's Trade in Value Added (TiVA) database and World Input–Output tables which provide information on the backward linkage from manufacturing to services in exports and final demand, respectively, and also highlights the nature of this linkage, that is, whether it is domestic or foreign.[1] Hence, the focus of these core sections is on assessing the role played

---

[2] Available at http://unctadstat.unctad.org/ReportFolders/ reportFolders.aspx?sCS_referer=&sCS_ChosenLang=en (accessed on 10 March 2015).

by services in enabling India's participation in the global manufacturing value chain through exports, which is necessarily also related to how services strengthen domestic manufacturing production more generally. This focus is warranted by the government's goal of making India a bigger player in international production networks. The section 'Explaining the Trends: Some Inferences and Conclusions' assesses what the observed trends convey about prospects and challenges in leveraging the linkages between manufacturing and services in India, at the aggregate as well as sub-sectoral levels and possible reasons for the same. It concludes by outlining some policies that may be needed in services and also other areas so as to strengthen and deepen the contribution of services to the growth and competitiveness of Indian manufacturing.

SERVICIFICATION: BRIEF OVERVIEW OF THE EVIDENCE

Global value chains (GVCs) facilitate the integration of countries into the global economy by enabling them to join at any point of the production value chain based on their competitive advantage, rather than building a whole value chain within the country. Capturing value in GVCs requires competitiveness, skills, and innovation. However, what is the role of services in this participation?

Services are found through the manufacturing value chain. Services play a critical role in ensuring a seamless operation of GVCs by providing business and infrastructure support to production processes. For instance, logistics services, which include a variety of services such as cargo handling, storage, warehousing, and packaging are critical for the functioning of supply chains and the final delivery to the distribution sector. Communication services are a basic requirement for participation in GVCs as information and communication flows among interdependent stakeholders in value chains help reduce transactions costs, enable coordination and facilitate the off shoring and fragmentation of production across distant geographies. Most value- and knowledge-intensive services are found at the beginning and end of the value chain. The famous Smiley Curve of services value added in the global value chain shows how services contribute across the production process, from R&D and conceptualization of a manufactured product to the final sales, marketing, and branding of the product (ITC, 2014: 7, Figure 3).

Services are also important in manufacturing trade. Not only do they directly enable trade in goods in the form of transport, storage, and distribution services, they also indirectly enable trade in the form of embodied intermediate inputs in goods. According to the WTO, services value added accounts for about one-third of manufacturing exports in developed countries and for 26 per cent in developing countries. India shows very high services content in manufacturing exports, at 36 per cent, comparable to that in the most developed countries. Within this, the share of foreign services value added in manufacturing exports for both developed and developing countries is lower than that for domestic services at around 11 to 12 per cent, indicating that at present, domestic services inputs are more important for manufacturing export competitiveness and also the fact that there is scope to increase the international backward linkage of manufacturing with services through services reforms and liberalization (WTO, 2014).

Table 12.1 illustrates the range of contributions made by services in the manufacturing value chain.

Analysis of the embodied value of services in manufacturing exports based on the OECD's Trade in Value Added (TiVA) database shows that the services content in manufacturing exports has increased over the 1995–2011 period for most developed and developing countries and that distribution and transport services contribute the bulk of this value. Segments such as ICT and business services, however, show a much greater contribution in developed countries, most likely indicating the greater value addition embodied in the latter's manufacturing exports. Further, for most countries, while domestic services content remains more important, the contribution of foreign services content has increased over this period indicating the likely opening up of services around the world in the last two decades and greater integration of countries with world markets through trade and FDI flows (OECD, 2015: 203).

The implications of such 'servicification' are many for manufacturing firms. These spill-overs have been discussed in several cross-country and country-specific studies. Evidence suggests that productivity gains are generally larger for those manufacturing industries which use business services more intensively and that access to a wide range of high quality services promotes manufacturing competitiveness. For example, business services such as ICT give manufacturers the flexibility to specialize in certain activities and to outsource less productive tasks. Studies by the OECD indicate that liberalization of services trade can boost manufacturing competitiveness by lowering costs and increasing the variety of services available to manufacturers, with beneficial effects in industries such as automotives, which are well integrated into international production networks, where parts and components cross borders multiple times and are subject

Table 12.1   Illustrative Examples of the Role of Services throughout the Product Value Chain

Driver	Stages in the Value Chain	Services	Benefit to Producer
More efficiency and lower costs of product development, production and overhead	Design	Design services	Improves process efficiency
	R&D	R&D services, prototyping services	Improves products; reduces development costs and shortens product development cycle; increases product efficiency (in decreased cost of failure)
	Sourcing of intermediate inputs	Logistics and transportation services; supply chain management services; IT services production process management services; testing services; parts inventory tracking	Allows geographic dispersion of GVC with the aim of lowering costs
			Makes process more efficient
		Network and communications services; data services and processing services	Makes process more efficient
	Warehousing and distribution	Inventory management services; logistics and transportation services	Allows geographic dispersion of GVC with the aim of lowering costs
	Management of the firm	Human capital management services	Lowers overhead costs and improves coordination of the enterprise
		IT services	
		Financial and treasury services	
		Legal, accounting and other professional services	Lowers financing costs
			Lowers overhead costs
More product differentiation and customer satisfaction; enabling higher sales margins and more product positioning	Marketing, branding and sales	Online sales	Facilitates outreach to customers and offers ways to access new markets
		Sales force management services	Enables faster and more efficient customer targeting
		Financial services (such as customer finance or equipment leasing services)	Enables sales of large-ticket items such as aircraft via customer franchising solutions

Source: Based on USITC (2013), Chapter 3, Table 3.1, 3–6.

to numerous border and behind-the-border restrictions. Although the literature on GVCs and specifically on servicification is rather new and is still evolving, it is clear that factors beyond the conventional sources of comparative advantage matter if we consider a country's participation in global manufacturing production networks and such interdependencies between sectors. Factors affecting the services sector and especially those services that are used intensively by manufacturing companies are also critical determinants of a manufacturing firm's competitive advantage in the domestic and global market.

SERVICIFICATION TRENDS IN INDIAN MANUFACTURING

In order to understand whether India can leverage its service sector to participate more effectively in global manufacturing value chains and enhance manufacturing competitiveness, we need to understand the visible as well as the invisible, that is, the direct as well as indirect or embedded contribution of services in the Indian economy. As is well known, the share of services in India's GDP and exports has increased significantly over the past two decades. Inclusive of construction services, its share in output has risen from around 50 per cent in 1995 to over 60 per cent in 2012 and its contribution to exports has risen from a little less than 20 per cent to around 33 per cent over this same period (although its share in total imports has remained almost the same). Furthermore, the composition of services exports has changed considerably, with a declining share of traditional segments such as travel and transport and a growing contribution of 'other commercial services', which include segments such as IT, business process outsourcing (BPO), and various business services. The share of other commercial services exports in India's GDP, which is indicative of the trade orientation of these segments, has risen from around 1 per cent in 1990 to 8 per cent in 2012, much above the developing country average of 4.5 per cent and even the developed country average share of 7 per cent.[3]

But beyond this direct and visible role is the embedded contribution of services to India's exports, which is much greater than that revealed by conventional balance of payments statistics. The following discussion highlights this embedded role of services in economy-wide exports and its salient characteristics. It then delves into the nature of this contribution with regard to manufacturing exports.[4]

Services Contribution in Overall Exports

As discussed earlier, production and trade of manufactured goods increasingly requires a combination of domestic and foreign intermediate inputs, including services such as transportation, communications, insurance, finance, distribution, and business support activities. Figure 12.1 shows the decomposition of value added content in India's gross exports across the three sectors of the economy, while Figures 12.2 and 12.3 further highlight the relative importance of traditional versus modern services and the significance of specific service segments in this breakdown, respectively.

Figures 12.1, 12.2, and 12.3 highlight some important features regarding the role of services in overall exports. As seen in Figure 12.1, the share of services value added contribution in India's gross exports across all sectors was close to 50 per cent in 2011, significantly greater than the balance of payments (BoP) based share of services exports in total exports. This is also much greater than in other emerging countries and is comparable to the value added share for service sector-oriented economies such as Singapore and Hong Kong as well as developed countries such as the UK and the USA. Figures 12.2 and 12.3 further show that over the 1995–2011 period, modern services and in particular business support services have come to contribute more than traditional segments such as transport and distribution services in India's gross exports. This is consistent with the shift in the pattern of India's services exports towards modern segments noted earlier but may also be indicative of

differences in competitiveness between modern and traditional services, changes in production formats which require greater use of business support services, and differences in the nature of linkage between other parts of the economy and different service segments. What is interesting to note is that computer and related ser-

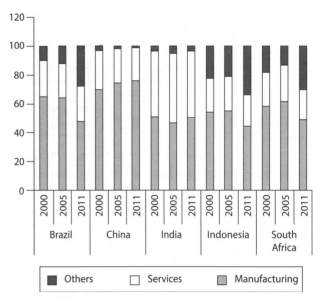

Figure 12.1   Decomposition of Value Added Content of Gross Exports by Sectors (Percentage), Selected Years

Notes: Others includes agriculture, hunting, forestry, fishing, mining, and utilities.
Source: Author's construction based on http://stats.oecd.org/ (accessed 30 June 2015).

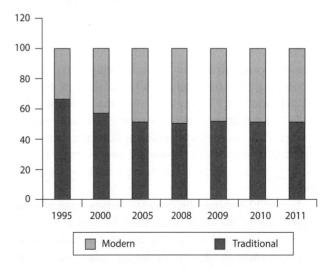

Figure 12.2   Traditional vs Modern Services VAD (Value Added) in Gross Exports (%)

Source: Author's construction based on http://stats.oecd.org/ (accessed 30 June 2015).

---

[3] Based on http://unctadstat.unctad.org/ReportFolders/report Folders.aspx?sCS_referer=&sCS_ChosenLang=en (accessed 10 March 2015).

[4] Throughout the discussion, services are inclusive of construction, wholesale and retail trade and distribution services. The analysis is based on the OECD TiVA database unless otherwise specified.

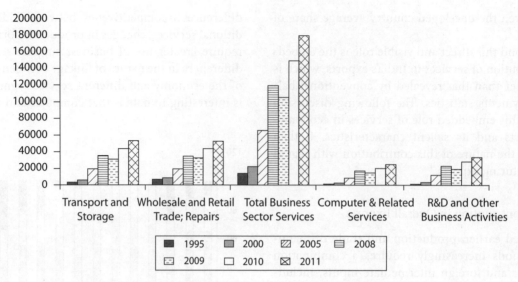

Figure 12.3   Service Segment-wise Contribution to VAD Content of Gross Exports (US $mn)

Source: Author's construction based on http://stats.oecd.org/ (accessed 30 June 2015).

vices, which occupy the major share of India's services exports, account for a much smaller share in value added terms in gross exports. This would indicate that these services are mostly directly exported as opposed to being embedded in exports of other parts of the economy and thus the scope to leverage certain services far more in the country's exports in other sectors. The very low level of contribution of R&D and other business activities is also striking and may be indicative of the likely presence of Indian manufacturing exports at the lower end of the value chain where the scope for the integration of services may be more limited.

Further analysis of the origin of this services value added contribution based on the OECD TiVA database reveals that across all services, around 90 per cent was of domestic origin in 2011 (comparable to that seen in most developing countries) and much higher than the roughly 60 per cent share in the case of manufacturing value added contribution to overall exports.[5] The latter would suggest that the competitiveness of domestic services is particularly important for overall export competitiveness, given the sector's sizeable contribution to gross exports.

Figure 12.4 shows the domestic versus foreign value added shares for selected services in overall exports. From the observed trends, we find that although there has been some increase in the foreign value added share

of services in gross exports, this remains low at less than 20 per cent across all services, while the share of foreign manufacturing value added has risen much more sharply. The difference between the sourcing pattern in manufacturing and services is likely to indicate the difference in the degree of openness and the degree of competitiveness between the two sectors. Further, differences in the share of foreign value added contribution within the service sector also suggests a similar mix of reasons, with competitive segments like computer and related services and less liberalized segments such as financial and distribution services showing a continued high share of domestic content. The rising foreign share of R&D and other business services and the almost nonexistent domestic contribution of this segment in overall exports is also noteworthy.[6] Another way of interpreting these trends is to recognize the scope for increased participation of foreign service suppliers in India's exports through further liberalization and deregulation, with possible spill-over benefits to the economy.

Services Contribution to Manufacturing Exports

The trends highlighted only capture services contribution to overall exports and final demand in the

---

[5] Available at http://stats.oecd.org/ (accessed on 15 October 2015).

[6] Similar trends are observed for the value added contribution of services in domestic final demand as for overall exports. The most striking aspect is the negligible role of R&D and other business activities and within this the dominance of foreign service suppliers.

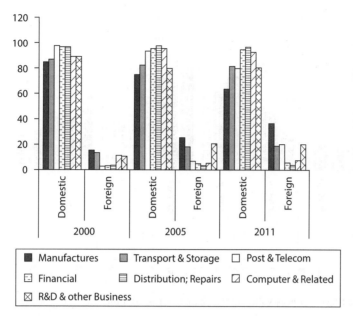

Figure 12.4   Value Added Shares of Manufacturing and Selected Services in Gross Exports by Source (Percentage)
Source: Author's construction based on OECD.Stat.[7]

economy. From a Make in India perspective, we need to understand the extent to which it contributes to manufacturing exports and final demand and which are the services segments primarily involved in this linkage. The latter would enable us to assess whether the 50 per cent or so value added share of services in India's gross exports largely reflects its use within the service sector or whether there is a strong and growing relationship with manufacturing exports over time. Figures 12.5 and 12.6, respectively, show the services–manufacturing linkage in exports and final demand and the domestic versus foreign origin of this linkage.[8]

According to Figure 12.8 and Figure 12.9, services value added constituted around 34 per cent of gross manufacturing exports in 2011, with two-thirds being

of domestic origin and accounted for around 18 per cent of domestic final manufacturing demand (after netting out exports from total final manufacturing demand). It is worth noting that the foreign component of this contribution in both manufacturing exports and manufacturing final demand has been rising over the 1995–2011 period, possibly reflecting issues of quality, standards, liberalization, regulatory changes, competitiveness, and the scope for integration of services in the manufacturing export basket. These trends compare with a manufacturing value added share of around 38 per cent in manufacturing exports and 29 per cent in manufacturing domestic final demand (after netting out exports) in 2011, as shown in Figures 12.7 and 12.8, respectively. Thus, services contribute a comparable share of value added as the manufacturing sector in India's manufacturing exports.

It is also interesting to note that with regard to the foreign versus domestic sourcing of this value added content of services China is different in the pattern of its services use in manufacturing exports. It exhibits a higher foreign as opposed to domestic services value added contribution in its manufacturing exports, while all other developing countries shown earlier exhibit the reverse. However, it shows a similar pattern in the sourcing of services value added as other developing countries in the case of final demand. This latter feature raises an interesting question. Is the higher intensity of services use of foreign

[7] Available at http://stats.oecd.org/ (accessed on 30 June 2015).

[8] These value added contributions to exports are based on input-output coefficients which are applied to trade figures. The total forward and backward linkage coefficients for India's services sector were 0.37 and 040, respectively and 0.62 and 0.58 for manufacturing, based on the mid 2000 input-output table for India. The corresponding coefficients for China were 0.52 and 0.55 for services and 0.72 and 0.65 for manufacturing as per their mid 2000 input-output table. Thus, for both manufacturing and services, India's backward and forward linkage in production has been lower. This is seen for modern as well as traditional services where China's total backward as well as forward linkage is higher than for India.

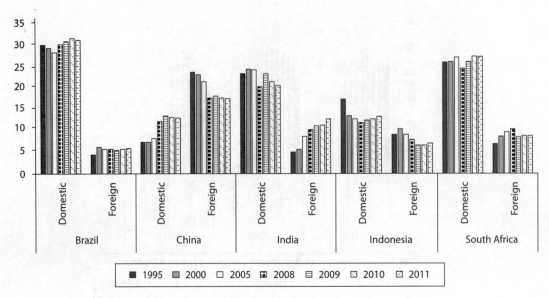

Figure 12.5   Services Value Added Share in Gross Manufacturing Exports (Percentage)

Source: Author's construction based on OECD.Stat.[9]

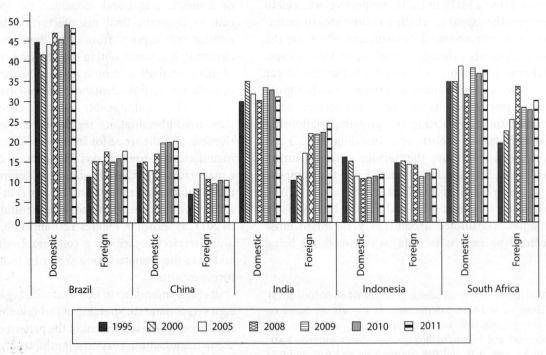

Figure 12.6   Services Value Added Share in Manufacturing Final Demand (Percentage)

Source: Author's construction based on OECD.Stat.[10]

[9] Available at http://stats.oecd.org/ (accessed on 5 August 2015).
[10] Available at http://stats.oecd.org/ (accessed on 9 July 2015).

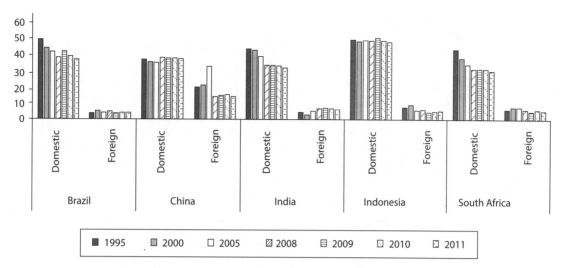

Figure 12.7 Manufacturing VAD Contribution in Gross Manufacturing Exports, by Source (Percentage)
Source: Author's construction based on OECD.Stat.[11]

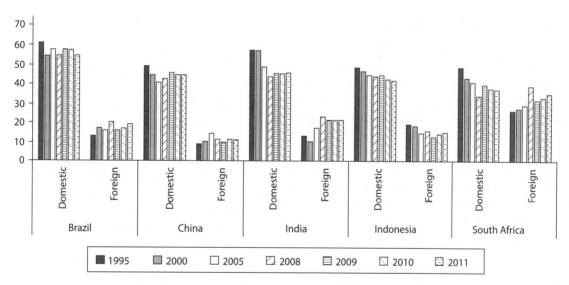

Figure 12.8 Manufacturing VAD Contribution in Manufacturing Final Demand
Source: Author's construction based on OECD.Stat.[12]

origin related to China's highly export-oriented strategy in manufacturing and the need to be competitive in the global market? What might this suggest in terms of a strategy for the service sector for India, which is seeking to increase its participation in global manufacturing value chains? The Chinese case may be indicative of the importance of a competitive services sector in areas which directly support manufacturing exports and the need to simultaneously focus alongside manufacturing on issues of services quality, efficiency, availability and variety and associated regulations and policies to boost manufacturing competitiveness in international markets.

[11] Available at http://stats.oecd.org/ (accessed on 5 August 2015).
[12] Available at http://stats.oecd.org/ (accessed on 5 August 2015).

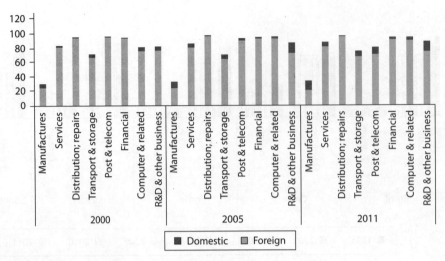

Figure 12.9   Services Value Added Shares of Manufacturing and Services Gross Exports (Percentage), India

Source: Author's construction based on OECS.Stat.[13]

DECOMPOSING SERVICES CONTRIBUTIONS TO MANUFACTURING EXPORTS

From the services–manufacturing linkage at the aggregate level, we next turn to examine the relationship between the two sectors at the sub-sectoral level to see which services contribute to manufacturing exports, to what extent some of the key Make in India manufacturing industries rely on services and the domestic versus foreign nature of this linkage. If one examines these disaggregated linkages, then some interesting observations arise which raise concerns about the nature of our service sector's contribution to other parts of the Indian economy and its competitiveness.

Analysis of OECD TiVA data reveals that services value added in manufacturing exports accounted for 29.4 per cent of services value added in total exports in 2011. Hence, the bulk of services VAD in India's exports was embodied in services exports. At the sub-sectoral level, this pattern is stronger. For example, the value added content from a competitive service sub-sector such as computer and related services in manufacturing exports was a mere 12.8 per cent of the segment's total contribution to exports in 2011, that is, 87 per cent contribution to India's exports was to services exports. Moreover, 94.6 per cent of this contribution to services exports was accounted for by the subsector itself, that is, computer services value added content within the same subsector. Likewise, the value added contribu-

tion of R&D and business services to manufacturing exports constituted only 15 per cent of the segment's total contribution to exports and thus the bulk 85 per cent contribution was to the service sector. Again, within services, business services value added contribution to the segment itself was 97 per cent. In the case of transportation and storage services, the contribution to manufacturing exports was higher than for the other services at around 30 per cent, but this contribution has declined over the 1995–2011 period.

Figure 12.9 highlights the much greater within services linkage in gross exports than between services and manufacturing exports. Within services value added shares were a little under 80 per cent in 2011 and across all service subsectors, the shares were 70 per cent or more, with this contribution being largely domestic in nature.

However, what is the origin of this services value added and how broad-based is services contribution to manufacturing exports? How does it compare with the manufacturing sector's value added contribution to its own exports? Figure 12.10 shows the source of value added in India's gross manufacturing exports by origin and by industries and services. The industries chosen are groupings based on the OECD TiVA database and have been selected keeping in mind their relevance to the Make in India programme (even though the groupings are broader and do not correspond one-to-one with the Make in India categories).

The picture that emerges is that the individual value added contribution of the selected manufacturing indus-

[13] Available at http://stats.oecd.org/ (accessed on 30 June 2015).

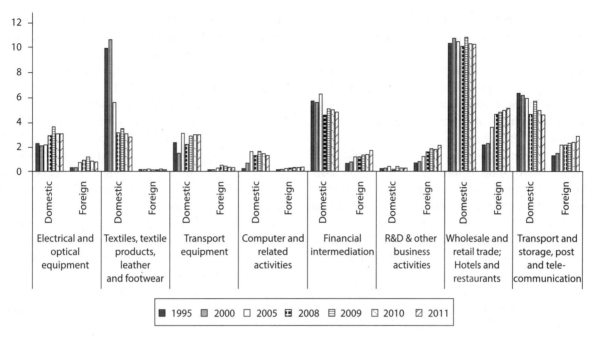

Figure 12.10   Value Added Source in India's Gross Manufacturing Exports for Selected Industries and Services (Percentage), Selected Years

Source: Author's construction based on OECD.Stat.[14]

Note: Wholesale and retail trade; hotels and restaurants include repairs.

tries in India's gross manufacturing exports is quite low. Even in the case of textiles, textile products, and leather and footwear products, the contribution has come down over time. It is also worth noting that emerging manufacturing industries such as transport equipment and electrical equipment show very little value added contribution, indicating that they rely heavily on imported parts and intermediates. This itself is quite informative as it suggests that domestically generated manufacturing content in India's manufacturing exports is low, which has implications for policies concerning foreign direct investment (FDI), scale and quality in Indian manufacturing. However, if we examine the contribution of the service sector to overall manufacturing exports, we find that it is concentrated in trade and distribution services and to a lesser extent in transport and storage and financial intermediation services. The service sector's linkage to manufacturing exports is thus dominated by traditional services.[15] The only exception to this is the

growing role of financial intermediation services which is noteworthy as it signifies the importance of access to financial services and the quality of the financial sector in supporting manufacturing activity. However, the main point of concern is that emerging areas such as R&D and business services and IT services, which can potentially create more value, increase business sophistication and raise technological depth in production—some of the stated goals of the Make in India programme—show very low levels of contribution to manufacturing exports.

Several inferences can be drawn from these subsectoral trends in value added contributions and associated with these inferences some related questions can be raised. First, we find that globally competitive segments like IT services are not contributing in any significant way to India's manufacturing exports and further that India's IT services exports are largely directly exported (given the high share of within segment exports). What

[14] Available at http://stats.oecd.org/ (accessed on 30 June 2015).

[15] Based on the country-wise input-output tables for the mid 2000s, service sector inputs to manufacturing is more heavily dominated by transport followed by distribution services in the case of China, compared to the case of India. But in both cases,

services such as computer and related activities or business activities play an insignificant role in manufacturing as per the input-output matrices. The main difference between the two is in the case of financial services whose input contribution is much greater in the case of India.

would this imply about the leveraging of IT in improving manufacturing processes, raising efficiency, increasing productivity and automation, issues, which would certainly be important if India is to play a bigger role in international production networks? Does this reflect on the nature of Indian manufacturing which perhaps due to issues of scale, infrastructural and regulatory hurdles shows a low IT intensity in its exports? Does it reflect on the pattern of our manufacturing export basket and might this change going forward with greater emphasis on value added manufacturing? Clearly, there is a need to examine how to leverage India's strength in IT services in order to add value to its manufacturing sector.

Second, the very low contribution of R&D and business services indicates the inadequate utilization of business support activities in India's manufacturing exports. This is noteworthy as a number of studies highlight the efficiency and competitiveness-enhancing role played by business services. Might this indicate lack of globally competitive business services in India, which can add value to its manufacturing exports? Might this be due to regulatory barriers and standards and quality related issues in various business services in India, which may be weakening this relationship with manufacturing exports? Might this be due to the less business services-intensive nature of our manufacturing exports to begin with? The numbers also suggest the relatively low R&D services intensity in India's manufacturing exports. What does this imply about the role of innovation and the unrealized potential to move up the value chain into more R&D intensive manufacturing?

Third, the declining contribution of domestic transport and storage services value added in manufacturing exports suggests a weakening link between the two. This may suggest high costs of domestic services, inefficiencies, regulatory barriers, and changes in the structure and dispersion of production that reduce the dependence on transport and storage services.

The reason for highlighting the three aforementioned services subsectors with regard to their links to manufacturing exports is because they capture different kinds of issues and concerns in the context of a Make in India initiative. They raise concerns about whether manufacturing exports in India are sufficiently integrating successful services such as IT, whether they are focusing enough on innovation and value creation, and whether they are being hindered by high logistics costs.

However, if one examines the contribution of individual service subsectors in the exports of specific manufacturing industries that are important for the Make in India programme, within overall manufacturing exports, the picture is different. There is an upward trend in the contribution of services as a whole and of specific services such as distribution, transport, business and IT services to exports of transport equipment, electrical equipment and textile and textile products, three important Make in India industries within the manufacturing sector. For instance, the share of R&D and business services value added in the exports of the transport equipment and the electrical equipment industries has risen 1.4 per cent to 5.8 per cent and from 1.1 per cent to 4.4 per cent, respectively between 1995 and 2011. Similarly, the value added contribution of computer and related services in the exports of these same industries has risen from less than 1 per cent to around 4 per cent, and 3 per cent, respectively. This contribution, however, is significantly smaller than the sub-sector's value added contribution to its own exports, which stood at over 80 per cent in 2011. On the other hand, the value added contribution of traditional services such as transport and storage services and in particular trade and distribution services far exceeds that of emerging services such as R&D, business, and IT services. These traditional services have also experienced a significant increase in their contribution to the exports of all three manufacturing industries over the 1995–2011 period, particularly in the case of the textile and footwear industry. Thus, while the contribution of new services in manufacturing exports is on the rise, their value added shares are very low indicating that their link with key manufacturing industries remains weak, that is, services which relate to adoption of new technologies, business practices and innovation continue to play a small role in manufacturing exports. The intra-services as opposed to services-manufacturing linkage and the traditional services-manufacturing linkage are much stronger. Of course, with the changing pattern of India's manufacturing export basket and the government's thrust on more skill- and technology-intensive emerging industries like automotives and electronics, the scope for integrating services in manufacturing production and exports can be expected to increase.[8]

EXPLAINING THE TRENDS: SOME INFERENCES AND CONCLUSIONS

The key insight that emerges from the trends is that there is potential to create value in India's exports through the integration of services. This unexploited potential may be due to various reasons. The weak linkage between manufacturing and services may indicate constraints in the manufacturing sector, which hinder its ability to draw upon the service sector. These constraints are likely to be the usual ones that are discussed in the context of Indian manufacturing, such as issues of scale and fragmentation, which may make it difficult to integrate IT, R&D, and business services in production and exports, or issues of infrastructure. However, the low embedded contribution of services in manufacturing may also reflect challenges affecting the service sector as a whole and individual services, an issue that does not receive adequate attention in debates over how to boost Indian manufacturing. These challenges confronting services may be related to issues of capacity, quality, regulation, and the degree of liberalization and modernization in services. While our preceding analysis does not allow us to pinpoint specific challenges in services, such an inference is in line with existing evidence and literature which suggests that trade and FDI policies that shape the regulatory environment in services and the degree of contestability in services markets and policies which facilitate improvements in quality, productivity, efficiency, and capacity in the services sector can benefit manufacturing and also the economy as a whole (Escaith, 2014; Miroudot, Rouzet, and Spinelli, 2013; USITC, 2013).

Constraints in the Services Sector

Drawing upon various competitiveness and regulatory indices which are relevant to gauging the service sector's efficiency and capacity to contribute effectively to other parts of the economy, we find that India does not perform very well on several aspects which are important for enabling servicification of manufacturing. This is notwithstanding the fact that services have grown more rapidly than other sectors and some services segments are globally very competitive and have grown in importance in the export basket.

India's rankings in the Enabling Trade Index where one of the sub-indices on transport and communication infrastructure, which is directly a reflection of the quality of such services, stood at 52 in 2008 and declined to 67 in 2014 compared to China's rank at 36 in both these years, out of 108 and 114 countries in these two years, respectively.[16] Thus, India ranks in the middle for the quality of transport and communications infrastructure. Another relevant indicator for assessing trade efficiency that is dependent on services quality and capacity is the logistics performance index. In 2014, India's ranking in

the sub-index for logistics services was 52 among 160 countries, and on the infrastructure sub-index, its rank was 58. There has also been deterioration in both these sub-indices between 2007 and 2014. India's overall ranking on logistics performance declined from 39 to 54 over this period.[17] On the innovation and sophistication sub-index, another indicator which in part captures the country's capacity and quality in R&D services, India shows a decline in its rank, from 27 to 41 to 52 between 2008, 2013 and 2014, out of around 140–50 countries over this period.[18] The latter suggests that the ecosystem for innovation is not particularly strong and has deteriorated in recent years. Altogether, although these various indices are not always specific to the service sector, they are broadly indicative of constraints that exist in various services segments, such as in producer services like transport and communications that are key inputs to trade in manufactured goods.

Indices which capture the incidence of regulatory barriers in India's services sector highlight the likely policy-induced constraints to exploiting the linkages between services and manufacturing. Figure 12.11 shows the FDI regulatory restrictiveness indices for the secondary, manufacturing, and tertiary sectors as well as for overall FDI in India, in selected developed and developing countries. This index is relevant to the discussion on the services-manufacturing linkage as the internationalization of many services requires FDI presence and hence the efficiency and competitiveness of the services sector and a country's participation in the global manufacturing value chain can be shaped by FDI activity in important areas such as transport, communication, and business services. The indices presented in Figure 12.11 suggest that services FDI in India is more restricted than FDI in manufacturing and the economy as a whole and although the incidence of these restrictions has declined over the 2006–14 period, the overall level of protection still remains quite high.

Figure 12.12 provides a disaggregated overview of the regulatory environment affecting different services. Clearly, in sub-sectors such as transport and logistics, legal, accounting, and distribution services, all of which are key enablers to participation in manufacturing GVCs and for enhancing manufacturing competitiveness, India is much more restrictive than other countries.

---

[16] Based on the World Economic Forum's, 'The Global Enabling Trade Report' (various years).

[17] Based on the World Bank's, 'Connecting to Compete: Trade Logistics in the Global Economy' (various years).

[18] Based on the World Economic Forum's 'Global Competitiveness Report' (various years).

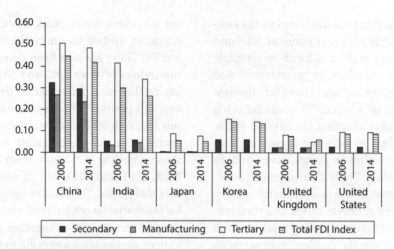

Figure 12.11 FDI Regulatory Restrictiveness Index

Source: Author's construction based on OECD.Stat.[19]

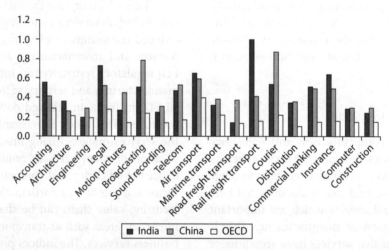

Figure 12.12 Trade Restrictiveness Indices for Specific Services Sub-sectors, 2014
Source: Author's construction based on OECD 'Compare your Country'.[20]

Way Forward

As India embarks on a range of initiatives to boost its manufacturing sector, it is important to recognize that a singular focus on manufacturing alone would not be appropriate. Any holistic policy framework must recognize the interdependence between manufacturing and other sectors of the economy. The trends in servicification discussed in this chapter indicate the scope to increase services content in Indian manufacturing output and exports. However, in order to realize this, apart from focusing on issues of skilling, land acquisition, taxes, and other measures pertaining directly to the operating environment in the manufacturing sector, the government will also need to focus on increasing efficiency in India's services sector as an input to the manufacturing sector.

If India is to move into higher value added manufacturing for the global market, the government must pay attention to developing capacity across two broad

[19] Available at http://stats.oecd.org/ (accessed on 28 July 2015).

[20] Available at http://www.compareyourcountry.org/service-trade-rictions?cr=average&cr1=oecd&lg=en&page=1# (accessed on 6 May 2015).

clusters of services. First, those services such as transport and logistics which directly enhance connectivity and efficiency in trade; and second, those services such as R&D and business support services which add value to manufacturing and enable product differentiation and internationalization. Such a focus would require investment in transport and digital infrastructure. It would require measures aimed at reducing regulatory restrictions that affect services at both the border and behind the border and which hurt the quality of services. It would also require steps to strengthen and sustain India's advantage in knowledge and skill-intensive business and professional services where India's competitiveness has declined in recent years, through the opening of some of these segments to foreign providers, through the harmonization and internationalization of domestic standards, and through greater emphasis on innovation and intellectual property.

In sum, India needs to leverage its growing services sector more effectively than it has done so far. Its development strategy should adopt a services-cum-manufacturing rather than a services-versus-manufacturing approach, where the two-way linkages between the sectors are strengthened. This integrated, twin-pillar approach to development is unfortunately not evident in the current policy discourse on Indian manufacturing and Make in India. Each sector tends to be viewed as a silo, as if the growth of one is at the expense of the other. The earlier paradigm of development, from primary to manufacturing to services still prevails. The time is right to change this perspective and to recognize that a competitive and vibrant services sector would be an enabler for the manufacturing sector and would facilitate its movement up the value ladder. In fact, sectors such as IT services, whose growth has till date been driven by external demand, will be better able to buffer the effects of global downturns, external shocks and growing competition overseas if they become more integrated with domestic manufacturing and are boosted by domestic demand drivers. A growing, competitive, and vibrant manufacturing sector would create demand for a wide range of services and would strengthen India's service sector overall. Such a philosophy should underpin any initiative to bolster Indian manufacturing.

REFERENCES

Escaith, Hubert. 2014. 'Participating and Upgrading in Trade in Value-added: The Services Perspective'. Paper presented at the Third Conference of Latin America Network for Research in Services (REDLAS): Innovation and Internationalization in Services: New Sources of Economic Development in Latin America, 13–14 March, Mexico City.

International Trade Centre (ITC). 2014. *Global Value Chains in Services: A Case Study on Costa Rica.* Geneva.

Miroudot, Sébastien, Dorothée Rouzet, and Francesca Spinelli. 2013. 'Trade Policy Implications of Global Value Chains: Case Studies'. OECD Trade Policy Paper No. 161, Paris.

National Board of Trade. 2010. *Servicification of Swedish Manufacturing.* Stockholm: National Board of Trade.

OECD. 2015. *Competing in the Global Economy: Services–Manufacturing Linkages.* Paris.

Powers, William. 2012. 'The Value of Value Added: Measuring Global Engagement with Gross and Value-added Trade'. U.S. International Trade Commission (USITC) Office of Economics Working Paper No. 2012–11A.

Schreyer, Paul. 2013. 'The OECD–WTO Trade in Value-Added Database'. WTO Trade Data Day, Geneva, 16 January.

US International Trade Commission (USITC). 2013. 'Economic Effects of Significant US Import Restraints (8th update)—Special Topic: Services' Contribution to Manufacturing'. Investigation Number 332–325. Washington, DC. December. Available at http://docplayer.net/268749-U-s-international-trade-commission.html (accessed on 10 July 2017).

World Bank. Various years. *Connecting to Compete: Trade Logistics in the Global Economy.* Washington, DC.

World Economic Forum. Various years. *The Global Competitiveness Report.* Geneva.

———. Various years. *The Global Enabling Trade Report.* Geneva.

World Trade Organization. 2014. *World Trade Report: Trade and Development: Recent Trends and the role of the WTO.* Geneva.

13

One Size Does Not Fit All

An Analysis of the Importance of Industry-Specific Vertical Policies for Growing High Technology Industries in India

Sunil Mani

INTRODUCTION

India, currently (c. 2015) is one of the fastest growing countries in the world. But this growth is largely
driven by its services sector. From around 2006 or so,
the country has been striving to industrialize through
the manufacturing route as growth driven by the
manufacturing sector has a number of long-lasting
economic benefits. First of all, manufacturing sector
has many more linkages with the other two sectors of
the economy, namely the primary and tertiary sectors.
Second, most of the innovations that are used in the
primary and tertiary sectors emanate from the manufacturing sector. For these reasons and more, countries
across the world, including that of India, are on a conscious drive to increase the size and technical content
of its manufacturing sector. The manufacturing sector,
in turn, consists of a number of disparate industries. One way of grouping them is in terms of their
respective employment content and another way is to
group them according to their technology content.
Although the manufacturing sector in most developing

countries are supposed to be dominated by labour-
intensive or low technology industries, the current
emphasis is on increasing the share of high technology
industries. This emphasis on high technology manufacturing is for three specific reasons at least. First, high technology industries have very high levels of productivity,
both capital and labour. So, even if their share is small,
their contribution to GDP of the country is expected to
be much larger. Second, high technology industries have
much better linkages with downstream and upstream
industries as most high technology manufactured
products are based on an assembly of components. So
their multiplier effects on growth in the region where
they are located is supposed to be much higher. Third,
world trade in manufactured products is dominated
by high technology products (Lall, 1998; Mani, 2004)
and if a country wants to increase its share of exports,
it must encourage the production of high technology
manufactures. Given the capital-intensive nature of
production, use of very often-proprietary technology,
high failure rates, and so on, the role of the state in high

technology production is very well accepted. Even in advanced countries such as the USA or Japan, where the market is perceived to be more efficient in the allocation of resources, high technology production has been supported through concerted state intervention. For instance, the role of the state in the SEMATECH project in the USA or the VLSI one in Japan is now very well accepted as the main reason for the supremacy of both the USA and Japan in semiconductor production. Having successfully achieved its original target, the programme is now moving towards the development of other high technology industries such as biomedicine, cyber security, and alternative energy. The specific way in which the state intervenes in the development of high technology industries can vary in terms of its content. There are at least three ways in which the state intervenes. The first mode is a direct one in which the state establishes a state owned-enterprise (SOE) which then manufactures the high technology product. The second mode is for the state to establish a public Research and Development (R&D) programme either exclusively or in partnership with the market, develop the high technology, and then transfer it to production enterprises whether owned by the state or the private sector. The third mode is for the state to craft the ecosystem for high technology production by having explicit policies and instruments for this to be developed by both public and private sector enterprises. Most industrializing countries such as India have actually used all the three modes. First mode and second mode were very popular in the pre-liberalization phase while the third mode is the preferred one in the post-liberalization phase characterized by a paring down of state intervention in economic activities.

In the context, the purpose of the study is to analyse the growth of high technology manufacturing industries in India. Our hypothesis is that whichever mode is employed, each high technology industry requires a specific policy that is crucial for its sustained growth. In short, one size rarely fits all. Let us consider two different high technology manufacturing industries, namely aerospace and pharmaceutical. For the aerospace industry the most important instrument for its promotion will be public technology procurement, which manifests itself in the form of an offset policy. Such a policy assures a certain amount of demand for the new product, which encourages the manufacturers to be venturesome. On the contrary, for the pharmaceutical industry, the most important policy is the one on patents, as patents are extremely important for chemical industries in general and pharma in

particular.[1] However, a policy for financing R&D and policies on increasing the quantity and quality of science and engineering human resource is important for both the industries. We refer to the former set of specific policies as vertical policies (VP) and the latter set as horizontal policies (HP). The study proposes to verify the hypothesis of the crucial importance of VP by taking three successful cases and one unsuccessful case from India's manufacturing industry. The three successful cases are aerospace, pharmaceutical, and automotive industries, and the one unsuccessful case is the telecommunications equipment industry.

The motivation for the study springs from two sources. First is the growing emphasis on the need for and importance of industrial policy in promoting and nurturing industrialization in especially late industrializing countries. Industrial policy is an important area in which there has been major rethinking. The standard argument was that markets were efficient, so there was no need for government to intervene either in the allocation of resources across sectors or in the choices of technique. Also, even if markets were not efficient, governments were not likely to improve matters. But the 2008–09 global financial crisis showed that markets were not necessarily efficient and, indeed, there was a broad consensus that without strong government intervention—which included providing lifelines to certain firms and certain industries—the market economies of the USA and Europe may have collapsed. Today, the relevance and pertinence of industrial policies are acknowledged by mainstream economists and political leaders from all sides of the ideological spectrum (Stiglitz, Lin, and Monga, 2013). Second motivation is the growing emphasis in India of the size and composition of its manufacturing sector. India has become *one of the fastest growing economies* in the world and there is great emphasis on public policies for maintaining and improving this growth performance. Although India has emerged as the sixth largest manufacturing country in the world in terms of the relative size of its Manufacturing Value Added (MVA), the manufacturing sector accounts for only 17 per cent of the GDP—between 1991and 2014, the share has increased only by 2 per cent or so. But there has been a conscious effort to increase the size and sophistication of India's manufacturing

---

[1] The importance of patents to pharmaceutical innovation has been reported in several cross-industry studies by economists. See for instance Levin et al. (1987), Cohen, Nelson, and Walsh (1997), Mani and Nelson (2013).

sector during recent times (the enunciation of the National Manufacturing Policy of 2011 and the Make in India programme of 2014). Thus, both the general debate on industrial policies and the specific policy in India of promoting the manufacturing sector has highlighted the importance of specific vertical policies.

Rest of the chapter is structured into three sections. Next section maps out the growing importance of high technology products in India's commodity export basket. The section titled 'The Four High Technology Industries' identifies four high technology products that are important contributors to India's high technology exports, namely aerospace, pharmaceutical, and automotive and telecommunications equipment and identifies the key policies that have contributed to the growth performance of these high technology sectors. Of these four, telecommunication is a failure in as much as that India is very much dependent on imports for its requirement, while in the other three, India has a growing positive trade balance and innovative activity by domestic enterprises. The fourth and final section sums up the main findings of the chapter and identifies the key policies that are responsible for the growth performance of each of these chosen four high technology industries.

GROWING IMPORTANCE OF HIGH TECHNOLOGY MANUFACTURING

India has now (c. 2015) emerged as the sixth largest manufacturer in the world defined in terms of share in world MVA (see Figure 13.1). According to the latest estimates by the Central Statistical Organization (CSO), the share of the manufacturing sector in overall GDP works out to about 18 per cent (CSO, 2015). The government is pursuing a strategy for increasing both the share of manufacturing and an improvement of its technology content through a number of high profile strategies; the most recent version of it is the Make in India strategy announced in 2014.

For quite some time, and precisely since the start of the current millennium, India has been trying to improve its small manufacturing sector both in terms of its size and in terms of its technological content. There are two visible manifestations of this 'growing high technology manufacturing industry' strategy. First, a number of policy statements pertaining to specific high technology manufacturing sectors have been enunciated. Examples of this are the aerospace manufacturing (contained in the civil aviation), automotive, biotechnology, chemical, electronics and

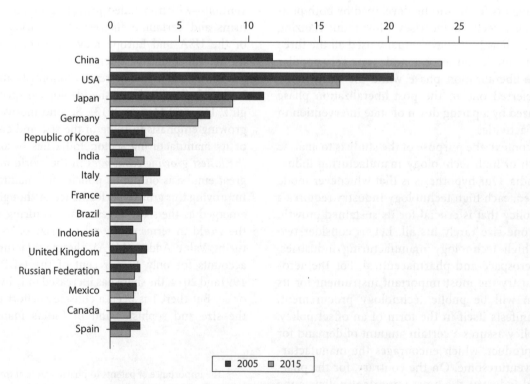

Figure 13.1   Share of India in World MVA at Constant 2010 Prices

Source: United Nations Industrial Development Organization (UNIDO), 2016.

Table 13.1 Share of High Technology Products in Total Manufactured Products (Values in Rs crore, based on Gross Value Added at Constant 2011–12 Price)

	2011–12	2012–13	2013–14
Electronic component, consumer electronics, magnetic and optical media	15652	14966	15957
Computer and peripheral equipment	3330	3822	4256
Communication equipment	3315	5273	5680
Optical and electronics products n.e.c	6567	7452	8166
Electrical equipment	48255	54278	59139
Machinery and equipment n.e.c	108555	119145	127476
Transport equipment	128665	147584	158346
Chemical and chemical products except pharmaceuticals, medicinal and botanical products	134782	121173	130846
Pharmaceutical; medicinal chemicals and botanical products	85099	87924	96923
Total high technology	534220	561617	606789
GVA unadjusted for FISIM	1358625	1400815	1490556
Share of high technology manufactures in total manufactured products (in per cent)	**39.32**	**40.09**	**40.71**

Source: Central Statistical Organization, 2015.

telecommunications, pharmaceutical, and semiconductor policies, announced from time to time during the period. Second is the growing importance of high technology products in both the gross value added and exports of the manufacturing sector. The quantitative dimensions of both these are presented in Tables 13.1 and 13.2 respectively.

Growing Importance of High Technology Products in India's MVA

It is interesting to note that high technology manufactures account for about 40 per cent of gross value added of the manufacturing sector. Unfortunately, lack of availability of consistent disaggregated data for earlier periods are not available, and so one cannot track how much of an improvement in the high technology intensity of domestic manufacturing has actually taken place. Further, our way of defining the high technology sector does fully correspond to the Organisation for Economic Co-operation and Development (OECD) definition,[2] and so, we do not foresee any overestimation of high tech output. This means that India's manufacturing sector has a high share of technology-intensive industries such as chemicals, in general, pharmaceuticals, automotive and machinery, and equipment, in general.

However, most of the high technology products are targeted at the domestic market and as we can see from the next section, India's high technology intensity (high

Table 13.2 Growing High Technology Exports from India, 1988–2013

	Value (Millions of USD)	Intensity (%)
1988	402.15	4.07
1989	512.08	4.20
1990	497.83	3.94
1991	604.23	4.69
1992	615.24	4.05
1993	695.84	4.25
1994	959.20	4.78
1995	1351.22	5.80
1996	1662.49	6.87
1997	1685.90	6.54
1998	1414.83	5.62
1999	1679.11	5.74
2000	2062.49	6.26
2001	2286.51	6.97
2002	2353.67	6.24
2003	2710.12	5.95
2004	3355.93	6.00
2005	4139.24	5.80
2006	4876.30	6.07
2007	5997.79	6.40
2008	7738.41	6.78
2009	10728.45	9.09
2010	10086.63	7.18
2011	12870.673	6.87
2012	12434.267	6.63
2013	16693.424	8.07

Source: World Bank, 2016.

[2] See the OECD definition at http://www.nsf.gov/statistics/seind93/chap6/doc/6s193.htm (Accessed on 7 April 2016).

tech exports measured as a percentage of manufactured exports) although doubled itself over time, is still less, much less, compared to other high technology promoting countries such as that of China.

Growing Importance of High Technology Products in India's Manufactured Exports

As a late industrializing country, deficient in both disembodied technology and management and organizational skills, India's export basket was, to a large extent, dominated by labour-intensive manufacturers such a cotton textile, ready-made garments, gems and jewellery, and leather and leather manufactures. However, India's export basket has slowly undergone a qualitative change with more high technology products taking a discernible position in it. In fact, the high technology product intensity has virtually doubled itself during 1988 through 2013 (Table 13.1). In value terms it has been growing at a rate of 17 per cent per annum during this period. The growing importance of high technology production is evident even in Indian patenting abroad as almost the entire patents granted to Indian inventors at the United States Patent and Trademark Office (USPTO), during the same period, is in high technology areas such as pharmaceuticals and computer software.

High technology exports from India are driven by four items, namely automobiles, pharmaceuticals, electronics (read as telecommunications equipment), and aerospace (Figure 13.2). Of these four, exports of three of them have been increasing (although there is decline

in aerospace exports in 2015 compared to 2014). Exports of electronic products have been steadily declining. However, India has a consistent positive trade balance in only three of them, namely, aerospace, automobiles, and pharmaceuticals, while it has a growing negative trade balance in telecommunications products. This is a bit counterintuitive as India had a long strategy of developing local technological capability in telecommunications equipment where considerable amount of state investments in manufacturing and R&D were done. Further, with a total subscriber strength of nearly 1 billion telephone subscribers, growing India has one of the largest markets in the world for telecommunications equipment, but it has virtually no serious manufacturer of telecom equipment but only assemblers of equipment based on imported components. It was seen that gross value added to gross value of output ratio is very low in the case of this industry (Mani, 2012).

Of these four industries, only the success achieved in pharmaceutical industry has merited any detailed attention. Although there are some studies available on the automobile and telecommunications equipment industries, there are practically no studies on the aerospace industry in the country. While the role played by the policy on patents in explaining the growth of India's pharmaceutical industry has been debated, the role of public policies in shaping the growth trajectory of the other three high technology industries have hardly attracted any attention in the scholarly literature. In fact, in India, there has been an erroneous tendency to equate high technology with luxury consumption goods, which

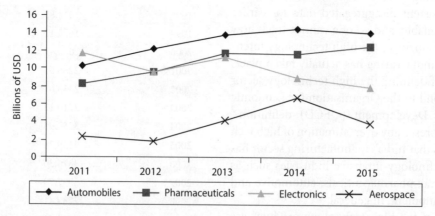

Figure 13.2 Exports of High Technology Products Disaggregated during 2011 through 2015
Source: ITC Trade Map-International Trade Statistics.[3]

---

[3] Available at http://www.trademap.org/tradestat/Product_SelCountry_TS.aspx?nvpm=1|699|||TOTAL|||2|1|1|2|2|1|1|1| (accessed on 29 March 2016).

are hardly suited for bulk of the consumers with very low purchasing power. But as recent events and discussions have showed rather conclusively that each of these four high technologies have made a perceptible difference to the living conditions of an average Indian citizen. For instance, having a successful and innovative generic drug industry has made many lifesaving drugs at affordable prices, having one of the cheapest telecommunications services and indeed equipment (although much of the latter is imported) has increased the affordability of telecommunication services and reduced the rural urban digital divide by a significant amount. Likewise, having a successful aerospace industry has increased communications services and have increased the diffusion of tele-medicine and education in unreachable physical locations, and having a domestic automobile industry has increased both the movement of passengers and goods across large tracts of the country. In other words, the growth of high technology industries has gone towards improving the quality of life of an Indian citizen. In the following section, we analyse the role of public policies in explaining the growth performance of four chosen high technology industries, although it has not resulted in successful outcomes in all the four cases.

THE FOUR HIGH TECHNOLOGY INDUSTRIES

We discuss the four cases separately, beginning with the aerospace case.

Aerospace Industry

The aerospace industry in India consists of two distinct industries: aeronautical and astronautics. While the success of the astronautics is fairly well understood as India has demonstrated time and again, its technological capability to design and manufacture and successfully launch both satellite launch vehicles and satellites, its forays in aeronautics is hardly recognized. Although India has one of the most profitable aerospace enterprises in the world, its technological activities are almost entirely in the defence space. However, what is most interesting is that India has started becoming an important exporter of aeronautical products since 2010 (see Table 13.3). Currently (c. 2013) India accounts for over 2 per cent of the world exports and it is also significant to note

Table 13.3   Exports of Aerospace Products from India

	Exports (in millions of USD)	Share in world exports (%)	Ratio of India to China
2010	1534.6	1.1	1.22
2011	2302.3	0.9	1.42
2012	1775.5	0.6	1.14
2013	4151.3	1.3	2.15
2014	6721.2	201	2.54
2015	3815.8	na	1.10

Source: Computed from UN Comtrade

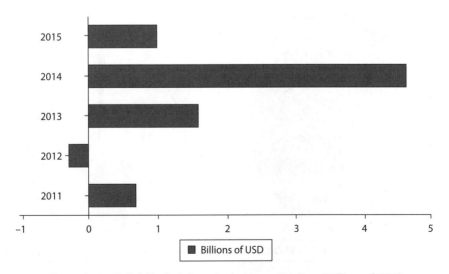

Figure 13.3   India's Trade Balance in Aerospace Products (Billions of USD)

Source: Computed from ITC, Trade Map-International Trade Statistics.[4]

---

[4] Available at http://www.trademap.org/tradestat/Country_SelProduct_TS.aspx (accessed on 24 March 2016).

that its level of exports is twice that of China's. India is increasingly getting inserted into the global value chain for aeronautical products. In fact, most of the leading aircraft manufacturers like Airbus and Boeing have started manufacturing and R&D operations in India, although the scale of it may be low.

Types of Aerospace Products Exported

India's aerospace exports is largely composed of aircraft parts (Figure 13.4). However, exports in 2015 are largely composed of aircraft to Sri Lanka. According to Engineering Export Promotion Council, Sri Lanka has been importing engineering items from India and the current increase in exports is due to various reasons including the free trade agreement with India and some big orders received in the recent past. However, the traditional market for India's exports of aerospace products is to the UAE, USA, UK, France, and Germany in that order.

Aerospace product manufacturing is taking place through firms located in five aerospace clusters of which, quantitatively speaking, the most important one is in Bangalore. This is because one of the largest aerospace manufacturing firms in the country, the state-owned Hindustan Aeronautics Limited, is located in Bangalore; besides, a number of sector specific research establishments, such as the National Aerospace Laboratory, are also located in the city. Mani (2013) had discussed the evolving sectoral system of innovation of this high technology industry in terms of its three building blocks namely the

lead actors, the technology domain, and demand. At the sub-national level, the state governments of both Karnataka and Andhra Pradesh have very explicit policies for establishing aerospace manufacturing clusters in their respective states (Government of Andhra Pradesh, 2013; PWC, 2015).

What can possibly explain this phenomenal growth in exports of aeronautical products from India?

Contribution of the Offset Policy

Our hypothesis is that this could possibly be traced to a vertical policy known as Offset Policy (OP).[6] The OP of a country defines the mechanism for routing procurement funds paid to international contractors back into the spending country. OP can manifest itself in three ways: direct, semi-direct, and indirect.

Offset Policy in India

The policy was introduced in India for the first time in 2005. Since then, the Defence Offset Guidelines have been revised in 2006, 2008, 2011, 2012, 2013, 2015, and

---

[6] The key objective of the Defence Offset Policy is to leverage capital acquisitions to develop Indian defence industry by (i) fostering development of internationally competitive enterprises, (ii) augmenting capacity for Research, Design, and Development related to defence products and services, and (iii) encouraging development of synergistic sectors like civil aerospace and internal security.

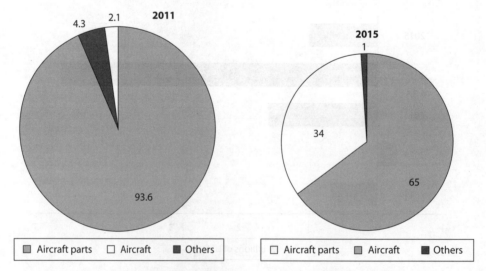

Figure 13.4 Distribution of Aerospace Products Exported from India According to Type

Source: Computed from ITC, Trade Map-International Trade Statistics.[5]

---

[5] Available at http://www.trademap.org/tradestat/Country_SelProduct_TS.aspx (accessed on 24 March 2016).

2016 based on difficulties faced in their implementation and feedback from stakeholders and the same have been made more comprehensive and user friendly to derive maximum advantage from offsets in defence contracts (see Figure 13.5).

According to the OP when the value of either a defence or civilian contract exceeds the threshold of Rs 3 billion, 30 per cent of the value of the equipment imported will have to be co-produced or manufactured in India by the exporter. The OP then implies a direct and positive correlation between import and exports of the equipment or product covered by the policy. The Defence Acquisition Council (DAC), the apex decision-making body of the ministry, approved changes to its Defence Procurement Procedures (DPP) in January 2016 to introduce a new category for indigenously made products. The DAC has revised the defence offset clause, which will now be applied only to contracts of more than Rs 2,000 crores instead of the current Rs 300 crores. The rationale for this change is to encourage more foreign companies to do business with India, but it has the greatest danger of negating the success achieved through the present policy in jump starting a domestic aerospace industry. However, in order to minimize this negative effect, the government has introduced a new category under the new category for Indigenously Designed, Developed and Manufactured (IDDM) equipment, it will be mandatory for 40 per cent of the content to be sourced locally. According to industry sources (PwC-Assocham, 2016), this category is expected to bring two benefits to the fledgling aerospace industry in India: (i) significant investments in R&D; and (ii) it will ensure that the human resource in India is engaged in developing cutting-edge technologies in defence.

Routes through Which Offsets Can Increase Domestic Production and Exports

The precise routes through which offsets can create an aerospace industry is mapped out in Figure 13.6. Hitherto (c. 2014) a total of 24 offset contracts have been concluded amounting to approximately $5 billion. These offset contracts are currently under implementation stage with the execution period of certain contracts extending till 2022, although the status of most of the contracts, at the moment, is not known in any detail. The Indian government announced some years ago its plans to implement a fully automated system to monitor, account for, and audit offsets in real time, however, to date, this system has not been realized. The Indian Offset Partners (IOP) through which the vendors are executing offset obligations are both from public and private sector. In those cases where foreign vendors are not adhering to implementation schedule of signed offset contracts, penalties at the rate of 5 per cent of the unfulfilled obligations are being levied as per the provisions of the offset guidelines. But, as pointed out by successive Comptroller and Auditor General (CAG) reports that the actual offsets implemented is short of what was expected to be implemented.

Offsets and Aerospace Exports

The offset policy can explain much of the aerospace exports till 2013 as most of the offsets are actually in

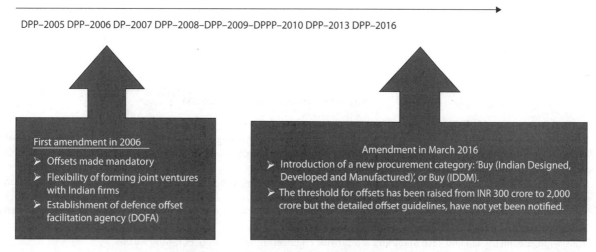

DPP–2005 DPP–2006 DP–2007 DPP–2008–DPP–2009–DPPP–2010 DPP–2013 DPP–2016

First amendment in 2006
➤ Offsets made mandatory
➤ Flexibility of forming joint ventures with Indian firms
➤ Establishment of defence offset facilitation agency (DOFA)

Amendment in March 2016
➤ Introduction of a new procurement category: 'Buy (Indian Designed, Developed and Manufactured)', or Buy (IDDM).
➤ The threshold for offsets has been raised from INR 300 crore to 2,000 crore but the detailed offset guidelines, have not yet been notified.

Figure 13.5   Major Trends in India's Offset Policy

Source: Department of Defence Production, Government of India.

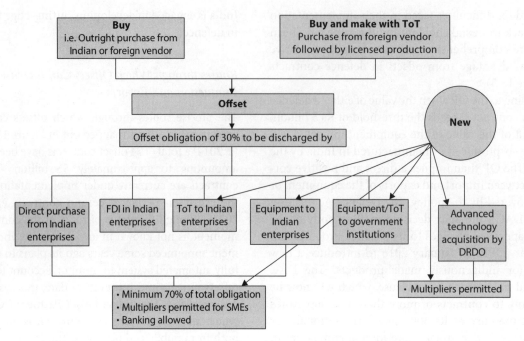

Figure 13.6   Routes through which an Offset Policy can Create Domestic Aerospace Industry

Source: PWC, undated.

the aerospace arena with foreign buyers such as Boeing, Airbus, Lockheed Martin, and Dassault Aviation and the Indian beneficiaries of these offsets are aerospace companies such as Hindustan Aeronautics and private companies such as the Tata, Reliance group, Mahindra, and the Larsen and Toubro. During the period, 2008 through 2010, for which data are available, a cumulative sum of USD 2.64 billion was the offset amount (Figure 13.7). The largest offsets is from Boeing. Of late, Airbus has also become a very large contractor to Indian aerospace companies (see Box 13.1).

Apart from Airbus, Boeing too is concerned with sourcing components worth about $1 billion from India

as part of an offset obligation linked to the purchase of $3 billion-helicopter deal.

With the ongoing acquisition spree of India's airline carriers such as Indigo, Go Air, and Spice Jet, the amount of offsets that will be implemented is likely to increase manifold, although raising the threshold for offsets to a much higher level is likely to dampen it as well. Success will now depend on IDDM policy. If the daily announcement of domestic manufacturing activity by foreign aerospace firms is anything to go by, domestic manufacturing of aerospace components is bound to increase by a significant amount in the years to come.

Box 13.1   Airbus Procurement from India (c2015)

- In 2015, Airbus exceeded $500 million in annual procurement from India from over 45 suppliers.
- Hindustan Aeronautics Ltd makes half of the Airbus A320 family forward passenger doors produced worldwide, while Dynamatic Technologies Ltd makes flap-track beams for A320 on a global single-source basis and has been contracted to manufacture them for the A330 family.
- Mahindra Aerospace Ltd is in a contract to supply a million aero-components per year, while Aequs Pvt Ltd recently added to a pre-existing sheet metal, assembly and forging facility.
- Tata Advanced Materials Ltd provides composite parts for the wing for the A350 XWB and the A320, while another Tata unit TAL Manufacturing Solutions Ltd is supplying some parts for the A320.
- Infosys Ltd, Geometric Ltd and Tech Mahindra Ltd provide engineering and IT services for the Airbus.

Source: Sanjai, 2016.

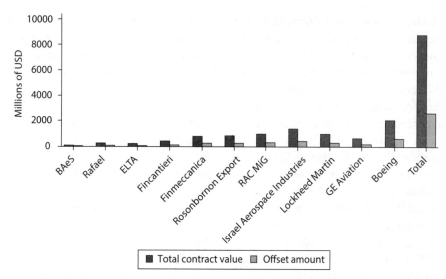

Figure 13.7   Offset Amount vs Total Contracted Value in Aerospace Contracts in India, 2008–10

Source: Lucintel, 2012.

Other Policies Promoting Aerospace Exports

Apart from the offset policy, which creates the condition for a number of small- and medium-sized enterprises (SMEs) to emerge in the country, three other factors also have led to the emergence and growth of the aerospace industry in India. The first factor is India's growing emphasis on space research and also its growing techno-logical capability in designing and manufacturing satel-lites and satellite launch vehicles. This policy has spawned a large number of private sector aerospace component manufacturers in the private sector located mostly in the South Indian cities of Bangalore and Hyderabad. The second one is the increasing opening up of India's manu-facturing sector and specifically the defence equipment-manufacturing sector that has resulted in increasing inflows of foreign direct investment (FDI) to the sector. This policy has also resulted in a large number of joint ventures in aerospace manufacturing in the country. The third factor is the increasing technological sophistication of India's computer software industry. We now discuss each of these three factors in some detail below.

Growing Emphasis on Space Research

Since the 1960s, India has an active programme of space research. Approximately a third of India's total expenditure is on space research. Unlike many other space agencies across the world, the Indian Space Research Organisation (ISRO) assembles satellites and launch vehicles from parts supplied by ISROs eleven centres spread around the coun-

Table 13.4   Space Budget as a Per Cent of GDP

	2013		2008
Russia	0.25	Russia	0.09
USA	0.23	USA	0.29
France	0.10	France	0.09
Japan	0.07	Japan	0.06
China	0.07	China	0.11
India	0.06	India	0.06

Source: OECD, 2014.

try. It also has a commercial branch—Antrix—which, among other things, exports satellite components. How-ever, increasingly over time, ISRO has been able to transfer the technology for manufacture of satellite components to a whole host of private sector space manufactureres. According to various estimates (OECD, 2014), about 80 per cent of the parts of Polar Satellite Launch Vehicles (PSLVs) are now produced by the industry.

India's satellite communication sector has experi-enced significant growth over the period 2009 through 2014, driven by explosive demand from Direct to Home (DTH) pay-TV platforms and growing telecommunica-tion needs in the country. The satellite communications (satcom) value chain is strongly influenced by the ISRO that is present all along the satcom value chain, includ-ing satellite manufacturing, launch, satellite operations, regulations, and partially services. On the manufactur-ing level, roughly half of the country's satellite manu-facturing sector spending is dedicated to developing communications satellites. While ISRO dominates the satcom manufacturing landscape, outsourcing to foreign and national companies will continue to provide growth opportunities for a number of manufacturers. Dhruva Space, Xovian, and Transpace are new private sector manufacturers that have come up during the period since 2010. However, much of India's exports of satellite manufactures and services are exported by ISROs commercial wing, Antrix Corporation. Exports by Antrix Corporation, however, has been fluctuating as most of the satellite components manufactured within the country are exclusively meant for ISRO's consumption (Figure 13.8). Antrix has also been rendering a number of other technical services such as launching satellites built by foreign customers on ISROs PSLVs and these are not included in the export data depicted in Figure 13.9. Hitherto (c. 2015), 57 foreign satellites from 21 countries have been successfully launched by PSLV.[7] During 2013 through 2015, a total of 28 international customer satellites belonging to nine countries, namely Austria (2), Canada (5), Denmark (1), France (1), Germany (1), Indonesia (1), Singapore (7), UK (6), and USA (4) were launched, and Antrix has earned Euro 80.3 million from these launches. Further, it has signed agreements with clients in seven countries for launching 25 satellites during 2016–17. These include 12 from the USA, four from Germany, three from Canada, three from Algeria, and one each from Indonesia, Japan, and Malaysia.

This growing emphasis on space research and indeed manufacturing is also a factor explaining India's arrival on the world market for aerospace products.

Linkages with Foreign Buyers

Increasingly, India has managed to insert itself into the global value chain of international aeronautical manufacturing. This is very evident in two of the world's largest aircraft manufacturers establishing their operations in the country. Both have manufacturing and research collaborations with a number of Indian public and private sector aerospace manufacturers. For instance, Airbus has an agreement with Hindustan Aeronautics Limited (HAL) to manufacture forward passenger doors for the A320 aircraft. HAL now produces half of all A320 forward passenger doors. In addition, Airbus' list of Indian partners and suppliers has expanded to encompass engineering, IT services, technical publications, research and technology and manufacturing of aero-structures, detail parts and sub-assemblies. In March 2009, Boeing launched a research and technology centre for sustained collaboration with Indian R&D organizations—both government and private, universities and companies. Since 2007, Boeing has been working together with the Indian Institute of Science and Wipro and HCL, as part of the Aerospace Network Research Consortium. Boeing also has manufacturing contracts with Indian

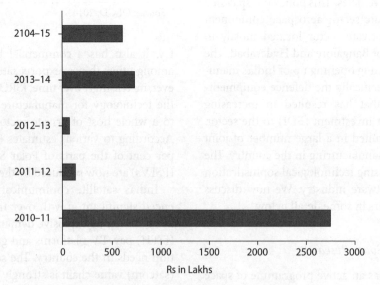

Figure 13.8 Exports of Antrix Corporation

Source: Annual reports of Antrix Corporation (various issues).

---

[7] See answers to questions in India's upper house of the parliament, Rajya Sabha, http://164.100.47.4/newrsquestion/Search_minwise.aspx (Accessed on 4 April 2016).

aeronautical companies such as HAL and Dynamatics for manufacturing aircraft parts and components and has now a joint venture with Tata Advanced Systems Limited (TASL). In fact, TASL has a number of other joint ventures with world's leading aerospace manufacturers. Mahindra Aerospace is another domestic manufacturer having manufacturing facilities for air frame parts and assemblies. The firm also has a number of foreign associations, primarily in Australia. Thus, the Indian aerospace manufacturing industry is developing both its production and technological capability by being able to associate itself with some of the leading aircraft manufacturers abroad. This capability is now manifested in increasing exports of aerospace products from India.

Finally, there are two governmental initiatives which will have potential implications for developing the civil aerospace industry in India. First is the National Civil Aircraft Development project (NCAD) and second is the most recent policy on civil aviation. Although the NCAD project was initiated in 2007 to design and fully develop a 90 seater Regional Transport Aircraft (RTA), nothing much is known about its actual progress. The draft National Civil Aviation Policy released in 2015 by the Ministry of Civil Aviation (MoCA) has also a number of provisions for increasing aircraft production in India (Box 13.2).

Increasing Technological Sophistication of India's Computer Software Industry

India's computer software industry has become the world leader in rendering of computer and information services since 2005 (Mani, 2014). It has managed to maintain and improve its leadership position during the last 11 years

or so, and has also been going up the technology ladder in terms of rendering IT services to customers abroad. Aerospace design is one of those areas in which all the mainstream IT services providers and a few niche services providers have been showing their technological competences. This crucial capability is also going to give a fillip to India's aerospace industry. A proxy for this capability is the increasing exports of architectural, engineering, and technical services (see Figure 13.9).

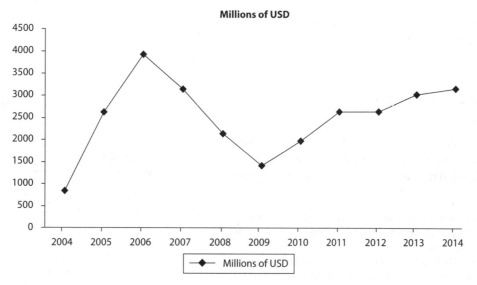

Figure 13.9 Exports of Architectural, Engineering, and Technical Services from India
Source: Computed from UN Trade in Services Database.

Pharmaceutical Industry

The pharmaceutical industry is one of India's main high technology industries. The industry has three characteristics that are worth noting:

- India is an important player in the production and supply of generic drugs;
- India is virtually self-sufficient in most drugs;
- The drug industry is very innovative.

In the following sections, we discuss each of these three features in some more detail.

An Important Generic Drugs Manufacturer in the World

India's pharmaceutical production falls into three broad categories: (i) generic drugs, accounting for 72 per cent, over the counter (OTC) medicines accounting for 19 per cent, and patented drugs, the remaining, 9 per cent. Generic drugs are the largest share and India alone accounts for 20 per cent of the global exports in terms of volume, making the country the largest supplier of generic medicines in the world. This has earned the country the sobriquet of 'pharmacy of the developing world'. The country manufactures and sells over 60,000 generic brands across 60 therapeutic categories. The number of Abbreviated New Drug Applications (ANDA)[9] approved by the US FDA can be taken as a good indicator of the innovation capability of generic drugs manufacturers. Going by this indicator, over 40 per cent of the ANDAs issued by the US FDA have gone to Indian pharmaceutical firms. Historically, too, this has been the case (Mani and Nelson, 2013; see Table 13.5). The country has more than 100 manufacturing facilities approved by US FDA. The US FDA official figures indicate that 6,300 active Drug Master Files (DMFs) with the regulatory body, of which 26 per cent or 1,700 are from Indian companies.

India Is Self-Sufficient in Drugs

India is self-sufficient in most drugs except for a small number of patented lifesaving drugs. Exports have been continuously rising and in 2014 it stood at 11.56 billion of US dollars. As a result of increase in exports,

[9] ANDAs were introduced in the Hatch-Waxman Act and are used by foreign generic drugmakers to challenge a USA patent before its expiry. If successful, the applicant gets a 6-month (180 day) exclusive right to sell its generic version. At the end of that period, other generic drug companies can enter other versions of the molecule, and generally, the price of the generic version falls sharply.

Table 13.5 Number of ANDAs Granted to Indian Pharmaceutical Firms in the USA

	Number of ANDAS Approved	Share of the World (%)
2004	26	6.8
2005	49	14.2
2006	72	19.5
2007	98	24.6
2008	126	29.1
2009	126	31.3
2010	130	30.9
2011	154	34.8
2012	201	40.3
2013	158	42.7

Source: Based on USFDA data cited in CRISIL, 2014: 7.

trade balance too has been rising and it remained positive all through the years. Pharmaceuticals is one of the few manufactured products where the trade balance has been consistently positive and that too rising over time (Figure 13.10). This increase in exports is the

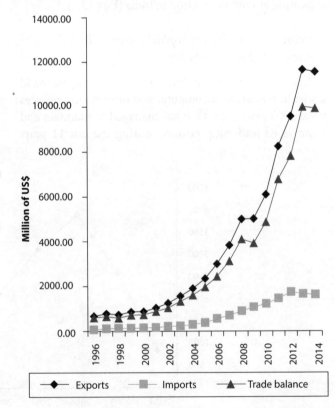

Figure 13.10 Trends in Trade Balance of India's Pharmaceutical Industry

Source: Computed from UN Comtrade.

result of India's considerable technological capability in the design, manufacture, and sale of essentially generic drugs which are off patent. Chaudhuri (2005) has shown that this capability, to a large extent, is explained by the Indian Patents Act of 1970 which enabled the domestic firms to do reverse engineering. In short, the role of the state in enabling the domestic firms to acquire this important capability hardly needs to be reemphasized.

Pharmaceutical Industry Is Very Innovative

The pharmaceutical industry is one of the leading innovative industries in India. In fact, the industry dominates both in terms of conventional measures of innovation such as in R&D expenditure incurred and in patents granted. In fact, the industry alone accounts for over 20 per cent of the business enterprise R&D (Mani, 2015). The number of patents granted to the industry, even after TRIPS compliance has increased manifold (Figure 13.11). In short, the main VP that was crucial for the growth and evolution of the pharmaceutical industry was the patents policy.

Factors Explaining the Emergence and Growth of India's Pharmaceutical Industry

The growth performance of this high technology industry has fairly well been documented (Chaudhuri, 2005).

There is now enough consensus that the growth of a world-class generics industry in India has been contributed, to a great extent, by the non-TRIPS compliant Indian Patents Act of 1970 which did not recognize product patents in pharmaceuticals, agrochemicals, and food products. Only process patents in these three products were recognized by the prevailing intellectual property regime. Even in this case, the patent term was only seven years from the grant of the patent and the burden of proof for any possible infringement of the process patent lay with the patentee whose patent was infringed upon. Such an intellectual property rights (IPR) regime enabled, first of all, a number of Indian pharma companies to emerge, and once emerged, grow very fast by developing own technological capability through reverse engineering and imitation. So the crucial one policy which made the difference for India's generic drug industry is the patent policy. Even though the policy has been made TRIPS compliant in 2005, the Indian drug industry continues to grow and innovate as evidenced by increases in the exports, positive trade balance, increase in direct employment, and increases in innovative activity (measured through increases in R&D expenditure, patents granted, number of ANDAs secured, and so on; see Mani and Nelson, 2013). This is because the industry has managed to develop fair amount of domestic technological capability, which enabled it to stand on its own feet when a

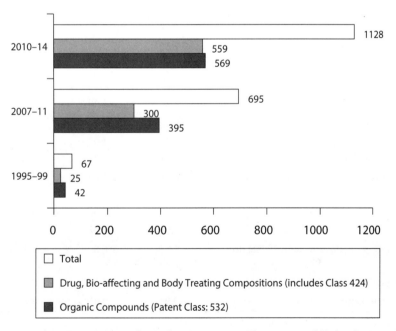

Figure 13.11   Trends in Patents Granted to Indian Inventors in Pharmaceutical Technologies at the USPTO

Source: Computed from USPTO.

product patent regime was re-imposed in 2005. Exploiting variation in the timing of patent decisions, a recent paper by Duggan, Garthwaite, and Goyal (2016) estimated that a molecule receiving a patent experienced an average price increase of just 3–6 per cent, with larger increases for more recently developed molecules and for those produced by monopoly firms when the patent system began. Their results also show little impact on quantities sold or on the number of pharmaceutical firms operating in the market. In other words, TRIPS compliance does not seem to have had any negative effects on the Indian pharmaceutical industry. Our argument is that this is essentially due to the build-up of domestic technological capability that happened during the non-TRIPS compliant. Further, in addition to this, the policy of providing R&D tax incentives and research grants to this industry has also been another important policy that contributed the growth performance of the industry very favourably.

Automotive Industry

India's automotive industry is one of the successful cases of India's economic liberalization strategy set into motion since 1991. The industry, which was dominated by a few domestic manufacturers, was hardly known for any innovations before 1991, but is now one of the fastest growing manufacturing industries (real GVA of the industry grew at 7 per cent in 2013–14) not just in India but globally as well. In 2015, India emerged as the second fastest growing car market in the world next only to China. Sales of two wheelers is touching 20 million units during the year, a first, with all major two-wheeler manufacturers registering high double-digit growth and passenger vehicle sales have touched almost 2.6 million in 2015. India, in 2015, was the largest tractor manufacturer, second largest two-wheeler manufacturer, fifth largest heavy truck manufacturer, sixth largest passenger vehicle manufacturer, and seventh largest commercial vehicle manufacturer in the world. Gross turnover of the industry has increased from just $30.5 billion in 2007 to $74 billion in 2015.[10] Exports of cars and auto parts together now make up for a large share of India's exports—even crossing the shares of its traditional exports such as gems and jewellery, readymade garments, and so on.

[10] The source of this data is the website of Society for Indian Automobile Manufacturers (SIAM), http://www.siamindia.com/statistics.aspx?mpgid=8&pgidtrail=10 (accessed on 8 April 2016).

Table 13.6 Shares (in Per Cent) of Various Products Exported at Four Digit Level of Disaggregation

	2011	2012	2013	2014	2015
Petroleum oils, not crude	18.11	18.22	19.93	19.16	11.36
Diamonds, not mounted or set	10.69	7.72	8.6	7.58	8.3
Medicament mixtures (not 3002, 3005, 3006), put in dosage	2.32	2.9	3.06	3.24	4.25
Articles of jewellery parts thereof	4.77	6.29	3.15	4.12	3.78
Rice	1.35	2.12	2.43	2.49	2.41
Cars (including station wagon)	1.2	1.46	1.65	1.82	2.04
Gold unwrought or in semi-manufactured forms	0.15	0.01	0.73	0.77	2.01
Meat of bovine animals, frozen	0.85	1.02	1.31	1.49	1.52
Parts and access of motor vehicles	0.91	1.21	1.16	1.26	1.47
Cotton yarn (not sewing thread) 85 per cent or more cotton, not retail	0.91	1.09	1.42	1.29	1.42
Crustaceans	0.55	0.62	0.88	1.21	1.21
T-shirts, singlets and other vests, knitted or crocheted	0.69	0.72	0.77	0.86	1.08
Light vessel, dredger; floating dock; floating/submersible drill platform	1.57	0.8	0.39	1.05	1.06
Women's suits, jackets, dresses skirts, and shorts	0.84	0.78	0.73	0.81	1.02
Aircraft (helicopter, aeroplanes) and spacecraft (satellites)	0.02	0.01	0.77	1.65	0.94

Source: Computed from ITC, Trade Map-International Trade Statistics.[11]

[11] Available at http://www.trademap.org/tradestat/Country_SelProduct_TS.aspx (accessed on 8 April 2016).

The fact that India has emerged as one of the leading manufacturers of especially passenger cars is a fascinating story and our argument here is that this too can be related to industry specific policies which the government put in place beginning with the auto policy of 2002. A chronological evolution of these policies that were directed at the automotive industry is mapped out in Figure 13.12. The success of the industry could be explained by the liberalization of the industry in general. Although this was a horizontal policy, it affected the automotive industry much more than any other industry. Further, there were many VPs for the first time like the Auto Policy of 2002, the Automotive Mission Plan of 2006–16, National Automotive Testing and R&D Infrastructure Project (NATRiP), and the specific taxation proposals contained in various union budgets. All these VPs aided the firms in the industry,

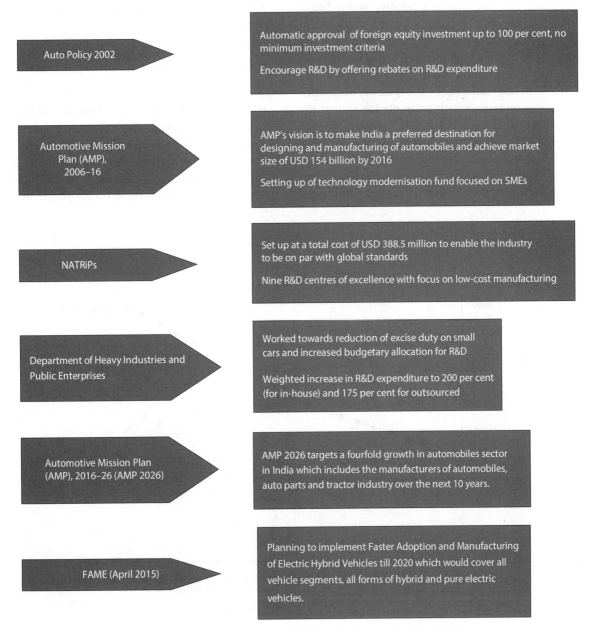

Figure 13.12   Specific Policies that have Supported the Growth of the Industry

Source: Adapted from India Brand Equity Fund, 2016.

both domestic and foreign to grow and improve both its domestic and export performances as well.

Along with growing exports, the industry has also become one of the strong R&D spenders in India's manufacturing sector: the industry accounts for about 8 per cent of business enterprise R&D in the country and is ranked number two in terms of its level of R&D spending.

Telecommunications Equipment Industry

There are two facets to the telecommunication industry growth story. The first one is a positive story; India, in 2016, was one of the world's largest markets for telecommunications equipment. The second one is a negative story of that large market being largely met through imports primarily from China as the country does not have any technological capability to manufacture mobile phones, which accounts for almost the entire share of the market. The total number of telecom subscribers, which was just 5 million in 1991, now stands at over 1 billion, and every month India is adding subscribers which are more than the total number of subscribers in a number of Western European countries. Figure 13.13 traces the trends in total number of subscribers and the monthly additions to it in India. Although India had pursued a policy of self-reliance in telecommunications technology, due to severe limitations in its actual implementation, the country has got into a situation of importing its telecom requirements from especially China. These large-scale imports have resulted in a growing negative trade balance in telecommunications equipment. Our argument here is that both the positive and negative sides of the story can be ascribed to government policies. We now propose to analyse the two sides of the telecommunications equipment coin by beginning with the positive side of the story.

How Did the State Create Such a Large Market for Telecom Equipment?

Historically speaking, right through Independence in 1947, the government has sought to create a domestic manufacturing base in telecom equipment, although the size of this market was only a minute fraction of what it is now. Over the period from 1947 and up until now, one can identify three broad phases in the extent

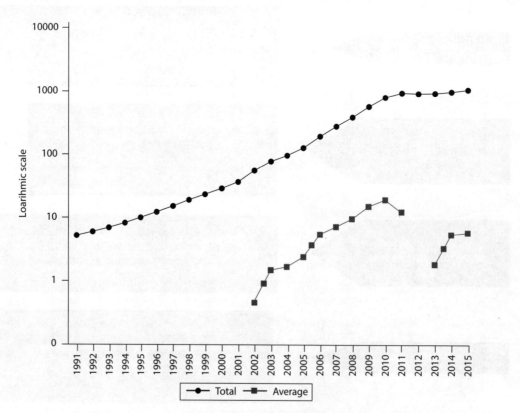

Figure 13.13   Emergence of India as a Huge Market for Telecommunication Equipment

Source: Compiled from monthly press releases of Telecom Regulatory Authority of India (TRAI).

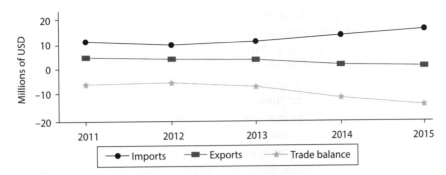

Figure 13.14   Exports, Imports and Trade Balance in Telecommunications Equipment

Source: Compiled from ITC, Trade Map-International Trade Statistics.[12]

and nature of government intervention in the telecom equipment industry. The first phase covers the long period of 1947 through 1985, when state intervention took an extreme form of manufacturing being under the exclusive purview of state-owned undertakings but with imported technology. The second phase covers the period 1985 through 1991, when the manufacturing of some of the equipment were deregulated and opened up to private sector participation and the state establishing a public laboratory to generate state-of-the-art technologies domestically. The third phase is the period since 1991, when the market was opened up to private and indeed foreign participation. The main difference between the first two and the third phase is in the size of the market. During the first two phases, the market for telecom equipment were extremely small as there was only one technology, namely fixed line and only one service provider, which too was owned, by the state. Mani (2005) had shown that during this period the main instrument for market creation was public technology procurement as the demand for these equipment emanated from just one state-owned provider. During the third phase there are two technologies, namely fixed and mobile and a large number of private sector service providers. Our argument here is that the state increased the size of the market by first promoting competition between service providers and then by regulating their market conducts through an independent regulatory agency. This increased competition coupled with regulation reduced telecom tariffs. In the previous section, we charted the phenomenal growth of the mobile services industry in India. Although mobile communications

started to make their mark in the late 1990s, the growth picked up and accelerated over the last five years and to be very specific, since 2006 or so. This has led to demand for a variety of telecommunications equipment, most of which, especially the handsets, was not being domestically manufactured. As Mani (2005) has shown, this is because the domestic manufacturing industry and indeed the sectoral system of innovation that the state built up over time focused almost entirely on fixed line technology and indeed products. So the initial growth in the services segment was met through imports of equipment leading to very high import dependence in the economy. However, with the domestic market becoming sizeable, with an average of six million subscribers per month (say in 2015), the monthly demand for telecom equipment in India is almost three or five times the annual demand for such equipment in countries such as Finland, South Korea, and the USA (homes of some of the largest mobile handset manufacturers in the world). Such being the case, there has been a steady increase in the establishment of domestic manufacturing capacities in India by all leading multinational companies (MNCs) in the telecommunications equipment industry. However, most of the equipment were either imported or assembled locally with imported components. India has always been eager to create a domestic telecom manufacturing industry. Its history can be traced back to 1948, when the very first public-sector enterprise created turned out to be the leading telecom equipment manufacturer, ITI, set up in Bangalore. This was followed by the establishment of a public laboratory in the name of C-DOT in 1985 to enhance the country's domestic technological capability in the area of equipment manufacturing. Mani (2005) had shown that the main public policy instrument used for domestic

[12]   Available at http://www.trademap.org/tradestat/Country_SelProduct_TS.aspx (accessed on 8 April 2016).

manufacturing was public technology procurement. However, with the deregulation and consequent privatization of the distribution of services, the ability of the state to practice this has been compromised. So during the 1990s, we find two discernible routes adopted by the state for encouraging the new desire of the government to make India a manufacturing hub. The first one is through the provision of a variety of fiscal incentives, including through the creation of Special Economic Zones (SEZs). The second is through opening up the sector to FDI in telecom equipment manufacturing.

Mani (2012) showed that the way the telecom service providers were licensed ensured that there was intensive competition between them. The national market was divided into several circles or service areas and in each of the service areas, a number of service providers were licensed. There are, at present, at least 10 service providers in most service areas, although four of them are very recent entrants and are too small in size to infuse any competitive pressure on the market. We measure competition in terms of the Herfindahl Index (HI). The HI at the national level during the period 2003 through 2015 was within a narrow range of 0.14 to 0.16 with the HI in most years at 0.14. Most of the service providers have focused on specific regional markets, with the exception of the last four service providers. In fact, there are only four service providers that have a presence in all the service areas. It is also interesting to see that the service areas where the state-owned BSNL has a monopoly position are also those with very low revenue potential. In other words,

the private-sector providers have positioned themselves in the most revenue-earning markets. Also, it is evident that it is in the circles with high revenue-earning potential that one sees an increase in the intensity of competition, such as the metropolitan areas of Delhi, Mumbai, and Chennai.

One of the more direct effects of this competition is lower prices. Before the deregulation of the telecom services industry and indeed the entry of mobile service providers, the telecom consumers were periodically subjected to increases in the tariff. This has now been effectively checked. Although it is not easy to talk about the price of telecom services, basically it follows a two-part tariff, both in the case of fixed and mobile services, first an activation charge followed by a charge for each type of call. For mobile communication consumers, there is the additional cost of calls according to whether it is post-paid or pre-paid. Based on estimates made by TRAI we have obtained average revenue per user for GSM services during the period 2009–13 (Figure 13.15). It shows a continuous reduction for every category of markets and by service providers (SPs). The implication of this continuous reduction is that with the price of mobile services falling so rapidly, this has given rise to an ever-increasing number of subscribers. Further, this reduction can also give an additional fillip to the growth of the information and communications technology (ICT) industry in the country. Although the aforementioned data refers only to tariffs for mobile telecommunications services, a similar trend may hold true even for fixed services. If one were to plot the price of telecom services and the number of subscribers, one can see an inverse

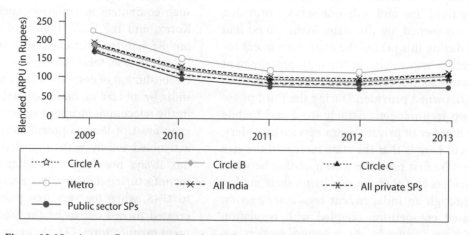

Figure 13.15 Average Revenue per User (ARPU) across Markets and Service Provider

Source: Based on Open Government Data Platform India.[13]

Note: Blended ARPU is average monthly ARPU of postpaid and prepaid subscribers.

[13] Available at https://data.gov.in/catalog/arpu-average-revenue-user (accessed on 8 April 2016).

relationship in the case of mobile services, although in the case of fixed services such an inverse relationship is not visible. This is because of the relative advantages which mobile technology can bestow on its user.

What Went Wrong with the Policy on Manufacturing of Telecom Equipment?

In the previous section, we charted the phenomenal growth of the mobile services industry in India.

But these policies have failed to create a local manufacturing industry. So when the market for telecommunications equipment in India grew rapidly, these increased domestic demand were met through imports. Due to paucity of data, we measure the share of domestic output in total availability (total availability is domestic output + imports – exports), only for the three years 2012–14 (Figure 13.16). The self-sufficiency rate has been steadily falling and now stands only at 20 per cent, signifying the heavy dependence of the country on imports. Although the country has a few domestic manufacturers, all of them are basically assemblers of imported components. In fact, some of the leading domestic handset manufacturers such as Samsung, Micromax, Xiaomi, Gionee, Lenovo, and OnePlus have only set up assembly units in the country.

SUMMING UP

The study is primarily concerned with the growth of the high technology sector in India and the role

that specific policies have played in promoting the growth performance and especially the trade performance (growth in exports and sign of trade balance) of the industry. The argument in the chapter is that each industry, given the nature of its technology and demand for it, requires a specific policy for nurturing its growth apart of general and horizontal policies like liberalization and easing the way business is done. The specific policies range from offset policy in the case of aerospace to public technology procurement in the case of telecommunications equipment. India has been, through these specific or VPs, successful in establishing and nurturing three of the four high technology sectors considered (Table 13.7). It is also interesting to note that government's intervention in the successful cases is, by and large, indirect. The policies have actually been implemented at the ground level by private sector enterprises, although in the case of the aerospace industry, there were public sector entities too in the form of HAL and ISRO.

Public policies for growing the telecommunications, although having the longest history, has failed because the government had on the basis of, on hindsight, weighty non-technical considerations, implemented contradictory policies, which essentially nullified the positive effects of the specific VP.

An important dimension of the growth performance story that is analysed in the present chapter is the factor that while having sharply focused and implemented VPs are a necessary condition for a high technology industry to emerge and grow (best exemplified by the

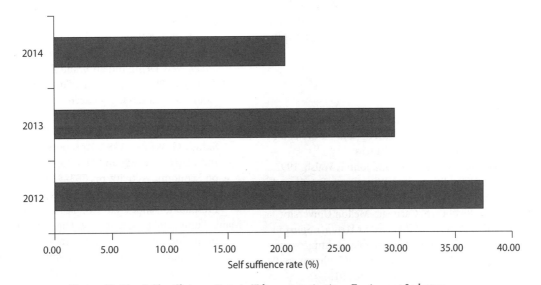

Figure 13.16   Self-sufficiency Rate in Telecommunications Equipment Industry

Source: Computed from CSO (2015) and ITC, Trade Map-International Trade Statistics.

Table 13.7   Summary of the Four Cases of High Technology Industry Development in India

High Technology Industry	Specific Vertical Policy That Has Been Crucial	Export Rank in the World for the Most Recent Year	Qualitative Assessment of Domestic Technological Capability	Nature of Government Intervention
Aerospace	Offset policy	6th rank, 2.1 per cent of the world in 2014	Fair amount for manufacturing aerospace components, and also for designing, manufacturing and launching satellites and satellite launchers	Indirect for component, Direct for satellites and satellite launch vehicles
Pharmaceutical	Patent policy	12th, 2.4 per cent of the world in 2014	High technological capability for designing and manufacturing generic versions of known drugs	Indirect
Automobile	Automotive policy	22nd, 1 per cent in 2014	High capability in designing and manufacturing latest models of fuel efficient cars, two-wheelers and a range of commercial vehicles	Indirect
Telecommunication equipment	Public technology procurement earlier, off late the National Telecom Policy	No rank at all	No capability at all in mobile phones- only assembling capability based on imported components	Was direct in the design and manufacture of fixed line telephones

Source: Author's own compilation.

growth and continued success of Indian generics drug industry), the sufficiency condition is in terms of key actors like business enterprises with good corporate strategy and have themselves taken advantage of government policies and built up considerable internal technological capability. So the success depends on the existence of both the necessary and sufficient conditions, although in the present study, we focused only on the former, as this is very often not highlighted in the role of public policies for growing a sophisticated manufacturing sector. Finally, the study also emphasises the important role of government, which simply cannot be wished away.

REFERENCES

Chaudhuri, Sudip. 2005. *The WTO and India's Pharmaceuticals Industry, Patent protection, TRIPS and Developing countries*. Delhi: Oxford University Press.

Cohen, Wesley M., Richard R. Nelson, and John P. Walsh. 1997. 'Appropriability Conditions and Why Firms Patent and Why They Do Not in the American Manufacturing Sector.' Working Paper, Pittsburgh: Carnegie-Mellon University.

CRISIL. 2014. *Indian Pharma Well Placed to Weather Spurt in FDA Actions*. CRISIL Insight. Available at http://www.crisil.com/Ratings/Brochureware/News/V5-Pharma%20Article%20EdV3.pdf (accessed on 8 June 2015).

Duggan, Mark, Craig Garthwaite, and Aparajita Goyal. 2016. 'The Market Impacts of Pharmaceutical Product Patents in Developing Countries: Evidence from India.' *American Economic Review* 106(1): 9–135.

Government of Andhra Pradesh. 2015. *Aerospace and Defence Manufacturing Policy 2015–2020*. Department of Industries and Commerce, Government of Andhra Pradesh. Available at https://www.apindustries.gov.in/APIndus/Data/GO/2015INDS_MS54.pdf (accessed on 5 April 2016).

Government of Karnataka. 2013. *Karnataka Aerospace Policy 2013–2023*. Bangalore: Department of Industries and Commerce, Government of Karnataka. Available at http://gubbilabs.in/demo/investkarnataka/sites/default/files/Aerospace%20Policy_Final.pdf (accessed on 5 April 2016).

India Brand Equity Fund. 2015. *Automobiles, Presentation Slides*. New Delhi: Indian Brand Equity Fund.

Lall, Sanjaya. 1998. 'Exports of Manufactures by Developing Countries: Emerging Patterns of Trade and Location.' *Oxford Review of Economic Policy* 14(2): 54–73.

Levin, Richard C., Alvin K. Klevorick, Richard R. Nelson, and Sidney G. Winter. 1987. 'Appropriating the Returns from Industrial Research and Development.' Brookings Papers on Economic Activity, pp. 783–820.

Lucintel. 2011. *Aerospace Offset Market Opportunity in India*. Presentation slides, Las Colinas: Lucintel.

Mani, Sunil. 2004. 'Exports of High Technology Products from Developing Countries: Are the Figures Real or Are They Statistical Artefacts?' In *Innovation, Learning and Technological Dynamism of Developing Countries*, edited by Sunil Mani and Henny Romijn. Tokyo: United Nations University Press.

Mani, Sunil. 2005. 'Innovation Capability in India's Telecommunications Equipment Industry.' In *ICT's and Indian Economic Development*, edited by A. Saith and M. Vijayabaskar, 265–322. New Delhi: Sage Publications, 2005.

———. 2012. 'The Mobile Communications Services Industry in India: Has it Led to India Becoming a Manufacturing Hub for Telecommunication Equipment?' *Pacific Affairs* 85(3): 511–30.

———. 2013. 'Evolution of the Sectoral System of Innovation of India's Aeronautical Industry.' *International Journal of Technology and Globalization* 7(1 and 2): 92–117.

Mani, Sunil and Richard Nelson. 2013. *TRIPS Compliance, National Patent Regimes and Innovation*. Cheltenham, UK and Northampton, Mass.: Edward Elgar.

PwC. Undated. *Decoding the Indian Aerospace and Defence Sector, Domestic and Foreign Investments and Offset Obligations*. Available at https://www.pwc.in/assets/pdfs/industries/aerospace-and-defence-services.pdf (accessed on 30 March 2016).

———. 2015. *Aerospace Manufacturing Attractiveness Ranking*. Available at https://www.pwc.com/us/en/industrial-products/publications/assets/aerospace-manufacturing-attractiveness-rankings-2015.pdf (accessed on 6 April 2016).

PwC-Assocham. 2016. *Make in India: Achieving Self-reliance in Defence Production*. Available at http://www.pwc.in/assets/pdfs/publications/2016/make-in-india-achieving-self-reliance-in-defence-production.pdf (accessed on 6 June 2016).

Sanjai, P.R. 2016. 'Make in India at Centre of our Business Strategy: Airbus', *Mint*, 29 March. Available at http://www.livemint.com/Companies/h5JDsmLG8kivRcD2PCG1uI/Make-in-India-at-centre-of-our-business-strategy-Airbus.html (accessed on 31 March 2016).

Stiglitz, J., Justin Yifu Lin, and Celestin Monga. 2013. 'The Rejuvenation of Industrial Policy'. Available at http://papers.ssrn.com/sol3/papers.cfm?abstract_id=2333944 (accessed on 25 August 2016). Also Stiglitz, J.E., and J.Y. Lin, 2013, eds. *The Industrial Policy Revolution I: The Role of Government beyond Ideology*. New York, Palgrave Macmillan.

UNIDO. 2016. *International Yearbook of Industrial Statistics*. Cheltenham, UK: Edward Elgar.

14

Make Where in India?

Sanjoy Chakravorty

One of the first major policies of the BJP-led National Democratic Alliance (NDA) government that swept to power in May 2014 was the Make in India initiative, announced in September 2014.[1] The stated goal of the initiative was to make India a global manufacturing hub that would compete with China to produce high-quality goods for the global market and for the domestic economy, and, in the process, create millions of jobs in the manufacturing sector (100 million by 2022 to be exact) and generate *smart* urbanization that would enable the inevitable and much-desired rural-urban transition. Twenty-five priority sectors were identified;[2] foreign direct investment (FDI) norms were relaxed, allowing 100 per cent FDI in all sectors (except Space, Defence, and News Media); and several more limited and specific new policies were announced or existing policies brought under the overall purview of the Make in India

initiative.[3] It is too soon to assess whether the initiative has had much impact on the ground, but the initial reactions appear to be mixed; there is enthusiasm associated with investment promises/intentions declared by some big brands, such as General Motors, Lenovo, Foxconn, Xiaomi, and Huawei, but also some dismay by 'India Inc.' at the hesitant pace of reforms.

This chapter evaluates the Make in India initiative from a spatial perspective—that is, it asks the question 'where in India will things be made under the new policy direction?' Since there is no evidence yet on the effects of the initiative, this assessment will be based on theory from economic geography and the history of past policies and their effects. A spatial perspective may appear to be

---

[1] Much of the details of the Make in India initiative that is part of the chapter is from the official website http://www.makeinindia.com/home (accessed on 11 July 2017).

[2] These 25 sectors are: automobiles, automobile components, aviation, biotechnology, chemicals, construction, defense manufacturing, electrical machinery, electronic systems, food processing, IT and BPM, leather, media and entertainment, mining, oil and gas, pharmaceuticals, ports and shipping, railways, renewable energy, roads and highways, space, textiles and garments, thermal power, tourism and hospitality, and wellness.

[3] For example, consider the different policies and institutional adaptations made under the *automobile* sector of the Made in India initiative: (i) automatic approval for foreign equity investment up to 100 per cent with no minimum investment criteria; (ii) manufacturing and imports in this sector exempted from licensing and approvals; (iii) encouragement of research and development (R&D) by offering expenditure rebates on R&D; (iv) an Automotive Mission Plan adapted from a preexisting approach; (v) a National Automotive Testing and R&D Infrastructure Project (NATRIP); (vi) a National Mission For Electric Mobility 2020; (vii) Pilot Electric Vehicle Projects; (viii) Faster Adaptation and Manufacturing of Hybrid and Electric Vehicles (FAME); and (ix) a new Merchandise Exports from India Scheme (MEIS).

narrow, but that sort of thinking, as is discussed further, is part of the Indian policymaking tradition, one that has always focused more on sectors than space, which, in turn, has led to weak outcomes—so much so, that it has become necessary to imagine a new Make in India initiative. The chapter argues that spatial principles are central for both growth and distribution. That is, spatial principles are, at the same time, fundamental to the outcomes of the Make in India initiative (which, one presumes, will be evaluated by results on economic growth and industrial investment) and crucial to India's regional structure and competitive federalism.

The remainder of this chapter is divided into five sections. The first section provides some basic guidelines from spatial theory that are relevant to this analysis. The second reviews the history of spatial policymaking for industrial development in India. The third section presents some basic information on the long-term trends in industrialization and regional development in India, including the current industrial structure and geography of the country using recent data. The fourth section discusses some details of the Make in India initiative (as arguably the first industrial policy that is based on explicit spatial considerations), specifically the industrial corridor and manufacturing cluster approaches. The final section critically examines the implications and shortcomings of the Make in India initiative and makes two recommendations: to 'think small in big', and to 'innovate for the isolated'.

IMPERFECTIONS, IMMOBILITIES, AND LOCATION

Consider the core issues. The economics of location, or the economic geography of production, is built on three basic principles that arise from the complete or partial immobility of land and other productive factors. As any textbook on regional economics or economic geography tells us, these three core imperfections or immobilities lie at the heart of the comparative advantage that various regions enjoy for specialization in production and trade:

1. Imperfect factor mobility (or natural-resource advantages that exist because some things, like coal and oil and rivers and natural harbours, are where they are).
2. Imperfect mobility of goods and services (which is the central tenet of geographical economics—that distance causes friction and has to be overcome by spending on transportation and communication).

3. Imperfect divisibility, which leads to two important ideas; one of them—the economies of scale—is well known; the other—the economies of concentration, which are the increasing returns from density—is less known and understood.

It is necessary also to underline two spatial elements—first, the relationship between urbanization and industrialization, and second, the macro- and micro-geography of production. The history of modern growth is a history of industrialization-led urbanization. In fact, the modern developed economies had been marked precisely by a progressive model in which industrialization, urbanization, and economic growth moved in the same direction. Therefore, it is important to understand the structural and spatial aspects of urbanization to prognosticate on the prospects of Make in India. At the same time, it is necessary to understand that any analysis of regional growth has to take into account two different scales—the macro-geography and micro-geography of production—or what is also conceptualized as the interregional and intraregional scales. The first, for India, answers the question 'in which state will new investment locate?', whereas the second answers the question 'where, specifically, in that state will new investment locate?'

The former has traditionally been thought of as the more important question ('why Gujarat and not Bihar?') and it is reasonable to argue that from the perspectives of political economy and welfare it is indeed the more important question. The second question on specific location, however, is the one that excites contemporary scholars in economic geography, especially those studying the leading and innovative sectors and regions of the global economy (see McCann and Ortega-Argilés, 2013 among many others). It may not be as pertinent a question for Indian manufacturing (because it has no leading or innovative industrial sectors at a global scale), but there are issues related to the benefits of localization that should matter, but do not seem to, in analysis and policymaking on industrial location in India.

The bottom line is this: a growth-oriented strategy should seek to maximize the comparative advantage of regions. But therein lies the rub. A growth-oriented strategy, one that is built upon spatial principles to maximize growth, will, if successful, almost inevitably increase regional inequality.[4] The questions we must ask then

[4] The chapter argues that we need not concern ourselves with the idea of regional 'convergence' that builds on the endogenous growth literature and emphasizes diminishing returns. Barro and Sala-i-Martin (1992, 1995) argued for two types of regional

are twofold: First, is the Make in India initiative built upon good spatial principles that will maximize growth? Second, what are the likely outcomes for comparative regional development of the Make in India initiative?

It goes without saying that this initiative is not going to be applied to tabula rasa. There is an existing economic geography of industry in India and an ideology of industrial development that created it. These existing investments in cities, infrastructure, and factories are sticky, in the sense that they are not easily altered. At the same time, new investments are path dependent and tend to flow where there are already existing investments in cities, infrastructure, and industry.

There are two broad realities in the existing structure of cities and industry: First, the urbanization level in India is low (about 31 per cent in 2011), the growth rate of the urbanization level is slow (it is slower in India than in almost all developing regions and slower than its own rate during the slow-growth decades of the 1960s through the 1980s), and the distribution of urban areas is regionally lopsided (significantly more widespread in western and southern states such as Maharashtra, Gujarat, Tamil Nadu, and Kerala and much less so in eastern states such as Bihar and Odisha).

Second, the industrial sector in India is small (the formal or licensed manufacturing sector employs less than 13 million out of a labour force of close to half a billion), capital intensive, and has a large state-owned component. Informal industry, which is entirely private and small-scale, employs about four times as many people but the labour is about one-eighth as productive. Formal and informal industry together employ about 11–12 per cent of the labour force and produce 26 per cent of the national output. The formal industrial sector is heavily biased to the western and southern states (like urbanization is) and tends to locate in non-metropolitan, even non-urban settings.

What will be the effects of the Make in India initiative on this setup? This review suggests that the initiative is built upon some solid spatial principles, especially the first and second principles discussed earlier (imperfect factor mobility and imperfect mobility of goods and services), but lesser on the third principle (imperfect

---

convergence in the long run: when the dispersion of real per capita income across a group of economies falls over time, there is σ-convergence. When the partial correlation between growth in income over time and its initial level is negative, there is β-convergence. Empirical tests of these ideas have generally been successful with North American and European data (σ-convergence is seen to be more likely), but far less so with data from the rest of the world (Milanovic, 2005).

divisibility). In other words, the initiative pays serious attention to transportation costs but not to external or agglomeration economies. By the standards of contemporary understandings of spatial processes, this could be called old-fashioned thinking. As a result, in some key sectors, especially those that rely on internal scale economies and seek reduced transportation costs, the Make in India initiative has the potential to succeed to some extent—but only in the domestic economy; the declared objective of challenging China in the global market for manufactured goods is a fantasy. However, whether or not there is substantial success in attaining high growth rates, it is likely that the already high and increasing regional inequalities will be sharply exacerbated.

INDUSTRIAL POLICIES IN SPATIAL FOG

The Make in India initiative is based on a relatively clear spatial strategy. One could go so far as to argue that at the heart of the initiative is its spatial strategy. This is rather radical because almost all past policy planning in India had little or no spatial strategy. Development planning in independent India was marked by the relative absence of an explicit spatial perspective: 'Indian planning ... has been limited to [the] allocation of investment over time, sectors and sub-sectors, whereas there is no explicit spatial dimension in the formal planning models' (Awasthi, 1991: 27; also see Chakravarty, 1979). The policymakers, led by the Planning Commission and Soviet-inspired input-output macroeconomic models, concentrated on the factors of production to the exclusion of any spatial context. It was a sectoral strategy linked to specific projects. Of course, all projects have to be located somewhere, but there is little evidence that much thought had been put into the role of space itself in realizing a policy (that is, some locations are more efficient than others) or that policies have spatial consequences.

Johnson (1970: 167–69) argued that there were three extenuating or explanatory factors: first, a belief in the 'redemptive mystique' of large industry, wherever it may be located; second, the 'emulative desire to attain the demographic patterns of the more developed countries'; and, third, what John Lewis (1995: 224) called a 'village fetish'. Lewis argued that two other factors were particularly important: one, that 'any implementation of a positive spatial strategy would cost a lot of money', and two, 'the spatial dimension (of development) was most obviously and blatantly political'. But fundamentally, there was poor recognition of the inherently spatial nature of all development.

Often, there was a denial of the role of geography or hubristic attempts to overcome it by brute force. The most infamous example of the latter was the Freight Equalization Policy that was part of the Industrial Policy Resolution of 1956 (which laid out the guiding principles of industrialization in Nehru's India). This policy, which equalized the prices of 'essential' items like steel, coal, and cement throughout India, 'robbed the producing areas of Southern Bihar and Bengal, Western Orissa and Eastern Madhya Pradesh of their comparative advantage in industries using these products' (Mohan, 1983: 51). It is possible that the industrialization of western and southern India was fundamentally enabled by it.

A recent example of the denial of the role of geography in economics was the Special Economic Zone Act, 2006, which borrowed the name SEZ from China, but not the principles that made the policy special. At the core of China's SEZ policy was the theory of 'imperfect divisibility', or the benefits of industrial clustering enabled by massive concentration of infrastructure in a few key locations. China created five SEZs to start with and poured significant resources into each. The explicit goal, surpassed beyond expectations, was to realize external economies through clustering (Sahling, 2008; Zheng, 2011). This was the singular reason for the success of China's SEZs. The Indian approach took the label SEZ but not the underlying economic principle (Chakravorty, 2013; Sivaramakrishnan, 2009).[5] Within two years after the passage of the SEZ Act, over 580 SEZs had been approved in principle, thereby obliterating the main reason that made China's SEZs, especially Shenzhen, so successful. It is perhaps the principal reason for the stillbirth of the policy—a failure to understand the core principles of economic geography.[6]

Time and again, policymakers in India have acted as if space did not exist, as if they could not see through a fog. The initial post-Independence policy thrust that was oriented strongly towards creating an industrial nation, was inspired by the Soviet rather than the Euro-American model of industrialization. This model was based on a mistrust of and discomfort with large cities, a deep belief in the productive power of internal scale economies (that is, the large, vertically integrated plant), and what we can now recognize as a complete blindness to the productive power of external and agglomeration economies (that is, dense collections of small, interacting plants). In other words, industrialization was led by state-owned firms with large, capital-intensive plants located in non-metropolitan, even non-urban settings. Later, these could be recognized as 'growth poles' (Darwent, 1975; Friedmann 1974; Perroux, 1955), though the term itself had barely been invented. 'Import substitution' and 'infant industry protection' and 'balanced regional development' were the explicit goals and these were very much the accepted and desirable objectives at the time. This was the Rosenstein-Rodan 'big push' model of industrialization. The big private business houses of the time—like the Tatas and Birlas—also supported this strategy (why would they not, if they were to be protected from external competition?). It was common sense at the time.

The limitations of this strategy were obvious by the mid-1970s, by which time a 'license-permit-quota' system of state control/supervision of all enterprise was producing what the economist Raj Krishna called a 'Hindu rate of growth'. Extended discussions of this period and its industrial miasma are available in several sources, notably Isher Ahluwalia (1991). Despite widespread misgivings about the strategy and direction of the Indian economy and its manufacturing sector, changes were slow and hesitant, till a foreign exchange crisis in 1991 became the ostensible reason to begin structural reforms.

The reforms placed commercial considerations above government mandates in investment decisions, including ownership, location, local content, technology, capital goods imports, and so on. The central government began to divest its interest in the ownership of capital-intensive and 'sick' industry. The spatial or urban dimension of reforms received some attention, but not much. The restrictions on locating industry in metropolitan areas were lessened, but only marginally, for some 'non-polluting' industry. The Freight Equalization Policy was finally abandoned. New strategy documents were generated, such as by the National Commission on Urbanization in the late 1980s and a series of infrastructure reports by different expert groups of the government of India. New urban initiatives were created, such as the Mega City Programme in the mid-1990s and the JNNURM (Jawaharlal Nehru National Urban Renewal Mission) in the mid-2000s.

MADE IN INDIA—BEFORE AND AFTER LIBERALIZATION

How did these policies combine with spatial *immobilities* and *imperfections* to create India's industrial geography? The

---

[5] For example, the minimum contiguous area requirement for certain sectors (electronics hardware or software, IT, gems and jewellery, biotechnology, non-conventional energy, including solar energy equipment, and solar cells) was a mere 10 hectares.

[6] Also see Mukhopadhyay (2009) and Chakravorty (2013) on what may have been the *real* reason the SEZ policy turned out the way it did—that it became (and perhaps all along was meant to be) a device to make money from land and real estate.

most extensive work on the subject covering the period up to 2000 are available in Chakravorty (2000, 2003a, 2003b), Chakravorty and Lall (2007), and Lall and Chakravorty (2005). Some of these findings, especially on the continuing decentralization and de-urbanization of manufacturing, are confirmed in Ghani, Goswami, and Kerr (2012). A selection of the findings, on the region- and state-level distribution of

industrial employment from 1961–94 (which can be considered the pre-reform period)[7] are shown in Figure 14.1.

[7] Though the reforms began in 1991, Chakravorty and Lall (2007) argue that their effects would not have been realized on the ground in terms of actual work in factories before about 1994.

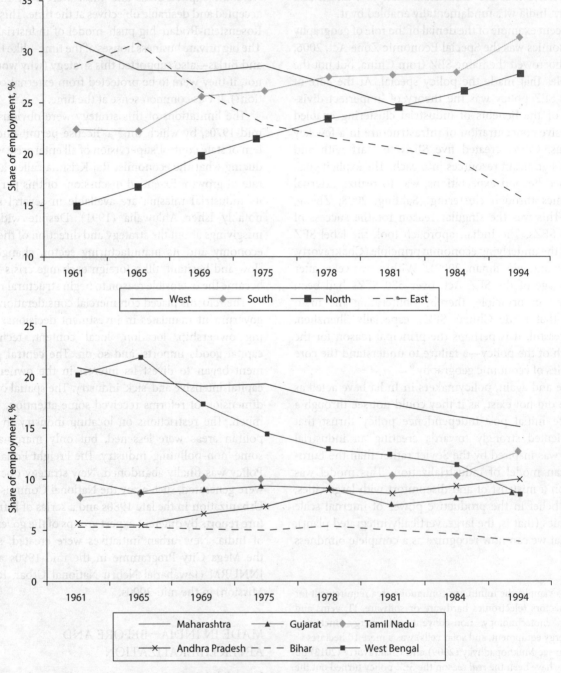

Figure 14.1   Distribution of Industrial Employment in Regions and Selected States, 1961–94
Source: Adapted from Chakravorty and Lall (2007).

In early post-Independence India, industrialization was regionally unbalanced (Mitra, 1965). In 1953–61, of the 4,971 industrial licenses granted in the country, over one-third went to the three industrial metropolises Calcutta, Bombay, and Madras, and fully one-fifth went to a single district: Bombay. Over half the licenses were given to firms in the three leading states: Maharashtra, West Bengal, and Tamil Nadu. By the late 1950s, however, a slight trend toward deconcentration of industry could be noticed, that became more strongly evident through the following two decades. By the end of the 1970s and into the early 1980s, industry locations had spread to many states and cities beyond the initial three leaders.

Broadly, it is possible to divide the post-Independence period into two phases: the first lasted up to 1980 and was characterized by industrial decentralization and declining regional inequality; the second started in the mid-1980s, and was characterized by increasing regional industrial concentration and income inequality. This U-shaped pattern appeared to defy theoretical expectations of an inverted-U curve (Alonso, 1980; Williamson, 1965) and was catalyzed by a major shift in the 1960s when the leading state (West Bengal) began to decline precipitously.

From the 1980s the overall trend did not change. Chakravorty and Lall (2007) called this a pattern of 'concentrated decentralization', or 'interregional divergence with intraregional convergence'.[8] Industries continued to locate within larger and more expanded leading industrial regions (with the exception of Calcutta) so that there was deconcentration within these leading regions, at the same time that there was increasing interregional concentration. These trends accelerated after the structural reforms of 1991, driven to a considerable extent by the decline of the state industrial sector and the rise of the private sector, where the latter had a demonstrated bias towards locating in coastal regions and existing industrial regions (Chakravorty, 2003b). Both private and public sector industries were capital intensive during this period, but the latter, in the form of large metal and energy plants, were considerably more so.

[8] What took place in India (and continues today) was not *spread* or *polarization reversal* of industrial location as had been theorized by some scholars (Richardson, 1980) in that there was increasing interregional polarization of industry at the same time that there was intraregional dispersal inside the leading regions (Chakravorty, 1994). In other words, the situation was one of concentration with dispersal, or to make an ironic use of the term, of concentrated decentralization, where the new growth centers were in advanced regions rather than in lagging ones.

Snapshots of the structure and spatial distribution of the industrial economy in 2012–3 (the most recent data available) are shown in Figure 14.2 and Tables 14.1 and 14.2. Figure 14.2 shows the distribution of employment, wages, investment in plant and machinery, and output in the four regions of India and 13 leading states. About 85 per cent of total industrial output was produced in these 13 states. Table 14.1 shows the distribution of industry by two-digit industrial sector and Table 14.2 shows the state-level distribution of the six leading sectors by output (coke and refined petroleum products; basic metals; food products; chemicals and chemical products; motor vehicles, trailers and semi-trailers; and textiles). These six leading sectors produced over 61 per cent of total industrial output and employed about 42 per cent of all workers.

The spatial processes that were identifiable in the first years after the reforms of 1991 became more deeply entrenched in the two decades that followed. The decline of the east continued at the same time that the west and south became more strongly industrialized. The deindustrialization of the east is a matter of serious concern; we return to the subject later in the chapter. Just four states—Gujarat, Maharashtra, Tamil Nadu, and Andhra Pradesh (including Telangana)—were home to about half of Indian industry (measured by any variable, from employment to output). Within this leading front, it was possible to discern one clear regional difference: the western states of Gujarat and Maharashtra were home to more capital-intensive and resource-based industries (exemplified by India's largest sector: coke and refined petroleum products) than the southern states of Tamil Nadu and Andhra Pradesh.

Maharashtra had the most diversified industrial base; it was ranked first or second for all six of the leading sectors. Tamil Nadu, on the other hand, had the highest concentration of labour-intensive industry; the largest industrial labour force was in Tamil Nadu, though Gujarat and Maharashtra had significantly higher total output and investments in plant and machinery. Gujarat led in both total output and investments in plant and machinery but employed a labour force that was barely larger than in Andhra Pradesh, which was far behind it in the other categories. The Gujarat model of industrial development was by far the most capital-intensive in India, and also more resource-based than in the other leading states. If the designers of Make in India were inspired by the so-called 'Gujarat model', disappointment is sure to follow because that model is neither transferable to nor appropriate for the rest of the nation.

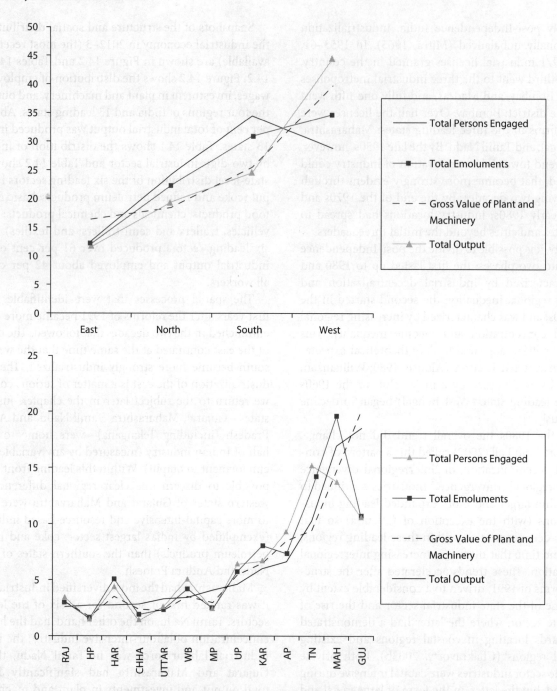

Figure 14.2 Distribution of Industry, by Region and Leading States, 2012–13

Source: From data in *Annual Survey of Industries, 2012–13*.

Notes: AP includes Telangana. The cut-off used to choose states was a minimum share of 2.5 per cent of national output.

MAKE IN INDIA—INDIA'S FIRST SPATIAL STRATEGY FOR GROWTH

In light of the history of indifference and/or incompetence in spatial thinking outlined earlier, the Make in India policy is a clear departure. Since Make in India is a concept or initiative rather than an act or law or even

a clearly enunciated policy, which means that there is no statutory documentation of its ambit, it is necessary to rely on material on the initiative's website (which appears to be the most detailed source available). This website material suggests that there are two major elements of spatial thinking in the initiative.

Table 14.1   Structure of Industry by Sector (Share of National Total, in Per Cent)

NIC-08	Description	Operating Factories	Fixed Capital	Total Persons Engaged	GVA	Total Output
19	Coke and refined petroleum products	0.66	7.39	0.77	12.54	17.50
24	Basic metals	5.58	22.21	7.85	10.19	12.75
10	Food products	16.30	6.15	11.95	6.59	11.59
20	Chemicals and chemical products	5.12	6.79	4.89	8.87	7.85
29	Motor vehicles, trailers, and semi-trailers	2.66	5.65	5.90	7.03	6.61
13	Textiles	7.43	5.45	10.88	5.76	5.15
OT	Other industries	4.68	13.81	3.23	5.44	4.66
28	Machinery and equipment nec	5.44	2.85	5.18	6.59	4.23
27	Electrical equipment	3.46	2.18	3.87	4.01	3.54
23	Other non-metallic mineral products	11.93	9.25	6.89	5.33	3.24
22	Rubber and plastics products	5.62	2.79	4.16	3.08	3.22
21	Pharmaceuticals, medicinal chemical, and botanical products	2.36	3.18	4.11	6.09	3.16
25	Fabricated metal products, except machinery and equipment	7.17	2.16	4.91	3.63	2.70
32	Other manufacturing	1.43	0.48	2.06	1.38	2.62
30	Other transport equipment	1.12	2.04	2.27	2.47	2.20
26	Computer, electronic and optical products	1.16	1.02	1.69	2.10	1.77
14	Wearing apparel	3.63	1.11	7.13	1.90	1.50
17	Paper and paper products	2.86	1.96	1.82	1.06	1.14
01	Cotton ginning, cleaning, and bailing; seed processing for propagation	1.90	0.22	0.81	0.47	0.97
11	Beverages	0.94	1.14	1.10	1.43	0.87
15	Leather and related products	1.69	0.33	2.20	0.64	0.68
18	Printing and reproduction of recorded media	2.09	0.64	1.29	0.94	0.56
12	Tobacco products	1.53	0.25	3.31	1.28	0.55
16	Wood and products of wood and cork, except furniture	1.95	0.22	0.59	0.26	0.31
31	Furniture	0.63	0.29	0.50	0.29	0.24
33	Repair and installation of machinery and equipment	0.34	0.15	0.26	0.22	0.15
58	Publishing activities	0.13	0.18	0.20	0.33	0.12

Source: *Annual Survey of Industries, 2012–13.*

By far the more important of these is an *industrial corridor approach*, specifically the following five: Delhi-Mumbai Industrial Corridor (DMIC); Bengaluru-Mumbai Economic Corridor (BMEC); Chennai-Bengaluru Industrial Corridor Project (CBIC); Vizag-Chennai Industrial Corridor as the first phase of the East Coast Economic Corridor (ECEC); and the Amritsar–Kolkata Industrial Corridor (AKIC).[9] This is a further commitment to the 'golden quadrilateral' project of high-quality highways to link India's four largest metropolitan regions that was launched in 2001 by the BJP-led NDA government and continued under the two Congress-led United Progressive Alliance

---

[9] The Delhi-Mumbai Industrial Corridor seems to be the one that has received the most attention (and the Amritsar-Kolkata Industrial Corridor the least—actually none, other than being named and listed). The website states that: 'Initially, eight nodes/cities in the six DMIC states have been taken up for development.' These include the Dadri-Noida-Ghaziabad Investment Region in Uttar Pradesh, Vikram Udyogpuri near Ujjain in Madhya Pradesh, Neemrana in Rajasthan, Shendra Bidkin Industrial Park in Maharashtra, and Dholera Special Investment Region in Gujarat.

Table 14.2 State-Level Concentration of Leading Industrial Sectors

			Share of Output	Share of GVA
19	Coke and refined petroleum products	Gujarat	46.9	47.8
	Output: Rs 10.54 trillion (17.5% of all industrial output)	Maharashtra	14.3	35.7
	GVA: Rs 1.26 trillion	Karnataka	6.7	0.9
		Tamil Nadu	5.1	3.8
		Kerala	5.0	1.3
		West Bengal	4.1	0.2
24	Basic metals	Maharashtra	16.3	6.6
	Output: Rs 7.68 trillion (12.75 per cent of all industrial output)	Odisha	9.7	17.5
	GVA: Rs 1.03 trillion	Chhattisgarh	9.1	9.9
		West Bengal	8.2	6.0
		Jharkhand	7.9	9.6
		Gujarat	7.5	2.2
		Tamil Nadu	6.9	8.9
		Karnataka	6.0	9.1
		Haryana	4.7	2.0
		Uttar Pradesh	4.6	3.3
10	Food products	Maharashtra	16.1	12.7
	Output: Rs 6.98 trillion (11.59 per cent of all industrial output)	Uttar Pradesh	11.3	7.1
	GVA: Rs 0.66 trillion	Gujarat	10.4	6.4
		Karnataka	7.7	9.8
		AP	7.6	6.8
		Tamil Nadu	7.0	9.0
		Haryana	5.7	7.4
		MP	4.7	5.1
		West Bengal	4.5	4.0
		Punjab	4.1	4.5
		Rajasthan	3.5	2.3
20	Chemicals and chemical products	Gujarat	29.4	31.8
	Output: Rs 4.73 trillion (7.85 per cent of all industrial output)	Maharashtra	16.5	21.0
	GVA: Rs 0.89 trillion	Rajasthan	7.4	4.3
		Uttar Pradesh	5.6	5.0
		Tamil Nadu	5.1	4.6
		West Bengal	4.9	0.6
		AP	3.7	2.9
		HP	3.7	5.9
		Uttarakhand	2.6	3.9
		Goa	2.3	2.9

(Cont'd)

Table 14.2 (*Cont'd*)

			Share of Output	Share of GVA
29	Motor vehicles, trailers and semi-trailers	Tamil Nadu	28.8	28.6
	Output: Rs 3.98 trillion (6.6 per cent of all industrial output)	Maharashtra	21.7	17.3
	GVA: Rs 0.71 trillion	Haryana	19.5	22.5
		Karnataka	7.6	6.4
		Uttarakhand	6.5	8.7
13	Textiles	Gujarat	18.6	14.1
	Output: Rs 3.1 trillion (5.15 per cent of all industrial output)	Tamil Nadu	17.2	17.5
	GVA: Rs 0.58 trillion	Maharashtra	12.6	20.7
		Punjab	10.6	11.0
		D&N Haveli	10.3	5.3
		Rajasthan	6.3	5.6
		West Bengal	3.9	5.2
		MP	3.8	4.0

Source: *Annual Survey of Industries, 2012–13.*

(UPA) governments that followed. According to the Make in India website:

In each of these corridors [identified, planned and launched by the Government of India in the Union Budget of 2014–2015], manufacturing will be a key economic driver and these projects are seen as critical in raising the share of manufacturing in India's Gross Domestic Product from the current levels of 15 per cent to 16 per cent to 25 per cent by 2022.… Along these corridors, the development of 100 Smart Cities has also been envisaged in the Union Budget of 2014–2015. These cities are being developed to integrate the new workforce that will power manufacturing along the industrial corridors and to decongest India's urban housing scenario.

Though 'smart cities' have been incorporated into the Make in India vision, it is not clear that the two initiatives are compatible.[10] The objectives of this initiative appear to be directed towards improving basic urban infrastructure (especially in water, sanitation, and transportation) using intelligent IT-embedded design and enabling e-governance at various levels. Twenty cities were selected for funding in the first round, and 13 more were added in a second list released in mid-2016. The first round cities were heavily biased to the western and

southern states (15 of the 20 are located there), whereas there were just two in the east (Bhubaneshwar in Odisha and Guwahati in Assam). The second round list went the other way, oriented more toward the northern and eastern states. The five-year commitment to this initiative is reportedly around Rs 50,000 crore, but the project has been a slow starter and reportedly only about Rs 100 crore have been spent in the first two years.[11]

Taken together, the industrial corridor and smart city initiatives resemble what Joel Garraeu (1997) called the 'pig in a python' design of edge cities in the US. Garreau, however, was describing a circular feature—nodes of employment that had developed along ring highways around old central cities, whereas the vision in Make in India is decidedly linear. To the best of my knowledge, this is the only instance of a linear design for industrial

[10] The most detailed information on Smart Cities is on the website http://smartcities.gov.in/ (accessed on 11 July 2017).

[11] More recent media reports state that each Smart City will get 'central assistance of Rs. 200 crore in the first year and Rs. 100 crore each during the subsequent three financial years. State governments and respective urban local bodies will also provide the same amount' (NDTV, 2016). If this is correct, then the total money from central and state sources that each Smart City will receive over four years is Rs 1,000 crore, which, if media reports are to be believed, is the same amount that Bollywood star Salman Khan is charging for the satellite rights to his recent films. One wonders how much smartness can be added for this amount of money.

development. Everywhere else—from the US to Germany to Japan to China—market driven industrial development is imagined in circular form around the leading cities.

This anomaly brings us to the second and unquestionably lesser element in the Make in India initiative's spatial vision: a *manufacturing cluster approach*. The language used appears to be mindful of the competitive advantages of clusters, but the understanding of the concept, the chapter argues, is inadequate. There is a very large literature on the subject (see Chakravorty, 2010 and World Bank, 2009 for recent reviews of this literature), but the main point is one that engages a significant fraction of professional economic geographers. In Michael Porter's words (1995: 57): 'The competitive advantage of a location does not usually arise in isolated companies but in clusters of companies—in other words, in companies that are in the same industry or otherwise linked together through customer, supplier, or similar relationships. Clusters represent critical masses of skill, information, relationships, and infrastructure in a given field.' Moreover, these 'critical masses' of skill and information create ecosystems in which innovations are most likely to be fostered. As a result, clusters are now considered the most important source of the competitive advantage of regions and nations.

But, as far as it is possible to tell, automobiles are the only industry for which the Make in India initiative explicitly discusses clusters. Specifically: Delhi-Gurgaon-Faridabad in the north, Mumbai-Pune-Nashik-Aurangabad in the west, Chennai-Bangalore-Hosur in the south, and Jamshedpur-Kolkata in the east. All of these are too large to be called clusters, but the latter's inclusion in this list suggests that the concept of clusters is poorly understood. Jamshedpur and Kolkata are about 300 km apart, much too far for the external economies that generate cluster advantages to function. What is missing from the list is also revealing. The leather industry (which is one of the 25 sectors identified in Make in India) is one that benefits greatly from clustering—not only because of external economies, but because a part of the process (tanning) is polluting, it is best to segregate the land use. In India, there are at least three well-known leather clusters—in Chennai, Kolkata, and Kanpur—and the industry itself has an estimated 2.5 million workers, a majority of whom are in the unorganized household and small scale sectors. Yet, or perhaps as a consequence of its unorganized structure, nowhere in the discussion of the leather sector in Make in India is there mention of clusters at all or any of the three existing ones.

These are signs that the cluster concept is being used as a label without an understanding of its organic content (like SEZ in the recent past). These are signs also of the continuation of an industrial ideology that favours big plants over small, which produced the industrial structure that exists now. Spatial scale is of vital importance here and needs to enter the imagination of policymakers in new, more useful ways. A real cluster depends, above all else, on proximity, on density. It operates at the scale of local labour markets. In its ideal form, workers in a cluster should be able to leave one firm and join another in the same or a related industry without having to change residence. This—the increasing returns to scale of large, local labour markets—is what analysts from Jane Jacobs (1970) to Paul Krugman (1996) to Edward Glaeser (2012) have identified as the fundamental advantage of metropolitan areas, the core reason for their continued and rising importance. Also, the firms that produce these large labour markets are not the big plants with thousands of workers that Indian policymakers tend to imagine when they think of industry (the integrated steel plants of Durgapur and Rourkela in the Nehruvian days, or the Jamnagar refinery of Reliance Industries in the Modi days), but numerous small units—nimble, adaptable, competitive—that generate the productive and creative juices that make clusters work. Exactly the kind that the Chennai leather cluster is and the Jamshedpur-Kolkata automobile 'cluster' is not.

This brings us to a final point about the persistence of a peculiar industrial vision in India in which the big capital-intensive plant or project is the ideal form, in contrast to the historical evidence and expert understanding of the far more important contribution of the small plant and small entrepreneur operating in an ecosystem of similar units.[12]

---

[12] It is an interesting question: why this fascination with the large plant, the capital-intensive industry? It is possible to see why this fascination would have existed in the early days. Between the need to jump-start industrialization and the seeming success of the Soviet model, before it fell apart, the large plant could have seemed to have been the more attractive option. That is why in a capital-constrained nation, capital was made relatively cheap, especially by keeping the exchange rate low to ease the import of plant and machinery. But why has this model persisted, despite its failure to create mass industrialization and urbanization in a society with abysmal rural incomes and an abundance of unskilled, low-wage labour? Perhaps it has something to do with the image of success (it has to be big and visible), especially for the political class. Perhaps it has something to do with the potential for higher rents for the political class because rent-collection is easier in a single-payer than a fragmented system (in a fragmented system, rents tend to go to retail politicians, whereas in a centralized system it goes to *big* leaders). Speculation is all that is possible,

This becomes obvious when we consider the data in Tables 14.1 and 14.2. The sector 'coke and refined petroleum products' (NIC code 19) produces 17.5 per cent of total industrial output (by far the highest among all sectors) but employs only 0.77 per cent of the industrial labour force. This industry is resource-based and its plants are located where the resource is found; the best known current example being Jamnagar in western Gujarat. Compare this with 'textiles' (NIC code 13), the industry that is intimately linked with urbanization and industrialization in world history, that produces just 5.2 per cent of the industrial output but employs 10.9 per cent of the formal industrial workforce; if we add the 'wearing apparels' sector to 'textiles', the total produces 6.65 per cent of industrial output while employing about 18 per cent of the industrial labour force (more than 2.3 million workers). In contrast, the textiles sector alone employs about four million workers in Bangladesh (45 per cent of all industrial workers in that country) and well over 10 million in China (which has over 100,000 textile factories of *decent* size).

In a recent study of global value chains in the BRICS economies, Gereffi and Sturgeon (2013) show that India's industrial export structure is very similar to Brazil's—39 per cent of it is resource-based, and only 9 per cent is high-tech—rather than China's (which is 9 per cent resource-based and 33 per cent high-tech). Not only that, the value of China's exports in 2011 ($1.9 trillion) was more than six-times larger than India's $301 billion. It is clear that the structure of India's industrial economy—which is resource-based, capital-intensive, and produces low-tech goods—is reflected in the structure of its exports.[13] Competing with China, which is an obsession in Delhi's policy circles, seems to be nothing less than a fantasy.

SUCCESS AND FAILURE

What would constitute success for Make in India? What benchmarks or targets should be set up now, before things really get going? Should these benchmarks be defined by growth of output or growth of the size of the industrial labour force, or its wages? Or is it necessary to look at Make in India not in isolation but as a vital part of a larger policy regime that includes Smart Cities and Mahatma Gandhi National Rural Employment Guarantee Act (MGNREGA) that together create the foundations of the occupation and location choice set for Indian labour? The overall effort should, after all, be directed towards changing the basic structure of society and space. The surplus rural labour that struggles with miniscule quantities of land and earns incomes that barely rise to subsistence level (averaging less than Rs 6,500 per month per family in the most recent survey of Indian agriculture by the National Sample Survey (NSS) in 2012–13) must urbanize into more livable cities, that are not overrun by slums and abysmal infrastructure, where there is work that pays living wages for semi- and unskilled labour.

It is too much to expect that Make in India alone can deliver these outcomes. Therefore, the immediate goals should be more modest, and perhaps, can be taken from the policymakers own declared objectives: to make India a global manufacturing hub that can compete with China in the global market; make a range of products for the domestic economy; create 100 million jobs in the manufacturing sector by 2022; and enable 'smart' urbanization and a better absorption of rural labour in cities.

As the discussion in the preceding section makes clear, it is doubtful that the Make in India strategy will make Indian manufacturing more competitive in the global economy.[14] We know that the industrial success stories of the far past (in the USA and Western Europe) and recent past (in China, Taiwan) were based on small-scale, labour-intensive manufacturing that relied on external economies such as labour-pooling, local supply chains, and innovations in large urban centers. There appears to be no such vision in the Make in India initiative, which remains in the thrall of large-scale, capital-intensive manufacturing in small urban centers. One is afraid that the label Make in India may be new, but the wine is old. In fact, there is a temptation to look at Make in India as simply a rebranding exercise because it

---

because there is no systematic work on the political economy or behavioral psychology of *bigness* in India.

[13] The share of capital-intensive manufactures in Indian production and exports is not only high, but has been increasing in the post-reform period. The worker-to-fixed-capital ratio in the registered manufacturing sector has declined from 10.9 in 1990–91 to 3.2 in 2009–10, according to Seth (2012), which suggests that the manufacturing sector as a whole has become significantly more capital-intensive. As far as exports are concerned, Veeramani (2012) shows that in the post-reform period (1993–94 to 2010–11), the share of capital-intensive products doubled from about 25 per cent to about 54 per cent, while the share of unskilled, labour-intensive products halved from 30 per cent to 15 per cent.

[14] Raghuram Rajan, then Governor of the Reserve Bank of India, famously made the same argument, albeit from different angles—that the global economy was too tepid to admit a new manufacturing power and that it was unwise to pick a winner, manufacturing in this case, rather than let entrepreneurs work it out (livemint.com, 2014). This critique is believed to be one of main reasons for his subsequent *ouster* from the RBI governorship.

is based on the same ideology that produced India's existing industrial structure. It is hard to imagine that in the short or medium term, it can be globally competitive any more than it is now—in the manufacture of a small list of resource-based and/or capital-intensive products.

But it is likely that production for the domestic economy will increase, led by increasing demand for consumer durables like cars, two-wheelers, TVs, refrigerators, and washing machines by a growing middle class in a growing population—Prime Minister Modi's 3Ds: democracy, demography, and demand.[15] It is important to note that this had been happening without Make in India and would continue without it. But the Make in India initiative has very likely ensured that this industrialization for the domestic economy will take place in the spatial economy imagined in it—small-to-medium-sized cities along the golden quadrilateral of highways, with a distinct bias toward the southern and western states, especially three special axes: the Pune-Mumbai-Surat-Vadodra-Ahmedabad corridor, the Ghaziabad-Delhi-Jaipur corridor, and the Chennai-Bangalore corridor. Industrialization in these southern and western states will continue to rise, along with per capita income and urbanization levels, and most of the eastern and

northern states will fall further behind. This is the condition now and the Make in India initiative will, at best or worst, hasten the trend toward regionally polarized industrialization, urbanization, and development.

The one thing that is missing from the Make in India language is any mention of balanced regional development. At one level, this is to be lauded—for its honesty. It is simply not possible to make the argument that Make in India will lead to regional balance. But at the level that matters—of real development—this is deeply worrisome. The eastern region, with over 28 per cent of the nation's population, and much of its mineral reserves, is home to around only 12 per cent of the industrial economy, down from around 31 per cent in 1965 and 23 per cent in 1975. Similarly, whereas the large states in the west and south (Maharashtra, Gujarat, Tamil Nadu, Kerala) are almost half urban, several large eastern states are barely urban, especially Bihar (11.3 per cent), Assam (14.1 per cent), and Odisha (16.7 per cent). The per capita state domestic product in Gujarat and Maharashtra is about five-fold and in Tamil Nadu and Kerala about four-fold that of Bihar. The spatial design of Make in India, with its significant bias toward the southern and western industrial corridors, will open up this growing chasm even more widely, perhaps to politically unsustainable levels.

Certainly, Make in India is not responsible for the political economy of regional backwardness in the nation. Neither is it responsible for the creation of the cultural perception of intangibles—like Gujarat's entrepreneurial society, the south's knowledge economy, virtual statelessness in Bihar, and extreme labour militancy in West Bengal—on which interregional outcomes often turn. But, we must ask, who then is responsible to enhance the development prospects of the lagging east? If the state will not or cannot be any more involved in the ownership of industry, and the private sector cannot be induced to invest till fundamental local political–economic problems are resolved, and these local problems may not be resolved without investment and growth, how can development reach the lagging regions? Is it necessary to think of a 'freight equalization' policy in reverse, a new 'freight subsidy' policy for the east?

This idea may be anathema to most economists, but there are few good tools in the regional planner's box. Traditional regional development policies have typically taken the form of location incentives like investment subsidies (in Brazil), tax and import duty exemptions (in Mexico), tax holidays (in Thailand), or revenue sharing (in Korea). In India, the usual method has been to provide financial incentives (typically in the form of tax holidays) for private industrial investment

---

[15] The automotive industry, in particular, may have the potential for significant growth, driven not only by the 3Ds, but the rising symbolic value of personal automation. According to the Make in India website, this industry 'accounts for 45% of the country's manufacturing gross domestic product (GDP), 7.1% of the country's GDP and employs about 19 Million people both directly and indirectly.' The numbers are highly questionable (as are many other figures on the Make in India website), especially the employment figure (which, one suspects, must have been arrived at by including the thousands of repair shops in India's cities and along its highways; because according to *Annual Survey of Industries* (*ASI*) figures, there are just one million workers in the added categories 'Motor Vehicles, Trailers and Semi-Trailers' and 'Other Transport Equipment'). But there is no doubt that if one industry more than any other was shaken up and reconstituted by liberalization, it was this. Many of the leading global players (or brands) are either already in India or trying/planning to be, not to make cars for export, but for the Indian market. The growth potential of the industry was underlined recently by the rapid emergence of Sanand, near Ahmedabad, as an auto hub. As recently as 2007 Sanand was a greenfield site, till Tata Motors' Nano small car project was driven out of Singur in West Bengal and enticed to locate there in a fascinating tale of land acquisition politics (Chakravorty, 2013). Now, in less than 10 years, the Sanand-Becharaji-Halol triangle in Gujarat includes operational or planned factories of Tata, Maruti Suzuki, Ford, GM, Honda, and Hero (Das, 2015). The appetite for cars and two-wheelers in India can only grow for years to come, and this industry, without selling a single unit abroad, has the potential to grow by double digit figures annually.

in designated lagging districts (about 60 per cent of all the districts in India). State governments also enacted their own policies to attract capital to lagging districts (for instance, West Bengal and Maharashtra created three- and five-category systems for identifying which districts should receive tax and duty abatements and to what degree). All these approaches share a common outcome—failure. Location incentives simply do not work, especially in the lagging districts of lagging regions (Chakravorty and Lall, 2007).

TWO RECOMMENDATIONS

The Make in India initiative faces several serious challenges. Most are inherited—like regional imbalance, capital intensity in a labour-abundant society, and distrust of large cities. Some are relatively new—like the booming land market that has made land in India arguably the most expensive in the world, at the same time that land acquisition has become a serious challenge in the political economy. Some challenges are in the design of the initiative—like the overreliance on scale economies in production and transportation, and lack of understanding of external and agglomeration economies. But all these will probably be swept under the carpet as demographic forces create more and more demand for manufactured goods, a demand that must largely be met by making in India.

If that is the case—that is, whether or not there is a Make in India initiative, there will be more things made in India simply because there is a growing demand for things by a growing and more prosperous population—then the following two recommendations should receive serious consideration.

First, *think small in large*. That is, give serious attention to the potential of the clustering of small firms in large cities. Which also means: give serious attention to the textiles, garments, leather, and other small-to-medium–scale labour-intensive sectors. This is what has always succeeded … everywhere that industrialization has taken root. History cannot be so wrong, neither can the rest of the world. This will require Indian policymakers to go against their timeworn instinct of thinking large in small—the big plant in the small town. That has been tried before, over and over again—it is a recipe for jobless growth.

Second, *innovate for the isolated*. The deepening regional polarization of industry and development cannot be a good outcome for the nation's political economy. Granted that there are almost no good options available in the usual toolbox of location incentives. It is necessary then to think anew, perhaps in the domain of transportation and freight subsidies, with a focus not on the lagging districts in lagging regions (which is what has been tried so far—with no success) but the leading districts in lagging regions—try to grow Patna because Chhapra simply cannot; try to grow Kolkata and Durgapur because Dinajpur is impossible. Given the location choices available in India, private capital simply will not locate in Chhapra or Dinajpur; but it may, with the right incentives, be willing to do so in Patna or Kolkata or Durgapur.

The look and feel of the Make in India initiative suggests something new in Indian policymaking—that ideas and plans are adaptable and contingent. Therefore, when policymakers retool and recraft the initiative, they will do well to admit the inherent tension in spatial development, one that has been recognized from time of Gunnar Myrdal and Albert Hirschman. That is the problem of cumulative causation: growth is more likely in growing places, so lagging places fall further behind. The second generation of Make in India ideas should focus more clearly on this inherent tension. The place to begin is in the large cities and existing urban centers on both sides of the divide.

REFERENCES

Ahluwalia, I.J. 1991. *Productivity and Growth in Indian Manufacturing*. Delhi: Oxford University Press.

Alonso, W. 1980. 'Five Bell Shapes in Development'. Papers of the Regional Science Association, 45: 5–16.

Awasthi, D. 1991. *Regional Patterns of Industrial Growth in India*. New Delhi: Concept Publishing.

Banerjee, A. and L. Iyer. 2005. 'History, Institutions and Economic Performance: The Legacy of Colonial Land Tenure Systems in India'. *American Economic Review* 95: 1190–1213.

Barro, R.J., and X. Sala-i-Martin. 1992. 'Convergence'. *Journal of Political Economy* 100: 223–51.

————. 1995. *Economic Growth*. New York: McGraw Hill.

Chakravarty, S. 1979. 'On the Question of Home Market and Prospects for Indian Growth'. *Economic and Political Weekly* Special Issue, 4.

Chakravorty, S. 1994. 'Equity and the Big City'. *Economic Geography* 70: 1–22.

————. 2000. 'How Does Structural Reform Affect Regional Development? Resolving Contradictory Theory with Evidence from India'. *Economic Geography* 76: 367–94.

————. 2003a. 'Industrial Location in Post-Reform India: Patterns of Interregional Divergence and Intraregional Convergence'. *Journal of Development Studies* 40: 120–52.

————. 2003b. 'Capital Source and the Location of Industrial Investment: A Tale of Divergence from Post-Reform India'. *Journal of International Development* 15: 365–83.

Chakravorty, S. 2010. 'Clusters and Regional Development.' In *The International Studies Encyclopedia Volume 1*, edited by R.A. Denemark, 323–42.

———. 2013. *The Price of Land: Acquisition, Conflict, Consequence.* Oxford University Press.

Chakravorty, S., and S. Lall. 2007. *Made in India: The Economic Geography and Political Economy of Industrialization.* Oxford University Press.

Darwent, D.F. 1975. 'Growth Poles and Growth Centers in Regional Planning: A Review.' In *Regional Policy: Readings in Theory and Applications*, edited by Friedmann and Alonso. Cambridge, Mass.: The MIT Press.

Das, S. 2015. 'Sanand: The New Global Auto Hub.' *Business Standard.* March 23. Available at http://www.business-standard.com/article/companies/sanand-the-new-global-auto-hub-115032200818_1.html (accessed on 11 July 2017).

Friedmann, J. 1973. 'A Theory of Polarized Development.' In *Urbanization, Planning and National Development*, edited by J. Friedmann, 41–64. Beverly Hills: Sage.

Garreau, J. 1991. *Edge City: Life on the New Frontier.* New York: Anchor books.

Gerrefi, G. and T. Sturgeon. 2013. 'Global Value Chains and Industrial Policy: The Role of Emerging Economies.' In *Global Value Chains in a Changing World*, edited by Deborah K. Elms and Patrick Low. Geneva: World Trade Organization.

Ghani, E., A.G. Goswami, and W.R. Kerr. 2012. 'Is India's Manufacturing Sector Moving Away from Cities?' NBER Working Paper No. 17992.

Glaeser, E. 2012. *Triumph of the City: How Our Greatest Invention Makes Us Richer, Smarter, Greener, Healthier, and Happier.* New York: Penguin.

Jacobs, J. 1970. *The Economy of Cities.* New York: Vintage.

Johnson, E.A.J. 1970. *The Organization of Space in Developing Countries.* Cambridge, Mass.: Harvard University Press.

Krugman, P. 1996. 'Urban Concentration: The Role of Increasing Returns and Transport Costs.' *International Regional Science Review* 19: 5–30.

Lall, S. and S. Chakravorty. 2005. 'Industrial Location and Spatial Inequality: Theory and Evidence from India.' *Review of Development Economics* 9: 47–68.

Lewis, J.P. 1995. *India's Political Economy: Governance and Reform.* New Delhi: Oxford University Press.

Livemint.com. 2014. Available at http://www.livemint.com/Politics/nEPZGnUMtLN3o86upKbPsI/Raghuram-Rajan-questions-Modis-Make-in-India-strategy.html (accessed on 11 July 2017).

McCann, P. and R. Ortega-Argilés. 2013. 'Modern Regional Innovation Policy.' *Cambridge Journal of Regions Economy and Society.* doi: 10.1093/cjres/rst007.

Milanovic, B. 2005. *Worlds Apart: Measuring International and Global Inequality.* Princeton: Princeton University Press.

Mitra, A. 1965. *Levels of Regional Development in India.* New Delhi: Census of India. 1961.

Mohan, R. 1983. 'India: Coming to Terms with Urbanization.' *Cities* 1: 46–58.

Mukhopadhyay, P. 2009. 'The Promised Land of SEZs.' In *Special Economic Zones: Promise, Performance, and Pending Issues*, 39–60. CPR Occasional Paper Series. New Delhi: Centre for Policy Research.

NDTV. 2016. Available at http://www.ndtv.com/india-news/lucknow-warangal-2nd-list-of-smart-cities-is-out-10-facts-1409414 (accessed on 11 July 2017).

Perroux, F. 1950. 'Economic Space: Theory and Applications.' *Quarterly Journal of Economics* 64: 89–104.

Richardson, H.W. 1980. 'Polarization Reversal in Developing Countries.' *Papers of the Regional Science Association* 45: 67–85.

Sahling, Leonard. 2008. *China's Special Economic Zones and National Industrial Parks—Door Openers to Economic Reform.* ProLogis Research Bulletin.

Sivaramakrishnan, K.C. 2009. 'Special Economic Zones: Issues of Urban Growth and Management.' In *Special Economic Zones: Promise, Performance, and Pending Issues*, 85–106. CPR Occasional Paper Series. New Delhi: Centre for Policy Research.

Williamson, J.G. 1965. 'Regional Inequality and the Process of National Development.' *Economic Development and Cultural Change* 13: 3–45.

World Bank. 2009. *Reshaping Economic Geography: The World Development Report 2009.* Washington DC: World Bank.

Zheng, D.Z. 2011. *How Do Special Economic Zones and Industrial Clusters Drive China's Rapid Development?* The World Bank. Policy Research Working Paper No. 5583.

15

Evolution of the Insolvency Framework for Non-financial Firms in India

Rajeswari Sengupta, Anjali Sharma, and Susan Thomas

INTRODUCTION

Since the economic reform process of the 1990s, there has been significant progress in the development of financial markets and services in India (Thomas, 2005). However, this development has been skewed largely towards equity markets. Despite considerable policy initiatives, the development of debt markets has seen little progress (Table 15.1). While many factors have contributed to the lack of development of a debt market in India, one that clearly stands out as a large missing piece is the absence of a coherent and effective mechanism for resolving insolvency.

The limited liability company is a contract between equity and debt. Unlike an equity contract, where there are no promised returns to investors, in a debt contract, the borrower (or the 'debtor') promises a 'return' as well as a 'repayment of the original capital' to the lender (or the 'creditor') at a defined time in the future. All debt contracts contain a possibility that at the time of repayment, the debtor may not make the payment as promised and 'defaults'.

Non-payment by a debtor firm may be due to a short-term cash-flow stress even when the underlying business model is generating revenues or due to a fundamental weakness in the business model because of which the business is unable to generate sufficient revenues to make payments. As long as the debt obligations are met, equity owners have full control and the creditors of the firm have no say in the running of the business. When the debtor defaults on payments, the control transfers to the creditors and the equity owners should have no further say. Upon default, the creditors have the incentive to be the first to recover their amounts. Consequently, a race to collect may ensue, with firm liquidation as the inevitable outcome. What should ideally happen is that the creditors and the debtor should negotiate a financial rearrangement to preserve the economic value of the business and keep the enterprise running as a going concern. If, however, the default is due to a business failure, then the enterprise should be shut down as soon as possible. The insolvency and bankruptcy law of the country provides a framework through which these decisions can be taken and hence it assumes great importance.

The insolvency and bankruptcy law of a country lays down a process by which firms in financial distress can seek a resolution or an exit. The three different states of distress, insolvency and bankruptcy are presented in Figure 15.1.

When implemented efficiently, the law provides protection to the creditors in the event of a firm insolvency. It

Table 15.1   Financial Market Development in India, 1996–2015

As Percentage of GDP	1996	2008	2015
Equities	32.1	108.4	80.0
Government bonds	14.3	36.1	34.3
Corporate bonds	0.9	3.9	14.0
Bank assets	46.5	73.8	89.0

Source: SEBI, RBI, IMF World Economic Outlook.

provides certainty to parties in a debt contract about the expected outcomes and this, ex ante, enables the creditors to take better credit decisions in the pre-insolvency stage. An insolvency law, therefore, impacts both pre-insolvency and post-insolvency actions of the debtors and the creditors and is a critical element of the financial environment of a country.

With a clear and coherent insolvency and bankruptcy law, there is lower contention between the creditor and the debtor, and financial distress can be resolved rapidly. Debtors can re-enter the enterprise arena quickly and with lower costs and creditors get incentivized to repeatedly provide credit. An empirical analysis of domestic bond market development in 49 countries around the world finds

that the size of local debt markets is larger when countries have better rule of law and better creditor rights (Burger and Warnock, 2006). The chapter also shows that countries where creditors' incentives to lend are low, and have poorly developed bank-based and market-based lending.

The current Indian framework for corporate insolvency resolution is characterized by a complex system with fragmented laws accompanied by an inadequate institutional set-up. The origin of such a complex framework can be traced back in the history of its evolution. In this chapter, we describe the evolution of the corporate insolvency framework, with the objective of linking it back to the policy directive of the time. We conclude that when policy adopts a piecemeal approach focusing on solving a part of a complex problem, one at a time, it most often leads to non-optimal outcomes on the overall objective.

THE EVOLUTION OF INSOLVENCY LAWS IN INDIA

The Origins of Indian Insolvency Law

Insolvency law in India has its origin in the English law. In India, the need for a legal framework to deal with insolvency was first felt in the three Presidency towns—

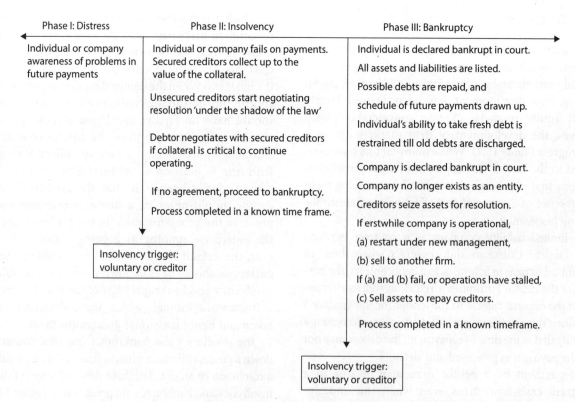

Figure 15.1   Distress, Insolvency, and Bankruptcy in Debt Relationships

Source: Author's compilation.

Bombay, Calcutta, and Madras—where the British carried on trade.

The earliest insolvency provisions can be traced back to Sections 23 and 24 of the Government of India Act, 1800, Statute 9 enacted in 1828, the Indian Insolvency Act, 1848, and the Presidency-towns Insolvency Act, 1909. The Presidency towns Insolvency Act, 1909 continues to be in force for Bombay, Calcutta, and Madras and covers the insolvency of individuals, partnerships and associations of individuals.

Till the early 1900s, there was no insolvency law for the non-Presidency town areas. The 1907 Provincial Insolvency Act which was eventually replaced by the 1920 Provincial Insolvency Act was the first insolvency law for the other areas. It continues to be the insolvency law in force in areas other than the Presidency towns of Bombay, Calcutta, and Madras and deals with insolvency of individuals, which may also include individuals as proprietors.

In 1964, the Law Commission of India[1] recommended combining the two laws to create a common insolvency law that would be applicable to the entire country. However, this was not implemented. Till today, the Presidency towns Insolvency Act, 1909 and the Provincial Insolvency Act, 1920 continue to be the relevant laws for insolvency resolution of individuals and associations of individuals.

The First Law for Corporate Insolvency: The Companies Act, 1956

In the Indian Constitution enacted in 1950, the terms 'bankruptcy' and 'insolvency' were specified in the Concurrent List.[2] However, incorporation, regulation, and winding up of corporations[3] were under the Union List.[4] With these powers, the Parliament enacted the Companies Act in 1956. This act governed all aspects of the functioning of companies, including their winding up.[5] The act had no definition of the terms insolvency or bankruptcy and dealt only with the 'inability to pay debts'. However, for all practical purposes, it was the only law available for dealing with corporate insolvency.

The high courts constituted the adjudicating authority for winding up related matters under this law. Creditors with unpaid dues above a defined threshold[6] could petition the court for winding up a company. Winding up was preceded by liquidation, a process managed by an Official Liquidator (OL), appointed by the high court. The OL was responsible for collecting the assets of the company, and managing the sale and the distribution of the proceeds in accordance with the priority defined in the act. This act, passed in the early periods of India's policy of industrialization, prioritized workmen dues and dues to the government over secured creditors' dues.

The Companies Act, 1956 contained certain provisions through which the company or its creditors could seek to reorganize it.[7] However, these were general provisions and not specific to insolvency or bankruptcy situations.

In 2013, there were approximately 14 lakh registered companies in India of which only 9.5 lakh were active.[8] In contrast, on an average, between 2008 and 2010, not more than 6,500 cases of winding up were registered with the high courts. Only about 250–350 cases were added every year and about 300–600 completed every year. This highlights the low use of the Companies Act procedures for dealing with corporate insolvency. It also points to a lack of capacity at the high courts to deal with case volumes. Anecdotal evidence suggests that winding up under the act, on an average, takes around 5–8 years to complete and in extreme cases even 25–30 years.

The Companies (Amendment) Act, 2003 proposed significant changes to the insolvency related provisions of the Companies Act, 1956. However, these could not be notified due to legal challenges. In 2013, the new Companies Act was passed. Most of the provisions of the 2013 Act are in line with those proposed under the Second Amendment in 2002. Implementation challenges with respect to the corporate insolvency provisions continue even with the new Companies Act, 2013.

---

[1] 26th Report of the Law Commission of India.

[2] As Entry 9 of List III of the Seventh Schedule. Both centre and state governments can make laws relating to this subject.

[3] Entry 43 and 44 of List I of the Seventh Schedule. There are some exceptions such as incorporation, regulation, and winding up of cooperative societies, which is covered in List II of the Seventh Schedule.

[4] Subjects on which only Parliament can make laws.

[5] The Act covered the process of winding up registered companies (in Part VII of the Act, covering Section 425(560). It also covered the winding up of foreign companies, partnerships, societies, and associations with more than seven members under Part X of the Act.

[6] Rs 1 lakh.

[7] Sections 390, 390A, and 391. Any creditor or member of a company could approach the court with a scheme of arrangement or a compromise. The court would order a meeting of the creditors to consider the scheme. If three fourths of the creditors agreed to it, the court could enforce it on the remaining creditors. The court enabled this action without judging the merit of the scheme.

[8] Data from Ministry of Corporate Affairs Annual Report.

As a result, the provisions of the Companies Act, 1956 continue to be in force.

Strengthening Debtor's Rights: Sick Industrial Companies Act (SICA), 1985

From 1956 to 1985, the Companies Act was the only law dealing with corporate insolvency. The early policies of the government after Independence involved the development of manufacturing industries in the economy, which required significant investments. As was typical in several emerging economies, the government made these investments through large development finance institutions (DFIs), which were set up with the objective to encourage industrial development. In return for credit, the DFIs were given a seat on the board of these firms. This was expected to give these creditors a direct control on the management of these firms. In turn, this resulted in poor allocation of economic capital. There is evidence that large firms with banks as creditors and the latter on the boards have higher leverage, lower investment, and tend to be in greater financial distress. This turned out to be true in India as well (Bubna and Gopalan, 2012).

By the early 1980s, the problem of sickness among the industrial companies had become widespread. From 1981 to 1985, the number of sick industrial units rose from 26,758 to 119,606.[9] In 1980, an empowered committee (Tiwari Committee) was set up to recommend legislative and administrative remedies to the problem of industrial sickness. As an outcome of this, the Sick Industrial Companies Act (SICA) was passed in 1985 with the objective of identifying 'sickness' in industrial companies and reviving them. The act was supported by the setting up of a new legal forum, the Board of Industrial and Financial Reconstruction (BIFR) and the Appellate Authority for Industrial and Financial Reconstruction (AAIFR).

The SICA was the first law which focused solely on restructuring of companies. However, its coverage was narrowly defined to include only 'industrial companies' that were deemed 'sick'.[10] The act put the onus of reporting sickness on the board of the firm. Once sickness was reported, the act provided an automatic stay on all suits, claims and proceedings against the company. This procedure differed from that in the Companies Act, where a stay was not automatic and was granted at the discretion of the high court. The SICA also empowered the

debtor company to control its assets and operations even after being adjudged sick. Over time, the law developed a distinct rehabilitation bias (Van Zwieten, 2015). Key provisions of the act were interpreted and reinterpreted by judges in an attempt to rescue companies that were bankrupt and hence destined for liquidation, and to protect some types of stakeholders (especially employees) in the interim period.

An additional challenge with SICA was that there was only one bench of the BIFR, in Delhi. As enterprises grew manifold in number all over the country, the lack of capacity at the BIFR became a bottleneck. Further, if the BIFR judged the company to be sick, it recommended winding up. However, the winding up order as per the Companies Act, 1956, was issued by the high court. Often, winding up recommendations by the BIFR were re-opened by the high court's afresh and many a time, even reversed, thereby causing inordinate delays and associated loss in firm value.

An analysis of BIFR cases between 1987 to 2014 shows that a total of 5,800 cases were reported to the BIFR. Of these cases, 53 per cent were either dismissed or abated; 22 per cent of the cases were recommended for liquidation; in 9 per cent of the cases, a rehabilitation plan was implemented; and the remaining 15 per cent cases remain pending in BIFR. The average time taken for the closure of a case is around 5.8 years. This highlights fact that eligible companies often used BIFR as a mechanism to seek protection from their creditors. It also points to the capacity challenge at BIFR in dealing with case volumes.

The 2003 Amendment of the Companies Act sought to repeal SICA. However, due to legal challenges this amendment could not be notified.

POLICY FOCUS ON STRENGTHENING CREDITORS' RIGHTS

In the decade of 1990, there was a general acknowledgement of the failure of insolvency resolution process under the Companies Act, 1956 and the SICA, 1985. Procedures under both these acts were plagued with significant delays and did not lead to productive outcomes. In order to rectify this several committees were set up between 1991 and 2008 to reform the framework for corporate insolvency resolution. Table 15.2 lists the numerous government committees that have worked on this subject, for many decades. A noticeable feature of this reform push was the attempt to strengthen the 'individual' recovery rights of banks and financial institutions, the dominant lenders at the time, rather than all creditors in general.

---

[9] *Economic Survey 1987–88*, Ministry of Finance.

[10] Industrial companies and sickness were defined under the Act, though the definition of sickness was amended over time.

Table 15.2   Government Committees on Bankruptcy Reforms

Year	Committee	Outcome
1964	24th Law Commission	Amendments to the Provincial Insolvency Act, 1929.
1981	Tiwari Committee (Department of Company Affairs)	SICA, 1983.
1991	Narasimham Committee I (RBI)	RDDBFI Act, 1993.
1998	Narasimham Committee II (RBI)	SARFAESI Act, 2002.
1999	Justice Eradi Committee (GOI)	Companies (Amendment) Act, 2002, Proposed repeal of SICA.
2001	L.N. Mitra Committee (RBI)	Proposed a comprehensive bankruptcy code.
2005	Irani Committee (RBI)	Enforcement of Securities Interest and Recovery of Debts Bill, 2011. (With amendments to RDDBFI and SARFAESI Acts.)
2008	Raghuram Rajan Committee (Planning Commission)	Proposed improvements to credit infrastructure.
2014	Bankruptcy Law Reforms Committee (Ministry of Finance)	Insolvency and Bankruptcy Code (Replacing extant laws with a single consolidated code).

Source: Authors' compilation.

As an outcome of the policy reform push of the 1990s and early 2000s, laws focusing solely on strengthening the recovery rights of the banks and public financial institutions were brought about. A consequence of this, and of the general failure of the collective resolution mechanisms under Companies Act, 1956 and SICA, 1985, is that credit in India continues to be dominated by secured lending and reputation based lending by banks. This thwarts the development of alternative sources of credit such as corporate bond market and in turn makes it difficult for new firms and firms without collateral to access credit.

The Recovery of Debts due to Banks and Financial Institutions Act, 1993

The recommendations of the High Level Committee on the Financial System (Narasimham Committee I, 1991) led to the enactment of the Recovery of Debts due to Banks and Financial Institutions Act, 1993 (RDDBFI, 1993). The committee highlighted that the banks and

DFIs found it difficult to recover their dues from borrowers using the Civil Court system. It recommended the setting up of specialized tribunals that would speed up these recoveries. Accordingly, the RDDBFI Act paved the way for setting up of the Debt Recovery Tribunals (DRT) and the Debt Recovery Appellate Tribunals (DRAT). The DRTs and the DRATs were intended to be specialized tribunals that would facilitate expeditious recovery of debt from the defaulters by banks and a defined set of financial institutions.[11]

The DRTs were given the power to order recovery through sale of the debtor's assets and also to imprison or detain the debtor. DRTs were the first court of appeal for aggrieved debtors, but any appeal to the DRT could only be made after depositing 75 per cent of dues beforehand with the DRATs.

While the DRTs were set up for speedy adjudication of matters pertaining to the recovery of dues, they suffered from several weaknesses. This included the lack of resources available to the tribunals, which in turn led to delays in deciding cases beyond the prescribed timeframe of six months. The DRT recovery rates in 2012 and 2013 were at 17 per cent and 14 per cent respectively of the amounts involved.[12] Further, since this law did not apply to creditors other than banks and specified financial institutions, the DRTs created a special class of creditors with greater recovery rights. This limited the confidence of other types of creditors to enter into the debt market, and limited the size of these markets.

Securitisation and Reconstruction of Financial Assets and Enforcement of Security Interest Act, 2002

The second Narasimham Committee (Narasimham Committee II, 1998) on banking sector reforms raised concerns around the rising non-performing assets (NPAs) of the banking sector. The committee's recommendations led to the enactment of the Securitisation and Reconstruction of Financial Assets and Enforcement of Security Interest Act in 2002 (SARFAESI, 2002).

The act provided sweeping powers to the banks and financial institutions to recover against non-performing secured loans. Since the DRTs had not proved to be as

[11] The DRTs are one-member tribunals that have sole jurisdiction over matters related to the recovery of dues to banks and specified financial institutions, with the exception of the Supreme Court. Appeals against the orders of the DRT were to be heard in the Debt Recovery Appellate Tribunals (DRATs).

[12] Source: *RBI Report on Trends and Progress of Banking in India*, 2008–13.

effective in enabling recovery as expected, the SARFAESI Act provided an alternative route for recovery. The act allowed banks and FIs to take possession of the collateral security without court intervention. Its intent was to reduce the growing size of NPAs at banks and large public financial institutions. After its implementation, the number of new cases led with DRTs went down by almost 40 per cent (Rajan, 2008).

The Narasimham Committee I and II also recommended setting up of Asset Reconstruction Companies (ARCs). Banks could offload their bad debts at a discount into the ARCs for the purpose of resolution. Accordingly, SARFAESI, 2002 paved the way for the creation of Securitisation Companies/Asset Reconstruction Companies (SC/ARC). These financial firms are specialized institutions that buy NPAs from the banks, for the purpose of recovering and resolving them.

The SARFAESI vested extraordinary enforcement powers, but only with certain class of secured creditors, that is, the banks. In addition, enforcement actions under the SARFAESI Act took precedence over BIFR proceedings in the high courts, if agreed upon by 60 per cent of the creditors in value. This meant that rehabilitation under SICA or winding up under the Companies Act, could be delayed or even abated using SARFAESI enforcement.

The performance of SARFAESI in enabling recovery of banks' secured dues was at first promising, but has worsened over time. The recovery rate declined from 61 per cent in 2008 to 21.9 per cent in 2013. The sale of NPAs by the banks to the ARCs has also remained stagnant.[13]

BANKING REGULATION AND CORPORATE INSOLVENCY

In 2001, the RBI set up the Corporate Debt Restructuring (CDR) process as an out-of-court mechanism between the debtor and the creditor banks to negotiate new terms on their existing loans. The CDR mechanism is based on the 'London Approach' which is founded upon the principles of collective and coordinated efforts to rescue a defaulting firm that has multiple creditors. Comprehensive guidelines for the CDR mechanism were first issued in 2008, and subsequently augmented in 2012 and 2013. The key feature of the CDR process was that the RBI would permit lower provisioning on loans made to companies that were restructured under this mechanism.

As of March 2016, out of 655 applications, 530 cases were approved for CDR.[14] The aggregate debt outstanding of these companies is approximately Rs 4.03 trillion.

In 2014, RBI introduced the Joint Lenders' Forum (JLF) mechanism, to facilitate the adoption of a comprehensive banking system-wide view of loans made to a company. In 2015, it introduced the Strategic Debt Restructuring (SDR) mechanism, which enables banks to convert their debt to a firm to equity and execute a change in the management of the firm.

The CDR, JLF, and SDR are all mechanisms through which RBI has allowed the banks to recover their dues from corporate borrowers. Since all these mechanisms are accompanied by some amount of regulatory forbearance on NPA provisioning, over time these have become the preferred mechanisms for collective recovery of corporate dues.

LEGAL AND ECONOMIC OUTCOMES

The evolution of the laws for corporate insolvency resolution, as described, has resulted in a complex and fragmented environment for both creditors and debtors. The reforms that have sought to strengthen creditors' rights, give benefit only to the banks and a subset of FIs. Non-bank creditors can only enforce debt recovery action using the civil courts. Collective action by these lenders can only be under the provisions of SICA, 1985 and the Companies Act, 1956.

Among debtors, there are limitations on the firms that get covered under the two main laws—Companies Act, 1956 and SICA, 1985. A large number of small, unregistered enterprises with less than seven members may not be covered under the Companies Act, 1956 or 2013. The SICA, 1985 is only applicable to a subset of 'sick industrial companies'.

In a landscape dotted with multiple laws and special provisions, there is a lack of clarity on what holds precedence in a given situation. In India, this has been a subject of significant litigation. This has also given rise to the concept of 'forum shopping', where both the creditor and the debtor firm can opt for the judicial mechanism that suits their individual needs, at the cost of maximizing the economic value of the business (Ravi, 2015). Added to this complexity, is the dearth of timely mechanisms that are consistently available to all categories of creditors to resolve the insolvency of all categories of debtor firms.

Figure 15.2 attempts to capture this scenario, where each column represents the fragmentation of the laws

---

[13] These figures have been compiled from the *RBI Report on Trends and Progress of Banking in India*, for 2008 to 2013.

[14] Source: www.cdrindia.org.

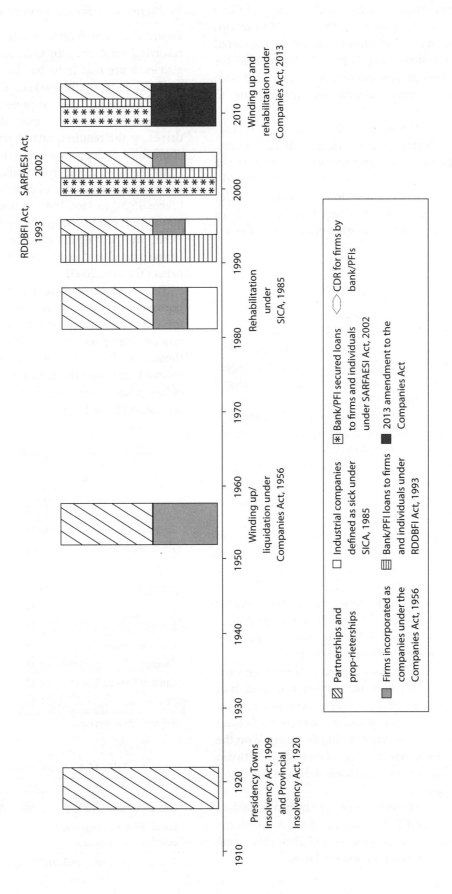

Figure 15.2 Evolution of Insolvency Resolution Mechanisms in India

Source: Authors' own.

across entities (horizontally), and across creditors (vertically). It starts from a single law in 1920 to two laws in 1956, with Companies Act for all registered entities and the Insolvency Acts of 1909 and 1927 for partnerships and proprietorships. It ends in 2013 with two acts across entities, but with three separate laws to initiate debt recovery.

The current insolvency resolution framework is characterized by deficiencies in the definitions of the laws, their procedures, their implementation as well as the capacity and capability of the institutional frameworks supporting them. A typical winding up process under the Companies Act, 1956 takes anywhere between 3–15 years leading to a complete erosion of the value of assets of the company.

Problems in Legal Outcomes

- There is no common framework for all firms.
- The trigger for filing a petition differs across different laws. (For example, Companies Act, 1956 considers the incidence of default as the trigger while SICA, 1985, accepts a balance sheet trigger of negative net worth.)
- There is no clarity on whether there is a moratorium on actions against and by the debtor after a petition has been filed in court.
- There are no procedural timelines defined in any of the laws. Even where the timelines are defined, these are not adhered to (for example, RDDBFI, 1993).
- The supporting infrastructure of dedicated benches in courts and tribunals or the official liquidators do not yet have the required capacity to support a diverse set of creditors.
- The law does not encourage interim-financing for debtors that have led for insolvency resolution.
- Banks and specified FIs have superior enforcement rights under debt recovery laws.
- There is no clarity on the interaction of the various insolvency laws and debt-enforcement laws between themselves as well as with other major laws, for example, the Industrial Disputes Act and Transfer of Property Act. The dependence on the courts for a resolution of the conflicts between these laws causes significant delays in the insolvency process.
- Out-of-court mechanisms used by banks, such as the CDR and SDR processes distorts the incentives in the credit process and skews the same towards large debtors and creditors.

Problems in Economic Outcomes

Figure 15.2 demonstrates the lack of a clear process for resolving insolvency. In such an environment, there is also evidence that India has faced significant problems in developing credit markets. Given the state of corporate insolvency laws, at present, bond investors plan for near-zero recovery upon default, which in turn drives up the required rate of return. This leads to few companies finding it cost effective to issue bonds. As a result, secured credit from banks and FIs continues to be the dominant source of debt financing for companies (Table 15.3). In fact, India is unique in that equity is a larger source of financing than debt for firms on average. While the debt-equity ratio tends to be around 3 for firms in developed economies, it is around 0.5 for Indian firms (Thomas, 2005).

Table 15.3 shows that out of 29.48 per cent of total borrowings by Indian firms in 2009–10, banks account for 17.83 percentage points. In the absence of a well-functioning insolvency resolution framework, banks themselves continue to be vulnerable to poor recovery against loans when the debtor firms fail. The size of NPAs of banks has grown over the years along with their loan portfolios (Table 15.4).

Table 15.3 Sources of Funds Aggregated for All Non-financial Firms

	1991–92	2009–10	2012–13
Equity	22.60	34.87	37.21
Retained earnings	10.56	21.05	6.85
Fresh issuance	12.04	13.82	30.36
Depreciation	17.64	9.69	3.56
Borrowing	35.32	29.48	21.57
Banks	17.14	17.83	15.20
Bonds	7.87	3.94	0.96
Inter-corporate	1.28	2.28	3.32
Foreign	5.51	3.22	0.74
Current liabilities	24.42	24.19	37.65
D:E	1.56	0.85	0.58

Source: CMIE Prowess.

Table 15.4 NPAs of the Banking System

	2008	2010	2013	2015
Gross Advances (Rs Cr)	23,318	32,719	59,883	67,423
Gross NPA + restructured advances (percentage)	3.59	6.90	8.82	10.91

Source: Report on Trends and Progress of Banking in India.

RECENT REFORMS

Bankruptcy Law Reforms Committee, 2014

In 2014, a significant effort at comprehensive bankruptcy reform was undertaken when the Ministry of Finance set up the Bankruptcy Law Reforms Committee (BLRC) under the Chairmanship of T.K. Viswanathan. The mandate of the BLRC was to recommend an Indian Bankruptcy Code that would be applicable to all non-financial corporations and individuals, and would replace the existing framework. The committee submitted its report and a comprehensive draft Insolvency and Bankruptcy Code (IBC) to the government in November 2015. In May 2016, the IBC was enacted in the Parliament. This implies that India now has a new insolvency law that would supersede the existing laws for all categories of debtors and creditors. The new law is yet to be notified by the government.

The Insolvency and Bankruptcy Code, 2016

The Insolvency and Bankruptcy Code, 2016 is different from the labyrinth of extant Indian laws dealing with corporate insolvency, both in principle and in the design of the resolution framework. It incorporates the recommendations of several past committees that were not taken into consideration earlier.

It is a single, consolidated code for insolvency resolution of all entities unlike the existing laws such as Companies Act, 1956, SICA, 1985, or SARFAESI, 2002, that apply selectively to a certain group of debtors and creditors. Once implemented, it will supersede all existing legislation pertaining to the insolvency and bankruptcy of firms as well as individuals. This will address the problem of 'forum shopping' that creditors and debtors resort to under the current system given the plethora of laws and statutes in place.

Under IBC, an insolvency resolution process (IRP) can get triggered when a debtor defaults on her credit contract. Any financial or operational creditor can initiate the insolvency proceedings. The debtor herself can also apply for an IRP once a default has occurred. In other words, the IBC empowers all creditors (secured, unsecured, financial, and operational) to initiate insolvency proceedings. This is a significant departure from the existing framework. Unsecured financial creditors and operational creditors including the employees of the debtor firm have no rights to seek resolution of an insolvent firm under the prevalent laws. The idea of using default as a trigger for IRP makes the initiation process under IBC cleaner and also creates scope for early detection of insolvency. This is a major improvement on the existing laws. For example

under SICA 1985, restructuring proceedings can be initiated only when the firm has been reported 'sick' which might be too late to recover any value.

The IBC proposes a linear resolution process starting from a default-triggered IRP which can continue for a maximum period of 180 days. During the IRP, the debtor and the creditors negotiate with each other and the negotiations are intermediated by a regulated and qualified insolvency professional (IP). This paves the way for collective recovery and resolution. It gives opportunity to all key stakeholders to participate in the insolvency proceedings and collectively assess the viability of the defaulting firm. This is different from the individual recovery rights accorded to secured financial creditors by laws such as the SARFAESI, to the detriment of other creditors.

Once the resolution process begins, there is an automatic moratorium on all suits and claims against the debtor firm. This is to enable a calm period where other proceedings do not derail existing ones. While SICA 1985 has this provision as well, it permits the promoter/management of the debtor firm to retain control of the firm's assets even in 'sickness'. This has often led to pilferage and siphoning off of assets by the promoters/management, at the cost of the creditors. The debtor-in-possession regime promoted by SICA has been criticized by several committees in the past. The IBC rectifies this by replacing the existing management during insolvency proceedings. An IP will run and manage the firm as a going concern during the period of the IRP.

The IP will also seek potential resolution plans from interested parties. The resolution plan will be deliberated upon by a committee of financial creditors. The voting rights of the creditors depend upon the value of their claims. Once a resolution plan is voted upon by majority of the creditors, the adjudicating authority declares the IRP as completed and the plan is thereafter implemented. The IBC does not go into the details of the form and manner of resolution that can be included in the plan because the market participants and the creditors' committee are the best judge of this.

In case no resolution plan is agreed upon by majority of the creditors, the firm automatically goes into liquidation. In other words, if the creditors' committee assess the firm to be unviable and bankrupt, the firm enters the liquidation process. Liquidation under IBC is led by the adjudicating authority and conducted by a regulated liquidator. The IBC outlines a clear waterfall of priorities for the payment of dues to all claimants once the bankrupt firm's assets are sold off.

In addition to the 180 days' time limit for the IRP, the IBC stipulates finite time limits for completing various stages of the resolution process. This will improve the timeliness of insolvency proceedings—a major shortcoming of the existing framework. In the current system, judicial involvement in business decisions often causes inordinate delays in resolving insolvency. Under IBC, the adjudicator's main role is to see that the processes follow the law. All business decisions will be taken by the creditors' committee.

Thus the IBC once implemented will bring about a number of significant improvements to the way insolvency and bankruptcy cases are dealt with in India. The IBC also proposes to set up new institutions to support the implementation of the law and ensure efficient outcomes. These include a cadre of regulated IPs and IP agencies, regulated information utilities, an insolvency and bankruptcy regulator, as well as a specialized tribunal to adjudicate upon insolvency related matters. It has been decided that individual insolvency cases will be referred to the DRTs and DRATs whereas the newly set up NCLT and NCLAT will deal with corporate insolvency matters. Allocating all corporate insolvency matters to designated tribunal will hopefully address the problem of delays caused due to an overburdened judiciary.

With this framework, the IBC seeks to achieve the objectives of low time to resolution, higher recovery rate and higher levels of debt financing across diverse sources.

WAY FORWARD FOR INDIA

Aghion, Hart, and Moore (1994) document how the development of bankruptcy law, 'as a series of attempts to solve perceived immediate problems', has led to 'a widespread dissatisfaction with bankruptcy procedures throughout the world'. This accurately describes the manner in which insolvency laws came about in India. One flaw in the development of the legal framework for insolvency resolution is that it has addressed the interests of a single participant at every point in the evolution. There tended to be a bias towards certain constituencies, either the Indian business houses as the dominant debtors, or the banks and public financial institutions as the dominant creditors, or labour and state dues. These biases in development are reflected in the debt markets that are in place today.

Policy instead needs to develop to protect the interests of all parties involved in debt contracts. These include unsecured creditors, and operational as well as financial creditors such as banks or non-banking finance companies. The unsecured creditors form a strong emergent class of creditors to a wide range of debtors in India today. These include firms that produce services but do not have collateral such as the services sector or young firms. Debt markets that are restricted to a homogenous set of creditors are typically not able to provide credit to this broader mass of potential debtors. In such a market, debtors are limited in the diversification of their credit access, and creditors are limited in how well they can diversify their debt portfolio.

For a robust credit market to develop in India, there needs to be a single unambiguous law that covers insolvency of all classes of debtors and gives clarity to all classes of creditors about their rights when a debtor becomes insolvent. Creditors and the debtor have tangential preferences in insolvency. Creditors would prefer to liquidate the firm as quickly as possible to preserve existing economic value. Debtors would prefer to take on more risk within the enterprise in the hope of earning higher future revenues. While clarity on the individual rights of the debtor and the creditors is important, a good bankruptcy law should also incentivise collective action in assessing the economic value of the enterprise in distress.

The IBC, 2016 is based on this principle of collective action and according rights to all the key stakeholders. Once implemented, the law will potentially change not only the manner in which insolvency is resolved in India but also the entire credit landscape of the country. It will pave the way for the development of alternative sources of credit that are crucial if India is to transition to a mature, market economy. For this to happen energy and resources need to be devoted to a full-edged implementation plan that will work through the establishment of the institutional pillars envisaged by the law and also create the requisite state capacity. Anything short of this will result in an incomplete bankruptcy reform initiative.

REFERENCES

Aghion, Phillippe, Oliver Hart, and John Moore. 1994. 'Improving Bankruptcy Procedure.' *Washington Law University Quarterly* 72(3): 849–72.

Bubna, Amit, and Radhakrishnan Gopalan. 2012. *Bank Involvement in Firm Management: Panacea or a Pain?* Tech. rep.

Burger, John D., and Francis E. Warnock. 2006. 'Local Currency Bond Markets.' IMF Staff Paper 53.

Ravi, Aparna. 2015. 'The Indian Insolvency Regime in Practice: An Analysis of Insolvency and Debt Recovery Proceedings.' *Economic and Political Weekly* 50(51).

Thomas, Susan. 2005. 'How the Financial Sector in India was Reformed.' In *Documenting Reforms: Case Studies from India*, edited by S. Narayan. Observer Research Foundation.

Van Zwieten, Kristin. 2015. 'Corporate Rescue in India: The Influence of the Courts.' *Journal of Corporate Law Studies* 1.

A Statistical Profile of India's Development

A1 NATIONAL INCOME

Table A1.1 Key National Accounts Aggregates—2004–05 Series (at Constant Prices)

(Rupees, Crore)

Year	GDP at Factor Cost	CAGR	Net Factor Income from Abroad	GNP at Factor Cost (2+3)	CAGR	Consumption of Fixed Capital	NNP at Factor Cost (4–5)	NDP at Factor Cost (2–5)	CAGR	Indirect Taxes Less Subsidies (9–2)	CAGR	GDP at Market Prices (2+8)	CAGR	NDP at Market Prices (7+8)	CAGR	GNP at Market Prices (4+8)	CAGR	NNP at Market Prices (6+8)	CAGR
1	2		3	4		5	6	7		8		9		10		11		12	
1950–51	279618	..	–941	278677	..	23272	255405	256346	..	14319	..	293937	..	270665	..	292996	..	269724	..
1960–61	410279	3.9	–1540	408739	3.9	22978	385761	387301	4.2	25758	6.0	436037	4.0	413059	4.3	434497	4.0	411519	4.3
1970–71	589786	3.7	–4115	585672	3.7	43805	541867	545981	3.5	54603	7.8	644389	4.0	600584	3.8	640275	4.0	596470	3.8
1980–81	798506	3.1	–2	798504	3.1	71144	727359	727362	2.9	67834	2.2	866340	3.0	795196	2.8	866338	3.1	795193	2.9
1990–91	1347889	5.4	–16849	1331040	5.2	128735	1202305	1219154	5.3	139726	7.5	1487615	5.6	1358880	5.5	1470766	5.4	1342031	5.4
2000–01	2342774	5.7	–23800	2318974	5.7	244116	2074858	2098658	5.6	211230	4.2	2559711	5.6	2309888	5.4	2530204	5.6	2286088	5.5
2010–11	4918533	7.7	–54647	4863886	7.7	570301	4293585	4348232	7.6	363853	5.6	5282386	7.5	4712085	7.4	5227739	7.5	4665438	7.4
2011–12 (RE.2)	5247530	6.7	–46367	5201163	6.9	627834	4573329	4619696	6.2	385520	6.0	5633050	6.6	5005216	6.2	5586683	6.9	4958849	6.5
2012–13 (RE.1)	5482111	4.5	–65452	5416659	4.1	687884	4728775	4794227	3.8	417736	8.4	5899847	4.7	5211963	4.1	5834395	4.4	5146511	3.8
2013–14 (AE)	5748564	4.9	–67737	5680827	4.9	753674	4927153	4994890	4.2	424969	1.7	6173533	4.6	5419859	4.0	6105796	4.7	5352122	4.0

(Contd.)

Table A1.1 (Contd.)

(Rupees, Crore)

Year	GDP at Factor Cost				Private Final Consumption Expenditure in Domestic Market (PFCE)		Government Final Consumption Expenditure (GFCE)		Gross Domestic Capital Formation (Adjusted)		Net Domestic Capital Formation (Adjusted)		Per Capita GNP at Factor Cost (in Rupees)		Per Capita NNP at Factor Cost		Per Capita NDP at Factor Cost		Population (million)	
	Public Sector	Per Cent of GDP	Private Sector	Per Cent of GDP		CAGR		CAGR		CAGR		CAGR		CAGR		CAGR		CAGR		CAGR
	13		14		15		16		17		18		19		20		21		22	
1950–51	..	..	..	..	252210	..	17979	..	37952	..	14680	..	7763	..	7114	..	7141	..	359	..
1960–61	34181	8.3	376099	91.7	368492	3.9	25473	3.5	71204	6.5	48226	12.6	9418	2.0	8889	2.3	8924	2.3	434	1.9
1970–71	84379	14.3	505407	85.7	491979	2.9	61370	9.2	114805	4.9	71000	3.9	10826	1.4	10016	1.2	10092	1.2	541	2.2
1980–81	166492	20.9	632014	79.1	681341	3.3	95196	4.5	190472	5.2	119327	5.3	11760	0.8	10712	0.7	10712	0.6	679	2.3
1990–91	324105	24.0	1023784	76.0	1025024	4.2	183488	6.8	379436	7.1	250701	7.7	15865	3.0	14330	3.0	14531	3.1	839	2.1
2000–01	573221	24.5	1769553	75.5	1618072	4.7	324727	5.9	630056	5.2	385940	4.4	22757	3.7	20362	3.6	20595	3.5	1019	2.0
2010–11	na	na	na	na	3109170	6.7	583544	6.0	2100497	12.8	1530197	14.8	41011	6.1	36202	5.9	36663	5.9	1186	1.5
2011–12 (RE.2)	na	na	na	na	3394871	9.2	623574	6.9	2183259	3.9	1555425	1.6	43271	5.5	38048	5.1	38433	4.8	1202	1.3
2012–13 (RE.1)	na	na	na	na	3569463	5.1	662032	6.2	2297807	5.2	1609925	3.5	44508	2.9	38856	2.1	39394	2.5	1217	1.2
2013–14 (AE)	na	na	na	na	na	na	698548	5.5	na	na	na	na	46073	3.5	39961	2.8	40510	2.8	1233	1.3

Note: RE.1: First Revised Estimate; RE.2: Second Revised Estimate; AE : Advance Estimate.
Growth for 1960–61, 1970–71, 1980–81, 1990–91, 2000–01 and 2010–11 are compounded annual growth rate (CAGR).
Source: Central Statistics Office (CSO).

Table A1.2 Key National Accounts Aggregates—2004–05 Series (at Current Prices)

(Rupees, Crore)

Year	GDP at Factor Cost	CAGR	Net Factor Income from Abroad	GNP at Factor Cost (2+3)	CAGR	Consumption of Fixed Capital	NNP at Factor Cost (4-5)	NDP at Factor Cost (2-5)	Indirect Taxes less Subsidies	CAGR	GDP at Market Prices (2+8)	CAGR	NDP at Market Prices (7+8)	CAGR	GNP at Market Prices (4+8)	CAGR	NNP at Market Prices (6+8)	CAGR
1	2		3	4		5	6	7	8		9		10		11		12	
1950–51	10036	..	−41	9995	..	531	9464	9505	365	..	10401	..	9870	..	10360	..	9829	..
1960–61	17049	5.4	−72	16977	5.4	808	16169	16241	893	9.4	17942	5.6	17134	5.7	17870	5.6	17062	5.7
1970–71	44382	10.0	−284	44098	10.0	2804	41294	41578	3256	13.8	47638	10.3	44834	10.1	47354	10.2	44550	10.1
1980–81	136838	11.9	345	137183	11.9	11422	125761	125416	12804	14.7	149642	12.1	138220	11.9	149987	12.2	138565	12.0
1990–91	531813	14.5	−7545	524268	14.3	52650	471618	479163	54399	15.6	586212	14.6	533562	14.5	578667	14.5	526017	14.3
2000–01	1991982	14.1	−22733	1969249	14.1	206892	1762358	1785091	176670	12.5	2177413	14.0	1961761	13.9	2145919	14.0	1939028	13.9
2010–11	**7248860**	**13.8**	**−81807**	**7167053**	**13.8**	**760218**	**6406834**	**6488641**	**535255**	**11.7**	**7784115**	**13.6**	**7023896**	**13.6**	**7702308**	**13.6**	**6942089**	**13.6**
2011–12 (RE.2)	8391691	15.8	−76830	8314861	16.0	879896	7434965	7511795	618031	15.5	9009722	15.7	8129826	15.7	8932892	16.0	8052996	16.0
2012–13 (RE.1)	9388876	11.9	−116766	9272110	11.5	1016132	8255978	8372744	724405	17.2	10113281	12.2	9097149	11.9	9996515	11.9	8980383	11.5
2013–14 (AE)	10539605	12.3	−128500	10411105	12.3	1173462	9237643	9366143	780858	7.8	11320463	11.9	10147001	11.5	11191963	12.0	10018501	11.6

(Contd.)

Table A1.2 (Contd.)

(Rupees, Crore)

Year	GDP at Factor Cost				Private Final Consumption Expenditure in the Domestic Market		Government Final Consumption Expenditure		Gross Domestic Capital Formation	Net Domestic Capital Formation	Gross Domestic Savings	Net Domestic Savings	Per Capita GNP at Factor Cost	CAGR	Per Capita NNP at Factor Cost	CAGR	Population (million)	CAGR
	13		14		15		16		17	18	19	20	21		22		23	
1950–51	..	..	..	..	10047	..	608	..	968	437	989	458	278	..	264	..	359	..
1960–61	1665	9.8	15384	90.2	16996	5.4	1240	7.4	2560	1752	2079	1271	391	3.5	373	3.5	434	1.9
1970–71	6006	13.5	38376	86.5	41149	9.2	4479	13.7	7215	4411	6821	4017	815	7.6	763	7.4	541	2.2
1980–81	25833	18.9	111004	81.1	125129	11.8	15179	13.0	28684	17262	26590	15168	2020	9.5	1852	9.3	679	2.3
1990–91	132378	24.9	399436	75.1	408583	12.6	69525	16.4	152604	99954	134408	81758	6249	12.0	5621	11.7	839	2.1
2000–01	488871	24.5	1503111	75.5	1412970.108	13.2	273399.6064	14.7	528299	321407	515545.1211	308653.34	19325	12.0	17295	11.9	1019	2.0
2010–11	**1505281**	**20.8**	**5743579**	**79.2**	**4384396**	**12.0**	**890136**	**12.5**	**2841457.139**	**2081239**	**2621742.139**	**1861523.967**	**60430**	**12.1**	**54021**	**12.1**	**1186**	**1.5**
2011–12 (RE.2)	1698975	20.2	6692716	79.8	5167446	17.9	1025895	15.3	3200633.055	2320737	2824459.055	1944563.436	69175	14.5	61855	14.5	1202	1.3
2012–13 (RE.1)	1919806	20.4	7469070	79.6	5808733	12.4	1189132	15.9	3521399.019	2505267	3043474.019	2027342.358	76188	10.1	67839	9.7	1217	1.2
2013–14 (AE)							1372649	15.4					84437	10.8	74920	10.4	1233	1.3

Note: RE.1: First Revised Estimate; RE.2: Second Revised Estimate; AE: Advance Estimate.

Growth for 1960–61, 1970–71, 1980–81, 1990–91, 2000–01 and 2010–11 are compounded annual growth rate (CAGR).

Source: Central Statistics Office (CSO).

(Rupees, Crore)

Table A1.3 Key National Accounts Aggregates—2011–12 Series

Year		Gross Value Added (GVA) at Basic Prices	Taxes on Products	Subsidies on Products	Gross Domestic Product (GDP) (3+4+5)	Consumption of Fixed Capital (CFC)	Net Domestic Product (NDP) (6-7)	Primary Income Receivable from Rest of the World (ROW) Net	Gross National Income (GNI) (6+9)	Net National Income (NNI) (7+8)	Private Final Consumption Expenditure (PFCE)	Government Final Consumption Expenditure	Gross Capital Formation (GCF)	Per Capita GDP at Factor Cost	Per Capita GNI at Factor Cost	Per Capita NNI at Factor Cost	Per Capita PFCE	Population (million)
1	2	3	4	5	6	7	8	9	10	11	12	13	14	15	16	17	18	19
At Constant Prices																		
2011–12	RE(NS)	8106656	890060	260677	8736039	917141	7818898	−76824	8659215	7742074	4910447 [56.2]	968375 [11.1]	3457506 [39.6]	71607	70977	63460	40250	1220
2012–13	RE(NS)	8546552 (5.4)	974172 (9.5)	293845 (12.7)	9226879 (5.6)	1009204 (10.0)	8217675 (5.1)	−108170	9118709 (5.3)	8109505 (4.7)	5170252 [56.0]	973498 [10.6]	3602348 [39.0]	74712 (4.3)	73836 (4.0)	65664 (3.5)	41864 (4.0)	1235 (1.2)
2013–14	RE(NS)	9084369 (6.3)	1025799 (5.3)	270734 (−7.9)	9839434 (6.6)	1101753 (9.2)	8737681 (6.3)	−122372	9717062 (6.6)	8615309 (6.2)	5520068 [56.1]	977521 [9.9]	3562698 [36.2]	78653 (5.3)	77674 (5.2)	68867 (4.9)	44125 (5.4)	1251 (1.3)
2014–15	RE(NS)	9727490 (7.1)	1108339 (8.0)	283679 (4.8)	10552150 (7.2)	1192674 (8.3)	9359476 (7.1)	−124449	10427701 (7.3)	9235027 (7.2)	5864283 [55.6]	1102607 [10.4]	3776533 [35.8]	83285 (5.9)	82302 (6.0)	72889 (5.8)	46285 (4.9)	1267 (1.3)
2015–16	PE	10427191 (7.2)	1190986 (7.5)	267929 (−5.6)	11350248 (7.6)	1278464 (7.2)	10071784 (7.6)	−136920	11213328 (7.5)	9934864 (7.6)	6310565 [55.6]	1138558 [10.0]	3804349 [33.5]	88472 (6.2)	87405 (6.2)	77431 (6.2)	49186 (6.3)	1283 (1.3)
At Current Prices																		
2011–12	RE(NS)	8106656	890060	260677	8736039	917141	7818898	−76824	8659215	7742074	4910447 [56.2]	968375 [11.1]	3457506 [39.6]	71607	70977	63460	40250	1220
2012–13	RE(NS)	9210023 (13.6)	1057977 (18.9)	311658 (19.6)	9951344 (13.9)	1733669 (89.0)	8217675 (5.1)	−116763	9834581 (13.6)	8774615 (13.3)	5670929 [57.0]	1061360 [10.7]	3807551 [38.3]	80578 (12.5)	79632 (12.2)	71050 (12.0)	45918 (14.1)	1235 (1.2)
2013–14	RE(NS)	10380813 (12.7)	1201322 (13.5)	309371 (−0.7)	11272764 (13.3)	2535083 (46.2)	8737681 (6.3)	−139887	11132877 (13.2)	9934405 (13.2)	6507932 [57.7]	1152993 [10.2]	3907273 [34.7]	90110 (11.8)	88992 (11.8)	79412 (11.8)	52022 (13.3)	1251 (1.3)
2014–15	RE(NS)	11472409 (10.5)	1350361 (12.4)	334565 (8.1)	12488205 (10.8)	3128729 (23.4)	9359476 (7.1)	−147433	12340772 (10.8)	11007592 (10.8)	7193046 [57.6]	1365463 [10.9]	4257586 [34.1]	98565 (9.4)	97402 (9.5)	86879 (9.4)	56772 (9.1)	1267 (1.3)
2015–16	PE	12279410 (7.0)	1612197 (19.4)	315522 (−5.7)	13576085 (8.7)	3504301 (12.0)	10071784 (7.6)	−157340	13418745 (8.7)	11969428 (8.7)	8077560 [59.5]	1439198 [10.6]	4394306 [32.4]	105815 (7.4)	104589 (7.4)	93293 (7.4)	62958 (10.9)	1283 (1.3)

Note: RE: Revised Estimates, PE: Provisional Estimates, RE(NS): Revised Estimates (New Series).

Data in round brackets are percent growth over the year.

Data in square brackets are percent to GDP (Rate).

Source: Press note dated 8 February 2016 and 31 May 2016, Central Statistical Office, Ministry of Statistics and Programme Implementation, GoI.

Table A1.4 Gross Domestic Savings and Capital Formation (2011–12 series) (At Current Prices)

(Rupees, Crore)

Year	GDP	Gross Domestic Savings				Gross Fixed Capital Formation			Gross Capital Formation					
		GDS	Household Sector	Private Corporate Sector	Public Sector	GFCF	Private Sector	Public Sector	GCF	Private Sector	Public Sector	Valuables	Errors & Omissions	GCF (adjusted)
1	2	3	4	5	6	7	8	9	10	11	12	13	14	15
2011–12*	8736039	3026724	2065453	826805	134466	2997619	2356359	641260	3457506	2546031	658442	253033	–54612	3402894
2012–13*	9951344	3364823	2233950	992094	138778	3321413	2623805	697607	3807550	2816572	717203	273775	35193	3842743
2013–14*	11272764	3725046	2360936	1218356	145754	3564320	2769332	794988	3907272	2940946	803345	162982	4329	3911601
2014–15@	12488205	4116700	2380488	1585120	151092	3844366	2907688	936678	4257585	3140981	923941	192663	18573	4276158
						As a percentage of GDP								
2011–12*	100.0	34.6	23.6	9.5	1.5	34.3	27.0	7.3	39.6	29.1	7.5	2.9	–0.6	39.0
2012–13*	100.0	33.8	22.4	10.0	1.4	33.4	26.4	7.0	38.3	28.3	7.2	2.8	0.4	38.6
2013–14*	100.0	33.0	20.9	10.8	1.3	31.6	24.6	7.1	34.7	26.1	7.1	1.4	0.0	34.7
2014–15@	100.0	33.0	19.1	12.7	1.2	30.8	23.3	7.5	34.1	25.2	7.4	1.5	0.1	34.2

*: Second Revised Estimates   @: First Revised Estimates

Note: Figures in italics are as percentages to GDP prices.

Source: Press note dated 29 January 2016, Central Statistical Office, Ministry of Statistics and Programme Implementation, GoI.

A2 PRODUCTION

Table A2.1 Production Trends in Major Agricultural Crops

(Million tonnes)

Year 1	Rice 2	Wheat 3	Coarse Cereals 4	Cereals 5	Pulses 6	Foodgrains 7	Oil-seeds# 8	Cotton Lint@ 9	Jute & Mesta* 10	Sugarcane 11	Tea 12	Coffee 13
1950–1	20.58	6.46	15.38	42.42	8.41	50.83	5.16	3.04	3.31	57	275	24
1960–1	34.57	11.00	23.74	69.31	12.70	82.02	6.98	5.60	5.26	110	321	68
1970–1	42.22	23.83	30.55	96.60	11.82	108.42	9.63	4.76	6.19	126	419	110
1980–1	53.63	36.31	29.02	118.96	10.63	129.59	9.37	7.01	8.16	154	570	119
1990–1	74.29	55.14	32.70	162.13	14.26	176.39	18.61	9.84	9.23	241	754	170
2000–1	84.98	69.68	31.08	185.74	11.07	196.81	18.44	9.52	10.56	296	847	301
2010–1	95.98	86.87	43.40	226.25	18.24	244.49	32.48	33.00	10.62	342	967	302
2011–12	105.30	94.88	42.01	242.20	17.09	259.29	29.80	35.20	11.40	361	1095	314
2012–13	105.24	93.51	40.04	238.79	18.34	257.13	30.94	34.22	10.93	341	1135	318
2013–14	106.65	95.85	43.29	245.79	19.25	265.04	32.75	35.90	11.69	352	1209	305
2014–15	105.48	86.53	42.86	234.87	17.15	252.02	27.51	34.81	11.13	362	1197	327
2015–16(4AE)	104.32	93.50	37.94	235.76	16.47	252.22	25.30	30.15	10.47	352	1233	348
2015–16(1AE)	90.61	na	27.88	118.49	5.56	124.05	19.89	33.51	10.80	341	na	na
2016–17(1AE)	93.88	na	32.45	126.33	8.70	135.03	23.36	32.12	10.41	305	na	320
Decadal Growth Rates in Per Cent per Annum												
1950–1 to 1960–1	5.32	5.46	4.44	5.03	4.21	4.90	3.07	6.30	4.74	6.79	1.56	10.98
1960–1 to 1970–1	2.02	8.04	2.55	3.38	–0.72	2.83	3.27	–1.61	1.64	1.40	2.70	4.95
1970–1 to 1980–1	2.42	4.30	–0.51	2.10	–1.06	1.80	–0.27	3.95	2.80	2.01	3.12	0.74
1980–1 to 1990–1	3.31	4.27	1.20	3.14	2.98	3.13	7.10	3.45	1.24	4.57	2.84	3.67
1990–1 to 2000–1	1.35	2.37	–0.51	1.37	–2.50	1.10	–0.09	–0.33	1.36	2.07	1.17	5.88
2000–1 to 2010–11	1.22	2.23	3.40	1.99	5.12	2.19	5.82	13.24	0.06	1.47	1.33	0.03
2010–11 to 2015–16	1.68	1.48	–2.65	0.83	–2.02	0.62	–4.87	–1.79	–0.28	0.56	4.98	2.88

Notes: Decadal Growth Rates is simple CAGR (y-o-y).

AE: Advance estimate.   na : not available

* Production in million bales of 180 kgs each. @ Production in million bales of 170 kgs each. # Total of nine oilseeds out of eleven.

Source: GOI (2016), Press note dated September 22, 2016. and *Agricultural Statistics At A Glance*, Ministry of Finance.

Table A2.2 Index of Industrial Production with Major Groups and Sub-groups
Full Fiscal Year Averages Based on 2004–05=100

	Weight	Annual Average Growth	2005–6	2006–7	2007–8	2008–9	2009–10	2010–11	2011–12	2012–13	2013–14	2014–15	2015–16
			Index										
General Index	1000.00	5.7	108.6	122.6	141.7	145.2	152.9	165.5	170.3	172.2	172.0	176.9	181.1
			8.6	*12.9*	*15.6*	*2.5*	*5.3*	*8.2*	*2.9*	*1.1*	*-0.1*	*2.8*	*2.4*
1 Mining and Quarrying	141.57	-4.8	102.3	107.5	112.5	115.4	124.5	131.0	128.5	125.5	124.5	126.5	29.3
			2.3	*5.1*	*4.7*	*2.6*	*7.9*	*5.2*	*-1.9*	*-2.3*	*-0.8*	*1.6*	*-76.8*
2 Manufacturing	755.27	6.2	110.3	126.8	150.1	153.8	161.3	175.7	181.0	183.3	181.9	186.1	189.8
			10.3	*15.0*	*18.4*	*2.5*	*4.9*	*8.9*	*3.0*	*1.3*	*-0.8*	*2.3*	*2.0*
3 Electricity	103.16	5.9	105.2	112.8	120.0	123.3	130.8	138.0	149.3	155.2	164.7	178.6	188.6
			5.2	*7.2*	*6.4*	*2.8*	*6.1*	*5.5*	*8.2*	*4.0*	*6.1*	*8.4*	*5.6*
Use Based Classification													
1 Basic Goods	456.82	5.2	106.1	115.6	125.9	128.1	134.1	142.2	150.0	153.6	156.7	167.8	173.7
			6.1	*9.0*	*8.9*	*1.7*	*4.7*	*6.0*	*5.5*	*2.4*	*2.0*	*7.1*	*3.5*
2 Capital Goods	88.25	9.7	118.1	145.6	216.2	240.6	243.0	278.9	267.5	251.6	242.3	258.0	250.6
			18.1	*23.3*	*48.5*	*11.3*	*1.0*	*14.8*	*-4.1*	*-5.9*	*-3.7*	*6.5*	*-2.9*
3 Intermediate Goods	156.86	4.3	106.6	118.8	127.5	127.6	135.3	145.3	143.9	146.7	151.1	153.8	157.6
			6.6	*11.4*	*7.3*	*0.1*	*6.0*	*7.4*	*-1.0*	*1.9*	*3.0*	*1.8*	*2.5*
4 Consumer Goods	298.08	5.9	110.7	128.6	151.2	152.6	164.3	178.3	186.1	190.6	185.7	178.9	184.3
			10.7	*16.2*	*17.6*	*0.9*	*7.7*	*8.5*	*4.4*	*2.4*	*-2.6*	*-3.7*	*3.0*
Durables	84.60	9.8	116.2	145.6	193.8	215.4	252.0	287.7	295.0	301.1	264.4	231.0	256.8
			16.2	*25.3*	*33.1*	*11.1*	*17.0*	*14.2*	*2.5*	*2.1*	*-12.2*	*-12.6*	*11.2*
Non-durables	213.47	4.2	108.6	121.9	134.3	127.7	129.5	135.0	143.0	146.9	154.5	158.3	155.6
			8.6	*12.2*	*10.2*	*-4.9*	*1.4*	*4.2*	*5.9*	*2.7*	*5.2*	*2.5*	*-1.7*
Major Industry Groups of Manufacturing Sector (2-Digit Level)													
NIC Code													
15 Food Products and Beverages	72.76	5.0	113.2	131.2	147.5	135.4	133.5	142.9	164.8	169.5	167.3	175.7	165.3
			13.2	*15.9*	*12.4*	*-8.2*	*-1.4*	*7.0*	*15.3*	*2.9*	*-1.3*	*5.0*	*-5.9*
16 Tobacco Products	15.70	1.0	101.0	102.9	98.4	102.7	102.0	104.1	109.7	109.2	111.0	111.2	111.9
			1.0	*1.9*	*-4.4*	*4.4*	*-0.7*	*2.0*	*5.4*	*-0.5*	*1.6*	*0.2*	*0.6*
17 Textiles	61.64	4.2	108.3	116.8	124.6	120.1	127.4	135.9	134.0	142.0	147.9	152.4	156.3
			8.3	*7.8*	*6.7*	*-3.6*	*6.1*	*6.7*	*-1.4*	*6.0*	*4.2*	*3.0*	*2.6*
18 Wearing apparel, dressing and dyeing of fur	27.82	6.6	114.1	137.2	149.9	134.6	137.1	142.2	130.1	143.6	176.0	180.4	192.5
			14.1	*20.2*	*9.3*	*-10.2*	*1.9*	*3.7*	*-8.5*	*10.4*	*22.6*	*2.5*	*6.7*
19 Luggage, handbags, saddlery, harness & footwear; tanning and dressing of leather products	5.82	3.7	90.9	104.0	110.0	104.4	105.8	114.3	118.5	127.1	133.4	147.5	145.5
			-9.1	*14.4*	*5.8*	*-5.1*	*1.3*	*8.0*	*3.7*	*7.3*	*5.0*	*10.6*	*-1.4*

No.	Category													
20	Wood & products of wood and cork except furniture, articles of straw & plating materials	10.51	106.8	126.0	148.0	155.3	160.1	156.5	159.2	147.9	144.8	150.9	155.8
		4.4	*6.8*	*18.0*	*17.5*	*4.9*	*3.1*	*-2.2*	*1.7*	*-7.1*	*-2.1*	*4.2*	*3.2*
21	Paper and paper products	9.99	106.3	111.0	112.6	118.0	121.1	131.4	138.0	138.7	138.8	143.1	147.5
		3.6	*6.3*	*4.4*	*1.4*	*4.8*	*2.6*	*8.5*	*5.0*	*0.5*	*0.1*	*3.1*	*3.1*
22	Publishing, printing & reproduction of recorded media	10.78	113.7	122.8	140.2	142.4	133.8	148.8	192.8	183.0	183.5	175.9	160.1
		4.9	*13.7*	*8.0*	*14.2*	*1.6*	*-6.0*	*11.3*	*29.6*	*-5.1*	*0.3*	*-4.1*	*-9.0*
23	Cork, refined petroleum products & nuclear fuel	67.15	100.6	112.6	119.6	123.4	121.8	121.5	125.8	136.4	143.5	144.7	153.4
		4.0	*0.6*	*11.9*	*6.2*	*3.2*	*-1.3*	*-0.2*	*3.5*	*8.4*	*5.2*	*0.8*	*6.0*
24	Chemicals & chemical products	100.59	101.0	110.4	118.4	115.0	120.7	123.1	122.7	127.3	138.6	138.2	143.4
		3.4	*1.0*	*9.3*	*7.2*	*-2.9*	*5.0*	*2.0*	*-0.3*	*3.7*	*8.9*	*-0.3*	*3.8*
25	Rubber & plastics products	20.25	112.3	119.6	135.7	142.6	167.4	185.2	184.6	185.0	180.8	189.3	190.4
		6.2	*12.3*	*6.5*	*13.5*	*5.1*	*17.4*	*10.6*	*-0.3*	*0.2*	*-2.3*	*4.7*	*0.6*
26	Other non-metallic mineral products	43.14	107.8	119.5	130.6	134.9	145.4	151.4	158.6	161.6	163.2	167.4	169.9
		5.0	*7.8*	*10.9*	*9.3*	*3.3*	*7.8*	*4.1*	*4.8*	*1.9*	*1.0*	*2.6*	*1.5*
27	Basic metals	113.35	115.5	132.6	156.3	159.0	162.4	176.7	192.1	195.8	196.3	221.4	223.6
		7.8	*15.5*	*14.8*	*17.9*	*1.7*	*2.1*	*8.8*	*8.7*	*1.9*	*0.3*	*12.8*	*1.0*
28	Fabricated metal products, except machinery & equipment	30.85	111.1	133.3	143.8	144.0	158.6	182.8	203.3	193.8	179.8	179.1	181.6
		5.9	*11.1*	*20.0*	*7.9*	*0.1*	*10.1*	*15.3*	*11.2*	*-4.7*	*-7.2*	*-0.4*	*1.4*
29	Machinery & equipment nec	37.63	126.1	150.9	185.0	171.0	198.0	256.3	241.3	230.0	218.9	227.9	232.8
		8.8	*26.1*	*19.7*	*22.6*	*-7.6*	*15.8*	*29.4*	*-5.9*	*-4.7*	*-4.8*	*4.1*	*2.2*
30	Office acounting & computing machinery	3.05	145.3	155.5	164.8	148.8	154.4	146.3	148.7	128.1	107.9	67.0	67.8
		-1.6	*45.3*	*7.0*	*6.0*	*-9.7*	*3.8*	*-5.2*	*1.6*	*-13.9*	*-15.8*	*-37.9*	*1.2*
31	Electrical machinery & apparatus nec	19.80	116.8	131.6	373.0	530.8	459.2	472.1	367.1	369.2	422.2	511.6	453.4
		22.5	*16.8*	*12.7*	*183.4*	*42.3*	*-13.5*	*2.8*	*-22.2*	*0.6*	*14.4*	*21.2*	*-11.4*
32	Radio, TV & communication equipment & apparatus	9.89	122.7	312.8	604.2	726.7	809.1	911.5	950.5	1003.7	730.1	332.7	345.4
		22.5	*22.7*	*154.9*	*93.2*	*20.3*	*11.3*	*12.7*	*4.3*	*5.6*	*-27.3*	*-54.4*	*3.8*
33	Medical, precision & optical instruments, watches and clocks	5.67	95.4	104.8	111.4	119.8	100.9	107.8	119.5	117.1	111.3	108.6	105.9
		0.8	*-4.6*	*9.9*	*6.3*	*7.5*	*-15.8*	*6.8*	*10.9*	*-2.0*	*-5.0*	*-2.4*	*-2.5*
34	Motor vehicles, trailers & semi trailers	40.64	110.1	138.0	151.2	138.0	179.1	233.3	258.6	244.8	221.3	226.8	243.8
		9.3	*10.1*	*25.3*	*9.6*	*-8.7*	*29.8*	*30.3*	*10.8*	*-5.3*	*-9.6*	*2.5*	*7.5*
35	Other transport equipment	18.25	115.3	132.9	129.0	134.0	171.1	210.7	235.8	235.7	248.8	265.5	269.0
		9.8	*15.3*	*15.3*	*-2.9*	*3.9*	*27.7*	*23.1*	*11.9*	*0.0*	*5.6*	*6.7*	*1.3*
36	Furniture manufacturing nec	29.97	116.2	111.7	132.7	142.5	152.7	141.2	138.6	131.5	113.3	121.7	175.6
		6.3	*16.2*	*-3.9*	*18.8*	*7.4*	*7.2*	*-7.5*	*-1.8*	*-5.1*	*-13.8*	*7.4*	*44.3*

Notes: Figures in *italics* are percentage variations over the previous year.

Source: Central Statistical Organisation (CSO), (GOI), Ministry of Statistics and Programme Implementation.

A3   BUDGETARY TRANSACTIONS

Table A3.1   Budgetary Position of Government of India

(Rupees crore)

Budget Heads (1)	1990–1 Actuals (2)	2000–10 Actuals (3)	2010–11 Actuals (4)	2011–12 Actuals (5)	2012–13 Actuals (6)	2013–14 Actuals (7)	2014–15 Actuals (8)	2015–16 Revised (9)	2016–17 Budget (10)
(1) Revenue receipts	54954	192605	788471	751437	879232	1014724	1101473	1206084	1377022
(a) Tax revenue(net to centre)	42978	136658	569869	629765,	741877	815853	903617	947508	1054102
(b) Non-tax revenue	11976	55947	218602	121672	137355	198870	197857	258576	322921
(2) Capital receipts	50344	132987	402428	568918	582152	563894	484448	601645	587843
(a) Non-Debt Capital Receipts of which:	5712	14171	35266	36938	40950	41865	51475	44217	67134
(a.1) Recovery of loans	5712	12046	12420	18850	15060	12497	13738	18905	10634
(a.2) Other Receipts of which:	0	2125	22846	18088	25890	29368	37737	25312	56500
(a.2.1) Disinvestment of equity of PSEs	0	2125	22846	18008	25890	29369	37737	25312	56500
(b) Debt Receipts	44632	118816	367162	531980	541202	522029	432973	557174	520709
(3) Draw down of Cash Balance			6430	-15990	-51012	-19171	77752	-22084	13195
(3) Total Receipts (1+2-3)	105298	325592	1190899	1320355	1461384	1578618	1663673	1785391	1978060
	[18.0]	[15.0]	[15.3]	[15.1]	[14.7]	[14.0]	[13.3]	[13.2]	[13.1]
(4) Non-plan expenditure	76198	242942	818299	891990	996747	1106120	1201029	1308194	1428050
(a) On revenue account of which:	60850	226782	726491	812049	914306	1019040	1109395	1212669	1327409
(a.I) Interest payment	21471	99314	234022	273150	313170	374254	402444	442620	492670
% to Total Expenditure	20.4	30.5	19.5	20.9	22.2	24.0	24.2	24.8	24.9
(a.II) Pension	2138	14379	57405	61166	69478	74896	93611	95731	123368
% to Total Expenditure	2.0	4.4	4.8	4.7	4.9	4.8	5.6	5.4	6.2
(a.III) Subsidies	12158	26838	173420	217941	257079	254632	258258	257801	250433
% to Total Expenditure	11.5	8.2	14.5	16.7	18.2	16.3	15.5	14.4	12.7
(b) On capital account	15348	16160	91808	79941	82441	87080	91634	95525	100641
(5) Plan expenditure	29118	82669	379029	412375	413625	453327	462644	477197	550010
(a) On revenue account	12666	51076	314232	333737	329208	352732	357597	335004	403628
(b) On capital account	16452	31593	64797	78639	84417	100595	105047	142193	146382
(6) Total expenditure (4+5)	105316	325611	1197328	1304365	1410372	1559447	1663673	1785391	1978060
	[18.0]	[15.0]	[15.4]	[14.9]	[14.2]	[13.8]	[13.3]	[13.2]	[13.1]
(7) Revenue deficit	18562	85234	252252	394348	364282	357048	365519	341589	354015
	[3.2]	[3.9]	[3.2]	[4.5]	[3.7]	[3.2]	[2.9]	[2.5]	[2.3]

(8) Fiscal deficit	44650	118816	373591	515990	490190	502858	510725	535090	533904
	[7.6]	[5.5]	[4.8]	[5.9]	[4.9]	[4.5]	[4.1]	[3.9]	[3.5]
(9) Primary deficit	23134	19502	139569	242840	177020	128604	108281	92469	41233
	[3.9]	[0.9]	[1.8]	[2.8]	[1.8]	[1.1]	[0.9]	[0.7]	[0.3]

Notes: (1) Figures in square brackets are percentages to GDP at current market prices.

(2) GDP for 2016–17 is estimated to be Rs 15069455 crore assuming 11% increase (Budget document) over the provisional estimates for 2015–16 of 13576086.

(3) GDP data for the years up to 2011–12 are of 2004–05 series.

Source: Budget at a Glance and Expenditure Budget, 2015–16, Ministry of Finance, Government of India.

Table A3.2 Consolidated Budgetary Position of State Governments at a Glance

(Rupees crore)

Year	1990–1 Accounts	2000–10 Accounts	2010–11 Accounts	2011–12 Accounts	2012–13 Accounts	2013–14 Accounts	2014–15 Revised	2015–16 Budget
Total Revenue Receipts	66467	232509	935347	1098530	1252020	1369190	1805830	2011890
% change over the year	(17.6)	(14.6)	(21.8)	(17.4)	(14.0)	(9.4)	31.9	11.4
% to GDP	11.3	10.7	12.0	12.6	12.6	12.1	14.5	14.8
Revenue Expenditure	71776	287825	932297	1074570	1231700	1379750	1824160	1958170
% change over the year	(19.2)	(11.8)	(16.7)	(15.3)	(14.6)	(12.0)	32.2	7.3
% to GDP	12.2	13.2	12.0	12.3	12.4	12.2	14.6	14.4
Surplus(+)/Deficit(–)	–5309	–55316	–3050	–23960	–20320	10560	18330	–53720
Total Capital Receipts	24693	109705	238230	269385	305314	318860	405637	438334
% change over the year	(22.9)	(7.6)	(–0.5)	(13.1)	(13.3)	(4.4)	27.2	8.1
% to GDP	4.2	5.0	3.1	3.1	3.1	2.8	3.2	3.2
Capital Expenditure	19312	52010	226430	277041	302553	326394	444264	486781
% change over the year	(16.6)	(3.0)	(4.7)	(22.4)	(9.2)	(7.9)	(36.1)	9.6
% to GDP	3.3	2.4	2.9	3.2	3.0	2.9	3.6	3.6
Surplus(+)/Deficit(–)	5381	57695	–11800	7656	–2761	7534	38627	48447
Total Receipts	91160	342214	1173577	1367915	1557334	1688050	2211467	2450224
% change over the year	(19.0)	(12.3)	(16.5)	(16.6)	(13.8)	(8.4)	(31.0)	10.8
% to GDP	15.6	15.7	15.1	15.7	15.6	15.0	17.7	18.0
Total Expenditure	91088	339835	1158727	1351611	1534253	1706144	2268424	2444951
% change over the year	(18.6)	(10.3)	(14.1)	(16.6)	(13.5)	(11.2)	(33.0)	7.8
% to GDP	15.5	15.6	14.9	15.5	15.4	15.1	18.2	18.0
Overall Surplus(+)/Deficit(–)	72	2379	–14850	–16304	–23081	18094		
Fiscal Deficit	18787	87923	161461	168350	195470	247850	365460	333330
% to GDP	0.0	0.1	–0.2	–0.2	–0.2	0.2	0.0	0.0
Revenue Deficit	5309	55316	–3051	–23960	–20320	10560	18340	–53720
% to GDP	0.0	0.0	0.0	0.0	0.0	0.0	0.0	0.0
Net RBI Credit	420	–1092	2515	–1196	–1246	990	2420	–

Source: RBI (2013), State Finances – A Study of Budgets 2013–14 and previous issues.

Table A4.1 Money Stock Measures

(Rupees crore)

31st March	Components of Money Supply								Money Supply (M3)	Sources of Change in Money Supply (M3)						
	Currency in Circulation	Cash with Banks	Currency with the Public	'Other' Deposits with the RBI	Bankers' Deposits with RBI	Demand Deposits	Time Deposits	Reserve Money (3+4+5+6)	Money Supply (M3)	Net Bank Credit to Government	Bank Credit to Commercial Sector	Net Foreign Exchange Assets of Banking Sector	Government's Currency Liabilities to Public	Net Non-monetary Liabilities of Banking Sector	Net Non-Monetary Liabilities of RBI	RBI's Gross Claims on Banks
1	2	3	4=2-3	5	6	7	8	9	11	12	14	15	16	17	18	19
1950-1	.	.	1405	24	59	591	331	1494	2352	808	588	860	241	145	68	..
1960-1	2154	56	2098	13	71	757	1095	2239 (6.1)	3964 (2.1)	2489	1503	178	206	413	250	..
1970-1	4557	186	4371	60	205	2943	3646	4822 (9.8)	11020 (14.3)	5455	6522	551	384	1892	866	642
1980-1	14307	881	13426	411	4734	9587	32350	19452 (17.4)	55774 (18.1)	25718	36641	4730	618	11934	5360	1276
1990-1	55282	2234	53048	674	31823	39170	172936	87779 (13.1)	265828 (15.1)	140193	171769	10581	1621	58336	27022	10007
2000-1	218205	8654	209550	3613	81477	166270	933771	303295 (8.1)	1313204 (16.8)	511955	679218	249831	5354	133155	79374	12965
2001-2	250974	10179	240794	2831	84147	179199	1075512	337952 (11.4)	1499336 (14.1)	589565	759647	311044	6366	168286	101248	10748
2002-3	282473	10892	271581	3219	83346	198757	1244379	369038 (9.2)	1717936 (14.7)	676523	898981	393720	7071	258358	127170	7160
2003-4	327028	12057	314971	5097	104365	258626	1426960	436490 (18.3)	2005654 (16.7)	742904	1016151	526593	7296	287289	107613	5419
2004-5	368661	12347	356314	6454	113996	286998	1595887	489111 (12.1)	2245653 (12.0)	752436	1275912	649259	7448	439402	119804	5258
2005-6	429578	17454	412124	6843	135511	407423	1893104	571932 (16.9)	2719493 (21.1)	759416	1688681	726197	7656	462459	122492	5795
2006-7	504099	21244	482854	7467	197295	477604	2342113	708861 (23.9)	3310038 (21.7)	827626	2128862	913179	8161	567790	177047	7635
2007-8	590801	22390	568410	9027	328447	578372	2862046	928275 (31.0)	4017855 (21.4)	899518	2578990	1295132	9224	765008	210250	4590
2008-9	691153	25703	665450	5533	291275	588688	3535105	987961 (6.4)	4794776 (19.3)	1277333	3014893	1352176	10054	859681	387958	10357
2009-10	799549	32056	767492	3806	352299	717970	4113430	1155653 (17.0)	5602698 (16.9)	1669186	3491409	1281464	11270	850630	301643	1169
2010-11	949659	37823	911836	3653	423509	722856	4865771	1376821 (19.1)	6504116 (16.1)	1983896	4236676	1393343	12724	1122523	368350	5159
2011-12	1067230	43560	1023670	2822	356291	710902	5647437	1427240 (3.7)	7384831 (13.5)	2373731	4992338	1543780	13444	1538462	603841	4847
2012-13	1190975	49914	1141061	3240	320671	753225	6492293	1514886 (6.1)	8389819 (13.6)	2709011	5667867	1633659	15340	1639058	692502	40354
2013-14	1301074	55255	1245819	1965	429703	811978	7457624	1732742 (14.4)	9517386 (13.4)	3044870	6445296	1923948	17339	1914067	843319	48650
2014-15	1448312	62131	1386182	14590	465561	891632	8257764	1928463 (11.3)	10550168 (10.9)	3007394	7049724	2250649	19429	1777029	785273	187658
2015-16	1663463	65368	1598095	15451	501823	997021	9043773	2180740 (13.1)	11654340 (10.5)	3238484	7803069	2533722	21905	1979565	954173	284454

Note: 1 Figures in brackets are percentage change over the year.   ..:Not avaiable

Source: Reserve Bank of India, 2015–16, Handbook of Statistics on Indian Economy.

Table A4.2 Selected Indicators of Scheduled Commercial Banks Operations (Year-end) (Outstandings)

(Rupees crore)

Year	Aggregate Deposits	CAGR	Demand Deposits	CAGR	Time Deposits	CAGR	Bank Credit	CAGR	C/D Ratio	Food Credit	Non-food Credit	Invest-ments	I/D Ratio	Govt. Securities	Other Approved Securities	Cash in Hand	Balances with RBI	Borrowings from RBI
(1)	(2)		(3)		(4)		(5)		(6)	(7)	(8)	(9)	(10)	(11)	(12)	(13)	(14)	(15)
1960–61	1736		710		1026		1336		76.7			559	32.2	559		46	71	95
1970–71	5906	13.0	2626	14.0	3280	12.3	4684	13.4	79.3	214	4469	1772	30.0	1362	410	167	197	368
1980–81	37988	20.5	7798	11.5	30190	24.9	25371	18.4	66.8	1759	23612	13186	34.7	9219	3967	766	4092	589
1990–91	192541	17.6	33192	15.6	159349	18.1	116301	16.4	60.4	4506	111795	75065	39.0	49998	25067	1804	23861	3468
2000–01	962618	17.5	142552	15.7	820066	17.8	511434	16.0	53.1	39991	471443	370159	38.5	340035	30125	5658	59544	3896
2001–02	1103360	(14.6)	153048	(7.4)	950312	(15.9)	589723	(15.3)	53.4	53978	535745	438269	39.7	411176	27093	6245	62402	3616
2002–03	1280853	(16.1)	170289	(11.3)	1110564	(16.9)	729215	(23.7)	56.9	49479	679736	547546	42.7	523417	24129	7567	58335	79
2003–04	1504416	(17.5)	225022	(32.1)	1279394	(15.2)	840785	(15.3)	55.9	35961	804824	677588	45.0	654758	22830	7898	68997	0
2004–05	1700198	(13.0)	248028	(10.2)	1452171	(13.5)	1100428	(30.9)	64.7	41121	1059308	739154	43.5	718982	20172	8472	88105	50
2005–06	2109049	(24.0)	364640	(47.0)	1744409	(20.1)	1507077	(37.0)	71.5	40691	1466386	717454	34.0	700742	16712	13046	127061	1488
2006–07	2611933	(23.8)	429731	(17.9)	2182203	(25.1)	1931189	(28.1)	73.9	46521	1884669	791516	30.3	776058	15458	16139	180222	6245
2007–08	3196939	(22.4)	524310	(22.0)	2672630	(22.5)	2361914	(22.3)	73.9	44399	2317515	971715	30.4	958661	13053	18044	257122	4000
2008–09	3834110	(19.9)	523085	(-0.2)	3311025	(23.9)	2775549	(17.5)	72.4	46211	2729338	1166410	30.4	1155786	10624	20281	238195	11728
2009–10	4492826	(17.2)	645610	(23.4)	3847216	(16.2)	3244788	(16.2)	72.2	48489	3196299	1384752	30.8	1378395	6358	25578	281390	42
2010–11	5207969	(15.9)	641705	(-0.6)	4566264	(18.7)	3942083	(21.5)	75.7	64282	3877800	1501619	28.8	1497148	4471	30346	319163	5031
2011–12	5909082	(13.5)	625330	(-2.6)	5283752	(15.7)	4611852	(17.0)	78.0	81304	4530549	1737787	29.4	1735018	2770	36129	323271	8755
2012–13	6750454	(14.2)	662299	(5.9)	6088155	(15.2)	5260459	(14.1)	77.9	96422	5164037	2006105	29.7	2003653	2452	40491	282267	21588
2013–14	7705560	(14.1)	713921	(7.8)	6991639	(14.8)	5994096	(13.9)	77.8	98447	5895649	2212821	28.7	2211194	1627	45870	316344	41613
2014–15	8533285	(10.7)	794029	(11.2)	7739256	(10.7)	6536420	(9.0)	76.6	94418	6442002	2491825	29.2	2489751	2074	53355	373074	158202
2015–16	9327290	(9.3)	888996	(12.0)	8438294	(9.0)	7249615	(10.9)	77.7	105254	7144361	2625509	28.1	2623933	1576	57438	387442	232467

Note: Data in brackets are pecentage change over the year.   Growth rate for the years 1970–71, 1980–81, 1990–91 and 2000–01 are Compounded annual growth rate (CAGR).

Data relate to amount outstanding as on last Friday of March up to 1984–85 and last reporting Friday of March thereafter.

Source: Reserve Bank of India, 2015–16, Handbook of Statistics on Indian Economy.

A5 CAPITAL MARKET

Table A5.1 Resources Mobilization from the Primary Market

(Rupees crore)

Year	Total		Category-wise				Issue Type				Instrument-wise									
			Public		Right		Listed		IPOs		Equities				CCPS		Bonds		Others	
											At Par		At Premium							
	Number	Amount	Number	Amount	Number	Amount	Number	Amount	Number	Amount	Number	Amount	Number	Amount	Number	Amount	Number	Amount	Number	Amount
(1)	(2)	(3)	(4)	(5)	(6)	(7)	(8)	(9)	(10)	(11)	(12)	(13)	(14)	(15)	(16)	(17)	(18)	(19)	(20)	(21)
2000–1	151	6108	124	5379	27	729	37	3386	114	2722	84	818	54	2408	2	142	10	2704	1	36
2001–2	35	7543	20	6502	15	1041	28	6341	7	1202	7	151	8	1121	0	0	16	5601	4	670
2002–3	27	4070	14	3639	12	431	20	3032	6	1038	6	143	11	1314	0	0	8	2600	2	13
2003–4	57	23273	35	22265	22	1007	36	19838	21	3434	14	360	37	18589	0	0	6	4324	0	0
2004–5	60	28256	34	24640	26	3616	37	14507	23	13749	6	420	49	23968	0	0	5	3867	0	0
2005–6	139	27382	103	23294	36	4088	60	16446	79	10936	10	372	128	27000	0	0	0	0	1	10
2006–7	124	33508	85	29796	39	3710	47	5002	77	28504	2	12	119	32889	0	0	2	356	1	249
2007–8	124	87029	92	54511	32	32518	39	44434	85	42595	7	387	113	79352	2	5687	2	1603	0	0
2008–9	47	16220	22	3582	25	12637	25	12637	21	2082	5	96	40	14176	1	448	1	1500	0	0
2009–10	76	57555	47	49236	29	8319	34	30359	39	24696	1	9	71	54866	1	180	3	2500	0	0
2010–11	91	67609	68	58105	23	9503	28	22599	63	35559	2	50	78	57617	1	490	10	9451	0	0
2011–12	71	48468	55	46093	16	2375	17	6953	54	41515	4	104	47	12753	0	0	20	35611	0	0
2012–13	69	32455	51	15942	16	8945	34	18359	33	6528	10	6176	39	9297	0	0	20	16982	0	0
2013–14	70	44903	75	51429	15	4575	52	57768	38	1236	19	824	36	12446	0	0	35	42735	0	0
2014–15	89	19202	70	12455	18	6750	42	15892	46	3311	8	49	55	8740	1	1000	24	9413	0	0
2015–16	108	58167	95	48928	13	9239	34	43351	74	14815	13	672	74	23382	0	0	21	34112	0	0

Note: Instrument-wise break up may not tally with the total number of issues, as for one issue there could be more than one instruments.

Source: SEBI (2014), SEBI Bulletins.

(Rs. crore)

Table A5.2 Trends in Resource Mobilization by Mutual Funds (Sector-wise)

Year	Gross Mobilization					Redemption*				Net Inflow				Assets at the end of Period
	Private Sector	Public Sector	UTI	Total		Private Sector	Public Sector	UTI	Total	Private Sector	Public Sector	UTI	Total	
(1)	(2)	(3)	(4)	(5)		(6)	(7)	(8)	(9)	(10)	(11)	(12)	(13)	(14)
2000–1	75009	5535	12413	92957	(4.3)	65160	6580	12090	83830	9849	–1045	323	9127	90586
2001–2	147798	12082	4643	164523	(7.0)	134748	10673	11927	157348	13050	1409	–7284	7175	100594
2002–3	284096	23515	7096	314707	(12.4)	272026	21954	16530	310510	12070	1561	–9434	4197	109299
2003–4	534649	31548	23992	590189	(20.8)	492105	28951	22326	543382	42544	2597	1666	46807	139616
2004–5	736463	56589	46656	839708	(25.9)	728864	59266	49378	837508	7599	–2677	–2722	2200	149600
2005–6	914703	110319	73127	1098149	(29.7)	871727	103940	69704	1045370	42977	6379	3424	52779	231862
2006–7	1599873	196340	142280	1938493	(45.1)	1520836	188719	134954	1844508	79038	7621	7326	93985	326292
2007–8	3780753	346126	337498	4464377	(89.5)	3647449	335448	327678	4310575	133304	10677	9820	153802	505152
2008–9	4292751	710472	423131	5426354	(96.4)	4326768	701092	426790	5454650	–34018	9380	–3658	–28296	417300
2009–10	7698483	1438688	881851	10019023	(154.7)	7643555	1426189	866198	9935942	54928	12499	15653	83080	613979
2010–11	6922924	1152733	783858	8859515	(113.8)	6942140	1166288	800494	8908921	–19215	–13555	–16636	–49406	592250
2011–12	5683744	1135935	522453	6819679	(78.1)	5699189	1135935	525637	6841702	–15445	6578	–3184	22024	587217
2012–13	5892356	1375529	633350	7267885	(73.0)	5828566	1362780	628720	7191346	63790	12749	4629	76539	701443
2013–14	8049397	1718703	802352	9768101	(86.7)	8000559	1713759	801951	9714318	48838	4944	401	53783	825240
2014–15	9143962	1942297	815592	11086260	(88.8)	9040262	1942710	816870	10982972	103700	–412	–1278	103288	1082757
2015–16	11126277	2639279	1115823	13765555	(101.4)	13765555	11034883	2596492	1100407	91394	42787	15416	134181	1232824

*: Includes repurchases as well as redemption   na: Not Available

Notes: 1. Figures in brackets are percentages to GDP at current market prices. Series 2004–05 was used till 2011–12 thereafter Series 2011–12 was used to calculate the percentages.

2. IDBI principal has now become principal MF a private ector mutual fund.

3. Erstwhile UTI has been divided into UTI mutual fund (registered with SEBI) and the specified undertaking of UTI (not registered with SEBI).

Above data contain information only of UTI mutual fund.

4. Net assets pertaining to funds of funds schemes is not included in the above data.

Source: Securities and Exchange Board of India, 2014, SEBI Bulletins.

Table A5.3 Trends in FII Investments

Year	Gross Purchases (Rs crore)	Gross Sales (Rs crore)	3 as % 2	Net Investment Total (Rs crore)	4 as % 2	Eqity	Debt	Net-Investment (US $ mn)	Cumulative Net-Investment (US $ mn)
1	2	3		4		5	6	7	8
	17	4	23.5	13	76.5	13	na	4	4
1992-3									
1993-4	5593	467	8.3	5127	91.7	5127	na	1634	1638
1994-5	7631	2835	37.2	4796	62.8	4796	na	1528	3167
1995-6	9694	2752	28.4	6942	71.6	6942	na	2036	5202
1996-7	15554	6980	44.9	8546	55.1	8546	29	2432	7635
1997-8	18695	12737	68.1	5959	31.9	5267	691	1650	9285
1998-9	16116	17699	109.8	-1584	-9.8	-717	-867	-386	8899
1999-2000	56857	46735	82.2	10122	17.8	9670	453	2474	11372
2000-1	74051	64118	86.6	9933	13.4	10207	-273	2160	13531
2001-2	50071	41308	82.5	8763	17.5	8072	690	1839	15371
2002-3	47062	44372	94.3	2689	5.7	2527	162	566	15936
2003-4	144855	99091	68.4	45764	31.6	39960	5805	10005	25942
2004-5	216951	171071	78.9	45880	21.1	44123	1759	10352	36293
2005-6	346976	305509	88.0	41467	12.0	48801	-7334	9363	45657
2006-7	520506	489665	94.1	30841	5.9	25237	5607	6821	52477
2007-8	948018	881839	93.0	66179	7.0	53403	12776	16442	68919
2008-9	614579	660389	107.5	-45811	-7.5	-47706	1895	-9838	58167
2009-10	846438	703780	83.1	142658	16.9	110221	32438	30253	89335
2010-11	992599	846161	85.2	146438	14.8	110121	36317	32226	121561
2011-12	921285	827562	89.8	93725	10.2	43737	49988	18923	140482
2012-13	904845	736481	81.4	168364	18.6	140031	28333	31047	171529
2013-14	958576	908274	94.8	51649	5.4	79709	-28060	8876	180405
2014-15	1521346	1243887	81.8	277460	18.2	111333	166127	45698	226103
2015-16	1324418	1342593	101.4	-18175	-1.4			-2523	223588

Note: na: Not Available   Net Investment in US $ mn at monthly exchange rate.

Source: Securities and Exchange Board of India (SEBI), (Website: www.sebi.gov.in).

Table A5.4 Business Growth of Capital Market Segment of National Stock Exchange

Month/Year	No. of companies listed*	No. of companies permitted to trade $	No. of companies available for trading	No. of trading days	No. of trades (million)	Traded quantity (million)	Turnover (Rs crore)	Average daily turnover (Rs crore)	Average trade size (Rs)	Demat securities traded (million)	Demat turnover (Rs crore)	Market capitalisation (Rs crore)	% to GDP
(1)	2	3	4	5	6	7	8	9	10	11	12	13	14
2000–1	785	320	1029	251	168	32954	1339510	53367	79923	30722	1339510	657847	30.3
2001–2	793	197	890	247	175	27841	513167	2078	29274	27772	513167	636861	27.1
2002–3	818	107	788	251	240	36407	617989	2462	25771	36405	617989	537133	21.2
2003–4	909	18	787	254	379	71330	1099534	4329	29088	71330	1099534	1120976	39.5
2004–5	970	1	839	255	451	79769	1140072	4471	25279	79769	1140072	1585585	48.9
2005–6	1069	0	929	251	609	84449	1569558	6253	28781	84449	1569558	2813201	76.2
2006–7	1228	0	1084	249	785	85546	1945287	7812	24793	85546	1945287	3367350	78.4
2007–8	1381	0	1236	251	1173	149847	3551038	14148	30281	149847	3551038	4858122	97.4
2008–9	1432	37	1291	243	1365	142635	2752023	11325	20160	142636	2752023	2896194	51.4
2009–10	1470	37	1359	244	1682	221553	4138024	16959	24608	221553	4138024	6009173	92.8
2010–11	1574	61	1450	255	1551	182452	3577412	14048	23009	182452	3577412	6702616	86.1
2011–12	1646	73	1533	249	1438	161698	2810893	11289	19551	161698	2810893	6096518	69.8
2012–13	1666	76	1542	250	1361	165916	2708279	10833	19907	165916	2708279	6239035	62.7
2013–14	1688	75	1540	251	1443	153372	2808489	11189	19460	153372	2808488	7277720	64.6
2014–15	1733	4	1514	243	1833	236178	4329655	17818	23623	236178	4329655	9930122	79.5
2015–16	1808	4	1563	247	1852	220177	4236983	17154	22881	220177	4236983	9310471	68.6

Note: Figures in brackets are percentages to GDP at current market prices. GDP data are as per revised series from 2011–12 and as per 2004–05 series before 2011–12.

na: not available.

Source: National Stock Exchange (www.nse.india.com).

Table A5.5a Settlement Statistics of Capital Market Segment of NSE of India

(1)	No.of trades (million) (2)	Traded Quantity (number) (3)	Number of Shares (Deliverable) (4)	Per cent of Shares Delivered to Total Trade (5)	Trading Value (Rs. crore) (6)	Value of Shares Deliverable (Rs. crore) (7)	Percentage of Delivered to Value of Shares Traded (8)	Short delivery (million) (9)	Per cent of Short Delivery to Total Delivery (10)	Funds Pay in (Rs. crore) (11)
2000–1	161	30420	5020	16.5	1263898	106277	8.4	34	0.68	45937
2001–2	172	27470	5930	21.6	508121	71766	14.1	36	0.61	26208
2002–3	240	36541	8235	22.5	621569	87956	14.2	47	0.57	25889
2003–4	375	70453	17555	24.9	1090632	221364	20.3	101	0.58	81588
2004–5	449	78800	20228	25.7	1140969	277101	24.3	87	0.43	97241
2005–6	600	81844	22724	27.8	1516839	409353	27.0	89	0.39	131426
2006–7	786	85051	23907	28.1	1940094	544435	28.1	77	0.32	173188
2007–8	1165	148123	36797	24.8	3519919	972803	27.6	100	0.27	309543
2008–9	1364	141893	30330	21.4	2749450	610498	22.4	63	0.21	220704
2009–10	1679	220587	47395	21.5	4129214	916406	22.2	86	0.18	278387
2010–11	1548	180769	49737	27.6	3565195	978105	27.5	90	0.18	293357
2011–12	1437	160521	44323	27.6	2803889	784407	28.0	70	0.2	251754
2012–13	1357	164426	45935	28.0	2700656	796784	29.5	66	0.1	251034
2013–14	1428	150513	42342	28.1	2771237	822446	29.7	60	0.1	271842
2014–15	3496	444468	121959	27.4	8214629	2422737	29.5	168	0.1	694577
2014–16	1848	217786	61936	28.4	4202927	1252658	29.8	113	0.2	388405

Source: National Stock Exchange (www.nse.india.com).

Table A5.5b Settlement Statistics of Capital Market Segment of NSE of India

(1)	No. of Trades (million) (2)	Traded Quantity (number) (3)	Number of Shares (Deliverable) (4)	Per cent of Shares Delivered to Total Trade (5)	Trading Value (Rs. crore) (6)	Value of Shares Deliverable (Rs. crore) (7)	Percentage of Delivered to Value of Shares Traded (8)	Securities Pay-in (Rs. crore) (9)	Short delivery (million) (10)	Per cent of Short Delivery to Total Delivery (11)	Funds Pay in (Rs. crore) (12)
2009–10											
Mar-10											
Feb-10	115	12591	2536	22.52	253467	58767	23.19		8	0.18	18354
Jan-10	136	17572	4428	25.20	324584	85206	26.25		8	0.18	25887
Dec-09	127	15073	3429	22.75	298215	68853	23.09	68748	7	0.19	17995
Nov-09	133	16104	3559	22.10	332248	74650	22.47	74565	5	0.14	22913
Oct-09	140	17321	4022	23.22	373953	89940	24.05	89834	7	0.17	26965
Sep-09	134	19160	4344	22.67	349940	82209	23.49	82124	6	0.14	24853
Aug-09	148	19171	3961	20.66	371474	78662	21.18	78561	7	0.18	23751
Jul-09	169	21682	3976	18.34	419077	80194	19.14	80078	6	0.15	25433
Jun-09	182	28112	5311	18.89	496589	98889	19.91	98761	8	0.15	29632
May-09	144	21907	4555	20.79	357932	74436	20.80	74317	11	0.25	25219
Apr-09	126	17934	3441	19.19	261310	48149	18.43	48072	7	0.20	16269
2008–09	1364	141893	30393	21.42	2749450	611535	22.44	610498	63	0.21	220704
2007–08	1165	148123	36797	24.84	3519919	972803	27.64	970618	100	0.27	309543
2006–07	786	85051	23907	28.11	1940094	544435	28.06	543950	77	0.32	173188
2005–06	600	81844	22724	27.77	1516839	409353	26.99	407976	89	0.39	131426
2004–05	449	78800	20228	25.67	1140969	277101	24.29	276120	87	0.43	97241
2003–04	375	70453	17555	24.92	1090632	221364	20.30	220341	101	0.58	81588
2002–03	240	36541	8235	22.54	621569	87956	14.15	87447	47	0.57	34092
2001–02	172	27470	5930	21.59	508121	71766	14.12	64353	36	0.61	28048
2000–01	161	30420	5020	16.50	1263898	106277	8.41	94962	34	0.68	45937
1999–2000	96	23861	4871	20.42	803050	82607	10.29	79783	63	1.3	27992
1998–9	55	16531	2799	16.93	413573	66204	16.01	30755	31	1.09	12175
1997–8	38	13522	2205	16.31	370010	59775	16.15	21713	33	1.51	10827
1996–7	26	13432	1645	12.25	292314	32640	11.17	13790	38	2.32	7212
1995–6	6	3901	726	18.62	65742	11775	17.91	5805	18	2.46	3258
1994–5 (Nov–Mar)	0.3	133	69	51.74	1728	898	51.98	611	1	0.85	300

Source: National Stock Exchange (www.nse.india.com).

Table A5.6 Business Growth and Settlement of Capital Market Segments, Bombay Stock Exchange

Month/Year	No. of Companies Listed	No. of Trading Days	No. of Trades (lakhs)	Total Shares Traded (crore)	Total Turnover (Rs crore)	Total Average Daily Turnover (Rs crore)	Market Capitalization		Total deliveries			
							(Rs crore)	% to GDP	Number of Shares (crore)	Percent of Total Shares Traded	Value (Rs crore)	Percent of Total Turnover
(1)	(2)	(3)	(4)	(5)	(6)	(7)	(8)	(9)	(10)	(11)	(12)	(13)
2000–1	5869	251	1428	2585	1000032	3984	571553	26.2	867	33.5	166941	16.7
2001–2	5782	247	1277	1822	307292	1244	612224	26.0	577	31.7	59980	19.5
2002–3	5650	251	1413	2214	314073	1251	572197	22.6	699	31.6	48741	15.5
2003–4	5528	254	2028	3904	503053	1981	1201207	42.3	1332	34.1	107153	21.3
2004–5	4731	253	2374	4772	518715	2050	1698428	52.4	1875	39.3	140056	27.0
2005–6	4781	251	2639	6644	816073	3251	3022191	81.8	3164	47.6	320111	39.2
2006–7	4821	249	3462	5608	956185	3840	3545041	82.5	2310	41.1	298885	31.3
2007–8	4887	251	5303	9860	1578856	6290	5138015	103.0	3642	36.9	478034	30.3
2008–9	4929	243	5408	7396	1100074	4527	3086076	54.8	1966	26.6	230332	20.9
2009–10	4977	244	6056	11365	1378809	5651	6165619	95.2	3636	32.0	311364	22.6
2010–11	5067	255	5285	9908	1105027	4333	6839084	87.7	3769	38.0	302126	27.3
2011–12	5133	249	3944	6541	667498	2681	6214941	71.1	2560	39.1	181560	27.2
2012–13	5211	250	3235	5672	548774	2195	6387887	64.2	2432	42.9	168490	30.7
2013–14	5336	251	3632	4800	521664	2078	7415296	65.8	2312	48.2	180243	34.6
2014–15	5624	243	7111	8568	854845	3518	10149290	81.3	4321	50.2	299835	34.9
2015–16	5911	247	4117	7625	740089	2996	9475328	69.8	3570	46.9	246883	33.3

Source: Securities and Exchange Board of India, 2014, SEBI Bulletins.

Table A5.7 Working of Clearing Corporation of India Limited (CCIL)

	Outright			Repo			Forex*			CBLO**		
	Number of Trades	Volume	Average Volume	Number of Trades	Volume	Average Volume	Number of Trades	Volume	Average Volume	Number of Trades	Volume	Average Volume
2002–3	191843	1076147	3623	11672	468229	1577	100232	136102	1496	159	852	15
2003–4	243585	1575133	5303	20927	943189	3208	330517	501342	2161	3060	76851	251
2004–5	160682	1134222	3884	24364	1557907	5335	466327	899782	3813	29351	976757	3345
2005–6	125509	864751	3215	25673	1694509	5803	489649	1179688	5020	67463	2953134	10045
2006–7	137100	1021536	4187	29008	2556501	8755	606808	1776981	7466	85881	4732271	16096
2007–8	188843	1653851	6696	26612	3948751	13523	757074	3133665	13167	113277	8110828	27588
2008–9	245964	2160233	9192	24280	4094286	14266	837520	3758904	16414	118941	8824784	30748
2009–10	316956	2913890	12243	28651	6072829	21308	883949	2988971	12996	142052	15541378	54531
2010–11	332540	2870952	11623	27409	4099284	13943	1150037	4191037	17463	145383	12259745	41700
2011–12	412266	3488203	14656	29806	3763877	12934	1283178	4642573	20185	143949	11155428	38335
2012–13	658055	6592032	27353	41566	5402765	18695	1396138	4830933	20823	156099	12028040	41620
2013–14	820330	8956699	37011	46395	7228127	24669	1512215	4743321	20358	177918	17526192	59613
2014–15	977948	10156162	42853	42853	7875246	27440	1731706	5297790	23236	207241	16764597	58413
2015–16	883167	9728541	40367	40367	8621665	31125	1885129	5489286	23458	215151	17833529	64381

* Commenced operations from November 12, 2002, cash and Tom settlement is with effect from February 5, 2004.

** Commenced operation from January 20, 2003.

Source: Rakshitra, CCIL.

A6 PRICES

Table A6.1 Wholesale Price Index: Point-to-Point and Average Annual Changes

Year	Point-to-Point (Mar-Mar)				Average			
	All Commodities	Annual Change (per cent)	Food Index	Annual Change (per cent)	All Commodities	Annual Change (per cent)	Food Index	Annual Change (per cent)
Base Year 1993–4 = 100								
1994–5	116.9	16.9	114.1	14.1	112.8	12.8	115.3	15.3
1995–6	122.2	4.5	120.3	5.4	121.6	7.8	122.8	6.5
1996–7	128.8	5.4	135.0	12.2	127.2	4.7	132.4	7.8
1997–8	134.4	4.3	140.3	3.9	132.8	4.3	137.8	4.1
1998–9	141.6	5.4	153.8	9.6	140.7	6.0	154.2	11.9
1999–2000	149.5	5.6	160.6	4.4	145.3	3.2	155.7	1.0
2000–1	159.1	6.4	157.8	-1.7	155.7	7.2	156.7	0.6
2001–2	161.9	1.8	162.7	3.1	161.3	3.6	163.2	4.1
2002–3	171.6	6.0	168.8	3.7	166.8	3.4	167.9	2.9
2003–4	179.8	4.8	174.9	3.6	175.9	5.5	175.2	4.3
2004–5	189.4	5.3	180.1	3.0	187.3	6.5	181.4	3.5
Base Year 2004–05 = 100								
2005–6	105.7	5.7	103.9	3.9	104.5	4.5	103.7	3.6
2006–7	112.8	6.7	113.9	9.6	111.4	6.6	111.8	7.9
2007–8	121.5	7.7	121.6	6.7	116.6	4.7	118.1	5.6
2008–9	123.5	1.6	130.5	7.3	126.0	8.1	128.7	8.9
2009–10	136.3	10.4	154.6	18.5	130.8	3.8	147.5	14.6
2010–11	149.5	9.7	165.1	6.8	143.3	9.6	163.8	11.1
2011–12	161.0	7.7	179.5	8.7	156.1	8.9	175.7	7.2
2012–13	170.1	5.7	194.2	8.2	167.6	7.4	192.0	9.3
2013–14	180.3	6.0	207.7	7.0	177.6	6.0	210.1	9.4
2014–15	176.1	-2.3	216.8	4.4	181.2	2.0	220.4	4.9
2015–16	175.3	-0.5	226.7	4.6	176.7	-2.5	226.0	2.6

Note: With effect from October 17, 2009 Office of the Economic Adviser discontinued dessimination of price data on a weekly basis and started giving monthly data from September. Hence in this table point-to-point basis has been worked out by using March data instead of end March data for all the years.

Source: Office of the Economic Adviser, Ministry of Commerce and Industry, G of India (GOI).

Table A6.2 Cost of Living Indices

(A) Consumer Price Index for Industrial Workers

Year	Point-to-Point						Annual Average					
	Total Index	Annual Change (per cent)	Food Index	Annual Change (per cent)	Total Index	Annual Change (per cent)	Total Index	Annual Change (per cent)	Food Index	Annual Change (per cent)		
(1)	(6)	(7)	(8)	(9)	(2)	(3)	(2)	(3)	(4)	(5)		
Base Year 1982 = 100												
1990–1	201		207		193		193		199			
1991–2	229	13.9	241	16.4	219	13.5	219	13.5	230	15.6		
1992–3	243	6.1	253	5.0	240	9.6	240	9.6	254	10.4		
1993–4	267	9.9	281	11.1	258	7.5	258	7.5	272	7.1		
1994–5	293	9.7	311	10.7	279	8.1	279	8.1	297	9.2		
1995–6	319	8.9	339	9.0	313	12.2	313	12.2	337	13.5		
1996–7	351	10.0	373	10.0	342	9.3	342	9.3	369	9.5		
1997–8	380	8.3	401	7.5	366	7.0	366	7.0	388	5.1		
1998–99	414	8.9	445	11.0	414	13.1	414	13.1	445	14.7		
1999–2000	434	4.8	446	0.2	428	3.4	428	3.4	446	0.2		
2000–1	445	2.5	446	0.0	444	3.7	444	3.7	453	1.6		
2001–2	468	5.2	462	3.6	463	4.3	463	4.3	446	-1.5		
2002–3	487	4.1	479	3.7	482	4.1	482	4.1	477	7.0		
2003–4	504	3.5	494	3.1	500	3.8	500	3.8	495	3.8		
2004–5	525	4.2	502	1.6	520	3.9	520	3.9	506	2.2		
Base Year 2001 = 100												
2004–5	113	3.7	na	na	112	3.9	112	3.9	na	na		
2005–6	119	5.3	na	na	117	4.3	117	4.3	na	na		
2006–7	127	6.7	129	na	125	6.7	125	6.7	126	na		
2007–8	137	7.9	141	9.3	133	6.4	133	6.4	136	7.9		
2008–9	148	8.0	156	10.6	145	9.0	145	9.0	153	12.5		
2009–10	170	14.9	181	16.0	163	12.4	163	12.4	176	15.0		
2010–11	185	8.8	196	8.3	180	10.4	180	10.4	194	10.2		
2011–12	201	8.6	212	8.2	195	8.3	195	8.3	206	6.2		
2012–13	224	11.4	240	13.2	214	9.7	214	9.7	230	11.7		
2013–14	239	6.7	258	7.5	236	10.3	236	10.3	257	11.7		
2014–15	254	6.3	276	7.0	251	6.4	251	6.4	276	7.4		
2015–16	268	5.5	293	6.2	265	5.6	265	5.6	293	6.2		

Note: na: not available.

Source: Labour Bureau.

Table A6.2 Cost of Living Indices

(B) Consumer Price Index for Agricultural Labourers

| July–June | Point-to-Point | | | | Annual Average | | | |
	Total Index	Annual Change (%)	Food Index	Annual Change (%)	Total Index	Annual Change (%)	Food Index	Annual Change (%)
(1)	(2)	(3)	(4)	(5)	(6)	(7)	(8)	(9)
Base Year 1986–87 = 100								
2000–1	306	–1.3	299	–3.5	304	–1.7	299	–4.7
2001–2	314	2.6	306	2.3	311	2.2	304	1.6
2002–3	330	5.1	324	5.9	323	3.8	316	4.0
2003–4	336	1.8	329	1.5	332	3.0	326	3.0
2004–5	345	2.7	336	2.1	342	2.9	335	2.8
2005–6	370	7.2	365	8.6	358	4.7	351	4.9
2006–7	392	5.9	389	6.6	380	6.1	376	7.0
2007–8	423	7.9	422	8.5	409	7.6	406	8.2
2008–9	484	14.4	488	15.6	462	13.0	464	14.2
2009–10	547	13.0	555	13.7	530	14.7	540	16.4
2010–11	598	9.3	593	6.8	579	9.2	582	7.8
2011–12	646	8.0	630	6.2	622	7.4	610	4.8
2012–13	729	12.8	718	14.0	692	11.3	679	11.3
2013–14	785	7.7	766	6.7	764	10.4	750	10.5
2014–15	820	4.5	790	3.1	808	5.8	783	4.4
2015–16	869	6.0	845	7.0	847	4.8	820	4.7

Note: * Average based on Agricultural year i.e., July–June of every year.

**June over June every year.

na: not available.

Base is revised to 1986–7 w.e.f November 1995,.

Table A6.2 Cost of Living Index

(C) Consumer Price Index- All India (New Series) 2012 = 100

	Annual Average*					Point-to-Point**			
	Total Index	Annual Change (%)	Food Index	Annual Change (%)	Total Index	Annual Change (%)	Food Index	Annual Change (%)	
(1)	(2)	(3)	(4)	(5)	(6)	(7)	(8)	(9)	
Rural									
2010–11					87.8		88.2		
2011–12	92.8		92.3		96.0	9.3	94.6	7.3	
2012–13	102.7	10.7	103.0	11.6	106.0	10.4	106.2	12.3	
2013–14	112.6	9.6	115.1	11.7	114.6	8.1	115.8	9.0	
2014–15	119.5	6.1	122.7	6.6	121.1	5.7	122.7	6.0	
2015–16	126.1	5.5	128.9	5.1	128.0	5.7	129.8	5.8	
Urban									
2010–11					89.1		89.8		
2011–12	93.8		94.1		96.8	8.6	95.9	6.8	
2012–13	102.7	9.5	103.7	10.2	105.0	8.5	106.8	11.4	
2013–14	112	9.1	117.1	12.9	113.7	8.3	115.3	8.0	
2014–15	118.1	5.4	124.5	6.3	119.1	4.7	123.1	6.8	
2015–16	123	4.1	129.7	4.2	123.5	3.7	128.0	4.0	
Combined									
2010–11					88.4		88.9		
2011–12	93.3		93.0		96.4	9.0	95.2	7.1	
2012–13	102.7	10.1	103.3	11.1	105.5	9.4	106.6	12.0	
2013–14	112.3	9.3	115.8	12.1	114.2	8.2	115.7	8.5	
2014–15	118.9	5.9	123.2	6.4	120.2	5.3	122.8	6.1	
2015–16	124.7	4.9	129.2	4.9	126.0	4.8	129.2	5.2	

Source: Central Statistical Office.

A7 EXTERNAL SECTOR

Table A7.1 Foreign Exchange Reserves (End Period)

(Million tonnes)

End of	SDRs			Gold		Foreign Currency Assets		Reserve Tranche Position in IMF		Total	
	In million SDRs	Rupees Crore	In millions of US Dollar	Rupees Crore	In millions of US Dollar	Rupees Crore	In millions of US Dollar	Rupees Crore	In millions of US Dollar	Rupees Crore	In millions of US Dollar
(1)	(2)	(3)	(4)	(5)	(6)	(7)	(8)	(9)	(10)	(11)	(12)
1990–1	76	200	102	6828	3496	4388	2236			11416	5834
2000–1	2	11	2	12711	2725	184482	39554			197204	42281
2001–2	8	50	10	14868	3047	249118	51049			264036	54106
2002–3	3	19	4	16785	3534	341476	71890	3190	672	361470	76100
2003–4	2	10	2	18216	4198	466215	107448	5688	1311	490129	112959
2004–5	3	20	5	19686	4500	593121	135571	6289	1438	619116	141514
2005–6	2	12	3	25674	5755	647327	145108	3374	756	676387	151622
2006–7	1	8	2	29573	6784	836597	191924	2044	469	868222	199179
2007–8	11	74	18	40124	10039	1196023	299230	1744	436	1237965	309723
2008–9	1	—	1	48793	9577	1230066	241426	5000	981	1283865	251985
2009–10	3297	22596	5006	81188	17986	1149650	254685	6231	1380	1259665	279057
2010–11	2882	20401	4569	102572	22972	1224883	274330	13158	2947	1361013	304818
2011–12	2885	22860	4469	138250	27023	1330511	260069	14511	2836	1506130	294398
2012–13	2887	23540	4328	139740	25692	1412630	259726	12510	2301	1588420	292046
2013–14*	2887	26790	4458	130210	20978	1661190	276406	11010	1831	1829200	303674
2014–15	2889	24940	3985	119160	19038	1985460	317324	8080	1292	2137640	341638
2015–16	1066	9950	1488	132600	19325	2209070	332147	17390	2600	2369010	355560

Notes: 1. Gold was valued at Rs.84.39 per 10 grams till October 16, 1990. It has been valued close to international market price with effect from October 17, 1990.

2. Conversion of SDRs into US dollar is done at exchange rates released by the IMF.

3. With effect from April 1, 1991 the conversion of foreign currency assets into US dollar is done at week end rates for week end–data and or month–end rate for month end–data based on New York closing exchange rates. Prior to that it was done by using representative exchange rate released by the IMF.

4. Since March 1993, foreign exchange holdings are converted into rupees at rupee–US dollar market exchange rates.

5. Reserve tranche position has been reported as part of reserves since 2002–03.

*Outstanding as on March 28, 2014.

Source: RBI: Monthly Bulletin, Various Issues.

Table A7.2 Balance of Payments 2000–1 to 2015–16

(US $ million)

Year/Item	2004–05	2005–06	2006–07	2007–08	2008–09	2009–10	2010–11	2011–12	2012–13	2013–14	2014–15	2015–16
A. Current Account (I+II)	-2470	-9902	-9565	-15738	-27917	-38180	-48053	-78155	-88163	-32397	-26800	-22151
% of GDP**	(-0.4)	(-1.2)	(-1.0)	(-1.3)	(-2.3)	(-2.8)	(-2.8)	(-4.2)	(-4.8)	(-1.7)	(-1.3)	(-1.1)
I. MERCHANDISE (Net)	-33702	-51904	-61782	-91468	-119521	-118204	-127322	-189759	-195656	-147609	-144940	-130079
II. INVISIBLES (a+b+c) [Net]	31232	42002	52217	75730	91603	80023	79269	111604	107493	115212	118139	107928
a. Services	15426	23170	29469	38853	53916	36014	44081	64098	64915	72965	76588	69676
b. Transfers	20785	24687	30079	41945	44798	52046	53140	63494	64034	65276	65692	62627
c. Income	-4979	-5855	-7331	-5068	-7110	-8038	-17952	-15988	-21455	-23028	-24140	-24375
B. Capital Account (1 to 5)	28022	25470	45203	106585	7396	51634	63740	67755	89300	48787	89286	41128
1. Foreign Investment	13000	15528	14753	43326	8342	50363	42127	39231	46711	26386	73456	31891
2. Loans	10909	7909	24490	40653	8315	12447	29135	19307	31124	7765	3184	-4634
3. Banking Capital	3874	1373	1913	11759	-3246	2085	4962	16226	16570	25449	11618	10630
4. Rupee Debt Service	-417	-572	-162	-121	-101	-97	-68	-79	-58	-52	-81	-73
5. Other Capital	656	1232	4209	10969	-5918	-13162	-12416	-6929	-5047	-10761	1109	3315
C. Errors and Omissions	607	-516	968	1317	440	-13	-2636	-2432	2689	-931	-1080	-1073
D. Overall Balance	26159	15052	36606	92164	-20080	13442	13050	-12831	3826	15459	61406	17905

Notes: 1. Data stated above are the net figures (Credit-Debit).

2. Data for 2012–13 are preliminary estimates and for 2011–12 are partially revised.

3. Totals may not tally due to rounding off.

AE: Advance estimate. na: not available.

**–Current account balance as a percentage of Gross Domestic Product at current market prices.

Source: RBI; compiled by EPW Research Foundation.

Table A7.3 India's Foreign Trade

(US $ million)

Year	Exports			Imports			Trade Balance		
	Oil	Non-Oil	Total	Oil	Non-Oil	Total	Oil	Non-Oil	Total
1	2	3	4	5	6	7	8	9	10
1970–1	11	2020	2031	180	1983	2162	-169	38	-131
1980–1	32	8453	8485	6655	9212	15867	-6623	-758	-7382
1990–1	523	17623	18145	6028	18044	24073	-5505	-422	-5927
2000–1	1870	42691	44560	15650	34886	50537	-13780	7804	-5976
2001–2	2119	41708	43827	14000	37413	51413	-11881	4295	-7587
2002–3	2577	50143	52719	17640	43773	61412	-15063	6370	-8693
2003–4	3568	60274	63843	20569	57580	78149	-17001	2694	-14307
2004–5	6989	76547	83536	29844	81673	111517	-22855	-5127	-27981
2005–6	11640	91451	103091	43963	105203	149166	-32323	-13752	-46075
2006–7	18635	107779	126414	56945	128790	185735	-38311	-21011	-59321
2007–8	28363	134541	162904	79645	171795	251439	-51281	-37254	-88535
2008–9	27547	157748	185295	93672	210025	303696	-66125	-52277	-118401
2009–10	28192	150559	178751	87136	201237	288373	-58944	-50678	-109621
2010–1	41480	209656	251136	105964	263805	369769	-64484	-54149	-118633
2011–2	56039	249925	305964	154968	334511	489320	-98929	-84427	-183356
2012–3	60860	239541	300401	164041	326696	490737	-103181	-87155	-190336
2013–4	62687	249934	312621	165154	284929	450082	-102467	-34995	-137461
2014–5	56794	253544	310339	138326	309708	448033	-81531	-56164	-137695
2015–6	30424	231580	262004	82880	297476	380356	-52456	-65896	-118353

Source: RBI Bulletins.

Table A7.4 Foreign Investment Inflows

Year	Direct Investment (I+II+III)	I. Equity (a+b+c+d+e)	a. Government (SIA/FIPB)	b. RBI	c. NRI	d. Acquisition of Shares	e. Equity Capital of Unincorporated Bodies	II. Reinvested Earnings	III. Other Capital	Portfolio Investment	a. GDRs/ADRs	b. FIIs	c. Offshore Funds and Others	Total (A+B)
1990–1	97	0	0	0	0	0	0	0	0	6	0	0	6	103
1991–2	129	129	66	0	63	0	0	0	0	4	0	0	4	133
1992–3	315	315	222	42	51	0	0	0	0	244	240	1	3	559
1993–4	586	586	280	89	217	0	0	0	0	3567	1520	1665	382	4153
1994–5	1314	1314	701	171	442	0	0	0	0	3824	2082	1503	239	5138
1995–6	2144	2144	1249	169	715	11	0	0	0	2748	683	2009	56	4892
1996–7	2821	2821	1922	135	639	125	0	0	0	3312	1366	1926	20	6133
1997–8	3557	3557	2754	202	241	360	0	0	0	1828	645	979	204	5385
1998–9	2462	2462	1821	179	62	400	0	0	0	-61	270	-390	59	2401
1999–2000	2155	2155	1410	171	84	490	0	0	0	3026	768	2135	123	5181
2000–1	4029	2400	1456	454	67	362	61	1350	279	2760	831	1847	82	6789
2001–2	6130	4095	2221	767	35	881	191	1645	390	2021	477	1505	39	8151
2002–3	5035	2764	919	739	—	916	190	1833	438	979	600	377	2	6014
2003–4	4322	2229	928	534	—	735	32	1460	633	11377	459	10918	—	15699
2004–5	6051	3778	1062	1258	—	930	528	1904	369	9315	613	8686	16	15366
2005–6	8961	5975	1126	2233	—	2181	435	2760	226	12492	2552	9926	14	21453
2006–7	22826	16481	2156	7151	—	6278	896	5828	517	7003	3776	3225	2	29829
2007–8	34835	26864	2298	17127	—	5148	2291	7679	292	27271	6645	20328	298	62106
2008–9	41874	32066	5400	21332	—	4632	702	9032	776	-13855	1162	-15017	—	28019
2009–10	37745	27146	3471	18987	—	3148	1540	8668	1931	32376	3328	29048	—	70121
2010–1	34847	22250	1945	12994	—	6437	874	11939	658	31471	2049	29422	—	66318
2011–2	46553	35854	3046	20427	—	11360	1021	8205	2494	17410	597	16813	—	63963
2012–3	34298	22884	2319	15967	—	3539	1059	9880	1534	27769	187	27582	—	61592
2013–4	36396	25283	1185	14869	—	8245	984	9047	2066	5030	20	5010	—	41426
2014–5	45148	31911	2219	22530	—	6185	978	9988	3249	42205	1271	40923	—	87354
2015–6	55559	41112	3574	32494	—	3933	1111	10413	4034	-4130	373	-4016	—	51429

Note: Adjustment for repatriation investment & foreign direct investment by india not effected both in FDI and portfolio investment.
Source: RBI Bulletin.

Table A7.5 Human Development Characteristics of Some Selected Countries

Countries	HDI Rank 2014	Human Development Index 2000	Human Development Index 2014	Life Expectancy at Birth (years) Person 2014	Female 2014	Male 2014	Adult Literacy Rate (% aged 15 & above) Person 2005–13	Gross Enrolment Ratio in Education (%) Primary 2008–14	Secondary 2008–14	Tertiary 2008–14	GDP per capita (2011 PPP US $) 2013	Gender Inequality Index Rank 2012	Value 2012	Total Population (millions) 1990	2014	Total Dependency Ratio (per 100 people ages 15–64) 2000	2012	Total Fertility Rate (birth/women) 2000	2012
(1)	(2)	(3)	(2)	(3)	(4)	(5)	(6)	(7)	(8)	(9)	(10)	(11)	(12)	(13)	(14)	(15)	(16)	(17)	(18)
Australia	2	0.898	0.935	82.4	84.5	80.3	—	105	136	86	42831	19	0.110	17.1	23.6	49.6	49.3	1.7	2.0
Netherlands	5	0.877	0.922	81.6	83.3	79.7	—	106	130	77	44945	7	0.062	15.0	16.8	47.3	50.6	1.7	1.8
Germany	6	0.855	0.916	80.9	83.3	78.5	—	100	101	62	43207	3	0.041	79.4	82.7	47.0	51.7	1.3	1.4
United States	8	0.883	0.915	79.1	81.4	76.7	—	98	94	94	51340	55	0.280	254.9	322.6	51.0	50.7	2.0	2.1
Canada	9	0.867	0.913	82.0	84.0	80.0	—	98	103	—	41894	25	0.129	27.7	35.5	46.3	45.1	1.5	1.7
New Zealand	9	0.874	0.913	81.8	83.6	80.0	—	99	120	80	32808	32	0.157	3.4	4.6	52.7	51.4	1.9	2.1
Singapore	11	0.819	0.912	83.0	86.0	79.9	96.4	—	—	—	76237	13	0.088	3.0	5.5	40.5	35.4	1.4	1.3
Hong Kong	12	0.825	0.912	84.0	86.8	81.2	—	105	99	67	51509	—	—	5.7	7.3	39.3	32.3	0.8	1.1
UK	14	0.865	0.907	80.7	82.6	78.7	—	109	95	62	37017	39	0.177	57.2	63.5	53.4	52.7	1.7	1.9
Korea Rep of	17	0.821	0.898	81.9	85.0	78.5	—	103	97	98	32708	23	0.125	43.0	49.5	39.5	38.0	1.3	1.4
Japan	20	0.857	0.891	83.5	86.7	80.2	—	102	102	61	35614	26	0.133		127.0				
France	22	0.848	0.888	82.2	85.1	79.2	—	107	110	58	37154	13	0.088	56.8	64.6	53.6	55.7	1.8	2.0
Spain	26	0.827	0.876	82.6	85.3	79.8	97.9	103	131	85	31596	16	0.095	38.8	47.1	46.3	48.4	1.2	1.5
Italy	27	0.829	0.873	83.1	85.5	80.6	99.0	99	99	62	34167	10	0.068	57.0	61.1	48.3	53.8	1.2	1.5
Saudi Arabia	39	0.744	0.837	74.3	75.7	73.0	94.4	106	116	58	52068	56	0.284	16.3	29.4	72.5	49.0	4.0	2.7
Argentina	40	0.762	0.836	76.3	80.1	72.4	97.9	124	107	80	—	75	0.376	32.5	41.8	60.7	54.4	2.5	2.2
UAR	41	0.797	0.835	77.0	78.5	76.3	90.0	108	—	—	57045	47	0.232	1.9	9.4	36.3	20.9	2.6	1.7
Chile	42	0.752	0.832	81.7	84.5	78.6	98.6	104	89	74	21714	65	0.338	13.2	17.8	54.0	45.2	2.1	1.8
Kuwait	48	0.804	0.816	74.4	75.8	73.5	95.5	106	100	28	82358	79	0.387	2.1	3.5	42.3	41.1	2.6	2.3
Russia	50	0.717	0.798	70.1	75.8	64.4	99.7	101	95	76	23564	54	0.276	148.1	142.5	44.1	39.8	1.2	1.5
Malaysia	62	0.723	0.779	74.7	77.1	72.4	93.1	101	71	37	22589	42	0.209	18.1	30.2	59.1	52.8	3.1	2.6
Turkey	72	0.653	0.761	75.3	78.5	72.0	94.9	100	86	69	18660	71	0.359	56.1	75.8	56.0	46.8	2.4	2.0
Sri Lanka	73	0.679	0.757	74.9	78.2	71.5	91.2	98	99	17	9426	72	0.370	17.3	21.4	48.9	50.6	2.2	2.3
Mexico	74	0.699	0.756	78.8	79.2	74.4	94.2	105	86	29	16291	74	0.373	83.4	123.8	62.5	53.5	2.6	2.2
Brazil	75	0.683	0.755	74.5	78.3	70.7	91.3	136	105	26	14555	97	0.457	149.6	202.0	54.0	46.8	2.4	1.8
China	90	0.588	0.727	75.8	77.3	74.3	95.1	128	89	27	11525	40	0.191	1142.1	1393.8	48.1	37.6	1.7	1.6

(Contd.)

Table A7.5 (Contd)

Countries	HDI Rank	Human Development Index		Life Expectancy at Birth (years)			Adult Literacy Rate (% aged 15 & above)	Gross Enrolment Ratio in Education (%)			GDP per capita (2011 PPP US $)	Gender Inequality Index		Total Population (millions)		Total Dependency Ratio (per 100 people ages 15–64)		Total Fertility Rate (birth/women)	
		2014	2000	Person 2014	Female 2014	Male 2014	Person 2005–13	Primary 2008–14	Secondary 2008–14	Tertiary 2008–14	2013	Rank 2012	Value 2012	1990	2014	2000	2012	2000	2012
(1)	(2)	(2)	(3)	(3)	(4)	(5)	(6)	(7)	(8)	(9)	(10)	(11)	(12)	(13)	(14)	(15)	(16)	(17)	(18)
Thailand	93	0.726	0.648	74.4	77.9	71.1	96.4	93	87	51	13932	76	0.380	56.7	67.2	44.7	41.1	1.7	1.5
Colombia	97	0.720	0.654	74.0	77.7	70.5	93.6	115	93	48	12025	92	0.429	33.2	48.9	60.1	51.5	2.6	2.3
Jamaica	99	0.719	0.700	75.7	78.1	73.3	87.5	92	78	29	8607	93	0.430	2.4	2.8	67.0	55.9	2.6	2.3
Egypt	108	0.69	0.622	71.1	73.4	69.0	73.9	113	86	30	10733	131	0.573	57.8	83.4	67.9	57.2	3.3	2.7
Indonesia	110	0.684	0.606	68.9	71.0	66.9	92.8	109	83	32	9254	110	0.494	177.4	252.8	54.7	47.3	2.5	2.1
Philippines	115	0.668	0.623	68.2	71.8	64.9	95.4	106	85	28	6326	89	0.420	62.4	100.1	71.5	62.4	3.8	3.1
South Africa	116	0.666	0.632	57.4	59.3	55.2	93.7	101	111	20	12106	83	0.407	36.7	53.1	81.3	70.0	4.4	3.8
India	130	0.609	0.496	68.0	69.5	66.6	62.8	113	69	25	5238	130	0.563	862.2	1267.4	63.8	53.8	3.1	2.6
Bangladesh	142	0.570	0.468	71.6	72.9	70.4	58.8	114	54	13	2853	111	0.503	115.6	158.5	70.4	53.0	3.1	2.2
Nepal	145	0.548	0.451	69.6	71.1	68.2	57.4	133	67	14	2173	108	0.489	—	28.1	80.5	64.1	4.1	2.6
Pakistan	147	0.538	0.444	66.2	67.2	65.3	54.7	92	38	10	4454	121	0.536	115.8	185.1	82.8	63.4	4.5	3.2
Myanmar	148	0.536	0.425	65.9	68.0	63.9	92.6	114	50	13	—	85	0.413	40.8	53.7	55.2	43.0	2.4	2.0

Note: For details about the data see source.

Source: Human Development Report 2015, UNDP.

A8 SOCIAL SECTOR

Table A8.1 Human Development Index for India by State

State/UTs	HDI-1981		HDI-1991		HDI-2001		HDI-1999–2000		HDI-2008		HDI-2015	
	Value	Rank	Value	Rank	Value	Rank	Value	Rank	Value	Rank	Value	Rank
(1)	(2)	(3)	(4)	(5)	(6)	(7)	(8)	(9)	(10)	(11)	(12)	(13)
India	0.3020		0.381		0.4720		0.3870		0.4670		0.6087	
Andhra Pradesh	0.2980	23	0.377	23	0.4160	10	0.3680	15	0.4730	14	0.6165	15
Arunachal Pradesh	0.2420	31	0.328	29	*		*		*		*	
Assam	0.2720	26	0.348	26	0.3860	14	0.3360	16	0.4440	15	0.5555	16
Bihar	0.2370	32	0.308	32	0.3670	15	0.2920	18	0.3670	21	0.5361	21
Chhattisgarh							0.2780	20	0.3580	22	*	
Goa	0.4450	5	0.5750	4	*		0.5950	3	0.6170	4	*	
Gujarat	0.3600	14	0.4310	17	0.4790	6	0.4660	9	0.5270	10	0.6164	11
Haryana	0.3600	15	0.4430	16	0.5090	5	0.5010	6	0.5520	8	0.6613	9
Himachal Pradesh	0.3980	10	0.4690	13	*		0.5810	4	0.6520	3	0.6701	3
Jharkhand					*		0.2680	22	0.3760	18	*	
Jammu and Kashmir	0.3370	19	0.4020	21	*		0.4650	10	0.5290	9	0.6489	10
Karnataka	0.3460	16	0.4120	19	0.4780	7	0.4320	11	0.5190	11	0.6176	12
Kerala	0.5000	2	0.5910	3	0.6380	1	0.6770	2	0.7900	1	0.92	1
Madhya Pradesh	0.2450	30	0.3280	30	0.3940	12	0.2850	19	0.3750	19	0.5567	20
Maharashtra	0.3630	13	0.4520	15	0.5230	4	0.5010	7	0.5720	6	0.6659	7
Manipur	0.4610	4	0.5360	9	*		*		*		*	
Meghalaya	0.3170	21	0.3650	24	*		*		*		*	
Mizoram	0.4110	8	0.5480	7	*		*		*		*	
Nagaland	0.3280	20	0.4860	11	*		*		*		*	
Odisha	0.2670	27	0.3450	28	0.4040	11	0.2750	21	0.3620	21	0.5567	22
Punjab	0.4110	9	0.4750	12	0.5370	2	0.5430	5	0.6050	5	0.6614	5
Rajasthan	0.2560	28	0.3470	27	0.4240	9	0.3870	13	0.4340	16	0.5768	17
Sikkim	0.3420	18	0.4250	18	*		*		*		*	
Tamil Nadu	0.3430	17	0.4660	14	0.5310	3	0.4800	8	0.5700	7	0.6663	8
Tripura	0.2870	24	0.3890	22	*		*		*		*	
Uttar Pradesh	0.2550	29	0.3140	31	0.3880	13	0.3160	17	0.3800	17	0.5415	18
Uttarakhand							0.3390	15	0.4900	13		
West Bengal	0.3050	22	0.4040	20	0.4720	8	0.4220	12	0.4920	12	0.6042	13
Andaman & Nicobar	0.3940	11	0.5740	5	*		*		*		*	

(Contd.)

Table A8.1 (*Cont'd*)

State/UTs	HDI-1981		HDI-1991		HDI-2001		HDI-1999–2000		HDI-2008		HDI-2015	
	Value	Rank	Value	Rank	Value	Rank	Value	Rank	Value	Rank	Value	Rank
(1)	(2)	(3)	(4)	(5)	(6)	(7)	(8)	(9)	(10)	(11)	(12)	(13)
Chandigarh	0.5500	1	0.6740	1	*		*		*		*	
Dadra & Nagar Haveli	0.2760	25	0.3610	25	*		*		*			
Daman and Diu	0.4380	6	0.5440	8	*		*		*			
Delhi	0.4950	3	0.6240	2	*		0.7830	1	0.7500	2		
Lakshadweep	0.4340	7	0.5320	10	*		*		*		*	
Pondicherry	0.3860	12	0.5710	6	*		*		*		*	

*Not available

Note: The HDI is a composite of variables capturing attainments in three dimensions of human development viz. economic, educational and health. This has been worked out by a combination of measures: per capita monthly expenditures adjusted for inequality; a combination of litracy rate and intensity of formal education and a combination of life expectancy at age 1 and infant mortality rate.

For details see the technical note in the source for the estimation methodology.

Source: India *Human Development Report, 2015 and earlier issues.*

Table 8.2 Number and Percentage of Population below Poverty Line and Poverty Line in Rs (in Rs)

State	Rural			Urban			Combined	
	No. of persons (Lakh)	% of persons	Poverty Line (Rs)	No. of persons (Lakh)	% of persons	Poverty Line (Rs)	No. of persons (Lakh)	% of persons
				1973–74				
Andhra Pradesh	178.21	48.41	41.71	47.48	50.61	53.96	225.69	48.86
Arunachal Pradesh	2.57	52.67	49.82	0.09	36.92	50.26	2.66	51.93
Assam	76.37	52.67	49.82	5.46	36.92	50.26	81.83	51.21
Bihar	336.52	62.99	57.68	34.05	52.96	61.27	370.57	61.91
Goa	3.16	46.85	50.47	1.00	37.69	59.48	4.16	44.26
Gujarat	94.61	46.35	47.10	43.81	52.57	62.17	138.42	48.15
Haryana	30.08	34.23	49.95	8.24	40.18	52.42	38.32	35.36
Himachal Pradesh	9.38	27.42	49.95	0.35	13.17	51.93	9.73	26.39
Jammu & Kashmir	18.41	45.51	46.59	2.07	21.32	37.17	20.48	40.83
Karnataka	128.40	55.14	47.24	42.27	52.53	58.22	170.67	54.47
Kerala	111.36	59.19	51.68	24.16	62.74	62.78	135.52	59.79
Madhya Pradesh	231.21	62.66	50.20	45.09	57.65	63.02	276.30	61.78
Maharashtra	210.84	57.71	50.47	76.58	43.87	59.48	287.42	53.24
Manipur	5.11	52.67	49.82	0.75	36.92	50.26	5.86	49.96
Meghalaya	4.88	52.67	49.82	0.64	36.92	50.26	5.52	50.20
Mizoram	1.62	52.67	49.82	0.20	36.92	50.26	1.82	50.32
Nagaland	2.65	52.67	49.82	0.25	36.92	50.26	2.90	50.81
Odisha	142.24	67.28	46.87	12.23	55.62	59.34	154.47	66.18
Punjab	30.47	28.21	49.95	10.02	27.96	51.93	40.49	28.15
Rajasthan	101.41	44.76	50.96	27.10	52.13	59.99	128.51	46.14
Sikkim	1.09	52.67	49.82	0.10	36.92	50.26	1.19	50.86
Tamil Nadu	172.60	57.43	45.09	66.92	49.40	51.54	239.52	54.94
Tripura	7.88	52.67	49.82	0.66	36.92	50.26	8.54	51.00
Uttar Pradesh	449.99	56.53	48.92	85.74	60.09	57.37	535.73	57.07
West Bengal	257.96	73.16	54.49	41.34	34.67	54.81	299.30	63.43
All India	2612.90	56.44	49.63	600.46	49.01	56.64	3213.36	54.88

(*Contd.*)

Table A8.2 (*Cont'd*)

| State | Rural | | | Urban | | | Combined | |
	No. of persons (Lakh)	% of persons	Poverty Line (Rs)	No. of persons (Lakh)	% of persons	Poverty Line (Rs)	No. of persons (Lakh)	% of persons
				1983–84				
Andhra Pradesh	114.34	26.53	72.66	50.24	36.30	106.43	164.58	28.91
Arunachal Pradesh	2.70	42.60	98.32	0.12	21.73	97.51	2.82	40.88
Assam	73.43	42.60	98.32	4.26	21.73	97.51	77.69	40.47
Bihar	417.70	64.37	97.48	44.35	47.33	111.80	462.05	62.22
Goa	1.16	14.81	88.24	1.07	27.00	126.47	2.23	18.90
Gujarat	72.88	29.80	83.29	45.04	39.14	123.22	117.92	32.79
Haryana	22.03	20.56	88.57	7.57	24.15	103.48	29.60	21.37
Himachal Pradesh	7.07	17.00	88.57	0.34	9.43	102.26	7.41	16.40
Jammu & Kashmir	13.11	26.04	91.75	2.49	17.76	99.62	15.60	24.24
Karnataka	100.50	36.33	83.31	49.31	42.82	120.19	149.81	38.24
Kerala	81.62	39.03	99.35	25.15	45.68	122.64	106.77	40.42
Madhya Pradesh	215.48	48.90	83.59	62.49	53.06	122.82	277.97	49.78
Maharashtra	193.75	45.23	88.24	97.14	40.26	126.47	290.89	43.44
Manipur	4.76	42.60	98.32	0.89	21.73	97.51	5.65	37.02
Meghalaya	5.04	42.60	98.32	0.57	21.73	97.51	5.62	38.81
Mizoram	1.58	42.60	98.32	0.37	21.73	97.51	1.96	36.00
Nagaland	3.19	42.60	98.32	0.31	21.73	97.51	3.50	39.25
Orissa	164.65	67.53	106.28	16.66	49.15	124.81	181.31	65.29
Punjab	16.79	13.20	88.57	11.85	23.79	101.03	28.64	16.18
Rajasthan	96.77	33.50	80.24	30.06	37.94	113.55	126.83	34.46
Sikkim	1.24	42.60	98.32	0.10	21.73	97.51	1.35	39.71
Tamil Nadu	181.61	53.99	96.15	78.46	46.96	120.30	260.07	51.66
Tripura	8.35	42.60	98.32	0.60	21.73	97.51	8.95	40.03
Uttar Pradesh	448.03	46.45	83.85	108.71	49.82	110.23	556.74	47.07
West Bengal	268.60	63.05	105.55	50.09	32.32	105.91	318.69	54.85
All India	2519.57	45.65	89.50	709.40	40.79	115.65	3228.97	44.48

State	Rural			Urban			Combined	
	No. of persons (Lakh)	% of persons	Poverty Line (Rs)	No. of persons (Lakh)	% of persons	Poverty Line (Rs)	No. of persons (Lakh)	% of persons
				1993–94				
Arunachal Pradesh	3.62	45.01	232.05	0.11	7.73	212.42	3.73	39.35
Assam	94.33	45.01	232.05	2.03	7.73	212.42	96.36	40.86
Bihar	450.86	58.21	212.16	42.49	34.50	238.49	493.35	54.96
Goa	0.38	5.34	194.94	1.53	27.03	328.56	1.91	14.92
Gujarat	62.16	22.18	202.11	43.02	27.89	297.22	105.19	24.21
Haryana	36.56	28.02	233.79	7.31	16.38	258.23	43.88	25.05
Himachal Pradesh	15.40	30.34	233.79	0.46	9.18	253.61	15.86	28.44
Jammu & Kashmir	19.05	30.34	233.79	1.86	9.18	253.61	20.92	25.17
Karnataka	95.99	29.88	186.63	60.46	40.14	302.89	156.46	33.16
Kerala	55.95	25.76	243.84	20.46	24.55	280.54	76.41	25.43
Madhya Pradesh	216.19	40.64	193.10	82.33	48.38	317.16	298.52	42.52
Maharashtra	193.33	37.93	194.94	111.90	35.15	328.56	305.22	36.86
Manipur	6.33	45.01	232.05	0.47	7.73	212.42	6.80	33.78
Meghalaya	7.09	45.01	232.05	0.29	7.73	212.42	7.38	37.92
Mizoram	1.64	45.01	232.05	0.30	7.73	212.42	1.94	25.66
Nagaland	4.85	45.01	232.05	0.20	7.73	212.42	5.05	37.92
Odisha	140.90	49.72	194.03	19.70	41.64	298.22	160.60	48.56
Punjab	17.76	11.95	233.79	7.35	11.35	253.61	25.11	11.77
Rajasthan	94.68	26.46	215.89	33.82	30.49	280.85	128.50	27.41
Sikkim	1.81	45.01	232.05	0.03	7.73	212.42	1.84	41.43
Tamil Nadu	121.70	32.48	196.53	80.40	39.77	296.63	202.10	35.03
Tripura	11.41	45.01	232.05	0.38	7.73	212.42	11.79	39.01
Uttar Pradesh	496.17	42.28	213.01	108.28	35.39	258.65	604.46	40.85
West Bengal	209.90	40.80	220.74	44.66	22.41	247.53	254.56	35.66
All India	2440.31	37.27	205.84	763.37	32.36	281.35	3203.67	35.97

Source: Planning Commission.

Table 8.2A Number and Percentage of Population below Poverty Line and Poverty Line in Rs (in Rs)

2004–05 (Based on MRP Consumption)

State	Rural			Urban			Combined	
	No. of persons (Lakh)	% of persons	Poverty Line (Rs)	No. of persons (Lakh)	% of persons	Poverty Line (Rs)	No. of persons (Lakh)	% of persons
Andhra Pradesh	180.00	32.30	292.95	55.00	23.40	542.89	235.10	29.60
Arunachal Pradesh	3.20	33.60	387.64	0.60	23.50	378.84	3.80	31.40
Assam	89.40	36.40	387.64	8.30	21.80	378.84	97.70	34.40
Bihar	451.00	55.70	354.36	42.80	43.70	435.00	493.80	54.40
Chhattisgarh	97.80	55.10		13.70	288.40		111.50	49.40
Delhi	1.10	15.60		18.30	12.90		19.30	13.00
Goa	1.80	28.10	322.41	1.70	22.20	560.00	3.40	24.90
Gujarat	128.50	39.10	362.25	42.90	20.10	665.90	171.40	31.60
Haryana	38.80	24.80	353.93	15.90	22.40	541.16	54.60	24.10
Himachal Pradesh	14.30	25.00	414.76	0.30	4.60	504.49	14.60	22.90
Jammu & Kashmir	11.60	14.10	394.28	2.90	10.40	504.49	14.50	13.10
Jharkhand	116.20	51.60		16.00	23.80		132.10	45.30
Karnataka	134.70	37.50	391.26	51.80	25.90	553.77	186.50	33.30
Kerala	42.20	20.20	366.56	19.80	18.40	451.24	62.00	19.60
Madhya Pradesh	254.40	53.60	324.17	61.30	35.10	599.66	315.70	48.60
Maharashtra	277.80	47.90	430.12	114.60	25.60	559.39	392.40	38.20
Manipur	6.70	39.30	327.78	2.30	34.50	570.15	9.00	37.90
Meghalaya	2.90	14.00	362.25	1.20	24.70	665.90	4.10	16.10
Mizoram	1.10	23.00	387.64	0.40	7.90	378.84	1.50	15.40
Nagaland	1.50	10.00	387.64	0.20	4.30	378.84	1.70	8.80
Odisha	198.80	60.80	387.64	22.80	37.60	378.84	221.60	57.20
Puducherry	0.80	22.90		0.70	9.90		1.50	14.20
Punjab	36.70	22.10	387.64	16.90	18.70	378.84	53.60	20.90
Rajasthan	166.40	35.80	325.79	43.50	29.70	528.49	209.80	34.40
Sikkim	1.50	31.80	410.38	0.20	25.90	466.16	1.70	30.90
Tamil Nadu	134.40	37.50	374.57	59.70	19.70	559.63	194.10	29.40
Tripura	11.90	44.50	387.64	1.50	22.50	378.84	13.40	40.00
Uttar Pradesh	600.50	42.70	351.86	130.10	34.10	547.42	730.70	40.90
Uttarakhand	23.10	35.10		6.60	26.20		29.70	32.70
West Bengal	227.50	38.20	387.64	60.80	24.40	378.84	288.30	34.20
A & N Island	0.10	4.10		0.01	0.80		0.11	3.00
Chandigarh	0.20	34.70		0.90	10.10		1.10	11.60
Dadra & Nagar	1.11	63.60		0.14	17.80		1.26	49.30
Daman & Diu	0.02	2.60		0.13	14.40		0.15	8.80
Lakshwadeep	0.001	0.40		0.04	10.50		0.04	6.40
All India	3258.10	42.00	365.84	814.10	25.50	483.26	4072.20	37.20

State	Rural			Urban			Combined	
	No. of persons (Lakh)	% of persons	Poverty Line (Rs)	No. of persons (Lakh)	% of persons	Poverty Line (Rs)	No. of persons (Lakh)	% of persons
				2009–10 (Based on MRP Consumption)				
Andhra Pradesh	127.90	22.80	693.80	48.70	17.70	926.40	176.60	21.10
Arunachal Pradesh	2.70	26.20	773.70	0.80	24.90	925.20	3.50	25.90
Assam	105.30	39.90	691.70	11.20	26.10	871.00	116.40	37.90
Bihar	498.70	55.30	655.60	44.80	39.40	775.30	543.50	53.50
Chhattisgarh	108.30	56.10	617.30	13.60	23.80	806.70	121.90	48.70
Delhi	0.30	7.70	747.80	22.90	14.40	1040.30	23.30	14.20
Goa	0.60	11.50	931.00	0.60	6.90	1025.40	1.30	8.70
Gujarat	91.60	26.70	725.90	44.60	17.90	951.40	136.20	23.00
Haryana	30.40	18.60	791.60	19.60	23.00	975.40	50.00	20.10
Himachal Pradesh	5.60	9.10	708.00	0.90	12.60	888.30	6.40	9.50
Jammu & Kashmir	7.30	8.10	722.90	4.20	12.80	845.40	11.50	9.40
Jharkhand	102.20	41.60	616.30	24.00	31.10	831.20	126.20	39.10
Karnataka	97.40	26.10	629.40	44.90	19.60	908.00	142.30	23.60
Kerala	21.60	12.00	775.30	18.00	12.10	830.70	39.60	12.00
Madhya Pradesh	216.90	42.00	631.90	44.90	22.90	771.70	261.80	36.70
Maharashtra	179.80	29.50	743.70	90.90	18.30	961.10	270.80	24.50
Manipur	8.80	47.40	871.00	3.70	46.40	955.00	12.50	47.10
Meghalaya	3.50	15.30	686.90	1.40	24.10	989.80	4.90	17.10
Mizoram	1.60	31.10	850.00	0.60	11.50	939.30	2.30	21.10
Nagaland	2.80	19.30	1016.80	1.40	25.00	1147.60	4.10	20.90
Odisha	135.50	39.20	567.10	17.70	25.90	736.00	153.20	37.00
Puducherry	0.00	0.20	641.00	0.10	1.60	777.70	0.10	1.20
Punjab	25.10	14.60	830.00	18.40	18.10	960.80	43.50	15.90
Rajasthan	133.80	26.40	755.00	33.20	19.90	846.00	167.00	24.80
Sikkim	0.70	15.50	728.90	0.10	5.00	1035.20	0.80	13.10
Tamil Nadu	78.30	21.20	639.00	43.50	12.80	800.80	121.80	17.10
Tripura	5.40	19.80	663.40	0.90	10.00	782.70	6.30	17.40
Uttar Pradesh	600.60	39.40	663.70	137.30	31.70	799.90	737.90	37.70
Uttarakhand	10.30	14.90	719.50	7.50	25.20	898.60	17.90	18.00
West Bengal	177.80	28.80	643.20	62.50	22.00	830.60	240.30	26.70
A & N Island	0.01	0.40		0.00	0.30		0.01	0.40
Chandigarh	0.03	10.30		0.92	9.20		0.95	9.20
Dadra & Nagar	1.02	55.90		0.25	17.70		1.27	39.10
Daman & Diu	0.22	34.20		0.54	33.00		0.75	33.30
Lakshwadeep	0.03	22.20		0.01	1.70		0.04	6.80
All India	2782.10	33.80	672.80	764.70	20.90	859.60	3546.80	29.80

(Contd.)

Table 8.2A (Contd)

2011–12 (Based on URP Consumption)

State	Rural			Urban			Combined	
	No. of persons (Lakh)	% of persons	Poverty Line (Rs)	Poverty Line (Rs)	No. of persons (Lakh)	% of persons	No. of persons (Lakh)	% of persons
Andhra Pradesh	61.80	10.96	860.00	1009.00	16.98	5.81	78.78	9.20
Arunachal Pradesh	4.25	38.93	930.00	1060.00	0.66	20.33	4.91	34.67
Assam	92.06	33.89	828.00	1008.00	9.21	20.49	101.27	31.98
Bihar	320.40	34.06	778.00	923.00	37.75	31.23	358.15	33.74
Chhattisgarh	88.90	44.61	738.00	849.00	15.22	24.75	104.11	39.93
Delhi	0.50	12.92	1145.00	1134.00	16.46	9.84	16.96	9.91
Goa	0.37	6.81	1090.00	1134.00	0.38	4.09	0.75	5.09
Gujarat	75.35	21.54	932.00	1152.00	26.88	10.14	102.23	16.63
Haryana	19.42	11.64	1015.00	1169.00	9.41	10.28	28.83	11.16
Himachal Pradesh	5.29	8.48	913.00	1064.00	0.30	4.33	5.59	8.06
Jammu & Kashmir	10.73	11.54	891.00	988.00	2.53	7.20	13.27	10.35
Jharkhand	104.09	40.84	748.00	974.00	20.24	24.83	124.33	36.96
Karnataka	92.80	24.53	902.00	1089.00	36.96	15.25	129.76	20.91
Kerala	15.48	9.14	1018.00	987.00	8.46	4.97	23.95	7.05
Madhya Pradesh	190.95	35.74	771.00	897.00	43.10	21.00	234.06	31.65
Maharashtra	150.56	24.22	967.00	1126.00	47.36	9.12	197.92	17.35
Manipur	7.45	38.80	1118.00	1170.00	2.78	32.59	10.22	36.89
Meghalaya	3.04	12.53	888.00	1154.00	0.57	9.26	3.61	11.87
Mizoram	1.91	35.43	1066.00	1155.00	0.37	6.36	2.27	20.40
Nagaland	2.76	19.93	1270.00	1302.00	1.00	16.48	3.76	18.88
Odisha	126.14	35.69	695.00	861.00	12.39	17.29	138.53	32.59
Puducherry	0.69	17.06	1301.00	1309.00	0.55	6.30	1.24	9.69
Punjab	13.35	7.66	1054.00	1155.00	9.82	9.24	23.18	8.26
Rajasthan	84.19	16.05	905.00	1002.00	18.73	10.69	102.92	14.71
Sikkim	0.45	9.85	930.00	1226.00	0.06	3.66	0.51	8.19
Tamil Nadu	59.23	15.83	880.00	937.00	23.40	6.54	82.63	11.28
Tripura	4.49	16.53	798.00	920.00	0.75	7.42	5.24	14.05
Uttar Pradesh	479.35	30.40	768.00	941.00	118.84	26.06	598.19	29.43
Uttarakhand	8.25	11.62	880.00	1082.00	3.35	10.48	11.60	11.26
West Bengal	141.14	22.52	783.00	981.00	43.83	14.66	184.98	19.98
A & N Island	0.04	1.57			0.00	0.00	0.04	1.00
Chandigarh	0.00	1.64			2.34	22.31	2.35	21.81
Dadra & Nagar	1.15	62.59			0.28	15.38	1.43	39.31
Daman & Diu	0.00	0.00			0.26	12.62	0.26	9.86
Lakshwadeep	0.00	0.00			0.02	3.44	0.02	2.77
All India	2166.58	25.70	816.00	1000.00	531.25	13.70	2697.83	21.92

Note: 2004–05 data revised on the basis of 2011 population and population as on March 1, 2005 has been used for estimating number of persons

Source: Planning Commission

Table A8.3 Education Statistics

Year	Number of Educational Institutions (in '00)					
	Primary	Upper primary	Secondary	Senior Secondary	Colleges	Universities/ Deemed Univ. etc
1950–1	2097	136	na	74	578	27
1960–1	3304	497	na	173	1819	45
1970–1	4084	906	na	371	3277	82
1980–1	4945	1186	na	516	6963	110
1990–1	5609	1515	na	798	5748	184
2000–1	6387	2063	877	384	10152	254
2001–2	6640	2196	na	na	na	272
2002–3	6514	2453	na	na	na	304
2003–4	7122	2623	na	na	na	304
2004–5	7675	2747	na	na	na	407
2005–6	7726	2885	1060	536	16982	350
2006–7	7849	3056	1122	574	19812	371
2007–8	7878	3252	1138	592	23099	406
2008–9	7788	3656	1221	642	27882	440
2009–10	8199	3941	1222	717	25938	436
2010–11	7485	4476	1312	720	32974	621
2011–12	7143	4788	1283	841	34852	642
2012–13	8359	4103	1036	1196	35829	665
2013–14	7906	4011	1313	1026	36671	712

Year	Level-wise Ennrolment in lakhs				
	Primary	Upper primary	Secondary	Senior Secondary	Higher Education
1950–1	192	31	na	15	4
1960–1	350	67	na	34	10
1970–1	570	133	na	76	33
1980–1	738	207	na	110	48
1990–1	974	340	na	191	49
2000–1	1138	428	190	99.0	86.0
2001–2	1139	448	na	na	na
2002–3	1224	468	na	na	na
2003–4	1283	487	na	na	na
2004–5	1308	515	na	na	na
2005–6	1321	522	250	134.0	143.0
2006–7	1337	545	259	140.0	156.0
2007–8	1355	573	282	163.0	172.0
2008–9	1353	584	294	169.0	185.0
2009–10	1336	595	307	178.0	207.0
2010–11	1348	619	319	195.0	275.0
2011–12	1399	630	341	210.0	292.0
2012–13	1321	643	343	198.0	296.0
2013–14	1300	657	370	222.0	na

(Contd.)

Table A8.3 (*Cont'd*)

Year	Drop-Out Rates of All Student		
	I–V	I–VIII	I–X
1950–1	na	na	na
1960–1	64.9	78.3	na
1970–1	67	77.9	na
1980–1	58.7	72.7	82.5
1990–1	42.6	60.9	71.3
2000–1	40.7	53.7	68.6
2001–2	39.0	54.6	66.0
2002–3	34.9	52.8	62.6
2003–4	31.5	52.3	62.7
2004–5	29.0	50.8	61.9
2005–6	25.7	48.8	61.6
2006–7	25.6	45.9	59.9
2007–8	25.1	42.7	56.7
2008–9	27.8	39.3	54.2
2009–10	30.3	42.5	52.7
2010–11	27.4	40.8	49.2
2011–12	22.3	40.8	50.3
2012–13	21.3	39.0	50.4
2013–14	19.8	36.6	47.4

Year	Pupil Teacher Ratio (PTR)				
	Primary	Upper Primary	Secondary	Senior Secondary	Higher Education
1950–1	24	20	na	21	na
1960–1	36	31	na	25	na
1970–1	39	32	na	25	na
1980–1	38	33	na	27	na
1990–1	43	37	na	31	na
2000–1	43	38	31	35	na
2001–2	na	na	na	na	na
2002–3	na	na	na	na	na
2003–4	na	na	na	na	na
2004–5	na	na	na	na	na
2005–6	46	34	32	34	26
2006–7	44	34	31	34	20
2007–8	47	35	33	37	20
2008–9	45	34	32	38	21
2009–10	41	33	30	39	24
2010–11	43	33	30	34	26
2011–12	41	34	32	33	24
2012–13	30	30	30	40	23
2013–14	28	30	28	40	na

Year	Gross Enrolment Ratio (GER)				
	Primary	Upper Primary	Secondary	Senior Secondary	Higher Education
1950–1	42.6	12.7	na	na	na
1960–1	62.4	22.5	na	na	na
1970–1	78.6	33.4	na	na	na
1980–1	80.5	41.9	na	na	na
1990–1	83.8	66.7	na	na	na
2000–1	95.7	58.6	na	na	na
2001–2	na	na	na	na	8.1
2002–3	na	na	na	na	9.0
2003–4	na	na	na	na	9.2
2004–5	na	na	51.7	27.8	10.0
2005–6	109.4	71.0	52.2	28.5	11.6
2006–7	111.4	73.8	53.5	28.9	12.4
2007–8	114.0	78.1	58.2	33.5	13.1
2008–9	114.3	79.8	60.4	34.5	13.7
2009–10	113.8	81.7	62.9	36.1	15.0
2010–11	115.5	85.2	65.2	39.4	19.4
2011–12	106.5	82.0	66.6	45.9	20.8
2012–13	100.7	84.5	67.7	43.6	21.1
2013–14	99.3	87.4	73.6	49.1	na

Source: Department of Education.

Table A8.4 Indian Health Statistics

| Year | Central Sector Expenditure on Health (Rs crore) | | | Allopaathic Medicine | | Ayush - Indian System of Medicine | | | | | | |
| | Family Welfare | Central Sector Health | ISM&H/ AYUSH | Number of Medical College | Number of Admission | Total Ayush Hospital | | | | Dispensaries | Ayush Practitioners | No. per Crore Population |
						Number	No. per Crore Population	No. of Beds	No. of Beds/ Hospitals			
1991–2				146	12199	2723	31.5	37826	13.9	20879	562016	6506
1992–3	1000	291	11	146	11241	2777	31.5	38661	13.9	21120	568486	6448
1993–4	1270	462	21	146	10400	2807	31.2	42043	15.0	21221	573226	6373
1994–5	1430	552	26	152	12249	2845	31.0	42831	15.1	21496	581703	6341
1995–6	1581	646	24	165	7039	2848	30.4	48484	17.0	20904	586998	6275
1996–7	1535	792	23	165	3568	2856	30.0	51328	18.0	19464	591510	6203
1997–8	1822	706	33	165	3949	2930	30.2	52088	17.8	19762	602036	6194
1998–9	2343	818	50	147	11733	3045	30.8	55421	18.2	20075	609404	6154
1999–2000	3100	930	49	147	10104	3880	38.5	74611	19.2	20707	681124	6753
2000–1	3090	1095	79	189	18168	3845	38.3	69476	18.1	20627	688802	6696
2001–2	3614	1290	82	na	na	3842	37.4	65763	17.1	20627	691470	6613
2002–3	3917	1360	90	na	na	3794	30.4	64920	17.1	20229	695024	6542
2003–4	4409	1326	134	na	na	3100	29.1	66076	21.3	20973	699883	6486
2004–5	4862	1772	199	229	24690	3006	27.6	59326	19.7	21234	706586	6488
2005–6	5673	2254	291	242	26449	3019	27.3	60137	19.9	21132	713684	6453
2006–7	7487	1982	317	262	28928	3194	28.5	61261	19.2	21435	725568	6467
2007–8	10380	2184	383	266	30290	3207	28.2	62863	19.6	21548	754985	6634
2008–9	11260	3008	471	289	32815	3223	27.9	61260	19.0	21801	762072	6603
2009–10	13306	3262	679	300	34595	3252	27.8	62350	19.2	23514	752254	6430
2010–11	14697	4666	849	314	29263	3277	27.6	62649	19.1	24289	712121	6004
2011–12	16509	4160	611	356	39474	3193	26.6	58321	18.3	24146	628634	5230
2012–13	16763	4145	581	381	43576	3195	26.1	58321	18.3	24392	686319	5609
2013–14	18215	4261	750	381	48567	3605	29.3	57858	16.0	26102	736538	5945
2014–15	17628	6772	468	398	46456							

Note: Reported Data for admission.

Source: National Health Profile 2015 and Ministry of Health.

Table A8.5 Household Indebtedness in India: A Profile

	Amount of Debt by Occupational categories of Households (Rs. crore)							Proportion of Households Reporting Debt					
	Rural Households			Urban Households			All Households (4+7)	Rural Households			Urban Households		
	Cultivator	Non-Cultivator	All	Self-Employed	Others	All		Cultivator	Non-Cultivator	All	Self-Employed	Others	All
Year	2	3	4	5	6	7	8	2	3	4	5	6	7
1													
2013	153640	89221	103457	303221	391724	378238	481695	45.9	28.9	31.4	35.9	21.0	22.4
2002	81709	29759	111468	24341	40977	65327	176795	29.7	21.8	26.5	17.9	17.8	17.8
1991	17668	4543	22211	6306	8805	15232	37443	34.6	26.8	32.0	28.5	25.9	26.9
1981	5737	456	6193	1406	1617	3023	9216	21.7	12.0	19.4	16.6	17.4	17.2
1971	3374	474	3848	na	na	na	na	44.4	33.3	41.3	na	na	na

Percentage Share of Outstanding Debt According to Credit Agency: Rural and Urban

	Rural							Urban			
	2013	2002	1991	1981	1971	1961	1951	1981	1991	2002	2013
A. Institutional	56.0	57.1	56.6	61.2	29.2	17.3	7.2	59.9	64.3	75.1	84.5
Government	1.2	2.3	5.7	4.0	6.7	6.6	3.7	14.6	9.3	7.6	1.8
Co-op Scty/Banks	24.8	27.3	18.6	28.6	20.1	10.4	3.5	17.5	14.2	20.5	18.0
Commercial Banks	25.1	24.5	29.0	28.0	2.2	0.3	0.0	22.5	17.7	29.7	57.1
Insurance	0.2	0.3	0.5	0.3	0.1	0.0	0.0	2.1	1.4	3.5	1.6
Provident Fund	0.1	0.3	0.9	0.3	0.1	0.0	0.0	3.2	3.3	2.0	0.3
Other Institutions	4.6	2.4	1.9	0.0	0.0	0.0	0.0	0.0	18.5	11.9	5.8
B. Non-institutional	44.0	42.9	39.6	38.8	70.8	82.7	92.8	40.1	32.0	24.9	15.5
Landlords	0.7	1.0	4.0	4.0	8.6	1.1	3.5	1.0	0.8	0.2	0.1
Agrl. Moneylenders	5.0	10.0	6.3	8.6	23.1	47.0	25.2	3.6	1.2	0.9	0.1
Proff. Moneylenders	28.2	19.6	9.4	8.3	13.8	13.8	46.4	8.9	7.9	13.2	10.5
Traders	0.1	2.6	6.7	3.4	8.7	7.5	5.1	4.8	5.8	1.0	0
Relatives/Friends	8.0	7.1	6.7	9.0	13.8	5.8	11.5	15.2	10.4	7.6	4.2
Others	1.9	2.6	9.9	5.5	2.8	7.5	1.1	6.6	5.9	1.9	0.6

Cash Debt of Households Classified By Purpose of Loan (per cent)

	Rural Households				Urban Households			
	2013	2002	1991	1981	2013	2002	1991	1981
1. Farm Business								
Capital Expenditure	13.2	26.8	12.0	42.4	1.0	3.3	2.5	5.6
Current Expenditure	15.4	14.2	2.7	17.6	1.1	1.9	0.1	4.4
2. Non-farm Business								

(*Contd.*)

Table A8.5 (Cont'd)

Year	Amount of Debt by Occupational categories of Households (Rs. crore)							Proportion of Households Reporting Debt					
	Rural Households			Urban Households			All Households (4+7)	Rural Households			Urban Households		
	Cultivator	Non-Cultivator	All	Self-Employed	Others	All		Cultivator	Non-Cultivator	All	Self-Employed	Others	All
1	2	3	4	5	6	7	8	2	3	4	5	6	7
Capital Expenditure			8.7	9.2	5.8	7.2		8.4	16.5	10.8	23.2		
Current Expenditure			2.6	2.8	2.0	1.7		7.7	3.2	4.0	8.3		
3. Households													
Capital Expenditure in Residential Bldg			20.1	35.0	6.5	22.4		58.8	57.5	37.9	35.0		
Current Expenditure			31.9	na	0.5	na		17.7	na	1.5	na		
4. Productive Purposes (1+2+3)*			91.9 (39.9)	88.0 (53.0)	29.0 (22.5)	91.3 (68.9)		94.7 (18.2)	82.4 (24.9)	56.8 (17.4)	76.5 (41.5)		
5. Other Purposes			2.7	12.0	48.0	8.5		5.3	17.6	41.4	23.2		
Repayment of Debt			2.6	1.4	na	0.8		0.9	0.0	1.8	0.2		
Expend. on Litigation			0.0	0.3	na	0.2		0.0	na	na	na		
Fin. Investment Expe.			0.1	0.7	na	0.9		0.4	na	na	na		
Other purposes			na	9.6	na	6.6		4.0	na	na	na		
6. Unspecified			na	0.1	22.8	0.2		na	na	na	na		

*: Figures in brackets relate to those given by NSSO for productive purposes (1+2).

na: Details are not available.

Source: NSSO (2005), Household Indebtedness in India as on 30-6-2002, AIDIS Report No.501(59/18.2/2), December.

NSSO (2006), Household Borrowing and Repayments in India during 1.7.2002 to 30.6.2003, AIDIS Report No.502(59/18.2/3), January.

NSSO (2013), Key Indicators of Debt and Investment in India NSS KI(70/18.2), AIDIS Report No.502(59/18.2/3), (January–December 2013).

Table A9.1 Trends in Employment in Agricultural (excluding crop production and plantation) and Non–Agricultural Enterprises, 1980–2013

Total Employment in Thousands

	2nd Economic Census 1980			3rd Economic Census 1990			4th Economic Census 1998			5th Economic Census 2005			6th Economic Census 2013		
	Rural	Urban	Combined	Rural	Urban	Combined	Rural	Urban	Combined	Rural	Urban	Combined	Rural	Urban	Combined
All-India	24474	29194	53668	33296	38780	72076	39901	43399	83299	50185	48782	98968	67895	63398	131294
1 Andhra Pradesh	2658	2054	4712	4082	2652	6734	4635	2877	7512	5718	3152	8871	5901	2690	8591
2 Arunachal Pradesh	32	13	44	62	31	93	52	28	81	64	43	107	60	49	109
3 Assam	Census not conducted			1120	570	1689	1551	644	2195	1792	943	2735	2746	1207	3954
4 Bihar	1532	1245	2777	1743	1710	3454	1775	1654	3429	1383	893	2276	2171	1073	3244
5 Chhattisgarh				Included in Madhya Pradesh						1014	597	1610	1158	703	1861
6 Goa	136	116	252	98	121	219	98	118	216	120	125	246	85	204	289
7 Gujarat	1528	2124	3652	2022	2704	4726	2351	2929	5280	2569	3245	5814	5108	4500	9608
8 Haryana	370	604	974	524	829	1353	595	964	1559	1074	1138	2212	1464	1772	3237
9 Himachal Pradesh	236	108	344	312	156	469	387	189	577	462	205	667	744	233	977
10 Jammu and Kashmir	247	242	489	Census not conducted			217	256	474	364	387	752	599	496	1096
11 Jharkhand				Included in Bihar						580	589	1169	768	685	1453
12 Karnataka	2003	1863	3866	2588	2495	5083	2757	2496	5253	3320	2659	5978	3545	3601	7146
13 Kerala	1603	849	2452	1889	1400	3289	2760	1089	3849	3684	1876	5559	3287	3632	6919
14 Madhya Pradesh	1601	1689	3290	2363	2522	4886	2441	2815	5256	1868	2352	4220	2122	2425	4548
15 Maharashtra	2145	4605	6750	2847	6113	8960	3688	6756	10445	4625	7201	11827	6062	8450	14512
16 Manipur	46	59	105	77	80	157	97	104	201	121	114	235	251	159	410
17 Meghalaya	49	59	109	85	85	170	97	87	184	137	107	245	191	98	289
18 Mizoram	18	27	46	21	51	72	23	54	77	32	69	101	42	80	122
19 Nagaland	39	36	75	50	80	130	64	111	175	73	111	184	88	73	162
20 Odisha	1250	699	1949	1716	896	2612	2158	937	3095	2572	1004	3575	3194	1124	4318
21 Punjab	415	921	1336	580	1190	1770	743	1357	2100	1059	1628	2688	1675	1972	3647
22 Rajasthan	1138	1179	2317	1318	1520	2838	1793	1749	3542	2271	1969	4240	3646	2616	6262
23 Sikkim	15	15	31	28	19	47	27	21	48	41	28	69	51	41	91
24 Tamil Nadu	2305	2841	5146	2882	3354	6236	3583	3608	7191	5188	4678	9867	5587	6108	11695
25 Telangana										Included in Andhra Pradesh			2364	3173	5537
26 Tripura	83	52	134	132	89	220	168	101	268	249	130	379	233	171	404
27 Uttar Pradesh	2621	3122	5743	2949	3959	6909	3232	4248	7480	4196	4344	8540	7953	6165	14118
28 Uttarakhand				Included in Uttar Pradesh						396	353	749	539	511	1051
29 West Bengal	2242	3101	5343	3636	3811	7448	4374	4397	8771	4921	4397	9318	6067	5837	11904

(Contd.)

Table A9.1 (*Contd.*)

Total Employment in Thousands

	6th Economic Census 2013			5th Economic Census 2005			4th Economic Census 1998			3rd Economic Census 1990			2nd Economic Census 1980		
	Rural	Urban	Combined	Rural	Urban	Combined	Rural	Urban	Combined	Rural	Urban	Combined	Rural	Urban	Combined
Chandigarh	4	243	247	13	239	252	6	212	218	8	195	203	4	117	121
Delhi	28	2992	3020	73	4007	4080	86	3415	3501	73	2012	2085	96	1375	1471
Pondicherry	69	151	219	64	129	193	49	132	182	30	90	120	26	55	81
A & N Islands	38	31	69	28	36	64	37	25	63	31	21	52	21	17	38
D & N Haveli	37	57	94	47	18	65	28	5	33	12	3	14	5	2	7
Daman and Diu	15	67	81	57	10	68	21	11	32	11	10	21	Included in Goa		
Lakshadweep	2	8	10	7	5	12	5	11	16	6	10	16	8	6	14

Table A9.1 (*Contd.*)

Annual Growth Rate - Employment (per cent)

	2005–2013			1998–2005			1990–1998			1980–1990		
	Rural	Urban	Combined	Rural	Urban	Combined	Rural	Urban	Combined	Rural	Urban	Combined
All-India	**(3.85)**	**(3.33)**	**(3.60)**	**(3.33)**	**(1.68)**	**(2.49)**	**(2.15)**	**(1.34)**	**(1.71)**	**(2.88)**	**(2.81)**	**(2.84)**
1 Andhra Pradesh	(0.39)	(−1.96)	(−0.40)	(3.05)	(1.32)	(2.40)	(1.60)	(1.02)	(1.38)	(4.38)	(2.59)	(3.64)
2 Arunachal Pradesh	(−0.93)	(1.74)	(0.20)	(3.07)	(6.02)	(4.17)	(−2.13)	(−1.23)	(−1.82)	(6.97)	(9.65)	(7.80)
3 Assam	(5.48)	(3.14)	(4.71)	(2.08)	(5.61)	(3.19)	(4.15)	(1.54)	(3.32)	Not available		
4 Bihar	(5.80)	(2.31)	(4.53)	(1.79)	(−1.77)	(0.27)	(−0.95)	(−0.42)	(−0.68)	(1.30)	(3.23)	(2.20)
5 Chhattisgarh	(1.68)	(2.07)	(1.83)	(3.82)	(1.19)	(2.78)	Not available			Not available		
6 Goa	(−4.24)	(6.25)	(2.04)	(2.99)	(0.88)	(1.87)	(0.04)	(−0.34)	(−0.17)	Not available		
7 Gujarat	(8.97)	(4.17)	(6.48)	(1.27)	(1.48)	(1.39)	(1.90)	(1.01)	(1.40)	(2.84)	(2.44)	(2.61)
8 Haryana	(3.95)	(5.70)	(4.87)	(8.80)	(2.40)	(5.12)	(1.60)	(1.90)	(1.79)	(3.56)	(3.21)	(3.34)
9 Himachal Pradesh	(6.15)	(1.61)	(4.89)	(2.54)	(1.13)	(2.09)	(2.73)	(2.43)	(2.63)	(2.85)	(3.73)	(3.13)
10 Jammu and Kashmir	(6.42)	(3.14)	(4.82)	(7.65)	(6.08)	(6.82)	Not available			Not available		
11 Jharkhand	(3.57)	(1.91)	(2.76)	(0.66)	(−1.21)	(−0.32)	Not available			Not available		
12 Karnataka	(0.82)	(3.87)	(2.25)	(2.69)	(0.91)	(1.86)	(0.79)	(0.01)	(0.41)	(2.60)	(2.96)	(2.77)
13 Kerala	(−1.42)	(8.61)	(2.77)	(4.21)	(8.08)	(5.39)	(4.85)	(−3.09)	(1.99)	(1.66)	(5.13)	(2.98)
14 Madhya Pradesh	(1.61)	(0.38)	(0.94)	(1.69)	(0.54)	(1.04)	(0.41)	(1.38)	(0.92)	(3.97)	(4.09)	(4.03)
15 Maharashtra	(3.44)	(2.02)	(2.59)	(3.29)	(0.91)	(1.79)	(3.29)	(1.26)	(1.93)	(2.87)	(2.87)	(2.87)
16 Manipur	(9.53)	(−4.28)	(7.21)	(3.24)	(1.28)	(2.25)	(2.85)	(3.32)	(3.09)	(5.26)	(3.16)	(4.13)
17 Meghalaya	(4.21)	(−1.08)	(2.12)	(5.05)	(3.02)	(4.12)	(1.76)	(0.26)	(1.03)	(5.55)	(3.71)	(4.58)
18 Mizoram	(3.47)	(1.83)	(2.37)	(4.96)	(3.45)	(3.91)	(1.15)	(0.74)	(0.86)	(1.27)	(6.51)	(4.67)
19 Nagaland	(2.36)	(−5.00)	(−1.60)	(1.95)	(0.02)	(0.75)	(3.27)	(4.08)	(3.78)	(2.44)	(8.46)	(5.70)
20 Odisha	(2.75)	(1.42)	(2.39)	(2.54)	(0.99)	(2.08)	(2.90)	(0.56)	(2.14)	(3.22)	(2.51)	(2.97)

Annual Growth Rate - Employment (per cent)

	2005–2013			1998–2005			1990–1998			1980–1990		
	Rural	Urban	Combined	Rural	Urban	Combined	Rural	Urban	Combined	Rural	Urban	Combined
21 Punjab	(5.90)	(2.42)	(3.89)	(5.19)	(2.64)	(3.59)	(3.15)	(1.65)	(2.16)	(3.40)	(2.60)	(2.85)
22 Rajasthan	(6.09)	(3.62)	(5.00)	(3.44)	(1.71)	(2.60)	(3.92)	(1.77)	(2.81)	(1.48)	(2.57)	(2.05)
23 Sikkim	(2.63)	(4.67)	(3.50)	(6.41)	(4.32)	(5.52)	(–0.81)	(1.33)	(0.08)	(6.36)	(2.22)	(4.48)
24 Tamil Nadu	(0.93)	(3.39)	(2.15)	(5.43)	(3.78)	(4.62)	(2.76)	(0.91)	(1.80)	(2.26)	(1.68)	(1.94)
25 Telangana	Not available											
26 Tripura	(–0.83)	(3.47)	(0.79)	(5.84)	(3.71)	(5.07)	(3.05)	(1.60)	(2.48)	(–4.80)	(5.50)	(5.07)
27 Uttar Pradesh	(8.32)	(4.47)	(6.49)	(4.98)	(1.40)	(3.03)	(1.76)	(0.88)	(1.27)	(1.19)	(2.40)	(1.87)
28 Uttarakhand	(3.94)	(4.73)	(4.32)	(7.06)	(2.04)	(4.45)	Not available			Not available		
29 West Bengal	(2.65)	(3.61)	(3.11)	(1.70)	(–0.00)	(0.87)	(2.34)	(1.80)	(2.07)	(4.95)	(2.09)	(3.38)
Chandigarh	(–13.22)	(0.19)	(–0.24)	(12.11)	(1.71)	(2.07)	(–4.30)	(1.07)	(0.89)	(6.94)	(5.25)	(5.31)
Delhi	(–11.46)	(–3.58)	(–3.69)	(–2.26)	(2.31)	(2.21)	(2.12)	(6.84)	(6.70)	(–2.81)	(3.88)	(3.55)
Pondicherry	(0.86)	(1.95)	(1.60)	(3.83)	(–0.37)	(0.88)	(6.21)	(5.00)	(5.31)	(1.66)	(4.93)	(3.99)
A & N Islands	(3.67)	(–1.83)	(0.86)	(–3.90)	(5.15)	(0.35)	(2.25)	(2.26)	(2.25)	(4.02)	(2.39)	(3.33)
D & N Haveli	(–2.88)	(15.37)	(4.69)	(7.56)	(22.03)	(10.33)	(11.82)	(5.85)	(10.81)	(8.28)	(3.86)	(7.23)
Daman and Diu	(–15.49)	(26.02)	(2.35)	(15.32)	(–0.06)	(11.49)	(9.01)	(0.60)	(5.50)	Not available		
Lakshadweep	(–12.95)	(5.90)	(–1.57)	(3.53)	(–9.60)	(–4.00)	(–2.17)	(0.91)	(–0.20)	(–2.99)	(5.89)	(1.40)

Notes: (i) Annual growth rate for all-India between 1990 and 2005 is worked out after excluding Jammu and Kashmir as Economic Census for 1990 was not conducted.

(ii) Annual growth rate for Bihar, Madhya Pradesh and Uttar Pradesh for 1990 to 2005 are worked out after including Jharkhand, Chhattisgarh and Uttranchal, respectively.

(iii) Similarly growth rate between 1980–90 and 1990–98 for all-India excludes Assam and Jammu and Kashmir as Economic Census of Assam was not conduted in 1980 and that of J&K in 1990.

Source: GOI (2006), Press note dated June 12 on Fifth Economic Census 2005 and earlier Economic Census Reports.

Table A9.2 Trends in Number of Agricultural (excluding crop production and plantation) and Non-Agricultural Enterprises: 1980–2013

Number of Enterprises in Thousands

	2nd Economic Census 1980			3rd Economic Census 1990			4th Economic Census 1998			5th Economic Census 2005			6th Economic Census 2013		
	Rural	Urban	Combined	Rural	Urban	Combined	Rural	Urban	Combined	Rural	Urban	Combined	Rural	Urban	Combined
All-India	**11141**	**7220**	**18362**	**14722**	**10280**	**25002**	**17707**	**12641**	**30349**	**25809**	**16314**	**42124**	**34796**	**23700**	**58496**
1 Andhra Pradesh	1152	462	1614	1737	749	2487	2007	895	2903	2896	1128	4023	3138	1104	4243
2 Arunachal Pradesh	9	2	11	16	5	21	15	6	21	19	10	29	20	16	36
3 Assam	census not conducted			353	143	495	404	189	593	633	293	926	1456	574	2030
4 Bihar	713	331	1045	783	445	1228	872	571	1443	872	418	1290	1201	507	1707
5 Chhattisgarh	Included in Madhya Pradesh									454	202	656	519	255	773
6 Goa	32	21	53	34	27	61	38	34	72	43	38	81	32	64	97
7 Gujarat	699	490	1188	842	656	1498	1084	830	1915	1343	1075	2419	2407	1566	3973
8 Haryana	159	161	320	209	248	457	237	295	533	453	375	828	648	517	1165
9 Himachal Pradesh	115	24	139	148	35	183	182	44	225	219	52	272	334	78	412
10 Jammu and Kashmir	125	71	197	census not conducted			111	105	216	185	139	324	295	207	502
11 Jharkhand	Included in Bihar									294	197	491	355	283	639
12 Karnataka	883	492	1375	1033	661	1694	1152	760	1912	1598	902	2500	1714	1166	2881
13 Kerala	659	213	872	827	402	1229	1241	324	1565	2117	731	2848	1805	1550	3355
14 Madhya Pradesh	867	474	1341	1154	720	1873	1207	917	2124	953	826	1778	1136	1017	2153
15 Maharashtra	965	874	1839	1308	1315	2624	1613	1621	3234	2262	2113	4375	3294	2843	6137
16 Manipur	19	16	35	34	27	61	43	37	80	58	46	104	144	86	230
17 Meghalaya	21	12	33	32	18	50	36	20	56	56	28	85	73	33	106
18 Mizoram	8	6	13	10	13	23	10	15	25	18	29	47	21	37	57
19 Nagaland	9	7	16	13	11	24	14	16	30	21	17	38	33	27	61
20 Odisha	629	174	804	853	240	1094	1157	293	1450	1425	367	1791	1606	483	2089
21 Punjab	202	261	463	254	345	599	303	415	717	497	576	1072	785	728	1513
22 Rajasthan	606	357	964	689	481	1169	911	620	1531	1210	746	1957	1855	1040	2895
23 Sikkim	5	3	8	7	3	11	8	5	13	14	6	19	21	16	37
24 Tamil Nadu	981	787	1767	1167	944	2111	1408	1106	2514	2737	1710	4447	2687	2342	5029
25 Tripura	39	14	54	61	25	85	70	34	104	136	52	188	1197	890	2087
26 Telangana	Included in Andhra Pradesh									Included in Andhra Pradesh			145	91	237
27 Uttar Pradesh	1151	1015	2166	1291	1342	2633	1479	1564	3043	2194	1822	4016	4159	2525	6684
28 Uttranchal	Included in Uttar Pradesh						Included in Uttar Pradesh			200	128	329	232	162	394
29 West Bengal	1044	659	1704	1818	932	2750	2044	1191	3234	2831	1455	4286	3428	2478	5906

Number of Enterprises in Thousands

	6th Economic Census 2013			5th Economic Census 2005			4th Economic Census 1998			3rd Economic Census 1990			2nd Economic Census 1980		
	Rural	Urban	Combined	Rural	Urban	Combined	Rural	Urban	Combined	Rural	Urban	Combined	Rural	Urban	Combined
Chandigarh	2	81	84	8	58	66	3	37	40	5	29	33	1	15	16
Delhi	12	863	875	28	726	754	30	656	686	23	432	455	28	262	290
Pondicherry	18	41	59	17	33	50	13	29	43	10	21	31	10	13	23
A & N Islands	15	9	23	6	7	12	9	5	14	8	3	12	5	2	7
D & N Haveli	4	7	11	5	4	9	3	1	4	2	1	3	1	0	2
Daman and Diu	2	9	11	7	4	11	3	3	6	2	3	5	Included in Goa		
Lakshadweep	1	3	3	2	1	3	2	3	5	2	3	5	3	1	5

Table A9.2 (*Contd.*)

Annual Growth Rate – Number of Enterprises (per cent)

	2005–2013			1998–2005			1990–1998			1980–1990		
	Rural	Urban	Combined	Rural	Urban	Combined	Rural	Urban	Combined	Rural	Urban	Combined
All-India	(3.81)	(4.78)	(4.19)	(5.53)	(3.71)	(4.80)	(2.27)	(2.50)	(2.36)	(2.83)	(3.60)	(3.14)
1 Andhra Pradesh	(1.01)	(–0.26)	(0.67)	(5.37)	(3.35)	(4.78)	(1.82)	(2.25)	(1.95)	(4.19)	(4.96)	(4.42)
2 Arunachal Pradesh	(0.90)	(6.43)	(3.06)	(3.65)	(7.08)	(4.74)	(–1.14)	(2.96)	(–0.07)	(5.72)	(10.25)	(6.61)
3 Assam	(10.97)	(8.79)	(10.31)	(6.62)	(6.46)	(6.57)	(1.72)	(3.58)	(2.28)	Not available		
4 Bihar	(4.08)	(2.44)	(3.57)	(4.50)	(0.50)	(3.07)	(1.35)	(3.15)	(2.03)	(0.94)	(3.00)	(1.63)
5 Chhattisgarh	(1.69)	(2.97)	(2.08)	(3.24)	(2.64)	(3.06)	Not available			Not available		
6 Goa	(–3.40)	(6.71)	(2.24)	(1.75)	(1.75)	(1.75)	(1.46)	(2.85)	(2.09)	Not available		
7 Gujarat	(7.56)	(4.81)	(6.40)	(3.11)	(3.77)	(3.40)	(3.22)	(2.99)	(3.12)	(1.88)	(2.96)	(2.34)
8 Haryana	(4.57)	(4.10)	(4.36)	(9.68)	(3.46)	(6.50)	(1.62)	(2.19)	(1.93)	(2.78)	(4.43)	(3.64)
9 Himachal Pradesh	(5.41)	(5.06)	(5.34)	(2.73)	(2.60)	(2.71)	(2.63)	(2.70)	(2.64)	(2.49)	(4.00)	(2.76)
10 Jammu and Kashmir	(6.02)	(5.10)	(5.63)	(7.64)	(4.06)	(5.99)	Not available			Not available		
11 Jharkhand	(2.40)	(4.63)	(3.34)	(3.44)	(2.41)	(3.02)	Not available			Not available		
12 Karnataka	(0.88)	(3.26)	(1.79)	(4.78)	(2.49)	(3.91)	(1.37)	(1.76)	(1.52)	(1.59)	(2.98)	(2.11)
13 Kerala	(–1.97)	(9.85)	(2.07)	(7.93)	(12.33)	(8.93)	(5.21)	(–2.66)	(3.07)	(2.29)	(6.56)	(3.49)
14 Madhya Pradesh	(2.23)	(2.63)	(2.42)	(1.74)	(1.40)	(1.58)	(0.57)	(3.07)	(1.58)	(2.90)	(4.27)	(3.40)
15 Maharashtra	(4.81)	(3.78)	(4.32)	(4.95)	(3.86)	(4.41)	(2.65)	(2.65)	(2.65)	(3.09)	(4.17)	(3.61)

(*Contd.*)

Table A9.2 (Contd.)

	Annual Growth Rate - Number of Enterprises (per cent)											
	2005–2013			1998–2005			1990–1998			1980–1990		
	Rural	Urban	Combined	Rural	Urban	Combined	Rural	Urban	Combined	Rural	Urban	Combined
16 Manipur	11.95	8.14	(10.39)	4.46	2.92	3.76	(3.05)	(3.97)	(3.47)	(6.01)	(5.62)	(5.84)
17 Meghalaya	3.28	1.69	(2.77)	6.48	5.05	5.98	(1.54)	(1.56)	(1.55)	(4.44)	(4.43)	(4.24)
18 Mizoram	1.84	2.80	(2.45)	8.40	10.39	9.60	(0.91)	(0.98)	(0.95)	(2.23)	(8.77)	(5.53)
19 Nagaland	6.13	6.07	(6.10)	6.05	1.22	3.64	(1.02)	(4.51)	(2.75)	(3.91)	(4.64)	(4.24)
20 Odisha	1.51	3.50	(1.94)	3.02	3.26	3.07	(3.88)	(2.51)	(3.59)	(3.09)	(3.25)	(3.13)
21 Punjab	5.89	2.99	(4.40)	7.34	4.80	5.91	(2.19)	(2.33)	(2.27)	(2.35)	(2.81)	(2.61)
22 Rajasthan	5.48	4.23	(5.02)	4.15	2.69	3.57	(3.55)	(3.24)	(3.42)	(1.28)	(3.01)	(1.95)
23 Sikkim	5.76	13.56	(8.47)	8.39	1.16	5.83	(0.74)	(5.89)	(2.54)	(3.40)	(1.08)	(2.62)
24 Tamil Nadu	–0.23	4.01	(1.55)	9.96	6.43	8.49	(2.38)	(2.00)	(2.21)	(1.75)	(1.84)	(1.79)
25 Tripura	31.26	42.47	(35.08)	9.85	6.37	8.79	(1.87)	(4.05)	(2.53)	(4.41)	(5.72)	(4.77)
26 Telangana	Not available											
27 Uttar Pradesh	–28.78	–31.20	(–29.80)	7.07	3.14	5.14	(1.71)	(1.93)	(1.83)	(1.15)	(2.83)	(1.97)
28 Uttranchal	46.11	45.12	(45.73)	7.72	4.16	6.21	Not available			Not available		
29 West Bengal	–26.86	–23.98	(–25.79)	4.77	2.90	4.10	(1.48)	(3.11)	(2.05)	(5.70)	(3.52)	(4.90)
Chandigarh	114.44	59.81	(75.41)	15.57	6.67	7.46	(–6.01)	(3.22)	(2.25)	(15.16)	(6.92)	(7.72)
Delhi	–26.84	–23.94	(–24.04)	–0.91	1.45	1.36	(3.07)	(5.38)	(5.27)	(–1.84)	(5.12)	(4.60)
Pondicherry	–3.74	50.36	(43.05)	3.37	1.67	2.22	(3.99)	(4.47)	(4.32)	(–0.31)	(4.99)	(2.94)
A & N Islands	15.30	25.35	(21.48)	–6.16	–4.92	–1.36	(0.82)	(3.86)	(1.78)	(4.70)	(5.08)	(4.81)
D & N Haveli	13.14	11.93	(12.68)	8.65	20.98	12.31	(3.69)	(4.82)	(3.94)	(4.14)	(2.29)	(3.71)
Daman and Diu	–7.27	8.77	(0.69)	13.64	1.39	7.85	(2.49)	(0.66)	(1.42)	Not available		
Lakshadweep	0.27	27.51	(16.17)	1.80	–11.31	–5.02	(–1.30)	(0.94)	(0.02)	(–4.73)	(5.77)	(–0.25)

Source: Economic Census.